I0187570

Robert G. Ingersoll

A LIFE

Frank Smith

Prometheus Books

BUFFALO, NEW YORK

To Ann
"Roses, roses all the way."

ROBERT G. INGERSOLL: A LIFE. Copyright © 1990 by Frank Smith. All rights reserved. No part of this book may be reproduced in any manner whatsoever without written permission, except in the case of brief quotations embodied in critical articles and reviews. Inquiries should be addressed to Prometheus Books, 700 East Amherst Street, Buffalo, New York 14215, 716-837-2475.

Library of Congress Cataloging-in-Publication Data

Smith, Frank, 1907-
   Robert G. Ingersoll : a life / Frank Smith.
     p. cm.
   Includes bibliographical references.
   ISBN 978-0-87975-588-1
   1. Ingersoll, Robert, 1833-1899. 2. Lawyers—United States—
Biography. I. Title.
KF368.I54S65   1990
340'.092—dc20
[B]   89-70238
                                                  CIP

Table of Contents

Acknowledgments

In writing this book I have come under obligation to various persons and institutions. My friend David Henley started it all when he introduced me to the Ingersoll Papers at the Library of Congress, and he has liberally and literally shared with me his acquisitions as a collector of Ingersolliana. My sister-in-law Hazel Ralston put one chapter through the word-processor, and as the book progressed over the months my friends Sim Shanks and Nancy Osgood completed the word-processor transcript. None of them has received any compensation except my boundless gratitude and a few dinners out. Before I submitted the manuscript to Prometheus Books, Dr. Gordon Stein gave me counsel and encouragement, and he has graciously contributed a brilliant Foreword on the influence of Ingersoll. Patricia Pederson-Lawton, my editor at Prometheus, has a genius for style and organization as well as persuasion, and the reader and I have profited greatly from her suggestions.

In the course of my work I have knocked on other doors and have always found welcome. My friend Edward L. Ericson, formerly Chairman of the Board of Leaders of the New York Society for Ethical Culture, read my final chapter and gave it his benediction. My friends Helen Bergan and Monica O'Connell of the Martin Luther King Library in the District of Columbia made it almost a pleasure to call upon them time and again for help. I had an evening-long discussion with Reverend Roger E. Greeley, formerly Minister of the People's Church of Kalamazoo, Michigan, whose dramatic impersonations of Ingersoll have delighted thousands, and he loaned me his special materials. At Ingersoll celebrations I have enjoyed meeting Fred Ingersoll Harmon, great-grandson of Dr. John Ingersoll, and I am indebted to him for access to the moving letter from Robert to John describing the death of their father. Dr. Mark A. Plummer, professor of history at Illinois State University and trailblazer in the Ingersoll and Oglesby fields, has been a generous fellow worker. I have been enriched by contacts with Ruth ("Dixie") Jokinen, a formidable one-person movement for preserving Ingersoll mementoes and furthering his proper place in history. The personnel whom I met face to face at the several depositories of primary materials were invariably eager to help me in exploring their treasures.

This book partakes of a family venture. My wife Ann has worked with me, not only in our hometown, Washington, D.C., but in Peoria and Springfield, New York and Dobbs Ferry, researching and collating data and rescuing me from gaucheries of expression. My debt to her in this project and in my life is reflected in the dedication.

My benefactors share a large responsibility for the merits of this book but not for its failings. On that plateau I stand alone.

Foreword

The Influence of Ingersoll

Gordon Stein

Rarely will a high school student of today encounter the name Robert G. Ingersoll. Those college undergraduates who take courses on speech may occasionally see his name. Most college history students (unless they take an advanced course on nineteenth-century America) will not. Yet, during the latter part of his lifetime Robert G. Ingersoll (1833–1899), was perhaps the single best known and most listened to American. From about 1880 to his death in 1899, Ingersoll probably spoke to more Americans *in person* (there was no radio, television, or film) than anyone before or since. He had daily audiences of as many as three thousand people a night while he was on tour—several months a year for many years. Why then is Ingersoll not better remembered today? Did his ideas have any lasting influence, even if he did not?

We need to first briefly discuss how we are going to measure influence. Ingersoll invented nothing, for example, as Edison did, so we can't gauge the use of such an invention to measure his influence. Ingersoll wrote and spoke about a great many topics, but we would be hard pressed to find many original ideas among his writings and speeches. He was a popularizer; he had a unique and often poetic way of putting things that caused many people to remember what he said. To Ingersoll goes the credit for popularizing in a memorable way ideas that had not been popular before.

Does the subsequent popularity of some of these ideas mean that Ingersoll should be given all the credit? Hardly, although he certainly played a role. We can give Ingersoll credit only when those who make direct contributions to their fields acknowledge that Ingersoll's speaking or writings have helped shape their thinking. What *did* Ingersoll say, and are there any modern ideas for which he can be given credit?

Women's Issues

Let's start with birth control. Every historian credits Margaret Sanger with the promotion and successful establishment of the idea of birth control in America, but Sanger has revealed Ingersoll's contribution to her beliefs. Ingersoll recognized that a woman's role in society would always be a captive one unless she could control her childbearing. Sanger's father was an Irish freethinker whose announced heroes were Robert G. Ingersoll and Henry George.[1]

Ingersoll himself had the following to say about birth control:

> Why have the reformers failed? . . . I will tell them why. . . . Ignorance, poverty, and vice are populating the world. The gutter is a nursery. People unable even to support themselves fill the tenements, the huts, and hovels with children. . . . The babe is not welcome, because it is a burden. . . . The real question is, can we prevent the ignorant, the poor, the vicious from filling the world with children? . . . To accomplish this there is but one way. Science must make woman the owner, the mistress of herself. Science, the only possible savior of mankind, must put it in the power of woman to decide for herself whether she will or will not become a mother.[2]

Ingersoll spoke and wrote extensively about women. He was devoted to his wife and two daughters, and shared his home with his wife's immediate family. Ingersoll was close friends with Susan B. Anthony, Carrie Chapman Catt, Lucretia Mott, and Matilda Joslyn Gage. Although, again, it is difficult to know to what extent Ingersoll influenced these women (and they him), he certainly helped publicize their message. The most direct statement (of many) of Ingersoll's on women's rights is probably the following:

> In my judgement, the woman is the equal of the man. She has all the rights I have and one more, and that is the right to be protected. If there is any man I detest, it is the man who thinks he is the head of a family—the man who thinks he is "boss."[3]

Ingersoll thought that the Bible was largely to blame for the nineteenth century's attitude toward women. He said:

If we wish to find what the Bible thinks of women, all it is necessary to do is read it. We will find that everywhere she is spoken of simply as property—as belonging absolutely to the man. We will find that whenever a man got tired of his wife . . . [she] became a houseless and homeless wanderer.[4]

Further, Ingersoll held women to be men's intellectual equals.

Nothing gives me more pleasure, nothing gives greater promise for the future than the fact that woman is achieving intellectual and physical liberty. It is refreshing to know that here, in our country, there are thousands [!] of women who think and express their own thoughts— who are thoroughly free and thoroughly conscientious. Woman is not the intellectual inferior of man.[5]

With regard to women's right to vote, Ingersoll, of course, was for it.

I am willing that every woman in the nation who desires the privilege and honor shall vote. If any woman wants to vote, I am too much of a gentleman to say she shall not. She gets her right, if she has it, from precisely the same source that I get mine. There are many questions upon which I deem it desirable that women should vote, especially upon the question of peace and war.[6]

Ingersoll was in favor of divorce, initiated by either party, with just cause. He said:

When the civilized man finds his wife loves another, he does not kill, he does not murder. He says to his wife, "You are free." When the civilized woman finds that her husband loves another, she does not kill, she does not murder. She says to her husband, "I am free."[7]

Religion

It is hard for the average person to imagine what mainstream Protestant Christianity was saying in the last half of the nineteenth century. The concepts of eternal hellfire, the necessary immorality of unbelievers, and the literal truth of the Bible were commonplace. Very rarely was an unbeliever allowed to speak publicly. Therefore, the phenomenon of Ingersoll lecturing nightly to thousands of people against organized religion, and receiving front-page newspaper coverage, was a new one.

All of this publicity, and the size and enthusiasm of Ingersoll's audiences, struck fear into the hearts of many clergymen. Their first instinct was to strike back, and the easiest way appeared to be by *ad hominem* attacks. (At least then they wouldn't have to deal with his ideas.) Ingersoll had such a "squeaky clean" life and personality that no mud would stick. No past scandal could be unearthed (although people like Clark Braden were not averse to making up such scandals for the glory of God).[8] A few tried to attack his ideas.[9] They seem to me to have failed miserably.

Ingersoll believed that nothing was "sacred" or immune from discussion. He felt that mild satire could often make people consider the error of their views when straight discussion could not. His attack upon the inerrancy of the Bible was relentless. He blamed the Bible for the then-current attitudes toward blacks and women, and for much of the hypocrisy and injustice in the world. Through his repeated criticisms of the Bible, he reinforced people's existing doubts about its value as a moral guide. There can be no doubt that some of the liberalization of Protestant theology in America came about as a direct result of Ingersoll's attacks upon it, especially when he was later joined by a small army of other freethought lecturers, such as Samuel P. Putnam, B. F. Underwood, and John E. Remsburg.

The concept of eternal punishment, especially when meted out for what Ingersoll viewed as relatively minor offenses, was particularly disturbing to him. He minced no words as to the immorality of any Being who would want his creatures to suffer eternally.[10] Again, no doubt in part due to Ingersoll, the concept of eternal hellfire left mainline Protestantism and is now confined to the theology of fundamentalist groups. Similarly, the literal acceptance of the Bible, which Ingersoll fought so hard against, is currently found almost exclusively in fundamentalist groups.

The idea that belief in the Bible or possession of some religious belief was somehow necessary to being moral or worthy as a human being was disturbing to Ingersoll. His lecture "The Great Infidels" was designed, at least in part, to show that nonbelievers were moral and notable contributors to civilization.[11]

Ingersoll was also quick to point out what he thought was wrong with the "design" of the world (if indeed there was design). He always said, and it is one of my favorite quotes, that if *he* were designing the world, he "would make good health catching instead of disease."[12]

Ingersoll's whole approach to life could be termed *caring rationalism*. Although he generally allowed himself to be called an agnostic ("The Great Agnostic" was the way the press commonly referred to him), Ingersoll took the meaning of agnostic in a more precise way than most people use it today. To him an agnostic was someone who could say that he or she didn't know about God's existence, adding that neither did *you* know, because it was not possible for anyone to know whether God existed. Ingersoll also called himself an atheist, but usually not in public. In a moment of complete candor during a newspaper interview, he did admit publicly: "The Agnostic is an Atheist. The Atheist is an Agnostic. The Agnostic says, 'I do not know, but I do not believe there is any

God.' The Atheist says the same. The orthodox Christian says he knows there is a God; but we know that he does not know. He simply believes. He cannot know. The Atheist cannot know that God does not exist."[13]

This quotation demonstrates that Ingersoll correctly understood the classical meaning of the terms *agnostic* and *atheist*, that he recognized that one can be *both* an atheist and an agnostic, that he was an atheist himself, that the agnostic knows that one cannot know whether there is a God, and that Christians, even though they claim to know that there is a God, really do not and cannot *know*: Christians (and theists in general) can only *believe* that there is a God. Ingersoll proved that he was aware of the traditional way in which atheists have defined atheism and also used the word *agnostic* in the pure sense.[14] Finally, he showed that he correctly understood the epistemological problems inherent in the word *know*. In all of this, Ingersoll was far ahead of his contemporaries, and also ahead of some of today's atheists, who do not understand these important distinctions.

Finally, Ingersoll made a contribution to the field of organized freethought. He was largely responsible for the growth of the organized freethought movement in the United States from 1880 to 1899. This was the "Golden Age" of freethought. Robert Ingersoll's influence and participation enabled the movement to grow rapidly to a size it has never again achieved. He spread the message of the "good infidel," contributing money and articles to the freethought press, speaking to freethought congresses, and serving as an officer of various freethought organizations.[15]

The Role of Science

Ingersoll was a strong supporter of science, going so far as to call it "the only possible savior of mankind,"[16] recognizing that science is nonsectarian. He said that

> Nature, so far as we can discern, without passion and without intention, forms, transforms and retransforms forever. She neither weeps nor rejoices. She produces a man without purpose and obliterates him without regret. Only through man does Nature take cognizance of the good, the true, and the beautiful. So far as we know man is the highest intelligence.[17]

Ingersoll promoted evolution as an explanation of the origin of the present forms of life on earth:

> When I first heard of that doctrine [evolution], I did not like it. My heart was filled with sympathy for those people who have nothing to be proud of except ancestors. I thought how terrible this will be upon the nobility of the old world. Think of their being forced to trace their

ancestry back to the duke Orang Outang, or to the princess Chimpanzee. After thinking it over, I came to the conclusion that I liked that doctrine.[18]

Ingersoll also recognized early on that science and religion were in an inevitable and serious conflict. He states:

There is an irrepressible conflict between Christianity and science, and both cannot long inhabit the same brain. You cannot harmonize evolution and the atonement. The survival of the fittest does away with original sin.[19]

Politics and Civil Rights

Ingersoll was for many years the confidant of presidents. Among his close friends were James A. Garfield and Rutherford B. Hayes. Ingersoll had first come to national attention when he gave the nominating speech for James G. Blaine at the Republican Convention of 1876. Although Ingersoll was often interviewed by the press about his views on politics, only once did he seek political office himself. There was some talk that Hayes was going to nominate him to be ambassador to Germany, but this never happened. In short, it is difficult to know what sort of influence Ingersoll had on politics by means of private talks with individual politicians. On the issue of civil rights, however, we know exactly where Ingersoll stood. He was for equality of the races long before it was respectable: He said

I am willing to be on an equality in all hotels, in all cars, in all theaters, with colored people. I make no distinction of race. . . . I am willing to associate with all good, clean persons, irrespective of complexion. . . . Any government that makes a distinction on account of color, is a disgrace to the age in which we live.[20]

The Role of Government

In discussing the role of *government*, I use the term in a very broad sense, and will combine here a number of concerns that do not fit in neatly elsewhere. Again, we will see that Ingersoll was saying things that now seem to be commonplace, but were then distinctly minority viewpoints.

While ecology and the environment were not concerns of the last century, Ingersoll gave voice to at least the concern that man be responsible for his planet.

Being satisfied that the supernatural does not exist, man should turn his entire attention to the affairs of this world, to the facts in nature.

And, first of all, he should avoid waste—waste of energy, waste of wealth.[21]

Although Ingersoll died long before Prohibition was instituted, he did make a comment about it that turned out to be correct.

I am opposed to prohibition and always have been, and hope always to be. I do not want the legislature to interfere in these matters. I do not believe that the people can be made temperate by law.[22]

Ingersoll was a civil libertarian, although the term was not used back then. He was opposed to any limitation of free speech, especially speech criticizing religion. He was opposed to any laws against "blasphemy," for example.[23] However, there was one area in which Ingersoll showed his Victorian background: He was not in favor of allowing "obscene literature" to be sent through the mail. Naturally he was strongly against including freethough literature in the classification of the obscene, as Anthony Comstock wished to do.[24]

Social welfare was handled mostly by private charitable organizations and individuals in the last century. Robert Ingersoll was always quick to point out that unbelievers were often generous in their charitable contributions. The idea that a religious outlook was a prerequisite to charitableness was foolish.[25] Similarly, there should be no religious test for public office.[26]

Ingersoll's "creed" was a sort of a summation of his view of life. It was issued as a wall hanging after his death.

Happiness is the only good. The place to be happy is here. The time to be happy is now. The way to be happy is to make others so.[27]

No humanist of today could have said it better or more concisely.

Ingersoll's influence, as I have tried to show, was broad yet subtle. He spread the modern humanist outlook to vast groups of people before it was easy to do so, and before many were ready for that type of world view. Still, his vast popularity enabled him to help do what so few of us have ever been able to do, namely, to mold the world into a better place than the one that currently exists. Sticking to this "mission," born of honesty and concern, cost Ingersoll dearly. He effectively prevented himself from obtaining political office after he became attorney general of Illinois. That troubled him somewhat, as he viewed politics as a way of helping him accomplish his aims even more effectively. Still, how fortunate we are to have lost a politician and gained a true hero. Ingersoll attained the only immortality that humans can probably have: He remains in our memories long after he is gone from this world.

Notes

1. James Reed, *From Private Vice to Public Virtue: The Birth Control Movement and American Society Since 1830*, New York: Basic Books, 1978, p. 129. See also *Margaret Sanger: An Autobiography*, New York: W. W. Norton, 1938, pp. 20–21.

2. R. G. Ingersoll, *Works* (Dresden Edition), New York: Dresden Publishers, 1900, (12 volumes), volume 4, pp. 502–504.

3. *Works*, 1, p. 365.

4. *Works*, 5, p. 125.

5. *Works*, 12, p. 39.

6. *Works*, 9, p. 306.

7. *Works*, 12, p. 296.

8. Clark Braden, *Ingersoll Unmasked: A Scathing and Fearless Exposé* of His Real Life, Lexington, Ky.: Blue Grass Publ. Co., 1900.

9. See, for example, The Field/Ingersoll Discussion (*Works*, 6, pp. 121–218); The Ingersoll/Gladstone Discussion (*Works*, 6, pp. 221–462); and the discussion with Cardinal Gibbons (*Works*, 6, pp. 397–452).

10. See, for example, *Works*, 3, pp. 311–319.

11. *Works*, 3, pp. 307–395.

12. *Works*, 1, p. 73.

13. *Works*, 8, p. 247.

14. See "Atheism" and "Agnosticism" in Gordon Stein, ed., *The Encyclopedia of Unbelief* (Buffalo, N.Y.: Prometheus Books, 1985).

15. See his talks before the Congress of the American Secular Union, *Works*, volume 4, pp. 211–235 and volume 12, pp. 239–244. Also, see his talk to the Convention of the National Liberal League, *Works*, volume 12, pp. 233–235. Ingersoll served as the president of the American Secular Union and of the National Liberal League for several years.

16. *Works*, 4, p. 505.

17. *Works*, 1, pp. 59–60.

18. *Works*, 1, p. 393.

19. *Works*, 8, p. 225.

20. *Works*, 8, p. 136.

21. *Works*, 4, p. 124.

22. *Works*, 11, p. 271.

23. For example, in *Works*, 5, pp. 49–50.

24. *Works*, 7, p. 346; volume 12, pp. 215–230.

25. *Works*, 7, p. 315.

26. *Works*, 5, pp. 303–304.

27. *Works*, 8, p. 478.

I

The Minister's Son

Robert Green Ingersoll was born on August 11, 1833 in Dresden, New York, and died on July 21, 1899 in Dobbs Ferry, New York. He lived out his sixty-six years in the nineteenth century, one of the grand centuries for weal and woe in the nation and the world.

In America the great event of that century was the Civil War: It took the lives of more than half a million men, North and South, devastated wide areas, and left a legacy of enduring hatred. It decided that the Union would be united and all blacks would be free. The agricultural South, shorn of the slavocracy, lay prostrate, and the industrial North could flourish without interference. Villages bloomed into towns and cities, and the wheels of industry turned out a profusion of comforts and luxuries without precedent. Steam railroads crisscrossed the nation from the Atlantic to the Pacific; the telegraph and the telephone penetrated every community; transocean cables reached out to faraway lands. The United States, newly united in spite of tensions between its sections, became the richest country in the world. It broke the bonds of continental restraint, acquired Hawaii and the Philippines, and joined the struggle among the established powers for hegemony over the planet.

The post-war epoch is known as the Reconstruction Period and as the Gilded Age after the satiric novel of that name by Mark Twain and Charles Dudley Warner. Progress and Poverty walked hand in hand. The moral tone of government was notoriously low; offices and votes were bought and sold. There would be nothing comparable until the Teapot Dome scandals of the twenties. Four million emancipated blacks, aspiring to human dignity, were abandoned by their liberators to peonage and terrorism. The titans who created modern America have gone down in history as the Robber Barons for their no-holds-barred extermination of competitors, corruption of government officials, and pursuit of profit in disregard of employees and the public. Debt-burdened farmers fought a losing battle with the railroads and bankers; workers plunged into nationwide strikes, particularly those employed in railroads and mines. Government stood by, wedded to old ideas that such troubles were beyond political accommodation excepting suppression by police and the army. The country did not lack for reformers who proclaimed all sorts of remedies including free love and anarchism. There was no calm sanctuary in the churches, for here too the air was full of turbulence.

Robert Ingersoll was a child of the century, a man of his times, the product and agent of its social forces. He earned his credentials as a colonel in the Union Army. In the Reconstruction period no man, not even the president, was more conspicuous and better known, more loved and more hated.

Ingersoll burst on the national scene at the Republican convention of 1876, when he nominated James G. Blaine, his Plumed Knight, for the presidential candidacy. His speech is enshrined in history as the greatest nominating speech ever made (not in competition with Bryan's Cross of Gold speech, which was on a committee report). He was instantly recognized as a great orator and soon thereafter recognized as the greatest orator of the age. Politicians who would not nominate him for the proverbial position as dog-catcher implored him to speak for them, and he seldom refused when he was on their side. He took the stump for every Republican presidential candidate from Grant to McKinley, excepting Blaine himself (with whom he had fallen out over the Star Route prosecution). In streets and fields, in tents and under the open sky, rain or shine, he exhorted the masses to vote Republican and save the country. His political speeches on the national stage reflect the issues of the period and the sectionalism, ideology, demagogy, and idealism of the Republican party. On Decoration Day and the Fourth of July no man was in more demand to stir holiday patriots with visions of battle-scarred Old Glory waving over the land of the free and the home of the brave.

The most sensational courtroom battle of the Gilded Age was the Star Route prosecution, the first trial being held in 1882 and the second in 1883. The Star Route case is a microcosm of the age in its shabbier aspect. The Garfield–Arthur administrations, led by Blaine, Garfield's Secretary of State, mounted a spectacular enterprise to cleanse the reputation of the Republican party as a cesspool of corruption by sacrificing at the altar of purity a handful of marginal profiteers. The government was so certain of victory that it undertook verbatim publication of transcripts of the trials; they stand as monuments of its bad judgment and hypocrisy. Ingersoll and other counsel represented the defendants, and the best lawyers of New York and Philadelphia were special counsel for the government. The charge was conspiracy to defraud the government on contracts for mail deliveries in the hinterland. The odds were heavily against the defendants. The whole weight of government was against them and a public sickened by corruption was ravenous for culprits. Nevertheless, the formidable prosecution was unable to prove guilt to a jury of ordinary citizens inspired by Ingersoll to think for themselves. The Star Route record is the only full length exhibit available of Ingersoll's versatile brilliance at the bar. (Another notable but less well-known case is the Reynolds blasphemy trial in 1887, which Ingersoll lost although his summation is a masterpiece of courtroom eloquence for freedom of the mind.)

It is not because of his prowess at the bar, his journeyman work for the Republican party, and his celebration of the American dream that Ingersoll deserves a substantial place in history, however. He was the greatest freethinker of modern times. Paine the pamphleteer, the deist of the eighteenth century, leads to Ingersoll the orator, the agnostic of the nineteenth. To the rationalistic arguments of his predecessors against revealed religion Ingersoll added the higher criticism, nineteenth-century science, and his own reservoirs of rhetorical power, bringing freethought to a new plateau of radicalism. His principal target in the old orthodoxy was the doctrine of damnation and hell. He took on the whole religious establishment and held it at bay. Over and over he traveled up and down and through the entire country, New York to California, Maine to Florida, preaching to thousands, who gladly paid the price of admission to hear a new gospel—the religion of humanity, of science, of usefulness. He was not dismayed by personal abuse, boycott, or the hazards of prosecution and physical violence. His devotion to the cause, his courage, his perfect unflappability drew admiration even from some of his critics. He did not convert the nation or a large part of it, but when his work was done the specter of fire and brimstone had vanished from many minds. No one was afraid to declare himself a freethinker and a member of the ongoing crusade against belief in supernaturalism.

Ingersoll was born to an old American family. He could, if he wished, trace his ancestry back some eight generations to a Puritan commoner forbear from whom descended farmers, millers, craftsmen, and traders. His father, John Ingersoll, was a graduate of Middlebury College and an ordained Congregational minister. His mother, born Mary Livingston, the daughter of Judge Livingston, was related to the prominent Livingston family of colonial and revolutionary days. She is described as a tall, beautiful woman, devoted to her family, and holding compassionate views on the "Negro question." Robert was the last of five children, in order: Ruth Anne, John Livingston, Mary Jane, Ebenezer Clark (familiarly Ebon or Clark), and Robert Green. His middle name was in honor of Beriah Green, a minister friend of the Reverend John and a prominent abolitionist (L. D. Avery, *A Genealogy of the Ingersoll Family of America*, 1-217; Herman E. Kittredge, *Ingersoll: A Biographical Appreciation*, 8-14; Edward Garstin Smith, *The*

Life and Reminiscences of Robert G. Ingersoll, 5–26).

Dresden is situated in the beautiful lake country of south central New York near Seneca Falls, where the first women's rights convention was held in 1848. These facts of his birthplace were unimportant to Ingersoll himself, for he left the village as an infant and seldom returned.

Excepting a year in New York City during Robert's infancy the Reverend Ingersoll's career as minister and active head of his family was spent under frontier conditions. His income never amounted to more than two hundred dollars a year; a parsonage was not always available. The family living style was plain. The children studied the three Rs at the common school, did their chores, played in the woods and along the streams in the summers, skated and rode sleds in the snow-bound winters. Early to bed and early to rise. No liquor or tobacco disgraced the home. There were no public amusements for the family, no frivolous private entertainments, hardly any socializing. Occasionally a revivalist might drop in and soon host and guest were engaged in long discussions on such anxious issues as infant baptism.

The Reverend Ingersoll was an evangelical, or, to use the language of the twentieth century, a fundamentalist Protestant. He believed in the literal inerrancy of the Bible, the divinity of Christ, the virgin birth, original sin, vicarious atonement, physical resurrection, and heaven and hell. A strict Congregationalist (or a New Presbyterian when the parish was organized on Presbyterian lines), he believed that it was better not to go to church at all than to attend a Methodist meeting. He did not subscribe to Calvinism or predestination, but preached a very real and eternal hellfire awaiting unrepentant sinners. He had no sympathy for the newfangled doctrine of perfectionism (that faith in Jesus purified the believer of sin), and he opposed slavery on religious grounds.

The Reverend Ingersoll, like his son Robert, was a big, strong man, and he preached a vigorous gospel. He moved dramatically right and left behind the pulpit, walking down the aisles to confront the congregation *en masse* or an unfortunate individual face to face. The world was full of sin, and his task was to save sinners, not please them. Some parishioners were entranced by the total commitment and could hardly abide the interval between morning and evening sermons. Others balked at the high standards or at opposition to slavery as a Christian duty. The Reverend Ingersoll served some congregations only for six months, others no more than two or three years. He was continually on the move to new pastures.

The Ingersolls came to Dresden three months before Robert was born and left three months afterwards. In 1835 the Reverend Ingersoll was called to the Free Church at Cazenovia, New York. Here Mrs. Ingersoll, worn out, died at the age of thirty-six. The preservation of the family fell to the girls, Ruth Anne and Mary Jane, ages fourteen and nine respectively, whom their brother Dr. John Ingersoll would describe as "noble Sister Ruth" and "loving tho impulsive Mary" (To Robert, Aug. 11, 1895, L.C.).

Robert was not three years old when his mother died, but in mature years he referred to her death as one of the climactic events of his life. "My mother died when I was but a child, and from that day—the darkest of my life—her memory has been within my heart a sacred thing, and I have felt, through all the years, her kisses on my lips" (*Works*, V, 149; Interviews on Talmage). In his first encounter with death he had lost his mother, who had shown him the meaning of love. Perhaps here began the obsession with death that was at the core of his being, as well as his adoration of women in general and the domestic life of a complete family.

The Reverend Ingersoll was not a happy man. His portrait reflects a fine sad face, smooth shaven, the lower lip slightly forward like his famous son's. There was much for him to be sad about. The world was headed for perdition and there was little he could do about it. He worried about the spiritual health of his flock, and sometimes he worried about the daily bread for his family. He loved his children but they were always getting into trouble, especially Robert and Clark. (John was all right, ten years older than Robert and eight years older than Clark, a dear brother but not a pal in their escapades.) At the house Clark and Robert did their chores without evasion or complaint, sat quietly cheek by cheek poring over the *Useful Book of Knowledge*. On the loose they were different. They did not always arrive at school when they set out in the morning, too often they turned up as unwelcome guests in other people's orchards, and, worst of all, they lied about their misdeeds. The desperate widower believed in the biblical adage: Spare the rod and spoil the child. With heavy heart and heavy hand he laid on the punishment.

It would be said by some of his critics that Ingersoll's entire warfare against revealed religion was a reaction against a sadistic father who personified Christianity. This Ingersoll vigorously denied. He loved his father and could look back with a smile at the paddle in the minister's hand. "My father was a man of great natural tenderness, and loved his children almost to insanity. The little severity he had was produced by his religion. Like most men of his time, he thought Solomon knew something about raising children. For my part, I think he should have known better than to place the least confidence in the advice of a man so utterly idiotic as to imagine he could be happy with seven hundred wives" (Letter, *Utica Herald*, Nov. 5, 1877).

Of all his lectures, Robert Ingersoll was fondest of "Liberty of Man, Woman, and Child." Here he describes with disarming drollery what it was like to be a minister's son Sunday after Sunday in rural antebellum America.

In the olden time, they thought some days were too good for a child to enjoy himself. When I was a boy Sunday was considered altogether too holy to be happy in. Sunday used to commence then when the sun went down on Saturday night. We commenced at that time for the purpose of getting a good ready, and when the sun fell below the horizon Saturday evening, there was a darkness fell upon the house ten thousand times deeper than that of night. Nobody said a pleasant word; nobody laughed; nobody smiled; the child that looked the sickest was regarded as the most pious. That night you could not even crack hickory nuts. If you were caught chewing gum it was only another evidence of the total depravity of the human heart. It was an exceedingly solemn night. Dyspepsia was in the very air you breathed. Everybody looked sad and mournful. I have noticed all my life that many people think they have religion when they are troubled with dyspepsia. If there could be found an absolute specific for that disease, it would be the hardest blow the church ever received.

On Sunday morning the solemnity increased. Then we went to church. The minister was in a pulpit about twenty feet high, with a little sounding-board above him, and he commenced at "firstly" and went on and on and on to about "twenty-thirdly." Then he made a few remarks by way of application; and then took a general view of the subject, and in about two hours reached the last chapter of Revelation.

In those days, no matter how cold the weather was, there was no fire in the church. It was thought to be a kind of sin to be comfortable while you were thanking God. The first church that ever had a stove in it in New England divided on that account. So the first church in which they sang by note was torn in fragments.

After the sermon we had an intermission. Then came the catechism with the chief end of man. We went through with that. We sat in a row with our feet coming in about six inches off the floor. The minister asked us if we knew that we all deserved to go to hell, and we all answered "yes." The minister then asked us if we would be willing to go to hell if it was God's will, and every little liar shouted "yes." Then the same sermon was preached once more, commencing at the other end going back. After that, we started for home, sad and solemn—overpowered with the wisdom displayed in the scheme of the atonement. When we got home, if we had been good boys, and the weather was warm, sometimes they would take us out to the graveyard to cheer us up a little. It did cheer me. When I looked at the sunken tombs and the leaning stones, and read the half-defaced inscriptions through the moss of silence and forgetfulness, it was a great comfort. The reflection came to my mind that the observance of the Sabbath could not last always. Sometimes they would sing that beautiful hymn in which occurs those cheerful lines:

> "Where congregations ne'er break up
> And Sabbath never ends."

These lines, I think, prejudiced me a little against even heaven.

A different mood pervades another memory. Once Robert and Clark on their own attended a revival service conducted by a Free Will Baptist preacher. The text was the parable of Dives and Lazarus. The homespun preacher was eloquent and terrifying. He depicted the luxury of Dives and the misery of Lazarus on earth, the suffering of Dives in hell and the bliss of Lazarus in heaven. He assumed the personality of Dives and screamed in vain, as he had been screaming for eighteen centuries and would scream for endless ages hence, for Lazarus to come and dip his finger in water and bring a moment of relief to the parched tongue of the eternally doomed sinner.

> For the first time I understood the dogma of eternal pain—appreciated "the glad tidings of great joy." For the first time my imagination grasped the height and depth of the Christian horror. Then I said, "It is a lie, and I hate your religion. If it is true, I hate your God."
>
> From that day I have had no fear, no doubt. For me, on that day, the flames of hell were quenched. From that day I have passionately hated every orthodox creed. That sermon did some good. (*Works*, IV, "Why I am an Agnostic," 15)

In the early 1840s Reverend Ingersoll and his children were living in Ashtabula, Ohio. It was here in the declamation exercises at school that Robert tried his wings at public speaking. He recited Praed's song of childhood, "I remember, I remember" (*Letters*, 580), and it was probably here in his first original speech, laboriously memorized, that he forgot his lines and left the stage in disgrace (Interview, *Indianapolis News*, Feb. 19, 1892). He was a spirited, outgoing, popular boy. More than fifty years later, a classmate, Dr. Samuel Wetmore, could recall how attractive he was: "Life seemed to burst out with all the effulgence that intelligence and goodness could portray in a noble character" (Kittredge, 26). Ashtabula was the last place where the family would live under one roof. Reverend Ingersoll had married again but the marriage was not a success. When the Ingersolls moved to Aurora, Illinois, in November 1844, the second Mrs. Ingersoll was not with them, a scandalous state of affairs for a man of the cloth. The family was broken up and boarded around and the pastorate ended the following May (*Aurora Beacon News*, April 8, 1928; April 15, 1928; "Lutz" White, "Now and Then").

Reverend Ingersoll appears as pastor of the Old Presbyterian Church in Greenville, Illinois, in 1851. Robert attended school in the basement of the church, and "his old classmates, several of whom still live in Greenville, say that he was an exceptionally bright scholar, a fine grammarian and linguist, especially gifted in the use of metaphor" (*Boston Transcript*, Aug. 19, 1903). His ambition exceeded his talent. His gift for metaphor was still in the bud, as witness the lines "April 13" signed RGI on the beauties of the Midwest, where he says

> Thou glorious world of bloom,
>   Where bending flowers gently blow
>   And o'er thy breast their leaflets throw,
> In beauty's soft perfume.
>   (*Greenville Journal*, June 1852)

The family was falling apart—too many mouths to feed—and the hapless Reverend Ingersoll could not hold it together. Robert hit the road, wandering about. At age nineteen he was a vagrant in Pennsylvania, at the end of his tether. He poured his heart out to his brother John: "I am hard up for money I tell you. I have not got a cent in the world and I owe for board and I can't get away and can get nothing to do" (Conneautville, Pa., April 12, 1852, *Letters*, 509). He had planned to meet his father in Toledo, but neither father nor son had money for the trip.

The clouds lifted. Soon he was back in Illinois, teaching school in Mount Vernon. He did not like the town. Some fifteen years later, being briefly in Mount Vernon as attorney general of Illinois, he indulged in a "vision" of how desolate life had been and still was there.

> I see shapeless felt hats, surmounting heads covered with long lank "yaller" hair—the hair falling down upon a shirt open in front showing a breast covered with dirty frowsy moss—and there are knit suspenders holding up jean breeches, and below the breeches I see brogans with the toes of the wearers thrust through the upper leather. I see dogs "follering"— I see women in sun bonnets, and homespun dresses—I see sore eyes, and long flabby breasts, hanging down upon leathery bellies—the bellies supported by dirty legs and the legs sustained by spraddling feet—I hear people say "I have saw" and "I've hearn" and "I seed." They talk about "his'n" and "her'n" and "your'n"—I see meeting houses without windows, graveyards without fences—dooryards without grass—without vines, without flowers. I see people without education, without thought—without ambition, who seem to be waiting for death. I see young women without beauty and without youth—the youngest are as old as the oldest (To Clark, June 6, 1867, *Letters*, 140).

Robert was not happy with his own conditions in Mount Vernon. He told John that the pay was not much: thirty "scholars" at $2.50 each for a six-weeks quarter. "I am not making money very fast but can manage to get enough to eat & that's all." He weighed 153 pounds and, though nearly six feet tall, considered himself fat (Jan. 14, 1853, *Letters*, 379). He had one benefit: He had time to read. The world of great writers was opening to him. He enjoyed Goldsmith, Shelley, Poe, Coleridge, Keats. His favorite authors were Burns and Shakespeare. "I know more than three fourths of all Burns ever wrote by heart. I like him the best of all because he wrote the most natural of all. . . . I read in old Billy Shakespeare almost every night. I like to read Richard 3rd, the Taming of the Shrew. I have read them so often that I have learned them by heart" (To John, Sept. 29, 1852; Jan. 14, 1853, *Letters*, 373, 379).

Burns and Shakespeare were more than favorite authors. They were lifelong inspirations. Ingersoll could never forget the great moments when he learned of them. He discovered Burns when he went to the cobbler to have the shoes he was wearing, his only shoes, repaired. The old Scottish cobbler put down the book he was reading and Ingersoll picked it up to pass the time. It was Burns. "The first man that let up the curtain in my mind, that ever opened a blind, that ever allowed a little sunshine to struggle in, was Robert Burns." In a few days he had his own copy. At a village inn in Illinois, waiting for supper, he and other travellers listened to an old man reading from Shakespeare. "I was filled with wonder." He had to have a copy, no matter the cost. "The next day I bought a copy for four dollars. My God! more than the national debt" (*Works*, XII, Speech in Honor of Anton Seidl, New York, Feb. 2, 1895, 172). Now in possession of Shakespeare, the greatest student of humanity, and Burns, the greatest singer of common life, Ingersoll called Shakespeare his Bible, Burns his prayer-book.

Again on the move, in late 1853 Ingersoll was teaching school in rural Tennessee. He reported to his brother John, chiding him for not answering his letters. He gave some family news, was "doing very well" at the school, but was lonesome. It was his first contact with a slave state, a different kind of civilization, a shocking experience. "The very air seems to be chained. Nothing but nigers [sic], nigers all the time." He had seen a slave auction where a mother was separated from her children of about two and three years old. He had checked the law of the state and quotes it to the effect that no slave child under the age of eight shall be separated from its mother. But what can you expect in a state where all the grand jurors are slaveholders and stick together? He noted that *Uncle Tom's Cabin* was playing well in New Orleans, St. Louis, Memphis, and Nashville; perhaps it would improve the condition of the slaves, which was bad enough but not as bad as it was twenty years ago. "People here ask me 'once and a while' if I think slavery wrong & I tell them I do & that I believe it is wrong enough to damn the whole of them and they take it in good part." He sent some verses and begged for gentle criticism (Waverly's Humphrey's Co., Dec. 29, 1853, *Letters*, 106).

Robert Ingersoll was not destined to be a village schoolmaster, a village Hampden. His mental life was bursting at the seams; he had ideas on the times; he was ambitious. The conventional path to fame and fortune, to a role in public affairs, the path of Douglas and Lincoln, was the law. It was easy to become a lawyer. By 1854 Ingersoll was back in Illinois, reading law at Marion in the offices of William Allen, a former member of Congress, and his son William Justine Allen, and at the same time holding a job as clerk in the county government. He had settled down but not in a rut. He did not appear to be working or studying too hard

(Kittredge, 37). There was always time to lounge about in the courthouse or at the hotel, entertaining and edifying one and all with jokes and stories and readings and reviews of great books. He was living with his sister Mary Jane, and when she married and had a daughter, who but Uncle Bobby would teach Ciss to walk, to talk, to read. On December 20, 1854, he appeared at the courthouse in Mount Vernon bearing a certificate of good character, answered a few elementary questions of law, according to custom stood his examiners to a round of drinks at a tavern, and became a member of the Illinois bar.

To learn the practical ropes of the profession, Robert and Clark started a law practice in a small town, Shawneetown. There they joined the Masons.[1] Reverend Ingersoll had been divorced, had remarried, was again a widower, and was on his own as an evangelist in the Old Northwest, now Minnesota and Wisconsin. On June 20, 1857, Robert wrote to John, anxious about their father. "He is well & apparently contented and happy. I hope he is, God knows it makes me unhappy to think that father is so far away, no one to care for him—no one to take care of him should he be sick." Legal business was prospering. Robert was liberal in praise of his older brother at the bar: "Clark is well and doing well as ever and he always will do well and nothing can stop him. The secret of his success is Energy. He is as energetic as Napoleon ever was. I am lazy, careless and fat" (*Letters*, 108). Robert always disparaged himself by comparison with Clark.

All work and no play would have made Bob a dull boy. If one looked at the big tow-headed youngster and his boon companion Buck Casey at play or horseplay in Shawneetown, one might have supposed that Bob was portraying himself accurately as an indifferent lawyer (*Chicago News*, Nov. 11, 1897). Bob and Buck might warm up with convivial refreshment and then venture out on the little town shut up for the night. They might march up and down the streets, reciting alternate parts from Shakespeare at the top of their lungs, or they might stop at corners for Buck to cry hosannahs to the sky and Bob to roar amens. In fact Robert was no less diligent than Clark; it was simply in his nature never to be or to seem to be under pressure or in a hurry. It could be said of him, adapting Chaucer:

> Never so busy a man as he there was,
> And yet he never seemed busy as he was.

In the late 1850s the Ingersoll brothers moved their office to a metropolitan center. Peoria was the second largest city in Illinois, a railroad and shipping station set in rich farmland in the central part of the state on the Illinois River. It was a thriving community of some fifteen thousand inhabitants. Robert came to Peoria in February 1858. Clark, who had married, had preceded him and was settled in his own housekeeping.

Robert contracted for his meals at the Peoria Hotel at fifteen dollars per month and slept in the office.

The city had been waiting for the firm of Ingersoll and Ingersoll. People found their way in increasing numbers up the outside staircase to the new lawyers on Main Street. The legal fees were a real bargain. You could get a deed for a dollar, a chattel mortgage for five dollars, a lease for a dollar and a half, a power of attorney for two dollars. A divorce might cost you $25. If the fee for defending you was $50, you could pay $3.50 down and sign a note for $46.50. If you had a case in Pekin requiring a continuance (Pekin being about fifteen miles away) that would cost you $10 for the lawyer and $2 for the horse and carriage. Business expenses were correspondingly low: a lot of oats, $15; gas fixtures, $50; office stove, $8. Ingersoll and Ingersoll had to keep up appearances of youth and vigor. As if with an eye to history Clark notes in the Day Book on March 12, 1858, "I pulled from Robert's head about 20 silver gray hairs" (Library of Congress, hereinafter L.C.). The new lawyers were as competent as they were inexpensive. Their practice grew, particularly in the criminal field, where they had no competition.

Robert Ingersoll came to legal practice in Peoria fully equipped with the arts of the profession. He knew at least as much law as his brethren at the bar and had a self-confidence that could not be shaken. He was nearly six feet tall and built in proportion. As a gregarious man he knew people, could coddle friendly witnesses and cajole hostile ones, talk to juries face to face, and treat judges with respect but not subservience. He went straight to the heart of the matter, molding the rules of the law to the natural justice of the case, which invariably coincided with the interest of his client. A great advocate had come to judgment. "He played with words," said a fellow lawyer, George Foster, "as a child plays with flowers, an artist with the keys of a piano. His voice now painted a word picture of tender thoughts, now sent forth grand harmonies that shook the souls of strong men and insensibly drew them close and closer still to this matchless orator" (Quoted in E. G. Smith, 123). Adlai Stevenson, future vice-president of the United States and grandfather of the Adlai Stevenson of the twentieth century, met Ingersoll at the Peoria bar in April 1859. "He was then," wrote Stevenson in his memoirs, "under thirty years of age, of splendid physique, magnetic in the fullest significance of the word, and one of the most attractive and agreeable of men." Through the mist of years Stevenson looked back to Metamora, the old county seat: "Rarely at any time or place have words been spoken more eloquent [sic] than fell from the lips of Lincoln and Ingersoll in that now departed Court House, in the years gone by" (*Something of Men I Have Known*, 225).

We glimpse two criminal cases. Two adjoining farmers got into an argument over their boundary; one struck the other on the head with a spade, killing him. At the trial, in representing the defendant, Ingersoll did not bring in the wife and children. Instead, he painted a portrait of the wife at the cottage gate, one child in her arms, two clinging at her side, waiting, waiting, for husband and father. There was not a dry eye in the courtroom. Judge and jury were crying. "I was crying myself," said Ingersoll. He swept the jury with his gaze and asked them, Would they send this man home to the poor woman waiting at the gate? "We will!"shouted the foreman, and they did (*Truth Seeker*, Dec, 12, 1896. Editor Foote's Letters). The liberated defendant obtained pictures of Ingersoll and the jury and hung them on his wall, his Jesus Christ and the Twelve Apostles.

The young barrister was not always victorious. An unhappy farmhand set fire to his employer's barn. Ingersoll had his client given a very close haircut and argued in court, with a lecture on phrenology, that the defendant's cranium showed him an idiot not responsible for his actions. The jury was not impressed and the defendant went to the penitentiary for six years (*Peoria Journal*, March 20, 1881, reporting on the trial of Feb. 18, 1859).

What to do with energy overflowing? Ingersoll was a bachelor, and his free time, which he always found, was his own. One night he and his pals celebrated some unrecorded event or other. Leaving the tavern they requisitioned empty boxes and barrels in front of stores closed for the day and built a huge bonfire in the public square. They were not arrested but they had to appear in court the next morning, where Bob talked the authorities out of punishment (Macdonald, Appendix, 177).

Then there was the phenomenal meeting of the bar association held in Woodford in 1859. Stevenson described it in a straight-faced chapter entitled "A Bar Meeting Still in Session." The bar had met to consider a revision of the rules of court. When there was no further business, a motion for adjournment was made. Ingersoll and his faction were in the majority, and voted No. The venerable chairman inquired, "What is the further pleasure of the meeting?" Absolute silence, as in prayer. Motion to adjourn. Defeated. Silence. Motion to adjourn. Defeated. The chairman muttered an exclamation "not to be found in the Methodist book of discipline," stood up, and stormed out of the meeting. The other members straggled out. That meeting has never been officially adjourned (Stevenson, 381).

Ingersoll emerged in Peoria resembling Sabatini's Scaramouche, as he was born with a gift of laughter and a sense that the world was mad. Starting life with an innate sense of humor he would find much to laugh at in the world around him, and some would be offended by his levity. But if life was a comedy, it was a tragi-comedy. An Ingersoll audience might laugh at one moment and melt in tears at the next.

In letters to John, now a village physician in Wisconsin, Robert rambles on about personal and public themes. He has been ailing but is guardedly optimistic. "I have had the ague all winter although as soon as spring comes I shall get clear of that and probably take something worse" (Feb.

26, 1859, *Letters*, 109). He is worried (and this worry would be a life-long undercurrent of his mind) about death and dying. "My hair is growing gray right fast. I believe that by the time I am thirty I shall be real gray. . . . There is no thought more dreadful to me than that of getting old except death" (March 23, 1859, *Letters*, 509). He has a strong sense of family; they have known hard times together: "As a family we have had a great deal of trouble—more than almost any other, but I hope that our troubles are nearly at an end, that we are going to have at least a tolerable share of comfort the remainder of our lives. Dear father however is still adrift, I do not know what is to be done—after a little while I want him to come here and live with us, but some way he cannot content himself unless preaching, and preaching in revivals all winter" (March 23, 1859, *Letters*, 509). He asked his brother to "spank or kiss the baby for me, I rather you would kiss." Legal business is coming along fine. "We have a very nice office & lighted with gas. Gas as you know is an excellent thing in law, in fact indispensable" (Feb. 26, 1859, *Letters*, 109). The firm has had much success in criminal practice but the real rewards of the profession are elsewhere. They are beginning to meet the right people and receive larger fees. "We already have the confidence of the substantial men—by substantial I mean those who have the spondoolicks, and of all men they are the men to have on your side" (March 21, 1859. *Letters*, 510).[2] He had not been a grind at the law. He had enjoyed sleigh riding until the snow turned to mush (Feb. 26, 1859, *Letters*, 109). He traced the course of spring as it came up in locust trees and peach trees and went on from Shawneetown to Peoria to the northern country where John lived (May 6, 1859, *Letters*, 58).

On the growing political crisis in state and nation Ingersoll had taken his general bearings as a Douglas Democrat. Slavery was an evil but the question of slavery in the territories should be handled with due regard for the preservation of the Union and the rights of the free inhabitants of the territories to self-determination. The idea of pushing for the exclusion of slavery from the territories as a national program made him angry, so angry that he overstated his opposition with a splutter of Shakespearean rhetoric: "As for myself I think Douglas is right on the 'Great Bugger-boo' though I don't care one cent whether Kansas is a slave state or not. I never want to live there, and I am not going to bother myself about people 'clothed in the livery of the Sun' " (March 23, 1859, *Letters*, 510; Angell, 258).

Robert was sensitive to John's conventional beliefs in religion. Whatever skepticism Robert may have been developing in 1858, he looked upon religion with an amused detachment that left room for pious amenities. He reported that the town was full of "preaching drinking praying [sic] and swearing" (*Letters*, 109). Pious prayer meetings were held every day and night in every church; he had been to services three times in two years, and never in Peoria. "I suppose God has heard more nonsense in the last six months than he ever heard before in the whole course of his life, and by this time likely regrets that he made man—at least with the power of speech" (March 23, 1858, *Letters*, 510). These letters to John end with pious tags: "May the Good God be with you all is the prayer of Your Aff Bro" (March 3, 1858, *Letters*, 510). "God bless you all is the prayer of your brother" (May 6, 1858, *Letters*, 111).

The elder Ingersoll finally retired from his labors for the church and came to live with Clark's family in Peoria. He had always encouraged his children to be honest in their opinions even if the opinions were repugnant to him. In conversations with Robert and Clark during the winter months of 1858–1859 he showed that he had travelled some distance from the rigidities of his original creed. He no longer believed in the literal inerrancy of the Scriptures and the dogma of eternal punishment.

He died in Peoria on May 1, 1859, at the age of sixty-seven. It fell to Robert, not Clark, to send the news to John.[3] A sudden lung seizure had taken the elder Ingersoll away in a few hours. He had died serene and confident in his redemption from sin. "He went away as peacefully and quietly as when a child he sank to rest upon his Mother's bosom. And we were all orphans." Robert and Clark stayed with the body two days and two nights, declining the offers of friends to watch with them. The funeral sermon at the Congregational Church was on the text from the Psalms, "Precious in the sight of the Lord is the death of his saints."

Brother spoke to brother in common grief. Comforting was the thought that the minister's earthly troubles were over. "He is freed from all sorrow—from all suffering & from all care. He has escaped from an unfriendly and unappreciative world, from malice, slander & detraction." The head of the family was gone and the son spoke in the old spirit of the family. "He sleeps with the Patriarchs and Apostles, with Abraham, Isaiah, and Paul. . . . He has conquered the grave, he has robbed death of its sting, and Death has robbed him of nothing but his sorrows." He hoped that his father would look down from heaven upon his children "for whom he has made the very air tremulous with prayer from our cradles to his grave." Let them follow his example, "inspired by the same spirit of universal kindness and love." And so, "goodbye, May God and the spirit of our Father be with you."

Thirty-nine years to the day after his father's death—Ingersoll had a religious feeling about anniversaries—he wrote to his daughters from Chicago, where he was on a lecture tour against the religion of his father. "Thirty-nine years ago today my dear father died. It all comes back to me now—all that he said and did. I see again the ashen pallor of his face—hear his last words—his last sigh—his last farewell. It all comes back—how grand he looked in death—how serene and how satisfied. Death is a wonderful sculptor. The absolute repose—the dignity—the perfect content are far beyond all human art. How sad my father's life was! It almost breaks my heart to think of it—Well—it has happened—

nothing can change the past" (May 1, 1898, *Letters*, 592). The minister's son mourned his father afresh but had long since left his father's religion forever.

Notes

1. Clark's application is among the Ingersoll Papers, Illinois Historical Society. I exhibited Robert's ceremonial sword at the Ingersoll Sesquicentennial Anniversary Celebration held in Peoria, August 11–13, 1983.

2. *Spondoolicks* (or *spondulics* or *spondulix*) is a slang term for money.

3. The letter, dated May 3, 1859, was exhibited by Fred Ingersoll Harmon, great-grandson of Dr. John Ingersoll, at the Ingersoll Centennial Celebration in Peoria, August 11–13, 1983.

II

"The Coming Man
of the Northwest"

Bob Ingersoll was a young man in a hurry. In 1860, at the age of twenty-seven, he became the Democratic candidate in the Fourth Congressional District of Illinois.

In that fateful year, the most fateful in the history of the Republic, the electorate nationwide was called upon to choose among four presidential candidates—Lincoln (Republican), Douglas (Democrat), Breckenridge (Constitutional Democrat, having broken away from the regular Democrats), and Bell (Constitutional Union). Did the people want to exclude slavery from the territories, leave the determination of slavery or freedom to the inhabitants of each territory respectively, open all the territories to slavery, or just come out for law and order? There was no abolitionist candidate; no national candidate advanced a program directly affecting slavery in the slave states. The ultimate status of the "peculiar institution" was not on the surface an issue.

Bob Ingersoll was a regular Democrat. He fended off any long-range commitment on the irrepressible conflict with jokes and funny stories (Peoria *Transcript*, April 25, 1860). By mid-summer he led the field in the race for the Democratic nomination to Congress.

The Fourth of July approached. Owing to mismanagement and false signals, the celebration committee in Peoria found themselves without a scheduled speaker or much prospect of finding one as the third of July wore on. In desperation they appealed to the young politician. Bob was willing.

The Fourth was a hot and clear day. A motley procession—Hibernians, city council, fire companies, butchers, coal diggers, boom-booming bands—

wound down Main Street. A national salute was performed; boys and men fired off a variety of guns. The speaker briskly ascended the platform and the heavily Democratic crowd whooped it up in expectation of a rip-roaring partisan declamation. They did not get it. Ingersoll spoke from notes and the speech was not recorded verbatim, but it is clear that the orator of the day was, it turned out, not a Democrat—he was an American. He proclaimed freedom as the birthright of every man. He looked into the future and saw the day "when the dweller on the slopes of the Rocky Mountain shall look down the plains of the Pacific coast and the valleys of the Mississippi and behold them teeming with a population as dense as that of Belgium today and not hear the clanking of the chains of a single slave." At a bound the newcomer to political life had become the consummate orator of patriotic occasions—making the eagle scream, purple, fervid—in a word, grandiloquent. His achievement could not be denied. The local Republican paper grudgingly conceded that "he acquitted himself quite creditably," for he had "thrown off the limited range of his political visions" (*Transcript*, July 6, 1860).

What had happened? Had Ingersoll gone Republican, abolitionist? Not at all. A few days later, speaking in the village of Washington, he set the record straight. The people of the respective territories, he insisted, had the same right to allow or prohibit slavery within their borders as the original colonies had. He had heard that the Republicans were scheming to buy up the slaves in the slave states. He would have none of it. You could be sure that he would refuse to pay his portion of any tax demanded of him. The crowd huzzahed (*Transcript*, July 16).

Having easily won the Democratic nomination, Ingersoll delivered an acceptance speech tearing the Republicans apart. The Republicans were the enemies of constitutional freedom in the territories. Their program was absurd. "The Republicans believe that Congress should act as wet nurse and go over into the territories and bind diapers on the people. Judging from the character of the most of that party, they are well constituted to go into the diaper business." As for Lincoln, he was a man "of no character—no reputation" (*Transcript*, Aug. 3; Cramer, *Royal Bob*, 271.) In his political debut Ingersoll was already the perfect master of the art of stump speaking—we are right, they are wrong. A-B-C-logic and folksy wit left the opposition dead on the battlefield—at least to the satisfaction of the speaker and his cohorts.

Ingersoll's opponent was the incumbent, Judge William Kellogg, an elder statesman of the Republican party. As the underdog Ingersoll challenged Kellogg to debate, and Kellogg accepted. There would be an extensive series of joint appearances throughout the district. The candidates would alternate in speaking order from place to place, the opening speaker taking one hour, the opponent an hour and a half, the opener closing for half an hour.

Before the debates began, the local papers had done their best and worst on the challenger, who had lost no time in making himself visible. The *Transcript* published a less than enthusiastic impression from out of town:

> Bob, as he is familiarly called by his Democratic associates, rejoices in a full muscular frame (about equal in proportions to his competitor for congressional honors) and a loud, clear, sonorous voice, well adapted to stump speaking. His address is not remarkably graceful, yet animated, the most frequent gesture being the working up of each coat sleeve with the opposite hand, as if preparing to butcher an ox. . . . A large part of his speech consisted of puerile stories and lame attempts at wit, to catch the popular ear, interspersed with offers to bet, which were promptly taken. (Aug. 9)

On the other hand the *Democratic Union* rhapsodized over him.

> Well may the democracy of this district be proud of their candidate for Congress. Cold and prejudiced indeed must that man be who can listen to such impassioned eloquence poured forth today, in the vindication of Democratic principles, and not be ready to exclaim, from the impulse of his heart, Surely that man is a patriot and a statesman. There is not a pulse in his heart but what beats for freedom and no man living deplores more than he does the institution of human slavery. Yet he possesses that trueness of character to direct him in the path to do no injury or violence to a sister state. (Aug. 21)

In the debates the candidates stated and restated in detail wearisome to themselves, if not their listeners, their basic positions. Kellogg argued that slavery was a national evil affecting all the people and could be curbed only by national action excluding it from all the territories. Ingersoll contended that slavery, though evil, was a local state institution, sanctioned by history and the Constitution, and that its future in any territory should be freely determined by the people of that territory. In his first appearance as opening speaker, in Lacon on August twenty-eighth, he threw a jumble of hard questions at Kellogg: "Would you, as a member of Congress, vote for the admission of a slave state into this Union? . . . Would you vote for the repeal of the Fugitive Slave Law, or are you in favor of supporting its provision? . . . Are you in favor of the immigration of free Negroes into the free territories and the free states?" Kellogg was ready. He would vote for the admission of a slave state into the Union; he would not vote for the repeal of the Fugitive Slave Law and he believed in enforcing it; and he was opposed to the emigration of free Negroes into the free states or territories. Ingersoll countered that Kellogg differed on important issues with the leaders of his party, Lincoln and Chase, and that he really belonged with the regular Democrats. Each party had its gang of young toughs—the Republican Wide-

Awakes, the Democratic Ever-Readies—organized to encourage right thinking. That night in Lacon the Ever-Readies took the field. About one hundred and fifty of these stalwarts, dressed in "drab morocco and hickory shirts and red pantaloons," waving flags and banners and stabbing the darkness with torches and transparencies, roistered through the streets. They halted at the Marshall House, where their young leader came out and "made a few bright and happy remarks" (*Democratic Union*, Aug. 30).

Ingersoll's adherence to the doctrine of territorial rights did not preclude him from saying that he was against slavery and had always been against slavery, and that he was opposed to the most odious instrument of its enforcement. The Fugitive Slave Law had been conceived by the Democrats and blessed by the Republicans. It was not a national issue in 1860. Ingersoll could have conducted his congressional campaign within comfortable party lines, avoiding the statute that was the talisman of his own party. Instead, he chose to denounce it.

We have two eyewitness accounts, both recorded long after the events but assuredly not in error as to the essential facts. Clark E. Carr, Republican politico and later a close friend of Ingersoll's, was campaigning in the Peoria region in 1860 (*Transcript*, July 15; *Democratic Union*, Sept. 14). Years later, giving his first impression of Ingersoll, he depicted the young Democratic aspirant sitting impassive and apparently downcast as Judge Kellogg declared that the Republican party was not an abolitionist party but was against the extension of slavery; that it supported the guarantees of the Constitution and the Fugitive Slave Law. Then Ingersoll rose, a lion rampant. "It seems to me now," wrote Carr, "after the lapse of all these years, that even then he was the most brilliant, the most inspiring, the most majestic, and withal the most convincing of orators." Ingersoll blazed away at the law and its defenders. "The Fugitive Slave Law is the most infamous that ever disgraced a statute book. . . . The man that apologizes for that infamy is a brute." His imagination soared. According to Carr, Ingersoll "pictured a poor black woman with her child, her baby boy, whom she was hugging to her throbbing bosom, her only ambition to make him free, running by that hall and the United States marshal in close pursuit summoning us to join in the chase, and Judge Kellogg springing to his feet in obedience and calling upon these young men [probably pointing to the Wide-Awakes and Ever-Readies in the audience] to join in the cruel chase, and hue and cry, and then finally succeeding in dragging the poor wretch back to slavery." Ingersoll inveighed not only against Kellogg but all others damned for defending the Fugitive Slave Law including "the trusted leaders of your boasted Republican party" and "your Abe Lincoln himself" (*My Day and Generation*, 336). Strange argument for a Democrat to make against the Republicans!

Another witness described the confrontation over the Fugitive Slave Law in even more vivid colors. Here Ingersoll is represented as depicting a slave in flight for freedom and asking Judge Kellogg point-blank what he would do. Kellogg responded that he would abide by the law, whereupon Ingersoll "raised his clenched hand toward heaven, and bringing it down with emphasis exclaimed, 'I'll be God damned if I would' " (Captain John McGinnis in *The Truth Seeker*, Oct. 7, 1899). Such outcries may have cost him the election.

The partisan press knew where to throw bouquets and brickbats. To the *Transcript* it was a contest between a statesman and a rabblerouser. Judge Kellogg had given Ingersoll "one of the direst excoriations that any poor fellow ever received. It was evident to everyone that Ingersoll was no match for his competitor in that which goes to make the public debater and statesman. In the arts and trickery of the politician and demagogue Ingersoll was at home" (Sept. 28, 1860). And young Ingersoll had always been a gross ne'er-do-well requiring attention from the police (Sept. 13). From the opposite corner the *Democratic Union* beheld a decaying politician in an unequal struggle with a magnificent young gladiator: "Mr. Ingersoll, though young in years, has already shown himself the overmatch of his experienced competitor, and every discussion only brings the fact more vividly before the whole public, Republicans as well as Democrats. As a keen, logical debater he has few equals—as an effective stump-speaker he has no superior—as a man it is only necessary to know him to admire his fine qualities of heart" (Oct. 4). And the sanctimonious Judge was nothing but a high-flying gambler who neglected his illegitimate children (Aug. 29).

It was rough-and-tumble hurly-burly politics at the edge of civilization. The press could portray the brash young Democrat as a perfect ruffian. On October twentieth he made a speech (not in the debates) at Maquon. To the *Democratic Union* it was a perfect job, where "he displayed himself to his usual good advantage as one of the most able, eloquent, and effective speeches which nobody but Bob Ingersoll can make" (Oct. 24). The *Transcript* presented an entirely different picture. In a letter signed "Observer," Ingersoll was quoted as saying at Maquon that "he didn't give a god damn whether he was elected or not, but would carry out the principles or bust. If there were any there that did not want to vote for him they might go to hell and be god damned." Observer described "the veritable, dignified, gentlemanly Bob" as helping himself at the public table with his bare hands to the preserves, butter, and meat, and when called out in the evening by the Ever-Readies, he mounted a dry-goods box, where "attempting to lay down his views in a strong manner [he] lost his balance, and lay down himself but ever-ready hands soon raised him to the perpendicular." The *Transcript* elucidated Observer's message with boldface headlines:

GREAT "DEMOCRATIC BUST" AT MAQUON
Bob Ingersoll Gloriously Inebriated

BLACKGUARDISM RAMPANT
A Regular Blow Out

DISCRACEFUL EXHIBITION

(Oct. 24)

Ingersoll was infuriated. Stopping the editor on the street Ingersoll informed him that he was spared from a thrashing only because he was fifty pounds too light (*Democratic Union*, Nov. 1).

His fame spread. Ingersoll spoke at numerous places outside his congressional district. He was indefatigable. He spoke in Chicago and on October sixteenth he shared the platform at Springfield with Douglas before a crowd estimated at between thirty and forty thousand. On the seventeenth he made two speeches at Pekin and on the eighteenth he was on the train ("the cars") to Burlington, Iowa. To while away the ninety-mile ride from Peoria to Burlington he made a three-hour speech to his captive audience. Arriving at Burlington he was greeted by a reception committee and escorted to the Barnet House, where he conferred with local Democrats. In the evening he was escorted to Marion Hall by a drum-beating, torch-bearing procession of Highlanders, Little Giants, and plain citizens. His speech was the by now typical Ingersollism-on-the-stump. He had found a formula suited to his nature. "Bob, if possible," reported the *Democratic Union*, "exceeded himself—now holding his hearers spellbound by the fervor of his eloquence—and now bringing down the house by that keen quick-and-cracking wit which has made him the terror of his antagonists and the favorite of political friends. Never was audience more delighted—never was a speaker more successful. At the conclusion of his speech, which was of an hour and a half's duration, large numbers of enthusiastic admirers, as well as many ladies, lingered to take him by the hand" (Oct. 23). His future seemed wide and clear. If he won the election, "the time is not far distant when the name of Bob Ingersoll will be known and honored throughout the land" (*Democratic Union*, Oct. 4). The people of the Peoria district "should stand boldly for him as the coming man of the northwest" (Oct. 30).

The election figures tell their own story. Kellogg beat Ingersoll by 25,664 to 20,957, though trailing him in Peoria County by 3,538 to 3,784 (*Democratic Union*, Nov. 9, Dec. 13). In the national election the popular vote was Lincoln, 1,866,452; Douglas, 1,376,957; Breckenridge, 849,781; Bell, 588,879. The combined vote of Douglas and Breckenridge was 2,226,738. If the ultras had not split from the regular Democrats, Douglas might have been elected and war may not have broken out in 1861. Extremists were in the saddle North and South, and the two sections were on the road to Armageddon.

III

Colonel Ingersoll

Within three months of the election, the states of the lower South—
South Carolina, Georgia, Alabama, Florida, Mississippi, Louisiana, Texas
—had seceded. Douglas held Lincoln's hat while the new president proclaimed in his inaugural address that the Union was perpetual. In April
the assault on Fort Sumter precipitated a crisis that could be resolved
only on the field of battle. The upper South—Virginia, Arkansas, North
Carolina—rushed to join the Confederate States of America.

The coming of the war threw the Democratic party of the North
into disarray. The War Democrats believed in the Union; the Peace Democrats favored peace at any price. Peoria dramatized in miniature the torment
of the nation. The owner of the *Democratic Union* raised the American
flag; the editor threatened to tear it down (*Peoria Journal*, Oct. 20, 1911).
A crowd of Union adherents, assembled on Main Street, called for Bob
Ingersoll. He appeared on the balcony of his office. There was no doubt
where Bob stood—he was for the Union first and last. His words blazed
out. He hoped that the North would never crawl in the dust before
southern demagogues and traitors, and that his fellow countrymen would
have backbone enough to avenge any insults to the American flag. If
the government of Washington and Jefferson was not good enough for
Davis and his clan to live under, it was good enough for them to be
hanged under (*Peoria Journal*, Oct. 20, 1911). When Fort Sumter fell, the
Democrats of Peoria met in the courthouse. A resolution was made and
seconded sympathizing with the South and denouncing the president for
the call to arms. Ingersoll then entered and, catching the drift of the
proposition, mounted one of the benches and "bursting with indignation,
with all his manhood aroused, with an eloquence never surpassed, supported the Union, defended the president, and defeated the resolution"[1]

(*Peoria Journal*, Feb. 13, 1900). Peoria was saved for the Union.

Ingersoll did not wait for conscription. He and his friend and fellow-lawyer Basil D. Meek agreed to form a volunteer cavalry regiment. Ingersoll was commissioned colonel and Meek lieutenant colonel on October 22, 1861, and the Eleventh Cavalry was mustered into United States service on December 20, 1861 (*The Truth Seeker*, Aug. 9, 1924). War seemed the greatest adventure, the noblest of sports. An early war photo shows Colonel Ingersoll in uniform, sporting mustache and goatee, his right hand thrust into the tunic in Napoleonic style. Perhaps he was thinking of Shakespeare as well as Napoleon:

> Then a soldier,
> full of strange oaths, and bearded like the pard,
> jealous in honor, quick and sudden in quarrel,
> seeking the bubble reputation
> even in the cannon's mouth.

The recruits trained haphazardly under their inexperienced leaders in the open space at Camp Lyon in Glen Oak Park (where Ingersoll's statue now stands). They lived in barracks made out of cow-sheds, got their provisions free or by contract, and cooked in black kettles over tripods. Wives and sweethearts brought more pies, cakes, and other delicacies than they could consume. On pleasant days crowds came to watch the maneuvers and mix with the soldiers. It was all fun and games; a holiday spirit filled the air (*Peoria Journal*, Oct. 28, 1911).

Ingersoll's letters to his brothers reflect his military experiences. He had never known such responsibilities. He saw the comic mingled with the grim. He had charge of 144 mules, 1,158 horses, 24 wagons, 1,143 men, and 54 officers.

I never knew what work was before. Nearly 3000 mouths of horses, mules, & men must be filled every day. 1158 backs and twice that number of feet have to be kept covered. Something happens every moment. Somebody has lost something—broken something—stolen something—something is missing—something has run away—something is bad—something is rotten. The contractors do not feed us. They feed us too much. There is not wood & coal enough. There is too much used. Some officer has been insulted. Somebody has the measles, mumps, fever, broken head, black eye, sprained ankle. Somebody is drunk. Somebody raising Hell on the general plan. Somebody is sick—wants a pass—wants a furlough—wife about to be confined—two young men at the point of death—business must be attended to—wants to go 500 miles—man owes him six bits. No matter. A light heart and a thin pair of breeches will take any man through the world. (To John, Jan. 24, 1862, *Letters*, 112)

He had been able to get away for a visit with John. It was only for a day but emotionally draining, long enough "to remember old times—

our partings—our meetings—our joys & sorrows, . . . long enough to weep for the past and gather strength for, and faith in, the future." He was awaiting marching orders, and he felt swept along by history: "I have thrown myself into the great tide of the times, willing to let it bear me wherever it will—willing to accept the decree of my fate, and may the same God who watches over you watch over me, if not for my sake, for yours."

Robert Ingersoll married Eva Parker on February 13, 1862. He had met her in the summer of 1859, when he was trying a criminal case in Groveland, Illinois. A local dignitary, Judge Benjamin Weld Parker, enjoyed Ingersoll's histrionics in the courtroom and invited him to dinner. The Parkers had two marriageable daughters, Eva and Sue. The guest sat next to Eva, a handsome young woman. "It was a case of love at first sight," wrote Sue (later Mrs. Clinton Farrell) (Letter, *Minneapolis Times*, March 14, 1902). Robert and Eva were married in the Parker home. His first comments on the marriage were off-hand and temperate. He wrote to John from St. Louis: "I suppose you know that I was married on the 13th of last month. My wife is now at Peoria, but will be here this week. She is a good sweet natured woman, one that loves me and one that I love. This is enough" (March 9, 1862, *Letters*, 113). On the fifth anniversary of the wedding he called the day "the luckiest day of my life" (to Clark, Feb. 13, 1867, L.C.). And on the fifteenth anniversary he admonished his elder daughter, also named Eva: "I want you to know how much you owe to your sweet mother. You think I am good. She made me so. We all owe everything to her. She is the air, the earth, and sunshine in which all our joys have grown and blossomed. Love her with all of your heart. Worship her. Adore her" (Feb. 13, 1877, Ill. Hist. Soc., hereinafter IHS). Mrs. Ingersoll would give her husband two devoted daughters and a beautiful and sociable home. She would travel with him on his lecture tours, strengthen his resolve, modulate his manners. As the arch-infidel Ingersoll would have no really private life; if there was anything amiss in his domestic style or sexual morality it would have been shouted from the housetops. If ever a marriage was made in heaven, it was the Ingersoll marriage (though he would deny it with a smile, not believing in heaven).

On the twenty-second of February, nine days after the Ingersolls were married, the Eleventh Illinois Cavalry broke camp and headed for Benton Barracks near St. Louis to join the Army of the West under Halleck and Grant. Fifteen years later, glorifying the Union dead at a mass meeting for Republican candidate Hayes, Ingersoll relived that momentous expedition in a romantic passage that has gone down in the annals of declamation as "A Vision of War."

> We see them part with those they love. Some are walking for the last time in quiet woody places, with the maidens they adore. We hear the whisperings and the sweet vows of eternal love as they lingeringly part

forever. Others are bending over cradles, kissing babes that are asleep. Some are receiving the blessings of old men. Some are parting with mothers who press them to their hearts again and again, and say nothing. Kisses and tears, tears and kisses—divine mingling of agony and love! And some are talking with wives and endeavoring with brave words, spoken in the old tones, to drive from their hearts the awful fear.

And so the boys in blue leave home. "We see them all as they march proudly away under the flaunting flags, keeping time to the grand, wild music of war—marching down the streets of the great cities—through the towns and across the prairies—down to the fields of glory, to do and to die for the eternal right" (*Works*, IX, Indianapolis Speech, 1876, 167).

Not all was, in fact, pageantry and romance. The raw recruits had never known anything like it. For two weeks at winter's end the Eleventh Cavalry, one thousand men in a caravan of seventeen wagons drawn by four-mule teams, plodded two hundred miles down central and southern Illinois. At nightfall they pitched tents in the fields, a form of lodging whimsically described by their leader as "comfortable but not desirable" (To John, March 9, 1862, *Letters*, 114).

On March eighth the regiment was assembled at the Mississippi and ready to board six transports. The young colonel, not yet twenty-nine years old, supervising the transit was heart-sick. He admired the buoyant spirit of the youngsters under his command, but he dreaded the future carnage. He prayed to God. As the boats pulled off, "the boys gave three cheers for glorious Illinois and our band played 'Sweet Home,' and as the sounds floated away over the countless waves, I thought, How many of us will recross—how many again meet father, mother, brother, sister, child, wife? How many will return to their own firesides, how many be maimed, killed, how long left on the field of battle to suffer and die? And then raising my eyes to the [sky] where the great clouds floated over us I asked the blessing & protection of any Father's God" (*Letters*, 114).

The newcomers found St. Louis agog with jubilation over Grant's victories at Henry and Donelson, a flag-decorated town of parades and parades, old men and children "singing at the top of their voices our most shining & glorious National airs," and all over camp thousands of troops in ferment of preparation and departure, "Infantry, Cavalry & Artillery all commingled, going down the great river" (*Letters*, 114).

The Eleventh Cavalry stayed at Benton Barracks about a month to acquire training and supplies. The men were impatient and eager for combat. "They almost fear," Ingersoll mused, "that the war will be over before our regt. gets into the field. For my own part the sooner the war closes the better I shall be pleased" (To John, March 20, 1862, *Letters*, 115). He had ridden into the country. The fields were green, the trees in bud, the weather delightful, as in Wisconsin about the first of May.

He spoke of new arrivals from Wisconsin, "healthy large men." He told his physician brother that he had no faith in the Army medical services. He had visited the graves of soldiers who died in the hospitals; in one graveyard he counted over fifteen hundred graves. General Hospital was a killer. Most of the surgeons were "quacks." "Of all things I am going to avoid Hospitals. They are far more dangerous than shot & shell." He sent love from his wife, who had been visiting. Within a few days a large river steamboat carried the whole regiment—men, animals, equipment—down the river to Pittsburg Landing in Tennessee, where they pitched camp near the old Shiloh church.

In the Battle of Shiloh, the first major battle of the war, 63,000 Union troops under Grant and Sherman fought 40,000 Confederates under A. S. Johnson, for two days, from Sunday, April sixth through Monday April seventh, 1862. The Eleventh Cavalry served as rearguard reenforcement. In two letters to Clark (both dated April 11 and captioned "Seat of War") Robert Ingersoll describes in detail his experience in "awful Terrible battle, the most horrible I ever conceived of—a perfect Austerlitz."[2] The Eleventh Cavalry formed a line of battle on the edge of an open field. The Union forces had been taken by surprise and the Confederates were driving them back. The battle being fought in the woods, horses could not maneuver. The task of the Union cavalry was to retreat slowly, ready to change course and join in pursuit at any time. "The shot and shell were tearing through the woods at this point in the most fearful manner. Trees as large as my body were shattered to pieces and great limbs came crashing around where we were formed." The line of battle was shaped like a crescent six or seven miles long, its center three miles from Pittsburg Landing.

> The roar of the guns was almost deafening. No thunder that I ever heard was at all comparable to this. Hundreds of cannon and in the neighborhood of two hundred thousand muskets were discharged simultaneously and incessantly. There was no lull, no pause. They did not even wait a moment as great storms do to gather fresh strength, but the Rebels rushed us with the fury of Hell and our soldiers disputed every bloody inch with more courage and more dauntless desperate heroism than I before imagined possessed by men.

All day under attack the Union soldiers had been buoyed by expectation of reinforcements from General Buell. At long last they beheld "the sacred flag" emerging from the woods, and "high over the volleys of musketry, over the roar and boom of the guns rose cheers of a hundred thousand tired and desperate men." Buell checked the enemy advance and "along the whole of the line firing ceased and both armies lay down upon the terrible bloody field surrounded by thousands of dead and wounded and slept upon their arms."

The Confederates had overrun and occupied the tents, leaving the

Union troops without shelter in the fields. "The rain fell all night, slowly and sadly, as though the heavens were weeping for the dead. All night long I stood with my blanket around me, drearily by the side of a dead tree watching the shells of the gunboats. Every fifteen minutes would come a flash like heat lightning—then the boom—then the bluish line bending over the distant wood—then the roar of the bursting, and then last of all the double echo dying over the far hills." In the morning shortly after daybreak the battle resumed, but "thank God, we commenced the attack." As demoralized Union stragglers fell back to the Eleventh Cavalry Colonel Ingersoll tried to rally them to return to combat. (Lieutenant Colonel Meek was to say, "He made wonderful appeals to their patriotism, to take up arms, turn back and help their comrades who were fighting" [*Truth Seeker*, Aug. 9, 1924].) "At four o'clock cheer after cheer went up from our forces. The enemy had not only fallen back, had not only retreated, but was flying in the wildest confusion. The day was ours. The greatest Battle for the Union had been fought, the greatest, the bloodiest in American history, and had been won by the gallant arms of the Grand West." Ingersoll estimated the casualties as not less than 20,000 killed and wounded on each side. Official figures were nearer to 13,000 Union, 11,000 Confederate. "We [Eleventh Cavalry] lost four killed, one 1st lieutenant, twenty wounded and missing and had sixty-seven horses killed or wounded so as to be worthless" (*Letters*, 116).

In the aftermath of the great battle there was time to reflect on the baptism of fire and slaughter and bereavement. There was no glamor in it.

War is horrid beyond the conception of man. It is enough to break the heart to go through the hospitals & see gray-haired veterans with lips whitening under the kiss of death—hundreds of mere boys with thoughts of home—of sister and brother—meeting the dark angel alone, nothing but pain, misery, neglect, and death. Every day I hear some band playing a funeral march—in a little while a few muskets are discharged and I know some officer sleeps in the earth—to see death around you, everywhere nothing but death—to think of the ones far away expecting the dead to return and hoping for one more embrace—listening for footsteps that never will be heard on earth—it makes one tired—tired of war. (To Clark, May 5, 1862, *Letters*, 118)

And yet so is human nature constituted that men who have survived one battle soon crave another. The colonel marveled at how morale springs back after combat. "It is wonderful how soon an army regains its spirit—no matter how many dead—how many comrades are gone—who wounded—who maimed for life—in a few days all is forgotten, and the fortunate who escaped are anxious for another battle" (To Dear Bro, April 17, 1862, IHS).

Camp routine followed as in every war. Robert wrote to John,

"Nothing ever happening here. Camp life continues as dull as ever" (April 2, 1862, IHS). And on the same day he wrote to Clark about rumors, another universal and insidious feature of war. "One day we hear that Pope has taken Memphis, another day that McClellan has surrendered his whole command at Yorktown, another than Jeff Davis has sued for peace. Again, that Lincoln has said that the war had been prosecuted long without accomplishing anything but to convince him that our cause was hopeless and that in spite of all our efforts the Southern Confederacy would have to be recognized. And then we hear about England having sent a fleet to break the blockade"

> And more of horrible and awful
> Which to name would be unlawful.

There was work to be done—reconnaissance, and pursuit incidental to the campaign for Corinth. On maneuvers in ravaged northern Mississippi Colonel Ingersoll assured frantic housewives at his horse's side that their homes were safe from burning, that the Union soldiers were not "vandals and cut-throats" (Dearest Bro, May 2, 1862, IHS). The colonel had a low opinion of the southern countryside and its people. The Eleventh Cavalry encamped "in a little miserable town called Monterey." The fields had been stripped by the southern army; food was scarce and costly, and the people were starving.

> I asked several of them what they expected to do. One old butter-nut cuss said he "reckoned the Lord would take care of" him. I thought he expected the Lord to turn his attention to very small things. All the people I have seen are of the very meanest description. Lower if possible than the negroes—they look and the country looks like Southern Illinois and its people. The country is certainly not worth fighting for—not worth one life, and the prospect of a union with such ignorant dogs is disgusting rather than pleasing. (To Clark, May 5, 1862, Letters, 118)

Small pursuit missions by cavalry made no sense. The woods were full of Confederate infantry and artillery installations, for whom the Union men in the saddle were moving targets. On such a mission, at the foot of a hill the road turned to the right and as one fourth of the column completed the turn "bang! bang went the cannon of the masked battery, crash came the shell," scattering the men to unavailable cover as "like the hail of Hell came the cannon and grape." The next day Ingersoll's men rode all night until midnight over hills, through swamps, and over damaged bridges where they dismounted and walked their horses. At the break of dawn they received an order from General C. T. Smith to advance two miles down the road. It could not be done. "I was not quite a fool, and so I put the order in my pocket and went to sleep."

On the morrow his men moved forward under fire which "got d--d lively." He sent General Smith a note explaining his disobedience, and the General approved. The whole pursuit strategy was "a miserable failure." Ingersoll minced no words about it. "A pursuit planned by idiots and carried out by infantry without legs would have been equally successful. In fact, I believe he could have caught them quicker if he had gone the other way" (Dearest Bro, June 9, 1862, IHS).

No longer a Democrat and not yet a Republican, Ingersoll's mind was independently busy with the high politics of a nation at war. In his family letters he shows that he had formed positive opinions on the most important questions. He denounced the peace-at-any-price advocates among the northern Democrats. He compared them to the Jews under Moses as hankering for the flesh-pots of a strong united political party rather than rejoicing in separation from the slavocracy.[3] For once his metaphors tumbled over one another. The northern Democrats assembled in convention "throw cold water upon the present enthusiasm of the North. It is a fire in the rear; it dampens the ardor of the army" (To Clark, Sept. 22, 1862, *Letters*, 124).

Abraham Lincoln was not yet enshrined in hagiography, before which Ingersoll would lay many a wreath. He was a minority president grappling with a terrible problem, and to men like Ingersoll he seemed to be doing a poor job. He was filling high positions with incompetents like the "jackass" Pope, who had wasted the lives of hundreds of thousands of men. When would Lincoln stop appointing "idiots because they come from Ills. or are related to his charming wife. . . . Lincoln may be honest but when you are fighting smart scoundrels, honesty is worth but little, especially when possessed by an idiot" (To John, Oct. 7, 1862, *Letters*, 128). Was Ingersoll calling Lincoln an idiot—or, to take a more charitable view— was he referring to incompetent subordinates in general?

Threatening the very heart of the Union cause was Lincoln's usurpation of legislative and judicial powers, an action without precedent in American history (and not matched by Wilson in World War I or Franklin Roosevelt in World War II). The suspension of the writ of habeas corpus made a travesty of government by the people. Better that the Union be dissolved, that society revert to barbarism than "trampling into the earth every principle of government made holy by the best blood of the world," substituting "anarchy, dictation, distrust, cruel cowardice, tyranny." Suicide cannot prolong life; a free government cannot be sustained by the murder of personal liberty. "Must there be an American Bastille?" The Executive had gone too far; a revolution threatened to break out in the North, and "the President and Cabinet may themselves be petitioning for the most gracious writ of Habeas Corpus" (To John, Oct. 2, 1862, *Letters*, 128). In these violent phrases Ingersoll is not an eccentric, but is expressing the troubled spirit of many of his compatriots (Morison and Commager, *The Growth of the American Republic*, I, 595).

On the future of slavery Ingersoll reasoned that the outbreak of the rebellion had made the abolition of that institution an absolute war aim of the national government. As long as the South stayed in the Union she was entitled under the Constitution to the security of all her institutions. Now that she had defied the Constitution she had forfeited her rights under it. "The North now has the right and it is her duty to act according to the dictates of humanity—of necessity—She has no right to acknowledge property in man. It is not her duty to protect the institutions of an enemy even if they are good—If bad it is her imperative duty to destroy them—Slavery is unspeakable—detestable—Destroy it" (To Clark, Sept. 22, 1862, *Letters*, 124). In his view the Emancipation Proclamation, whereby Lincoln declared "forever free" all slaves in states and territories still engaged in rebellion as of January 1, 1863, would not hasten a just peace. It would only embitter the deep South and give cases of heartburn to the Border States. "I would like to see all the slaves free and forever, but proclamations will not do anything towards their emancipation" (To John, Oct. 2, 1862, *Letters*, 128).

Colonel Ingersoll was homesick, for his brothers, his sisters, his wife. He told them that he had a premonition that he would survive the war, that he would not take foolish chances, that he was thinking of them day and night; his eyes filled with tears (To Dearest Bro, May 2, 1862, IHS). He daydreamed about his wife's birthday, which was on May fourth, and, in the privacy of a family letter, he felt sorry for himself. "I hope you had a happy Sunday on Eva's birthday. At that time I was on the march, the rain falling in torrents and that night I slept on the ground, in a tent, and not a dry thread within a mile of me, and the rain coming harder every moment" (To Clark, May 9, 1862, *Letters*, 122). He regretted being unable to meet with his sister Ruth, who was on a family visit in Wisconsin and Illinois and whom he had not seen in ten years (To John, Sept. 10, 1862, *Letters*, 124). He asked Clark to send a watch and chain to John; for himself he would like to have a copy of Shakespeare (May 9, 1862, *Letters*, 120).

Ebon (Ebenezer) Clark Ingersoll (member of the House of Representatives, 1864–1870) began his political career with an unsuccessful bid for election to Congress in 1862. A War Democrat, he had come out strongly for the abolition of slavery. "I am proud of your position," Robert wrote to Clark (Sept. 22, 1862, *Letters*, 124). "Stand by it. Our sainted father if living would be proud of you." Robert greeted Clark's nomination by the Republicans with a brotherly endorsement that was not without a trace of envy. "They could not have made a better choice. I glory in you much more than in myself. I had rather see honors crown your head than mine" (Sept. 29, 1862, *Letters*, 126). His own defeat in 1860 had rankled. He was sure that he would never again submit his fate to the electorate. On the eve of the election he prepared Clark for the defeat that might lie ahead. It was no great distinction to be a member of Congress, "a collection of fools and knaves." A politician's life is not a happy one. He has to be "the skillet of grease in which little hungry puppy editors drop their miserable crumbs." How much better it is for a man "to make his own bread and eat it with his family—to let the Government take care of itself, to let the dear people—the garlic-breathed, greasy-capped multitude go to the Devil" (Nov. 1, 1862, *Letters*, 130).

On the evening of December sixteenth the Eleventh Cavalry was on a combat mission. District Headquarters at Jackson, Tennessee, had given the order: "Engage with the enemy whatever his forces may be. Keep him back if possible long enough for Jackson to be reenforced" (To John, March 16, 1863, *Letters*, 135). Under Colonel Ingersoll's command were two artillery pieces and about 650 men assembled from the Eleventh Cavalry and other units, many of whom had never heard gunfire. After an all-night march they encountered enemy pickets near Lexington, about twenty-eight miles east of Jackson. Skirmishing occupied the next day, and they slept that night "with our eyes open" (*Letters*, 136). He had placed his artillery at the edge of Beech Creek to prevent enemy crossing. He had rejected the advice of Lieutenant Colonel Meek that the cannon be moved to the rear. "We must keep the guns," he explained to Meek. "The great Napoleonic battle will be fought tomorrow morning and we will use artillery. Napoleon always used artillery" (Meek, 504). This strategy may have staved off defeat temporarily, but defeat was inevitable with a handful of Union defenders pitted against five to six thousand Confederates. The Tennessee volunteers sent to destroy the lower bridge and close the access road were overwhelmed and staggered back in terrified confusion. Attacked from front and flank, the Union force crumbled. The colonel fled, the enemy in hot pursuit. "They shot at me it seemed hundreds of times" (*Letters*, 135). His horse cleared a high fence but landing on the other side its knees gave way and it "fell flat," throwing the rider to the snow-covered ground. The men in gray closed in and Colonel Ingersoll surrendered in imperial phrases: "Stop that shooting and I'll recognize your damned Confederacy" (Meek, 504). The Confederates took 124 prisoners.

The Confederates were under the command of the redoubtable General Nathan B. Forrest, known to history for his slogan for military success, "Fust with the Most." The Union troops, huddled under close guard, awaited their doom. "We all wondered," Ingersoll reminisced years later, "whether we would be hung, drawn and quartered, or shot, and I tell you for a fact that we all felt uneasy" (Interview, *Ithaca News*, Jan. 26, 1893). Suddenly a mounted Confederate officer charged toward them, "and those of the boys who once knew how to pray doubtless ran their minds over their boyhood days in search of some religious balm" (*Ithaca News*). All that was wanted was that the field and line officers fall into a double line and march to the headquarters tent. There Forrest kept them waiting for a while, then emerged, "looked us over in a stern sort of way," and asked, "Who's in command of this regiment?" No response. Forrest gruffly ordered the field officers to step forward, which they did, feeling that their time had come. He looked them over "with another withering and somewhat contemptuous look" and repeated, "Who's in command of this regiment?" Ingersoll stepped forward, saluted, and said, "I *was* in command, General." Forrest smiled slightly at the distinction, then sat down with Ingersoll on opposite ends of a log and tried to examine him on the strength and location of Union forces. To his inquiry from where Ingersoll came, Ingersoll is said to have answered, "From everywhere but here, and I hope to be free from here just as soon as I can receive your genial approbation to that effect" (*Confederate Veteran*, XV, Feb. 1, 1907, 54–55). Back in captive huddle and expecting an order to the infamous prison camp at Andersonville, Ingersoll dashed off a note to Forrest (on both sides of a scrap of brown paperbagging) that he parole a captain about sixty-five years old and spare him from the rigors of prison camp. Summoning Ingersoll, Forrest shook hands and said that he would grant the request. As Ingersoll thanked him and turned to the guard to indicate that he was ready to go back, Forrest said, "Colonel Ingersoll, you made a splendid appeal to save your old captain from prison. Why don't you make a request for all your officers and yourself while you are about it?" The startled Ingersoll so requested orally and the request was granted. The prisoners were exempted from all restraint on their word of honor pending transfer.

Sociability was free and easy between captors and captives. Ingersoll charmed his hosts. He played draw poker with them and managed to lose; when his Union money ran out they staked him with Confederate bills (Henry, *"Fust with the Most" Forrester*, 110). The story is in character if a little hard to believe that he fraternized with them around a stove in a general store and that when the crowd got too large, they adjourned to the outdoors where he was invited to make a speech, which he promptly did from a box as he "effused with good will and the milk of human kindness." He said that the North had regretfully taken up arms, only in self-defense, after the assault on Fort Sumter and that negroes and poor whites had much in common. Like an evangelist he pictured the awful judgment day on slave-owners and altogether was wielding such hypnotic power over his listeners that Forrest, rushing up, exclaimed, more amused than angry, "Here Ingersoll, stop that speech and I'll exchange you for a government mule" (E. M. Macdonald, *Col. Robert G. Ingersoll As He Is*, 31).[4] Released on parole after three days Ingersoll returned to Camp Jackson, where his wife greeted him and General Sullivan praised him.

On parole Ingersoll awaited early exchange and return to combat. But nothing happened. Winter and spring came and went. He was in limbo; he could not fight and he could not attend to his family needs. His wife wanted him to quit. He still had some desire to pursue his reputation at the cannon's mouth but the opportunity was not likely.

"I rather hate to throw away the chance of rendering myself a little famous but Eva feels so terribly about my absence that I think on the whole I had better get out of the service" (To John, June 16, 1863, IHS). Apparently he need not inform his brother that his wife was expecting their first child in September. On June eighteenth he submitted his "complete and unconditional resignation as Colonel, the Eleventh Illinois Volunteer Cavalry," citing the shrinkage of the regiment, his pressing personal affairs, and his uselessness to the cause while on parole. Eight days later he explained his thoughts and confided his feelings to Clark. "Not that I think the rebellion ought not to be squelched. Not that I believe in the craven cowardly peace advocated by the Democracy of the North. Not that I think that Slavery ought for a moment to be preserved and protected. Not that I have come to the conclusion that two nations can exist in peace. Not that I think the North has not the ability to conquer, but because I have seen enough of death and horror. Because I have seen enough of bloodshed and mutilation" (Rogers, *Colonel Bob Ingersoll*, 168). He had done his part; he had had enough of war. On June 30, 1863, he was free.

In its greatest ordeal Ingersoll had served the nation on the field of battle. He would come to be called many things—Pope Bob, Pagan Bob, Champion Blasphemer, even Royal Bob—but his public name would be established as Colonel Ingersoll. He wore his Americanism proudly. No matter what he might say about the most sacred beliefs of the people, it would be hard for any American (that is, in the North) to throw mud at Colonel Ingersoll.

Notes

1. John S. Starr recounted these events in his speech to the Kickapoo Club on Lincoln's birthday (*Peoria Journal*, Feb. 13, 1900).

2. Austerlitz was one of Napoleon's more horrific major battles in his 1805 campaign.

3. Ingersoll wrote "d---d Jews" (IHS). The *Letters*, compiled and edited by Eva Ingersoll Wakefield, deletes *d---d*. Mrs. Wakefield obviously believed that her grandfather's reputation would benefit from such alterations of his occasionally reckless rhetoric.

4. Macdonald's account is allegedly based on a story that appeared in the *New York Sun* as told to them by a fellow prisoner of Forrest's.

IV

"All My Greatness"

Back in Peoria with his wife and his law partner Clark, the business of the firm was flexibly handled by the partners. Robert found it not too heavy to preclude indulging in his other interests. On July twenty-third he took a horseback ride and wrote a letter to John, stating again his new thinking, that the South had by rebellion forfeited any legal protection of slavery. "I send love to all hoping that you are all well & enjoying vegetables in abundance. I have had green corn for several weeks—plenty ripe tomatoes, cucumbers & some beans" (*Letters*, 136).

Ingersoll had, as he said, thrown himself into the great tide of the times. Once again he would woo the "grease-capped and garlic-breathed" masses, this time for nationality and freedom and his own rejuvenated career. He spurned a disgraceful peace. The North must never bend its knees to the rebels (Larson, *American Infidel: Robert G. Ingersoll*, 21; *Transcript*, Sept. 1, 1863 [speech in Pekin]). "There is a great gulf between the North and the South, as wide as that between Lazarus and the rich man" (Larson, 69; *Transcript*, Sept. 1, 1863 [speech in Smithville]). He had been a Democrat when the party's slogan had been "The Union must be preserved"; he had left it when its slogan became "The Union As It Was, the Constitution As It is." He was not a Democrat, a Republican, an Abolitionist, or "the other thing." "I am a free man, I intend to live and die free, nor will I stand between a man and his freedom. I am in favor of the emancipation of the whole world. They may call me an abolitionist or anything else they please, it matters not to me" (Larson, 69; *Transcript*, Sept. 1, 1869; Angell, *ISHSJ*, Winter 1966, 354). He debated man-to-man with hecklers and he squelched roughnecks with a double dose of their own rhetoric. In Macon a man under the influence shouted, "Wouldn't you help catch and sell a nigger if you could get half of the proceeds?" Ingersoll shot back, "If he wouldn't bring any more at auction than you would, it would not pay for the shoe leather worn out running after him. My friend, you had better dry up. If you desire information from me, get Balaam's ass to do your talking. He is smarter than you." The crowd shook with "immense laughter and uproar" (Larson, 71; *Transcript*, Oct. 21).

It was a principle with Ingersoll never to accept payment for political speech-making. The Union sympathizers of Lewiston, bent on showing their appreciation, had an elegant vest made for him by his tailors in Peoria. This had to be properly acknowledged, so he responded with an exhaustive medley of puns. "You made a good investment, at least for me," he wrote. Thanking his benefactors, he hoped that they would live long "in the enjoyment of all the vestal virtues of life, that your vested rights may never be wrested from you, at least not without legal investigation." He wished "that after your death you will not long be kept in the vestibule of the better world, be allowed to enter heaven at once," and he assured them that he was "in favor of prosecuting the war until not a vestige remains of the rebellion" (To J. W. Proctor, Oct. 21, 1863, *Truth Seeker*, July 24, 1909; Kittredge, 439).

One day in early March Ingersoll was in his office at ease expounding on the political situation to some friends, all partisans of the Union. The sheriff, entering on some routine business, disagreed vociferously. He opined that the sole war aim of the administration was to free the slaves, an action for which he plainly had no enthusiasm. Ingersoll replied with some heat that the slave had as much right to freedom as the sheriff and any other person. "A damned lie!" cried the sheriff. Ingersoll picked up a chair and went after his critic. At Ingersoll's trial on March fourteenth the jury deliberated three hours and failed to agree. The case was eventually dismissed (Larson, 72).

When Owen Lovejoy, abolitionist member of Congress from Illinois, died on March 25, 1864, the Republicans met in convention at Princeton to choose a candidate for the vacancy. Both Clark and Robert made fiery pro-Union speeches, Robert blasting the copperheads and vehemently proclaiming himself an abolitionist. "This Nation has been one of idolaters, worshiping slavery, now the image must be broken. Yes, I am an unconditional abolitionist. Copperheads may add damn if they wish" (*Peoria Daily Transcript*, April 14, 1864, cited in Plummer, *Peoria's Pagan Politician,* 19). Clark won the nomination and the special election (and would soon be running for a full term). Robert sought the Republican nomination for representative-at-large without success. The put-down rankled but was no surprise. In spite of his military record and his service on the stump his credentials as a newborn Republican did not impress the party leaders and the backwash of Clark's success worked against him. There was fear of an Ingersoll dynasty in the making. "I was the real choice of the convention had there been no trading," Robert grumbled. On the other hand, perhaps the rejection was justified. "I am too impatient to succeed as a politician with any certainty" (Letter to Clark, May 27, June 2, IHS).

Although he had no personal stake as a candidate Ingersoll plunged into the campaign. He often shared the platform with Richard Oglesby, Republican candidate for governor, and other Republican politicians including Clark Carr, then and forever afterward a close friend and ardent admirer. Robert wrote to his brother Clark on June second, "I just returned from Stark Penn township. Had a large meeting—three thousand at least were present. Everything went off in fine style, and every Union man was pleased to death with my speech" (IHS). On July fifth he reported, "Yesterday I was at Princeton. Oglesby and, Moulton were there. We had a splendid meeting. I spoke in the afternoon & at night. Oglesby said I made the finest speech he ever heard" (IHS).

During the summer Ingersoll found time for legal business, which he informed Clark was very good in spite of the usually slack season (July 25, Aug. 14, IHS). Peoria was under storm on behalf of the Confederacy. On August fifth he witnessed a Democratic mass meeting (*Works*, IX, 144). The speakers freely denounced the war as an "abolition nigger war" and branded Lincoln a tyrant. The Democrats paraded through the streets holding high an assortment of transparencies, one of which declared, "Is there money enough in the land to pay this nigger debt? Arouse, brothers, and hurl the tyrant Lincoln from the throne." Later that month the Democratic National Convention in Chicago nominated McClellan, called the war a failure, announced for peace, and attacked Lincoln for violating the constitutional rights of states and citizens.

Some of these strictures echoed Ingersoll's own private thoughts while in the service, but the only thing that mattered after three years of horror was the survival of the Republic. Ingersoll was one of the speakers at a Republican rally in Quincy. Some ten thousand people crowded the city park. The meeting was invaded by a gang of roughs from across the river in Missouri. They booed Clark Carr and yelled hurray for Jeff Davis. When Ingersoll rose they went after him but, as Clark Carr (always present at the right time) noted for history, Ingersoll immediately squashed them with "his irresistible wit, his withering scorn, and scathing denunciation." He then gave "a complete vindication of the administration of President Lincoln, an eloquent appeal to the people to stand by him, and the most resplendent tribute to the valor and sacrifices of the Union soldier." According to Carr the peroration of this battle veteran went something like this:

> God bless the soldiers of the army of the United States, wherever they may be—whether they are fighting on the hillside, the open plain, or in the dark valley, whether weary and footsore on the long march, whether parched with thirst they are dying in the field or are minis-

tered by loving hands in the hospital, whether they be writing letters to their friends by the dim light of the campfire, or reading letters from home. God bless the soldiers of the United States. God bless their friends and *God damn their enemies!*

Carr concludes: "Never did an orator express the intensity of feeling of a great audience more completely than Robert G. Ingersoll in that prayer and philippic, and never was there a greater demonstration of approval and applause. I noticed the Rev. Doctor Horatio Foote, a distinguished divine whom everybody knew, seated on the platform and enthusiastically pounding with his cane. Someone said to him, 'Doctor, is not that blasphemy?' 'Inspiration, gentleman, inspiration,' was his reply, and he continued to applaud" (Carr, 311).

At another meeting Ingersoll teased and rollicked with his audience. He was attacking Clement Vallandigham, leading northern spokesman of the South's Cause. He inquired, "If Vallandigham was here today, what would you do to him?" A moment's silence, then a burly farmer shouted, "I'd kick his --- -- --- ---." Everybody roared; Oglesby fell off his chair in laughter (E. G. Smith, 48).

On October twentieth the Republicans staged a torchlight parade and mass meeting in Peoria. Among the dignitaries on the platform were "Andy" Johnson, Governor Yates, and Robert and E. C. Ingersoll. Of the speeches by the Ingersolls the correspondent of the *Chicago Tribune* wrote: "The efforts of these gentlemen were able, manly, and convincing and exactly met the views of the large audience. They were frequently interrupted with applause" (Oct. 20, 1864).

The Republicans, including Lincoln, Oglesby, and E. C. Ingersoll, were victorious at the polls. Robert now sought a tangible acknowledgment of his services to the party. On November seventeenth he wrote to Governor-elect Oglesby, "After congratulating you, the State, the Country & the world upon the great victory won by Patriotism and Humanity, I want to say that I am anxious to be appointed U.S. Attorney for the Northern District of Ills. if the present incumbent M. E. C. Larned is removed" (Plummer, 80-81). Oglesby wrote on the back of the letter, "Would like to see him succeed but did not promise to sign or recommend him for the present." Nothing came of it. More acquaintance would have to develop before Oglesby would do such a favor for Ingersoll; then there would be no limit in personal dimensions to his liberality.

Clark being in Washington, all the burdens of the law practice fell upon Robert but there was always time to sit back and socialize. "This being St. Patrick's day in the morning, and having a few leisure moments," he wrote to John on March seventeenth, "I take my pen in hand etc. We are all well, never in better health any of us in the world. The little children [Eva and Maud] are perfectly well, growing up with all their might, and enjoying themselves 'beyont [sic] all telling' " (*Letters*, 137). He was ambivalent about political life; it was disgusting but he could not get free of it. It is "a low dirty scrambling, through misrepresentation, slander, falsehood and filth, and success brings nothing but annoyance & fear of defeat next time, and yet if one gets started in that kind of business it is very hard to get out. I find myself planning & scheming all the time." He had had dealings with the legislature at Springfield. "I suppose a more scaly set of one-horse-thieves & low-lived political tricksters never assembled on the earth." Please write: "Don't let the grass grow on the paths between our hearts." He enclosed ten dollars, one of many gifts over the years to the unprosperous physician in the Wisconsin village.

The war was winding down with the victorious march of the northern armies. In his Second Inaugural speech Lincoln advanced a policy of reconciliation "with malice toward none, with charity for all." Lee surrendered at Appomattox on April ninth. On April eleventh in his last public utterance Lincoln envisaged a nation that would be reunited when ten percent of the white citizens in the respective southern states had taken the oath of allegiance and were restored to their antebellum government. Lincoln was shot on April fourteenth and lingered until the next day. Ingersoll agreed with Clark, who had aligned with the Radical Republicans advocating a draconian enforcement of nationality and freedom. At the memorial meeting in Peoria four days after the assassination he grieved with his fellow-citizens at the terrible deed, so "contrary to the will and express command of the most high," and opposed a generous program of reunion. "Shall we offer them the same terms? Forbid it, Almighty God!" (Larson, 78; *Transcript*, April 20).

Speaking at the anniversary reunion of the eighty-sixth Illinois Regiment Ingersoll paid homage to the living, the dead, and the bereaved for their sacrifices in defense of national unity and human freedom. "We thank you that the deluge of blood has subsided, that the ark of our national safety is at rest, that the dove has returned with the olive branch of peace, that the dark clouds of war are in the far distance, covered with the beautiful bow" (*Works*, IX, 409). He saluted "the old banner of the stars" that "waves in triumph now and shall forever, from the St. Lawrence to the Rio Grande, and from the Atlantic to the Pacific" (410). Of blacks: "We thank you in the name of four millions of people whose shackles you have so nobly and generously broken, and by your efforts become men. We thank you in the name of this poor and hitherto despised and insulted race, and say that their emancipation was, and is, the crowning glory of this most terrible war" (412). Of the leaders of the rebellion: "If ever I vote to make them citizens of this great republic . . . may the Almighty on the morning of the resurrection forget my soul" (Larson, 78; *Transcript*, Aug. 30).

Ingersoll had taken into his law office Sabin Puterbaugh as junior partner. Puterbaugh's only claim to historic notice hitherto had been that as a major under Ingersoll he had bivouacked a detachment without sentries, leading to a bloody rout by the Confederates (Rogers, 155).

The business of the firm was booming. Ingersoll wrote to Clark, "Yesterday I got through at Metamora after two weeks hard steady work. The fees earned this term foot up at least a good sum—$1600" (Aug. 27, 1865, L.C.). There was family sorrow. Three days later he wrote a letter of condolence to John on the death of his infant son named for Uncle Robert. The letter is sweetly sad and religious. "I wish," Robert says, "that I could be with you that our tears might mingle, and that we might stand side by side at the grave of your little darling." The common fate had again struck the Ingersolls. "Death is becoming familiar in our family. Only a few days and we will have to join the dear ones on the other side. Another voice is calling you to heaven. You have one reason less for wishing to live." Little Robby was now "with our father and mother. He has only ceased to be mortal." And the child would be forever young in memory, the sweet baby in their hearts. Finally, "may the God of our Father be with you and give you strength to bear your great affliction" (Aug. 10, 1865, *Letters*, 511).

In writing to his religious brother John and in his political oratory the Robert Ingersoll of the mid-1860s remained within the religious tradition. His mind was not made up although he was moving from doubt to negation. Meanwhile the religion of his childhood was a bond between the brothers and also pulled the crowds to a speaker trying to express his politics in the most exalted language at his command.

Ingersoll had long since moved away from belief in the literal inerrancy of the Bible, its myths, and miracles. While visiting Clark in Washington in the winter of 1865–1866 he happened on an article in an Illinois newspaper describing Governor Oglesby's lectures on his travels in the Holy Land in 1857. Oglesby was reported as claiming among the proofs of the divine inspiration of Old Testament fables that he saw "leeks and onion" on the very spot mentioned in the book of Numbers' description of the Exodus, and that as he stood where the manna fell from the heavens to the Israelites, some quails flew up from their immemorial habitat. Oglesby recommended the Bible as "the best handbook for the traveller in that country" (Plummer, "Robert G. Ingersoll on Leeks and Onions in the Holy Land," Ill. Quarterly, Vol. 43).[1]

Ingersoll's letter to Oglesby dated January twenty-second is the first firecracker thrown off by the new laughing philosopher at revealed religion. "I think your new argument if properly applied," Ingersoll informed the governor, "will bring tears to the eyes of the most hardened and profane." Thank God, all doubts were now settled. "My Dear Governor, you do not know how delighted I am to learn that you actually stood on the identical spot where the manna fell. How touching it is to have the words of Moses verified by the Governor of Illinois. Who in the name of Credulity will deny that God in his goodness sent millions of quails, broiled, buttered, on toast, to satisfy the hunger of those patient, pious, and honest people, after it becomes generally known that your Excellency in the year 1856 or thereabouts saw in that same region of country some of the very same *kind* of birds?" Ingersoll asked Oglesby whether the burning bush was burning when he rode by on his camel, whether he crossed the stream which, in defiance of Newton's law, followed the Jews up and down for forty years, and whether he saw the clothes which "waxed not old" during that entire period (whereas a modern tailor like Andy Johnson would have suggested a plan of reconstruction along the way)? Ingersoll laughed at all the biblical fables that had captivated children through the ages. "How wonderful to think that God stopped the whole universe in order to give Joshua time to thrash a few wretches that he could have whipped just as well after dark." Ingersoll assured Oglesby that he believes the snake and apple story and the creation of Eve from Adam's rib, and he yearned for the good days before Newton, Kepler, Laplace, and Humboldt

> when Moses was God's clerk and geologist, when Joshua was his General and Astronomer, when the Earth was flat. . . . When Noah was secretary of the Navy, when God himself came down and cut and made Adam and Eve breeches and petticoat hoop skirts and a claw hammer coat. When jackasses made set speeches to angels that they met on the road. . . . And that intrepid mariner Mr. Jonah finding himself in the belly of a whale did not *blubber*. And although in the midst of the great and mysterious deep—without any compass, tracts, bibles, playing cards, or tobacco, with nothing but fish *balls* to eat—the subject of a scaly trick—without knowing what country he was near—only knowing that he was in Finnland—still had the presence of mind to thrust an oar out of the whale's alimentary canal and pull himself triumphantly ashore.

Ingersoll concludes gratefully, "In the name of Ancient Geography, Astronomy, Geology, and Navigation, I thank you again and again, And subscribe myself your convinced, converted and most obedient servant." (Plummer, "Leeks and Onions," 9).

Governor Oglesby, broad-minded and companionable, made a generous response. "I do not know," he wrote to Ingersoll on January twenty-eighth, "when I have read so good a letter. I would be willing to lecture once a week for such a letter. . . . You must not object to my reading it to my friends. . . . Come and see me on your way home." (Plummer, "Goodbye, dear Governor, you are my best friend," *ISHSJ*).

Progress

In politics as in legal practice Robert and Clark were in perfect harmony. Clark was a substantial person in his own right but recognized the superiority of his younger brother. As a member of Congress, Clark drew inspiration from him. Robert was ecstatic over the congressional resolution leading to the Thirteenth Amendment abolishing slavery throughout the land. "The glorious Resolution that Slavery shall be eradicated, destroyed, and utterly abolished forever is the grandest resolution ever passed by that body. The heart of the Nation has kept pace with its physical success on the field of battle. I am proud too that your name is so well connected with that great Measure of Liberty" (March 8, 1865, L.C.). Freedom for blacks had to include the right of suffrage. "I think the ground to take is that if the Negroes are too ignorant that they ought to have an equal opportunity with the whites to become intelligent" (April 3, 1865, L.C.). There was nothing to fear from an educated mind. "Intelligence cannot be dangerous except to errors, mistakes & crimes—whether the intelligence is in a brain bound in white or black leather." Robert was quick to endorse Clark's speech stating a basic thesis of radical Reconstructionism that proposed, however strained, that the defeated Confederates should be treated as alien enemies rather than wayward citizens amenable to prosecution for treason and to presidential pardon *en masse*, which would remove every disability and "inaugurate another rebellion more gigantic than the one just crushed" (May 12, 1866, L.C.). No matter that when war broke out Ingersoll had called from his office balcony for hanging Jefferson Davis as a traitor under the Constitution. The newfangled theory was high politics. It would paralyze Andrew Johnson, whom Clark had exposed, according to Robert's torrent of epithets, as "an impudent boaster, an egotistical ass, a shallow hypocrite & a malicious conspirator" (May 12, 1866, L.C.).

Ingersoll's mind was reaching out. He was well read, though self-educated. Realms of gold to travel in, and so little time! "How delightful it would be," the lawyer in Peoria fantasies to the member of Congress in Washington, "if you and I could pass a few months reading together" (May 5, 1866, L.C.). Of his reading in this period he specifically refers to Henry T. Buckle's rationalistic work *History of Civilization in England*. "I think it is the greatest work I ever read. He is a man of vast learning, and had the clearest and most logical head in the world" (To John, March 17, 1865, *Letters*, 137). He wrote of buying "a splendid copy of the Encyclopedia Britannica, 22 vols. the other day for $220" (To Clark, May 5, 1866, L.C.). His philosophy was taking shape. He needed no time to expand and refine it before giving it to the world or at least to Peoria. "On Monday night I am going to deliver a lecture on Progress. I have it all written" (To Clark, May 12, 1866, L.C.).

Years later, in 1893, Ingersoll would say in an interview, "My first lecture was entitled 'Progress.' I began lecturing because I thought the creeds of the orthodox church false and horrible, and because I thought the Bible cruel and absurd, and because I like intellectual liberty" (*Works*, VIII, 533). In fact "Progress" is not a direct challenge to the religious beliefs and practices of nineteenth-century America. It is concerned rather with enunciating the positive values of Ingersollism—the religion of democracy, science, and usefulness—in which the seeds of conflict with orthodoxy are present. Ingersoll defined progress as the increase of human happiness. Its necessary condition would be freedom of the mind and the body. He sketched the pre-modern times, the middle ages, as a dark period of bigotry, witchcraft, and persecution when priests and nobles exploited the ignorance of the people. He extolled the Reformation, though censuring the reformers for their own intolerance. He celebrated the French Revolution, "one of the greatest pages of all history" (*Works, IV, 466*), and moving with the tide said of the Emancipation Proclamation: "And on the 1st day of January, 1863, the grandest New Year that ever dawned upon this continent, in accordance with the will of the heroic North, by the sublime act of one whose name will be sacred through all the coming years, the justice so long delayed was accomplished, and four millions of slaves became chainless" (470).

The progress of mankind depends, in Ingersoll's view, upon the march of science, invention, printing, and education. "The inventors have helped more than any other class to make the world what it is: the workers and the thinkers, the poor and the grand, labor and learning, industry and intelligence. Watt and Descartes, Fulton and Montaigne, Stephenson and Kepler, Crompton and Comte, Franklin and Voltaire, Morse and Buckle, Draper and Spencer, and hundreds more that I could name" (*Works, IV, 452*).

"Progress" sparkles with eloquence. "There must be freedom in religion, for without freedom there can be no real religion" (432). "Without liberty the brain is a dungeon, where the chained thoughts die with their pinions pressed against the hingeless doors" (452). "Education is the most radical abolitionist in the world" (465). "We [defending slavery] made a whipping post of the cross of Christ" (462). And there are bits of Ingersollian humor. A pardonable pun on Luther throwing an inkwell on the Devil: "The devil, I believe, was untouched, he probably having an inkling of Luther's intention, made a successful dodge" (440). A sociable chuckle at the difference between the old and new times: "A majority of the people now live better than the king used to do. Poor Solomon with his thousand wives, and no carpets; his great Temple, and no gas light! A thousand women, and not a pin in the house; no stoves, no cooking ranges, no baking power, no potatoes—think of it! Breakfast without potatoes!" (451). The lecture ends with a startling flourish of rationalism: "Forward until superstition is a forgotten dream, forward until the world is free, forward until human reason, clothed in the purple of authority, is king of kings" (457).

The political papers made political judgments on the lecture, the Republican papers that the full house "listened attentively," and the Democratic that "people tried to keep awake." Neither appreciated that a great career in freethought had been launched (Larson, 89).

Now another game: The philosopher departs, the politician returns. In the summer of 1866 Robert managed Clark's campaign for renomination. Robert appeared as a sophisticated politician bent upon victory. "I have been working like a beaver" (To Clark, June 27, 1866, L.C.). In Peoria he hired a band and staged a mass meeting at Rouse's Hall to which he invited Clark's chief rival, McCoy, for debate. He had packed floor and galleries with an Ingersoll claque. As he approached the platform "the people cheered like Hell. I saw that I had him foul. We all had the discussion sufficient to say that I did not leave a gut in him" (To Clark, June 28, 1866, L.C.). To get out the vote for the party caucus in Peoria the next day Robert laid out four hundred dollars for carriages to bring the feeble to the polls and what in the jargon of a later day would be known as "walk-around money" for Clark workers. Clark was chosen by acclamation. "I would rather have died than to have been beaten. . . . All well, God bless you" (To Clark, June 28, 1866, L.C.). The opposition to Clark had claimed that he did not have the endorsement of Thaddeus Stevens, leader of the radical faction in the House. They also charged that Robert was seeking office as congressman-at-large and that the brothers aimed at establishing a dynasty in the state. At Galesburg Robert juggled old complimentary letters from Stevens to Clark, giving the impression of a current endorsement, and heatedly denied that he himself was a candidate. "You see I would not hurt your chances by saying that I was" (July 6, 1866, L.C.). Robert had spent about two thousand dollars on the party caucuses. "I shall spend no more money, the goose hangs high enough" (July 6, 1866, L.C.). Clark won the Galesburg caucus 3 to 1 and went on to overwhelming success in the primary and the election.

Relaxed and serene after the primaries Robert opened wide the workings of his mind to Clark (July 14, 1866, L.C.). He advised Clark on speech-making, voting in Congress, helping constituents. He rejected Clark's advice to run for the at-large seat: Not that he was afraid of competition but he was expecting a redistricting that would make it a one-term position; meanwhile his legal practice would be wiped out. Besides, his wife was objecting to state-wide canvassing, particularly as his holding public office would be "the end of *home*." Loftily he told his brother the congressman that he was not eager to join "the bread-and-butter brigade" and "trim my little sails to catch the breath of ignorant admiration and paid flattery." Politicians end miserably, witness Webster, Clay, Seward, and worst, of all, "A. Johnson, a political animal sporting in a very small drop of very mean rebel piss." The legal profession suited his needs. "I can make enough to get what books I want & get leisure enough to read them." He was reading great books, his mind expanding toward new horizons of thought. "I am keeping remarkably cool, and reading Comte's positive philosophy and the works of the Great Voltaire. I am steadfast in the faith and enjoying myself hugely. And feeling *infinitely* free. I feel as though I could exist without God just as well as he could exist without me—and I also feel that if there must be an orthodox God in Heaven I am in favor of electing him ourselves." A personal regimen for Clark: "Well dear Bro. be very careful of yourself. Keep your head cool & your bowels open. And every morning as you wake up say, 'I will be a little more radical today than I was yesterday.' " In August this erstwhile fugitive from politics was back on the stump, campaigning with Governor Oglesby for the anti-Johnson cause in Indiana, making more than a dozen speeches at various places including a big rally in Indianapolis (Plummer, *ISHSJ*, Summer, 1980, 81).

The elections over, the crowds gone, Ingersoll sank back into private life. He was not very happy. His cheerfulness was in conflict with his sense of the vanity of existence, the evanescence of all its values. His mind and heart opened to Clark like a book as the letters came. "I am in the best of health & spirits," he wrote, "only the town is lonesome without you, and the old lonely feeling that I am only a passenger in this world comes over me" (Dec. 6, 1866, L.C.). At the age of thirty-three he felt that his life was almost over. "It makes me shudder to think how old we are getting. The gray hairs are thickening on my head and our lives are touching the confines of the sombre. How I wish we could live with all we love forever here" (Dec. 14, 1866, L.C.). In this mood so much seemed to be going wrong. "I weigh 212 avoirdupois and my belly does not appear to have stretched to its full capacity. Peoria is infinitely dull and business is on the decline" (Dec. 20, 1866, L.C.). Yet there were compensations. "All my folks are in good health. I took a nice sleigh ride with your horse Robin & we went like birds. He is a perfectly splendid animal & has more sense than most members of Congress." He had found refreshment in the great writers of antiquity. "I have been reading a great deal this winter. I have been reading Eusebius, Polybius, Sallust, Herodotus" (Jan. 23, 1867, L.C.). Happily married, he marked the fifth anniversary of his marriage, "the luckiest day of my life" (Feb. 13, 1867, L.C.). Still, he was not content; he was not riding the tide of the times in Peoria. He was proud of his brother but could hardly hide his envy. "I am getting to be known as 'the brother of the Member.' Go ahead old Darling and be famous. I know that you will make a fair divide of your glory with me" (Feb. 20, 1867, L.C.).

In late 1866 the Illinois legislature created the position of attorney general. The first incumbent was to be appointed by the governor and successors chosen by popular vote. Having received assurances from Clark Carr that party leaders favored Ingersoll for attorney general (or any other post he might want), on February 27, 1867, Oglesby appointed Ingersoll to his first and, as it turned out, last public office. The Senate immediately confirmed without a dissenting vote (Robert to Clark, Feb. 27, 1867, *Letters*, 139). The position paid $3,500 per annum.

Should he move his family to Springfield? He thought the question over while organizing his new responsibilities at the state capital. He decided to keep them in Peoria as a continuing base for the brothers. "I am getting along first rate," he enthused to Clark after a week on the job. "I am giving satisfaction in my new office to everybody, I think." There was a hitch. "My wife has been a widow all winter & she is quite tired of my being away and I am as tired as she can be" (March 6, 1867, L.C.). Reluctantly Mrs. Ingersoll cooperated with her husband's plans.

The burdens of office were not heavy—that is, for Ingersoll. He accepted with good grace the ceremonial functions and his grumbling was not bitter at the "fool questions addressed to the atty general by people laboring under the impression that my whole business is to construe law for justices of the peace, town clerks, constables & men too poor to employ a lawyer" (To Clark, April 23, 1867, L.C.). Governor and Attorney General were great friends. Together they attended fairs, cornerstone layings, and such; together they travelled to Washington to lobby for internal improvements in Illinois at federal expense. They could consider enjoying a season of opera in Chicago (Ingersoll to Oglesby, Sept. 21, 1867, Plummer, *ISHSJ*, 94). Ingersoll, Oglesby, and Clark Carr attended a series of performances by Madame Ristori, reigning queen of European theater. Although the performances were in Italian, Ingersoll was entranced by the earthy passion and facial mobility of the great actress. He sent in his card. His companions asked to come along, and he sent in their cards. The next afternoon the three met her and through an interpreter lauded her wonderful acting, Italy, and the cause of freedom. As they were about to leave, Ingersoll grandly declared that Italy had furnished America with its first and last sensations, Columbus and Ristori, whereupon she shook both his hands and blew goodbye kisses at him. The report to Clark ends: "God bless and take care of you *if he can*" (April 1, 1867, L.C.). Ingersoll was a life-long aficionado of the stage, especially Shakespeare and Wagner, creators of dramatic and melodramatic larger-than-life personalities (Cf. Robson and Crane Dinner, Nov. 21, 1887; *Works*, XII, 95).

The attorney general could not repress his penchant for jokes, puns, and quips in writing to the governor. Good or bad they poured into his mind and he let them out. When the miners in La Belle County threatened to strike, Ingersoll advised the lieutenant governor, the governor being on vacation, to maintain order by warning the strikers that he would call out a local posse rather than the militia. The lieutenant governor acted accordingly. The announcement, Ingersoll reported, "will prevent any strikes in the future and for that reason fail to have any *striking* effect" (Ingersoll to Oglesby, Aug. 1, 1867, Plummer, *ISHSJ*, 93). He explained irreverently why he cancelled a trip to Chicago: "As soon as I heard that the martyr's widow was at the Hyde Park House, I concluded I would save my hide by staying at home" (Ingersoll to Oglesby, Sept. 21, 1867, Plummer, 96). On being invited to join the governor and his party for a vacation in the woods, he declined, lamenting the wonders of nature that he would miss: "I keep thinking of fishing, hunting the falls of Minnehaha, gnats, beautiful cool nights, beetles and fleas, moonlight excursions in canoes, mosquitoes, river flies, sand mud, poor hotels, tough steak, rye coffee, hay tea, a majority of the party always wanting to do the most stupid thing possible" (Ingersoll to Oglesby, Aug. 7, 1867, Plummer, *ISHSJ*, 93).

In a more serious vein Ingersoll conferred with Oglesby on legal problems of the state and on more general matters. The inflexible money supply and falling prices were leading to an economic problem with political implications. "Times are getting hard," he wrote from Peoria, "money getting scarce and consequently our party getting a little shaky. There must be an expansion of the currency. Men will never act good unless the times are good. When a man has his pocket full of money, he feels like a gentleman and when a man feels like a gentleman he votes our ticket. But when his pocket is empty and his shirt tail out he naturally slides over to the Democracy" (Dec. 22, 1867, Plummer, 97).

His official post did not bar Ingersoll from keeping up his private practice, and more and more he returned to business and family in Peoria, assuring the governor that he would return to Springfield on call. Unless called, why not stay in Peoria and avoid the heat and dust of travel? (July 22, 1867, Plummer, 94). In the summer of 1867 his junior partner Sabin Puterbaugh ran for a seat on the circuit bench, and Ingersoll electioneered extensively for him (Robert to Clark, June 6, 1867, *Letters*, 140). Puterbaugh being elected, they wound up the partnership.

One day, as the story goes, Ingersoll dropped into Judge Puterbaugh's court. The new judge was in the process of holding in contempt a young lawyer who had been caught sketching an uncomplimentary portrait of his honor. Ingersoll spoke up that it was all a joke, not to be taken seriously. Judge Puterbaugh replied sternly that when he needed Mr. Ingersoll's help he would call upon him. This was more than Ingersoll could take from his recent junior partner. He retorted that when the judge was "fishing for the ermine" he was glad to have Ingersoll's help. Promptly Judge Puterbaugh held him in contempt and fined him ten dollars. Ingersoll moved to comply. Groping through his pockets and coming out empty-handed, he strode to the bench and holding an empty palm under the judge's nose said, "Puterbaugh, lend me $10." Startled and shocked, the judge recovered quickly. "Mr. Clerk," he directed, "let the record show that Mr. Ingersoll's fine is remitted. Peoria county can better afford to lose $10 than I can" (*Chicago Mail*, Oct. 16, 1889; *Utica Observer*, March 21, 1900).

From the same period comes the story of Ingersoll and the newsboy. As Ingersoll was walking to the depot with his client Henry Mansfield, a barefoot newsboy asked him to buy a paper. "Yes," said Ingersoll, "give me a paper. What's the matter with you, you little cuss? Haven't you any shoes?" The boy replied, "No." Ingersoll inquired, "Can't you make enough money selling papers to buy shoes?" "No," said the boy. Ingersoll pressed, "Won't your parents buy you shoes?" The answer: "They don't got any money." Ingersoll took his hand out of his pocket holding a bill and gave it to the boy. "Here, you little cuss, go and buy yourself a whole outfit." When lawyer and client arrived at the depot Ingersoll reached into his pockets and found no money for a ticket. "Mansfield," he said, "I'm broke, lend me ten dollars." "No, I won't," replied Mansfield. "Do you know the denomination of the bill you gave that boy?" "No," said Ingersoll. Mansfield closed the discussion: "You gave that boy a twenty-dollar bill. Any man who will do such a thing should not be allowed to handle money" (E. G. Smith, 33).

Robert was Clark's representative in Peoria. He published Clark's speeches in the local papers, forwarded solicitations by constituents, counseled patience in dealing with the more obstreperous ones: "I would rather have the itch & no fingernails as to manage such people" (Feb. 27, 1868, L.C.). He advised Clark to make speeches in strategic parts of his district to enhance his reputation as a radical Republican. "I am prouder of you every day" (July 8, 1867, L.C.).

As a devoted older brother Clark was an unfailing source of support and inspiration. "You do not know how happy it makes me," wrote Robert, "to know that you think of me and love me" (June 2, 1867, L.C.). He faced so many questions, so many decisions to make: "My Lord, how I want to see you and take your advice about a lot of things." Nobody in Peoria was worth talking to: "The men of Peoria are stupid and rotten fish cast up by a sluggish tide on a muddy shore" (April 21, 1867, L.C.). He has been prospering: "I never was so well situated before and was never so happy in my life. Nothing troubles me now. I have enough to eat and wear, and my loved ones are in the same happy condition. So I say to Mr. Noah, 'Go ahead with your d---d ark. I don't think there will be much of a shower anyhow" (May 20, 1867, L.C.).

He was making his mark in public speaking. He spoke to the Turn Verein on the contributions of German-descent Union soldiers. "They were almost crazy with delight and I reckon that the German people are henceforth my friends" (June 20, 1867, L.C.). He quoted extensively from his bombastic Fourth of July speech in De Kalb County a few days after a Mexican firing squad executed Maximilian, ending Napoleon III's dream of empire in the New World. "This continent has virtually said to the despots of Europe, 'You cannot provide for your younger brothers here. If you have not land enough there to make them a kingdom, we have enough here to give them a grave. If you cannot build them a throne, we can erect a scaffold. If you cannot clothe them in the purple robe of authority, we can wrap them in the white shroud of death' " (July 8, 1867, *Letters*, 712.) Robert confessed to Clark that he was getting tired of the legal profession. "Court is dragging along its weary length as usual. It is impossible for me to get interested in a little law suit again. I feel disgusted to see all of them scrambling & almost fighting for a few dollars" (Feb. 27, 1868, L.C.). He basked in popular acclaim and saw a clear road ahead in public life, untroubled by rumblings of protest from orthodoxy: "The religious people are making quite a fight on me and begin to take delight in lying about me but it will all come right in the end" (June 20, 1867, L.C.).

The brothers also corresponded about literature and philosophy. In an office filled with the hubbub of legal business Robert wrote an essay of literary criticism. He agreed with Clark in downgrading Milton for his "mixture of Christian lies with pagan mythology." Greek religion was a temple, Christianity a barn. "Nothing but Hell & Heaven, Duty, looking bilious—Keeping Sunday & indulging in the fond hope that everybody but myself will be damned." He had no use for Petrarch and little for Rabelais. "Voltaire is the only man who never disappoints you. He is always fresh, sharp, to the point, and you never weary of the grand old autocrat of the world" (June 2, 1867, L.C.).

Ingersoll was meditating on the fundamental questions of life and death, and his heart was sick at what his mind told him. His love for Clark ran afoul of his preoccupation with death; in their correspondence, in time, Robert anticipated Clark's funeral. In mid-December, driving an open sleigh from court in Metamora to Peoria, there was time to think of the sweetness and pathos of life. The wind high, the snow flying, Robert's tears mingled with the snowflakes as he reflected on the life of the brothers together, of "how you made your appearance on a bleak December day in this bleaker world—of how I formed your acquaintance about twenty-one or twenty-two months after your arrival, and how we had been pretty well known to each other ever since" (Dec. 22, 1867, L.C.). The note of sadness insisted on returning. At thirty-six Clark's performance on the stage of life seemed almost over. Soon the play would end, the footlights dim out, the orchestra fade into weak discord and silence, "the Curtain will slowly fall, and no one will know that it will ever rise again. Dear Noble Brother, let us be together all we can while the play goes on. Let us enjoy together. I am losing my life while away from you." In his New Year's message he dwelt on the hopeless mystery of existence. "Will the Motion sometime cease? Did the Motion ever commence?" The Universe gave no answer. "What poor wretches we are. Ignorant alike of origin and destiny." They lived in hope, "borrowing sugar of tomorrow with which to take the pills of today—cheating ourselves at every step, yet expecting to get the best of the next bargain—doubling our bets but forever losing—and finally the poor man dies—the mouth of desire is full of dry sand & in his stiffened hands is found a forged certificate of immortality." Robert could not bear to think that he was one year nearer to death and separation from his loved ones, "the horrible—the terrible—the Unknown" (Jan. 1, 1868, L.C.).

Ingersoll could take advice from Lear: "Of that way madness lies." In his normal happy mood he was a man of the world and could not linger in the desert of cosmic despair. He enjoyed family life, went sleigh riding for pleasure, danced at parties. He found his acquaintances amusing and laughed at them—Carl Warner always standing beside the Indian Squaw in front of Newman and Ullman's tobacco shop, the "cuss" Puterbaugh thinking he can hold his breeches up without suspenders, Hugh Reynolds, whose coat is always too short "to cover his presbyterian stern." Politics was warming up. He would be with Oglesby in Washington in a couple of weeks. He would soon establish Grant clubs in every town in the country, preparing for the elections in 1868: *"Put our men your real friends* at the head of each one, and use the organization to carry the county without a struggle for you" (Jan. 1, 1868, L.C.).

A Political Battle

As the election year came on, Robert Ingersoll examined his own political prospects and found them not to his liking. His term as appointed attorney general was drawing to a close. To seek a second term seemed a pursuit of diminishing returns and not worth a thorough statewide canvass of the electorate (To Clark, Jan. 27, 1868, *Letters,* 142). He seemed to be at a standstill. He was not a party big-wig, and the indirect process of electing senators via the state legislature was beyond his reach. John ("Black Jack") Logan was ensconced in his congressional seat as representative-at-large and Clark held Peoria. Under the law at that time an incumbent governor could not succeed himself, so the office was up for grabs, but Ingersoll did not consider himself in the running. Party opinion had crystallized around John Logan and John Palmer as possible choices. "I suppose," Ingersoll had written to Governor Oglesby, "Palmer is prepared to accept your seat as soon as you vacate it & that Logan stands ready to push him away and sit down himself. Man proposes and God disposes, and maybe God will dispose of them both—otherwise I have no earthy objection to either of these gentlemen, except that I don't want a ring in the State so perfectly formed that it is known who is to be governor two years ahead" (Sept. 21, 1867, Plummer, *ISHSJ,* 94). As Union generals, Logan and Palmer each commanded heavy support from veterans and were separately invincible at the polls. In spite of just having won an important case for the state before the Illinois Supreme Court, Ingersoll was again in the doldrums. He was a politician and had nowhere to go. "I don't know what to do," he sighed to Clark. "I am pretty much tired of everything and feel as though the whole thing was a farce—but not to be laughed at" (Jan. 27, 1868, *Letters,* 142).

Suddenly a miracle! God seemed to dispose. Logan and Palmer began fading from the horizon as gubernatorial possibilities. The indications were that Logan was planning to run for reelection to Congress and looking forward to his Senate bid in 1870 (which proved successful). Palmer took himself out of consideration for personal reasons—the expense of a statewide canvass and a sick child. Nobody of any stature stood in the way of the attorney general to the executive mansion. "All our friends here," he wrote to Clark, "are crazy to have me run for governor " (March 3, 1868, IHS). He shared their enthusiasm. Professing indifference as to the outcome he threw himself into pursuit of the nomination with craft and energy. He spent a week in Chicago talking with politicians. He circularized Republican leaders throughout the state. They responded, endorsing him to a man, although some hedged their commitment in the event they were so instructed or if Palmer turned out to be a candidate (Ingersoll Papers, IHS). He solicited Governor Oglesby's "honest, square advice," couching his request with a not too subtle appeal to Oglesby's self-interest: "In that position I could help you more than in any other, and you know that I would do it" (Plummer, ISHSJ, 99). Oglesby, feet on the ground as usual, responded with prophetic insight that Palmer had not declared that he would refuse the nomination if offered. Nevertheless Oglesby had consulted party leaders and they were favorable to Ingersoll. "It is true to state however that you have not been supposed to be a candidate for Governor but once you are proclaimed to be I think you will be strong" (Oglesby to Ingersoll, March 19, 1968, Ingersoll Papers, IHS). The groundswell of enthusiasm rose in the press. The *Chicago Tribune* cited ten newspapers through the state, the *Peoria Transcript* two more, as endorsing Colonel Ingersoll, "able, logical, and convincing," "an uncompromising Radical" and believer in impeachment, one who would drive the copperheads to "hunting their holes before the canvass is half over" (*Transcript*, March 21, 1868). Swept by the euphoria of the moment, Ingersoll's imagination soared. "If I get the nomination, I will bet my ears that I break into the Senate in 1871" (To Clark, March 24, 1868, *Letters*, 146). Careless of his promise to Oglesby of his undivided support, he was ready for any deal that would benefit the Ingersoll brothers. "You must be re-nominated in the district," he told Clark, "& I am willing to make any sacrifice to accomplish that. You can tell Logan what you see fit & proper, but of one thing he may rest forever and forever assured & that is as you know that I am pledged to nobody in the world. Nobody has any mortgage on me but you. And if Logan wants to play fair & square I am willing to play with him" (March 29, 1868, L.C.). He would straddle Oglesby and Logan.

On that same day, March twenty-ninth, Ingersoll made his debut as gubernatorial candidate with a speech delivered in Springfield in the Hall of Representatives under the auspices of the Young Men's Republican Club. A correspondent for the *Chicago Journal* reported that in spite of a heavy rain the hall was "well filled with a highly intelligent and influential audience." Ingersoll spoke for an hour and a half and "kept the audience perfectly spell-bound, while the frequent sallies of wit and pungent home thrusts of the speaker elicited the most hearty rounds of applause." He glorified the Republican Party as "the grandest that ever existed upon the earth." It was the party of progress and religious values. "For bloodhounds it has substituted the schoolmaster and the missionary, & of the auction block it has constructed a pulpit." He excoriated the Democratic Party as "guilty of treason to the human race." He equated the Republican Party with the Grand Army of the Republic, triumphant over Democrats at home and rebels in the field, marching "*forward*, through the roar, and smoke, and fire, and hell of war—*forward*, to the very top of the mountain of universal victory, and there with proud hands they threw to the loving winds the banner of the stars, now floating from sea to sea." The parties having been identified and defined, the statement of issues took little effort:

> Shall Slavery be reestablished, or shall the Government be founded upon Justice? Shall the debt be paid, or the nation dishonored? Shall the loyal people of the South be protected, or abandoned to the mercies of those who hate and despise them? Shall liberty perish from the nation? Shall civilization stop, or sweep onward?

He championed equality. The white race was superior to the black but "by equality I mean the giving to every man in the race of life, without regard to birth or color, a fair and equal start. Honor to those who get ahead—kindness for those who fall behind, and justice for all." The correspondent apologized for giving "but a sketch of one of the most thrilling speeches delivered in our State capitol for a long time. At the conclusion a vote of thanks was passed by the club to the gifted orator of the evening, while cheer after cheer went up in honor of the prospective Governor of Illinois" (Quoted in *Peoria Transcript*, April 2, 1868).

On the morrow a cloud on the horizon. The *Chicago Tribune* quoted Palmer as saying that he would not seek the nomination but "if my name and services are essential to its [the Republican party's] success, I would waive all personal considerations and make the canvass" (Plummer, 101). A nervous Ingersoll came down from the clouds. "It seems that Palmer is not quite dead yet," he lamented to Oglesby, "that after all, 'Barkis is willing' " (April 1, 1868, Plummer, *ISHSJ*, 101). The *Illinois State Journal* of April seventh carried an exchange between Ingersoll and Palmer, Ingersoll saying that he never wanted to be a candidate against Palmer, and Palmer answering, "I am not, and do not intend to be a candidate for Governor" (Plummer, 101). "Palmer has been smoked out," a relieved Robert informed Clark. Nevertheless, he would take nothing for granted, he weighed the odds; he was fighting for a landslide victory over all his opponents.

Just got a letter from George A. Bangs of Aurora. He says I will carry
Farnsworth. I will carry most of Cooks district—all of Ross. Every County
in Moulton except the one he lives in. I will get at least half & I think
nearly all of Bromwells—I know that I will get Champaign, Macon, Piatt,
and Iroquois. I am told that I will carry Montgomery, but I don't know
a d---d man in that County or Piatt either. Gallatin, Salina, Bond, and
Alexander they say will be O.K. Sangamon, Mocoupin & Morgan I know
I will carry. I think the first ballot will settle the hash. I am growing
every day & the rest are growing small—I spoke in Jacksonville Saturday
& in Carlinville Monday. I speak at Bloomington on tomorrow night,
at Lincoln Monday, at Aurora Wednesday etc. So you see that I am
doing something. I will carry every County I speak in.

He had fallen out with Joseph Medill, editor of the *Chicago Tribune*. The
Tribune attacked Clark as being allied with the liquor interests and thieves
generally, and Robert had written Medill a bitter letter that he could
not accept support from a paper that opposed Clark. "Medill will likely
be against me. God damn him! Let him howl. I can beat him at his own
game. Well goodbye. Love to all" (April 19, 1868, *Letters*, 148). Palmer
joined Ingersoll at the Carlinville rally and pledged his support to the
choice of the party (*Transcript*, April 10, 1868, quoted from *Missouri Democrat*).

Palmer having expressly disclaimed any interest in the nomination,
the coast appeared clear. On April fourteenth the Peoria caucus voted
unanimously for Clark for Congress and Robert for the governorship.
"You and I have come up together and will continue to rise together,"
Robert wrote to Clark. He gloated, "The poor opposition is dead—I speak
of them in the singular because all of them would not make *one* man"
(April 14, 1868, L.C.). The Republican press all over the state played
a symphony of enthusiasm for the only serious candidate in the field,
the spellbinder from Peoria: "the first man after Palmer" (*Henderson Plain
Dealer*); "an active, able, and eloquent defender of the Union within the
members of the Republican party" (*Iroquois Republican*); "That he will be
a popular candidate and that, if elected, he will make an able and useful
Executive we have no doubt" (*Chicago Post*); "As a popular speaker familiar 'Bob Ingersoll' has few rivals in the country—and on the 'stump' he
stands preeminent—unrivalled. He is just the man for our State ticket.
It is no place to put *drones* or *fossil specimens*. It must be headed by an
able Commander—one that is able to stir up and keep awake enthusiasm
among the masses, and that Col. Ingersoll can do more effectively than
any other man in Illinois, Gen. Logan not excepted" (*Wilmington Independent*); "Since the declination of Gen. Palmer, nearly all our people are in
favor of Col. Ingersoll. Able, true, warm hearted, and popular, no one
else could incite so much enthusiasm in the Republican ranks" (*Galesburg
Free Press*, quoted in *Transcript*, April 18, 1868).

Suddenly the Palmer menace came to life again. As the date for the
state Republican convention drew near, well-founded rumors arose that

an attempt would be made to bulldoze Palmer's nomination through the convention. Not that the party leaders were disturbed by gossip that Ingersoll favored miscegenation, was a tool of the liquor interests, or held unpopular views on religion. He was a maverick, and his split with the *Tribune* showed that he could not be trusted as a team player. Besides, there were too many Ingersolls at the trough (Larson, 93).

To Ingersoll it all seemed a conspiracy to rob him of a prize he had fairly won, a conspiracy he could not overcome. He had statistics demonstrating that he could not beat Palmer in an open convention fight. Writing to Clark, in anticipating defeat and the end of his political career, he bitterly condemned Palmer and the stupid political system.

> It looks as though Palmer really wants to be Governor after all. He will likely beat me, but I am going to fight it out to the bitter end. If he allows himself to run, he will simply prove himself to be a dirty dog—To be beaten now I think will end me politically. I cannot afford to run any more for any thing. I will have been whipped too often. I don't think people know me. My friends are enthusiastic when I am helping them, but when I want something they generally prefer another man. This may be the experience of everybody. I am pretty nearly sick of the whole thing. . . . After the Convention is over I will settle down to the practice of that miserable profession known as the law, and bid goodbye to all political aspirations. Heartily disgusted—knowing that I have been throwing pearls before swine—that my party has not the sense to understand me. (April 29, 1868, *Letters*, 149)

In spite of his sense of almost certain personal defeat, Ingersoll kept on playing and enjoying his role as the jovial nemesis of the Democrats. Addressing a Republican rally at Rouse's Hall on the eve of the convention he was "frequently and loudly applauded" as he argued for human equality and redemption of the war-issue greenbacks in gold or silver, and ridiculed the Democratic party. The Democrats were always seeking new depths in which to sink and "the Lord help they may. The Democrats can never carry their record. If every one was a Samson with his hair to his heels they couldn't do it" (*Transcript*, May 6, 1868).

At the convention a tight-rope drama took place. The Palmer faction had spread the notion that his avowed noncandidacy had· merely "bolted the door of his inclination with a boiled carrot" (*Transcript*, May 6, 1868), and he would readily accept the nomination if offered on a platter. Although they held the convention in their grip the road to victory was not smooth. Ingersoll, Palmer, and S. W. Moulton were put in nomination. A motion to elect Ingersoll by acclamation was hooted down. Then General Rowett electrified the convention by reading a late exchange of telegrams with Palmer. Rowett: "It is certain that you will be nominated for Governor. Shall we after the nomination say that you will accept?" Palmer: "Do not permit this nomination. I cannot accept."

Rowett pleaded with the convention not to force Palmer into rejecting its mandate, which would simply damage his future in the party. The Palmer stalwarts were checked—for a moment. They engineered a dry run. If Palmer lost, no harm would be done to his future standing. The vote was Palmer 263, Ingersoll 117, others trailing. Palmer was clearly the choice of the convention. A delegate, one Eastman, read a letter a month old in which Palmer had informed the *Tribune* that if nominated for the candidacy he would be guided "by the duty of the hour" (Larson, 92; *Tribune*, May 7, 1868). The convention rushed to a regular vote that went 317 for Palmer, 118 for Ingersoll. The Ingersoll faction had stood firm but it was not enough. Palmer accepted.

There is a story of a preballot confrontation between Ingersoll and a convention committee in which he sacrificed his chances for the nomination with an eloquent affirmance of his antireligious beliefs. One Edward P. Fox, allegedly a member of the committee, was quoted as saying that five-sixths of the convention was predisposed for Ingersoll, and that the committee visited him for assurance that as the Republican nominee he would keep his unbelief out of the campaign. The story continues:

Mr. Ingersoll drew himself up and replied, "Gentlemen, I am not asking to be Governor of Illinois and it is a grave question with me whether I would accept the nomination if offered. I have in my composition that which I have declared to the world as my views on religion. My position I would not, under any circumstances, not even for my life, seem to renounce. I would rather refuse to be President of the United States than to do so. My religious belief is my own. It belongs to me, not to the State of Illinois. While I believe in the right of every man to think as he pleases, yet I have the moral honesty to declare from the housetops my conviction. I feel deeply the interests of the Republican party, yet, gentlemen, I must say to you again, my belief is my own. I renounce nothing, I promise nothing, I ask nothing of the Convention. (*Transcript*, Oct. 27, 1889, quoted from *St. Louis Democrat*; *Letters*, 77–80)

This has all the makings of a cherry-tree fable. It claims too much, and is full of holes. No contemporary record of the event has been found. A list of delegates as published in the *Transcript* (May 6, 1868), although not certifiably official or complete, does not include an Edward P. Fox. That Ingersoll entered the convention with five-sixths of the delegates behind him is not true, nor would he have dared to tell the committee that he was indifferent as to the outcome. Nonetheless, something had happened. A month after the convention Robert wrote to Clark: "You know I told you about the Methodist Conference pups sending down a letter against me. It turns out in evidence now that the man who brought the af'd letter heard me speak in the evening before the Convention & was so well pleased with the speech that he never showed me his letter—kept it in his pocket & used his influence for me" (June 10, 1868,

L.C.). Ingersoll did not mention such a momentous encounter to any-one. His biographer Cramer denies that the meeting took place (74); Larson disregards it entirely. Yet there must have been some such meeting. Captain John Hall, an identifiable Peorian, said at the memorial serv-ice for Ingersoll: "I was at his office when the committee from the state convention called upon him and told him he could have the nomination for governor of Illinois if he would keep his peculiar views out of the campaign. When the leader had finished Colonel Ingersoll stood erect like a giant and said to him, looking him full in the eye: 'I would not smother one sentiment of my heart to be president of the United States' " (Macdonald, 185). Ingersoll himself, years later, said to a reporter, "I was a candidate for that office, I am sorry to say, and a committee waited on me to know if I was an infidel. I told them I was and they said they would like to go for me, but they were afraid that their constituents would 'go' for them. I preserved my manhood and lost the office" (Interview, *New York Herald*, April 17, 1882; cf. *Six Interviews on Talmage*, in *Works*, V, 301).

Perhaps this matter calls for further comment. In 1867–1868 Inger-soll was an office-seeking politician who happened to be a student of religion. He had published no antireligious tracts nor made any antireli-gious public statements (excepting a few phrases in his lecture "Prog-ress," which was not published in his lifetime). However, his antipathy to revealed religion was well known. He was aware of disapproval from the churches but felt that he could accommodate his political career to it (To Clark, June 20, 1867, L.C., previously cited at p. 54). His oratory on the stump had been liberally sprinkled with biblical allusions and references to divine judgment, and his Springfield address in particular had lauded missionaries and pulpits. If he had pursued a political career it is fairly certain that he would never have become a famous apostle of freethought. As Paris was worth a mass to Henry of Navarre, so the Governor's Mansion, the Senate, the White House itself, were worth a bit of diplomacy to an ambitious politician. In high office Ingersoll could safely have advocated freedom of thought, though not freethought, and made theistic utterances in the manner of Jefferson and Lincoln. This was not to be. After the disastrous convention the *New York Times* car-ried a report on the religious factor in Ingersoll's defeat and the *New York Tribune* deplored a religious test for public office (Quoted in *Transcript*, May 16, 1868). Nevertheless, the religious test would grow and become an insurmountable barrier to Ingersoll as he became the outstanding spokesman of freethought.

The debacle in the convention was more than a defeat, it was a hu-miliation, a symbol of the hopeless struggle of existence. The young Ingersoll could explode at a radical difference of opinion, a challenge, a rebuff—Clark provided a safety valve. Again Robert was through with politics: "I am sick of the whole thing," and, in the grand style of

Shakespeare's Cardinal Wolsey, "I am thinking of bidding a 'long fare-well to all my greatness' " (May 14, 1868, *Letters*, 150). The grapes were sour anyhow: "Well I am glad that I was beaten. I would have been slan-dered by the other party and maligned by my own. God damn them both" (May 19, 1868, Carbondale Mss.). Governor Oglesby was another safety valve. What is the value of life itself after all? When Isham Hay-mie, adjutant general of Illinois, died, Ingersoll philosophized to the gov-ernor. Life is "a poor little play," where "we stand in the glare of the footlights and hear a little applause, mingled with a good many hisses," and then the play trails off. "Every day life seems more worthless than it did the day before" (May 27, 1868, Plummer, *ISHSJ*, 101).

Ingersoll was resilient. He never brooded. Soon he was again laughing at the human comedy, analyzing politics disinterestedly, accepting private life peacefully. His letters to Clark become cheerful. Perhaps he felt that the churches had been very instrumental in his defeat, for he laid a heavy lash upon them. He derided the Quadrennial Methodist Episcopal Con-ference for its first resolution, "Pray for Kings," and its fourth, proposing a constitutional amendment that the Bible be declared the Word of God. Is the secret coming out? "Do they [the churches] feel that the people are beginning to suspect the truth of that d-----d book? Do they want to bolster the old rotten lie? . . . From the bottom of my heart I hope to see the day when every church will be level with the earth." Grant had assured the Republican convention that if elected he would follow the wishes of the people on every matter. To Ingersoll this pledge was "a poor dirty letter, written by a man destitute of principle and devoid of enthusiasm" (June 7, 1868, *Letters*, 152). He was again in the law. "Court commences Monday and I am back in the races ready and anxious to make $20 in any way." He warned Clark that at a Sunday School conven-tion one Bill Reynolds had announced that Peoria County was emphatical-ly for Jesus Christ and would vote for him this fall. "If the aforesaid J. C. is running for Congress the statement may be of importance to you" (June 15, 1868, L.C.). Clark replied, "I rec'd yours of the 17th inst this morning. If J. C. don't run any better than he did *a long time ago*, I have no fear. Let him run" (June 19, 1868, L.C.). Robert recounted the story of a woman who was asked what she thought of the doctrine of total depravity and answered that it was a good doctrine if people would only live up to it. He then stated a conservative concept of mone-tary economics: The money supply could not be rationally expanded by fiat currency (as the government had attempted during the Civil War by issuing "greenbacks" with no backing). "I don't see how this argu-ment can be answered. The money of the world is gold and silver, and the bonds must be paid in the money of the world" (June 25, 1868, *Letters*, 154).

On August third "the colored people" of Peoria and vicinity gath-ered at the fairgrounds to celebrate the abolition of slavery in the West

Indies with music and feasting. Naturally they had invited Colonel Inger-soll to speak and naturally he had been glad to accept. He had been si-lent for three months, a painfully long time to hide his light under a bushel (*Transcript*, Aug. 4, 1868). He traced the history of slavery, its sanction by law and religion in every country. He quoted from Whittier:

> They bade the slave ship speed from coast to coast,
> Fanned by the wings of the Holy Ghost.

He saluted historic leaders of the antislavery movement—Wilberforce, Burke, Toussaint, Jefferson, and Paine, among others. Moving with the times he was a newborn abolitionist and eulogized persons for whom he had shown little affection in the past—William Lloyd Garrison, "that firm, consistent and faithful friend of your down-trodden race"; "old John Brown," who "struck the sublimest blow of the age for freedom"; Wendell Phillips; Senator Sumner; and "the immortal Lincoln," author of the glorious Emancipation Proclamation. Freed from politics he advised his listeners to be on guard against both parties. Democrats and Republi-cans had supported the Fugitive Slave Law. Once again he put upon the scene the female slave in flight for freedom, "the light of the North Star shining in her eyes, and her babe pressed to her withered breast," captured and dragged back to the hound and the lash. Emancipation had been a military necessity more than a humanitarian act. As a white man he apologized for the blood and tears of slavery, urged them to pursue education so that "the avenues of distinction will be open to you and your children."

> The great problem is solved. Liberty has solved it and there will be no more slavery. On the old flag, in every fold and in every star, will be liberty for all and Equality before the law. The grand people are marching forward, and they will not pause until the earth is without a slave and without a throne. (*Transcript*, Aug. 4, 1968)

In July Ingersoll had been solicited by James G. Blaine, member of Congress from Maine and a rising star in the Republican party, to spend two weeks in that state before their September elections and make speeches for the Republican cause. It was a seductive compliment. "What do you think? Had I better go?" (To Clark, July 28, 1868, L.C.). Why did he seek advice? If he was out of politics, there was no problem. If he was in politics, there was no problem. The problem was that he was neither in nor out. Clark probably urged him to accept the invitation. Inger-soll hesitated. "I hardly believe that I will go to Maine after all" (To Clark, Aug. 6, 1868, L.C.). Then he went.

Blaine had erred on the side of moderation in assessing Ingersoll. In Maine Ingersoll held public and politicians in his hand and gave them example after example of genius on the stump beyond their wildest dreams.

He spoke in Augusta for two and a half hours, and Senator William P. Fessenden, chairman of the Joint Committee on Reconstruction and formerly a member of Lincoln's cabinet, took him by both hands, saying, "That is the best speech I ever heard. There never was a better speech made in the world." Representative Blaine, Governor Harrison of New Hampshire, and other dignitaries on the platform agreed. "Yesterday I dined with Fessenden," Robert happily reported to Clark. "He seems to have taken a wonderful fancy to me. He came to hear me again Saturday night and says that he would like to hear me every day until election" (To Clark, Sept. 7, 1868, *Letters*, 155).

The newspapers swelled the acclaim. The *Augusta Journal* asserted, "It is the uniform testimony of all who have listened to him that Robert G. Ingersoll is the leading stump speaker of the country." The *Portland Press* found in him "a fine physical organization, a powerful voice, ready command of language, intense earnestness and fearlessness and unusual facility in the use of sarcasm," and savored "the health of the prairies in his statements—and occasionally in his stories." The *Portland Star* said that his hearers "were roused to a pitch of excitement not often attained in a campaign" (Quoted in *Transcript*, Sept. 21, 1868).

The floodgates were open. Briefly at home before sallying forth to combat in Indiana for Oglesby, Ingersoll was willing and ready to address a mass meeting on September nineteenth at Rouse's Hall. Rain had begun in the afternoon, but the citizens sloshed through rain and mud to the hall, where they occupied every seat on the floor and in the galleries, packing the aisles and even the space at the doorway. Ingersoll spoke for two hours. The reporter in the *Transcript* apologized that his two-and-a-half column summary "is only the dry thread of the argument, divested of the brilliant passages and the manner of the speaker" (Sept. 21, 1868). Nevertheless, it is the most detailed account of Ingersoll's Republicanism in 1868.

Thanking "the splendid audience" for braving the weather, Ingersoll proceeded to carve up the Democrats. He blended logic and humor, fact and fancy, sensational illustrations, sublime organ tones, and earthy wit. The audience listened entranced, clinging to every word, sighing, weeping, smiling, laughing, believing everything. He took up the Democratic arguments against Lincoln's repression of civil liberties on the home front. This had troubled Ingersoll before, but not now. The exercise of extraordinary powers had been necessary as a war measure. Sacred history supported this. In the founding fathers—Washington and Jefferson, the Continental Congress, the Committees of Public Safety—he found overwhelming precedent for summary imprisonment, confiscation, silencing dissident preachers and editors. That had been done to create the Union, this to preserve it.

Ingersoll celebrated Crispus Attucks, the runaway slave shot down by the British troops in the Boston Massacre, the first casualty of the

American Revolution. He called Attucks a greater man than Webster. "The people of Boston took that corpse and carried it to Faneuil Hall, and Faneuil Hall was honored that day more than when Daniel Webster afterwards stood up in it to defend the Fugitive Slave Law" (*a burst of applause*). He blasted Democratic criticism of the expenditures of the Freedmen's Bureau in serving the emancipated race: "Here are four million of negroes in the South, and we have spent for the Freemen's Bureau not to exceed $8,000,000. These men and their fathers have labored for us two hundred and fifty years for nothing—call it two hundred years. This would be $2 each for two hundred years, or a cent a year" (*laughter and applause*).

Ingersoll stressed the vital need of the hour, that of protecting the hard-won freedom of blacks from brutal assault. "There came a time in the history of the war when it became necessary to let black men fight in order to whip Democrats, and now there has come a time when it is necessary to let black men vote in order to whip Democrats. How is it now in the South? Murder in the South from one end to another. Men, masked, shooting down white men in the dead of night because they cared to hire negroes, and shooting negroes because they are negroes" (*sensation*). Ingersoll was not concerned about the rights of the Democrats. He waved the bloody shirt, castigating them for the sins of the past: "Every man who fired upon the flag was a Democrat. Every man who starved our heroes, who stole our arms and sent them to the rebels, who scattered our ships abroad upon the wide ocean, who was guilty of infinite acts of meanness, was a Democrat." Enough of grimness: Time for a joke. "What would happen if you got one idea of human freedom and progress into a Democratic head? The answer: It would make him vote the Republican ticket, or it would burst his head."

The national war debt was a debt of honor, and it must be paid in the money of the world—gold. Ingersoll explained the effect of the wartime greenbacks upon the level of prices. He told of a Democratic speaker in Maine holding up two bottles, one large, one small, each full of coffee. The large bottle held the amount of coffee that ten cents could buy before the war, the small bottle what it could buy after the war. An old farmer in the audience stood up to ask questions: How much coffee could you buy before and after for a pound of butter, a bushel of potatoes, a load of hay? To each the speaker answered that he did not know, he had never thought about it. " 'Butter and potatoes and hay,' says the old man, 'are all we sell, and if you never thought of these things, what the h--l are you talking about them for?' " (*great laughter and long continued applause*).

Ingersoll acted out comic dialogues ridiculing the futile Democratic pursuit of votes—a rebel and a black, a Democrat and a soldier. He closed with "a beautiful tribute to Gen. Grant, reciting his declaration, 'Let us have peace.' "

The reporter stated: "The night was dark, and it rained furiously, yet, in spite of all, the audience maintained the most unbroken attention, only interrupting him to burst into loud and long continued applause. We think the speech was the ablest and most powerful of any that we have ever heard from this gifted man."

Two days later Ingersoll was off for Indiana. He was lionized in the Hoosier towns and villages. Civil War veterans in military formation escorted him to packed halls, where he belted out his medley of logic, pathos, and humor to rhapsodic audiences (Speech in Indianapolis, 1868, *Works*, IX, 21). The *Evansville Journal* described his speech in Gibson County as "alternately convulsing the audience with laughter, thrilling them with deep emotion, lifting them up with its glorious flights of eloquence, and drawing out their appreciation with its solid and convincing declarations of the principles of the Republican party." On his speech in Evansville:

A very large number of the most intelligent, highly cultivated, and respectable ladies of the city were present, who, by the heartiness with which they joined in the frequent outbursts of applause, manifested their appreciation of the masterly effort, which was so temperate in tone, chaste in diction, sound in logic, and withal so full of genuine wit and pointed sarcasm, that it drew forth round after round of applause, and set all sides aching with laughter. (Quoted in *Peoria Transcript*, Oct. 7, 1868)

The *Lafayette Journal*, a neutral paper, said, "Mr. Ingersoll is one of the best speakers in the country, and his remarks were received with the most unbounded enthusiasm." The *Cincinnati Gazette* prefaced its verbatim report of the Indianapolis speech: "Among the prominent Republican speakers engaged in the present campaign none has a more enviable reputation than Col. R. C. Ingersoll, Attorney General of Illinois, and no one is laboring more zealously for the success of the Republican cause" (Quoted in *Transcript*, Oct. 7, 1868).

On October fourteenth, Illinois Republicans from Peoria, Akron, Rome, and Lacon came together for festivities at Chillicothe. The crowd included five hundred members of the social-political club the Tanners, the men from Rome wearing plug hats with "Union Forever" on the front, the women from Lacon in black dresses, red sack coats, and hats trimmed in white rosettes. At the speech-making in the public square Ingersoll held forth for two and a half hours and buffeted the opposition. How stupid were the Democrats! "They put cow-catchers on the rear of trains, and the slave society invented only one machine, a thrashing machine in the shape of a whip." An open-air banquet and a torchlight parade followed. Then the tireless Republicans again assembled at the speaker's stand and emitted shouts for Ingersoll. "After repeated solicitations he came forward and made a witty and telling speech, keeping the crowd convulsed with laughter for half an hour" (*Transcript*, Oct.

15, 1868). On the morrow he spoke for nearly three hours to a crowd of three thousand in the public square of Elmwood. The reporter marvelled that in spite of his exertions in Maine, Indiana, and Illinois his voice was as fresh and clear as at the beginning of the campaign (*Transcript*, Oct. 16, 1868).

The Republicans held a mammoth field day in Peoria on October nineteenth. Towards daylight the boom of cannon awakened the people (including Democrats, alas) and hardy enthusiasts ventured out into a town foggy, damp, and wind-swept. The paraders gathered in the open fields and at noon flocked to Adams Street, where they organized and began the march. Down Main Street they moved, taking fifty minutes to pass any one point—hundreds of lady and gentlemen Tanners, some on horseback, others on foot; martial bands; a company of German-Americans; hundreds of carpetbaggers, each carrying on his back a carpetbag with the name of his state of origin; a line of wagons decked with flags and banners. Some of the banners: "God Grant us peace. We are willing to forgive our enemies but not to appoint them our rulers"; "Soldiers vote for the Commander"; "The purest spirit of Democracy" [Old Rye in a bottle]; "E. C. Ingersoll our next Representative, Col. R. G. Ingersoll our next Senator"; "Democratic saints: Judas Iscariot, Benedict Arnold, Andy Johnson"; a picture of two dead ducks inscribed Seymour and Blair [the Democratic candidates for president and vice president]; "If General Grant is a despot, what kind of pot is Frank Blair?"

The celebration had hired every available meeting hall in town. Palmer and Ingersoll attended separate meetings. At the Wigwam Palmer gave an impassioned speech about the war in Kentucky and how he had proclaimed to twenty-five thousand black escapees in a field in Louisville, "In God's name you are free, and I'll stand by you." At the Court Square Ingersoll waved the bloody shirt at the Democratic party, "the party of every bounty hunter, draft sneak, rebel sympathizer, every man that starved our brothers." He called himself a missionary to the Democrats, warning of the wrath to come. He was not polite at all. The Democratic party, now dead, mistook the wiggling of the maggots devouring the carcass for signs of life. He thanked God "we live in the age we did," and he pleaded for votes for Grant, "who will lead our banners to victory now as he did in the war." For two and a half hours the crowd listened raptly, burst into sparks of applause, urging him to go on and on. It was hard for him to get away.

A free dinner was given to one and all at Rouse's Hall. In the evening two thousand Tanners carried torchlights in military step down Adams Street. Fireworks, concerts, more speeches. There was not much drunkenness, reported the *Transcript*, excepting a few Democrats who had imbibed too freely of benzene. By eleven o'clock the town was as quiet as usual. The *Transcript* said that it was the largest political demonstration ever held in Peoria (Oct. 20).

On October thirtieth the *Transcript* reprinted a dispatch in the *Chicago Tribune* on Ingersoll's speech at Morris. The report characterized the speech as "the most complete effort of the present campaign," a rare "combination of generous wit, severe criticism, and noble sentiment."

On November third Ingersoll was the final speaker at the Republican rally in Peoria ending the campaign. He hurled "shot and shell at the Democratic camp in such a manner as only the Colonel can do it." He was frequently cheered by an audience "appearing at times to be almost wild with enthusiasm" (*Transcript*, Nov. 4, 1868). Perhaps the people were not merely applauding a speech; they were also paying tribute to a man, this strange politician who was not running for office but had given body and soul to the Republican cause in three states. On the morrow they joined their fellow-citizens in electing the Republican ticket: Clark Ingersoll, Palmer, and Grant.

The 1868 elections over, it was high time for Robert Ingersoll to think about his future. Four years previously, after the 1864 elections, he had made a faint and unsuccessful effort to win appointment as U.S. attorney for the Northern District of Illinois in the post-election shake-up of patronage. Now he tried again. (Nothing in the state government interested him, whether or not Palmer was governor). Four years as U.S. attorney in Chicago would bring him a wide acquaintance, laying a basis for an extensive practice. He told Oglesby that his mind was more or less "made up to keep out of politics as *far* as possible. I am also in favor of making some money" (Nov. 22, 1868, Plummer, *ISHSJ*, 162). To Clark he wrote nonchalantly, "There will be in my opinion no trouble about my appointment but I am not very particular one way or the other. I can make a living in Peoria anyway." Suddenly he was emotionally depleted. The pyrotechnics of political oratory were gone. He was a man without a cause and without enthusiasm. "This is a sad world and there is not laughter enough to drown the groans. I am losing interest in things— there is a feeling in me that there is hardly time enough to do anything" (Dec. 1, 1868, L.C.).

Pending appointment he applied himself to the bread-and-butter business of law. He headed for Bloomington, "to attend to several very important suits—and in which I will get first rate fees" (To Clark, Dec. 5, 1868, L.C.). From Bloomington he wrote that he had been occupied with several suits, "one about the county seat of Cass County and others for the T. P. and W. Railway," and that he "will be engaged here in this trial till next Wednesday. Then have to go to Woodford—and will be busy there for two weeks at least. Then on the 7th of January have to return here to try the railroad cases" (To Clark, Dec. 11, 1868, L. C). He spent a dismal Sunday "at work all day with all my might drawing pleas, answers, demurrers, and declarations, and all the other pleasant fictions known to the law" (To Clark, Dec. 20, 1868, L.C.). "Court is grinding away, with all the solemnity of dignified ignorance" (To Clark,

Feb. 18, 1869, L.C.).

Ingersoll was not inhibited in discussing politics, no matter who the addressee. He did not think much of President-elect Grant and he spoke his mind in the unrefined language known to his intimates. Grant's silence about whom he would choose for his cabinet elicited a sweeping comment to Oglesby.

> It is a little laughable to me how Grant fools all the editors and smart men on the cabinet question. Not a word can they get out of him. The old idea of getting farts out of dead men is feasible compared to getting a hint from Grant. Grant has the sense to see that popularity and applause are but for the moment. The great public—like a whore—will be quite as warm for the next comer. The people will enjoy their idols' disgrace even more than their elevation. Some old Frenchman said that he never was so heartily cheered as when the people saw him in the tumbril going to death.

He advised Oglesby not to worry about his own future; it did not matter. After all, life amounts to little, and "nearly all of us when we come to the skeleton clasp—the lipless kiss of death—will have to repeat the last will and testament of Dr. Rabelais—'I have nothing—I owe much—the balance I give to the poor.' Goodbye, dear Governor, You are my best friend" (Dec. 7, 1868, Plummer, ISHSJ, 103). Peoria was in the grip of the national crisis of tight money, for which there appeared to be no workable solution. "Everybody in business is afraid of specie payment. It is the nightmare of all traders, buyers & sellers. And it is the El Dorado of all who have their entire fortunes in money and bonds. The people begin to feel the oppression of taxation. Money here is very close indeed. The old money-lenders and note-shavers are as happy as undertakers in a cholera season" (To Clark, Dec. 20, 1868, L.C.).

On December twelfth Ingersoll was in the thick of a trial in Bloomington. But it was Clark's thirty-seventh birthday, so a few minutes had to be found for a greeting—philosophic if cheerless. How time and life rushed on! And what was beyond? Robert posed Job's immemorial question: "If a man die shall he live again?" And Robert, who was something of a poet manqué, responded with morbid lyricism: "Faith once believed in life eternal, but now on the lonely shores of time Faith lies dead, like the corpse of a maiden beautifully white, with the drifted bosom naked to the stars—her wide sweet mouth blown full of cruel sand and all the waves are joyous with her golden hair." There was no comfort to be found but love. He reached toward his brother. "I wish I could be with you this day and with my arms around your sweet neck give you thirty-seven kisses full of love, gratitude, and pride" (Dec. 12, 1868, L.C.). Four months later, on April first, he was more melancholy than ever. "I constantly ask, 'Is this all? Is there nothing more than I have seen?' The ancient pilgrim to the Cave of Buddha having waded through the wide and thirsty deserts, through forests filled with robbers and wild beasts, having endured every privation and experienced all but death—upon being shown the glimmering outlines of a God, exclaimed, Is it then all that is given to men—to see a shadow? One would think that all days are the first of April, and that we simply supply laughter for the feast" (April 1, 1869, L.C.).

Still he pursued prizes that he disdained. As the days and weeks wore on he remained confident that he would be appointed U.S. attorney. However, he mounted a strong campaign to refresh and improve his application. On December twentieth he instructed Clark to contact Vice President-elect Colfax on his behalf (Dec. 20, 1868, L.C.). On January fifteenth he sent Clark endorsements of the Illinois senators, to be followed by endorsements from the Illinois representatives. He was becoming restless with Peoria, "beginning to feel a little anxious to get away from this small pinched up town. The fact is that there is very little to do here" (Jan. 15, 1869, L.C.). The fees were small and most of his practice was elsewhere. "The whole practice of law here is simply odious to me." He paid a courtesy visit to Grant. "I am willing to swear," he reported to Oglesby, "that he never said a d----d word on any subject pertaining in the least to any political subject. He did not even give a knowing or suggestive wink" (Feb. 22, 1869, Plummer, *ISHSJ*, 105). On March sixth he wrote to Clark, "See Nelson of Massachusetts and find out what kind of a man Hoar is. I reckon Wilson can help me in that direction. In fact, all the Eastern Maine members of the House & the Senate ought to be able to help me *right smartly*" (March 6, 1869, L.C.). To Oglesby: "I thank you most sincerely, heartily and warmly for your letter of recommendation." (March 12, 1869, Plummer, 106). Late in March, regardless of consequences, he went blithely ahead to Bloomington and delivered a two-hour expanded version of his "Progress" lecture (Oglesby, now exgovernor, was in the audience). He reported cheerfully to Clark that since then "the preachers here have done nothing but preach sermons, 'answering Col. Ingersoll.' Two sermons have been published giving me the devil" (March 31, 1869, *Letters*, 157).

Ingersoll had sought the post openly, was qualified for it, had earned it, and was backed by some of the most important men in the party. All to no avail. He was spurned, passed over. There was nothing to do but thank his friends. To Senator Fessenden he wrote:

Allow me to thank you for the interest you were kind enough to take in my welfare. You have placed me under real and lasting obligation. Could I have had my choice between the office that I sought and your friendship, you certainly would have remained my friend. Your course has flattered me exceedingly and your kindness will never be forgotten. Thanking you again and again, . . . (April 10, 1869, Georgetown).

The lesson was clear. Robert Ingersoll was not eligible for public office, elective or appointive. The lesson would become more glaring as he assailed Christian orthodoxy and the religious establishment from hundreds of platforms. Unfortunately for him it would require further humiliation before he could accept the total taboo. The politicians wanted and exploited his voice on the platform but they had no place for him in seats of power. The constitutional separation of church and state did not apply to him. He must find his greatness in other ways.

Note

1. We are indebted to Professor Plummer for bringing to light Ingersoll's reaction to this incident as well as other valuable Ingersoll letters previously hidden in the Oglesby papers.

V

Infidelity and the Law

In 1869 Ingersoll thought that the political wars were permanently behind him. He was no longer a politician, no longer tied to scheming bosses and the fickle public. Any lingering uncertainty about political involvement was erased by Clark's defeat in his 1870 reelection bid, a defeat caused in part by association in the press with "his vulgar brother," and in part because of a circular diatribe gotten up by some Princeton (Illinois) clergymen exhorting the faithful: "The Christian people of this city, almost to a man, feel that the honor, purity, and security of the republican party, and the interests of Christianity, imperatively demand the defeat of Mr. Ingersoll . . . a thoroughly corrupt man, devoid of moral principle, profane, atheistic" (Larson, 165). "Well!" Ingersoll exclaimed to Oglesby, "goodbye politics. I have had all I want. From this day henceforth and forever I am out of the business" (Nov. 12, 1870, Plummer, *ISHSJ*, 107). "I am as busy as a bee—have nothing to do with politics—don't care a d--n what party succeeds—feel no interest in anything but [religious] infidelity and law—the former gratifies my mind—the second feeds and clothes my body & the bodies of those I love" (July 11, 1871, Plummer, *ISHSJ*, 108). And to Clark: "I live here [in Peoria] with fools, but d--n them I am independent and say what I want to say" (Oct. 24, 1870, IHS).

There was always time to write letters. Oglesby and Clark were his closest intimates and he kept no secrets from them. "I like you better," he confided to Oglesby, "than any other man (except my own brother) in the world" (April 12, 1872, Plummer, 116). He praised Oglesby lavishly, and gratefully accepted praise from him. "The applause of friends is the very best of pay" (Plummer, "Robert G. Ingersoll and the Sensual Gods," *Western Illinois Regional Studies*). He imparted to Oglesby an uninhibited erotic reverie and, anticipating a slogan of a later day, said, "I had rather make love than war." He invited Oglesby to visit: "I want you to come and stay with me a week, a month, a year. Fix your time. I will arrange my business so that I can be wholly yours" (Plummer, *W. Ill. R. S.*). The love between the brothers was as strong as ever. When Clark was in Congress and Robert in Peoria the distance was hard to overcome. "When you are away," Robert wrote to his congressman brother December ninth, 1869, "it seems to me that I am fighting the world alone, as though no one really was my friend. No one sympathizes with my ideas, ends, and hopes. I do hope the time will come when we can be together again" (IHS). With Clark out of Congress and opening a law office in Washington as an excongressman, the distance remained frustrating. How nice it would be to spend a vacation together at Cobb's Island "by the sounding sea. . . . You are in my mind almost continually. It does not seem possible that I can get along through the world without you" (Aug. 26, 1871, L.C.).

No longer enamored of the law Ingersoll travailed without enthusiasm at making a living at the bar. Alone or with various partners, and from his base in Peoria, he built up a busy legal practice. He had said at the start of his legal career that "gas was an excellent asset," and he had plenty of it, his adversaries protesting at his "wind," "brag," "bluster" (*Canton Register*, Larson, 104). His infidelism, moving out of back-door gossip to open and proud avowal, never damaged his legal business, as everybody knew that he could crush any opponent at the bar who ventured to exploit his freethought against him. He was mainly a corporation lawyer (particularly a railroad lawyer in that period of railroad building), and he handled routine commercial matters—organization, finance, taxes, rates, right of way. In letters to Clark he is always on the go, carrying his briefs and notes up and down the state and its environs, pursuing victory for a fee. "In the morning at six o'clock I start for Rockville in Schuyler Co., to try a mandamus suit. On Friday I have to be at Pontiac, and a week from Monday Court convenes here again. So you see that I have business enough" (Oct. 24, 1871, IHS). "I was in Davenport, Iowa, last week and tried a case for three days. I won it all right. Am busy every moment. I won all my Fairbury R.R. suits—not the free suits but about the bonds and the location of the R.R." (Nov. 22, 1871, IHS). "Tuesday I am going to Pittsfield to argue a case before Judge Higbee. Wednesday night I am to be in Rock Island to argue a case before the Common Council—i.e., to get an ordinance for the right of way for the P. & R.I. [Railway]. Tuesday I have to be in Springfield to try a case before Treat, and Saturday I shall come home" (Nov. 19, 1871, *Letters*, 514). He was beginning to make money, join corporate boards, invest in stocks and bonds, live well. Even on the road he was a gourmet. Stuck in a dreary little town he bemoaned the crude facilities: "A good meal lost is gone forever" (Dec. 20, 1871, *Letters*, 151).

The champion spellbinder had said goodbye to politics but that was easier said than done. He could not resist any public cause that excited him. In the spring of 1870 a convention was held in Peoria to form a county Woman Suffrage Association. Ingersoll shared the platform with a minister and Susan B. Anthony. Anticipating both the Nineteenth Amendment and ERA he submitted a resolution, which passed unanimously: "That we pledge ourselves, irrespective of party, to use all honorable means to make the women of America the equals of men before the law." At the first meeting of the new association in April he was speechifying again. He listed the standard battery of arguments against women's rights: Women are weak; liberty would corrupt them; they might want to become constables and jurors, to experiment with free love; they don't serve in the Army, why should they vote? Ingersoll countered with the basic principles of a free society.

> According to your argument the rights of a human being depend upon the strength of the being. On the contrary, I assert that the rights of human beings do not depend upon strength. Justice is not a matter of weight. . . . If the right of self-goverment is not a matter of right, our government is based on an infinitely insecure foundation.

He also seized the opportunity to show the connection between biblical taboos and the subjugation of women. The *Transcript* was not impressed. It scolded the speaker for his visionary ideals, "A good cause is quite as requisite as a good speaker" (April 30, May 3; Larson, 102).

Ingersoll did not participate in the electioneering of 1872. To his own grievances was added resentment against the Illinois Republican machine for passing over Oglesby for the Senate in 1870. Nor had he fallen in love with President Grant, whose administration was already wallowing in corruption and incompetence. "Grant has degraded everything he has touched. Honor has been banished from the administration of public affairs, and incapacity is at the helm of each party" (To Oglesby, July 11, 1871, Plummer, *ISHSJ*, 108). The Republican party had fallen from grace; there was no good in it. "The party was at one time perfectly grand. It had lofty aims, sacred objects, splendid courage and real enthusiasm for the right. It has now become mean, base, sordid—cowardly and treacherous. It has been utterly demoralized by power. It has placed little men in great places, and turned the really good men out of doors" (To Oglesby, July 16, 1871, Plummer, *ISHSJ*, 109). He advised Oglesby not to salvage the party by running for office under its banner. "No grand principle is at stake, and in my judgment you have the right to stand aloof. Let the party depend on its Logans, Palmers, and Trumbulls, for success. Why should you help carry the state in order to show that the people voted wisely in standing by the aforesaid Logans, Palmers, and Trumbulls?" (July 11, 1871, Plummer, *ISHSJ*, 109). He went so far as to hope that the state would go Democratic in the fall of 1871, so that

Grant might be eliminated and room provided for a decent presidential candidate in 1872. In a private letter to Oglesby, he was not fastidious: "If you are not forced by the people to run I shall give my vote to some d--d mean Democrat. All this I shall do on the principle that the fellow chewed *hen turd* to spit in his enemy's face" (July 24, 1871, Plummer, *ISHSJ*, 110). Finally, he entreated Oglesby not to run for governor on a ticket with Grant for president. "You know that Grant is utterly unfit to be president. You know that both his hands have been blistered with gifts that were intended as bribes" (March 29, 1872, Plummer, *ISHSJ*, 101). However, if Oglesby did run Ingersoll hoped that he would win and use his victory as a stepping-stone to the Senate.

Oglesby was by nature a politician. He had to be in office or seeking it. He chose to run with Grant. He asked Grant to enlist Ingersoll in the Republican campaign. Grant replied through a secretary that he had "feelings of utter kindness and respect" for Ingersoll but could not promise him any patronage. The record does not show whether Oglesby communicated this shabby reply to its object. He *did* solicit Ingersoll's help but could not press for it. "If you cannot do so I will heartily excuse you and go on alone" (Aug. 6, 1873, Plummer, *ISHSJ*, 89).

It was not easy for Ingersoll to restrain himself from leaping into the fray and doing all he could to bring Grant down. A faction belonging to the Liberal Republicans, a third party mishmash of the discontented, solicited him to address their convention in Cincinnati. He refused. "I am done," he positively declared to one of the petitioners. "I can conceive of no circumstances under which I would make a speech. If ever in this world a man was thoroughly sick of political speaking, I am that man." He did not get along well with politicians, he said, and his only ambition was to make a living for his family. Gratuitously, out of the ruin of his own political career, he went overboard in his contempt for the electorate: "The American people have lost the power to confer honor" (To Jesse W. Fell, April 6, 1872, *Letters*, 159). When, however, Horace Greeley won the nominations of both the Liberal Republicans and the Democrats he was sorely tempted and almost agreed to speak for Greeley. Encouraging him, Clark advised that he should speak no more than four times a week starting September first! (July 16, 1872, L.C.). Ingersoll wrestled further with conflicting impulses. He decided to abstain. Grant and Oglesby were elected, and Oglesby resigned to accept a seat in the Senate.

The Self-Proclaimed Infidel

Law was a living, politics was in the air. Freed of political careerism (or, rather, barred from it), vibrant with appetite and ambition, Ingersoll sought a new world to conquer. He found it in religion.

In his lecture "Why I Am an Agnostic" (1896) Ingersoll reviewed the roadway of experience and reflection that led him to freethought. He described the rigors and rigidities of childhood as the son of a Congregationalist minister, Christian orthodoxy with its vicarious atonement and salvation by faith, the cruelties of the Old Testament God, and the "infinite lie" of eternal hell-fire for finite sins in the New. He had studied "just a little" in astronomy, geology, and biology, and knew how Gallileo, Copernicus, Kepler, Newton, and Laplace had demolished the biblical earth-centered cosmos, how the evolutionary science of Darwin ("the greatest naturalist the world has produced"), Huxley, and Spencer had shattered the concept of special creation. He had explored the German scientists Haeckel and Buchner and their arguments against the existence of God. He could not reconcile the existence of a good, wise, and powerful God with the evils of the world—earthquakes, floods, famine, disease. He had studied comparative religion and had seen the same supernatural myths in all creeds. He had been thrilled by the skeptics of the Enlightenment—Volney, Paine, Voltaire. He had been liberated from religious gloom by Shakespeare and Burns, Byron, Shelley, and Keats. To the cosmic mystery he had discovered no answer. "I do not deny. I do not know and I do not believe." He extolled the heroes over the centuries who gave their lives for freedom of the mind and the body. "I vowed to grasp the torch that they had held and hold it high" that light might conquer darkness still, to "drive frightful thoughts from the mind," and "flood the world with sunshine."

In this lecture Ingersoll does not mention what part if any the religious establishment played in his political defeats. Certainly it was with some embittered defiance that he declared war against it.

Ingersoll gradually emerged as the chief spokesman of freethought in America, a position he would occupy without rival for more than twenty-five years. He proceeded in three steps, three lectures—"Humboldt" (1869), "Thomas Paine" (1871), and "The Gods" (1872).

September 14, 1869, was the one hundredth anniversary of the birth of Alexander von Humboldt, the great German naturalist. As guest speaker at the celebration in Peoria Ingersoll utilized the occasion to speak of the warfare between religion and science, superstition and intelligence, stagnation and progress. The age of ignorance, fear, and bigotry was gone, the advent of modern science promising a better life for all. Nature was found to be orderly and the free mind would master it.

> Slowly, beautifully, like the coming of the dawn, came the grand truth, that the universe is governed by law; that disease fastens itself on the good and on the bad; that the tornado cannot be stopped by counting beads, that the rushing lava pauses not for bended knees, the lightning for clasped and uplifted hands, nor the cruel waves of the sea for prayer; that paying tithes causes rather than prevents famine; that pleasure is not sin; that happiness is the only good; that demons and gods exist

only in the imagination; that faith is a lullaby sung to put the soul to sleep; that devotion is a bribe that fear offers to supposed power; that offering rewards in another world for obedience in this is simply buying a soul on credit; that knowledge consists in ascertaining the laws of nature; and that wisdom is the science of happiness. [He praised the great thinkers—Copernicus, Galileo, Descartes, Montaigne, Galvani, Voltaire, Comte—and the great soldiers of science—Guttenberg, Watt, Stephenson, Arkwright.] And today we are not honoring some butcher called a soldier—some wily politician called a statesman—some robber called a king, nor some malicious metaphysician called a saint. We are honoring the great Humboldt, whose victories were all achieved in the arena of thought, who destroyed prejudice and error—not men; who shed light—not blood; and who contributed to the knowledge, the wealth, and the happiness of all mankind. (*Works*, I, 93–115)

Two weeks later "the renowned lecturer Col. R. G. Ingersoll" appeared in Cincinnati to repeat the Humboldt eulogy. In a crowded opera house a committee of prominent citizens escorted him to the platform, where the mayor introduced him as "a brilliant, genial gentleman, a man of brains, a man greatly respected and admired by all those who know him and greatly detested by those who disagree with him." The speech was frequently interrupted by "applause and cheers" (*Cincinnati Times*, Sept. 28; Larson, 100).

After the hero of science came the historic opponent of revealed religion—Thomas Paine. On January 29, 1871, the 134 anniversary of Paine's birth, Ingersoll was invited to speak at the dedication of the Fairbury Hall to Freethought. It was, he told a crowded house, a labor of love and gratitude: "With his name left out, the history of liberty cannot be written." He sketched Paine's early career in America, *Common Sense*, and the *Crisis* papers from "the times that try men's souls." He depicted Paine carrying the message of liberty to England in *The Rights of Man*, "a magazine of political wisdom." In heroically serving as a guest of the people in the National Assembly in France, seeking to destroy the monarchy and save the monarch, Paine was himself imprisoned and barely escaped the guillotine. Had he died then he would have been universally acclaimed. But he went further and in *The Age of Reason* challenged revealed religion and the religious establishment in the light of modern intelligence. That great pamphlet "has liberalized us all. It put arguments in the mouths of the people; it put the church on the defensive; it enabled somebody in every village to corner the parson; it made the world wiser, and the church better; it took power from the pulpit and divided it among the pews" (*Works*, I, 153). Because Paine dared to deny the authority of bibles, creeds, and churches "the world shut the door in his face and emptied its slops on him from the windows." The church pursued Paine and his reputation in order to deter others, but there had always been brave men who were not intimidated by the pomp and glitter of domes and cathedrals, and so it was not successful. Infidels have persisted in attacking religion because it imprisons the human mind and brands dissent with infamy. Because religious leaders "have implored [their] God to torment us [Ingersoll had enrolled in the infidel cause] forever" (158). Although church leaders have said that freethinkers have accomplished nothing, they had, in fact, freed the mind, civilized mankind, and filled the world with light, with discovery, with science. "Is it a small thing to quench the flames of hell with the holy tears of pity?" (163). As the struggle continued, "we need have no fear of being too radical. The future will ratify all brave and grand predictions. Paine was splendidly in advance of his time, but he was orthodox compared with the infidels of today." Ingersoll ended optimistically: "A few more years—a few more brave men—a few more rays of light and mankind will venerate the memory of him who said, *'Any system of religion that shocks the mind of a child cannot be a true system.'* . . . *The world is my country, and to do good my religion."*

Among the speakers on the platform that day was B. F. Underwood, a member of the small company of itinerant lecturers for freethought. He recorded his impressions in a letter to the *Boston Investigator:*

> Colonel Ingersoll, of Peoria, Ill., one of the most eloquent and popular orators of the west, delivered the finest address on Paine that I have ever heard. His oration was a carefully written production, replete with good sense and sparkling with brilliant thoughts, evincing thorough acquaintance with Paine's career and just appreciation of his character and services. The audience listened to Colonel Ingersoll with the closest attention, and the bursts of applause which greeted his most radical utterances attested the satisfaction with which he was heard. ("Recollections of Colonel Ingersoll," *The Progressive Thinker,* Nov. 11, 1905)

Robert sent a copy of his oration to Clark, and Clark sent a copy to John, urging that conventional-minded physician to read without prejudice this latest effort of their wonderful brother. "How infinitely honest, earnest, and intense is his brain and how infinitely good is his noble heart is illustrated on every page. To me, the words are just pure gold, set in diamonds! Altogether, it is more than grand, it is sublime! I would rather be the author of those forty-one pages than to be President of the United States" (Nov. 15, 1871, *Letters,* 513).

Clark sent Robert a copy of his letter to John. The pair exchanged fulsome compliments. Robert said, "I am afraid you will flatter me to death," but that "every word is precious to my heart. When you open the very doors of your soul and show me the niche occupied by me it is impossible to keep back my tears" (Nov. 19, 1871, *Letters,* 514). He added that he has had "a local complaint," but feels better, that he weighs 227 pounds and is going on a self-purification regimen. "Now I drink no tea or coffee, no spirits of any kind and use no tobacco and I am going to continue in the good cause until I satisfy myself whether the effect upon me is good or bad." Weight had become a vexatious problem that he could never control.

And existence itself? Even in the hour of a perfect performance on the platform he was not happy. The jovial mask hid a sad man, sad at the vanity of life. "Sometimes in the darkness of night I feel as though surrounded by the great armies of effacement—that the horizon is growing smaller every moment—that the final surrender is only postponed—that everything is taking something from me—that Nature robs me with her countless hands—that my heart grows weaker with every beat—that even kisses wear me away, and that my every thought takes toll of my brief life" (Nov. 19, 1871, *Letters*, 514).

Poor Clark! How could he help Robert, his younger brother? He gave a bouquet of gratitude: "As my mind runs over the varied record of the almost eight years of congressional life that which gives me the greatest pleasure is the consciousness of the fact that I have done nothing to make you blush or to cause you to regret that you have fought so many of my political causes which resulted in returning me so many times to a seat in the House of Representatives" (Dec. 3, 1871, L.C.). And he gave love: "I love you tenderly and infinitely and my heart would rejoice this moment at how I would exult could I but vanquish the 'armies of effacement' that incessantly war against us." Alas, that was a prayer that could not be answered.

Meanwhile the world, trivial and tragic as it was, had to be saved from superstition and bigotry. He had praised a hero of science and a hero of the warfare against revealed religion. It was high time to make his own statement, his creed, his manifesto. He must take the leap. Writing to Clark from Monmouth ("Here I am in this ancient burgh trying a long and tedious case before the Hon. Judge who probably is the greatest fool on the woolsack"), for once he doubted his power. Was he equal to the task of formulating a comprehensive theory of religion? "The subject is a vast one, and requires a good deal more learning than I have." He regretted that he had not been able to spend a few days in study at the Library of Congress (To Clark, Dec. 3, 1871, Monmouth, *Letters*, 158). Nevertheless he went ahead.

He need not have doubted himself. Even though, like Paine, Ingersoll was not learned in either theology or philosophy, each man became a trailblazer of freethought in his own time under adverse conditions— the pamphleteer in the shadow of the guillotine, the lecturer under the pressure of making a living at the law and at the cost of a political career. But each knew enough, and each had two extra factors—a sense of mission and genius—that more than made up for any formal limitation. *The Age of Reason* presents eighteenth-century deism, "The Gods" and successor lectures and writings (Ingersoll never put all his ideas on religion in one book) nineteenth-century atheism-agnosticism.

On January 29, 1872, the 135 anniversary of Paine's birth, the train,

from Peoria (and way stations) released at Fairbury an overflow crowd
to hear what their favorite orator had to say on "The Gods."

Although Ingersoll would later settle down behind the fortification
of agnosticism, his first volley against religion, the explosion that proclaimed his new career, was plainly atheism. He denied the existence
of all gods, deplored the dominance of these mythical beings upon the
minds of men, inveighed against the religious establishment through the
ages that exploited the ignorance of the people, and prophesied a new
day, not far off, when men would throw off the yoke of superstition
and enter the millennium of intelligence.

Ingersoll developed his argument discursively.

Each nation, he began, has had its gods, each of which reflected the
appearance and ideas of its creators. Obedience to these gods was supposed to bring happiness on earth and in heaven, disobedience misery
on earth and in hell.

In the Christian system divine authority is based on the Bible, which
is held too sacred to be doubted. We must not use our intelligence on
it; we must accept it on faith. This is salvation through slavery, Ingersoll
stated; it is worthless. Instead we should read the Bible as we would
any other book, taking the bandage of reverence from our eyes. We would
then be grateful to Satan for giving Adam and Eve knowledge of good
and evil. Satan was the first schoolmaster, teaching inquiry, doubt, and
investigation. "Give me the storm and tempest of thought and action
rather than the dead calm of ignorance and faith. Banish me from Eden
when you will, but first let me eat of the fruit of the tree of knowledge"
(Works, I, 22).

The traditional purpose of the religious enterprise is to sustain good
relations with the gods and to ward off the evil spirits that would lead
men astray. Christ has been depicted as having supernatural powers over
evil spirits, able to cast them out of people and to prevail over the imps
of Satan. We should consider the story of Satan's temptation of Christ.
The devil offered Christ the whole earth, yet the devil did not have "even
a tax title to one foot of dirt"—the whole earth is but a grain of sand
that already belonged to Christ.

People pray to God. What do they pray for? "Some want health restored;
some ask that the loved and absent be watched over and protected; some
pray for riches, some for rain; some want diseases stayed; some vainly
ask for food; some ask for revivals, a few ask for more wisdom, and now
and then one tells the Lord to do as he may think best" (36). God is
considered a power superior to nature. Allegedly he can make animals
talk like men. He stopped the sun and moon in the heavens so that General
Joshua could commit more murder. He made clothes that would not wear
out for forty years. He put birds in the restaurant business so that they
could feed wandering prophets free of charge.

Men were beginning to reason, to investigate, Ingersoll continued.

They were driving the gods off the earth. The job was not finished. Cholera, yellow fever, and smallpox were still considered heavenly weapons, but measles, itch, and the ague are attributed to natural causes.

Some religious thinkers believe that God made the rules of the universe, and that if there were no such God we would indeed be in a bad situation. Only God determines that two objects cannot occupy the same space at the same time, that going around a circle is longer than going across, that two times one equals two. Without a god there would be no sunshine for the flowers. But what about cancer?

If God had created the universe, he could not have made it out of nothing; he would have had to create it out of himself. But if an infinite universe was made out of an infinite God, how much of the infinite God is left?

Energy is indestructible and cannot be created. Force cannot exist apart from energy. Energy and force must have existed from eternity.

A god existing outside of nature exists in nothing and is nothing. To prove that he exists, one would have to show his interference with nature, special providence, miracles. Ingersoll asserted that miracles had never been performed and never would be.

> Do not send us to Jericho to hear the winding horns, nor put us in the fire with Shadrach, Meschach, and Abednego. Do not compel us to navigate the sea with Captain Jonah nor dine with Mr. Ezekiel. There is no sort of use in sending us fox-hunting with Samson. We have positively lost all interest in that little speech so eloquently delivered by Balaam's inspired donkey. It is worse than useless to show us fishes with money in their mouths, nor call our attentions to vast multitudes stuffing themselves with five crackers and two sardines. We demand a new miracle, and we demand it now. Let the church furnish at least one, or forever after hold her peace. (52)

God as First Cause? Every cause must have a cause; each is the effect of a previous cause. As the sequence of cause and effect is endless, there was no first cause, and there will be no last effect.

Man must at last learn to rely upon himself. No supernatural being could help him. "If abuses are destroyed, man must destroy them. If slaves are freed, man must free them. If new truths are discovered, man must discover them. If the naked are clothed, if the hungry are fed, if justice is done, if labor is rewarded, if superstition is driven from the mind; if the defenseless are protected and the right finally triumphs, all must be the work of man. The grand victories of the future must be won by man, and by man alone" (59).

"Since Paley found his watch"[1] theologians had been trying to prove the existence of God by the presence of design in the universe. Evolutionary science had swept this argument away. There was no design to be found, only constant change, constant waste, constant evil. Suppose one found on an island a man a million years old who showed you his beautiful new carriage, perfect in every detail; he told you how it took the cumulative thought and labor of thousands of years to create it—inventing a light log base, two wheels, spokes, tires, linchpin, tongue, changing two wheels to four—would you consider that a perfect design for making a carriage? To create mankind, Ingersoll informed his audience, God began with the lowest forms of life. Species were born, died, and disappeared. Much of the earth was not habitable by man. Since animals feed on animals, "every mouth is a slaughterhouse and every stomach a tomb. Is it possible to imagine universal intelligence and love in universal and eternal carnage?" (71).

A pious friend once had challenged his idea that the world was full of imperfections. "Be kind enough," said his friend, "to show even one improvement that you would make if you had the power?" "Well," said Ingersoll, "I would make good health catching instead of disease" (72).

Religions came and went; there was no permanence in them. Ingersoll, a poet manqué, grieved in prose that could be set out as blank verse over beautiful religions dead and gone.

> The divine fires of Persia and of the Aztecs have died out in the ashes of the past, and there is none to rekindle, and none to feed the holy flames. The harp of Orpheus is still; the drained cup of Bacchus has been thrown aside; Venus lies dead in stone, and her white bosom heaves no more with love. The streams still murmur, but no naiads bathe; the trees still wave, but in the forest aisles no dryads dance. The gods have flown from high Olympus. Not even the beautiful women can lure them back, and Danae lies unnoticed, naked to the stars. Hushed forever are the thunders of Sinai; lost are the voices of the prophets, and the land once flowing with milk and honey is but a desert waste. One by one the myths have faded from the clouds; one by one the phantom host has disappeared, and one by one facts, truths, and realities have taken their places. The supernatural has almost gone, but the natural remains. The gods have fled, but man is here. Christianity will not endure. Christ sits upon the old throne. Who will be his successor?
>
> Reason, Observation, and Experience—the Holy Trinity of Science—have taught us that happiness is the only good; that the time to be happy is now, and the way to be happy is to make others so. This is enough for us. In this belief we are content to live and die. If by any possibility the existence of a power superior to and independent of nature shall be demonstrated, there will then be time enough to kneel. Until then, let us stand erect. (84–86)

Ingersoll and other infidels were charged with tearing down and not building up. But they were actually like the surgeon who cured the cripple so the cripple could throw his crutches away. They did not claim to have all the truth, but were trying to unchain the future to free the present. Doing away with gods and the supernatural was not an end in itself but a means to an end, the happiness of mankind. They looked to the regeneration of society in the light of reason, when all would be free and equal and live happily together.

The lecture ended with a battle cry for the new freedom:

> We are laying the foundations of the grand temple of the future—not the temple of all the gods, but of all the people—wherein with appropriate rites will be celebrated the religion of humanity. We are doing what little we can to hasten the coming of the day when society shall cease producing millionaires and mendicants—gorged indolence and famished industry—truth in rags, and superstition robed and crowned. We are looking for the time when the useful shall be the honorable; and when Reason, throned upon the world's brain, shall be the King of Kings and God of Gods. (89)

Having delivered his manifesto, his first and most important contribution to freethought, Ingersoll rested intermittently from his labors in theology. He had become the serene sage of a movement, enjoying the bubbles of protest and the applause of devotees alike. After spending a day with the Ingersolls sometime later, Underwood reported him "in excellent health and not the least disturbed by the harangues from the pulpits or the replies which his oration on 'The Gods' has begun calling forth from frightened theologians. He laughs good-naturedly over their impotent rage." The politician and the lawyer had been swallowed up in the philosopher. "Colonel Ingersoll, though full of business, finds time to give considerable attention to scientific and literary subjects. He is one of the most sociable of men and his house is always open to his friends. The Peorians are very proud of him and he is greatly regarded as 'the biggest man in the West.' Were he ambitious for office, he could have almost any position in the gift of the people of his state. But he would rather have a seat in his library than in Congress; he would rather give orations on 'Paine,' 'The Gods,' and 'Humboldt' than make political speeches, and he prefers to chat with his wife and play with his children than spend his time in caucuses and conventions or in wrangling about party politics" (*Boston Investigator*, May 28, 1872, quoted in "Recollections of Colonel Ingersoll").

In 1874 Ingersoll issued a slim volume entitled *"The Gods" and Other Lectures*. It was dedicated to "Eva A. Ingersoll, My Wife, A Woman without Superstition," and the frontispiece consisted of two sketches, the upper "For the Love of God" depicting crucifixions and burnings at the stake, the lower "For the Love of Man," a line of telegraph poles and wires. The book includes, besides the lectures discussed above, "Individuality" (1873) and "Heretics and Heresies" (1874). "Individuality," which bears comparison with Emerson's "Self-Reliance" and "The American Scholar," asserts the importance of the free mind as the *sine qua non* of human progress. "Who can imagine the infinite impudence of a church assuming to think for the human race? Who can imagine the infinite impudence of a church that pretends to be the mouthpiece of God and in his name threatens to inflict eternal punishment upon those who honestly reject its claims and scorn its pretensions? By what right does a man, or an organization of men, or a god, claim to hold a brain in bondage?" (*Works*, I, 177).

"Heresies and Heretics" reviews in vivid detail the history of heresy and persecution (especially under the Inquisition and Calvin), and files an impassioned brief for the defense in the pending heresy trial of the Reverend Swing (who, among other departures from orthodoxy, was charged with being sympathetic to the evolutionary doctrine [and therefore deserved damnation along with Darwin, Bastian, Huxley, and Tyndall] and with preferring not to preach the eternal damnation of the soul).

> Who can estimate the misery that has been caused by this most infamous doctrine of eternal damnation? Think of the lives it has blighted—of the tears it has caused—of the agony it has produced. Think of the millions who have been driven to insanity by this most terrible of dogmas. This doctrine renders God the basest and most cruel being in the universe. Compared with him, the most frightful of the most barbarous and degraded tribes were miracles of goodness and mercy. There is nothing more degrading than to worship such a god. Lower than this the soul can never sink. If the doctrine of eternal damnation is true, let us share the fate of the unconverted, let us have any place in hell, rather than in heaven with a god infamous enough to inflict eternal misery upon any of the sons of men.

The differences in the American reception of Paine and Ingersoll as freethinkers reflected the differences in the epochs. Paine was an outcast, Ingersoll only a controversial figure. The church-dominated society of the late eighteenth century regarded *The Age of Reason* as the mouthing of an imp of Satan. The post-Civil War period had its evangelicals who damned Ingersoll as vehemently as their grandfathers had damned Paine, but in general the spirit of the age, nurtured in the expanding thrust of democracy and individualism, emerging from a war of liberation, schooled in the revolutionary concepts of modern science, was tolerant of the Ingersollian message even while disapproving of it.

Midwestern journals ran the gamut. The *Chicago Times* praised it:

> One of the most marvelous books ever presented to the public is that just issued by Col. Ingersoll. It is remarkable for many things, the ability, the spirit of fairness that pervades it, but above all for its courage. It is also remarkable in another sense—no inherent quality to be sure— and that is that it marks an epoch in the world of thought, a new birth, for the book now everywhere read and reviewed on its merits would have been met by a howl of execration but a simple ten years ago.
>
> Col. Ingersoll is a man in earnest. He is a man of power. The rarest

gifts bountiful nature now and then bestows on mortals, seldom more than one at a time, she has showered on him in profusion. As an orator he stands probably without an equal; as a writer, considering that close application to the law has given him little opportunity for practice, he is almost equal to himself as an orator, and this in the most comprehensive sense, for his efforts present a rare combination of force, pure diction, poetical imagery, comprehensive and brilliant reasoning, and a logic that is inexorable. (July 5, 1874)

The *Chicago Evening Journal* and *St. Louis Republican*, respectively, were supportive but less effusive.

This book belongs to a class of publications which challenge attention by boldness and strength. Every statement is brilliant with the light of genius and based on sincerity.

There are in these days many books which assail in some way the accepted ethics of the day. Communism is a philosophy of robbery and free love is a synonym for licentiousness. Very many of the most radical thinkers of the day strike at the moral convictions and virtues on which civilization is built. It is a hopeful sign that while Mr. Ingersoll is an iconoclast of the most pronounced type, he is conservative in everything pertaining to morality and sociology. (July 3, 1874)

Many would call it a bad book, and yet it illustrates the grand principle of freedom of thought and opinion, and is perfectly decorous in language. (July 11, 1874)

The *Cincinnati Times* and *Evansville Journal* found both praiseworthy and blameworthy material in "*The Gods.*"

There isn't much piety in this book, but there is a good deal of strong, vigorous writing, some troublesome truths, some originality, and considerable weak philosophy and a little nonsense. (Aug. 4, 1874)

Robert G. Ingersoll is well known throughout this part of the country as a political speaker. We doubt whether a man has ever addressed the people of southern Indiana who made a more lasting impression upon their minds. The present lectures have in them the fire and humor and strong ways of putting things, which made his political speeches so attractive and effective, while, in addition, they have received a finish and polish which were necessarily denied the political audiences. It is one of the great defects of these lectures that there is apparent all through them an overruling desire to say something that will startle the religious world and arouse their antagonism. Consequently most extravagant declarations are conspicuous on every page and by the very multiplicity of superlatives the force of the argument is weakened and the beauty of the lecture tarnished. (Aug. 1, 1874)

Of course, not all were pleased:

> Mr. Ingersoll attacks the principles of Christianity with a vigor of intellect and a power of languages though not of argument, that causes one to grieve at their abuse.
>
> When Death takes hold of Mr. Ingersoll and he rests for a while in the great "divide between time and eternity," he may, as other infidels have done, change his notes of defiance to those of unavailing lament over the evils he has tried to accomplish. (*Chicago Post and Mail*, July 3, 1874)

> We have read only the lecture which gives title to the book, "The Gods." Of it little need be said. It is valuable chiefly as showing what a hopeless, muddy thing the human intellect is when without God and without hope in the world. Had the rage of authorship seized on some fellow writhing in the grip of delirium tremens, a similar work might have resulted. (*Chicago Christian Cynosure*, July 30, 1874)

The storm over *"The Gods"* did not faze Ingersoll's fellow citizens in Peoria. Most of them were his friends and admirers. They loved him whether or not they shared his explosive theories on the meaning of life and the universe. In March 1872 some of them crowded into his "capacious living room" to give him a silver service costing $375 as a tribute for "your honesty of sentiment and your fearless independence of character and expression." Ingersoll responded graciously. He reviewed the historic martyrdoms for intellectual liberty that sowed "a priceless harvest." "Most of all, I thank you for being the friends of mental freedom. I have no idea [whether] you agree with me in many of my religious, or rather irreligious opinions; but I know that you believe in liberty of thought and speech, and for that you have my thanks and respect" (*Transcript*, March 28, 1872, cited in Plummer, *Peoria's Pagan Politician*, 67).

In 1874 A. A. Avery was a young law student in Peoria selling *"The Gods" and Other Lectures* on commission. Nearly sixty years later he reminisced about the author, "the greatest and kindest man I ever knew" (*Topeka Journal*, Dec. 4, 1933). Receiving a notice from Mr. Bush, the white-haired keeper of the firm's records, that he owed $7.50 he presented himself to that grumbling gentleman and said that he did not have the money at the time. After this distressing encounter he was going down the narrow staircase when he met Ingersoll going up. The two faced each other sideways. To the young man's greeting Ingersoll replied, "What's the matter, Avery?" "Nothing at all, Colonel, why?" "Well, I thought you looked down in the mouth." Avery then spoke of the unpleasant debt and Ingersoll said, "Don't give yourself the least uneasiness about a little debt of $7.50. I wish that was all that I owed." They parted. Acquiring some cash Avery returned to "the sour company" of Mr. Bush and offered payment. Bush opened the ledger to check the account, then slammed it shut. "What's the matter, Mr. Bush?" "The account is cancelled," Mr. Bush replied. "I wish people would leave my books alone."

Ingersoll encouraged Avery to borrow books from his library, the best library in town. When Avery demurred that he did not have time to read the books and return them promptly, Ingersoll said, "Don't try to read every line. I don't read more than three lines on a page of any damn book." "But," Avery said, "you are all often away from home." "Well, in that case, break a window and go in and get them." Avery remembered some of the books as *Holbach's System of Nature*, Alfred Benet's *The Psychic Life of Micro-Organisms*, Spencer's *Synthetic Philosophy*, Adolf Bastian's *Spontaneous Generation*, and Thomas Huxley's *Protoplasm*.

Once Avery ran into Ingersoll returning from a lecture out of town. Declining Avery's offer to carry his bag Ingersoll invited him in, where he began sorting his mail in three piles while Avery brought him up on local events. When Avery slowed down Ingersoll said, "Just keep right on talking. Don't mind that I appear to be busy. I can hear every word you say." Simon J. Kilduff entered, "a dwarf of a man but the largest distiller in Peoria at the time." After a cordial greeting Kilduff asked whether Ingersoll had come to a conclusion on a pending matter. Ingersoll replied, "My advice is not to sue, Simon." "Very well," said the distiller, "that settles it. How much do I owe you?" "About a thousand dollars." Kilduff wrote out a check and left the office with a smile. Ingersoll turned to Avery and said, "I suppose you think that a large fee for some comparatively small service, but it saved him a loss of about $50,000."

Although Ingersoll was not yet a household name in the nation, his fame was spreading. On vacation and business in the east in 1874 he dropped in at the New York offices of *The Truth Seeker*, a recently founded magazine which would become the principal organ of freethought in America. It had characterized the "*Gods*" volume as "a gem of the first water," "pure gold," and was selling it at two dollars (plus twenty cents postage). Soon the magazine would be advertising an imitation bronze bust of the author, slightly larger than life-size, for twenty dollars (Sept. 1, 1874). "It does one good," the magazine declared, "to see and converse with such a noble and fearless defender of the truth." It went on to note that Ingersoll was busy with the law, but it hoped that he would from time to time be able to lecture on freethought. "He is a most genial gentleman—full of cheerfulness, earnestness, and vivacity. Long may he live to adorn the social circle in which he moves, and the ranks of Liberals and Free Thinkers to which he proudly belongs" (Sept. 15, 1874). Later *The Truth Seeker* would acknowledge a gift of thirty dollars from Ingersoll, which with an earlier donation of five dollars made him its most generous benefactor. *The Truth Seeker* later reported the formation of the Peoria Free Thought Association, with Ingersoll as president and sixty or seventy members at the start. The group was cheerfully patient with "the faithful ones" standing aloof and a hundred "mostly namby-pamby milk-

and-water, weak-kneed 'doubters' " who wanted to join but were afraid of the orthodox (Jan. 1, 15, 1875).

Ingersoll was already known as an outstanding friend of the black race, a reputation that would not falter but would grow and spread with the years. Frederick Douglass affords a striking illustration. On a lecture tour in the dead of winter Douglass had to lay over for train connections one night in Peoria. He was afraid he would find no accommodation there (it happened once before in that town) and would have to walk up and down the streets all night to keep from freezing. A friend advised him that he would have nothing to fear, that he would find a welcome at the Ingersolls' at any hour of the night and in any weather. However, Douglass was accepted overnight by the best hotel in Peoria. The next morning he went to check out the noted infidel and possible benefactor. "I gave him an early call, for I was not so abundant in cash as to refuse hospitality in a strange city when on a mission of good will to men." The experiment was a complete success. "Mr. Ingersoll was at home, and if I have ever met a man with real living sunshine in his face, and honest manly kindness in his voice, I met one who possessed those qualities that morning. I received a welcome from Mr. Ingersoll and his family which would have been a cordial to the bruised heart of any proscribed and storm-beaten stranger, and one which I can never forget or fail to appreciate." So began a life-long friendship. "Incidents of this character," Douglass reflected, "have greatly tended to liberalize my views as to the value of creeds in estimating the character of men. They have brought me to the conclusion that genuine goodness is the same, whether found inside or outside the church, and that to be an 'infidel' no more proves a man to be selfish, mean, and wicked, than to be evangelical proves him to be honest, just, and generous" (*Life and Times*, 1893 ed., 507 et seq.).

In 1874 Ingersoll was as happy as he could be. He enjoyed his role as the spokesman of freethought. To "my friend Shaffer," who had sent him a poem on the divine solicitude for the sparrow, he responded with a bit of doggerel entitled "The Song of the Tape-Worm":

> O, I live in his guts and laugh
> To see him work and eat
> Till he starves his wife and children
> To give a tapeworm meat.
>
> I am only a worm I know
> And a worm of low degree
> But I bless the God with all my might
> For making a man for me.
> (July 14, 1874, L.C.)

And he enjoyed his family. To his aunt Candice Sykes he sent the statistics: "I will tell you a little about myself. I am nearly forty-one years old—have been married nearly thirteen years—have the best and sweetest wife in the whole world—have two girls—one eleven, nearly, and one nine. They are both perfectly healthy, and as good as they can be. The youngest weighs 97, and the other 100. So you see they are not dwarfs. My wife weights 178, and I weigh 221. What do you say to that for a family?" (Jan. 18, 1874, *Letters*, 517).

In the summer Ingersoll combined business and pleasure and took his family to Long Beach, Long Island. They stopped off at Niagara Falls. He was not impressed. He wrote his sister-in-law Sue (his wife's sister) and her husband Clinton Farrell in Peoria, "All I have to say is that it is a d----d pokerish place, and I dreamed of going over the afd folly about twenty times the next night. I never want to go about that place again" (July 29, 1874, L.C.). He could not help gloating over the good food in New York: "I don't want to trifle with your feelings, but we had a few dozen Blue Point oysters raw last night for lunch and fried oysters and clams for breakfast. Wipe your mouths and forget this as soon as you can." From Long Beach he wrote them:

This morning we went down to the beach and watched the bathers. They looked like a lot of d----d Esquimaux [sic]. We looked a while and then I went and got four bathing suits and in a little while after three stacks of wool and one stack of hay might have been seen struggling with the waves. The children enjoyed it wonderfully. They had not a particle of fear but laughed at the waves dashing over their heads. Eva (big Eva) and I were old bathers in a few minutes. We never enjoyed anything so much. We sat down on the beach and let the waves come frothing and bubbling over us. (Aug. 16, 1874, L.C.)

In a few days he wrote that he "never felt so well and vigorous—so like running a race as I do now." He had found the key to happiness and told the Farrells that if they were not happy it was their own fault. "All I have to say is, Love one another—that is the height of all philosophy. It is beyond all religions. It is the secret of joy—the fountain of Perpetual Youth—the only rainbow on life's dark cloud" (Aug. 21, 1874, L.C.).

Nonetheless, the clouds lowered as the year drew to a close. He vented his mood on Clark. Happiness was an illusion. He was nostalgic, sad. There were tears on his face as he thought of sacred family graves. "Back over the days and years—over the weird and shadowy landscape called the Past—back upon the waveless sea, with but a single shore—searching the vain and vanished hours, those withered leaves beneath the tree of life—wandering sadly mid the ruined castle of the air, smiling at old hopes and expectations, and gathering again the tender remnants of half-forgotten dreams" (Dec. 12, 1874, *Letters*, 518).

In the summer of 1875 the Ingersolls went on their first trip to Europe, a two months' vacation in England and France. On the eve of the journey Robert's thoughts were of Clark in Washington, and Sue and Clint in Peoria. Clark had written a love-sick letter. "Life could be much more hopeful and charming could we work, live, and love in the light of each other's eyes. I shall see you and press you to my heart soon. We must live within the same horizon" (June 16, 1875, *Letters*, 518).

Clint's coffee and spice business was doing poorly, but Robert reported that he had obtained credit for a large shipment from a New York importer. "Saturday, away we go," he wrote, "and all that sets the least shade of sadness in my heart is that we leave the ones we love behind." He preached again his sermon on the good life: "Don't allow the smallest space of grass to grow on the paths between your hearts. Wealth, power, honor, fame are as dust in the street compared with the starry heaven of love." And the Farrells should live well. "I charge you to be sure and get enough meat from Eiser & plenty of truck from Hudson and Farrell." They should not worry about the bills, because the Farrells lived under the Ingersoll roof (Aug. 19, 1875, L.C.).

Ingersoll kept a diary (as yet unpublished) of the European trip. Early on the morning of August twenty-first a group of five Peorians waved goodbye from the pier and the *Adriatica* bearing the Ingersolls moved away from its mooring. Beautiful weather alternated with rain and storm. Mrs. Ingersoll was ill most of the time, staying in the cabin. They met fellow passengers, "all pleasant people," and saw porpoises and whales that spouted exactly as in the pictures in Olney's *Geography*. At midnight of the twenty-ninth they landed in Ireland "from a perfectly hellish little boat." The next day they saw the sights in Queenstown, Blarney Castle, and Cork. Across the Irish Channel and down to London, they took quarters at the Victoria Hotel, Euston Station. The next three days they spent riding about the city in a cab, viewing some of the historic and colorful places—Charing Cross, Trafalgar Square, the Tower, Billingsgate, Newgate, the Old Bailey, the National Gallery, the Prince Albert Memorial.

Leaving London they crossed the Channel on the well-travelled route from Dover to Calais, and after a hot and dusty ride arrived in Paris and took rooms at the Hotel L'Empire, "everything beautiful." They went shopping on the Champs Elysées, the women buying dresses and bonnets. Robert was measured for a black suit ($45), bought sleeve buttons and a chain for his vest, and loaned their travelling acquaintances the Hitchcocks $250. They visited the Pantheon, the final resting-place of the illustrious dead. "Over the grave of Voltaire the priests are mumbling while idiots kneel in prayer. The torch from Rousseau's tomb gives no light in France." At Notre Dame they "walked about and saw the confessional and a few fools with clasped hands adoring a stone Jesus in the arms of a marble virgin." At Napoleon's tomb "nobody at home." The diarist told himself, "There will be no liberty in France while the church has power and as long as the people have the least respect for what is called the Sacred. Damn the church, say I." They were impressed by the great statues at the Louvre. "The Venus de Milo has a majesty, a serenity, a kind of sublime repose that can never be excelled." They went to Saint Cloud, the Père Lachaise Cemetery, the Bois de Boulogne, the Luxemburg Palace, and the races at Longchamps.

On September sixteenth the Ingersolls returned to England via Dieppe and registered at the Grosvenor Hotel, Victoria Station. They visited Westminster Abbey, Parliament, Westminster Hall, took a boat ride on the Thames to Kew Gardens, and stood at Kendall Green before the graves of Sydney Smith, Thomas Hood, and Thackeray. They left the Grosvenor Hotel because of the bedbugs, going to 102 Jermyn Street: "we nearly starved and at supper ate everything in the house." Madame Tussaud's "Wax Works" was something special. They celebrated a birthday: "Today my darling Eva is twelve years old. We all gave her twelve kisses apiece and one to grow on. We gave her the same number of slaps and told her how dearly we loved her." In bad weather they stayed indoors, the elder Ingersolls recovering from chills. They were homesick but happy, played cards, wrote letters, and "cussed" the coffee and the English in general. Ingersoll shared the standard discontent of travellers with English cuisine. On September twenty-sixth "the landlady presented us with a plum pudding capable of killing a large family." On the twenty-eighth he wrote the folks back home in Peoria, "We are all in excellent health and doing our best to get enough to eat. The English have not the slightest idea how to cook anything. The beefsteak is perfectly infamous—they can't fry potatoes—nor make coffee—nor broil ham. They boil eggs very well, and the hot water here is about the same as we get at home" (L.C.).

Running short of cash he sent a request via the newfangled under-ocean cable to his friend R. G. Herney for a thousand dollars. Herney not responding, he comments in the diary "God damn Herney," then, "Damn R.G.H.," "D.R.G.H.." "G.D.R.G.H."

They visited the South Kensington Museum, saw ancient weapons, pioneer locomotives, paintings, and statues. Ingersoll was particularly impressed by a copy of Adam Krafft's statue on the descent from the cross. "Mary Magdalen lets the head of Christ fall upon her lips. Her face upturned in a kind of rapture. The most loving and affectionate thing I saw in the Christ business." At St. Paul's the graves of Benjamin West, Joshua Reynolds, Lawrence Wren, Wellington, Nelson, those of Wellington and Nelson in "utter and studied absence of taste." On October fourteenth the Ingersolls, accompanied by a Mr. and Mrs. Secor, took the train at Waterloo Station for Windsor Castle. There Ingersoll asked a guard whether he knew where Mrs. Ford and Mrs. Page lived. The guard did not but would inquire. They went through the church "where the Queen humors God on Sunday," and the castle, where most of the paintings were "not worth a damm." The poorly lighted tapestries looked like tablecovers at a country inn stained with coffee and eggs, and the banquet hall was "a kind of barn." Back in London some shopping, some bad weather, and finally on the twenty-first again on the *Adriatica.* Sunday, October twenty-fourth: "Didn't go to church. Several priests on board, bothered the Lord all day."

On November 16, 1875, responding to a request, Ingersoll made a speech in Peoria, "Some Things Seen, Heard, and Thought While in Europe," for the benefit of the National Blues, a military organization. He brought a bit of the glamor of the old world to the American hinterland in his rambling, humorous talk. He said that he did not kiss the Blarney Stone (he did not have to). He spoke of Shakespeare's Cordelia, "her eyes jewelled with pity's holy tears," and Caesar dead and Antony putting a tongue in every wound. He touched off some of Dickens's characters: "Mr. Pickwick with his hands placed philosophically under his coat-tails," Dr. Manette, "his daughter's golden hair bringing him back to sanity and love," Pecksniff the philanthropist. The only reference bearing on religion was his comment on a storm at sea. "I went up on deck and held the iron railing about the pilot house and I held on. There was not any hypocrisy about the way I grabbed that piece of railing" (E. G. Smith, *Life and Reminiscences,* 82).

One incident of this trip Ingersoll did not relate to his diary or his lecture audience. His visit to St. Paul's was long remembered there. The superintendent told Chauncey Depew: "Many Americans come here but the most remarkable of them was Colonel Robert G. Ingersoll. He was very inquisitive and wanted to know all about Wellington's tomb. I told him that the duke's body was first put in a wooden coffin, and this was incased in steel; that this had made for it a position in a stone weighing twenty tons and over that was a huge stone weighing forty tons. He gave me a slap on the back which sent me flying quite a distance and exclaimed, 'Old man, you have got him safe. If he ever escapes cable at my expense to Robert G. Ingersoll, Peoria, Illinois, U.S.A.' " (Depew, *My Memories of Eighty Years,* 309).

At the end of 1875 there was much reason for Ingersoll to be in relatively good spirits in this world of light and shadow, content if not grateful. He was in the prime of life, in excellent health and physical vigor, a prosperous lawyer, a happy family man with the best of friends, a scholar, a gentleman, and a good fellow. He was a ready and exuberant public speaker, available almost for the asking. He was—with some dissent, of course—the first citizen of Peoria and its favorite son. Politics? No, no, never again. He had found a more congenial career for serving humanity and fulfilling himself, where there was excitement enough and no such thing as failure. He was the primary champion of freethought in America.

Note

1. In his *Natural Theology* William Paley (1743–1805) said that if one found a watch on the ground its intricacy and suitability to its function would imply a watchmaker; likewise the organization of Nature implies a Creator. This is the classic argument from design, one of the principal targets of Ingersollism.

VI

Plumed Knights
and Plucked Feathers

The centennial and election year 1876 dissolved the self-created image of Ingersoll as a small-town lawyer and village atheist of moderate national renown. He returned to politics in a blaze of national fame leading to both personal triumph and personal defeat.

Ingersoll began the new year as usual in a depressed mood over the brevity of life and the vanity of human wishes, in which nothing was worth having except love. He wrote to Clark, "I feel that we have passed the crown of the hill, and that the milestones are getting nearer and nearer each other and now and then I catch a glimpse of the great wall where the road ends" (Jan. 1, 1876, *Letters*, 519).

He could not afford to wallow in hypochondria. On March first he argued a case before the Supreme Court in Washington. The hearing over and the court in recess he sat down in the vacant courtroom and wrote a cheering letter to Clint Farrell. "I hope business is good," he said, "and that ground coffee is on the rise—that the demand for sage is still unabated—that the cry is still for mustard—that everybody wants pepper and spice and everything nice." He sent his love to Clint's wife Sue and the baby "and to my children and to my wife. Tell them that they are my Holy Trinity composing the only Deity I worship." About the legal matter just argued, "I believe I am going to win my case" (To Clint, March 1, 1876, L.C.). He was engaged in behalf of the Toledo, Peoria, and Warsaw Railway Company, in conjunction with other claimants, in challenging the constitutionality of a complex state property tax on railroads. He had reason to be optimistic; he had won an injunction in the court below. But he guessed wrong about the Supreme

Court, as it voted unanimously against him (State Railroad Tax Cases, Oct. 1875 Term, 92 U.S. 375).

As a prominent midwestern lawyer, in May of 1875 Ingersoll was the leading defense counsel in a federal prosecution, United States v. Munn. It was an incident in one of the many scandals of the Grant administration, the Whiskey Ring affair, in which some midwestern distillers were charged with conspiring with government officials to cheat the federal government on excise taxes. In an age of corruption among government officials unparalleled until the days of President Harding, Ingersoll eventually would find himself representing defendants in three sensational trials of alleged corruption—the Munn case, the Star Route case in Washington, and the Kerr case on municipal bribery in New York. These cases—or at least the first two—were vigorously prosecuted, and the juries were not predisposed in favor of the defendants. Nevertheless, Ingersoll won each case, the government being unable to show beyond a reasonable doubt that his clients were culprits and not scapegoats.

Ingersoll brought his bag of lawyer tricks into the Munn case. Entering the crowded courtroom on the morning of May twenty-second for final arguments he was wearing a broad-brimmed felt hat which made him look (in the eyes of one reporter) like a prosperous Quaker. When he took it off, presto, he turned into a close-cropped liegeman of the house of Montague as in Romeo and Juliet. He balanced his ample form on a rickety chair and listened impassively without taking notes on the prosecution. His own presentation was a flamboyant, wide-swinging spectacle. The judge rebuked the audience for laughing at his wit and scolded Ingersoll himself for impugning the integrity of the prosecutor. The case against Munn, a deputy supervisor of the Internal Revenue, hinged on the testimony of a subordinate, Jacob Rehm. Ingersoll pilloried Rehm as a born perjurer, derided his "reputation" as contrasted with Munn's, and pleaded for consideration of Munn's eighty-year-old father "tottering on the verge of the grave," Munn's "pallid, invalid wife," his children. He asked the jurors one by one, eye to eye, whether they would want to be sent to the penitentiary by such a flimsy prosecution. "Do you? Do you? Do you? Does any man in the world imagine that twelve honest men can be found that can rob another of his citizenship, of his honor, of his character, of his home, and of his entire fortune simply on the testimony of such scoundrels?" Three days later, back in Peoria, he wrote Clark, "I have had a long and terrific trial, the United States v. Munn. It lasted fourteen days. Yesterday the jury acquitted. It was a great victory" (May 25, 1876, L.C.).

On the day of his triumph in Munn Ingersoll attended the funeral of his father-in-law Judge Parker, in Peoria, and spoke briefly. This in its entirety is what he said:

Friends and Neighbors: To fulfill a promise made several years ago, I want to say a word.

He whom we are about to lay in the earth, was gentle, kind, and loving in his life. He was ambitious only to live with those he loved. He was hospitable, generous, and sincere. He loved his friends, and the friends of his friends. He returned good for good. He lived the life of a child, and he died without leaving in the memory of his family the record of an unkind act. Without assurance, and without fear, we give him back to Nature, the source and mother of us all.

With morn, with noon, with night, with changing clouds and changeless stars; with grass and trees and birds, with leaf and bud, with flower and blossoming vine—with all the sweet influences of Nature, we leave our dead.

Husband, father, friend, farewell. (*Works*, XII, 385)

In some circles Ingersoll the freethinker was already noted (or notorious), and his private expressions of grief were news. This beautiful tribute was something for his critics to pounce upon. They said that it was void of Christian sentiment, that it was appropriate for "any respectable well-bred dog" and that "we do not anticipate that the Colonel will have a large number of engagements for funerals" (*The Christian Advocate*, undated clipping; *The Philadelphia Times*, undated clipping, L.C.). Their prediction was wrong. Ingersoll hated death and funerals and had hope merely for immortality, but time and again he would be called to speak at the last rites for the famous or the obscure and give what comfort he could find in nature and reason.

Long after the events of 1876 Ingersoll reminisced on how it happened that he became the spokesman for Blaine at the Republican convention of that year. He had, he said, been chosen a delegate without his knowledge or consent and was instructed to support Blaine. Here, he said, was an opportunity to defend the heritage of the Civil War, so when Blaine invited him to make his nomination speech, he readily accepted the honor.

There was more to the matter than that. What had become of his absolute declarations to one and all that he was through with the dirty game of politics forever? Obviously, whether he knew it or not, he had merely banked the fires of political ambition, not extinguished them. Blaine brought them to a blaze. In spite of a scandal purporting that Blaine had bargained off his votes in Congress for a pack of corporate securities, he was the head of the Republican party. His nomination seemed almost certain, since the Republicans had won every national election since 1860. For Ingersoll, to expend the talents of which he was justly proud at the very center of the Blaine campaign was quite different from assisting Grant in the Midwest in 1868. The national spotlight would be shining on him; the prospects for preferment in a Blaine administration seemed almost limitless. Who can say what combination of vanity, self-interest, and idealism prompted Ingersoll to say Yes?

As for Blaine—he wanted Ingersoll. He had seen Ingersoll in action and nobody else would do. He had struck pay dirt when he invited Ingersoll to make speeches for the party in Maine in 1868; he knew that Ingersoll was one of the greatest orators in America. He was not troubled by Ingersoll's peripheral contact with the Whiskey Ring. Nor was he put off by Ingersoll's infidelism. Ingersoll had sent him a copy of the *"Gods"* volume and Blaine had responded that he himself believed in the fatherhood of God but "that this does not prevent my admiring the brilliance of your style—still less does it prevent me from subscribing myself with sincere regards your friend, J. G. Blaine" (Oct. 7, 1874, L.C.). Blaine was a practical politician. He knew that the American electorate could be swept off their feet by a great orator who formulated their political sentiments, no matter what might be his religion (or lack thereof). In late May the Ingersolls were dinner guests of the Blaines in Washington (Mrs. Blaine's *Letters*, May 29, 1876, I, 129). On the floor of the House on June fifth Blaine staged a phenomenal self-exculpation from the charge of bribery. With a little effort the nomination would be his.

The Republican convention opened in Cincinnati on June fourteenth. The Ingersoll brothers shared a hotel suite. There is a legend that Robert arrived without manuscript or notes and that his apparent lack of preparation moved Clark to distraction. This is not inconsistent with Robert's reputation as a prankster. Kittredge, an early biographer and an intimate of the family, says that on the morning of Robert's speech Clark was frantic and demanded that Robert write something down immediately. Robert demurred, saying, "Let's have some breakfast first." "No, you shan't leave this room until you prepare your speech." "Will this do?" "When did you write it?" "Oh, last night while you were asleep" (Kittredge, *Ingersoll—A Biographical Appreciation*, 83). More credible is the story that Ingersoll told a reporter that at his brother's direction he wrote the speech out at midnight in ten minutes, having mulled over ideas and phrases for several weeks (C. J. Edwards, *The Blue Grass Blade*, Lexington, Ky., Dec. 13, 1909).

June fifteenth came and the nomination. As the clerk reached Maine and Maine looked to the Illinois delegation, the pro-Blaine delegates erupted into the standard demonstration, yelling themselves hoarse, stamping their feet, waving fans, hats, handkerchiefs. Ingersoll emerged from an obscure corner, moved briskly to the platform, and faced the crowd. They saw a man in early middle years, just under six feet, heavy-set, broad-shouldered, balding at the top and grayish at the sides, immaculate, handsome, perfectly poised, gray eyes beaming with friendship. The crowd toned down to listen to this comparative unknown who would speak for the leader of the party.

It was his shining moment and he made the most of it. Richard Henry Dana had just assured the convention that Benjamin H. Bristow, Secretary of the Treasury and zealous prosecutor of the Whiskey Ring, could carry Massachusetts. That was Ingersoll's cue. "Massachusetts may be satisfied with the loyalty of Benjamin H. Bristow; so am I; but if any man nominated by this convention cannot carry the State of Massachusetts, I am not satisfied with the loyalty of that State. If the nominee of this convention cannot carry the grand old Commonwealth of Massachusetts by seventy-five thousand majority, I would advise them to sell out Faneuil Hall as a Democratic headquarters. I would advise them to take from Bunker Hill that old monument of glory." Having taken the convention by storm with this assertion, Ingersoll extolled his candidate in violent, vibrant hyperbole, in majestic rolling phrases, as the personification of Republican virtues and the perfect standard-bearer of Republican ideals. The Republican party needed as leader in "the great contest of 1876 a man of intelligence, of integrity, a man of well known and approved opinions . . . a man who will preserve the financial honor of the United States" and "who knows that prosperity and the redemption" of greenbacks would come "hand in hand through the golden harvest fields," "the whirling spindles and the turning wheels," "the open furnace doors," "the flaming forges," "the chimneys filled with eager fire." The Republicans needed a man who would protect every citizen at home and abroad, for "any government that will not defend its defenders, and protect its protectors, is a disgrace to the map of the world." The Republicans "demand a man whose political reputation is spotless as a star, but they do not demand that their candidate shall have a certificate of moral character signed by a Confederate congress." Then the phrase that would fasten on Blaine for the rest of his life and history: "Like an armed warrior, like a plumed knight, James G. Blaine marched down the halls of the American Congress and threw his shining lance full and fair against the brazen foreheads of the defamers of his country and the maligners of his honor." The speech concludes:

> Gentlemen of the convention, in the name of the great Republic, the only republic that ever existed upon this earth, in the name of all her defenders and of all her supporters, in the name of all her soldiers living, in the name of all her soldiers dead upon the fields of battle, and in the name of those who perished in the skeleton clutch of famine at Andersonville and Libby, whose suffering he so vividly remembers, Illinois—Illinois nominates for the next President of this country, that prince of parliamentarians—that leader of leaders—James G. Blaine. (*Works*, IX, 55–60)

It is easy to criticize this great little speech. The stain on Blaine's character was national, not sectional; the linking of prosperity with contracted currency was dubious; the image of Blaine striding down the halls of Congress in a suit of armor and throwing a lance at the collective brow of his enemies was absurd. And the speech fell short of Ingersoll's

Gentlemen of the Convention: In the name of the great Republic, the only Republic that ever existed upon this earth; in the name of all her defenders and of all her supporters; in the name of all her soldiers living; in the name of all her soldiers dead upon the field of battle, and in the name of those who perished in the skeleton clutch of famine at Andersonville and Libby, whose sufferings he so vividly remembers, Illinois—Illinois nominates for the next President of this country that prince of parliamentarians, that leader of leaders, JAMES G. BLAINE.

COL. R. G. INGERSOLL

(From: *The National Weekly*, May 29, 1880)

own desire. He had written and crossed out "one who is in favor of the eternal separation of church and state," settling for the fuzzy "eternal separation and divorcement of church and school" (Georgetown). No criticisms, however, can detract from the magnificence of this forensic extravaganza. "Words can do but meagre justice to the wizard power of this extraordinary man. He swayed and impelled and restrained and worked in all ways with the mass before him as if he possessed some key to the innermost mechanism that moves the human heart, and when he finished, his fine, frank face as calm as when he began, the overwrought thousands sank back in exhaustion of unspeakable wonder and delight" (*Chicago Times*, June 16, 1876). The "Plumed Knight" speech has attained an absolute status as the greatest nominating speech ever made.

It was the general opinion among the delegates that if the convention had gone through to a night session Blaine would have been nominated on the first ballot. An effort was made in that direction, but the chairman ruled that the gaslights were not safe for such use (*Official Proceedings*, 302). That left the evening free for opponents of Blaine to concert a strategy for defeating him, while Ingersoll, heading the Blaine forces on the floor, won procedural points aimed at preserving and enlarging the Blaine vote. Blaine led on the first ballot at 285 votes, 92 short of a majority, his principal rivals being Senator Morton of Indiana (a pioneer at waving the bloody shirt) at 124 and Secretary Bristow at 113, Governor Rutherford B. Hayes of Ohio trailing at 61. Blaine kept the lead through the next 5 ballots, attaining 308 at the sixth. Then the scattered opposition collapsed and reformed, and on the seventh ballot the dark horse Hayes passed Blaine by 384 to 351 and was declared the winner.

No time for Ingersoll to lick his wounds, rest, or even earn his living. He could not let the centennial Fourth of July go by without making a speech. At the celebration in Peoria he made a freethinker's interpretation of the Revolution as an upheaval against divine right and priestly control. In the spirit of Paine in *Common Sense* and *The Rights of Man* he lambasted the monarchial system, the king, "tinsel crown upon his brazen head," who "could trace his pedigree back to antiquity's most successful robber" (*Works*, IX 67). He lauded the founding fathers for establishing the first secular government in the world, where authority came not from the clouds but from the people. "The fathers devoted their lives and fortunes to the grand work of founding a government for the protection of the rights of man. The theological idea as to the source of political power had poisoned the web and woof of every government in the world, and our fathers banished it from this continent forever" (85).

The speechifying done, sweet was the emotional plaudit sure to come from Clark. "Ever Dearest Brother: I have just rec'd your grand oration delivered on the 4th. I paid it the tribute of my tears. . . . Your thoughts have the irresistible and boundless sweep of the ocean, and the directness of a ray of light. I wish your oration could be read by every human being on the planet! The whole race would be elevated, except those 'robbers called kings' and those 'hypocrites called priests.' My dear splendid brother, I cannot tell you how proud I am of you, and how much

I love you" (July 11, 1876, *Letters*, 528; Kittredge, 128).

Blaine was a good party man, and so, by this time, was Ingersoll, who naturally was waiting for a call. It came—doubly. First from Blaine —an old record, asking Ingersoll to make some speeches in Maine. "No exaggeration to say that your coming may be turning point in national fight. Splendid victory awaits you here" (Telegram, Aug. 4, 1876. L.C.). Then a plea from candidate Hayes himself, a letter dated August eighth, marked *Private*. Blaine had expressed to Hayes some uncertainties about the prospects in Maine. "He feels, as I do, that you could do great good there. As Maine is the first contested state to hold an election, it is very important that we should do well there. I therefore have taken the liberty to write you to say that if it is possible for you to make a few speeches in Maine you will do the cause much service by doing so, and specifically gratify Sincerely, R. B. Hayes" (Muzzey, *James G. Blaine*, 133n). To this joint appeal there could be for Ingersoll only one answer. He joined the Hayes campaign for the duration, letting everything else go by the board.

Ingersoll and his family went to Maine. There they travelled on a barnstorming tour with Governor Connor and Senator Blaine by carriage inland and by yacht along the coast. The pace would have killed an ordinary man. "Last Monday I spoke at Rockland—had a fine meeting. No, I made a mistake. I spoke at Rockland Saturday the nineteenth, then at Lewiston on Monday—had a magnificent meeting there—Tuesday at Portland, Wednesday at Skowhegan, Thursday at Bangor, Friday at Dover and Dexter, and Saturday at Belfast" (To Clark, from Mt. Desert, Me., Aug. 27, 1876, Georgetown). At every place Ingersoll was the principal speaker, Mrs. Ingersoll and the girls sat on the platform with the dignitaries.

Republican papers were ecstatic. "The Colonel is a man of fine presence, such as you would select for the most popular stump-orator in America. His voice will go further, and probably tell more than any voice this side of the last trumpet. He can talk two hours, and the audience will hardly be aware that he has been talking thirty minutes. He has rare gifts of humor, of pleasantry, sarcasm, and eloquence, and he gives his audience such a variety that they know no weariness after standing a couple of hours on [the] City Hall floor" (*Lewiston Evening Journal*, Aug. 22, 1876). "Such a speech by such a man—if there is another—must be heard, the magnetism of the speaker must be felt; the indescribable influence must be experienced, in order to appreciate his wonderful power. The vast audience was alternately swayed from enthusiasm for the grand principles advocated, to indignation at the crimes of Democracy, as the record of that party was scorched with his invective; from laughing at the ludicrous presentment of Democratic inconsistencies, to tears brought forth by the pathos and eloquence of his appeals for justice and humanity" (*Bangor Whig and Courier*, Aug. 25).

The Democrats tried to smear him with religion. At the outskirts of meetings they passed out leaflets quoting, not always accurately, the most radical anti-Christian utterances of the speaker, the enemy of God. Ingersoll had expected this and he took it in stride. "This has done no harm, and has in fact increased the demand to hear me" (Letter to Clark, Aug. 27, 1786, Georgetown). In the stress of campaigning Ingersoll had not forgotten his kith and kin. He tells the hypochondriac Clinton not to get the blues, to laugh cares away, to say to the servants that he will give them fat jobs when he gets to be president (Rockland, Me., Aug. 20, 1876, L.C.). He wished that Clark could be with him for a few days to enjoy the grand scenery. "I give you my heart" (Letter to Clark, Aug. 27, 1876, Georgetown).

The speech at Bangor, as taken down by a reporter, shows how Ingersoll brought the Republican message to Maine in 1876. It is not the confession of a personal odyssey, his loves and hates of the party of Lincoln and Grant. It is campaign oratory at its best (or worst, depending on your point of view): We are good, they are bad. The speaker had looked down the vista of the years and found the Republican party perfect, always the party of physical and mental freedom, the torchbearer of reason, science, and progress. He began: "I have the honor to belong to the Republican party, the grandest, the sublimest party in the history of the world." The Republican party "bends no knee for the past. Its face is toward the future; it is the party of advancement, of the dawn, of the sunrise" (*Works*, IX, 99). For sixteen fortunate years the country had been in the hands of the unblemished party, which had preserved its territorial integrity and financial honor. The Democratic party had always been evil: in 1860 when it claimed a right of secession, in 1864 when it counselled surrender, in 1868 when it defended the persecution of the liberated Negroes, in 1872 when its candidate, the grand man Greeley, was the helpless pawn of a party with "itchy palms and empty pockets" (108). The Republican party would pay with real money the national debt represented by the greenbacks issued to finance the Union cause. The Republican party "put down the most gigantic rebellion in the history of the world; it expunged from the statute books of every State, and of the Union, all the cruel and savage laws that Slavery had enacted; it took whips from the backs and chains from the limbs of men; it dispensed with bloodhounds as the instruments of civilization; it banished to the memory of historians the slave pen, the auction block, and the whipping post; it purified a Nation; it elevated the human race." The Democratic party "has been, during all these years, the enemy of civilization, the hater of liberty, the despiser of justice." Not all the Democrats were bad. "Some fought for the Union [he had to find a haven for himself]; some are Democrats because their fathers were Democrats. . . . By the Democratic party I mean that party that sided with the South— that believed in secession—that loved slavery—that hated liberty—that denounced Lincoln as a tyrant—that burned orphan asylums—that gloried in our disasters—that denounced every effort to save the nation" (113).

He took apart the candidate of the Democratic party, the candidate who claimed to speak for honesty and reform. The crowd must have guffawed as the lawyer from Peoria answered his own question "Who is Samuel J. Tilden?" with a heavy sentence: "He is an attorney." Ingersoll faulted Tilden for never having married; for being tied to the Democrats of New York, the worst governed city in the world; for supporting the Confederacy; for believing in states' rights; for being weak and vague on redeeming the greenbacks.

Finally, Ingersoll summed up, the plain and simple difference between the parties should be obvious. 'The Republican party is the party of progress, of ideas, of work. To make a Republican you must have schools, books, papers. To make a Democrat take all these away. Republicans are the useful, Democrats the noxious, corn and wheat against dog fennel and Canada thistles" (122).

The campaign was young and already warming up. Ingersoll was riding high, enjoying acclaim and the furious pace. "I have had a continual and continuous ovation in Maine. I speak at Cooper Union next Monday evening—at Philadelphia next Wednesday evening, at Pittsburgh on Friday evening and Columbus, Ohio, Saturday evening—at Indianapolis Monday evening" (Portland, Me., Sept. 8, Dear Folks, L.C.).

On September tenth Ingersoll spoke at Cooper Union to an audience consisting largely of prominent merchants, lawyers, and public officials overflowing the main hall, the corridors, the platform, and any committee room to which his voice could reach. "His address," wrote a local reporter, "was in his happiest epigrammatic style, and was interrupted every few minutes either by the most uproarious laughter or enthusiastic cheering" (New York Tribune, Sept. 11, 1876).

He started his speech by reading a telegram aloud from Blaine, jokingly saying to the crowd, "If it were not good, you may swear I would not read it." The telegram announced an overwhelming victory in Maine. The Democrats would say to Ingersoll's audience, Let by-gones be by-gones. But would they hire an engineer proved incompetent, or lend money to a known deadbeat? Reversing history he saddled the Democrats with sole responsibility for the now-abhorrent slave law and took a crack at the southern clergy who had preached that God supported slavery. "Well, all I have to say is this, if God did this, he never chose a more infamous instrument to carry out a more diabolical object" (Works, IX, 134). He made sport of his religious critics: "I have done what no other man in the United States ever did—I have made the Democratic party come to the defense of Christianity. I have made the Democratic party use what time they could spare between drinks in quoting Scripture" (132). He poured bloody-shirt rhetoric over the Democrats of 1864 for declaring the Union cause a failure: "Rise from your graves, Union soldiers, one and all, that fell in support of your country—rise from your graves, and lift your skeleton hands on high and swear that when the Democratic party resolved that the war for the preservation of your country was a failure, that the Democratic party was a vast, aggregate liar" (146). He warned against the tendency of some Democrats to look to the government for handouts and inflated currency: "The people have to support the Government; the Government cannot support the people" (147). Hence only a hard money policy can serve a sound recovery. "The alchemists of the olden time who fancied that they could make gold out of nothing were not more absurd than the American advocates of soft money" (148). The government must protect its citizens. The government that could draft anyone has a duty to protect everyone. Only the party that gave freedom to the Negro could preserve his freedom.

Tilden belonged to the Democratic party of New York, Ingersoll went on, the worst party ever organized in a civilized country. Its rank and file were the riffraff of society: "I wish you could see it. The pugilists, the prize-fighters, the plug-uglies, the fellows that run with the 'masheen,' nearly every nose is mashed, half the ears have been chawed off, and of whatever complexion they are, their eyes are nearly always black" (132). Far from being the party of honesty and reform "the Democratic party of the city of New York never had but two objects— grand and petit larceny" (154). After the speech Ingersoll held a reception lasting half an hour on the platform and was then piloted through the applauding crowd to the outside, where three or four hundred enthusiasts sped his coach on its way with lusty cheers.

On the next night Ingersoll spoke at Newark, where a correspondent, either disinterested or leaning to honesty and reform, commented that he was "a leading counsel for the Whiskey Ring out west, and is therefore well competent to speak for the Republican party" (Special correspondent of the *Philadelphia Times*, Newark, N.J., Sept. 12, 1876).

Then the slow, roundabout way back home to Peoria. The people there, most of them, had been watching his progress with happy pride. "We do not believe there can be a man in Peoria who is not proud of the almost continuous ovation which Col. Ingersoll is receiving in the east" (*Transcript*, Sept. 13, 1876). In halls, public squares, open fields, at depots waiting for train connections, from hotel balconies, the man from Peoria was always ready and willing to address the crowd on Republican virtues, Democratic vices. For scheduled mass meetings, people from outlying areas poured into town or village in carriages or trains, the guest of honor was escorted from depot or hotel by Minute Men or Boys in Blue, and on the platform brass bands blared and glee clubs rendered songs like "Hold the Fort for Hayes and Wheeler" and "Grandly the Hosts are Marching." Ingersoll could be counted on to speak for at least two hours and usually there was a parade with flags, banners, and transparencies, a line of torchbearers on horse or on foot stretching for a mile or more. Rain could dampen but not extinguish the Republican hoopla.

In Philadelphia ten thousand persons crammed Forrest Mansion, and thousands more pressed in vain outside for admittance. "When a semblance of order had been restored, Colonel Ingersoll began, and for the next two hours held the immense audience spellbound with his eloquence, moved them to tears by his reference to the wrongs which the Republican party had been created to right, and threw them into convulsions of laughter by his ludicrous illustrations of pointed arguments and telling shafts of wit, directed at the manifested weak points of Democratic records" (*Philadelphia Press,* undated clipping. L.C.). The chairman had introduced Ingersoll with a clever dig at his religious critics: "If it is true, sir, as we all admit, that we have but one Robert G. Ingersoll, so must we conclude that a kind Providence placed him at a critical moment in the lead of a great party, and opened wide his path to matchless triumph." And a local editor commented, "The religious or irreligious opinions of any stump speaker in this contest seems to us to be of no particular consequence. A man may be an atheist and yet have very sound views of the political questions of the day. . . . When the corrupt old Democratic party, which is responsible for more than any political organization that ever existed in modern times, attacks a man because his theology is not sound, there is an instance of Satan rebuking sin which is impudent enough to be almost ludicrous" (*Philadelphia Bulletin,* undated clipping, L.C.). At Dayton Ingersoll addressed five thousand, at Cleveland twenty-five thousand.

The high point of Ingersoll's 1876 political oratory was the speech in Indianapolis on September twentieth. The event had been orchestrated as a veterans' reunion and Republican rally, and Ingersoll greeted the vast open-air assembly, "Ladies and Gentlemen, Fellow Citizens and Citizen Soldiers." He could add nothing to his old arguments, but his passion was more intense and more luridly conveyed.

In effect Ingersoll was saying that the Democrats of 1876 were the same monsters and traitors that had brought havoc to the nation in 1861. His rhetoric illustrated that the homicidal hatred between North and South at war had hardly waned in the eleven years since Grant said, "Let us have peace." Figuratively, he waved the bloody shirt with one hand, Old Glory with the other.

> Every enemy this great Republic has had for twenty years has been a Democrat. . . . The man that assassinated Abraham Lincoln was a Democrat. Every man that wept over the corpse of slavery was a Democrat. . . . Every man that cursed Abraham Lincoln because he issued the Proclamation of Emancipation—the grandest paper since the Declaration—every one of them was a Democrat. . . . Every man that believed this glorious nation of ours is a confederacy, every man that believed the old banner carried by our fathers over the fields of the

Revolution; the old flag carried by our fathers over the fields of 1812; the glorious old banner carried by our fathers over the plains of Mexico; the sacred banner carried by our brothers over the cruel fields of the South, simply stood for a contract, simply stood for an agreement, was a Democrat. . . . Soldiers, every scar you bear on your heroic bodies was given you by a Democrat. Every scar, every arm that is lacking, every limb that is gone, is a souvenir of a Democrat. I want you to recall it. Every man that was the enemy of human liberty in this country was a Democrat. Every man that wanted the fruit of all the heroism of all the ages to turn to ashes upon the lips—every one was a Democrat. (*Works*, IX, 158–160)

The speaker was proud to say that he belonged to the Republican party because it was the party of freedom, embraced all religions and no religion, believed in science and progress. The nation under the Republican party would always protect its protectors, never abandon them to the unrepentant South. As "the Government can come into your home while you are sitting by your fireside with your wife and children about you, and the old lady knitting, and the cat playing with the yarn and everybody happy and serene," and draft you for the army, so it has a duty to protect you when the war is over. He did not want the vote of any man who did not believe in liberty, in progress. But he had to have his little joke. "If there is any Democrat within hearing who expects to die before another election, we are willing that he should vote one Republican ticket, simply as a consolation on his death-bed" (162–164).

Gazing proudly at his old comrades in arms Ingersoll rose to heights of grandiloquence in a passage which has come to be separately known as "A Vision of War." The "Vision" casts a romantic glow over the Union soldiers and their families, their heroism and sacrifices. "I have one sentiment for soldiers living and dead, cheers for the living, tears for the dead." (We have applied this passage to wartime Peoria in an earlier chapter, "Colonel Ingersoll.")

He proceeded to state the central issue of 1876, but it was simply the old war in a new phase. "Shall a solid South, a united South, united by assassination and murder, a South solidified by the shot-gun; shall a united South, with the aid of a divided North, shall they control this great and splendid country? We are right back where we were in 1861. This is simply a prolongation of the war. This is the war of the idea; the other was the war of the musket."

Rumblings of a movement to inflate the currency and increase prices were finding favor among Democrats. (It would explode as the central issue of the Bryan-McKinley contest of 1896.) It was economic heresy, and Ingersoll was orthodox in economics. He ridiculed the idea of a flexible currency in a *reducto-ad absurdum:* "Some people tell us that the Government can impress its sovereignty on a piece of paper, and that is money. Well, if it is, what's the use of wasting it making one dollar bills?

It takes no more ink and no more paper—why not make one thousand dollar bills? Why not make a hundred million dollar bills and all be billionaires?"(178). A Roman gold coin had perpetual value, but Roman paper money would be worthless as modern currency.

Like many a soothsayer before and since the speaker had a vision. He beheld the Republican party on the march to the Promised Land. "I have a dream that this world is growing better and better every day and every year, and there is more charity, more justice, more love every day. I have a dream that prisons will not always curse the land; that the shadow of the gallows will not always fall upon the earth; that the withered hand of want will not always be stretched out for charity; that finally wisdom will sit in the legislatures, justice in the courts, charity will occupy all the pulpits, and that finally the world will be governed by justice and charity, and by the splendid light of liberty." This may have been inspiring, but how the Republican party could bring the millennium to a sorely divided nation and a troubled world was not clear. In the politics of 1876 the vision was at best mere fantasy.

It may be hard to imagine how Ingersoll's eloquence moved that mass of humanity standing in the gentle rain that September day in 1876. Witnesses on the spot give a hint. The leader of Spencer's Glee Club, which frequently travelled with Ingersoll on political safari, recorded that the speech

> sent the blood leaping through the veins and engendered an ecstasy of feeling too great for speech. The thrilling climax was reached when he delivered what has since become known as "A Vision of War." No words can describe the effect on the vast multitudes who gazed upon the great orator like one inspired, as indeed he was. When this part of the speech was reached no sound came from the enraptured thousands. Silent as the lips of death they drank in the music of his words. His voice, a rich musical high baritone, rose and fell with regular cadence. Words are inadequate to describe the effect of such eloquence. One must have heard it and witnessed its hypnotic and awe-inspiring influence upon those silent thousands who, unmindful of the drizzling rain, centered their admiring and sometimes tearful gaze upon the greatest orator of his time. ("Recollections of Ingersoll," *Peoria Star*, June 11, 1913)

A member of the Ohio legislature described how "step by step he led us on from Sumpter [sic] to Appomattox, until the climatic [sic] twist of the mysterious wand opened to us through the army yet living and the army of heroic dead, as he murmured and sobbed, with such an air of pride: 'Cheers for the living, tears for the dead' " (Private Dalziell, *Dayton Journal*, May 8, 1918). Ingersoll's message travelled far and wide. Robert M. LaFollette, twenty-one years old, read "A Vision of War" on a poster "as large as a door" in the post office at Madison and unabashedly wept (Autobiography, 17). Clark sent his regular accolade. "I have no adequate words in which to express the admiration I feel for your grand & incomparable speech at Indianapolis. It has exalted your name and fame to the very Zenith! In reading it I had to clear the tears before I could see to proceed. . . . I would like to hug you to my heart" (Oct. 24, 1876, Georgetown).

On October twentieth Ingersoll expounded the Republican doctrine at the huge Centennial Building in Chicago. The event had been eagerly awaited. When the doors were flung open at 7:30 thousands rushed in, instantly occupying all the seats on the main floor and in the gallery, and all the standing room space in the rear and the aisles, roosted in the elevators, and perched on trusses; others got on the roof and peered through the skylight—a swarm of humanity estimated at twenty thousand. Ingersoll delivered his standard argument with a few frills. He put a fraternal arm around the emancipated race in what has come to be known as the Oreo-cookie image. "For my part, I think more of a friend, black outside and white inside, than I do of a man who is white outside and black inside" (Works, IX, 197). In temperate phrases he portrayed Hayes as a good man, a loyal man, a veteran. He began his indictment of Tilden with a jibe so outrageous as to be funny.

> Now, my friends, the Democratic party, if you may call it a party, brings forward as its candidate Samuel J. Tilden, of New York. I am opposed to him, first, because he is an old bachelor. In a country like ours, depending for its prosperity and glory upon an increase of the population, to elect an old bachelor is a suicidal policy. Any man that will live in this country for sixty years, surrounded by beautiful women with rosy lips and dimpled cheeks, in every dimple lurking a Cupid, with pearly teeth and sparkling eyes—any man who will push them all aside and be satisfied with the embraces of the Democratic party, does not even know the value of time. (209)

Having waved the bloody shirt enough on previous occasions he concluded with a blend of conciliation and partisan sentiment: "I do not ask you to remember in revenge, but I ask you never, never to forget. As the world swings through the constellations, year after year, I want the memory, I want the patriotic memory of this country to sit by the grave of every Union soldier, and while his eyes are filled with tears, to crown him again and again with the crown of everlasting honor. I thank you, I thank you, ladies and gentlemen, a thousand times. Good night" (223).

On October twenty-fifth the Blaines visited the Ingersolls in Peoria. Arriving by train at dawn "I [Mrs. Blaine] heard Mrs. Ingersoll's well-remembered voice asking for us. . . . There she was at six in the morning, almost a dozen men in attendance, three carriages, herself dressed beautifully in a brown silk costume, all ready to take us to the very middle of her heart and home." At the house little Eva ran down to the gate to meet the guests, Maud greeted them at the door. They met Mrs. Parker and the Farrells. "The house is large and handsome and handsomely furnished, but it was as the small dust in the balance compared to the hospitality which was lavished upon us. Perhaps I never felt so welcome anywhere in my life." The table was laden with "three kinds of meat, not to mention fried oysters, potatoes in different styles, cakes, etc,." Who would carve the meat? Robert was out politicking, Clinton Farrell (who had struck Mrs. Blaine as nervous) had disappeared, Blaine begged off. Apparently nobody entertained the possibility that Mrs. Ingersoll, Mrs. Blaine, or Mrs. Farrell could handle such a task. Sue Sharkey, "a most wholesome, respectable looking woman," now thirteen years in service as the housekeeper, was called in, did the carving, set a portion on each plate asking no questions, and returned to the kitchen. Robert came in at ten and "nothing could exceed the warmth of his welcome." In the afternoon a stream of local citizens came through the parlor and in the evening there was a serenade (137 et seq.).

Ingersoll spent the last days of the campaign in a blitz of small towns in Illinois—Gilman, Champaign-Urbana, Aurora, Belleville, Quincy, Moulton—and in Madison, Milwaukee, and Davenport, Iowa. The towns vied among themselves in greeting "the prince of orators" with brass bands and escorts wearing the Union blue. In the afternoon he delivered to the enormous crowds—seven thousand in Gilman, ten thousand in Quincy, twelve thousand in Champaign-Urbana—what they had come to hear, a two-hour panegyric on the Republican ticket that held them spellbound regardless of inclement weather and tired standing (Gilman, Oct. 28; Champaign-Urbana, Oct. 30; Quincy, Nov. 1; all special dispatches to *Chicago Tribune*, undated clipping, L.C.). The *St. Charles Leader* made two trenchant comments. It remarked on the difference between the man on the platform and the bogeyman of religious critics:

For the past five years we have been reading descriptions of him from the same papers that are now deifying him. They told us he was a poor, miserable, whiskey-soaked, tobacco-bedaubed, illiterate, vulgar, blasphemous, red-faced atheist. We had read the descriptions often, and from papers of such pretended respectability, that we supposed there must be some little foundation at least for their black picture. You may judge somewhat then our surprise when we tell you that we saw a gentleman about five feet ten inches in height, over two hundred pounds weight, a big, smooth innocent looking, finely chiseled sweet face, and a great, large, magnificently formed head, getting bald on top, and the side covered with iron gray hair, in short, a perfect specimen of an elegant, brilliant gentleman.

And it noted a difference in tone between his words as spoken and in print. "There is one remarkable thing about his speeches which we cannot explain; his harsh words that sound so bitter and full of malignity when read, seem to lose all those characteristics when you hear him utter them. He has a peculiar facility of robbing all his harsh-sounding utterances of every particle of malice" (Nov. 5, 1876). The *Peoria Transcript* summarized his electioneering: "He has been on the stump almost continuously for three months, and it is not too much to say that to him more than to any other man will be due the success which the Republican party will achieve on the 7th of November. He has gained for himself a world-wide reputation and has largely aided in securing the success of the Republican party" (undated clipping, L.C.).

When it appeared that Tilden had won the popular vote but that the electoral results in several southern states were in dispute, Congress, having the responsibility of decision, was thrown into a battle verging on armed conflict between the parties. Ingersoll was in the midst of it in Washington, pushing for a Republican victory (and his own prospects in a new Republican administration). But February thirteenth was his wedding anniversary; it had to be celebrated. He wrote separate letters to Clinton Farrell ("Nothing excites my sympathy more than a poor old cuss who never had a wedding day."), to Sue Farrell ("I think of you always as one of the best friends I have in the wide world, and one without whom my house would not be complete."), and his housekeeper Sue Sharkey ("I thought I would thank you for the numberless acts of kindness that you have done for me & mine and tell you I feel your debtor.") (L.C.; L.C.; *Letters*, 520).

The Ingersolls, Robert and Eva, were in the gallery when the House declared the Louisiana vote for Hayes. They could hardly resist the impulse to stand up and cheer! Then they had lunch at the Capitol on "fancy roasts of oysters" (To Clinton, Feb. 20, 1876).

In a letter written after Hayes's victory, Ingersoll apologized to the folks in Peoria for staying away. "If I did not think it best for all of us I would not stay. In a certain sense my future is all depending upon what will happen within the next few days." In 1868, he continued, when he had aspired unsuccessfully to become governor or district attorney, he had not yet published antireligious tracts, but now he was known nationwide as an author of infidelism. Nonetheless, he did not think he had definitely disqualified himself for public office—at least he hoped not. "Of course, it is impossible to tell what may happen. Mr. Hayes may ignore me entirely. It may be that religious people will do what they can to block the wheels of Fortune's car so far as I am concerned" (Feb. 22, 1877, To Dear All of You, L.C.).

The commission appointed by Congress to settle the dispute strictly followed party lines, voting eight to seven that Hayes was the winner by 185 votes to 184. Ingersoll's hopes for himself rose, and he joked about his place among the office seekers. "The city of Washington is filled to overflowing with gentlemen willing to take any office within the gift of the President. I have not yet made up my mind whether to ask for the English mission or for Hayes to resign and let me take his place" (To Clint, March 3, 1877, L.C.). At the suggestion of Senator Blaine and Senator Morton, Ingersoll, accompanied by an independent party ideologue, called upon the new president on Inauguration Day and informed him that he wanted nothing for himself (a pious untruth), only Republican unity in a strong program for the South. Soon it became known that Hayes was appointing an un-Reconstructed rebel, David M. Key, as postmaster general and was otherwise leaning to a policy of conciliation that threatened the security and aspirations of the emancipated race.

To Ingersoll this was a blatant betrayal of the Republican cause that he would denounce regardless of mere personal consequences. He was scheduled to speak in New York on the volatile political situation; he decided he would align himself against the emerging policy of the administration. He regretted his labors against the Democrats and saw his own prospects going down the drain. "It would have been better to have elected Tilden. He would not have destroyed the Republican party, and I am afraid Hayes will. Well, just my luck! It always was that way" (To Dear Folks, March 9, 1877, L.C.). Then he had a long talk with Hayes, calmed down into the idea of conciliation without sacrifice of basic values, and changed his mind about a public break with the administration (To Sue, March 12, 1877, L.C.).

Ingersoll's decision to go along with Hayes coincided with an encouraging letter from Clark on sentiment in the administration. Clark had met with Senator Morton, who said that if he were president he would ask Colonel Ingersoll to name any place within his gift and that he believed Hayes would offer the Colonel the position of Minister to England or France on his own initiative. Clark had also called upon Secretary of State Evarts, who conveyed through him "many thanks for the very complimentary manner in which he referred to me in his New York speech." People at the White House had told him that "Hayes admires you greatly and that he really intends to do something handsome for you." So "keep cool, and smother down for the present at least" (IHS).

But Ingersoll could not "keep cool" and "smother down." Quite the contrary: He took the stump for Hayes and Reconciliation. His address, "Eight to Seven, or Political Questions and Answers," was his bouquet to the administration whose favor he sought. He regretted the bitterness and relentlessness of the late campaign, to which he had contributed, but it had been necessary to review the wartime grievances against the South and the post-war atrocities against blacks and their friends. The people of the North could still "hear the whip and could hear the drops of blood as they fell upon the withered leaves" (Works, IX, 225). Then he changed tack, tried to coax a smile out of everybody. "But to show you that my heart is not altogether wicked I am willing to forgive and do forgive with all my heart every person and every party that I have said anything against" (225).

Ingersoll spoke his own mind. He was a peacemaker trying to pull a nation together. In the post-war world the purity of the ballot must be reestablished. Civil service reform is not important—brave men should not discuss it "with tremulous lips and tearful eyes," women turn pale, or children sob. He admitted that he was not happy when Hayes appointed Key to the Cabinet, but he checked Key on a personal visit "and really he begins already to look a good deal like a Republican" (237). And Hayes had also appointed Frederick Douglass as Marshal of the District of Columbia, who "has been fighting for the liberty of his race, and at the same time for our liberty."

The time had come for reason, for discussion, for compromise, so that a prostrate nation could be revived. He pleaded with the South to accept Hayes's offer and, with the North, rise above the past. "Take it! The North will forgive if the South will forget. Take it! The Negro will wipe from the tablet of memory the strokes and scars of two hundred years and blur with happy tears the record of his wrongs. Take it! It will unite our nation. It will make us brothers once again" (263).

Old faithful brother Clark reacted to the "Eight-to-Seven" speech according to expectations: "Ever Dearest Brother, I rec'd yours with report of your speech at Chicago. I ran it over hurriedly and saw that you had made the best of your political speeches. I cannot tell you how proud I am of you. Your name and praise are in the mouth of everyone I meet." Clark had taken the paper to the White House and shown it to Rogers, chief of staff, who had insisted on showing it to the president, and Hayes himself sent "his best regards." And as might be expected, the letter ends, "I am lonesome without you, pretty blue, when shall I take you to my heart again?" (April 3, 1877, Kittredge, 103).

The Orator

Time dragged. With no word from Hayes, every passing day was a disappointment. Ingersoll's legal practice in Peoria had dried up while he was on the stump. How to replenish the resources of his extended family? Luckily he lived in the period of Chautauquas and lyceums, when an expanding literate public thirsting for entertainment and enlightenment flocked to hear lectures on philosophic and social themes in plain language. Could he duplicate his success as a day-after-day political orator with a commercial venture of equal proportions, lecturing on free thought? He found an entrepreneur who had faith in the project. He contracted with William B. Barton for a lecture tour from mid-April to early June. He would receive $250 per lecture, expenses paid, and all net profits would be divided equally between them. Flyers and newspaper advertisements would pave the way, offering "the incomparable orator" at fifty cents or seventy-five cents for the gallery, seventy-five cents or one dollar for the main floor and stage.

The tour was new as far as locale and topics. Ingersoll spoke in the principal cities of the western half of the country (Missouri, Kansas, Nebraska, Iowa, Michigan, Wisconsin, Minnesota, Wyoming Territory, Washington, Colorado, Nevada, California), an area where, excepting the banks of the Mississippi, he had not yet appeared as a public speaker. He spoke on "Progress," "The Ghosts," and "The Liberty of Man, Woman, and Child." Repetitions of "Eight to Seven" kept his political prospects warm or lukewarm. He did not seem concerned about what adverse effects his glaring infidelism might have in Washington.

Mrs. Ingersoll was a poor traveller and dreaded being away from the children. Starting for the depot on a trip to Chicago in January, as the elder Ingersolls got into the family coach and Ingersoll picked up the reins, she begged, "Drive fast, they feel badly to see us go" (Dear Children, Chicago, Jan. 9, 1877, Carbondale Mss). And Ingersoll could not bear being away from his entire family for a long time. On this western trip wife and children came along.

"The Ghosts" is an assault on belief in the supernatural, in good and evil spirits who rule the universe, confer authority, and sanction ignorance and persecution; on courtroom proceedings by magical signs; witchcraft; and treatment of disease by prayer. He eulogized the heroes of science and invention who had made the world a better place to live in. "The moment it is admitted that all phenomena are within the domain of the natural, the necessity for a priest has disappeared. Religion breathes the air of the supernatural. Take from the mind of man the idea of the supernatural, and religion ceases to exist" (Works, I, 288). Faith in the supernatural was still among his audience. "Only a little while ago the governor of Minnesota appointed a day of fasting and prayer to see if some power could not be induced to kill the grasshoppers or send them to some other state" (278). In tender and picturesque phrases he denied that belief in the natural order must absolutely negate belief in immortality. "The idea of immortality, that like a sea has ebbed and flowed in the human heart, with its countless waves of hope and fear, beating against the shores and rocks of time and fate, was not born of any book, nor of any creed, nor of any religion. It was born of human affection, will continue to ebb and flow beneath the mists and clouds of doubt and darkness as long as love kisses the lips of death. It is the rainbow—hope shining against the tears of grief" (270). It is a peculiar feature of Ingersollianism, as contrasted with the main stream of freethought, that it has hope for immortality—not faith but hope. On this issue Ingersoll combined reason and sentiment.

"The Liberty of Man, Woman, and Child" was Ingersoll's favorite lecture. It radiates a neighborly disposition. He wept and laughed his way into his audience's heart as he celebrated homespun virtues and inveighed against slavery, cruelty, and hypocrisy in religion and the social order.

"There is no slavery but ignorance. Liberty is the child of intelligence" (*Works*, I, 329). Kings had said that men could not work for themselves, priests that men were not to think for themselves. In the good old days uniformity of thought was enforced by ostracism and brutality. He had seen the older iron arguments of Christianity (the religion of love)—the thumbscrew, the Collar of Torture, the Scavenger's Daughter, the rack—and he had imagined himself in the place of the victim, suffering for honesty of opinion, his fingernails torn from his hands, the glittering axe falling upon him, the flames climbing about his limbs.

But the human race had progressed by intelligence. He pictured first primitive man and his dugout, his club, his yellow cave paintings, his tom-tom, and then the man-of-war and the steamship, the Krupps cannon (a dubious boon, he admitted), the artist's landscape, a Verdi opera. Man had advanced by mixing thought with labor. When a wheel refused to turn, the mechanic did not drop to his knees and seek the assistance of some divine power. He knew the nature of the problem and could solve it. The world was beginning to pay homage to intellect, to genius, to heart. Haeckel towered above King William, George Eliot above Queen Victoria. Abraham Lincoln was recognized as "the grandest man ever President of the United States."

> I have made up my mind to say my say. I shall do it kindly, distinctly, but I am going to do it. I know there are thousands of men who substantially agree with me, but who are not in a condition to express their thoughts. They are poor; they are in business; and they know that should they tell their honest thoughts, persons would refuse to patronize them—to trade with them; they wish to get bread for their little children; they wish to take care of their wives; they wish to have homes and the comforts of life. Every such person is a certificate of the meanness of the community in which he resides. And yet I do not blame these people for not expressing their thoughts. I say to them: "Keep your ideas to yourselves; feed and clothe the ones you love; I will do your talking for you. The churches cannot touch, cannot crush, starve, cannot stop or stay me; I will express your thoughts." (355)

The sections on the liberty of women and children generalize Ingersoll's domestic bliss into a social theory which seems at first challenging but is really conventional. Merriment abounds in the lecture, but sometimes there is a comfortable tear. He glorified women and the marital union of love; he had no use for the long-haired men and short-haired women who were against marriage. Religion blamed the evils of the world upon women: "Well, if that is true, I had rather live with the woman I love in a world full of trouble, than to live in heaven with nobody but men" (358).

He had read in a book how God made the first man Adam out of nothing. Poor Adam, all alone wandering about the Garden of Eden like a man waiting for a train—no papers, no politics, not even civil service reform to think about. Adam needed a companion, so God took a rib or, as the French say, a cutlet out of Adam and made Eve: "And considering the amount of raw material used, I look upon it as the most successful job ever performed" (359). Our first parents were told what they could do and the one thing they could not do, which they went ahead and did. They were turned out of the park and extra policemen were put on to keep them out. And all manners of devilment followed— mumps, measles, whooping cough, scarlet fever, toothache—all the troubles of the world. Then he read of human origins according to Brahma, who gave our ancestors a period of courtship before marriage: "Then they had their courtship, with the nightingales singing, and the stars shining, and the flowers blooming, and they fell in love. Imagine that courtship. No prospective fathers- or mothers-in-law; no prying or gossiping neighbors; nobody to say, 'Young man, how do you expect to support her?' and when they sinned, Brahma forgave them because of their love for each other. Honor bright, is not that the better and grander story?" (362).

He despised the man who wants to be "Boss"; the cross man whose brain power is spent in buying calico at five or six cents and selling it at seven while his wife is taking care of five or six children, one or two of them sick; the stingy man who demands, "What did you do with that dollar I gave you last week?" Once he looked down on the sarcophagus of Napoleon and had a vision of that restless man's career—Paris, Lodi, Egypt, the Alps, Marengo, Ulm, Austerlitz, Russia, Leipzig, Waterloo, and finally "St. Helena, with his hands crossed behind him gazing out at the sad and solemn sea"—and, thinking of the orphans and widows Napoleon had made and of the tears of the only woman who ever loved him and whom he abandoned, he would rather have been a French peasant wearing wooden shoes, "that poor peasant with my loving wife by my side, knitting as the day died out of the sky—with my children and their arms about me—I would rather have been that man and gone down to the tongueless silence of the dreamless dust than to have been that imperial impersonation of force and murder known as 'Napoleon the Great' " (370).

Children had the same rights as adults and should be treated like human beings. If they were to tell a lie, the world was not about to go into bankruptcy: "If someone thundered at you, 'Who broke that plate?' there is not a solitary one of you who would not swear you never saw it, or it was cracked when you got it" (373). Parents should be fair: "Just imagine a man who deals in stocks whipping his boy for putting false rumors afloat! Think of a lawyer beating his own flesh and blood for evading the truth when he makes half of his own living that way. Think of a minister punishing his child for not telling all he thinks. . . . When your child commits a wrong, take it in your arms; let it feel your heart beat against its heart; let the child know that you really and truly and sincerely love it" (373–374). He sketched with whimsical touches how stifling to a normal child were the conventional Sundays of the old-time religion (as we have quoted in an earlier chapter, "The Minister's Son").

He took another wallop at the doctrine of eternal punishment, that God would damn his children forever for expressing honest beliefs. "If there is a God who will damn his children forever, I would rather go to hell than go to heaven and keep the society of such an infamous tyrant" (382). He believed in evolution and development: "Upon that question I stand about eight to seven, which for all practical purposes is very near to certainty" (392).

The experiment of an extended lecture tour on freethought was a great success. The people of the West were by and large not afraid of unbelief. They welcomed the famous orator, crowded the meeting halls for intellectual entertainment. Even before he uttered a word he had won their goodwill. He was a big man alone on the platform, exuding cordiality. "Col. Ingersoll stepped promptly to the front, and stood like a grand genial whole-souled, happy, smiling Colossus, with his thumbs inserted in the armholes of his vest, beamed benignly on the assembled audience. His face is a benediction, and is an unquestionable certificate of character. Colonel Ingersoll is bald as to his dome-like skull and ruddy face. His eyes sparkled like those of a roguish boy and he seems to be as guileless and honest as a child" (San Francisco Daily Evening Herald, June 7, 1877). His oratorical style won praise even from political adversaries: "Colonel Ingersoll launched into his subject at once, talking in an easy, off-handed way, without water pitcher or notes. His topic is a broad one, his treatment pleasantly pungent, and his method of delivery the perfection of wit, and seems as easy to imitate as 'falling off a log' " (Denver Daily Democrat, May 14, 1877).

Whether you agreed with him or not this lay preacher was not a mere entertainer of an evening. Journalists ran the gamut of appraisal. One reporter, surveying the crowds of avid listeners, mused, "Less than a generation ago it would have been impossible for any man to have delivered that lecture without sacrificing his reputation and social standing" but now "everybody goes to hear him, everybody discusses him, and a good many people frankly applaud him." The reporter did not accept the explanation that the old religion remained intact while people became more tolerant. "Toleration as regards religious belief is only compatible with a decline of faith" (Savannah Record Union, undated clipping, L.C.).

Another distinguished between the old evangelicalism and a new undefined liberalism. People could laugh with Ingersoll at Old Testament fables and still believe in essential Christianity. "To love the good above all things and your neighbor as yourself is neither impeded by nor dependent upon Jonah's engagement with the whale." Therefore "in a word, Colonel Ingersoll came, amused, but did not conquer, for the church bells rang out yesterday morning as ever before, the Lord's Prayer was as kind and comprehensive as ever, and men went on in their allegiance to the ideal of perfection preached and lived over fifteen hundred years ago" (*Denver Democrat*).

Inevitably, one reporter condemned Ingersoll in spite of his charm: "Always and in everything downwards and degrading, the Ingersollian system would sink and drag and fairly burst in inextricable chaos. But the brilliant, reckless, bombastic 'Bob' describes it all so grandly, so eloquently, so magnificently, so majestically, why, who wouldn't follow him all the way to hell? The Examiner will not" (San Francisco, June 7, 1877). Nevertheless, the *Pantalumena Weekly Argus* would: "Those who expected to hear the churches vulgarly abused were disappointed, those who stayed away for fear of having 'the hollows of their ears' violated by sacrilegious utterances did not save their ears but missed a good thing. . . . We believe what he said came from the heart, and if he is in error let us demonstrate it by the logic of reason. To dismiss the arguments of this man with a wave of the hand and with an upturned nose of derision is either treating liberty of investigation with contempt, or a cowardly admission of the truth of his arguments. We say it, that Col. Ingersoll is the best orator of the nation, and we would like to hear him again and again" (June 8, 1877).

The higher dramatics of the tour centered in San Francisco. At two o'clock in the morning of May nineteenth the travellers arrived at the Palace Hotel bone-tired from the train ride, flopped on their beds, slept until eleven, got up, and braced themselves for the endless invasion of visitors. The *Daily Alta* blew hot and cold on the lecture on Liberty: "The lecture was frequently interrupted by the most enthusiastic applause— a tribute to his overpowering eloquence in spite of the unsoundness of the doctrines adduced, in some instances the boldest heresies, but uttered with faultless diction and the most magnetic manner" (May 23, 1877). Pulpit and press fell upon him, but he enjoyed the flurry. "I have stirred up a hornet's nest in this town and the preachers are making mincemeat of me," he gloated in a letter to Clinton. "The vials of wrath are being poured and all I can say is, 'Let 'em pour' " (May 28, 1877, L.C.). After lecturing in several other cities in California and Nevada he returned to San Francisco and delivered a standing-room-only lecture in response to his critics.

"My Reviewers Reviewed" begins with a salute to the audience: "Against the aspersions of the pulpit and the religious press, I offer in evidence this magnificent audience" (*Works*, VII, 5). What was his offense? "I believe in Liberty, Fraternity, and Equality, (the Blessed Trinity of Humanity); I believe in Observation, Reason, and Experience (the Blessed Trinity of Science); I believe in Man, Woman, and Child (the Blessed Trinity of Life and Joy)." He offered these as honest beliefs, not crimes. He denied that Voltaire and Paine recanted on their deathbeds. Dying men revert to childhood, like Falstaff, who, Mrs. Quickly says, "went away, an it had been any Christian child" and "babbled of green fields" (20). He was shocked at the attempt to justify the slaughter of the Canaanites and had nothing but contempt for the premise that whatever God decreed in the Bible must be right regardless of its gross injustice. He wondered at the extensive efforts put forth by the orthodox to refute his argument. "If all I have said is nothing, if it is all idle and foolish, why do they take up the time of their fellow-men replying to me? Why do they fill their religious papers with criticisms, if all I have said and done reminds them, according to the Rev. Mr. Girard, 'of some little dog barking at a railroad train?' Why stop the train, why send for the directors, why hold a consultation and finally say, we must settle with this dog or stop running the cars?" (40).

The main part of the lecture sets out, chapter and verse, the biblical image of God and the world as incompatible with modern science and humane values (93). "Is there an intelligent Christian in the world who would not with joy and pleasure receive conclusive testimony to the effect that all the passages in the Bible upholding and sustaining polygamy and concubinage, political tyranny, the subjection of women, the enslavement of children, establishing domestic and political tyranny, and that all the commands to destroy men, women, and children, are the interpolations of kings and priests, made for the purpose of subjugating mankind through the instrumentality of fears?" Once again he denounced his arch-enemy in Christian theology, the doctrine of eternal damnation.

> It is a doctrine so abhorrent to every drop of my blood, so infinitely cruel, that it is impossible for me to respect either the head or heart of any human being who teaches or fears it. This doctrine necessarily subverts all ideas of justice, to inflict infinite punishments for finite crimes, or rather for crimes committed by finite beings, is a proposition so monstrous that I am astonished it ever found lodgment in the brain of man. Whoever says that we can be happy in heaven while those we loved on earth are suffering infinite torments in eternal fire, defames and calumniates the human heart. (93)

"I believe the time will come when there will be charity in every heart, when there will be love in every family, and when law and liberty and justice like the starry sphere, will surround the world" (167). Ingersoll spoke not as a party politician selling utopia around the corner but as a freethinker whose millennium would come in good time with the triumph of freethought.

The audience applauded, and Ingersoll basked in his success. "We had a magnificent meeting last night," he wrote to the folks back home. "I delivered a lecture replying to the preachers. I made it hot for the dear old stupid theologians. I never made a better speech in my life" (Dear All, June 28, 1877, L.C.).

In letters to the household in Peoria, Ingersoll the faithful reporter said over and over that the travellers were homesick. However, they seemed to be enjoying themselves. Some trains stopped at every station. Once the Ingersolls got out and talked with the Indians; once they had an extra feast of strawberries and oxblood cherries; once the locomotive jumped the track but nobody was hurt. Cheyenne was appalling, "a town without a tree and without a garden." The rocks from Cheyenne to Laramie looked "like the ruins of the forts built by the Titans when they battled with the Gods." San Francisco Bay at moonlight was delightful. "The waves were all touched with silver and the ships looked like happy dreams and we were all as happy as the ships looked." Audiences were all cordial—"a fine house," "a splendid meeting"—although business conditions in California were depressed; "everybody dead broke, except a few, and those few own the State."

In Virginia City, Nevada, the superintendent of the Idaho Gold Mine invited the Ingersolls to inspect the mine eleven hundred feet below the surface. Ingersoll was not eager but the girls were and that settled it (Mrs. Ingersoll was not in the picture). The girls took off their hats and tucked up their dresses and the four (including the manager Barton), wearing makeshift waterproofs, huddled tight in the cable cage for the long ride down and up in the dripping darkness.

One cool summer day in San Francisco Ingersoll had not a care in the world and teased the unfortunate Peorians.

Is it hot where you are? Is it dusty—is it hellish? Well, if it is, think about us. Here we are cool as cucumbers sliced on ice—cool as the love of a Presbyterian God—cool as grass that grows upon the lips of a spring under a hill—cool as Sue Sharkey when she says, "The old scallawag has got home again, hasn't he?" Here we are cool as potatoes fried yesterday—cool as the audience at Quincy—cool as the bosom of a Boston old maid. Think of that & weep. (Dear All, June 30, 1877, L.C.)

In the fall Ingersoll was invited to speak on farming at the state fair in Peoria. The subject was not exactly in his line but he had no difficulty in accepting and doing more than a routine job. His speech is an upbeat sermon on "the good life" on the farm (Works, I, "About Farming in Illinois"). He told the farmers to turn away from the old life under "the blessed trinity of chance, accident, and mistake." It was time to leave behind isolation, ignorance, boundaries marked by dogs, dilapidated houses, the pig sty next to the home, working from before sun-up to after sun-down, careless cultivation of crops and animals, reliance upon spirits above for good harvests, hauling animals to market in wagons. The railroads had brought the Illinois farmers in touch with New York, London, Liverpool. They should raise their standards accordingly. They should live in villages, have communal cultural centers, decorate their homes, get more sleep!

He had definite ideas about improving the fare of the country kitchen. "The inventor of a good soup did more for his race than the maker of any creed. The doctrines of total depravity and endless punishment were born of bad cooking and dyspepsia" (432). Every farmer should own his own home because "few men have been patriotic enough to shoulder a musket for a boarding house" (419). Insofar as the farmer's problems were due to a contracting currency and falling prices, it seemed to Ingersoll that the demonetization of silver in 1873 was largely to blame (see p. 314, Note 1). "I do not say that money be made out of nothing. I do not ask for the prosperity born of paper. But I do ask for the remonetization of silver. Silver was demonetized by fraud. It was an imposition on every solvent man, a fraud upon every honest debtor in the United States. It assassinated labor. It was done in the interest of avarice and greed, and should be undone by honest men" (426). (This passage would haunt Ingersoll in the politics of the eighties and nineties when he was accused of turning coat on the silver cause. In that period, silver, cut away from governmental support, fell gradually in the commercial market to about 30 to 1. By then he was asserting for the Republican party that remonetization at 16 to 1 would be a fraud on creditors—that is, the moneyed interest he had previously denounced.)

Hayes had been in office for six months and had given Ingersoll nothing; Ingersoll had quietly made his peace with disappointment when suddenly his prospects came to life again. On November first he received a telegram from Oglesby, now a senator. The White House had given the Illinois delegation in Congress the choice of the new minister to Germany, and Ingersoll was their unanimous selection. Would he accept? It seemed fairly that all he had to do for the appointment was to say yes. Accepting, Ingersoll replied that the idea of receiving a place had long since "paid its bill and left my mind," but he was disposed to give the president "an opportunity of expressing himself in regard to me. I suppose the religious people or rather the people who want to be considered extremely pious will have but little hesitation about expressing their ideas" (Plummer, *ISHSJ*, 92). Oglesby sent a long, cautious reply. He and other Illinois members of Congress had had a cordial interview with Secretary of State Evarts. To Evarts's inquiry about Ingersoll's knowledge of the German language they had answered that they did not know but were sure that he could readily master it. Evarts had brought up Ingersoll's antireligion and they had replied that his personal character, his reputation as a lawyer, his sound Republicanism, and his service to the party should outweigh any religious sentiment against him. Evarts had concluded by saying that President Hayes himself must pass on all ambassadorial appointments. Oglesby was hopeful but restrained in his expectations (Nov. 3, 1877, IHS).

News of the impending appointment leaked out, and the White House was bombarded with letters pro and con. Some of Ingersoll's partisans emphasized his skill in negotiations between corporations. A typical nay vote came from a William Pater of New York. "I believe the appointment of such a man, who disregards and scoffs the sacred things, would shake the confidence of all Christian men in your administration, of which we now have such great hopes" (Kleber, *Magic of His Power*, 286).

Undaunted, Ingersoll went on with his crusade against religion—"I had a splendid meeting last night," he wrote from Utica, New York, (Nov. 15, 1877, L.C.)—not hesitating to express his political opinions as well. Ingersoll defended Hayes's conciliatory policy toward the South as a necessity but insisted that a nation that drafts a man into the army in time of war had a duty to protect him in time of peace. He had not sought the German mission and was not in the habit of accepting appointments before they were made. He derided opponents of the nomination. "There might be some objections. Some reverend idiot (be sure and say idiot, put that in sure) like De Witt Talmage [a noted evangelical with whom Ingersoll would tangle later] might object." Instead of avoiding opposition he gloried in it.

The administration, on the spot, became as silent as the grave. The long days dragged on as the White House wavered between honor and expediency. Ingersoll had had enough and took himself off the hook. He called on Evarts personally and told him that he was no longer interested in the Berlin appointment. To his family he took pride in not letting the matter just fade away. "The people here have a good deal to say about the Berlin mission," he wrote back home. "All consider that I am ahead. I flanked the gentlemen. I was bound that Mr. Evarts would not leave me with the bag in hand. I left him out in the cold. He is a dirty dog, without even good manners" (Nov. 25, 1877, L.C.). A load was off his mind. He need no longer defend Hayes's southern policy. Hayes was a coward, and most of his cabinet were like him. This is the administration of "Hypocrisy" and "Cant." "Between us girls, I hate the whole thing" (Dear All, Nov. 29, L.C.).

This was his most painful disappointment in his intermittent pursuit of public office. Never again would he risk himself on another "sure thing" in politics. It was done; he did not brood. He looked forward to enjoying winter's life with his entire family in Peoria—eating and drinking, laughing and singing, sitting at the fireside, playing with the Farrell baby. "We will ride out in the cold sharp wind, come home with cheeks like roses and hearts full of joy and love and hope" (Dear Folks, Nov.

21, 1877, L.C.). The Farrells had written about a rainstorm and flood so severe that it had driven them out of the house. Ah, it was like Captain Noah's adventure; perhaps the whole family had web feet now. He hoped that they tied a towel to the chimney so that they could find the house when the water subsided (Dear All of You, Nov. 24, 1877, L.C.). In Washington Maud had rented a piano and was banging away with all her might. Eva was reading about Macaulay, both girls were reading Charles and Mary Lamb, Maud a novel by Miss Thackeray, and he himself a history of French literature (Nov. 29, 1877, L.C.).

On December third Ingersoll wrote at least three personal letters. Again he counselled the melancholy Clint, "Be as cheerful as you can. D--n business. Enjoy your youth. There is nothing after all but love. Wherever love is, there is heaven" (L.C.). In a separate letter he thanked Clint for a big package of nuts: "We have had the dyspepsia since they came. I have just finished eating a pocketful. If you hear of my sudden death you will know the cause" (L.C.). To Thurlow Weed, prominent New York publisher and politician, he wrote: "I care nothing on earth about that protest signed by the thirty reverend incompetents. Goethe says, 'When you hear the dogs bark, you may know that you are travelling.' I am however, much obliged to you for having said a few words in my favor. Accept my sincere thanks" (IHS).

Ingersoll was at the crossroads. It was time to reorganize his life. On December twelfth he informed his daughters that he had finally decided to leave Peoria for Washington. Peoria was too small for him and required too much work for too little money. As Clint's business was not improving, Robert was confident that not only could he make plenty of money at law in Washington, but he also could find Clint plenty of work with a future. Incidentally, he was lecturing that night in Washington, expected a fine house, nearly all the seats were already sold (L.C.). He did not mention that he was tired of Illinois politics and that his long separation from Clark would end; the two would resume the practice of law together.

On the next day he wrote, at Mrs. Ingersoll's dictation, a letter to her sister Sue Farrell. Mrs. Farrell was planning a fancy polonaise dress. Mrs. Ingersoll made suggestions on materials and pattern, silk, lace, velvet, scallops, tassels. The letter is subscribed, "Love to all, Eva, by her secretary, Robert" (L.C.). Greater love hath no man—or woman—and the writer's heart was happy.

And there was the joy of lecturing, the communion of brave new ideas, the kindred spirits, the admiring faces. Praise was good, censure inspiring. On December seventeenth Ingersoll lectured to a packed house in Troy, New York. The *Daily Times* commented, "Such eloquence, we venture to say, whatever may be thought of the sentiments of the lecture, was never before heard in this city. . . . No one, unless wholly signed by prejudice, can deny that much of what he said is the essence of good sense, that the mind instantly feels must be the truth beyond a possibility of refutation" (Dec. 18, 1877).

Ingersoll had planned to speak in Richmond, Indiana, on the nineteenth. The local manager, A. P. Griffin, explained in *The Palladium* (undated clipping, L.C.) why the lecture was cancelled. Ingersoll had lectured in Albany under the auspices of the Young Men's Association, and twenty-six Albany ministers had signed a public letter protesting that such an endorsement was an insult and an outrage to many citizens of the city. Griffin wrote to Ingersoll inquiring whether he (Griffin) could give assurance to his audience that nothing offensive to Christianity would be in the lecture. Ingersoll had replied, "I will not lecture in Richmond under your auspices."

In the spring of 1878 appeared a small volume: *"The Ghosts" and Other Lectures* by Robert G. Ingersoll. It was published in Peoria by C. P. Farrell and was dedicated to Ebon C. Ingersoll, "My Brother, From Whose Lips I heard the First Applause, and with Whose Name I want My Own Associated Until Both Are Forgotten." The book included "The Ghosts," "The Liberty of Man, Woman, and Child," "The Declaration of Independence," "About Farming in Illinois," "Speech at Cincinnati" (nominating Blaine), and "The Past Rises Before Me Like A Dream" ("The Vision of War," from the Indianapolis speech for Hayes). Anyone looking for "Eight to Seven" or "My Reviewers Reviewed" would not find it. The book was in a sense the new testament of its patriot-prophet author, assembling his more general messages as citizen and freethinker since the *"Gods"* volume of 1874. Henceforth he would be not an ambitious politician but a Washington lawyer, and he would always find time to speak out on public affairs and to spread the religion of humanity.

VII

The "Happy" Warrior

The Ingersolls took a house at 25 Lafayette Place (now East Executive Avenue). The household consisted of the four Ingersolls, Clinton and Sue Farrell and their little daughter Eva, Mrs. Parker, and Sue Sharkey. (History does not record how they all got along together without friction due to two Sues and three Evas.) The spacious, brownstone house looked out westward on Lafayette Square, with its greenery and winding walks, and, at the center, the statue of Andrew Jackson on horseback. It was situated half a block north from the White House and a ten minutes' walk from the offices of Ingersoll and Ingersoll at 1417 G Street. Soon the family were friends with the local police, the newsboy, and neighbors, and were reputed an easy touch for panhandlers.

A Washington journalist would later describe Ingersoll as "the most popular man in town because he was never on stilts" (George C. Blanchard, *The Truth Seeker*, April 2, 1910). In the Capital City his sociability blossomed. Social evenings at 25 Lafayette Place became a well-known event. The doorsteps were well trodden; newspaper men enjoyed writing about the parties. Bigots and timid politicians might stay away, but there was never a lack of good and varied company—obscure friends and acquaintances, members of Congress, departmental heads, judges, diplomats, exotics of every kind, and notables like Frederick Douglass, Clara Barton, and the world traveller George Kennan.

On Saturday evenings when Robert was in town the Ingersolls were "at home." They greeted their guests at the door.

Theirs is the truly happy family, and all their home relations are beautiful and tender. Mrs. Ingersoll is a strikingly handsome woman, tall and a fine figure, flashing eyes, smooth black hair. . . . The two daughters are quiet, pretty girls, the oldest, Miss Eva, being the possessor of a clear and rich soprano voice, a wonderful crown of rippling brown hair, and a pair of soft, shy eyes. Miss Maud is a plump young lady with the roguishness of youth in her eyes and dimples. (*The Daily News*, Denver, Colo., Feb. 27, 1882, quoted from *St. Louis Post Dispatch*)

Taking off their "traps," the ladies keeping on their "bonnets," the guests may have noticed the life-size bust of Shakespeare in the hall before moving into the front room, which was done in deep red and lined with comfortable chairs and well-stacked book shelves (Mark Twain and Spinoza side by side). They then may have proceeded farther into the double reception room, which contained in tasteful arrangement a Steinway piano, a bust of Ingersoll, a three-foot replica of the Venus de Milo, and an edition of Shakespeare the size of a large family Bible, gold-lettered on the cover "The Book of the Brain" and on the spine "the Inspired Book." Near it was a handsome edition of Burns, his "Prayer Book."

The guests sat or stood about in groups conversing. Ingersoll circulated among them, making introductions and an occasional clever remark. The atmosphere was genteel. Once Ingersoll and Miss Thomas, sister of a congressman, engaged in a fifteen-minute literary duel, parrying remembered verses from Shakespeare and Burns to the delight of the congressman, the Japanese ambassador, and others. After about an hour of buzzing small talk Ingersoll would call for music. Some instrumentalists brought their own instruments. If there were no musicians among the guests, Sue Farrell might play the piano or Eva might sing solo or join Maud in duet (*Galveston News*, Feb. 15, 1881). At about ten-thirty Ingersoll would excuse himself briefly and soon the folding doors which set off the dining room would be opened, revealing a table laden with sandwiches, cold meats, cakes, and ices, and Ingersoll mixing champagne and claret in a huge punch bowl, from which he would serve each guest liberally. After more music and conversation, the party would begin to break up, the last guests leaving at about midnight, the gentlemen equipped with choice Havana cigars to smoke on the way home.

Ingersoll and his brother the excongressman were what were called "parliamentary lawyers"—lobbying on Capitol Hill and appearing before administrative agencies. The firm represented the state of Illinois in claims arising out of the Civil War and the North German Lloyd and Hamburg American Packet Company against discriminatory tonnage duties. It urged repeal of the tax on bank deposits and pressed for improvement in the status of reserve officers, promoted sale of refrigerators to the Navy and cancelling machines to the Post Office. Ingersoll was seen so often on the floors of Congress (where he had no right to be) that he was taken to be a member or a former member like his brother (Blanchard, April 2, 1910). He had no compunction about molding legislators to his purposes. He directed Senator Oglesby to exercise his subpoena powers in furthering an Ingersoll bill before his committee, and told Senators Blaine, Allison, and Windom what to do and how to do it on a pending bill. His clientele was largely from business and government, but he did not ignore the poor and unfortunate who sought his help. There is a story about a group of congressmen who called upon him at home. While they were waiting, a frail and shabbily dressed woman entered and took a seat in a corner. Bustling in, Ingersoll shook hands with the congressmen, and noticing the woman went to her and asked how he could help her. She appeared ill at ease in the presence of the important people, so he gave her his arm and led her off to another room, where she enlisted him in the cause of her pension rights as a widow while the important visitors tapped their fingers on their top-hats (*Daily News*, Denver, Colo., Feb. 7, 1872, quoted from *St. Louis Post Dispatch*).

It was no secret that Ingersoll was casual and generous about money. The banker Jesse Seligman, apologizing for delay in fee payment, sent $2,500 on account with a message: "You will probably be thankful to me that I have not sent you more, for I know that you have a big heart, as well as holes in your pocket" (June 3, 1881, L.C.). Not that the firm was indifferent about fees. They wrote to a client interested in a pending bill that would come up in the next session of Congress, "You had better be here at the opening of Congress prepared to stay until the end and do not fail to bring with you at least one thousand dollars" (A. L. Rawley, Nov. 23, 1878, L.C.).

A reporter asked Ingersoll, "Colonel, which do you prefer, the platform and its applauding audiences or the court-room with a practice which must be a lucrative one to a lawyer of your eminence?" He replied, "I can make more money in the practice of law, but I do far more good by lecturing. Personally, I like the business where I can do the most good. The world is in mental chains—intellectual dungeons. I want to break the chains and flood the dungeons with light" (*The Republic*, Washington, D.C., Jan. 30, 1880). A contrary view held that Ingersoll the lecturer was simply in business, making money the easier way. A Kendrick lithograph in *Chic* entitled "Where Should We Spend the Sabbath?" shows in the left foreground three cadaverous ministers exhorting a few people whose backs are turned, excepting one person identified as the Rising Generation who is thumbing his nose. On the platform Ingersoll is swallowing sulphur, Henry Ward Beecher balancing a Bible on his nose, and DeWitt Talmage on all fours breathing hell-fire, all competing with one another and two buxom, lightly-clad "Sisters Nautey-Nice" [sic].

Solicitations for lectures poured in from all sections of the country except the Deep South. Ingersoll either left the details to general managers or himself set out the precise terms upon which he would lecture (if available). He charged according to the size of the town, a flat amount for small places ranging from two hundred to four hundred dollars, or one-half or two-thirds of the gross receipts. Tickets must be priced at

WHERE SHOULD WE SPEND THE SABBATH?
The Shows that Pay, and the Shows that do not Pay

(From: Chic)

not less than fifty cents and might go to one dollar for the better seats. He furnished lithographs, posters, and press notices for advance promotion. He either specified the topic or offered a choice, and sometimes even indicated the relative coverage of religious and nonreligious themes, but he would never accept censorship.

In the Washington period Ingersoll lectured mainly on three new subjects: "Hard Times and The Way Out," "Some Mistakes of Moses," and "What Must We Do To Be Saved?"

In "Hard Times and The Way Out" Ingersoll grappled with problems of the economy and disputes between capital and labor. To resolve the economic welter of the late nineteenth century he could offer only a jumble of old and new ideas without a center. In "Hard Times," in spite of the railroad strike of 1877, one of the most violent and devastating struggles between the haves and have-nots in American history, he asserted, "There is no conflict, and there can be no conflict, in the United States between capital and labor; the men who endeavor to excite the envy of the unfortunate and the malice of the poor are the enemies of law and order" (*Works*, IX, 268). Property is the reward of industry, poverty usually of indolence. The extravagances of the rich give jobs to the poor.

In his absolute devotion to hard currency he expounded the extreme Republican doctrine that money is not a medium of exchange or a stan-

ROBERT J. INGERSOLL

TEN CENTS

Is all we ask for our "90 CHOICE
READINGS AND RECITATIONS."

OGILVIE & CO., Publishers,

29 Rose Street, New York.

Private Collection, David Henley

dard of value, for goods and services are traded for money and not for other goods and services. Money is not a yardstick of value because a yardstick does not measure value. Not that the government was powerless to stimulate the economy and relieve economic distress: A large internal improvement program would have the incidental benefit of providing jobs. The government had been under the control of demagogues and had pursued "a small, mean, and penurious course" (295). It should improve rivers and harbors, promote the completion of railroads. Forgetting that he had denied the existence of a class struggle he preached the danger of Armageddon between the classes.

For five years we have been wasting the labor of millions—wasting it for lack of something to do. Prosperity has been changed to want and discontent. On every hand the poor are asking for work. That is a wretched government where the honest and industrious beg, unsuccessfully, for the right to toil, where those who are willing, anxious, and able to work cannot get bread. If everything is to be left to the blind and heartless workings of the laws of supply and demand, why have governments? If the nation leaves the poor to starve, and the weak and unfortunate to perish, it is hard to see for what purpose the nation should be preserved. If our statesmen are not wise enough to foster great enterprises, and to adopt a policy that will give us prosperity, it may be that the laboring classes, driven to frenzy by hunger, the bitterness of which will be increased by seeing others in the midst of plenty, will seek a remedy in destruction. (294)

In October 1879 Ingersoll brought together his various lectures on the Pentateuch into a composition entitled "Some Mistakes of Moses" (*Works*, II). In the footsteps of Paine's *Age of Reason*, Colenso on the Pentateuch, Haeckel and Buchner on force and matter, modern science, and the theory of evolution, he constructed a comprehensive critique of the biblical account of creation and of how the ancient Jews treated their

✳MASS MEETING✳

—◦·◄AT►·◦—

POUGHKEEPSIE, N. Y.,

Friday, Oct. 29, 1880,

At 2 o'clock P. M.

The greatest orator in the world,

Col. ROBERT G. INGERSOLL,

and other eminent speakers will be present.
A general invitation is hereby extended
to all neighboring counties.

The Executive Committee.

(Library of Congress)

neighbors. (Some people today may consider Ingersoll as a quaint and outmoded iconoclast of the nineteenth century who tilted against the myths and fables of a dead creed. They are mistaken. The evangelical faith of his day has become fundamentalism and remains open to his ongoing criticism. He was more than a critic of fundamentalism. He was opposed to *any* belief in a supernatural power, no matter how attenuated or sophisticated.)

In "Some Mistakes of Moses" Ingersoll took his ax to the biblical account of creation, a narrative which his reason cannot accept: that God made the earth out of nothing, separated a heaven and earth by a "firmament," made leaves, birds, flowers, and fruits before the sun, set the sun and the moon in the sky for the convenience of the earth and without regard to other planets and interstellar space, put life in the waters after life on earth, and made man by special creation. Instead, Ingersoll contended that the interplay of force and matter in nature is persuasive of an eternity of existence without divine involvement. The telescope had annihilated the "firmament" and the cosmic system of the Bible. Modern science had demonstrated the evolution of all life, including man, from one-celled organisms.

Further, the idea of a god and that of a divinely inspired Bible rest on different foundations. "If there is a God, it is reasonably certain that he made the world, but it is by no means certain that he is the author of the Bible." If, as some modern-minded theologians had come to believe, the biblical story occurred over millions of years and not mere days, there was no reason to set apart one day out of seven as the Sabbath for meditating on damnation and hell-fire. "Let us throw away these superstitions and take the higher, nobler ground that every day should be rendered sacred by some loving act, by increasing the happiness of man, giving birth to noble thoughts, putting in the path of toil some flowers of joy, helping the unfortunate, lifting the fallen, dispelling gloom, destroying prejudice, defending the helpless, filling homes with light and love" (107).

Besides a little joshing about the creation of Eve there was little humor in the argument until Ingersoll changed his tone with a dramatic skit (in which as lecturer he played all the parts).

> Let me show you the result of unbelief. Let us suppose, for a moment, that we are at the Day of Judgment, listening to the trial of souls as they arrive. The Recording Secretary, or whoever does the cross-examining, says to a soul:
>
> Where are you from?
>
> I am from the Earth.
>
> What kind of a man were you?
>
> Well, I don't like to talk about myself. I suppose you can tell by looking at your books.
>
> No, sir. You must tell what kind of a man you were.
>
> Well, I was what you might call a first-rate fellow. I loved my wife and children. My home was my heaven. My fireside was a paradise to me. To sit there and see the lights and shadows fall upon the faces of those I loved, was to me a perfect joy.
>
> How did you treat your family?
>
> I never said an unkind word. I never caused my wife, nor one of my children, a moment's pain.
>
> Did you pay your debts?
>
> I did not owe a dollar when I died, and left enough to pay my funeral expenses, and to keep the fierce wolf of want from the door of those I loved.

Did you belong to any church?

No, sir. They were too narrow, pinched and bigoted for me. I never thought that I could be very happy if other folks were damned.

Did you believe in eternal punishment?

Well, no. I always thought that God could get his revenge in far less time.

Did you believe the rib story?

Do you mean the Adam and Eve business?

Yes! Did you believe that?

To tell you the God's truth, that was just a little more than I could swallow.

Away with him to hell! Next! Where are you from?

I am from the world too.

Did you belong to any church?

Yes, sir, and to the Young Men's Christian Association besides.

What was your business?

Cashier in a savings bank.

Did you ever run away with any money?

Where I came from, a witness could not be compelled to incriminate himself.

The law is different here. Answer the question. Did you run away with any money?

Yes, sir.

How much?

One hundred thousand dollars.

Did you take anything else with you?

Yes, sir.

Well, what else?

I took my neighbor's wife—we sang together in the choir.

Did you have a wife and children of your own?

Yes, sir.

And you deserted them?

Yes, sir, but such was my confidence in God that I believed he would take care of them.

Have you heard of them since?

No, sir.

Did you believe in the rib story?

Bless your soul, of course I did. A thousand times I regretted that there were no harder stories in the Bible, so that I could have shown my wealth of faith.

Do you believe the rib story yet?

Yes, with all my heart.

Give him a harp.

Ingersoll asked some hard questions about the biblical stories, subjecting them to common sense and humane feeling. Why should Adam and Eve have been forbidden to eat the fruit of the tree of knowledge? Why put the tree in the center of their garden? Why deny them immortality? Where did the Hebrew-speaking serpent come from? Who made him? (134). "Why was he not kept out of the garden? Why did not the Lord God take him by the tail and snap his head off?"

All in all, if the people of the ancient world had known as much astronomy and geology as we do now, they would never have believed the Bible inspired. "For the establishment of facts, the word of man is now considered far better than the word of God. In the world of science Jehovah was superseded by Copernicus, Galileo, and Kepler" (242).

In a section entitled "Dampness" Ingersoll took on Noah and the Flood. Why did not God create Noah and his family in the first place and avoid extermination of the rest of the human race and all the innocent animals except those admitted to the ark? (141). "Why did he fill the world with his own children, knowing that he would have to destroy them? And why does this same God tell me how to raise my children when he had to drown his." To state the logistics of the ark is to show its absurdity. He wonders how "eight persons attended to the wants of 175,000 birds, 3,616 beasts, 11,300 reptiles, and 2,000,000 insects, saying nothing of countless animalculae" (156). How were portions of the ark kept warm for tropical animals and cool for polar bears? "For me it is impossible to believe the story of the deluge. It seems so cruel, so barbaric, so crude in detail, so absurd in all its parts, so contrary to all we know of law that even credulity itself is shocked" (164).

Ingersoll derided belief in the confusion of tongues at the Tower of Babel and in God's invocation of frogs, lice, flies, boils, and the like as means of persuasion upon Pharaoh. "In any event it is infinitely more probable that the author was misinformed than that the God of the universe was guilty of these childish, heartless, and infamous things. The solution of the whole matter is this: Moses was mistaken" (207). Likewise he laughs at the adventures of the Exodus as an article of faith. "Is it possible that there is, in this country, an intelligent clergyman who will insist that these stories are true, that we must believe them in order to be good people in this world, and glorified souls in the next?" (220).

Ingersoll denied that the Ten Commandments were the foundation of all ideas on justice and law. People had always objected to being robbed and murdered; ancient codes of India and Egypt provided penalties for such behavior. In a section entitled "Inspired" Ingersoll struck at divine sanctions in the Bible for slavery, polygamy, indiscriminate slaughter of women and children, and religious persecution. He neither wanted the heaven nor feared the hell of a God who blesses slavery. As an orthodox believer in monogamy, the polygamy ordained in Old Testament times impelled him to alliterative outpouring against an institution "where crawl and hiss the slimy serpents of most loathsome lust" (251). He asked, "Who is the blasphemer, the man who denies the existence of God, or he who covers the robes of the Infinite with innocent blood?" (254). Citing the passage in Deuteronomy in which God is said to command that each individual shall be the first to stone to death one's own brother, son, or wife who would entice one to serve other gods, Ingersoll posed devastating questions:

> Can we believe that any such command was ever given by a merciful and intelligent God? Suppose, however, that God did give this law to the Jews, and did tell them that whenever a man preached a heresy or proposed to worship any other God that they should kill him, and suppose that afterward this same God took upon himself flesh, and came to this very chosen people and taught a different religion, and that thereupon the Jews crucified him. I ask you, did he not reap exactly what he had sown? What right would this God have to complain of a crucifixion inflicted in accordance with his own command? (259)

These are terrible questions, the most terrible that Ingersoll ever opposed to the Judeo-Christian tradition.

In "What Must We Do To Be Saved?" Ingersoll subjected salvation by faith to the test of reason. "A while ago," he said, playing with his audience, "I made up my mind to find out what was necessary for me to do in order to be saved. If I have got a soul, I want it saved. I do not want to lose anything that is of value. For thousands of years the world has been asking the question: 'What must we do to be saved?? Saved from poverty? No. Saved from crime? No. Tyranny? No. But 'What must we do to be saved from the eternal wrath of the God who made us all?' " (458).

He found the question absurd on its face. Infinite wisdom never made a poor investment, and would not waste its products by subjecting them to eternal suffering. If God is perfect, he is conditionless, wants nothing; nobody can offend him and incur his displeasure. (A joke was in order.) "A Jewish gentleman" went into a restaurant for dinner. Tempted by the devil, he partook of some bacon. When he had gone in, the weather had been delightful, the sky blue as in June. When he left, he was confronted with angry clouds, lightning, and thunder. His face "white as milk," he rushed back into the restaurant and cried out, "My God, did you ever hear such a fuss about a little piece of bacon?" (438).

The Christian religion relies on the New Testament: "Nobody ever saw anybody who had heard of anybody that had ever seen anybody that had ever seen one of the original Hebrew manuscripts" (454). The doctrine of salvation by faith rests upon certain passages in Mark: "He that believeth and is baptized shall be saved, but he that believeth not shall be damned"; and John: "God so loved the world that he gave his only begotten Son, that whosoever believeth in him shall not perish but have everlasting life." To reward or punish for belief made no sense to Ingersoll. Belief was the result of reasoning. One could not believe as one might wish but as one must. One might as well be rewarded or punished for having red hair.

And the Gospels were full of different assurances of salvation: that the merciful shall obtain mercy, that the forgiving shall be forgiven, that every man shall be judged according to his works and his keeping the Commandments, that the blessed who gave Christ food and drink shall inherit the kingdom. Surely God will not inflict eternal thirst upon a man who put a cup of cold water to the lips of his neighbor, or eternal pain to one who clothed his fellow man, so why all the fuss?

"Today thou shalt be with me in Paradise," Christ uttered to the thief on the cross alongside. Who was this thief? To what church did he belong? I do not know. Did he believe in the Old Testament? In the miracles? I do not know. Did he believe that Christ was God? I do not know. Why then was the promise made to him that he should meet Christ in Paradise? Simply because he pitied suffering innocence upon the cross.

Ingersoll assailed the Catholics and the Methodists but he reserved his special barbs for the Presbyterians, the heirs of Calvin and Knox, "a pestilence and a famine." These leaders expounded the dogma that God had a right to damn us because he made us. On the contrary, to Ingersoll that was the very reason why he did not have such a right. He had recently talked with a young Presbyterian who was trying to convert him. "Said I, suppose your mother were in hell, would you be happy in heaven then?' 'Well,' he says, 'I suppose God would know the best place for mother.' And I thought to myself then, if I was a woman, I would like to have five or six boys like that" (310). To the argument that he was waging war against dead ideas, storming a cemetery, he noted a recent conference of the Evangelical Alliance that affirmed the divine legitimacy of the Scriptures and the total depravity of human nature.

What did he offer instead? In the first place good fellowship, good friends, sincere men and women, mutual forbearance born of mutual respect, a sense of humor ("Whenever I see an exceedingly solemn man, I know that he is an exceedingly stupid man"), good living ("You cannot make any god happy by fasting"), good food ("It is a thousand times better to know how to cook than it is to understand any theology in the world"), the gospels of education and of justice ("We do not need the forgiveness of God, but of each other and of ourselves"), and the gospel of humanity ("God cannot hate anybody who is capable of loving anybody") (518–521).

Ingersoll neither believed nor disbelieved in immortality—he hoped for it. What he objected to was corruption of that idea by superstitious fear. "I want it so that when a poor woman rocks the cradle and sings a lullaby to the dimpled darling, she will not be compelled to believe that ninety-nine chances in a hundred she is raising kindling wood for hell" (522). If there were such a thing as immortality, it would be a fact in nature, not the product of any theology. And if there were no immortality he glorified eternal sleep in words that must have brought tears to the eyes of his audience as his own eyes glistened.

Next to eternal joy, next to being forever with those we love and those who have loved us, next to that, is to be wrapt [sic] in the seamless drapery of eternal peace. Next to eternal life is eternal sleep. Upon the shadowy shore of death the sea of trouble casts no wave. Eyes that have been curtained by the everlasting dark will not know again the burning touch of tears. Lips touched by eternal silence will never speak again the broken words of grief. Hearts of dust do not break. The dead do not weep. Within the tomb no veiled and weeping sorrow sits, and in the rayless gloom is crouched no shuddering fear (524). . . .

"Why," they say to me, "suppose all this should turn out to be true, and you should come to the day of judgment and find all these things to be true. What would you do then?" I would walk up like a man and say, "I was mistaken."

" 'And suppose God was about to pass judgment upon you, what would you say?" I would say to him, "Do unto others as you would that others should do unto you. Why not?" (489)

Leaving the legal business, its squabbles and pressures, to willing and faithful Clark, Ingersoll set out from time to time on lecture crusades through New York, New England, and the Midwest. He travelled by trains and horse conveyances and was constantly on the go. His schedule was not supernatural, but superhuman: Monday, March fourth, New Haven; Tuesday, March fifth, Boston; Wednesday, March sixth, Portland, Me.; Thursday, March seventh, Springfield, Mass.; Friday, March eighth, Boston; Saturday, March ninth, Worcester. He stayed at hotels rather than with friends so as to be master of his time and more accessible to the public. Sometimes he spoke on social issues but usually, regardless of title, it was the same basic message of freethought sprinkled with topical references and delivered day after day with the freshness of a new revelation.

A journalist named Gath had struck up an acquaintance with the Ingersoll brothers in a trolley car in Washington in January 1878. A month later, heading for the Pullman train from Washington to New York, he was told by the gate attendant, "Bob Ingersoll is on the train; you'll have good company." And of course he would have a story for his paper. Sitting down with Ingersoll and his current manager James Redpath, Gath said for a show of politeness, "Colonel, when you lecture again I will go hear you if I am anywhere near." Ingersoll took him up on it. "Come tonight to the Brevoort House with me and take some supper, and go with me to the lecture. Will you do it?" Although not too eager for such a close tie with the infidel Gath found himself agreeing, and the ride proceeded with steady conversation, mostly about John Brown, with whom Redpath had been associated.

In his hotel suite Ingersoll ran on about Voltaire, Beecher, Lincoln, and Stephen Douglas, and spoke disparagingly of Thier's *History of the French Revolution*, John Quincy Adams on Shakespeare, and the late pope. Though not admiring Hayes he philosophized on the president's critics. "They forget that when the ship is in port men are not wanted to go aloft and set the sails." He considered the English bench and bar stupid, and stated that "among the solemn follies of the world is believing that judges are anything but lawyers and human beings and talking about the sanctity of the Bench." After a bath Ingersoll put on a new suit of black broadcloth, in which he looked to Gath like "a deceased senator in swallow-tails." After dispatching "a brace of mutton chops" and some mushrooms on toast Ingersoll called for a cab and they rode to Gilmore's Garden, where a small group gathered about them eager to tell how they had been converted to freethought. Ingersoll mounted the platform alone and spoke without manuscript or water. "The sentences were so resonant and sparkling that, with natural fervor, they seemed to drop gems and to lead a battle. The subject was Liberty—for the mind, the thinker, the heretic, the wife, the children—freedom from form, dignity, tyranny, oppressive discipline, etc. An athletic, versatile, dramatic, communicating mind was at work. The style was not coarse or vituperative, but elevated, and less like an argument than a performance by Dickens."

Back at the hotel Ingersoll looked over his large amount of mail, much anonymous and full of abuse or pleas to repent and come to Christ. At daylight Ingersoll said, "Hello. Did you see any ghosts? Have any dreams? Why, you ain't more than half orthodox" (*Cincinnati Daily Enquirer*, Feb. 15, 1878).

A few days after Ingersoll lectured in Buffalo a female evangelist, Reverend Maggie van Cott, labelled him "a poor barking dog." When a reporter showed Ingersoll this remark in the morning paper Ingersoll read to him the rejoinder which he had already mailed to this critic (Feb. 25, 1878, *Letters*, 238).

Miss Van Cott

My dear madam:—
    Were you constrained by the love of Christ to call a man who has never injured you "a poor barking dog?" Did you make this remark as a Christian, or as a lady? Did you say these words to illustrate in some faint degree the refining influence upon women of the religion you preach?
    What would you think of me if I should retort, using your language, changing only the sex of the last word? I have the honor to remain,

Yours truly,

R. G. Ingersoll

The Reverend Van Cott did not respond.

Ingersoll spoke at Terre Haute on April 30, 1878. The lecture had been arranged by Redpath and a citizen of Terre Haute in his early twenties, Eugene Victor Debs, president of a mutual improvement circle, the Occidental Literary Society. Redpath had written Debs, "Boldly advertise him as the greatest orator in the world. He is" (Debs, "Recollections of Ingersoll," *Pearson's Magazine*, April 1917). Debs met Ingersoll at the depot and escorted him to the hotel. It was the beginning of a life-long relationship between saint and disciple. "He at once filled my eye," Debs wrote later, "captivated me completely. There was something intensely fascinating in his personality, an irresistible charm in his presence, a liquid melody in his voice—and withal he bore the stamp of genius and the towering majesty of a man! I felt that here was the greatest man in all the world" (304). Before a packed opera house and from a stage lavishly decorated with flowers and greenery Ingersoll delivered "The Liberty of Man, Woman, and Child." The *Daily Express* and Debs agreed that the impact of Ingersoll on the lecture platform could not be communicated. The *Express* said, "His style is indescribable. At one time his audience would sit in rapt attention drinking in his matchless eloquence, the next they exploded in roars of laughter at his inimitable humor" (May 1, 1878). In later years Debs would reminisce,

> Never until that night had I heard real oratory, never before had I listened enthralled to such a flow of genuine eloquence. The speaker was in his prime, not yet forty-five, tall, shapely, graceful, and commanding, the perfect picture of the beau ideal of his art. Never can I forget his features, his expressive blue eyes, his mellifluous voice, his easy, graceful gestures, and his commanding oratorical powers. He rippled along softly as a meadow brook or he echoed with the thunder of some mighty cataract. He pleaded for every right and protested against every wrong; he touched every emotion and expressed every mood of his enchanted listeners. His words fell as pure as sunshine from his inspired lips and his impassioned periods glowed with the fervid enthusiasm of their thrice-eloquent orator. Redpath was right, Ingersoll was the greatest orator in all the world. No pen or tongue could ever describe his brilliant eloquence or his matchless powers. (305)

Although Debs would have difficulty enshrining Ingersoll in the Socialist canon, he never diluted his adoration of the freethinker who had inspired him to think bravely.

On the circuit Ingersoll was alternately sinister and charming—according to the critics. America did not know what to make of him. Meriden, Connecticut, reacted with typical small-town revulsion. The *New Haven Evening Union* reported, "Colonel Robert G. Ingersoll of Illinois gave his three-hundred-dollar-a-night lecture on 'Skulls,' 'The Liberty of Man, Woman, and Child,' 'The Democracy of the Fireside,' or, whatever else you may call it, in Meriden last night to a select and appreciative audience, yet not a large one, many who would otherwise have attended having been frightened out of it by the howls that went up from the press and pulpit when it was announced that the famous and eloquent infidel was coming" (May 14, 1878).

In the big cities the story was different. Educated people of all classes, including members of the clergy, were not afraid of freethought. They did not believe that their happiness here or hereafter depended on clinging blindly to the old-time religion. Whether they were inclined to believe Ingersoll or not, they flocked to hear him. Long lines besieged the ticket offices, scalpers did a thriving business, standing room only was snatched up, and after the lecture some of the unfatigued repaired with the speaker to a party room at a hotel, where they enjoyed a temperate love-fest of freethought. The *Boston Journal*, March 9, 1878:

The audience which greeted Col. Robert G. Ingersoll at Music Hall on his second appearance here this week was fully as large as the hall could accommodate. Every seat was taken before the usual lecture hour, and while the platform was occupied by auditors many stood through the two hours that his genius held their attention. It was the largest gathering in the hall for the past five years and the advance sale of tickets has been unequaled in that period. It was a remarkable audience in character as well as number—as thoroughly metropolitan as ever assembled. Clergymen, men of science and letters, thinkers, and thoughtless people, all intermingled, and while the lecture was a radical one compared with the first there was no murmur heard except those of applause, which were liberally bestowed and often as he made a brilliant hit or uttered, with his stirring language, some humorous sentiments which seemed to well up from his soul.

The water was making its mark on the rock. Even in insulated Meriden the speaker's magnetism could not be completely denied. "He is perfectly audacious in his wicked and blasphemous onslaughts on the things we have been taught to revere and hold sacred, and yet, in the midst of his most impious perorations he interjects so much of brilliant wit and so much of legitimate native fun that we can scarcely suppress a hearty laugh. We are pained to recognize in so brilliant an intellect so powerful and dangerous an enemy of the Christian religion" (*West Meriden Daily Meriden Reporter*, May 14, 1878).

It was apparent to thoughtful believers that the Ingersollian challenge would not go away, that it had to be taken seriously. "It is not enough that ministers go about among easy-minded folks who will assent to every proposition, without ever thinking of the truths involved or the duties implied. It is not the end of the Christian's accountability to sing hymns already set to music, to repeat prayers by bell and book, to pronounce the routine phrases of orthodoxy, and then to intone an echoing Amen—to sigh, to groan, and go to sleep" (*Methodist Reporter*, Pittsburgh, June 29, 1878).

Ingersoll could be well pleased with himself. He was having a good time spreading the gospel of reason, winning admirers and baiting opponents, and he was making money at it.

In the summer of 1878 the Ingersolls took their second and last vacation trip to Europe. A reporter found Ingersoll on the quarter-deck of the *Reims*. Wearing a loose-fitting suit of blue flannel, a white beaver hat pushed back on his forehead, he was leaning against the rail, smoking a cigar, and watching the hurly-burly of preparations for departure. Nearby on a bench sat Mrs. Ingersoll and the girls, "blooming maidens, the youngest being an exact replica of her father."

Ingersoll was as usual relaxed and expansive, ready to talk about anything. The main purpose of the trip, he said, was to visit the native haunts of Robert Burns, the "cottage" of poetry as compared with

Shakespeare's "palace." He lectured the reporter on idle worry about the here and the hereafter.

> I don't take stock in any creed that keeps me worrying about what is beyond. No one can know what is to come afterwards. Why, it would be just as reasonable for me to worry about the future state as it would be for me to rush ashore, lay in a heavy stock of tales about appalling shipwrecks and the sufferings of shipwrecked men while clinging for their lives to spars and hen coops, and lose all the enjoyment I expect to derive from the voyage in reading them. This is a sound and trim ship, and there's plenty of beer aboard—though, by the way, the only beverages that I enjoy are champagne and claret—and I don't propose to make myself miserable.

Would he on his return make any more speeches in the political field? He could not say. The country had problems that must be faced. People had a right to live decently. "The party that is to carry the country in the future must do something for the workingmen. Their need is the vital demand of the hour. I think that a Government of the United States that cannot assure every industrious man a house of three or four rooms, a wife and three or four children, and plenty of food, clothing, and fuel, when we have millions of acres of land to yield food and articles of exchange with Europe, has no right to exist." Possible candidates? Grant will not run, although Hayes's weakness encourages Grant; Blaine will be the strongest Republican candidate (*New York Sun*, Aug. 4, 1878, quoted in *The Truth Seeker*, Aug. 10, 1878).

The voyage was pleasant and uneventful. The travellers looked forward and backward. "We can see you all in the house—in the park, sitting in the door" (To Clint and All, Aug. 13, 1878, L.C.). From the Langham Hotel in London they spent two busy days revisiting some old places— Westminster Abbey, the Tower, the British Museum, "and we are all homesick as the devil." The queen ignored them. "We have not seen the queen, nor any of the royal family. They treat us with the utmost cruelness. They pretend not to know that we are in town. All right! We will get even with them when we get home" (To Clark, Aug. 16, 1878, L.C.).

In Edinburgh they visited Carlton Hall, the Burns Monument, Salisbury Crags, Arthur's Seat, and other places. Ingersoll applauded the absence of religious restraints. "We were greatly pleased to see thousands of the people walking and riding here on Sunday. Even here the cursed church is losing her power" (Dear Folks, Aug. 18, 1878, L.C.).

On the next day they visited the cottage near Ayr where Burns was born, and "all went to Auld Kirk Alloway where Tam O'Shanter saw the devil and the witch with the shorn chemise (sark) on. There is buried Wm. Burns, father of the poet, and 'Souter' Johnny, the fellow who drank with O'Shanter, and then went to Burns's monument on the banks of the bonnie Doon, and over the bridge, and down to the mill where Burns went to school" (Aug. 19, 1878, *Letters*, 375). On the wall at Burns's birthplace now hangs one of Ingersoll's more felicitous efforts in formal verse, a paean to Scotland's "noblest, grandest" son, "the loving cotter-king."

> And here the world through all the years,
> As long as day returns,
> The tribute of its love and tears,
> Will pay to Robert Burns.

Back in England they visited Stratford-on-Avon. Robert wrote, "We are all in the best of health and lonesome enough." At the American Express they had found five letters from home. "I brought them out to the carriage and I read them aloud to the family. We were delighted to hear from you and especially from that baby Eva Farrell. Her little sweet letter brought tears into all eyes. . . . We will see you in a few days. Be sure and have a good time" (Aug. 24, 1878, *Letters*, 376). Then to Paris and the voyage back home.

On one or two occasions Ingersoll delivered a lecture on Burns, regaling the audience with his Scottish accent as he recited "Thou'll break my heart, my bonnie bird," "Should auld acquaintance be forgot," and "A man's a man for a' that." Redpath and Mrs. Ingersoll thought the Burns lecture his best; he preferred "Liberty of Man, Woman, and Child" (Boston, Oct. 2, 1878, L.C.).

It did not take long for Ingersoll to embrace Clark and check the firm's business before again hitting the road of secular evangelism. East of the Mississippi and above the South, wherever people could gather, they turned out in droves for him. He was, to put it mildly, popular. He could not help feeling exhilarated. On September twenty-eighth he wrote to his children from Burlington, Vermont. It seemed years since they all had been together on the seas. "I have had a successful trip so far. The houses have been good and enthusiastic. Had a splendid house at Watertown, also at Malone. Mr. Wheeler, the Vice President, escorted me to the fair grounds. He does not like Hayes. Everybody seemed to like my speech to the farmers. I had a splendid audience at the fair and the manager told me that they had made money out of me, and that I had drawn the largest crowd ever seen on the grounds. In the evening I lectured on Moses. The hall was jammed full and all appeared delighted." A doting father, his heart was full of love and longing for his children. He advised his daughters not to read too much but to read thoughtfully, improving their own skill in language by noting beautiful effects, and to take a walk every day. "I cannot tell how dearly I love you both—how proud I am of you and how happy I want you to be. Kiss all for me and don't forget the baby" (*Letters*, 523). On the same day he gave Clinton an assignment. "I am as lonely as hell would be with the fire out. Clint, be sure the dear folks have everything they want. Live high. Be happy as larks. We will have a splendid time this winter" (L.C.). The continuing pace was such as only Ingersoll could maintain. A slice of the schedule for early 1879: Trenton, N.J., March 5; New Brunswick, N.J., March 6; Paterson, N.J., March 7; Harrisonburg, Va., March 8; Pittsburgh, Pa., March 9; Youngstown, Ohio, March 10; Cleveland, March 11; Toledo, March 12; Fort Wayne, Ind., March 14; South Bend, Ind., March 14; Kalamazoo, Mich., March 15; Chicago, March 16 (*Seymour Weekly Times*, March 1, 1879).

Cincinnati was typical of the enthusiasm that permeated all classes. The *Enquirer* on March 18, 1879 said that

> Pike's Opera House was filled last night as it has not been filled since the season of Italian opera at that place a year ago. The house was not only liberally and abundantly full—parquet, dress circle, balcony, and gallery—but it was filled with an audience that, for marked intelligence and fineness of reasoning, is seldom, if ever, surpassed. Indeed the people who were there for two hours feasting their souls upon the rhetorical food that was flung them from the speaker's lips were, in point of number and powers of mental capacity, a great compliment to the eloquent man who stood on the rostrum before them.

The reporter enjoyed confessing his infatuation with "the most eloquent man who graces the American Continent." "Such words may sound too full of flattery to be really true, but it is hard for me to write less who is just fresh from the fascinating presence and glittering speech of this wonderful, powerful orator. Men went last night solely to hear the lecturer talk, not for an instant entertaining the idea that they would believe a word of his atheistical teachings. These men left the hall willing to admit that if the devil be as black as he is painted, Bob Ingersoll, at least, has been an unjustly abused and vilified person." The reporter admired his style. "Mr. Ingersoll does not require an introduction to his audience. He walks right out on the stage, takes hold of his theme, like a dog seizes a rat, and talks and talks and talks, for two hours, while the people laugh, and laugh, and laugh, and think they have known him ever since he was a little boy."

In the fall of 1878 Ingersoll returned to Terre Haute to lecture again under the auspices of the Occidental Literary Society. At the depot he was greeted by Debs, the members of the committee, and Senator Voorhees. Rain had been falling in torrents, and the committee was worried that they might lose money because of a poor house. Ingersoll relieved their fears. "Boys," he said, "don't worry in the least. If the rain keeps the people away I will charge you nothing for the lecture and pay my own expenses." As they boarded the street car the rain fell stronger than ever, but Senator Voorhees said, "The rain will make no difference tonight. Colonel Ingersoll is the only man in America who can draw against the elements and fill the biggest house on the rainiest night." "And," says Debs, "he was right." To a well-filled house Ingersoll delivered his lecture on Burns, described by Debs as "beautiful and poetic." From Terre Haute Ingersoll was going to Indianapolis by the midnight train. Debs went on the train to see him off, but found him "too magnetic, too kind, and hospitable," and stayed on. It was raining in Indianapolis. As Ingersoll looked out of the hotel window he shook his head and grumbled, "That rain is apt to cost me $500 and yet I haven't even been consulted about it." "But," Debs wrote later, "it didn't for the house could not have held more people" ("Recollections of Ingersoll," 305).

On the road Ingersoll was not merely a lecturer, but also a public personality offstage. His company was sought by many, his definitive opinions avidly solicited and reported, He was a national oracle who wore no man's collar. Perhaps he might sometimes have preferred some privacy at the hotel, to take a bath or a nap or to play parlor games with his wife and daughters, but he did not really miss these comforts. When people sent up their cards almost always the word was to come up. A typical example: "A representative of the *Express* called at the Mansion House yesterday morning and received a cordial greeting from Col. Ingersoll and his wife, a handsome and matronly-looking lady. Mrs. Ingersoll is travelling with her distinguished husband on his lecture tour. Laying aside a letter he was writing to his daughters, the Colonel leaned back in his chair and chatted away for an hour or more on public issues" (*Buffalo Express*, Nov. 4, 1878).

To another reporter, comments on the political scene: Of Republican candidates on the horizon he was all out for Blaine. "Oh, I love Blaine, I love him. He's a splendid fellow, Blaine is" (*Washington Post*, undated clipping, L.C.). In Cincinnati he enlarged on his choice: "I am for Mr. Blaine. I have not changed my opinion since 1876. I made at that time, in this city, a speech that was considered as friendly to Blaine." "Slightly, I believe," the reporter agreed. Ingersoll continued, "I would like an opportunity to repeat that speech in the same circumstances, with a different result. No man could harmonize the different sections of the country more than Blaine. He has the element of popularity. He is free, frank, candid, chivalric, intelligent—all in the highest degree." Yes, Grant was the greatest general ever of the Anglo-Saxon race, but the peacetime country doesn't need such leadership now (*Cincinnati Commercial*, Nov. 1878, L.C.). Hayes? "Mrs. Hayes is a worthy lady, and the smartest in the family." He took a dim view of civil service reform. "It is not in human nature to keep his enemy in office." He was opposed to the Greenback Party and fiat money. "I am not a believer in miracles. I do not believe something can be made out of nothing" (*Washington Post*, undated, 1878). The rights of the emancipated race were crucial. "Whether I act with the Republican party or not depends on how the Republican party believes and acts. If that party agrees with the statement recently made by one of its leaders that the government cannot protect its citizens at home, and nothing is left for the colored people than to submit and suffer—if that is Republicanism I am not a Republican" (*Cincinnati Daily Gazette*, undated, L.C.).

In reporting to his folks in Washington Robert did not glorify his travel as a crusade: He was, rather, a salesman selling a good product and relishing his success. "We had a good meeting last night and I gave Mr. Moses his stomach full" (Syracuse, Oct. 31, 1878, L.C.). Tension sharpened his appetites; he "cannot restrain them." "I did not smoke till to-day and I am so fat I can hardly breathe" (Buffalo, Nov. 3, 1878, L.C.). "I had a good breakfast this morning. Gridels and potatoes and beefsteak and chicken. Don't think I will need anything more for a week" (Springfield, Ohio, Nov. 25, 1878, L.C.).

A constant theme is his homesickness, his love for the entire family. "You must give our best love to Sue and Clint and to the darling little baby. We want to see her every day. Love to Sue Sharkey and tell her that the night shirts fit. They are long enough." The next day was Maud's birthday. "I wish we could be home. You must have a splendid dinner and lots of flowers and be as happy as larks. Well, goodbye. We leave here at six o'clock. Love to you and kisses by the thousand. You are the sweetest girls in the world" (Boston, Oct. 3, 1878, *Letters*, 524). In Grand Rapids a letter from Eva was given to him as he was about to go on stage. He let the audience wait until he read it. "They are indebted to your letter for a better speech than I could have made without it. That letter filled me with love and gratitude and joy." His love for his family occasionally was intense to the point of tears. "Sweet Eva you are too generous. Your letter made tears come into my eyes. You and Maud asking Mother to stay with me. You are the best children in the world" (Nov. 8, 1878, *Letters*, 527).

In Springfield, Ohio, a letter from Maud was delivered while he was in bed. "At first I thought it was my overcoat, or that Mother had sent me some shirts and a suit of clothes. You may judge of my surprise when I found that it was a letter from my sweet daughter. I got right up—put on my specs—sat down in my night shirt and did not stir until the last word was read" (Nov. 25, 1878, L.C.). He dreaded the time when she would marry or go away. "Whoever takes you away must be a splendid fellow with a head full of brain and a heart full of love." They must all be together always, Maud and her family, Eva and hers, Mother and Father, in one household. "We have to have a fireside large enough for all to sit around. What happy evening with the firelight falling on all the faces we love. That's my idea of heaven. To be separated, that's my idea of hell." He finished a letter to Maud: "It is now half past eleven. My cigar is nearly smoked and I am going to bed. I hope you are all asleep and that I will soon be dreaming of you all" (Cincinnati, Nov. 20, 1878, L.C.).

Love was the greatest good in the world, death and separation from loved ones the greatest evil. In May 1879, Clark Ingersoll was stricken with a fatal heart attack. Robert was at his bedside. Clark's last words were, "I am better now," a sign not of healing but of life yielding to death. Robert wrote to John, "The world looks dark to me. We were not only brothers, but we were friends." He added a phrase which must be understood in accordance with the rhetoric of the time: "We were not only friends, but we were lovers" (June 1, 1879, *Letters*, 329).

The funeral service was held in Clark's home in Washington. The house was crowded; hundreds could not get in. The service consisted of Robert's eulogy. He had not followed his custom of trusting for words to the impulse of the moment, but read from manuscript. This may be his richest and greatest speech—on the values of a life and on the human predicament in which there is no certain exit in fulfillment. As he began, his voice broke, his eyes filled with tears, he bowed his head over the coffin, and wept. Clark had died in the prime of life, forty-eight years old.

> Yet, after all, it may be best, just in the happiest, sunniest hour of all the voyage, while eager winds are kissing every sail, to dash against the barren rock, and in an instant hear the billows roar above a sunken ship. For whether in mid-sea or 'mong the breakers of the farther shore, a wreck at last must mark the end of each and all. And every life, no matter if its every hour is rich with love and every moment jeweled with joy, will, at its close, become a tragedy, as sad and deep and dark as can be woven of the warp and woof of mystery and death. (*Works*, XII, 390)

Clark Ingersoll had been a freethinker who practiced the religion of humanity. "He believed that happiness is the only good, reason the only torch, justice the only worship, humanity the only religion, and love the only priest. He added to the sum of human joy, and were every soul to whom he did some loving kindness to bring a blossom to his grave, he would sleep tonight beneath a wilderness of flowers" (390).

Existence was a mystery beyond understanding. Only a faint hope for eternal meaning endures. "Life is a narrow vale between the cold and narrow peaks of two eternities. We strive in vain to look beyond the heights. We cry aloud, and the only answer is the echo of our wailing cry. From the voiceless lips of the unreplying dead there comes no word, but in the night of death hope sees a star and listening love can hear the rustle of a wing"—the nearest Ingersoll ever came to avowing faith in immortality. The honorary pall-bearers included Senators Allison, Blaine, Davis, Voorhees, and Paddock, Congressmen Garfield, Boyd, and Adlai Stevenson. There was no further ceremony at the Oak Hill Cemetery in Georgetown (*National Republican*, Washington, D.C., June 3, 1879).

The office on G Street seemed to be waiting for somebody. The chair opposite Robert's was terribly empty. But Ingersoll never indulged in long depressions when the demands of life must be met. "Well, time is the great healer," he wrote to Clint, who was out of town. "We must wait" (June 6, 1879, L.C.). A pile of sympathy notes, some from kind people who were devout church-goers, had to be answered. To John W. Farwell, Chicago merchant and a pillar of the church, Ingersoll wrote: "Accept my warmest thanks for your kind and touching letter. I shall never forget that in my great sorrow I was remembered by you" (*Reminisces of John W. Farwell*, II, 89). Again to Clint, of odds and ends: "There is nothing to say except that the weather is very cool; that we are all in good health; that I am very busy, going from one dept. to another; that poor Bennett is in jail; that I am trying to get him pardoned; that all the pious frauds in the country are writing to the President asking him to keep Bennett in prison; that Clark's family are all well; that the town is very dull; that we all want to see you; . . . that the days are long and lonely; that we will probably have to stay here all summer; that it seems years and years since we saw you; that we all want you back; and that the world is mostly a stale flat and weary pasture" (June 7, 1879, L.C.).

"Poor Bennett is in jail." D. M. Bennett, publisher of *The Truth Seeker*, was one of the victims of the quasi-governmental Society for the Suppression of Vice headed by Anthony Comstock and dedicated to eradicating evil thoughts from the American consciousness. A book, *Cupid's Yoke*, by Ezra Haywood, was being offered for sale in *The Truth Seeker*. (Haywood had been convicted on a charge of obscenity but was pardoned by President Hayes.) It was not pornographic or erotic, but simply an abstract argument in favor of free love, stating that marriage was the yoke that repressed wholesome free love instincts. Here Comstock saw an opportunity to strike a blow against free love and freethought at the same time. By decoy he obtained a mail-order copy and commenced a campaign of prosecution against Bennett for mailing obscene matter. Eventually Bennett was convicted and sentenced to thirteen months at hard labor.

Ingersoll swallowed his dislike of Hayes and undertook to seek a presidential pardon. No man in American valued marriage (subject to liberal divorce laws) more highly or differed more deeply with Haywood's philosophy than Ingersoll, but here the issues were freedom of thought and free speech. He came away from an extensive meeting with Hayes with the impression that the president was wavering, did not consider the book obscene but felt bound by the decisions of five federal judges (To T. B. Wakeman, June 20, 1879, L.C.). Letters to the president for pardon were far outweighed by an avalanche against from bishops and ministers and "their cousins, aunts, and sisters."

The president was weighing his options. In his diary he recorded: "I have heard arguments by Ingersoll and Wakeman in favor of pardoning D. M. Bennett, convicted of sending obscene matter through the mails—viz., a pamphlet of a polemical character in favor of free love.

While I am satisfied that Bennett ought not to have been convicted, I am not satisfied that I ought to undertake to correct the mistakes of the courts consistently persisted in by the pardoning power. There is great heat on both sides of the question. The religious world are against the pardon, the unbelievers are for it" (July 1, 1879, 123).

Ingersoll fought hard. He had more personal interviews with the president, followed by memoranda on the difference between obscenity and abstract discussion and on the broad scope of presidential power but to no avail (Ingersoll Papers, Georgetown). Ingersoll the infidel had not been considered a safe appointee as ambassador to Germany; it would be impolitic to sustain him as the advocate of an infidel as prominent as himself. Hayes felt that the conviction of Bennett was an absolute disgrace, a gross violation of his constitutional rights, but it could not be overcome. Ingersoll despaired. "I have seen the President again today," he wrote to Bennett, "and I believe that he has concluded not to interfere in your behalf, but to let what he is pleased to call the law take its course." He wondered whether he had been the best man for the pardon effort, whether a religious lawyer might have fared better. He was sarcastic, bitter. "It is only just to you to know that a great number of ministers have protested against your pardon. That a great many ladies have written to Mrs. Hayes setting forth that you are an extremely bad man, and begging that you be allowed to go to the penitentiary. I had no idea hardly of the bigotry of this country until I read some of these letters" (July 22, 1879, L.C.). The politician in the White House washed his hands of the matter.

From prison Bennett proudly published in the September 25 issue of *The Truth Seeker* Ingersoll's comradely letter of August twenty-ninth. "I have thought of you every hour that I have been awake since your imprisonment. . . . You have violated no law, committed no wrong, and made no being unhappy. You have lived an honorable, useful life and in any country not governed by Christians you would be free and respected. Well, bear up as well as you can. Time goes on, and in a little while liberty will unlock your cell and give you back to home and friends." Bennett had pressed one hundred dollars on Ingersoll for his professional services (July 27, 1879, L.C.).

Early in October 1879 Van Buren Denslow, author of a liberal survey of modern philosophy entitled *Modern Thinkers*, paid an unscheduled visit to Ingersoll at his new law offices on New York Avenue. Ingersoll not being in, Denslow looked around. "Mr. Ingersoll's present offices are capacious, fairly stocked on all their walls with an ample law library, with which, as if by some accident, a stray copy of Bishop Colenso on the Pentateuch and one or two copies of 'Robert's' own lectures on 'The Gods' and the 'Ghosts' happens, as if to indicate that the philosophical bias of the 'attorney-at-law' who here receives his clients is something neither to be obtruded nor concealed." On his desk was a life-size bust of himself, against the fireplace a facsimile of Magna Carta bearing the seals and coats of arms of the barons in attendance, and on the mantel a portrait of Clark, flanked right and left by the "Vision of War" and Clark's funeral eulogy.

Denslow left. Returning, he found an office buzzing with lawyers and clients, Ingersoll attending thoroughly to each and all, simultaneously reading proof of *Mistakes of Moses* and riffling through a stack of unsorted letters. "The man was full of vitality. He had spoken during each of the preceding three evenings and had been riding through the mountains of Pennsylvania by rail the last night, yet was as fresh and ruddy as a school girl in June." Ingersoll was developing arguments and compromises with counsel when one letter in particular caught his eye, and glancing over it he dictated an apropos letter. It was to Colonel Thomas A. Scott, president of the Pennsylvania Railroad, telling him that an eccentric fellow traveller of theirs had died and that his destitute family would appreciate a pass to northern California, where friends would take care of them. Then two black men were announced: "Show 'em up." They had been cheated on a land purchase in North Carolina and were going north to try their fortunes in a society where black men could earn a living without sharecropping. Chuckling at their being cheated by Christians, Ingersoll advised them on conditions up north and sent them on with encouragement. He invited Denslow to sit down beside him and began talking.

> Did it every occur to you, Mr. D., what a luxury it would be to live a little while in a world where the people are not all crazy? I tell you the people of this world are all a little touched—some in one place, some in another, but they've all got it somewhere.
>
> For instance, I have been gone five days. Now, I know before I open this mail that there will be at least five challenges from as many reverend Billy-goats, scattered over the country, each defying me to debate with him the truth of the Bible, or the verity of the devil, or the need of hell, or some such crazy thing. Just about one a day these challenges are coming, what would become of me if all the damnphools [sic] buckled on their armor?

Ingersoll handed Denslow three of the challenges, barely literate scrawls on postcards. "I could see how," he continued, "if a man could live for a thousand years, it might pay to try to help lift the world out of its mire. But for poor, ephemeral creatures like you and me the serious question is, Does it pay for the cussing you get? I tell you, my candid and serious opinion is that the better thing to do is to bank on one's home, to save from the general wreck the domestic affections, to keep the happy birds singing together in their little cage and let the rest of the world drift in its idolatries, worshiping what they will."

Denslow had brought along a copy of his book. Ingersoll asked to

look it over. Oblivious to legal business—all the other visitors had gone—
he spent several hours with Denslow reading and commenting. He had
definite ideas on Swedenborg, Bentham, Paine, and Adam Smith. He
criticized the omission of Voltaire and Hume, and found fault with Four-
ier's theories on the family. (If Denslow had any responsive ideas he
does not seem to have expressed them.)

Ingersoll took Denslow home to dinner. Denslow had his story (*Chicago Times,* Oct. 25, 1879; Special Correspondent, New York, Oct. 20,
1879, By V. B. D.). Subsequently Ingersoll wrote an introduction to a
new edition of *Modern Thinkers.*

Ingersoll was scheduled to lecture in Pittsburgh on a Sunday. An
ordinance provided that no entertainment or performance could be given
on Sunday (except for charitable or benevolent purposes) where an
admission fee was charged. Zealous defenders of the faith besieged the
mayor to prevent the lecture. Counsel advised the mayor that the meeting could not be legally prevented; it could only be prosecuted after the
event, the maximum penalty being a fifty dollar fine. An enterprising
reporter canvassed the local clergy. Most of them could not be reached—
"absent from the city," "just stepped out," "gone to the Post Office," "in
attendance at a church dedication." Those who faced the reporter did
not enthuse for free speech, nor were they eager to sanctify the unwelcome visitor by throwing him to the lions. Reverend W. J. Robinson said,
"I have not the slightest sympathy with Ingersoll. . . . I believe the most
successful way to meet that sort of thing is to let it severely alone."
Reverend Ramsey declared, "I have always had the idea that the Sabbath had a right to be kept sacred. At the same time I rather incline
to the belief that it is not policy to suppress the utterance of religious
or irreligious ideas inasmuch as by so doing a man's notion may often
attain a notoriety of which he himself is not worthy." Dr. Scovelle would
rather not express an opinion because he was not conversant with the
circumstances. When the reporter persisted, stating the plain facts,
Reverend Scovell said, "With your permission I would rather not speak
further" (*Pittsburgh Dispatch,* Oct. 24, 1879.).

Ingersoll could have avoided a face-off with orthodoxy in the Smoky
City by giving a free lecture (that would be nothing new) or changing
the date to a weekday. Instead, he went ahead with the Sunday meeting.
What, reporters asked, did he think of the situation? He replied that
laws should be enforced or repealed, that he had no personal feeling
against the mayor for enforcing the law. He jibed at his adversaries. Ministers could not increase church attendance by shutting up other places
but only by saying something worth hearing. Why were they afraid of
him? He was charging fifty and seventy-five cents, while they were
speaking free; surely they could compete with him. Christians, Jews, deists,
and atheists should be exactly equal before the law. He had previously
lectured in all the principal cities of the country, including Pittsburgh,

on Sundays without incident, although once, in Baltimore, he had postponed the lecture at the request of the local manager. The interview
turned to politics. Now as before he favored Blaine. Did he have the
same opinion of Hayes that he had expressed in Pittsburgh in 1876?
He played with the question. "Not quite. I said more about him then
than I knew. And I know more about him now than I will say. *Requiescat
in pace.* You may put the Latin in silent letters" (*Pittsburgh Leader* and *Pittsburgh
Commercial Gazette,* Oct. 27, 1879).

The advance turbulence had guaranteed a large audience. The lecture
was scheduled for eight o'clock. By seven the sidewalks on both sides
of Fifth Avenue were held by lines waiting to buy tickets, and by eight
every seventy-five seat in the orchestra and dress circle, and most of
the fifty-cent seats in the gallery were occupied. When Ingersoll appeared
on stage, he was welcomed by a thunderous ovation and a bouquet from
the Pittsburgh Liberal League. The air was tense with the excitement
of an illegal assemblage.

Departing from the announced subject, "Human Rights" (probably
a variation of the "Liberty" theme), Ingersoll heaped ridicule on Sabbath
observance and threw potshots at orthodoxy. He asked, How could
anybody conclude that any God wanted him to be bleak and miserable
one-seventh of the time? Far better to attend an opera or a Shakespeare
play. "That day is the most sacred day on which the most good has been
done for mankind." If God exists, he is perfect, conditionless. Others
could add nothing to his greatness, hurt or please him on Sunday or
any other day.

The evil in the world was incompatible with the existence of a good
God. When one saw innocent men chained and burned at the stake for
loving God, one would have to ask why God did not interfere. It had
been said that all would come out for the best. "That may do very well
for God but it is awful rough on the man." The church said that God
ordained this world to build character. "Well, if that is the only way
character can be developed it is bad for children who die before they
get a character. What would you think of a schoolmaster who would
kill half his pupils the first day?"

Above all Ingersoll stressed the primacy of an honest mind. "Now
I read the Bible and I find that God so loved the world that he made
up his mind to drown the most of us. I have read this book, and what
shall I say of it? I believe it is generally better to be honest. Now I don't
believe the Bible. Had I not better say so?"

As Ingersoll was arguing for taxation of church property—"if the
property belongs to God he is able to pay the tax"—a voice broke out
from the crowd. Ingersoll: "What did the gentleman say?" Another voice:
"Oh, he's drunk." Ingersoll: "I don't think any Christian ought to get
drunk and come here to disturb us."

A reporter observed, "The lecture was attentively listened to by the immense audience from beginning to end, and the speaker's most blasphemous flights were the most loudly appl:.uded" (*Pittsburgh Commercial Gazette,* Oct. 27, 1879).

The owner of the building was fined fifty dollars, which Ingersoll paid (*Works: Interviews,* VIII, 19).

The flurry in Pittsburgh was not intimidating. Ingersoll wrote to his daughters from Canton, Ohio, that he had had a good house lecturing on "Liberty" even though the churches had been "howling" against him and urging the people to stay away. "We are getting along the best kind. Mother keeps talking about you. She says, 'They are in bed now,' or 'They are eating now,' or 'They are just getting up.' You are never out of her mind. I feel a little ashamed to take her away. Yesterday we met Mark Twain on the cars. He was on his way to Chicago. We had quite a visit with him. We leave here at six this evening and will reach Chicago in the morning. I am trying to think of something to say but hardly know whether I shall succeed or not" (Nov. 10, 1879, L.C.).

Ingersoll was referring to the banquet for the Army of the Tennessee, to be held at the Parker House in Chicago on November thirteenth. The banquet, chaired by General Sherman, would honor the former president, General Grant, following his triumphal tour of Europe. Ingersoll and Mark Twain were among the scheduled speakers who would offer toasts. Ingersoll need not have doubted his competence for the occasion. Luckily he had been assigned a fitting subject for the twelfth toast: "The Volunteer soldiers of the Union army, whose Valor and Patriotism saved the Nation," acting for "a Government of the People, by the People and for the People." When his turn came he climbed up on the table and proceeded to deliver a paean to the Union victory. The great Republic had prevailed against "the savagery of the lash, the barbarism of the chain and the insanity of secession." He did not blindly respect the original Constitution. "The Union soldiers had relighted the torch of the Revolution, had torn from the Constitution that infamous clause that made men 'the catchers of their fellow men,' " had fought that "mothers might own their babes and that arrogant idleness should not scar the back of patient toil." They dared to roll away the stone from the sepulchre of progress, freeing the shining angels of Nationality and Liberty. "Blood was water, money was leaves, and life was only common air until one flag floated over a Republic without a master and without a slave." The Union army united the whole nation, North and South. "They made us a nation. Their victory made us free and rendered tyranny in every other land as insecure as snow upon [a] volcano's lips."

The peroration was one of Ingersoll's most moving and glowing utterances as a patriot of the Republic.

And now let us drink to the volunteers—to those who sleep in unknown, sunken graves, whose names are only in the hearts of those

they loved and left—of those who only hear in happy dreams the footsteps of return. Let us drink to those who died where lipless famine
mocked at want; to all the maimed whose scars give modesty a tongue
[What a phrase!]; to all who dared and gave to chance the care and
keeping of their lives; to all the living and to all the dead; to Sherman,
to Sheridan, and to Grant, the laureled soldier of the world, and last,
to Lincoln, whose loving life, like a bow of peace, spans and arches all
the clouds of war. (*Works*, XII, 81)

Mark Twain wound up the banquet with a mildly humorous monologue on babies and their figurative kinship with Grant. At five o'clock
in the morning he left the festivities to write a letter to his wife. "I
have just come to my room. Livy darling I guess this was the memorable
night of my life." The greatest American prose master of the age was
almost at a loss for words about Ingersoll's eloquence. "Oh, it was just
the supremest combination of English words that was ever put together
since the world began. My soul, how handsome he looked, as he stood
on that table, in the midst of those 500 shouting men and poured the
molten silver from his lips! Lord, what an organ is human speech when
it is employed by a master!" (*Mark Twain's Letters*, I, 370). Later that day
he wrote to Howells, " 'They fought that a mother might own her child.'
The words look like any other print, but, Lord bless me! he borrowed
the very accent of the angel of mercy to say them and that vast house
rose to its feet, and you should have heard the hurricane that followed.
That's the *only* test! People may shout, clap their hands, wave their nap-
kins, but none but the master can make them *get up on their feet*" (Paine,
Mark Twain, a Biography, I, 365). Twain proudly recorded how he and Ingersoll ran into each other in the crowded halls. Ingersoll put his arms
around the younger man and said, "Mark, if I live a hundred years, I'll
always be grateful for your speech—Lord, what a supreme thing it was."
Twain felt that it was Ingersoll who "had walked off with the honors
of that occasion. Bully boy is Ingersoll—traveled with him the other day
in the cars, and you can make up your mind we had a good time" (To
his wife, *Twain's Letters*, 372).

The Chicago banquet was not only a tribute to Grant the Union
commander. It was also the opening gun of his bid for a third term in
the White House. In December Ingersoll was invited to attend a banquet
in Pittsburgh boosting the candidacy of "the laureled soldier of the world."
He respectfully declined (To Gen. A. L. Parson, Dec. 6, 1879, *Letters*, 169).

In early 1880 Ingersoll lectured extensively in the Midwest, New
England, the mid-Atlantic states, Ottawa, and Toronto. His fame had
gone before him, and he was greeted with more brickbats and bouquets
than ever. Evangelical ministers and the more ardent members of their
flocks tried to boycott his appearances, staged rival events, and pressured
storekeepers not to display his lithographs in their windows, all to no
avail. Seats were at a premium. Spectators easily unloaded tickets at twice

their regular prices. Crowds pushed past youngsters from the YMCA handing out scriptural quotations and anti-Ingersoll flyers. Seats and standing room were quickly filled; hundreds of would-be listeners were turned away. The prophet of irreligion could not be exorcised.

What was it about Ingersoll that drew paying crowds to his lectures? He was a charismatic speaker who appeared on the scene at the right time. His theology was subversive but exciting, while his moral values were conventional, reassuring, heart-warming. He could speak for two hours without being boring. An Englishman, hearing him at McVicker's Theater in Chicago on "What Must We Do To Be Saved?" analyzed this American phenomenon. He noted that there was not a vacant seat in the house and that the audience was well-dressed and intelligent-looking.

[Ingersoll] came out from the prompt side of the stage, and was received with round upon round of applause. A middle-aged man, he was attired in evening dress, "the custom of an afternoon," it seemed, on the American platform. He held some notes in his hand. They turned out to be the creed of the Athanasians and other extracts from the English Scriptures and from the New Testament. He began just as I would have fancied him sitting by my London fire, he tackled the subject in his first words, hit predestination a stunning blow in a telling epigram, and then told his favorite story of the Hebrew and "the bit of bacon" which has been already told in *The Times*. He spoke with happy facility. He was never at a loss for words. Sometimes he would pause for the purpose of emphasizing a telling phrase. His action is great when compared with the repose of English speakers. He walks about the stage as Father Gavazzi used to do; only the Italian was tragic, flinging his coat over his shoulders like a bandit, while Ingersoll is simply emphatic in his gestures. He laughs at his own jokes, laughs with the audience, they with him; it is as if he and his audience were on close and intimate terms; as if he slapped them on the back and they him, as if they were real intimates of nature; and it is moments when they are closed together over a good joke—the bacon story, for example—that he suddenly pours out upon them the eloquent warnings of his better nature, of the responsibility that rests upon every man of living a just and manly life. He is one of the most natural of all the orators I have heard. His voice is not musical; his manner is uncultivated; but his matter is original, his treatment unique, and he has the magnetism of all great speakers who sway and dominate multitudes. (*New York Times*, undated clipping, "The Apostle of Unbelief: An Englishman's View of Ingersoll," J. H.)

Wherever Ingersoll went lecturing he exhorted his enchanted audience to think for themselves, to use common sense, to follow the sound instincts of their hearts. "It is of more importance to you that you love your wife than that you love God. It is of far more importance that you love your children than that you love Jesus Christ. He who builds a home erects the holiest altar beneath the stars" (*Philadelphia Times*, May 26, 1880). At McVicker's J. H. saw tears in the eyes of many in the audience as Ingersoll contrasted the uncertain and formless bliss of heaven with the certain happiness of kind deeds and domestic duties well fulfilled on earth. He needled the contradiction in Christianity on forgiveness. "What a doctrine it is for God to say to me, 'Forgive your enemies, but I will damn mine; if your enemy spits upon one cheek, turn to him the other; but whoever does not keep my law shall suffer eternal agony' " (*Boston Herald*, Aug. 30, 1880). As Ingersoll was asserting at McVicker's that no God can afford to damn a forgiving man, a critic in the gallery piped up, "Will he forgive Democrats?" Ingersoll did not blink. " 'Oh, certainly,' replied 'the Pope.' Let me say right here (*laughter*) that I know lots of Democrats—great, broad, whole-souled, clever men and I love them (*applause*), and the only bad thing about them is that they vote the Democratic ticket (*great laughter and applause*), and I know lots of Republicans so mean and narrow that the only decent thing about them is that they vote the Republican ticket' " (*Chicago Tribune*, Sept. 20, 1880).

In Toronto a Reverend Clark invited Ingersoll to a dialogue on religion. Ingersoll consented. Reverend Clark maintained that the idea of a personal God was instinctive in human nature and the attempt to uproot it would always fail. Ingersoll replied, "I know the idea has been generally held, but that doesn't prove it to be correct. Mankind has had to give up many universal ideas." Did Ingersoll want to destroy the Christian church? "No, but I want to change the preachers into teachers, and the priests into men. I want to substitute the religion of humanity for the religion of priestcraft. In 1776 we Americans got God out of politics, and now we want to get God out of religion" (*Toronto Evening Telegram*, April 4, 1880).

As it was a presidential election year interviews naturally turned to politics. On a hot day in Philadelphia Ingersoll was asked what his role would be in the campaign. Wiping sweat from his forehead he made a perfect, two-part answer. "I am out of politics. Why? Simply because I am out. Who do I favor? Blaine, first, last, and all the time. If I happen to go to the convention, I shall support Blaine as heartily as I did four years ago" (*Philadelphia Press*, May 26, 1880). Of one thing he was sure: Hayes was politically dead; his chances were zero. "It's all folly. Hayes couldn't be elected if no one ran against him. There would be enough scattering votes to defeat him if he were the only candidate in the field" (*Cincinnati Enquirer*, May 10, 1880). He drew a careful line against Grant for a third term. "Say what you will, the administration of Gen. Grant was not a conspicuous success." By 1880, the nation needed a statesman, not a soldier (*Chicago Times*, undated, 1880). But was this giant of eloquence and conviction really "out of politics"?

VIII

Freethought and Politics

In the presidential election year of 1880 Robert Ingersoll could no more separate himself from the political scene than the proverbial leopard could change its spots. From 1860 to 1876 he had mounted the hustings as a candidate for public office or as a party worker expecting to share in the fruits of victory. He no longer sought an office of any kind, but was he really through with politics as he had known it? Was that one talent, which was death to hide, to be limited to courts and lecture halls during the nation's present quadrennial convulsion? The trial of warfare had determined that the course of American history would be for nationality and freedom, but the South still refused to accept that as a final verdict. To Ingersoll the Democrats were anathema, the Republicans emasculated by compromise and corruption. There was work to be done if one cared to do it. A man truly independent of both the people and the party leaders could make a difference. And Blaine was again running for the presidency. Ingersoll took the first step to full involvement and renewed his fight for Blaine.

Although he had made a strong speech for suffrage for the District of Columbia at an 1880 conference, Ingersoll did not seek election as a delegate to the Republican convention. Local party leaders, mostly blacks, passed him by in spite of his services to the District and the race.

Attending the Chicago convention as a nondelegate, Ingersoll could have no role in the official business, much less make a nominating speech. He promoted the Blaine candidacy behind the scenes in lobbies and caucuses. Grant was presented to the convention by Senator Roscoe Conkling, the brilliant and mercurial machine boss from New York, in an eloquent speech stressing the General rather than the ex-President.

And when asked what State he hails from,
Our sole reply shall be
He hails from Appomattox
and its famous apple tree.

The Plumed Knight—the hall was liberally spotted with posters depicting Blaine in medieval armor—was presented in a speech remarkable only for its utter insipidity. Grant led Blaine in the early balloting but could not win a majority. Blaine broke the deadlock by throwing his support to James A. Garfield, newly elected senator from Ohio. Garfield had made the nominating speech for Secretary of the Treasury John Sherman and felt committed to Sherman. Ingersoll joined those pressuring his friend Garfield to enter the race. "You have no right to give to a small man [Grant] what belongs to a great country. Do not allow Conkling to rule this country" (Ingersoll to Garfield, June 8, 1880, quoted in Kleber, 30). Garfield yielded, and beat Grant on the thirty-sixth ballot, 399 to 306. As a sop to Conkling his associate Chester A. Arthur, formerly Collector of Customs in New York, was chosen for the vice-presidency. Blaine would become Secretary of State, the gray eminence of the Garfield administration.

On July second Ingersoll, Mrs. Ingersoll, Eva, and Maud settled down for the summer—with occasional lecturing on the side—at Bass Rock House, Gloucester, Massachusetts. He wrote to John, "It is a very pleasant place—good surf bathing & plenty of walks and drives. We are all in the best of health. We bathe every day about noon, and we enjoy it like fish." He believed that the Republicans were frightened. He did not know whether he would take part in the campaign. He wanted no office, and the party, as it was, did not inspire him. "I do not intend to tear any of my underclothing whatever happens" (July 6, 1880, *Letters*, 169).

Judge Edgar J. Sherman of the Supreme Court of Massachusetts owned a cottage nearby and became a friend of the Ingersolls. He saw them almost every day and made a brief record of his visits. "I never saw a happier family," he wrote. Among the guests at the hotel were a group of Canadians who arrived after the Ingersolls. The Canadians proceeded to hold prayers in the parlor after breakfast. The manager tried to stop these prayers, thinking them objectionable to Ingersoll. The Canadians appealed to him. Ingersoll assured them that he did not mind, that he spent the mornings out of doors, on the piazza, in the fields, or at the beach.

The Ingersolls had a house guest, Edouard Remenyi, a Hungarian violin virtuoso and political romantic. At one of his free concerts of Mozart, Schubert, and Beethoven for the community, some women kept up a low-key conversation. Finally he put down his bow and exploded in broken English to the effect, "Here I am giving a free concert and pouring into it my best efforts, my very life, and there are a lot of old women cackling like so many hens." Ingersoll calmed both sides, the concert resumed, and, Sherman said, "It did seem as thought the artist poured his whole soul into the music" (*Some Recollections of A Long Life*, 256-257). Remenyi would become a close friend and moonstruck admirer of Ingersoll, frequently delighting his family and guests with his music.

On politics Ingersoll was torn between two roads—obscurity or prominence. He was leaning toward prominence but he had a precondition: He would not support a candidate who was not strong for religious freedom. On the same day as his letter expressing indifference to John he reached out to the Republican candidate. Garfield was an ordained minister. What was his position on freedom of thought? Speedily came the response:

> My Dear Colonel, Yours of the 6th inst. is received. I not only never introduced such a resolution as that to which you refer—but in several public speeches I have praised the wisdom of our fathers for prohibiting Congress from legislating on the subject of religion—and leaving it to the voluntary action of the people. I send you a copy of one my speeches in which allusion is made to the subject. I am well—always glad to hear from you—. As always your friend, J. A. Garfield. (July 9, 1880, L.C.)

Soon Blaine was pressing him again to make a lot of speeches in Maine. No, no, not so many this time. Blaine responded: "My Dear Robert, I want you and the 'woman without superstition' and the two girls to come to Maine about August 20-23 directly to our house for headquarters and general abiding place—and you to make us some speeches. But whether you make 40 speeches or not Mrs. Blaine and I want you to come— You can wake the State as no other man can. Don't say No. Regards to Madam and the girls. Yours devotedly, J. G. B." (July 26, 1880, L.C.).

Warming up for the fall campaign Ingersoll pulled away from his seaside vacation and spoke at a Garfield-Arthur rally in Gloucester. Banners fluttered: "A Free Ballot, the American Birthright," "Mechanic, Soldier, Statesman." For summer fare the orator glorified his candidate as the American myth personified. "I like this country because the boy who has worked on a canal, who has driven a mule on the towpath, who has cut wood at 25¢ a cord, is going to be [the] next President of the United States." It was the war over again: northern nationalism against southern sectionalism, freedom against slavocracy, transferred from the battlefield to the hustings, where compassion and fairness were the first casualties. He denounced the doctrine of states' rights (to which he had once subscribed), the doctrine of slavocracy, and the current oppression of the emancipated race. He waved the bloody shirt, first making sure that it was a blue shirt and not a gray one. "Every shot that was fired at the flag was fired by Democrats. Every northern man who got a scar on his body got it from a Democrat," and so forth. The Democratic party had no place in the ongoing life of the Republic. It was a party of the past, "a cemetery of ideas," with an epitaph on its flag. "Let us meet the solid South by a solid North. Is it any worse to be solid in favor of the right than solid for the wrong?" (*Cape Ann Advertiser*, Aug. 13, 1880).

Ingersoll's involvement with the Republican campaign was in tune with his battles and his split with the organized freethought movement, the National Liberal League. The ultimate disappearance of the League and its resurrection as the American Secular Union is an object lesson in the insufficiency of freethought (in later language, humanism) as a unifying basis for a comprehensive social program. Starting out agitating for the complete destruction of the gods of the sky, the League attracted radicals of every persuasion—advocates of "soft" money, government ownership of utilities, socialism, anarchism, free love, and such. Each faction believed that a movement aimed at the destruction of the idols of the sky naturally favored the destruction of its own particular devil on earth. The League was an uneasy brotherhood of motley forces, held together by hardly anything more than Ingersoll, the sun around which the whole movement revolved and which every member claimed as his or her own. These varied perceptions were grievous errors. They would lead time and again to bitter and painful discord.

Excepting religion Ingersoll was not a thoroughgoing radical. He believed in nationality and freedom and a "sound" laissez-faire economy humanized by a sense of social responsibility. Every man willing and able to work was entitled to a job and a decent living for himself and his family. He said that any society that could not satisfy these wants had no right to exist, but he did not hail in the storm and stress of the times any portents of revolutionary change. He lived in a state of helpless annoyance at seeing himself and freethought associated with every wind of doctrine that blew through the League.

Before 1880, the League was stirred by a strong current of opinion urging the formation of a new party, the Liberal party. Ingersoll sympathized with the general idea. In August 1879 Thaddeus Burr Wakeman, a dynamic free-thinking scholar, journalist, and lawyer, sent Ingersoll a draft of an agenda for a new party. Ingersoll was quick with objections. As he had never sought to steer the League away from the straight and narrow path of freedom of thought, he criticized Wakeman's intention to embrace additional objectives. What, he asked, did their movement have to do with the Mormon ulcer or expressions of sympathy for the Socialists of Europe? However, not all the developments were bad. "I am delighted to hear that the Free Lovers are against us. I want nothing to do with them. Let them spend their time examining each other's sexual organs and letting ours alone." The purpose of the new party should simply be "to secularize the gov't, to take the hand of superstition from the throat of progress" (Aug. 15, 1879, L.C.).

The rift between Ingersoll and Wakeman soon widened—by the nineteenth Ingersoll wrote to Wakeman, "We seem to be working at cross purposes." He thought that the call for a convention should simply propose consideration of forming a new party, not to join with the Democrats or Greenbackers or any other party or to encourage guerrilla warfare. He outlined a platform to eliminate religion from government. "I want to assist what little I can in the inauguration of a new political movement, for the purpose of accomplishing, first, the divorce of Church and State; second, the divorce of Church and School; third, the repeal of all Sunday laws; fourth, the repeal of all laws discriminating against persons on account of their religious or irreligious belief. In other words, I want to make the free-thinker the equal of every other man before the law" (Letters, 642). He sent a similar letter to Elizur Wright, grand old man of abolitionism and freethought, who had signed Wakeman's draft (Aug. 19, 1879, Letters, 642).

As Ingersoll arrived in mid-September in Cincinnati for the new-party convention a reporter asked whether he was abandoning the Republican party. "No, if they will help me and help the cause of human rights, I shall help them with all my might. But as for political speaking I do not hanker for it." But if the Republican party would not defend the rights of citizens he was not a Republican (Truth Seeker, Sept. 20, 1879, quoted from Cincinnati Gazette).

The convention opening on September fourteenth adopted a resolution offered by Ingersoll expressing sympathy with Bennett and his family, victims of "religious bigotry and ignorant zeal." Cries arose, "Ingersoll! Ingersoll!" A little speech was in order. It was a good time for stating his basic principles. "Allow me to say," he began, "that the cause nearest my heart, and to which I am willing to devote the remainder of my life, is the absolute, the absolute, enfranchisement of the human mind." The family was the unit of good government, he continued, and the real temple of the human heart was the hearth-stone. All human beings were entitled to human rights—the misery in the world pleaded for relief.

> When I look about upon the world and see how the children that are born today, in this year, in this age, come into a world that has nearly all been taken up before their arrival; when I see that they have not even an opportunity to labor for bread; when I see that in our splendid country some who do the most have the least, and those who do the least have the most, I say to myself there is something wrong somewhere, and I hope the time will come when every child that nature has invited to our feast will have an equal right with all the others.

A moral reformation was on the way. "Education not only of the head but of the heart will bring a time when a man who has amassed millions will not be respected until he uses his wealth to improve the condition of his fellow-men." In that spirit "let us all agree that we will stand by each other splendidly, grandly, and when we come into convention let us pass resolutions that are broad, kind, and genial." In that ecumenical spirit of abstract benevolence he led successful fights against motions favoring nationalization of the railroads and even outright socialism. Such positions would be offensive to many stockholders who were staunch freethinkers (*Works*, XII, 234; *Truth Seeker*, Sept. 29, 1879). As the convention was winding up, Ingersoll, in front of the platform, waved his hat in the air as he led three cheers for the new party (*Truth Seeker*, Oct. 4, 1879).

It was really "Hail and farewell." Ingersoll did nothing more for the Liberal Party. Within a month he was saying, "Wakeman is working away all the time about his party. My notion is that we need no party outside of the Liberal League" (To A. B. Morton, Oct. 23, 1879, L. C). With his support gone, the new party died aborning.

Consternation fell on the rank and file. They felt betrayed by their leaders. Where was their new Party? they mourned. What better opportunity than then to raise the standard of Liberalism, when the country was in the grip of two corrupt parties having no live issue but only scrambling for the spoils of office? Bennett and Wakeman were favoring the Democrats, Ingersoll the Republicans (naturally). Must the people choose between Garfield the stock swindler and Hancock the West Point aristocrat? What was the use of destroying all the gods and the devil when our leaders preached for a more damnable idol, the idol of gold? Liberals should vote for General James B. Weaver, the candidate of the Greenback party. Respectfully but bitterly they criticized Ingersoll for changing his mind. Vote for Blaine? Is that what Liberals must do to be saved? And how could Ingersoll stay with a party that had treated him so badly, denied him the governorship of Illinois, the Berlin mission, the Bennett pardon? (Letters in *Truth Seeker*, June 12, 1880; July 17, 1880; Aug. 28, 1880).

The League was heading for an explosion. At the convention of September 1880 the differences between Ingersoll and his opposition came to a crisis over the federal postal laws and pornography. The postal laws proscribing the transit of "immorality, lotteries, and other offensive matter" through the mails had been the instrument of sending Bennett to prison. Extreme libertarians opposed these regulations entirely, whereupon a public image developed of the freethinkers as defenders and purveyors of obscene literature. To a motion for outright repeal Ingersoll offered a moderating amendment that supported the prosecution of pornography and demanded freedom for the decent expression of ideas. Ingersoll and Wakeman headed rival camps debating the nature of pornography and the function of law. Ingersoll argued that the League as an organization had no more to do with the postal laws than with laws against selling stale eggs, but instead should vigorously declare against pornography and for freedom of thought. Earnestly, anxiously, almost tearfully, he pleaded—"I beg of you, I beseech you"—and he warned that if the convention voted for repeal "all I have to say is that, while I shall be for liberty everywhere, I cannot act with this organization, and I will not" (*Works*, XII, 230). The convention voted for repeal and he immediately resigned, taking some of his faction with him. As if to signal their relief at his departure the rump majority adopted a resolution calling for "the emancipation of the wage workers from the galling chain of industrial slavery" and declaring that "perfect religious freedom is an impossibility while the bodies of men and women are enthralled under the despotism of capital" (*Truth Seeker*, Oct. 2, 1880).

If Ingersoll had been a religious man he would have thanked God for liberating him from the Liberals. He breathed his own sigh of relief. "Dear Chicks," he wrote to his daughters, "I never saw such a perfect lot of idiots together. I left them and I think you will be glad. They have stained me enough and I want no more to do with them" (Sept. 19, 1880, L.C.). His popularity on the lecture platform had been enhanced by his defense of social conservatism. The crowds were larger than ever. "I had a great meeting yesterday. The house was packed and at least one thousand were turned away. . . . I made thousands of friends by leaving the dirty Liberal League, and by the lecture. The lecture is the talk of the town. The net proceeds were over $1,000" (Chicago, Sept. 20, 1880, L.C.). There were plaudits—"Your friends here rejoice at your course in leaving the League, now run by 'short-haired women and long-haired men' " (From Nathan French, Sept. 22, 1880, IHS)—and condemnations. The lost leader had chosen the biases of the politician and the lawyer rather than being "the grand master and heroic leader" of the people (*Truth Seeker*, Oct. 9, 1880, letter by J. H .W. Toohey).

In spite of the hot words of eternal damnation on both sides, the rupture did not last. Ingersoll and organized freethought needed each other, and there was no absolute reason why they could not work together. Within a few weeks Ingersoll was again pressing for a new structure confined to freedom of thought. His influence gradually prevailed. The National Liberal League went out of existence and the American Secular Union came into being. Later, in his inaugural address as president on September 13, 1885, Ingersoll would lavish praise upon his former opponents Wright and Wakeman. But the new harmony of freethought was destined to be broken again by the political passions of the age.

When Ingersoll resigned from the League he was already engaged in the Republican cause. Garfield had allayed his fears on religion and freedom of thought, and Blaine had easily persuaded him to do some speaking in Maine. Mrs. Blaine had seconded her husband's invitation. "If you will come you will receive for yourself a long night of rest and a short day's travel. And for me the unspeakable gratification of a little visit from a dear friend" (Sept. 2, 1880, Telegram, L.C.).

The thousand-fold crowd poured in from all directions, some eight thousand by special excursion on the Maine Central Railway, some three to four thousand by carriage or by foot. They packed the grounds at Lake Maranacook, some finding seats, most standing. Suddenly cries of "There's Bob!" and "There's Ingersoll!" went up, as "a portly, jolly looking, clean-shaven gentleman, with short gray hair and a nobly modelled chest and waist, dressed in a white and blue shirt, seersucker duster and vest, light pants, and straw broad-brim, edged through the crowd."

Introduced by a man of the cloth Ingersoll plunged into the themes of nationalism with a sectional twist that he had propounded in Gloucester and which could not fail to delight the Yankees before him. "Ladies and Gentlemen, this is in my opinion the greatest and best country in the world. (*A voice*, "Bully for you," *followed by cheers*) and when I speak of 'our country' I mean the North, East, and West. There are parts of the country that are not yet civilized." This country, excepting the South, was on the side of liberty. People had plenty to eat and to wear, and more kind husbands and more good women than any other country on the globe. Having captured the crowd with this hokum he asked, "Now, if that liberty is to be preserved, whom will you have preserve it? Honor bright, now (*tremendous applause and laughter*)." Certainly not the South, which had not yet learned that in this country the king was the will of the majority. He told a few more or less pertinent jokes depicting the South as a vast wasteland. A man wanted to buy a horse. The dealer directed him to a horse that he said looked exactly like the one shown in engravings of George Washington's horse. "Yes," said the man, examining the horse's teeth. "I'll be d----d if I don't believe it's the same horse" (*tremendous laughter*). Two ministers held a revival. After the service one of them passed around the hat, and the people threw in old nails, bits of sticks and paper, but no money. The minister turned the hat up and out came the trash. "Well," said the other, "let us thank God." "What for?" asked the first (*laughter*). "Because we got the hat back" (*uproarious laughter*). He spoke "a little sense" about monetary theory. The only real money was hard money, gold and silver, precious metal, or paper redeemable in precious metal; so that when a Hottentot saw an American dollar flying in the wind he would grab it as eagerly as if it were a lump of gold. "You might as well attempt to make fiat suns, moons, and stars as a fiat dollar" (*applause*).

Now the tried-and-true bloody shirt. "Every man that said slavery was a divine institution was a Democrat. Recollect it! Every man that shot a Union soldier was a Democrat. Every wound borne by you Union soldiers is a souvenir of a Democrat. You got your crutches from Democrats," and so forth.

Ingersoll defended himself. He had been asked, " 'Oh, ain't you ever going to forgive the Democratic party?' No! I'm not going to forgive them until I can speak as freely in one part of the country as another, protected by the old flag!" How could he vote for Garfield, a Christian? "I tell you, friends, why I can vote for him—because I am not a bigot and Gen. Garfield is not one."

For more than two hours Ingersoll held those thousands in his hand, reasoned with them, made them laugh, brought tears to their eyes. "The great orator fulfilled the expectations of everybody. Ingersoll's eloquence and wit Friday afternoon probably cannot be matched by any living orator. His originality and force and power of presenting facts in their fullest and most forcible senses made his speech something that his hearers will delight to tell their grandchildren about if they ever have any" (*Chicago Tribune*, Sept. 12, 1880, quoted from *Lewiston Journal; Boston Journal*, Sept. 4, 1880).

Ingersoll commenced a blitz above the Mason–Dixon line for the Garfield-Arthur ticket. Almost everybody who could walk, regardless of party, attended his rallies. Few stayed away because of religious scruples. The *Chicago Tribune* ridiculed the ultrapious who were urging a boycott of Ingersoll's candidates in the name of Christianity. It reprinted a piece from a religious journal asserting that the Christian religion was a thousand times dearer to millions of Christians than a political triumph, and a comment in a Democratic newspaper that Ingersoll was denouncing Democracy as he denounced the Bible. The *Tribune* observed, "The idea that the Republican party must bear the blame of Ingersoll's anti-religious views is as obnoxious to the impartial mind as the idea that the Christian religion must be condemned because it harbors some canting hypocrites" (undated clipping, L.C.). An Ingersoll rally was simply the best show in town. Most Democratic listeners would vote Democrat, and most orthodox Christians who were inclined to vote Republican would not be frightened by spiritual anxiety.

It was the 1876 campaign repeated. Almost every day a new town big or little and the same hoopla—flags and banners everywhere, parades, torchlight processions, brass bands and glee clubs banging out "John Brown's Body" and other Union songs, fireworks, and feasting. There were some differences. The message might be much the same but the speaker could now be advertised with some legitimacy as the greatest orator in the world. Everywhere immense crowds by train or wagon or foot, everywhere the newspapers, including the Democratic, acclaiming the demonstration as the greatest ever in that area, at least since 1860. Local committees strained for novelty. In Ligonier, Indiana, thirty-eight girls were arranged on a float in a pyramid representing the thirty-eight states; in Cincinnati huge calcium lights glowed at the intersection of Eighth and Pace Streets so that he could address a crowd a block long north, east, west, and south; in Springfield, Ohio, a whipping post and an auction block went on parade and then two oxen, twelve pigs, and forty sheep were sacrificed in a feast of the faithful.

Ingersoll was at the height of his genius, popularity, good health, and good spirits. Blessed by the chairmen—"I have the honor, fellow-citizens, to introduce to you the distinguished orator, Robert G. Ingersoll of Illinois," as "the first orator of the age, and its most fearless and eloquent champion of human rights"—he faced audiences ready to revel in a full-spectrum display of histrionics that would be described later in the friendly press: "Every sentence is a sledge-hammer, an eye-moistener, or a side-splitter" (*Albany Evening Reporter*, Oct. 26, 1880). In Cincinnati the crowd whooped as he mounted the platform to a cry "Go in, Peoria." In Batavia, Ohio, the committee drove out on the road to meet the Ingersoll carriage and escort the guest of honor in a clattering gallop to an uproarious welcome (*Cincinnati Commerical*, Oct. 3, 1880).

Ingersoll enjoyed being "hounded" by the press. In Chicago a reporter found him in a barber chair and pelted him with tasteless personal questions. He responded with jovial wit as usual. Did he ever use profane language at home? Well, he might sometimes refer to the residence of the devil when it was not a necessary part of the conversation, and "if by swearing is meant the use of God's name in vain, there are very few preachers who do not swear more than I do, if by 'in vain' is meant without any practical result." Was he drunk at a political meeting back in 1860? Well, he didn't remember what happened after the drinking. "I don't pretend to be a teetotaler. I heard a story the other day that illustrates my position. There was an Irishman who joined the Sons of Temperance, and, a few days afterwards, one of his friends saw him in a saloon with a glass about half-full of whisky in his hand. Said he: 'Pat, I though you were a teetotaler.' 'So I am,' said Pat, 'but, thank God, I am not a bigot' " (*Chicago Inter-Ocean*, Sept. 30, 1880).

He thrived in the limelight. "Colonel Ingersoll was early on the scene. His appearance was treated with a salvo of applause. He looked himself and tripped up to his seat lightly and buoyantly. From his jolly round face breathed health and happiness. He sat in the rear with his tall stove-pipe hat upon his head, and a muffler about his neck, fearful of a draft. He was dressed in black, a cut-away coat, and an unobtrusive cravat" (*Syracuse Standard*, Oct. 22, 1880).

Many years after the 1880 campaign oldtimers would recall through a haze of romance the great scene when Ingersoll came to town. It was a visitation. In the courthouse square in Lafayette a boy sat in the fork of a poplar tree and surveyed the crowd:

> members of all political parties, members of all churches—and those not members of any—youth and beauty, old age with its wisdom, the wealthy and the poor, the farmer and the mechanic, the banker, the doctor, the lawyer, the butcher, the baker, and the candlestick-maker. All had come to hear great oratory, and none were disappointed. . . . His voice was clear as a bell. His intellectual face was ruddy with the glow of perfect health. His gestures were the perfection of grace and at a climax he would throw his head back, thrust both his hands into his trouser pockets, as if to say, 'Answer that if you can.' His voice was like music, and his language more beautiful than I had ever heard before. At times his wit convulsed the audience. At times he was pathetic.

Throughout he was entertaining and logical, and that great audience, regardless of church creed or politics, was stirred and moved as the tree-tops in an April breeze. (Alvin O. Reese, *Indianapolis News*, Oct. 27, 1903)

In Ogdensburg, New York, Ingersoll began by inviting his listeners to ask questions at any time. As he spoke, the questions came, about a dozen, and he went right on with his speech. Hecklers demanded answers. He stopped, pointed to the first questioner, answered his question, then to the second, answered his, and so on, all twelve in order. He then resumed his speech (Canton, N.Y., *Plain Dealer*, Oct. 7, 1924).

Throughout the campaign Ingersoll was in close touch with Garfield. He scheduled his speeches according to the candidate's wishes and wrote cheery letters of support on the charges of personal misconduct a la Blaine, and informed him of the progress of the campaign. As he was about to leave home for Garfield and Ohio he sent a note across the hall to "My dear Madam," inviting Mrs. Ingersoll to accompany him. She would hear good singing, excellent speaking, and a vast amount of most patriotic noise. If she was not available, other ladies might like to go (Oct. 8, 1880, *Letters*, 531). She was available.

Garfield noted in his diary, "Bob Ingersoll is a good fellow after all. He reached here the other day just in time to break up a prayer-meeting in my office and bounce out seven or eight ministers who had come to interview me on my religious convictions. He chucked Mrs. Garfield under the chin, kissed the children, winked at the cook, and took half an hour to convince the hired man that Jonah was swallowed by a mule instead of a whale. If I am elected President and Robert wants a little office, he shall have it" (abstracted extract from General Garfield's diary, L.C.). Garfield appreciated Ingersoll's support. "I watch the track of your campaign by the light and lightening that flash along it" (Oct. 12, 1880, L.C.). "I have followed your shining track through the campaign and have seen with what hearty brotherhood of friendship to me you have poured your scorn upon these rascals. Thanking you again for your letter and your work in the campaign, I am as ever yours, J. A. Garfield" (Oct. 16, 1880, *Letters*, 170).

Ingersoll's most important contributions to the Garfield campaign were in his three forays into New York City.

At Cooper Union on October twenty-third the stampede for admittance overwhelmed the police and almost caused a disaster as the people in the rear came on like an ice-breaker, sweeping those in front down the stone staircase. Some three thousand found sitting and standing room, some five thousand could not get in. "At half past seven precisely the handsome though corpulent figure of Colonel Ingersoll was seen struggling through the masses filling the background of the platform. The Colonel, who seemed as fresh and hearty as ever, in spite of his recent campaign experiences, was accompanied by his wife and his daughters. His appearance called forth a thunder of applause, which did not die away until several minutes had elapsed. This demonstration elicited an acknowledgment from the Colonel which took the form of a bow, a slight wave of the hand, and a grand expression of countenance peculiar to the man" (*Daily Tribune*, Oct. 4, 1880). The standard speech, followed by the standard the riotous applause.

Five days later a daytime rally was held at the steps of the Sub-Treasury in Wall Street. An elaborate platform complete with sounding board had been erected, decorated with flags and bunting. Brass bands led hordes of men in loose parade to the platform, where they hung their banners. Soon the adjacent streets were dense with humanity, only buildings, lampposts, and telegraph poles visible above the chiefs (and Indians) of industry and finance. "It was a tremendous crowd in point of numbers, and its composition was entirely of gentlemen—men with refined, intelligent faces—bankers, brokers, merchants of all kinds—real business men, thousands and millions of dollars were represented in it" (*New York Times*, Oct. 29, 1880). To his standard arguments Ingersoll added a special allurement to this audience. He bluntly appealed to the class consciousness that he had once denied. "The farmers of Illinois," he proclaimed, as if still a resident of Peoria, "depend upon the merchants, the brokers, and the bankers, upon the gentlemen of New York, to beat the rabble of New York." (What a phrase from the apostle of the religion of humanity!) He warned that if the Democrats won, every kind of property in the country, including stocks and bonds, private and public, would depreciate.

Time for a joke, all the funnier perhaps for having nothing to do with the subject.

> There is not a university in the North and East or West that does not have in it a Republican majority. There is not a penitentiary in the United States (*cheers and applause and shouts of* "We know the rest" *and* "Go on")— How did you know what I was going to say! There is not a penitentiary that has not in it a Democratic majority, (*laughter*) and they know it. Two years ago there were about 283 convicts in the Maine penitentiary. Out of the whole number there was only one Republican (*laughter; a voice,* "It was the chaplain,") and he broke out. He said he didn't mind being in the penitentiary, but the company was a little more than he could stand. (*Times*, Oct. 29, 1880)

At the end of the speech the ecstatic audience gave a special sign of their pleasure. "When he had spoken for an hour and thirty minutes the immense crowd cried out for more, and insisted on having the great orator show himself where they could cheer him. And cheer him they did. The history of Wall Street tells of few if any such scenes as that which took the nature of an ovation to the greatest orator of the day.

Men shouted themselves hoarse, hats were flung wildly in air, while the subject of this extraordinary enthusiasm stood uncovered, bowing and smiling from the steps of the Treasury building" (*Herald Tribune*, Oct. 29, 1880).

The Garfields were delighted with the Wall Street speech. Garfield read it aloud to Mrs. Garfield, and she wrote to Ingersoll, "Your eloquent speech was grandly equal to the occasion. Though your theology may not be able to give me much comfort, your magnificent friendship does, and I thank you for every word you uttered. General Garfield joins me in admiration and gratitude, and in kindest regards to Mrs. Ingersoll and your daughters" (Oct. 31, 1880, *Letters*, 171).

Ingersoll's speech two days later at the Brooklyn Academy of Music was his crowning performance of the campaign. The setting tingled with the stuff of drama. The chairman was Henry Ward Beecher; the most prominent minister in the land introduced its most famous unbeliever. Beecher was magnanimity personified. He said that he stood there not as a minister but as a man among men and that he respected Ingersoll "as the man that for a full score and more of years has worked in the great, broad field of humanity, and for the cause of human rights. I consider it an honor to extend to him, as I do now, the warm, earnest, right hand of friendship." Ingersoll rose and took the hand in a clapping clasp that resounded throughout the hall. The crowd of six thousand rose to its feet and applauded. Beecher continued, "I now introduce to you a man who—and I say it not flatteringly—is the most brilliant speaker of the English tongue of all men on the globe. But as under the brilliancy of the blaze of light we find the living coals of fire, under the lambent flow of his wit and magnificent antitheses we find the glorious flame of genius and honest thought. Ladies and gentlemen, Mr. Ingersoll."

The Academy of Music speech is a comprehensive statement of Ingersoll's political orientation as of 1880. It is at once parochial and timeless, narrow and broad, true and false, in its pursuit of votes, which is the business of politics. First he proclaimed his independence. He was mortgaged to nobody. He praised the War Democrats (he had been one), who had been loyal to the Union. In a minute he is whimsical. "In its [the Republican party's] great efforts to do right it has sometimes by mistake done wrong. And I also wish to admit that the great Democratic party in its effort to get office has sometimes by mistake done right. You see that I am inclined to be perfectly fair" (*Works*, IX, 349).

He asked the crowd where they stood—"honor bright"—on the main issues of the election—free speech, honest ballot, vigorous enforcement of taxes, honest money, nationality versus states rights, protection of citizens. The South had always suppressed free speech because free speech contributed to knowledge and condemned slavery. The ballot when honest stood for the sovereignty of the people, the poorest man equal to the millionaire in shaping the course of the nation. "Can you trust it to the masked murderers who rode in the darkness of night to the hut of the freedman and shot him down, notwithstanding the supplication of his wife and the tears of his babe? . . . Do you want to put the ballot box in the keeping of the shot-gun, of the White Liners, of the Ku Klux?" (359–360).

The country absolutely needed honest money, gold and silver, and paper with gold and silver behind it. Silver was a great American product and its coinage should be encouraged. "But I want a silver dollar worth a gold dollar, even if you make it or have to make it four feet in diameter" (363). Inflation had to be resisted, as it would dilute real value.

Time for a poker joke, good for a laugh even if it were not strictly pertinent. "I have been told that along toward morning the man that is ahead suddenly says, 'I have got to go home. The fact is, my wife is not well.' And the fellow who is behind says, 'Let us have another deal; I have my opinion of the fellow that will jump a game' " (365–366).

They lived in one nation, indivisible, where each man was equal to every other man because they were men. The doctrine of state sovereignty had never been appealed to for any good. "It was made so that they could rob the cradle in the name of law. Think of it! Think of it!" (372). It was made "so that the bloodhound, with clots of blood dripping from his loose and hanging jaws, might traverse the billowy plains of Kansas. Think of it! It was made in defense of secession and treason, which cost us six thousand millions of dollars and four hundred thousand lives" (378–379).

In a brilliant sentence Ingersoll condensed his argument so far: "Free speech is the brain of the Republic; an honest ballot is the breath of its life; honest money is the blood of its veins; and the idea of nationality is its great, beating, throbbing heart" (382).

The speaker came out for the protection of American labor by tariff walls. A protective tariff, he contended, was necessary so that the American laborer would have enough to eat and wear and be enabled to see his wife well dressed, "a few blue ribbons fluttering about her children . . . the flags of health flying in their beautiful cheeks" (380). He carried the rationale of protection to its absolute conclusion: The walls had to be high enough to make America economically self-sufficient. "I want America to produce everything that America needs. I want it so that if the whole world should declare war against us, if we were surrounded by walls of cannons, bayonets, and swords, we could supply all our material wants in and of ourselves. I want to live to see the American woman dressed in American silk; the American in everything, from hat to boots, produced in America by the cunning hand of American toil" (384).

He rose to a fever pitch with inflammatory memories of the war— the tattered but still useful bloody shirt.

I say to you, that every man who tried to tear the flag out of heaven was a Democrat. The men who wrote the ordinances of secession, who fired upon Fort Sumter, the men who starved our soldiers, who fed them with the crumbs that the worms had devoured before, they were Democrats. . . . Who were joyful when your brothers and your sons and your fathers lay dead on the field of battle that the country had lost? They were Democrats. . . . That party was once the enemy of my country, was once the enemy of our flag, and more than that, it was once the enemy of human liberty, and that party tonight is not willing that the citizens of the Republic should exercise all their rights irrespective of their color. (389-390)

He was asked how long he would preach the doctrine of hate. He denied that he was preaching hate, but reaffirmed that "I am going to preach my doctrine until every American citizen is permitted to express his opinions and vote as he may desire in every State of this Union" (401).

He compared the candidates, General Garfield and General Hancock. Was Hancock more sincere when he was killing rebels or now that he was their candidate? General Garfield had been accused of being dishonest. The Democrats had tried to steal nearly half the country. They lived on the unpaid labor of four million people. How could he support Garfield, a minister? Because Garfield was not a bigot and because Garfield believed in freedom of speech and thought and in the absolute divorce of church and state. Ingersoll denounced the forgery that represented Garfield as favoring Chinese immigration on the Pacific coast. (He did not say that he himself had favored Chinese immigration in a satiric gem in *The Chicago Times* on March twenty-seventh.)

Ingersoll ended with a gush of love for America, the land of liberty. "Oh! I love the old Republic, bounded by the seas, walled by the wide air, domed by heaven's blue, and lit with the eternal stars. I love the Republic, I love it because I love Liberty. Liberty is my religion, and at its altar I worship, and will worship" (403).

Ingersoll and Beecher stood side by side at the front of the stage under a canopy of flags and with baskets of flowers to right and left. Beecher led three cheers for Ingersoll, and Ingersoll three cheers for Beecher.

At Garfield's request Ingersoll made a speech in Delaware the night before the election. He was, he said, proud to belong to the party of human liberty and human progress, the party that would keep the furnaces hot and the sky filled with the smoke of American industry, the party that had elected Lincoln and Grant and would elect Garfield. He flourished the bloody shirt. Vehemently and cheerfully—a typical Ingersollian mood— he sounded a death knell for the Democratic party. "Friends, this is the last speech I make in this campaign. I have done the best I could. I feel tonight as if I was delivering the funeral oration of the Democratic party. Standing by the open grave, I am moved to say, 'The Lord giveth and the Lord taketh away,' and as I listen to the clods fall upon the coffin I am happy as can be expected under the circumstances" (*Wilmington Morning News*, Nov. 2, 1880).

The knell was premature. The Democratic party—the white South augmented by machine bosses and some of the urban poor in the North— won 4,442,035 popular votes against the Republican 4,449,053, although the electoral vote was 155 to 214.

A period of euphoria followed for the triumphant orator. On November fifth the Garfield-Arthur Club of Washington, preceded by a section of the Marine Band, paraded through the streets for half an hour, ending with a celebration and serenade at the brightly lighted and decorated home of the Ingersolls. He came out and made a little speech, "that he had heard it said that the Democratic party had gone to a place that he did not believe in (*long and continuous applause*) but for the sake of argument if there was such a place and its tenant was the Democratic party all he could say was that he pitied the place" (*National Republican*, Nov. 6, 1880). As guest of honor at a banquet of the National Towpath Club (in swallowtail coat and white cravat) he offered a toast for the future citizenship of the District of Columbia. On a lecture tour in the East he was found by a reporter "smiling and jolly as usual, ready to give his views on any question to anybody who desired them" (*Pittsburgh Dispatch*, Dec. 11, 1880). The election had settled the issue of nationality and its implications; future campaigns must be on other issues. He would always be with the party that favored "a larger and grander liberty." He predicted population growth, industrial expansion, world trade, and "I must not forget the thing that is always closest to my heart. There is more intellectual liberty in the United States today than ever before. The people are beginning to see that every citizen ought to have the right to express himself freely upon any possible subject" (*Washington Post*, Nov. 14, 1880). He took a final happy swat at Hayes. What did he think of Hayes's views on civil service and polygamy? "I think that they are laughable. President Hayes has no right to speak about civil service reform or polygamy. He has never practised either" (*Pittsburgh Times*, Dec. 11, 1880).

The president-elect was appreciative, gracious. He wrote: "I cannot say it as well as Mrs. Garfield has said it, but yet I must tell you that no man was ever so royally defended as I have been by you. Though I know as you do the cause was worth more than either of us, yet, as far as I am personally concerned, I am inclined to care more about the friendship which this contest has developed than for the victory we have won. As ever yours, J. A. Garfield" (Nov. 10, 1880, *Letters*, 171). On the night of November twenty-third Garfield's train pulled into the depot at Washington. Ingersoll was there to greet him, to extend a hand and say heartily, "How do you do, General?" Garfield grasped the hand and responded with equal enthusiasm, "Royal Bob, how are you?" (*Washington Post*, Nov. 24, 1880).

Was the newly crowned Royal Bob a happy man? Not quite. Time's winged chariot was hurrying near, and vast deserts of eternity lay beyond. He wrote to John, "Nothing new is happening to me. The girls are studying music, German & French, reading a few books and talking a great deal. I am thinking a little and writing a few pages now and then and so the world goes on and the swift years pass and the end approaches. The wall in front of each life recedes day by day, but suddenly it will stop, and the darkness will cover all. After all, death seems natural enough. Life is the mysterious thing" (Nov. 28, 1880, *Letters*, 532).

On the day before the inauguration Washington was as usual flooded with visitors. Men in military uniform abounded. One New York militia regiment stayed up half the night having a good time. Among their songs:

> Ingersoll, Ingersoll, he's the man for me.
> We'll escort him to the White House
> And treat him to cold tea!
> Chorus: Yes, by God, we will!
> (Blanchard, April 2, 1910)

IX

A Champion at the Bar of Justice

With the election of Garfield, Ingersoll could look forward to a vista of prestige and influence, lucrative practice as a Washington lawyer, extensive lecture tours for the religion of humanity, and enjoying life. Unfortunately nothing would turn out as expected. Blaine would force a prosecution of Ingersoll's friend ex-Senator Dorsey of Arkansas for mail fraud, Garfield would be assassinated, Ingersoll would make his most magnificent triumph at the bar, and the Blaine–Ingersoll connection would come to a dead stop never to be resumed, a most unfortunate event for Blaine when Ingersoll sat out the Blaine-Cleveland contest for the presidency in 1884. Well might Ingersoll think with his beloved Burns:

> The best-laid plans of mice and men
> Gang aft agley.

In the interval between election and inauguration Garfield met often in Washington with his designated-Secretary of State Blaine, king-maker and soon-to-be prime mover in the short-lived Garfield administration. Since Ingersoll and Blaine were neighbors, Garfield frequently ran into Ingersoll at the Blaine residence (T. Smith, Garfield I, 901). It may be conjectured that if Ingersoll had requested a post in his administration Garfield would have complied (especially in view of Garfield's diary entry, cited in the precious chapter). However, the *Fond du Lac* (Wisc.) *Commonwealth* even reported that Blaine had actually crushed Garfield's intended appointment of Ingersoll as an ambassador (Oct. 25, 1895). There was a rumor that Blaine opposed such an appointment because of Ingersoll's antireligion, and a cartoon showed Blaine slamming the back door of the White House on Ingersoll as not sufficiently "orthodox." At any rate Ingersoll had good reason for not seeking an appointment in the government. It undoubtedly would have to be of cabinet or high diplomatic rank and might not survive a debate in the Senate. Besides, the constraints of public office were incompatible with his irreversible career in freethought. To the public Ingersoll appeared content. He told a reporter that he approved the Garfield cabinet but he himself held a higher office, Secretary of the Exterior, its only drawback being the precarious nature of the salary (*Chicago Tribune*, March 3, 1880).

The storm over the mail delivery business that would go down in history as the Star Route prosecution, the most sensational *cause célèbre* of the Gilded Age, was slow in developing. Congress had designated sparsely inhabited areas beyond reach by train or steamboat as postal routes for service under individual contracts. These outlying routes were indicated in official schedules by three asterisks for, hopefully, "celerity, certainty, and security" hence the name Star Routes, which has continued to be the nomenclature for such routes. During the Hayes administration they were under the jurisdiction of Second Assistant Postmaster General Thomas J. Brady, who awarded contracts on competitive bidding. For the fiscal year ending June 30, 1880, Congress appropriated the full amount requested by Brady—$5,900,000—but when he asked for a deficiency appropriation of $1,700,000, they balked, voting only $1,100,000 and intimating that his management might be worth investigation by the Department of Justice.

Was there skullduggery in high places? The American public, sensitized by memories of the Grant scandals, seized upon the Star Route incident and clamored for a thoroughgoing investigation. Suspicion focused upon Brady and ex-Senator Stephen W. Dorsey of Arkansas, formerly chairman of the Post Office Committee and secretary of the Republican National Committee in the recent campaign, who headed a group holding some Star Route contracts. Garfield inherited a mess that would not quietly go away.

The volatile situation was aggravated by Secretary Blaine. Here was a golden opportunity to erase the stigma of corruption from the Republican party and simultaneously eliminate a political foe on whom he placed a great deal of responsibility for his own sullied image in the public eye (T. Smith, I, 59.) Garfield wavered between Secretary Blaine, to whom he owed the nomination, and Dorsey and his friend Ingersoll, to whom he largely owed the election. During the campaign Garfield had written to Dorsey, "I rely greatly on your equipoise" (Sept. 29, 1880, T. Smith, II, 1035). On January 21, 1880, a high-riding Dorsey boldly laid down a course of action for Garfield. The selection of Blaine as first minister was a *fait accompli*. It could not be reversed, but perhaps his influence might be curbed. "No President has ever done a wiser thing than you

PUT NOT YOUR TRUST IN PRESIDENTS.

R.G.I.:—Where do I come in, Jim?
J.G.B.:—Guess you'll have to stay out, Bob.
You're not quite orthodox enough for us.
(National Weekly)

have done in placing Mr. Blaine at the head of your Cabinet. And no one ever has done or could do as unwise a thing as to permit him to have a hand in selecting the other members of your cabinet or in any degree to control it after it is selected. The pleasantest satisfaction I have in the midst of all the rumor and newspaper talk is the fact that I believe that General Garfield will be President himself and not Mr. Blaine" (T. Smith, II, 1058). From the other side Blaine accused Dorsey of plotting to control the office of the Second Assistant Postmaster General, "through which channel, in my judgment, there are cunning preparations being made to steal half a million a year during your administration" (Blaine to Garfield, Feb. 22, 1880, T. Smith, II, 1085). Sorely troubled over the issue a generous-minded president noted in his journal on May 14, 1881, "I was kept up until midnight by business connected with Dorsey's troubles. I have great sympathy with him and some doubts" (T. Smith, II, 1160).

The spur to prosecution was a confession made by M. I. Rerdell, a financial clerk to Dorsey, allegedly made to Thomas James and Wayne MacVeagh, Garfield's postmaster general and attorney general, professing intimate knowledge of a conspiracy between Dorsey and Brady against the federal Treasury. Ingersoll came to the defense of his friend Dorsey, with whom he had campaigned for the Garfield-Arthur ticket in Indiana. Rerdell recanted. On June twenty-eighth Garfield noted in his journal, "Dorsey and Ingersoll came and read me an affidavit by Rerdell recanting his pretended revelations to James and MacVeagh. I told them that he confessed himself a liar and a scoundrel and I did not believe a word of his stuff against James and MacVeagh" (T. Smith, II, 1162).

On July second Ingersoll spent the evening from eight to ten in conference with Garfield. In the morning, when they were to resume discussion, Ingersoll was late, driving up at the White House just in time to greet the president on his way to the trains to keep an out-of-town engagement. Ingersoll returned home. Some fifteen minutes later there were cries in the street: "The President has been shot! The President has been shot!" Hurrying to the depot Ingersoll was admitted to the upstairs room where the wounded president lay stretched out on the floor, several doctors ministering to him. Garfield recognized Ingersoll, they exchanged a few words, and Ingersoll returned home.

A stunned nation was agog with sorrow, anxiety, prayers, rumors. What did it all mean? Soon reporters were on the Ingersoll trail. Had he had any contact with Charles Guiteau, the assailant? Were Vice President Arthur and ex-Senator Conkling behind Guiteau? Would prayers be beneficial to the president?

Yes, Ingersoll answered, Guiteau, a complete stranger, had called upon him a few months ago seeking a letter to Secretary Blaine in support of his application for a consulate. Since Guiteau said that he was a personal friend of Senator Logan of Illinois, Ingersoll told him that if he could bring a testimonial from Logan he would do what he could for him. Guiteau could bring no such testimonial. During a later encounter Guiteau asked whether Ingersoll was biased against him because he had followed Ingersoll's lecture route in New England and had proclaimed from several platforms that the hot jaws of hell were waiting for the arch-infidel. "God bless you," Ingersoll had answered, "I never knew that you had said anything about me." A week before the shooting Guiteau had made a touch to him for twenty-five dollars. Ingersoll had turned him down.

Would prayers have any value? He would not brush them away. Prayer in general might help the person praying by putting him or her in a frame of mind to accept disappointment, and might benefit the president by the goodwill that it manifested. Beyond that it was useless. If God, who knows all, had wanted to get into the act he should have done something when he was allowing Guiteau to spend his time beating hotel bills; he should have made Guiteau turn the pistol on himself. Ministers were making reckless and absurd interpretations of the event—that it was a divine judgment against the spread of infidelity, that ignorant people and foreigners should not be allowed to vote, that there was too much religious liberty in general. In fact Guiteau was an educated man, a native-born American and a Christian, a member of the YMCA and a follower of the Reverends Dwight Moody and Ira Sankey.

The rumor that Vice President Arthur and ex-Senator Conkling were behind Guiteau? That was mischievous nonsense. The shooting of the president was the lone deed of a disappointed and malicious man.

A reporter who interviewed Ingersoll at home was liberal in praise of the Ingersoll family and Ingersoll's role in the national crisis:

> An hour or two spent in the attractive parlors of the Ingersoll homestead, around that rare group, lends a newer meaning to the idea of home and a more secure beauty to the fact of family life. During the past exciting three weeks Colonel Ingersoll has been a busy man. He holds

no office. No position could lend him an additional crown and even recognition is no longer necessary. But it has been well that amid the first fierce fury of anger and excitement, and the subsequent more bitter if not so noble factions' suspicions a counsel has been able to hold so positive a balance. (*Sunday Gazette*, Washington, D.C., July 21, 1881; *Works*, VIII, 100).

Garfield lingered for eleven weeks and died on September nineteenth. Blaine's funeral eulogy of the slain president is one of the great unknown masterpieces of American oratory. As far as Star Route was concerned, the new president, a protege of Conkling and intimate of Dorsey, was on the spot. As vice-president elect, at a Delmonico's victory banquet honoring Dorsey, he had imbibed too much and had blurted out a grateful compliment to Dorsey for the judicious distribution of party funds in the Indiana campaign. President Arthur had no viable alternative to continuing with the Star Route prosecution. The juggernaut ground on to indictment and trial.

The first Star Route trial went from June 1, 1882, to September 15, 1882, ending in acquittal of one minor defendant, conviction of two other minor defendants, and a hung jury on the remaining six defendents. The second lasted from December 4, 1882, to June 4, 1883, and ended in acquittal of all the defendants. (Since the entire Star Route case was one extravanganza incorporating related and repeated parts, we shall consider it later as one event. Meanwhile we shall review Ingersoll's other activities during the early eighties. Some of these activities, insofar as they impinged on Star Route proceedings, were incidentally intended by him to down-play the importance of the case. It was not, as the prosecution alleged, the greatest case ever, upon which—that is, with the defendants found guilty—the fate of the Republic depended. It was just another run-of-the-mill criminal case in which the jury should exercise its civic mission of independence and resist the pressure to magnify it to the detriment of the fellow citizens before them. Life went on as usual in and out of Judge Wylie's courtroom.)

In the early eighties Ingersoll sallied forth from time to time, for a day or several days, and even for a whole month between the Star Route trials, to preach his "gospel" over the eastern half of the country (excepting the South). He carried in his baggage two new lectures—"Some Reasons Why" and "The Great Infidels."

In "Some Reasons Why" he struck out against the bigotry that resulted from having a closed mind on religion. "Whenever a man believes that he has the exact truth from God, there is in that man no spirit of compromise. He has not the modesty born of the imperfections of human nature; he has the arrogance of theological certainty and the tyranny born of ignorant assurance. Believing himself to be the slave of God, he imitates his master, and of all tyrants the worst is a slave in power" (*Works*, II, 274).

In "The Great Infidels" Ingersoll was optimistic that we have "passed midnight" in the great struggle between fact and faith, science and superstition (*Works*, III, 307). He derided what he called "the appeal to the cemetery," by which the orthodox contended that revealed religion was true because great men long since dead had believed it. "Facts have no pedigree, logic has no heraldry, and the living should not be awed by the mistakes of the dead" (326). He lauded the great men of the ages—men like the Emperor Julian, Bruno, Spinoza, Hume, Voltaire, Diderot, Paine—who dared to challenge orthodoxy, serving intellectual freedom and the pursuit of truth (344–384).

A person reading "The Great Infidels" in the age of the atomic bomb, feeling briefly immersed in the naive optimism of the nineteenth century, may be shaken out of such condescension by this prophetic passage:

> It may be that the fabric of our civilization will crumbling fall into unmeaning chaos and to formless dust, where oblivion broods and even memory forgets. Perhaps the blind Samson of some imprisoned force, released by thoughtless chance, may so wreck and strand the world that man, in stress and strain of want and fear, will shudderingly crawl back to savage and barbaric night. The time may come in which this thrilled and throbbing earth, shorn of all life, will in its soundless orbit wheel a barren star, on which the light will fall as fruitlessly as falls the gaze of love upon the cold, pathetic face of death. (332)

Finally, in words of exquisite beauty whether one believes them or not: "The infidels have been the brave and thoughtful men; the flower of all the world; the pioneers and heralds of the blessed day of liberty and love; the generous spirits of the unworthy past; the seers and prophets of our race; the great chivalrous souls, proud victors on the battlefields of thought; the creditors of all the years to be" (394).

By 1881, Ingersoll had made peace with his opponents in the freethought movement and was ready to lead it again. On April 11, 1881, in Boston Robert and Eva quietly entered Paine Hall to attend a lecture on freethought by George Chainey. Their presence becoming known, the crowd burst into a rapturous ovation. After the lecture the chairman, Horace Seaver, called upon Ingersoll for a few words. For some fifteen minutes he stirred his fellow believers with a millennial vision of a world freed of superstition. That night he addressed several thousand at the Boston Theater on "Some Reasons Why" he did not believe in Christianity. He inveighed against the savagery of church-dominated societies as if he felt the agonies of their victims in his own flesh. "Hitherto," wrote a young enthusiast named Samuel Putnam, "he has wielded the sword of Saladin, but now he struck with the hammer of Thor" (*Truth Seeker*, April 23, 1881).

The people who flocked around Ingersoll, if not fully attuned to his preachment, left little to be desired in their welcome. He was famous and popular. They swarmed about him at the hotel, plied him with compliments and questions, allowing him no time for rest and hardly any time for his daily letters to the folks back home. He loved it all. "I have had 100 callers this morning. I started this letter in Saginaw. Fellow cried out 'Bus' and I had to stop" (Nov. 10, 1882, L.C.). On lecture days special trains brought in crowds from points as far as a hundred miles away. At five o'clock they were already assembled on the sidewalk outside the auditorium for an eight o'clock lecture. They passed their time by perusing religious tracts thrust upon them free or Ingersoll lectures at five cents a copy, then pushed their way to the box office, only to find quite often that all the seats and even standing room were sold out, that speculators were hawking tickets in the lobby at two or three times the regular price. When the doors of the auditorium opened, the standing-room ticket holders would charge in, occupying all the aisles in seconds, causing traffic jams. Order came as the crowd quieted down in place and awaited the new revelation.

Who were these people? Reporters repeated that they were a cross section of America, although by and large of literate America. In New York: "They were eminently respectable and clearly of the very best inhabitants of the city. No greater compliment could have been paid to Colonel Ingersoll or any other lecturer than the crowd who besieged Booth's Theater last night" (*Evening Express*, April 25, 1881). In Chicago: "The audience was a representative one, because in addition to a large number of recognized free thinkers and liberal-minded citizens, there were present many men whose names are household words in Chicago, and who are conspicuous in the vestries, prayer-meetings, and Sunday schools of the churches" (*Chicago Times*, May 21, 1881). In Kansas City: "It was not a fashionable, but very noticeably a very representative popular audience, just such as may be imagined Col. Ingersoll would be particularly pleased to address. Two thousand people and more of all creeds and nationalities were there, and paid the closest and most rapt attention to every word that fell from the speaker's lips" (*Kansas City Times*, Nov. 20, 1882).

Such were the Ingersoll audiences as seen by the daily metropolitan press. Other eyes perceived them differently. The devil's henchman could lure only the scum of the earth. For example: "The audience of Col. Ingersoll, when he gets up a tirade against the Bible, reminds one of the old adage that 'birds of a feather flock together.' All the riff-raff of society—profane men and bad women, thieves, and liars, and drunkards, and debauchees, and adulterers, and sportsmen, and fast women, and sensual pleasure-seekers, and apostates from churches—all rush to hear him, because bad men and abandoned women willingly believe those things they desire to be true" (*American Christian Review*, Cincinnati, Ohio, quoted in *Truth Seeker*, April 28, 1883). (There is another old adage: "All looks yellow to the jaundiced eye.")

Most of the audience was under the Ingersoll spell. Some looked about with uneasy and absent-minded expressions, some hissed softly now and then, some made early exits. Rarely did a heckler interrupt. In St. Joseph, Missouri, Ingersoll was pounding away at the biblical adjuration to unclasp the arms of a wife and fly to the desert for salvation. A Mr. Miller jumped to his feet. Would the speaker condemn a man who left wife and child to fight for his country? "You just sit down," said Ingersoll, "and I'll tell you. I am ready to cast my lot with my fellow-men and go to war to fight for my country. For my country needs my help, but God does not. He can fight his own battles." Miller persisted that the country of the Christian was in danger. Ingersoll replied, "Then let God take care of it" (*Herald*, Nov. 23, 1882).

Reporters everywhere described the man and his oratory in loving detail, with no caricatures. A reporter for the *New York Sun* wrote at length about his round head, his fat face, his thinning hair, his bright dark eyes. He was more theatrical than Beecher or Talmage, the reporter continued, the mobility of the upper part of his body, the movements of his forehead, and his nods punctuating his emphatic points. He noted the "Honor bright!" and "It won't do"; how he peopled the stage with imaginary dummies, like one of our primitive ancestors in the dugout, and from time to time pointed to them in their imaginary places. "Mr. Ingersoll's voice is soft and melodious. His manner and movements upon the stage, with his wonderful nod, are the elements of his success as a popular orator." (*New York Sun*, April 3, 1881, quoted in the *Chicago Journal*).

Reporters were concerned about his health. He seemed to be aging, putting on too much weight, slowing down physically, though he could still mesmerize audiences with lectures two or more hours long. After a day's journey on the rails from Grand Rapids he arrived at Indianapolis at 7 P.M. with hardly time for the horse taxi to bring him speedily to the hotel for a change of clothes. He departed for Chicago at 11:00, lectured there the next afternoon and then was on his way to St. Paul. A reporter offered him wholesome but useless advice. "Seeing that there is but one world for man it would seem the part of wisdom to go slow and make the most of it. But no man who is of any account ever does that" (*The Ages*, Indianapolis, Aug. 18, 1882).

Ingersoll was the most accessible of public figures, and reporters knew that a session with him was good for a story in tomorrow morning's paper. Typically in St. Joseph a reporter tapped timidly on the door and stuck his head in. Ingersoll was lying on the bed smoking a cigar after a long day's journey on the rails. He extended an arm full length for a firm handshake and said, "How d' ye do, Mr. *Herald*? Sit down, sit down, make yourself at home." Would he answer a few questions? "Fire away!" (Nov. 23, 1882).

What did he think of the political situation asked one reporter? "I am not a politician," he protested. "The gentlemen who have the offices must hold them, and the gentlemen who want the offices must get them. I belong to neither class. My principal business is to destroy the superstitions of the world—to augment the liberty of man and to add a little to the sum of human joy. It is part of my mission to civilize the orthodox, to put out the cruel fires of hell, and to laugh at the attacks of the doctors of divinity" (*Brooklyn Sunday Eagle*, April 21, 1881, Special Correspondent to the *Eagle*, Washington, April 23.) After every political campaign he had resolved to make no more political speeches, and this time he positively meant it. "There is no principle to fight for. The Democrats are doing all they can to hide their past, and the Republicans never tire of reading their epitaph. The Democrats are ashamed of the record, and the Republicans say, 'We were so good then that everybody should vote for us now.' It will be difficult to find a dividing line in the next election" (*New York Herald*, Aug. 14, 1882). To a select meeting of Republican leaders in a Chicago hotel he called for a new leadership in the party (*Inter-Ocean*, Nov. 13, 1882). When Senator Conkling, battling with President Garfield over patronage, resigned his office in a quixotic test of popular support, Ingersoll sided with Garfield and presidential prerogative. He said that Conkling was like a man who had swallowed poison and then would gladly pay all his wealth for a stomach pump, that in spite of personal honesty and talent Conkling had authored no legislation of any consequence and was "a swill politician." His office gone and beyond retrieving he was of no use politically beyond breaking a tie in the general election (*Brooklyn Sunday Eagle*, Nov. 24, 1881).

Ingersoll chatted with reporters and others in the smoking car of a train going through Missouri. After enthusing over the beauty of the sunset and the glorious future of the West he discussed a man in the news of the day, Frank James. The junior brother of the late Jesse James had recently surrendered to the authorities. Ingersoll's love of humanity fell short of persons like Charles Guiteau and the James boys. He opined that Frank "ought to have just one more bullet go through him that would make a hole one inch in diameter. He ought to be hung, and even that would be too good for him" (*Kansas City Journal*, Nov. 21, 1882). This unfriendly remark reaching Frank in jail, that gentleman retorted, "Any man who would assail the sacred book would dare do anything," adding, "the Lord is my helper. I care not what men shall do or say against me. Ingersoll is doing unspeakable injury to this nation. He is now sowing the seeds of iniquity in the minds of our youth" (*Kansas City Journal*, Nov. 27, 1882). "The champion blasphemer" was proud of his enemies, and of none could he be more proud than the assassin Guiteau and the train robber Frank James.

Not that Guiteau and the younger James were typical of Ingersoll's critics. Some adherents of orthodoxy, men and women ordinarily of goodwill, took up arms against him. This was not debate but vilification, outcries for boycott, suppression, imprisonment. Ingersoll laughed. All this was grimly funny. His off-the-cuff rejoinders crackled with serene wit.

In February 1881 Chief Judge Comegys of the Delaware Supreme Court called upon a grand jury to indict Ingersoll under blasphemy laws dating back to colonial days. The grand jury declined but warned Ingersoll that if he lectured again in Delaware he would be subject to prosecution. Ingersoll scoffed. Surely there were some good and sensible people in Delaware who had travelled in other states, heard Republican speeches, and did not subscribe to the taboos of 1740. He had heard, he said, that the Lord had originally equipped oysters with legs but had to take the legs off when it became evident that the people of Delaware would not run for anything (*Truth Seeker*, Feb. 26, 1881). To a group of reporters gathered around his fireside he expatiated on the implications of the blasphemy laws. Since God is conditionless and perfect, he could not be harmed by anybody or be displeased by any comment. Who was orthodox? Judge Comegys's ancestors had been Catholic; did they sin when they became Presbyterian? And the judge's more remote ancestors were tattooed savages; were they right in condemning "any gentleman" who did not bear a tattooed snake on his body? "The root, foundation, germ, and cause of nearly all religious persecution is the idea that some certain belief is necessary for salvation." The discussion or monologue over, he lighted a cigar and passed the box around. "I guess you have had enough for this evening" (*Truth Seeker*, March 12, 1881, quoted from *Brooklyn Eagle*). Nonetheless, thereafter Ingersoll stayed away from Delaware. He was not courting martyrdom.

On Sunday, May 31, 1881, a Brooklyn minister, the Reverend Dr. Buckley, speaking from the pulpit on "The Christian's Liberty and the Infidel's License," denounced Ingersoll's recent "irreverent and infidel" lecture on liberty under the auspices of the Central Young Men's Republican Club. He declared that the lecture, coming in Lent and the season of revival meetings, affronted "the Christian sentiment of the city," and called upon all members of the Club who laid any claim to decency to resign. The Club snapped back at the Reverend Buckley, and Ingersoll had his say. A Brooklyn reporter found him in his office going through the morning mail. "The colonel," noted the reporter, "is about the busiest man in Washington, is very quick of perception and in dispatch of business, and never loses his temper." Between instructing his clerks and answering telephone calls Ingersoll commented expansively on the Reverend Buckley and the requirements of Lent. (Was he prepared for this opportunity, perhaps?) "If they think that there is some subtle relation between hunger and heaven, or that faith depends upon and is strengthened by famine, or that veal during Lent is the enemy of virtue, or that beef breeds blasphemy, while fish breeds faith—of course, all that is nothing to me. They have the right to say that vice depends on victuals, sanctity on soup, religion on rice, and chastity on cheese, but they have no right to say that a lecture on liberty is an insult to them because they are hungry." Most of the world's troubles, the overweight speaker who had tried fasting hazarded, are caused by the nasty disposition that comes from self-imposed hunger and poor cooking.

> Your good cook is a civilizer, and without good food, well prepared, intellectual progress is simply impossible. Most of the orthodox creeds are born of bad cooking. Bad food produced dyspepsia, and dyspepsia produced Calvinism. Calvinism is the cancer of Christianity. Oatmeal is responsible for the worst features of Scotch Presbyterianism. Half-cooked beans account for the religion of the Puritans. Fried bacon and saleratus biscuit underline the doctrine of State rights. Lent is a mistake, fasting is a blunder, and bad cooking a crime. [How could his lecture interfere with revivals which did not have enough life in them to be killed?] Still, I think that if all the persons engaged in the revivals had spent the same length of time in cleaning the streets the good would have been more apparent. (*Brooklyn Sunday Eagle*, April 24, 1881, Special Correspondent to the *Eagle*, Washington, April 23)

Early in April 1881 the Reverend Isaac J. Lansing of old Meriden in Connecticut sermonized against Ingersoll for personal and intellectual faults and prevailed upon the managers of the Opera House to breach their contract and deny him their building. A reporter in New Haven, where Ingersoll was lecturing, provided a rebuttal platform. Ingersoll denied that he ever favored circulating obscene matter through the mails. He would be glad to debate any authorized minister of standing. What kind of man did he think the Reverend Lansing was? "I would take him to be a Christian. He talks like one and he acts like one. If Christianity is right, Lansing is right. If salvation depends upon belief, and if unbelievers are to be eternally damned, then an infidel has no right to speak. He should not be allowed to murder the souls of his fellow men. Lansing does the best he knows how. He thinks that God hates an unbeliever and like God Lansing knows that he has the right to slander a man whom God is to eternally damn." Lansing has called him a wolf with fangs sharpened by three hundred dollars a night to "tear the lambs of his flock." "All I have to say is, that I often get three times that amount, and sometimes much more. I guess his 'lambs' can take care of themselves. I am not very fond of mutton anyway. . . . The idea that he is a shepherd— that he is on guard—is simply preposterous. He has few sheep in his congregation that know as little on the wolf question as he does. He ought to know that his sheep support him—his sheep protect him, and without the sheep poor Lansing would be devoured by the wolves himself." He would not sue the managers of the Opera House but he might pay Lansing for the advertisement.

The reporter turned to general topics. Did any clergymen denounce him during the recent presidential campaign? Some did, but they would not if they had been running for office on the Republican ticket. "What is most needed in public men, Colonel?" "Hearts and brains." He was a Republican because he believed in liberty. of the body and an infidel because he believed in liberty of the mind. He was really not a bad fellow, and if Lansing knew him better they would surely be friends. Would the world be a better place because of disbelief in the Bible? "Yes. If any man really believes that God once upheld slavery; that he commanded soldiers to kill women and babes; that he believed in polygamy; that he persecuted for opinion's sake; that he will punish forever and that he hates an unbeliever, the effect in my judgment will be bad. It always has been bad. This belief built the dungeons of the Inquisition. This belief made the Puritan manacle the Quaker, and this belief has raised the devil with Mr. Lansing." A frequent question, always good for a quip: Would there be a millennium, and if so where would it start? "It will probably start in Meriden, as I have been informed that Lansing is going to leave." Is there anything else he could say that would make good reading? "Yes, goodbye" (*New Haven Sunday Union*, April 10, 1881).

The time had long since passed when the press could be cowed by the church. After Ingersoll had taken the town by storm, the *Omaha Bee* canvassed the local clergy for analyses of his popularity. The responses fell into three general categories: curiosity, desire to listen to eloquence and wit, and sinfulness seeking escape from its consequences. The *Bee* rebuked the ministers. "It is a little singular," it objected, "that no one has suggested that a large measure of Col. Ingersoll's popularity might arise from the fact that many of the intelligent and thinking public are dissatisfied with the character of the pulpit itself." Perhaps the pulpit was losing its grip on the community because of the incompetence of the ministry and the intolerance of new ideas. "The fault does not entirely lie with the people that Col. Ingersoll attracts—two thousand persons every night that he cares to lecture, and vulgar curiosity is a shallow explanation of the success of the arch-infidel" (Quoted in *Truth Seeker*, Dec. 30, 1882).

Beginning in August 1881 the *North American Review* published a debate between Ingersoll and Jeremiah Black, who had been attorney general under Buchanan, entitled "The Christian Religion." Black took a self-contradictory position—that the goodness of God is a given and not debatable and that its existence may be proved in debate. Ingersoll's contribution was mainly a scissors-and-paste job from his lectures, especially from "Some Reasons Why."

On January 8, 1882, occurred the funeral of Harry Miller, little son of Ingersoll's freethinking friend Detective George O. Miller of the Washington police force. Ingersoll was among the mourners at the gravesite. The mother sobbed. There was an awkward silence. The undertaker motioned to Ingersoll to say something. "Does Mrs. Miller desire it?" Yes. Then "in a voice of exquisite cadence," as the ubiquitous reporter said, Ingersoll, standing with head uncovered as the drizzle fell, spoke.

"How vain it is to gild a grief with words." Yet there need be no fear at a grave, the common fate of all. "From the wondrous tree of life," he said with poignant sweetness, "the buds and blossoms fall with ripened fruit, and in the common bed of earth patriarchs and babes sleep side by side." We do not know whether death is an end or a beginning, nor who is the more fortunate, the babe dying in its mother's arms or the aged tottering toward the end. Every cradle asks, "Whence?" and every grave "Whither?" and neither the poor barbarian nor the robed priest can answer, but no man is warranted in predicting an afterlife of pain and tears for anybody. It may be that death gives all there is of worth to life, for the knowledge of death cultivates love and weeds out selfishness and hate. "And I had rather live and love where death is king than have eternal life where love is not." Hearts were breaking, but in the common needs and duties of life grief would lessen day by day and the grave become at last a place of rest and peace. "The dead do not suffer. If they live again, their lives will surely be as good as ours. We have no fear. We are all children of the same mother, and the same fate awaits us all. We, too, have our religion, and it is this: Help for the living—Hope for the dead" (*Works*, XII, 339–340). The reporter concluded, "His invocation thrilled his hearers with awe, each eye that had previously dimmed with tears brightened, sobs became hushed" (*Washington Post*, Jan. 9, 1882; *Works*, XII, "At a Child's Grave," 395).

In the spring of 1882 Ingersoll issued his *Six Interviews on Talmage*. T. DeWitt Talmage, Presbyterian minister in Brooklyn and a leading exponent of the evangelical point of view, was a vehement critic of Ingersoll as "the champion blasphemer of America" (Talmage, "Ingersollian Infidelity Confuted," 35).[1] The *Interview* form illustrated Ingersoll's usual method of composition. His secretary would write: "Nearly everything he gave for publication was dictated. His legal briefs and papers, his magazine and review articles, press interviews, monographs, speeches, lectures—everything he wished to say—were delivered in faultless form through the portals of his facile lips. Wherever he happened to be,—in his office, at his home, on the boat, in the train, in the cab rolling through noisy streets, sitting, standing, reclining—he spoke the splendid words that the stenographer's art reproduced for him" (Baker, *An Intimate View*, 48–49).

In defending himself Ingersoll attacked the intellectual system espoused by Talmage. To the argument from authority, the argument from the "cemetery"—great men have believed in Christianity, therefore it is true—Ingersoll replied that in the realm of reason there are no serfs and no masters, that every man must think for himself. What is blasphemy? Every religious pioneer, including the Presbyterian, was considered a blasphemer in his own time. The Moslem considers the Christian a blasphemer. There could not be any blasphemy against God, who is infinite and perfect and cannot be injured. The real blasphemy is something else. "Any man who knowingly speaks in favor of injustice is a blasphemer. Whoever wishes

Birthplace of Robert G. Ingersoll, Dresden, N.Y. (E. C. Smith, *The Life and Reminiscences of Robert G. Ingersoll*)

One of Reverend Ingersoll's churches in Hume, Allegany County, N.Y. (Courtesy of David Henley)

Attorney General Ingersoll of Illinois, 1867-68 (Courtesy of Illinois State Historical Society)

Reverend John Ingersoll (E. C. Smith, *The Life and Reminiscences of Robert G. Ingersoll*)

The extended Ingersoll family, 1892: (*standing, left to right*) unidentified nurse, Sue Sharkey, Maud Ingersoll, Eva Ingersoll Brown, Walston Hill Brown, R.G.I., Sue (Parker) Farrell; (*seated*) Eva Farrell, Mrs. Harriette Parker, Eva (Ingersoll) Brown, Eva (Parker) Ingersoll. (Library of Congress)

Christian or Sceptic—The Tug of War. (*Chic*, undated)

THE TRUTH SEEKER

A JOURNAL OF FREETHOUGHT AND REFORM.

Vol. 15. No. 35. | PUBLISHED WEEKLY. | New York, Saturday, September 1, 1888. | 28 LAFAYETTE PL. | $3.00 per year

Here is our Goliath.—Bring on your David. (*The Truth Seeker*, Sept. 1, 1888)

Bob Ingersoll, the "Illustrious Infidel." (*Puck*, undated)

(*Top*) Colonel Ingersoll delivers the oration at Whitman's funeral. (*Inset*) The coffin. (*Center*) The funeral ceremonies. (*Lower left*) Whitman's tomb. (*Lower right*) At Whitman's residence. (*Frank Leslie's Weekly*, April 14, 1892)

May 9, 1899 (Dresden Publishing Co.)

A SUNDAY SHOW.—PROFIT FOR PAGAN AND PREACHER.

In this cartoon Talmage is depicted as Ingersoll's punching bag.

(Puck, *May 3, 1882, Library of Congress)*

to destroy liberty of thought, the honest expression of ideas, is a blasphemer" (*Works*, V, 52).

The natural evils of the universe, the evils of society, and the uselessness of prayer deny the existence of a good God. "I prefer to say that the universe is all the God there is. I prefer to make no being responsible. I prefer to say: If the naked are [to be] clothed, man must clothe them; if the hungry are [to be] fed, man must feed them. I prefer to rely upon human endeavor, upon human intelligence, upon the heart and brain of man" (49).

Ingersoll ridiculed Talmage's attempt to rationalize Bible stories in order that they be consistent with belief in the literal inerrance of Scripture. "He [Talmage] could have explained it [the Jonah story], called it an allegory, poetical license, a child of the oriental imagination, a symbol, a parable, a poem, a dream, a legend, a myth, a divine figure, or a great truth wrapped in the rags and shreds and patches of seeming falsehood. His efforts to belittle the miracle, to suggest that Jonah traveled in the mouth instead of the stomach—to suggest that Jonah took deck passage, or lodged in the forecastle instead of the cabin or steerage—to suggest motion as a means of avoiding digestion, is a serious theological blunder, and may cause the loss of many souls" (105).

Talmage had accused him of seeking to abolish the last best hope of man. But what hope could there be in a religion which damns most of the human race to eternal hell-fire? Talmage had said that infidelity lead to the penitentiary and perdition. Not at all. "My creed is this: 1. Happiness is the only good. 2. The way to be happy is to make others happy. Other things being equal, that man is happiest who is nearest just—who is truthful, merciful, and intelligent—in other words, the one who lives in accordance with the conditions of life. 3. The time to be happy is now, and the place to be happy is here."

Talmage had said that a Christian could be happy in heaven while his parents were suffering in hell. No, said Ingersoll. He would rather be in hell so that his parents might be in heaven, though even the prospect of heaven itself was a little dismaying. "I cannot truthfully say that I look forward with any degree of joy to meeting with Haggai and Habakkuk, with Jeremiah, Nemehiah, Obadiah, Zechariah, or Stephaniah; with Ezekiel, Micah, or Malachi, or even with Jonah. From what little I have read of their writings, I have not formed a very high opinion of the social qualities of these gentlemen" (154). He would rather be in hell with his loved ones and Bruno, Spinoza, and Humboldt.

Talmage retorted to freethought by smearing Ingersoll personally. He had accused Ingersoll of favoring the circulation of obscene matter through the mails and of dishonoring his parents by repudiating the religion of his childhood. He cited Ingersoll's failure to win the Illinois gubernatorial race in 1868 as an encouraging object-lesson in the war against infidelism. In response Ingersoll revealed his actual record on obscenity and praised his father as a good and honest man who taught him to think for himself. In politics he would rather be honest and lose than hypocritical and win. He warned against religious tests for public óffice. "Mr. Talmage makes the serious mistake of placing the Bible above the laws and Constitution of his country. He places Jehovah above humanity. Such men are not entirely safe citizens of any republic" (305).

A national mass meeting was planned to celebrate Decoration Day, May 30, 1882. As the orator par excellence of American patriotism Ingersoll was a natural if not the only choice for speaker, so the arrangements committee offered the honor to him. The first Star Route trial would begin two days later, on June first. As defense counsel, Ingersoll would be deep in preliminary motions and trial preparations. Nevertheless, he accepted. The anticipated controversy flared up. The *New York Sun* printed letters (reproduced in the *National Republican*, Washington, D.C., May 30, 1882), one calling the selection an insult to the great masses of the people and the other asking the critics whether they had objected to Ingersoll as a soldier in 1860 and volunteered to go in his place. Ingersoll invited the committee to reconsider. They did so and unanimously agreed that he was their man. Again he accepted. The committee chairman could only exclaim, "Glory Hallelujah!" (Telegrams, L.C.).

The Academy of Music, where Ingersoll and Beecher had shaken hands, was lavishly decorated with patriotic symbols, the first balcony in blue, the second in white, the third in red. High above center stage hung an enormous American flag. As the curtain rose, the audience beheld an assemblage of generals and admirals resplendent in brass and gold lace, and some distinguished civilians, among them Carl Schurz, August Belmont, Charles Scribner, Jesse Seligman, and George William Curtis. Generals Bainum and McQuade, nominally the temporary and permanent chairmen, entered the stage and took seats front and center, and then the principal guests entered and arranged themselves: Attorney General Brewster, Secretary of the Treasury Folger, General Hancock, President Arthur, and General Grant; and ex-Senator Conkling, Reverend J. P. Newman, and Mayor Grace. Ingersoll entered, manuscript in hand. The crowd burst into a cheer. As he moved to the lectern someone in a box yelled, "Three cheers for Ingersoll," which were lustily given.

Without introduction Ingersoll began, a bit huskily and with some constraint, but soon warmed up. His Decoration Day speech is one of the great speeches of the greatest speaker of the age. He celebrated in mellifluous words the eternal struggle for freedom and the heroes who fought and died for the American ideal. The heroes of the Revolution were all gone. "The last has been mingled with the earth and nearly all are sleeping now in unmarked graves, and some beneath the leaning, crumbling stones from which the names have been effaced by Time's irreverent and relentless hands" (*Works*, IX, 423). The Declaration of Independence was "the chart and compass of all human rights," but the Constitution departed from its principles, substituting "white" for "all." As the nation prospered, its cornerstones were crumbling. "But Pity pointed to the scarred and bleeding backs of slaves; Mercy heard the sobs of mothers reft of babes; and Justice held aloft the scales, in which one drop of blood shed by a master's lash outweighed a nation's gold" (428).

He gave a nation's thanks to the abolitionists, who dared to fight against the monstrous crime of slavery. In language anticipating President Kennedy he said, "Mere politicians wish the country to do something for them. True patriots desire to do something for their country" (429). The Civil War had been uniquely a revolt not by the oppressed but by the oppressors. He glorified the Union army, whose commander-in-chief was sitting behind him. "Let us proudly remember that in our time the greatest, the grandest, the noblest army of the world fought not to enslave, but to free; not to destroy but to save; not for conquest but for conscience; not only for us but for every land and every race" (430).

The triumphant American flag proclaimed equal rights, universal education, government by consent, a responsible citizenry, an honest ballot box, the perpetual right of peaceful revolution, the right of every citizen to protection, and the government as the arbiter of simple justice between the weak and the strong, between labor and capital. Finally, in a most moving fashion: "There is no language to express the debts we owe, the love we bear, to all the dead who died for us. Words are but barren sounds. We can but stand beside their graves, and in the hush and silence feel what speech has never told. They fought, they died; and for the first time since man has kept a record of events, the heavens bent above and domed a land without a serf, a servant, or a slave" (434).

After the first Star Route trial, which lasted practically all summer, Ingersoll went on an extensive lecture tour. On November twenty-fourth he was regaling some visitors in his hotel suite in Lincoln, Nebraska, when suddenly his manager rushed into the room to report that an attractive offer had come for an early lecture in Covington, Kentucky. Ingersoll thought for a moment, then said, "No, I cannot do it. I promised the folks that I would be home December first, and I'm going to do it." Couldn't he meet the family in Cincinnati? He shook his head. "Grandma [Parker] couldn't stand the trip, and the others would be too tired. No, I wouldn't make another engagement that would keep me from reaching home on time, not if I were assured $1,000. Why, there's Grandma and Wilt [Clint?] and Sue all waiting for me, so they'd be so disappointed, and I'd be disappointed too" (Correspondence, *Omaha Daily Herald*, Nov. 26, 1882). He did not mention the second Star Route trial, scheduled to start on Monday, December fourth. Not to worry about that!

One of the persons whom he would disappoint on the way home was Mr. Debs of Terre Haute, who had hoped for a lecture date on the tour. Debs wrote, "We heard you at Indianapolis the other night, and your lecture was the grandest thing we ever heard. Oh, that every living human being could have heard it—the world would have grown a thousand per cent better in one night" (Nov. 26, 1882, L.C.). How sweet it was!

Eager though he was to return to Washington, Ingersoll was not in a panic about it. He always appeared the most relaxed of men; he could not be rushed into disregarding the amenities. Heading home from Chicago, he responded to an epistle from his niece Eva Farrell, about five years old. It was probably her first message out of school, her first letter to anybody, a big event in her life, and it required a substantial response commensurate with its importance. His letter, November 26 (L.C.), was published after his death in *The Truth Seeker* (Jan. 13, 1900). So far as I know, it has not been reproduced elsewhere.

My dear Miss Eva Farrell

I received your large letter. Two waiters brought it to the room on a large truck. I heard the wheels creak and the waiters grunt as they came along the hall. When they got into the room they turned the truck on one side and let the letter drop. You ought to have heard the windows rattle when the letter struck the floor. I then sent for a pickaxe to open the letter with. When I got it open it was so large that it covered the whole floor and the corners stuck out of the windows. I put on my glasses and walked all over it, and read as I walked. Hundreds of people came to see the letter, and they were all struck dumb with amazement. It cost me about $200 to get it out of the Post Office. After I read it I sold it the ragman to make paper with again, and he gave me $201, so I made a dollar after all. You must write again. I thank you for all your good news. I will see your mother in a few days. I send you a good large kiss and one for each of your dollies. Give my love to your mother and father and to the canary bird.

Your loving uncle,
Robert

While the second Star Route trial was going on from December 1882 to June 1883 Ingersoll implied time and again that it was not the be-all and end-all of his concern but just a piece of legal business of no extraordinary importance in his busy life. On January 14, 1883, as chairman of a lecture on Lincoln the lawyer, he stated his preference for men and direct experience of life itself as better sources .of education than the colleges that Lincoln and he had not attended, "where brickbats are polished and diamonds dimmed" (*National Republic,* Jan. 15, 1883). Two days later, regretfully declining an invitation to be "in clover" with his friends in the Clover Club of Philadelphia (where his arrivals were usually greeted with renditions of "In the Sweet Bye and Bye"), he played with words. Clover meant honey and cream and dreams of happy times; "of dimpled babes; of wholesome, loving wives; of honest men; of springs and brooks and violets, and all there is of stainless joy and peaceful human life." He went on. "A wonderful word is clover. Drop the 'c' and you have the happiest of mankind. Drop the 'r' and there remains the warm, deceitful bud that sweetens breath and keeps the peace in countless homes whose masters frequent clubs. After all, Bottom was right: Good hay, sweet hay, hath no fellow" (Jan. 16, 1883, *Letters*, 470).

Early in February 1883 two big social events took place on the same evening in Washington—President Arthur's reception of members of Congress and the Ingersolls' celebration of their twenty-first wedding anniversary. Most of the high and mighty of Washington moved from the White House across the street to Lafayette Square and joined nonpolitical friends in a company of some five hundred persons, who trooped through the Ingersoll home and felicitated the Colonel and his lady on a marital union which, as one reporter said, "was made in Heaven, if ever a match was made there." The reporter also noted, "The Colonel was in his glory, and everybody remarked how specially splendid he looked" (Special Correspondent to the *Gazette*, Erie, Pa., Feb. 15, 1883).

On April 14, 1883, Ingersoll's neighbor and friend, John G. Mills, a free-thinking radical journalist, died at the age of thirty-eight. On the next day Ingersoll delivered the funeral oration. (He could not comfort himself, but he could comfort others.) He saw the Sphinx gazing silently on the desert of death. Mills's heart had stopped in the May-time of life, but he had lived, he had loved, and had been loved. "This is enough. The longest life contains no more." His virtues as husband, father, neighbor, and honest man, built a monument of glory over his grave. "He was my friend. He will remain so; the living oft become estranged; the dead are true. He was not a Christian. He believed with Auguste Comte that the human race was the Supreme Being and he held that immortality exists in the eternal consequences of our acts . . . that every pure thought, every disinterested deed, hastens the harvest of universal good." All wish for happiness beyond this life. "Immortality is a word that all through the ages Hope has been whispering to Love." But the secret of the afterlife had never been told.

> Here success and failure are the same. The rag of wretchedness and the purple robe of power all difference and distinction lose in the democracy of death. Character survives, goodness lives, love is immortal. . . . What can we say of death? What can we say of the dead? Where they have gone, reason cannot go, and from thence revelation has not come. But let us believe that over the cradle Nature bends and smiles, and lovingly above the dead in benediction holds her outstretched hands. (*Works*, XII, 403)

This beautiful eulogy offended some ministers. How could this infamous infidel dare to officiate at last rites! He should have been stopped. A reporter asked Ingersoll, in his office, What did he think of all that? Pushing aside Star Route (and an accumulation of other legal business), Ingersoll responded thoroughly and bitterly. The clergy have always tried to preserve their livelihood by monopolizing births, marriages, and deaths, frightening away unbelief by denying these rituals to unbelievers. Mills had been an unbeliever. How could an orthodox Christian minister comfort the family of a man who, according to Christian dogma, was going to hell? Far from advocating infidel despair as against Christian assurance, Ingersoll was proud that he presented eternal hope for all mankind rather than eternal division between the saved and the damned. "The minister asks, 'What right have you to hope? It is sacrilegious in you.' But, whether the clergy like it or not, I shall always express my real opinion, and shall always be glad to say to those who mourn: 'There is in death, as I believe, nothing worse than sleep. Hope for as much better as you can. Under the seven-hued arch let the dead rest' " (*Washington Post,* April 30, 1883; *Works,* VIII, 117).

The Mills family was grateful. "My Dearest Friend Ingersoll," wrote Mills's son, "Like the throb of a great warm heart came your brief but breathing lines of sympathy to me as I sat in the shadow of death, and they were balm indeed" (May 23, 1883, IHS).

Another situation, another mood. We should laugh at human strivings, our own included. His guest Judge Sherman, warning Ingersoll on the dangers of good living, advised him to exercise. Ingersoll complied, but effort proved worse than futile. He reported the sad consequences to his mentor.

Washington, D.C., April 26, 1883

Hon. E. J. Sherman
Lawrence, Mass.

My dear Colonel:

After you went away, the folks commenced. No one man ever received an equal amount of advice in an equal time.

"You must walk. Colonel Sherman says that you are liable to fall dead for want of exercise. Do you hear? You must WALK!"

"Yes," said Grandmother, "the apoplexy is lurking in your blood."

"You are liable to be paralyzed," said my wife.

"Or to die in your sleep," said Mrs. Farrell.

"Or after you wake up," chimed in the baby.

"You must walk," said Eva.

"You ought to run," added Maud.

"And never sit down again as long as you live," shouted Clint.

So I started for Georgetown and walked five miles before breakfast. Then I footed it to the Court, and walked home. After supper I took a stroll in the country, returning home a little before midnight. The next morning my calves were swollen so that they looked like yearlings. After being rubbed down with whiskey and red pepper, and oiling my principal joints, I started again about daylight, and walked to Bladensburgh—distance about eleven miles. On my return, about halfway home, I was taken with cramps and lockjaw. I managed by signs to attract the attention of some people on their way to market, and was kindly taken home in a cart laden with garlic, kale, and sassafras.

I was carried in very tenderly by the entire family, all of whom insisted that MORE WALKING was what I needed.

"He stopped and cooled off too suddenly," said Clint.

"Lying down in the road will give anybody the cramps," said Maud.

"I guess Colonel Sherman knows what he is talking about," said Mrs. Farrell.

"Limber him up and start him again," said Clint.

So I was put in bed—covered with mustard—my legs straightened out by putting weights on my knees—mouth filled with dried apples to swell my teeth apart.

As soon as I was able to speak, I sent for Baker [his secretary] that I might dictate a letter to you for further instructions. Of course it is necessary for you to know my general condition:

1. Both my feet are covered with blisters.
2. The cords of my legs are as tight as the strings of a bass viol.
3. Great pain in the small of my back.
4. Sudden flashes of heat running up and down the spine.
5. Knees badly swollen.
6. Mind wandering.
7. Pulse about 120.
8. Temperature of the body 115 degrees.
9. Fur enough on my tongue to make a sealskin saque.

I think I have walked enough. The rest say not. Telegraph your opinion. I am held up in bed to sign this letter.

I have looked through WALK-er's Dictionary without finding anything on the subject. I have also read "Plato on the Sole."

Yours till death,
R. G. Ingersoll

The Star Route

In the Star Route prosecution the government was out for blood and glory. Attorney General Benjamin Brewster, nominal head of the prosecution, made one summation but otherwise did not participate. The case was presented by three special prosecutors, the elite of the New York and Philadelphia bars—Richard F. Merrick, George Bliss, and William W. Ker. The government was so sure it would destroy the defendants and win everlasting acclaim that it set itself to recording and publishing the trial proceedings, amassing a phenomenal compilation of 3,286 pages on the first trial (3 volumes), and 6,033 on the second (4 volumes). In the final showdown, however, the government was completely routed.

What was to be a monument to Republican virtue stands as a memorial to one of the greatest fiascoes in the history of federal prosecutions. If one had the task of awarding a prize for superiority among the victorious defense counsel one would be hard put to choose between Ingersoll, attorney for Stephen W. and John W. Dorsey, and Judge Jeremiah Wilson, attorney for Brady. (Ingersoll and Wilson were ably supported by prominent counsel for the other defendants.) Both Ingersoll and Wilson were magnificently competent, and zealous on law and fact (not to derogate from government counsel). The prize might go to Ingersoll for his personal glamour and for making the strategic decisions for the whole defense, decisions full of dangerous potentialities like refusing to produce the Dorsey group's financial records and keeping Stephen Dorsey and Brady off the witness stand in the first trial. Ingersoll dominated the courtroom, whether speaking or silent—even when absent. Judge Andrew Wylie, although old, fragile, and hesitant of speech, nevertheless held the reins tight with frigid cordiality.

The trials were held in the old classical-style federal courthouse in Washington, the scene of many historic trials on malfeasance in public office (and later, the Teapot Dome trial in the 1920s). In that very courtroom Guiteau had been recently condemned; he would be executed as the trial got under way. A tense nation and a tense capital city shifted attention to Star Route, but interest soon waned under the cumulative testimony replete with minor details and abstract legal fencing between counsel—until such times as Ingersoll was expected to speak, when crowds including members of Congress, Cabinet ministers, and personalities like Frederick Douglass poured into the courtroom, and Judge Wylie permitted standing-room in the aisles and at the rear.

The trial was an inquest into the office of Second Assistant Postmaster General Thomas J. Brady. There were about ten thousand Star Routes under his jurisdiction, and his office was under constant pressure for enlargement of services at public expense. Naturally cattlemen, trappers, traders, and soldiers living in wide-open spaces wanted better and better mail service—more trips and more speed, addition and expedition. Petitions for increases signed by local residents and endorsed by local mayors, governors, judges, and generals flowed into Washington to be endorsed as a matter of form by members of Congress responsive to the wishes of their constituents. They were then forwarded for approval by an Executive having no interest in friction with the Legislature. The situation was ripe for abuse.

The Dorsey group held 134 contracts, less than 2 percent of the total (hardly a representative portion of the Star Routes), and the government selected 19 of these routes for prosecution. It claimed that the total contracted cost of operating them as of May 1879 was $41,135 annually, but that by April 1881 it had soared to $448,670, reduced by fines and other deductions to $300,165. It claimed losses of public money due to fraud on the 19 contracts of about $60,000 before the contracts finally were cancelled. In negotiations between contractors and Brady, increased costs had been proportioned to increases in men and horses required. This was a mere basis for convenience's sake and did not allow for such factors as maintenance of service facilities, wear and tear on vehicles, simultaneous uses of some vehicles (as stage coaches, for instance), how hard men and animals were worked, or how much of the extra work was actually done or if done how legitimate. The government might argue wastefulness but could not demonstrate it with objective precision. More to the legal point was the allegation that Brady and the Dorsey group had conspired so that the contractors would kick back to Brady 30 percent to 40 percent of every increase granted and 50 percent on every fine remitted.

The prosecution presented the case as Armageddon; nothing less than the fate of the Republic depended on a verdict of guilty. Ingersoll played the case as just another instance of the traditional tug of war between the forces of the State as prosecutor and the independence of the jury; nothing more, nothing less. At almost all times he seemed the most relaxed and casual person in the courtroom. A fresh bouquet of flowers adorned his table every day, he held an unlighted cigar or a wad of chewing tobacco in his mouth, spread out and read newspapers, chatted with his colleagues as if they were guests in his parlor, and went out for a smoke while the prosecution droned on. He absented himself for several days at a time, fleeing every weekend during the first trial, and again toward the end of the second trial, from the steaming heat of Washington summer to the family "cottage" on Long Beach in Long Island, to refresh himself in the waves and with the music of the German band and his virtuoso guests including Remenyi. In the courtroom he was a dozing lion on display, ready to spring into action: to tell a joke or make a wisecrack, to argue law with the judge within and almost beyond decorum, to grapple with opposing counsel, to examine his own witnesses with tact (particularly Dorsey in the second trial who, because of his bona fide eye ailment, could not read papers and so was easily coached for the best answers) and examine theirs with smiling sarcasm. He bared his heart to the jury, with special attention to the blacks, addressing each personally, as they held the fate of Union veterans in their hands.

The opposing counsel had sworn a vendetta, dispensing with the usual courtesies of the courtroom. They were enemies without quarter. Ingersoll asked to see papers in the custody of the prosecution. Some serio-comics followed:

MR. MERRICK. I shall not show them to you.
MR. INGERSOLL. I am not speaking to you. I am speaking to the court.
MR. MERRICK. I am speaking to the court, also.
MR. INGERSOLL. Then don't talk to me.
MR. MERRICK. I am not talking to you.
MR. INGERSOLL. Don't do it.
JUDGE WYLIE. You are both talking to each other (*laughter*).

(Second trial, Feb. 27, 1883, 2403.)

Breaking into Merrick's summation Ingersoll denied that Dorsey had advocated the dismissal of the attorney general and the postmaster general. Merrick had him there. He quoted from Dorsey: "But if I did not do all I could, my tongue has lost all its cunning."

MR. INGERSOLL. Oh, faugh!
MR. MERRICK. Oh, faugh, faugh! But this is not very creditable in a court of justice.
JUDGE WYLIE. Mr. Ingersoll, take your seat, if you please.
MR. INGERSOLL. I have taken my seat.
(Second trial, June 7, 1883, 5747)

Ingersoll's pose of nonchalance, throwing dust in their eyes, grated on the nerves of the prosecution and threw them off balance. Merrick sought to introduce a simple computation. Wilson had no objection.

MR. INGERSOLL. I object to it. It is a very dangerous paper.
MR. MERRICK. The gentleman is right. It is a very dangerous paper.
MR. INGERSOLL. Wonderfully dangerous!
MR. MERRICK. It shows the way the sum was done, and it shows that unless perjury gives the quantities, a losing route can never become a gaining one. Mr. Ingersoll cannot sneer it [the computation] away. He cannot laugh it away. He may smile his blandest smile, and shake his round red head and fat cheeks to the end of time, but this calculation, justly and honestly made by mathematics, shows the foundation of his case to be in falsehood, in perjury and in corruption.
(Second trial, May 31, 1883, 5551)

As Merrick was cross-examining a defense witness a piece of plaster fell from the ceiling on him.

MR. INGERSOLL. That is rather ominous.
MR. MERRICK. I will bring him down as I brought down that (laughter).
MR. INGERSOLL. Exactly, right on you (laughter).
(Second trial, March 22, 1883, 3678.)

Judge Wylie was prepared for a hard time with Ingersoll, and Ingersoll did not entirely disappoint him. In every case on which he served Ingersoll conformed to the judge's ruling once made, but he never fawned upon wearers of the judicial robe. He even poked fun at some of Judge Wylie's rulings. "Sometimes I think your honor decides perfectly right and sometimes I think your honor decides wrong. I may be mistaken both times" (Second trial, Dec. 7, 1882, 52). A burst of laughter rippled through the audience. Judge Wylie was not amused. This was no theater comique. Such laughter was contempt of court, and wrongdoers would be punished; if they could not be detected the sections where they sat would be cleared. At another time Ingersoll was into an argument on law to the jury. That was improper, the judge ruled: Such arguments must be addressed to the court. All right, "then I will discuss them with the court. It is immaterial to me which way I turn when I am talking" (Second trial, May 18, 1883, 5272).

An uneasy peace gradually developed between the two. At times Judge Wylie was affable. When Ingersoll said of himself that he was not half as smart as Dorsey, the judge interjected, "I don't think you are either" (Second trial, April 2, 1883, 5930). Ingersoll suggested a lunch recess. Judge Wylie: "Are you hungry?" Ingersoll: "I am always hungry" (It *was* one o'clock) (Second trial, March 22, 1883, 3696). On March 20, 1883, the following colloquy occurred:

> JUDGE WYLIE. As we have a few minutes before one o'clock I should like to consult the counsel and the jury as to their wishes in regard to Good Friday.
> MR. INGERSOLL. I call any day good that I don't have to work. If it is not Good Friday I would like to have it made so.
> JUDGE WYLIE. I propose to consult Mr. Ingersoll, especially. It will be an important point gained if Mr. Ingersoll can be converted.

It was agreed to recess for Good Friday.

Starting the first trial Judge Wylie remarked, apropos of the crowd waiting to hear Ingersoll, "There is a large audience this morning" (*Washington Star*, Sept. 6, 1882). During the Easter season of 1883 Ingersoll's friend Judge Sherman of Massachusetts visited the Ingersolls, and Ingersoll introduced him to Judge Wylie. Wylie told Sherman privately, "When I learned that he was to take part in the trial, I was unhappy. I regarded him as a blatant infidel. After three weeks of the trial of the case I have become a great admirer of his. He can bring more sunshine into a courtroom than any man I ever saw" (Sherman, 261).

Needless to say, reporters shared the judge's final impression. "One of the compensations of this tedious trial has been Ingersoll," one commented. "The attractive feature about Ingersoll is his genial, generous, unbounded good nature. His laugh must be seen to be appreciated. It is a study in itself, and every fibre of his being (and Robert is physically no sardine) takes a hand in the performance. Here is no insincere, soulless snicker, that is born and dies in the face, with no more effect on the inner man than a flash of light on an iceberg, but is hearty, contagious, and undeniably merry" (*Toledo* [Iowa] *Chronicle*, June 7, 1883).

The prosection had charted a wide field that they plowed thoroughly. They brought in from faraway places a parade of carriers, subcontractors, and postmasters to show costs skyrocketing without benefit to the taxpayers. Some of the petitions for increase were manifestly bogus, as they were not signed by residents or were rewritten after signature, and so forth. Some authorized increases were not wanted, not needed, not done, not possible, or not warranted by current traffic or revenue received (productiveness). The prosecution depicted the contractors sitting in idleness in Washington, making enormous profits out of the labor and risks (including Indian raids) of the subcontractors. Instances were spelled out in stupefying and soporific detail. On Route 46247, Redding, Pa., to Alturas, California, the contract speed was brought down from 108 hours to 72 (though previously the mail had always been carried in 44), the annual cost jumped from $6,000 to $36,000, of which $21,000 went to subcontractors and $15,000 to contractors. On Route 40104, Mineral Park to Pioche, Arizona, where the only mail carried two-thirds of the time was the bill for delivery, the annual cost had jumped from $3,000 to $52,000, of which $28,000 went to subcontractors, $24,000 to contractors.

Rerdell now testified that Dorsey and Brady met frequently. He had accompanied Dorsey on a payoff visit to Brady's office, though he did not see any actual payment. For the prosecution, this was proof enough that the nation was floundering in a sea of corruption, headed for disaster like the Fall of Rome or the French Revolution unless the defendants were convicted. The government wanted a guilty verdict, the people demanded it, the jurors had taken an oath, and if they desired to stand well with their Maker they should say Guilty.

The defense countered that the petitions were in the main in good order and where deficient had been purified by community leaders and members of Congress. It was not a sin to make money, and the government was not an idiot or an infant to complain of a bad bargain. The subcontractors had not been deceived and, at any rate, their dealings with the contractors had nothing to do with the case. The nation had undertaken to carry the mails from one end to the other not as a business but as a service, and the heroic pioneers in the West were entitled to as good service as the city dwellers in the East regardless of differences in costs. "Mr. Bliss talks as though he thought that all the mutton and beef of the United States was raised in Central Park, as though we get all our wool from shearing lambs in Wall Street" (Works, X, 187). The many references to meetings between Dorsey and Brady reminded Ingersoll of a story. A boy had killed a woodchuck and was pounding away at the carcass. When asked why he was doing this he replied that he was teaching the animal that there was punishment after death. Further, Ingersoll continued, Rerdell's testimony that he had accompanied Dorsey as far as the anteroom of a payoff to Brady was ridiculed (in the parlance of a later day, there was no smoking gun). Rerdell had confessed and recanted and confessed again and had had the gall to attend defense huddles on strategy while simultaneously in contact with the prosecutors. Rerdell had no chance with Ingersoll, a long-time master at demolishing turncoats. Ingersoll composed an epitaph for Rerdell:

MR. INGERSOLL. Up to this time I have been faithful to my trust. My prayer to Gabriel is, "When you pass over this grave, don't blow" (*laughter*).
MR. DONALDSON (the court crier). Come to order, gentlemen.
JUDGE WYLIE. Speak to the ladies.

(Second trial, May 23, 1883, 5374)

The republic was not teetering on the edge of perdition. It would endure no matter how this case was decided. It was the paramount moral duty of the jury as American citizens to repell directives from the administration and even the pressure of popular opinion in order to make a free and independent judgment.

Unfortunately for the Goddess of Justice, religion and irreligion became issues in the Star Route trials. There was no hiding the fact that the principal attorney for the defense was "the champion blasphemer of America"; he wore his infidelism on his sleeve, but he did not advance it on his own initiative in Star Route except in casual banter. It was the prosecution that tossed lighted matches into the tinder. The prosecution had sneered at Mrs. Dorsey sitting beside her husband every day at the trial. They had exhorted the jury to dismiss every impulse of mercy from their minds, to act like icicles, godlike. "A cool conception of Deity," Ingersoll remarked (First trial, Sept. 6, 1882, 3106). The master of pathos went on:

> There is a painting in the Louvre, a painting of desolation, of despair and love. It represents the night of the crucifixion. The world is represented in shadow. The stars are dead and yet in the darkness is seen a kneeling form. It is Mary Magdalene with loving lips and hands pressed against the bleeding feet of Christ. The skies were never dark enough nor starless enough. The storm was never fierce enough nor wild enough, and the arrows of slander never flew thick enough to drive a noble woman from her husband's side. And so it is, in all of human speech the holiest word is WIFE. (First trial, 3109)

Surely Ingersoll was rhetorically using a legend of devotion in which believer and unbeliever could find common ground. Attorney General Brewster himself responded with an appeal to bigotry. "What has he to do with the crucifixion? Does he believe in it, that he used it for the purpose of influencing your judgment?" (First trial, Sept. 7, 1882, 314).

At the second trial the defense presented Dorsey and Brady as witnesses. As Dorsey took the stand prosecutor Merrick asked him whether he believed in an oath binding on his conscience in view of the future state of rewards and punishments. Ingersoll sprang up with a vehement objection: At the first trial the government had taunted the defense for keeping the principal defendants off the stand. Now that the defense was producing them, the government was blocking their testimony in order to exploit religious bias. "Whether a man believes in the future state of rewards and punishments has nothing to to do with his testimony; nothing. If at this time we are to rebuild the fires of hell, if we are to bring into this courtroom a literal devil, with a three-pronged fork to stir up the conscience of the average Christian that he will tell the truth, it seems to me that we had better go back for three or four hundred years and throw away all of the literature of the present age, all of its spendid discoveries, and all there is of civilization" (March 26, 1883, 3693). Judge Wylie excused Dorsey from answering the question.

But the prosecution had made a personal attack on Ingersoll as holding in contempt all things holy and sacred. He had to respond, for his clients if not for himself.

It may be that I am guilty, according to Colonel Bliss, of sneering at everything that people hold sacred. But I do not sneer at justice. I believe that over all justice sits the eternal queen, holding in her hand the scales on which are weighed the deeds of men. I believe that it is my duty to make the world a little better because I have lived in it. I believe in helping my fellowmen. I do not sneer at charity. I do not sneer at justice, and I do not sneer at liberty. And why did he make that remark to you gentlemen? Is it possible that for a moment he dreamed that he might prejudice your mind against the case of my client because I, his attorney, am not what is called a believer? Is it possible that he has so mean an impression of a Christian that a Christian must violate an oath when upon a jury, simply to get even with a lawyer who happens to be an infidel? Is that his idea of Christianity? It is not mine, it is not mine. (May 24, 1883, 5438)

During the second trial a Congressman Belford, called as a witness by the defense, felt entitled to clear his name from the rumor that he had accepted a payoff from Dorsey. Judge Wylie ruled the testimony inadmissible, whereupon the witness proceeded to exculpate himself anyhow. Wylie held him in contempt and almost acted similarly against Ingersoll, who challenged him to examine his own conduct. He pleaded for leniency and paid the hundred dollar fine (March 7, 1883, 3258).

Some events were not included in the official record. The day after their testy encounter on talking to the judge or to each other Merrick called Ingersoll a "puppy" (quite a puppy!), Ingersoll shot back "dirty dog," and the court was in an uproar (*Washington Post*, March 1, 1883). Two months later, an attorney, one H. Clay England, hailing from Rockville, Maryland, twenty miles from Washington, ran through the courtroom scantily clad "like a Fegee prince in bad luck." Shortly he returned fully clothed to shriek his professional opinion agreeing with the defense. "There is no conspiracy. They are not guilty" (*Washington Evening Star*, May 14–15, 1883).

Ingersoll concluded his summation in the second trial:

I want a verdict in accordance with the evidence. I want a verdict in accordance with the law. I want a verdict that will relieve my clients from the agony of two years. I want a verdict that will drive the darkness from the heart of the wife. I want a verdict that will take the cloud of agony from the roof and the home. I want a verdict that will fill the coming days and nights with joy. I want a verdict that, like a splendid flower, will fill the future of their lives with a sense of thankfulness and gratitude to you, gentlemen, one and all. (May 25, 1883, 548)

On May 25, 1883, Robert wrote to John. He had been so busy with the Star Route trial that he had hardly had time to eat and drink. He made a speech to the jury lasting six days, "long enough to kill all concerned" (Wilson and the government counsel had spoken at equal length). He was hoping for an acquittal, and knew there would be no conviction. He felt complimented that counsel for the minor defendants had adopted his summation as their own. He reflected no feverish anxiety, but rather, his thoughts turned to the good old "sad and mournful" days when he and John were together with Father, Mary, Ruth, and Clark. His innate *Weltschmerz* rose to the surface. How poor the world was and after all how little there was to this human life. "I see a spectre coming all wrinkled and filled with pain. It is Age, and the spectre is myself that is to be. We must write oftener. We must see each other oftener. We are entering the twilight. The shadows are deepening and in a few days there will be only silence and darkness" (*Letters*, 175). In the most protracted and most agonizing trial of his life his primary thoughts were not about the verdict but the tragedy of existence. Such a man cannot be profoundly happy.

Ingersoll jotted in a little notebook his connection with history: "Tuesday June 12th 1883. At about 3 P.M. the Star Route case was given to the jury. R. G. I." (L.C.). Two crises, one minor and one major, disturbed the jury deliberations. One of the jurors was an alcoholic. In the jury room he fell to the floor in a fit due to thirst, and the deliberations were suspended until Judge Wylie, on medical advice, ordered a spirituous restorative.

More serious, going to the heart of the drama, was the inquiry of the jury foreman to the court that, if the jury did not agree on conspiracy, could they vote on the guilt or innocence of the defendants? The verdict hung in the balance of the ruling from the bench. No, said Judge Wylie. He did not care in what order the jurors considered the counts of the indictment but the offense being charged was conspiracy, and a valid guilty verdict must be based on a unanimous finding of conspiracy. On Thursday morning, June 14, the foreman declared, "We find the defendants not guilty." The prosecution must have been tipped off. Bliss and Merrick were absent; Ker stood in the doorway.

Needless to say, pandemonium reigned beyond the possibility of restraint, and Judge Wylie made no effort to restrain it. Mrs. Dorsey, clad in gray silk, was hysterical, jumped up and down, hands raised to

THE RESULT OF THE STAR ROUTE TRIALS.

(Puck, June 20, 1883, Library of Congress)

heaven, shaking, sobbing, crying, "Glory to God! Glory to God!" Dorsey, tears streaming down his cheeks under green goggles, tried to tone her down. Ingersoll's lips and chin quivered, tears filling his eyes, while Mrs. Ingersoll, Eva, and Maud, and the Farrells were simply wild. Brady's lawyer Wilson lit a cigar and put the wrong end in his mouth, burning off half his mustache. The defense gathered in an anteroom, where the Dorseys showered kisses on Ingersoll.

As Ingersoll came out on the broad steps of the main courthouse entrance a crowd gave him three cheers. He struck a characteristic pose— white straw hat with blue band pushed back, short black coat partially buttoned over white duck waistcoat, hands thrust into gray trousers— radiating good nature. Cries of "Speech!" "Speech!" No, he laughed, no little speech this time, as he climbed into the family carriage. It was a fresh sunny day and as the open carriage moved slowly down Pennsylvania Avenue to Lafayette Square, people scattered along the sidewalk cheering. Ingersoll doffed his hat continually, then took it off and waved to right and left. It was like an inaugural parade in miniature. At the house, as the *New York Sun* observed, "There was a procession of people all day long who had no sympathy at all with the defendants and who were perfectly indifferent whether they went to the penitentiary or not, but who were just heartily glad that their friend Col. Ingersoll had accomplished such a great personal victory" (June 15). That evening there was a serenade. The crowd filled sidewalk and roadway between the house and Lafayette Square, and Ingersoll, Wilson, other defense counsel, and friends made brief remarks on the triumph of the jury system over the power of government.

A popular cartoon of the day depicted a sleek Ingersoll emerging from a small front doorway of the courthouse with a money bag under each arm while two ragged urchins, Dorsey and Brady, scrambled away from a side door. No such transfer of wealth occurred. The rumor that Dorsey paid Ingersoll a fee of $100,000, which would not have been excessive even for that period, was a journalist's pipe dream. Two days after the acquittal Ingersoll signed an accommodation note for $15,000 for Dorsey (IHS). On December 11 he made a notation of some of Dorsey's trial expenses paid by him and still owing.

Notary Public's ackkt's [sic] of Dr.'s statement	1.50
Cash advanced to R. B. Carpenter (attorney)	200.00
Services of C. G. McLareno, stenog's	15.00
Printing Rerdell's affidavit	10.00

(Acct. Book beginning Sept. 1, 1882, L.C.)

Dorsey built and furnished for Ingersoll a ranch house near his own in New Mexico for about $15,000 and brought him into the ill-fated Palo Blanco Cattle Company. Such a client can ruin a lawyer.

Meanwhile euphoria. "I felt that it was life or death for me. The Govt. put forth every effort. The cost has been about a million dollars. I defied them from the first and wiped the floor up with them at last. We have had a perfect jubilee for the last four days. Thousands have called at the house to congratulate me. It has been a continual ovation" (New York, To John, June 17, 1883, *Letters*, 176).

And so to Long Beach. A venturesome reporter found him in the surf. A thunderstorm having started, they stayed in the water and the reporter had an exclusive interview. The willing captive spouted a pint of salt water, and then laughed and discoursed on Star Route and current politics while swimming and floating about. The storm ceased, the sun shone, Ingersoll said, "Let us get out." Ingersoll's ample figure rose "hard as a rock and firm as flint" (the hike to Bladensburgh must have done wonders!). The clinging flannels were in sharp contrast to his trim courtroom appearance. Half an hour later the interview resumed as the reporter found Ingersoll in the library, smoking a fragrant Havana and listening to music by his daughters.

The reporter could not help observing what impressed all visitors: the happy father and husband, the loving wife and mother, the affectionate children. Turning to matters political, Ingersoll opined that Arthur could not be elected president because he had been vice president, "a vice that people will not pardon." He praised the Illinois court for discouraging fraud by enforcing a contract made on Sunday. He predicted the election of Oglesby as again governor of Illinois, and he promoted General Gresham as the coming man in Indiana. At last:

Well, Colonel, what are you up to?

Nothing. I am surrounded by sand, sea, and sky. I listen to music, bathe in the surf, and enjoy myself. I am wondering why people want to climb the greased pole of office and then dodge the brickbats of enemies and rivals; why any man wishes to be President, or a member of Congress, or in the Cabinet, or do anything except live with the ones he loves, and enjoy twenty-four hours every day. I wonder why all New York does not come to Long Beach and hear Schreiner's Band play the music of Wagner, the greatest of all composers. Finally, in the language of Walt Whitman, I loaf and invite my soul. (*New York Herald*, July 1, 1883)

Note

1. Reverend Talmage had set forth his views in his *Trumpet Peals: A collection of timely and eloquent extracts from the sermons of Reverend T. DeWitt Talmage including Demosthenian philippics against Ingersollian infidelity.*

X

Royal Bob Takes a Walk

Having "loafed and invited his soul" during the summer at the seashore, Ingersoll was back in Washington in the fall to resume the practice of law and his battles as a public citizen.

Although there was never a break between Blaine and Ingersoll over Star Route, in due time Blaine would feel the consequences of Ingersoll's deep resentment. Meanwhile amicable relations continued. In fact, Mrs. Blaine was among the celebrants of the Star Route victory. Blaine had left government service after Garfield's death and was writing his *Twenty Years in Congress*, planning another try at the presidency in 1884. He called on Ingersoll at his home the day before Ingersoll was to leave on a lecture tour, but, not finding him, he sent "My Dear Colonel" a letter. Would Ingersoll help him in collecting a note (at 6 percent interest, please) signed by Dorsey, which Blaine had acquired in the course of a stock deal? He had refrained from pressing the matter on Dorsey "after his troubles came." Having failed in his monumental campaign to destroy Dorsey, now he solicited Dorsey's attorney to be a courier for collecting a commercial debt. "I hope," he wrote, "you are all 'having a good time' as we say in Yankee land, and that your trip may be prosperous" (March 1, 1884, IHS).

The Ingersolls had moved into a larger house on K Street facing, from the north, another patch of green in the city—Franklin Square. In the spring of 1884 the great violinist Remenyi was a houseguest, as had previously been, among others, the English freethinker and cooperative movement pioneer George Jacob Holyoke and the great actor John McCullough. Ingersoll invited some friends, the Blaines included, to hear the Hungarian virtuoso, and from ten to twelve in the evening the house resounded with renditions of Schubert's "Ave Maria," a polonaise, mazurkas, and nocturnes by Chopin, and some Hungarian pieces, among them "Andalusian Dances" composed by Remenyi especially for his host, his "Jupiter" Ingersoll. It was a full-house event, with standing room only in the capacious parlor. Ingersoll stood at a doorway, eyes closed, lips pursed in concentration. Beside him stood Justice Harlan of the Supreme Court, the two making an artist's dream of physical and intellectual stature. Poor persecuted Remenyi, friend of Brahms and Liszt! A military band marched by on the street, whistling and thumping with fife and drum. The great violinst lowered his bow in utter despair and groaned, "Oh, it was ze bootiful, ze love part." The band faded away and Remenyi raised his bow (*Nebraska Capital*, June 14, 1884).

Justice Harlan is remembered as the Great Dissenter on behalf of civil rights. By the Civil Rights Act of 1875 Congress proposed to banish racial discrimination on a national scale in inns, public conveniences, and places of public amusement. The Civil Rights Cases (109 U.S. 3, 1883) involved a set of challenges to the custom of such enterprises, especially in the South, of maintaining segregated facilities for blacks. The Court invalidated the Act, holding that the Thirteenth Amendment abolishng slavery did not apply and that the Fourteenth Amendment, extending civil rights, applied only to governmental transgressions by states, not individuals. Alone in dissent Harlan protested that racial discrimination was a badge of servitude in violation of the Thirteenth Amendment and that the Fourteenth Amendment, by creating a federal standard of public equality, implied a federal power of enforcement against not only states but individuals.

The Civil Rights Cases were decided on October 15, 1883. Instantly, even before seeing the court's opinion or the Harlan dissent, Ingersoll filed his own dissent (*The National Republican*, Washington, D.C., Oct. 17, 1883; *Works*, VIII, 135). "I think it is all wrong." It drew "a color line which is as cruel as the lash of slavery." Any government that tolerated a distinction based on race would be a disgrace to mankind. It was absurd that a man like Frederick Douglass could be denied equal admission to cars, hotels, and theaters, pushed into "some ignominious corner" under judicial sanction. It had been said that the Republican party had outlived its usefulness, that there was very little difference between the two parties. Now Ingersoll summoned the Republican party back to its historic mission, which began with protest against the Dred Scott Decision. "This decision is the tap of a drum. The old soldiers will fall into line. This decision gives the issue for the next campaign, and it may be that the Supreme Court has builded wiser than it knew. This is a question greater than the tariff or free trade. It is a question of freedom, of human rights, of the sacredness of humanity. . . . The real Americans, the real believers in Liberty, will give three cheers for Judge Harlan."

On October twenty-second a mass meeting against the Civil Rights decision was held at Lincoln Hall in Washington. Frederick Douglass was the chairman, Ingersoll the speaker. Douglass recited Leigh Hunt's poem about Abou Ben Adhem, who, when told by the angel writing in a book of gold that he was not listed among those who love the Lord, prayed that his name be written as one who loved his fellow men.

> The Angel wrote and vanished. The next night
> It came again, with a great wakening light,
> And showed the names whom love of God had blessed,
> And lo! Ben Adhem's name led all the rest.

I have the honor to introduce Robert G. Ingersoll" (*Works*, XI, 1).

Ingersoll's Civil Rights addresss was not a simple outcry put together in half an hour. Composed in a week of concentration this labor of love covers some fifty pages and should stand beside Justice Harlan's dissent as a statement, comprehensive and eloquent, in the cause of freedom. He struck an impassioned note of sympathy with his mostly black audience. "The masked wretches who, in the darkness of night, drag the poor negro from his cabin and lacerate with whip and thong his quivering flesh, will, with bloody hands, applaud the Supreme Court." But they must always remember that civilized government needed courts and that the odious decision governed only until changed by law, amendment, or an enlightened court—not by armed revolution but by "the perpetual peaceful revolution" that is the essence of a free society.

He reviewed the Declaration of Independence and its proclamation of the inalienable rights of all men to life, liberty, and the pursuit of happiness. He repeated his old argument that the sacred document was perverted by a Constitution that sanctioned slavery and could accommodate the Fugitive Slave Law. "Our forefathers planted the seeds of injustice, and we gathered the harvest." After the blood and flames of war we civilized the Constitution by adopting three amendments—the Thirteenth, Fourteenth, and Fifteenth—"the Trinity of Liberty." In developing the thesis of an implied federal power to enforce federal rights, he fired volley after volley of legal citations, precedents, and analogues that would have exhausted and lost the audience if not spoken by the master orator himself. Gracefully and with perfect accuracy he predicted Harlan's place in history. "The judge has associated his name with freedom, and he will be remembered as long as men are free" (44).

Ingersoll riddled the bugaboo of social equality. The question at issue concerned human equality and common experience. The Union prisoners escaping from Andersonville and Libby and rescued and fed by slaves were not perturbed about eating with blacks and finding rest and shelter under a black person's roof. "Charity has no color. It is neither white nor black. Justice and Patriotism are the same" (49). Some people, white and black, were so unclean and disgusting that they had no right to be in any place but a bathtub. He poured pitying scorn on whites who feared that a chance encounter with a black in a public place might lead to intermarriage.

> They are willing that colored women shall prepare their food—that colored waiters shall bring it to them—willing to ride in the same cars with the porters and to be shown to their seats in theatres by colored ushers—willing to be nursed in sickness by colored servants. They see nothing dangerous—nothing repugnant, in any of these relations—but the idea of riding in the same car, stopping at the same hotel, fills them with fear—fear for the future of our race. Such people can be described only in the language of Walt Whitman. "They are the immutable, granitic pudding-heads of the world." (47)
>
> It is very easy to see why colored people should hate us, but why we should hate them is beyond my comprehension. They never sold our wives. They never robbed our cradles. They never scarred our backs. They never pursued us with bloodhounds. They never branded our flesh. (51)

On October twenty-fifth a group of twenty-five citizens headed by Douglass begged Ingersoll for a repeat of his address. He complied (*The Evening Critic*, D.C., Oct. 27, 1883).

Let us for a moment leave the historical frame of our narrative and look down the vista of subsequent events. In 1896 *Plessy* v. *Ferguson* (163 U.S. 537) challenged a Louisiana statute mandating separation of the races in public facilities. The Court upheld the statute under a newfangled "separate but equal" doctrine. Again alone in dissent Harlan contended that separation was inherently unequal, declaring in an immortal phrase, "The Constitution is colorblind." Against fruitless opposition Jim Crow segregation persisted down the years. The Civil Rights Act of 1964 turned back the pages of history, reviving the protections of 1875, and was upheld by a unanimous Supreme Court (*Heart of Atlanta Motel* v. *U.S.*, 379 U.S. 241, 1964; *Katzenbach* v. *McClung*, 379 U.S. 294, 1964).

The lecture platform had not seen Ingersoll for more than a year. From time to time in the winter/spring of 1883–1884 he escaped from routine legal business to this more congenial rostrum. He had prepared a new lecture, "Orthodoxy." It is a broadside on the whole system of revealed religion as an outworn heritage from simpler days. The parson and the priest must go the way of the astrologer, the alchemist, the soothsayer. Supernatural religion must give way to the religion of reciprocity based on reason and science.

Ingersoll argued that faith in Christianity had been eroded beyond repair by the march of history. The failure of the Crusades, the revival of learning after the Middle Ages, the discovery of America, the research of Copernicus and Kepler—all had discredited the Christian view of the world and human destiny. Sensible and humane people no longer believed in a God who involved himself in human affairs. An example:

A man told him the other day that he had planned to go on a ship but had been detained on land. The ship was lost at sea with all aboard; he had been spared by God. "Think of the infinite egotism of such a doctrine. Here is a man that fails to go on a ship with five hundred passengers and they go down to the bottom of the sea—fathers, mothers, children, and loving husbands and wives waiting upon the shores of expectation. Here is one poor little wretch that did not happen to go! And he thinks that God, the Infinite Being, interfered in his poor little wretched behalf, and let the rest all go. This is special providence" (*Works*, II, 355).

The nineteenth century would be known as Darwin's century after one of the greatest men that ever lived. His theories of evolution, the survival of the fittest, and the origin of species had erased the last vestiges of orthodoxy from every thinking mind. "The church teaches that man was created perfect, and that for six thousand years he has degenerated. Darwin demonstrates the falsity of this dogma. He shows that man has for thousands of ages steadily advanced, that the Garden of Eden is an ignorant myth, that the doctrine of original sin has no foundation in fact, that the atonement is an absurdity; that the serpent did not tempt, and that man did not 'fall' " (359).

Ingersoll then took up his critics who asserted that contemporary Christians did not believe in the old dogmas. Then why did they repeat them in their formal profession of faith? The new Congregational creed reaffirmed traditional Christian tenets based on belief in "God, the Father Almighty, maker of heaven and earth, and of all things visible and invisible" through the fall of man, original sin, vicarious atonement, redemption by grace, and the divine inspiration and authority of the Scriptures, to "a final judgment, the issues of which are everlasting punishment and everlasting life." That is the conception of human destiny that he opposed. He spoke like Adhem born again. "If there is a God, then that creed is blasphemy. That creed is a libel upon him who sits on heaven's throne. If there be a God, I ask him to write in the book in which my record is kept, that I denied these lies for him" (375).

The Old Testament was full of moral abominations; the New Testament was "infinitely" worse with its dogma of eternal punishment. "I have concluded that I will never deliver a lecture in which I will not attack the doctrine of eternal pain. That part of the Congregational creed would disgrace the lowest savage that crouches and crawls in the jungles of Africa" (410). The world would not be perfectly civilized until there were no gallows or penitentiaries, but according to the Christian religion God was the eternal jailer in an eternal penitentiary. And what was the offense for which the punishment was imposed? Failure to believe what the mind denies.

He presented an example of the true love of and respect for humanity. During a recent flood a woman standing on top of a house floating down the Ohio declined an offer of rescue. The house contained her dead children and she could not leave them. "If there is another world, and if in heaven they wear hats, when such a woman climbs the appropriate bank of the Jordan, Christ should tip his to her" (417).

An Ingersoll lecture was not complete without some jokes and funny stories. As an example of the literal inerrancy of the Scriptures, he cited the fifteenth chapter of Cornithians which, slightly altered, provided interesting counsel.

> "Behold, brethren, I show you a mystery; we shall not all die, but we shall all be changed." . . . This boy had rubbed out the "c" in "changed." So when the old man put on his spectacles and got down the Bible, he read: "Behold, brethren, I show you a mystery; we shall not all die, but we shall all be hanged." The old lady said, "Father, I don't think it reads that way." He said, "Who is reading this? Yes, Mother, it says 'hanged,' and more than that, I see the sense of it. Pride is the besetting sin of the human heart, and if there is anything calculated to take the pride out of a man it is hanging." (451)

Ingersoll the freethinker was not an eccentric visionary meeting with small coteries in dark cellars. His audiences numbered in the thousands from coast to coast. The spirit of the times, the genius of the man, and the popularity of the lecture circuit for entertainment-education all combined to make "the champion blasphemer of America" a national force. His year's absence from the platform had not dimmed his power to attract multitudes to pay their money for a two-hour diatribe against revealed religion. The big cities—Chicago, Kansas City, St. Louis, Denver, Boston, New York, Philadelphia—were like stages along a royal progress when Ingersoll came to town. Local clerics might warn against him, but the folk swarmed to the hall or theater, brushed past the YMCA picketers handing out religious tracts, and snatched up the available tickets. Latecomers were glad to be assigned chairs put on the stage or in the musicians' pit, trodding upon one another's heels in the lobby, and jostling their way into the auditorium. They were as before people of all sorts and ranks from the literate majority. They enjoyed an evening with Ingersoll whether or not they subscribed to his views; some came simply for the entertainment. In Denver: "The audience was of a highly cultivated and intellectual character," Governor Grant and party in the front seats (*Daily News*, Jan. 21, 1884). In Chicago: "There was hardly standing room in the largest auditorium in Chicago. The occasion was a lecture by Robert G. Ingersoll: subject, 'Orthodoxy.' There was no display of costumes among the audience, no appearance of dress-coats or full toilets of an opera night, but the applause was more frequent than when Patti or Campanini sings, and neither Booth nor Irving, when portraying the thoughts of others, has ever awakened more enthusiasm" (*The Times*, March 20, 1884). In New York: "The most intelligent of the middle class seemed to form the greater part of the assemblage and the Hebrew and German element was largely represented. Henry George sat upon the stage and Prof. Adler was in an orchestra chair. The audience was at times largely enthusiastic, applauding more the humor of the lecturer than his assault on Christianity" (*The World*, April 28, 1884).

In Boston a reporter walking on Washington Street to the lecture glimpsed an unusual mass of humanity in front of the Boston Theater and figured that a street fight or some other extraordinary event was going on. As he came nearer he saw the sidewalks on both sides of the roadway teeming with people and the roadway itself substantially occupied by a man marching up and down with a placard aloft:

THE WICKED
SHALL BE TURNED INTO
HELL
AND ALL THE NATIONS THAT
FORGET GOD

Psalms IX, 17

(*Boston Globe*, May 12, 1884.) All to little avail. "My receipts [for the] Boston lecture were just $1786. Pretty good" (Ingersoll to Farrell, Providence, May 13, 1884, L.C.).

The audiences were eager for the standard Ingersoll performance. They would hear an inimitable blend of wit, sentiment, sledge-hammer logic, and purple flights. Actor and action, style and substance were a unit of charm and challenge. "The round, beaming countenance of Colonel Ingersoll appeared at the wings and was the signal for a round of applause. He came forward, laid his manuscript upon the desk and, without any introduction, proceeded at once to his lecture" (*Boston Daily Globe*, May 12, 1884). With the art that conceals art he wooed and captivated his listeners: "Mr. Ingersoll at once started off with his well-known magnetic style of oratory, and for over two hours held that vast audience in wrapped [sic] attention. Some of his first assertions were such stunners that the spectators hardly knew what to think, and every thing save the sound of his voice in the house was as still as the solitude of a dense desert. Finally some witty saying started the applause, and from that time on during the balance of the evening it was tears, cheers, and laughter. Those who attended were well entertained" (*Topeka Commonwealth*, March 18, 1884). The Boston reporter took delight in recognizing some of Ingersoll's stage mannerisms—his vigorously nodding his head and closing his lips in making a strong point, his face shaking with suppressed laughter when about to say something funny. "He rarely stood behind the desk, but addressed the audience first on one side and then on the other, making simple but strong gestures, clinching his fist and quivering with the excitement of his utterances in his controversial periods. He swayed his audience to laughter and applause continuously during the two hours and a quarter which his address occupied" (*Daily Globe,* May 12, 1884).

Speechmaking was only part of an Ingersoll visitation. The inevitable interviews evoked impromptu charm and wit. The mutual love affair between the press and the orator continued; his every remark was written down and published. "Col. Robert G. Ingersoll," said the *Chicago Times,* "is perhaps the pleasantest subject for the interviewer of all the men whose opinions are sought by the public" (Feb. 21, 1884). Even more enthusiastic was the reporter in Las Vegas, New Mexico, who caught his quarry at the railroad depot, "a robust form clad in a dark gray business suit and wearing a brand new pair of yellow hogskin slippers. No one who had seen it could forget that face, large, round, and good-natured, without a hair upon it, and with eyes which seemed to speak to you from beneath a broad, high forehead; the worst judge of human nature could not but be impressed with the man who wore it. Robert G. Ingersoll is possibly the best known man in the United States. He is certainly the most intelligent" (*The Weekly Optic,* Feb. 28, 1884). As the reporter introduced himself Ingersoll extended a large fat hand for a firm handshake and said, "I am glad to see you. I have just eaten my breakfast and I feel like talking." The reporter smiled, not intending any criticism of Ingersoll as a free-flowing talker. Ingersoll misconstrued the smile but took no offense. "Oh," he said, "you think that the breakfast was unnecessary to make me talk. Well, probably you are right. I acknowledge a weakness that way when I am well, and this morning I never felt better." He dug his hands deep into his pockets, lit a cigar, and said, "Oh, you have a glorious climate here, this is really a perfect day." He walked up and down the platform, puffing away and discoursing on politics and religion.

In Topeka *The Commonwealth* reported only that the Ingersolls had checked in at the Copeland Hotel and that Ingersoll had retired for a nap until the evening lecture. The more enterprising reporter for *The Capital* managed to get a full-length interview. In Buffalo Ingersoll shook hands with the reporter in "one of those grips that make one feel that the cream in the milk of human kindness has not yet been turned." A raging toothache had kept him awake until four in the morning, the room reeked of chloroform, but he lit a cigar, glanced briefly through some newspapers, and turned his swollen face to the reporter, who asked him, "Do you ever talk politics on Sunday?" Solemnly came the reply, "Never." "Not to please the public and the *Express?*" "That consideration of the question might involve an exception to the general rule," and he was off (*Express,* May 19, 1884).

The reporters could be sure that Ingersoll would say something interesting in response to any question; he had ideas on almost every subject. "Well, Colonel," a reporter wanted to know, "is the world getting better or worse?" Instantly the reply: "It is my opinion that while events, like the pendulum of a clock, go backward and forward, man, like hands, goes forward"; even "the churches are improving. Ministers are ashamed to preach the old doctrines with the old fervor" (*Truth Seeker*, March 15, 1884, quoted from the *Denver Republican*). What was his advice on the American hog problem of the day? "Well, I have always regarded universal education as the best remedy. I have never had much confidence in civil service reform. But I suppose things will go along the old way. He will get most of the offices" (*Chicago Times*, Feb. 21, 1884). What were his views on cremation? "I am opposed to it in the next world" (*Buffalo Express*, May 19, 1885). A reporter startled him: "What are you going to do to be saved?" Recovering quickly, he smiled and said, "Well, I think that I am safe, anyway. I suppose I have a right to rely on what Matthew says, that if I forgive others, God will forgive me. I suppose, if there is another world, I shall be treated very much as I have treated others. I never expect to have a perfect bliss anywhere. Maybe I should tire of it if I should. What I have endeavored to do has been to put out the fires of an ignorant and cruel hell; to do what I could to destroy that dogma, to destroy that doctrine that makes the cradle as terrible as the grave" (*Truth Seeker*, March 15, 1884).

Wherever Ingersoll went preaching the gospel of infidelity he elicited hostile recognition from the evangelical ministry and he gave them tit for tat. In Kansas City a reporter showed him some adverse comments by the local clergy. Responding, he first thanked them all for serving as his advance agents, then rattled off his rebuttals. The Reverend Mr. Matthews could not rationalize the biblical story of creation, which meant six ordinary days, otherwise Sunday as a sacred day of rest would have no foundation. Mr. Jardine professed to be a student of the evidences of Christianity, but "there are no evidences, consequently Mr. Jardine is a student of nothing." Mr. Haley and Mr. Weeks gave their fellow ministers good advice not to answer him: "It is better to say nothing than to talk absurdity." Mr. Woods was afraid that Ingersoll would hurt the children. "He thinks that the mother ought to stoop over the cradle and in the ears of the babe shout, Hell! So he thinks in all probability that the same words ought to be repeated at the grave as a consolation to mourners" (*Kansas City Journal*, Feb. 23, 1884; *Works*, VIII, 194).

When Ingersoll lectured in Utica, the morning following his lecture at breakfast he felt good, playful, "inviting his soul." The next Sunday a local minister, denouncing him as a sensualist, a gourmand, and a violator of common decency, said that in the hotel dining room Ingersoll had ordered everything on the bill of fare and then insulted the waitress because she had not brought something not on it. But Elbert Hubbard, who was on the scene, described it differently. "It was 'an early train breakfast,' " and the bill of fare had not yet been printed. The sleepy waitress dragged herself to the Ingersoll party and, standing at "the Colonel's" side, mumbled, "Ham and eggs, mutton-chops, beefsteak, break-fast bacon, codfish balls, and buckwheat cakes." "Bob" solemnly responded, "Ham and eggs, mutton-chops, beefsteak, breakfast bacon, codfish balls, and buckwheat cakes." The startled girl gasped, "What?" Bob repeated the list backward: "Buckwheat cakes, codfish balls, breakfast bacon, beefsteak, mutton-chops, and ham and eggs." Everybody in the dining room, including the waitress, laughed. "Haven't you anything else, my dear?" "the great man" continued, looking disappointed. "I think we have tripe and pig's feet," said the waitress. "Bring a bushel," said "Bob," "and say, tell the cook I'd like a dish of peacock-tongues on the side." Again everybody laughed. The waitress brought everything ordered except the peacock-tongues. After the meal "Bob" left a dollar under his plate. The cook stood in the kitchen doorway and, waving a big spoon, cried, "Goodbye, Bob," and got another dollar (*Little Journeys To The Homes Of Great Americans*, "Robert G. Ingersoll," 40).

In Buffalo a reporter asked him what he thought of a letter in *The Times* by one R. H. S. that contended that his doctrines deprived people of hope to meet father, mother, sisters, and brothers after death; that belief in Hell was necessary to keep society together; that murderers were punished in Hell; and that he preached not for the benefit of man-kind but for money. His rapid-fire answer: According to Christian doc-trine some will be in heaven, some in hell, and he wanted to be with his loved ones no matter where they might be; God did not make people so mean that they could not be held together without scaring them; according to Christianity a murderer repenting on the scaffold would go to heaven; the question was whether his arguments were sound, not what kind of person he was (*Buffalo Times*, May 19, 1884).

In Philadelphia, just in from New York and seated at dinner in Gay's Hotel, Ingersoll was fair game for a reporter with news about Reverend Irwin H. Torrence. The Reverend Mr. Torrence, general secretary of the Pennsylvania Bible Society, had declared that if Ingersoll indulged in blasphemy in Philadelphia he would be arrested under the Pennsyl-vania blasphemy law. Ingersoll laughed, and tore into the Reverend Mr. Torrence. He "humbly" apologized for visiting Philadelphia while the Methodist Conference was in session. Blasphemy? "If all that take the name of God in vain were imprisoned there would not be room in the jails to hold the ministers. They speak of God in the most flippant and snap-your-fingers way that can be conceived of. They speak of him as though he was an intimate chum, and metaphorically slap him on the back in the most familiar manner possible." Really, if he (Ingersoll) was going to suffer in hell, Mr. Torrence ought to let him have a good time here. "He can amuse himself through all eternity by seeing me wriggle on the gridiron of his revenge, and that ought to be enough to satisfy, not only an agent, but the whole Bible society. . . . Mr. Torrence is a fossil from the old red sandstone of a mistake. Let him rest. To hear these people talk you would suppose that God is some petty king, some lilliputian prince, who was about to be dethroned, and was nearly wild for recruits" (*Philadelphia Press*, May 24, 1884).

In early March the Ingersolls spent a week in New Mexico, where Ingersoll was investing heavily in Dorsey's Palo Blanco Cattle Company, an immense ranch containing at that time more than forty-five thousand head of cattle, and where Dorsey was building a ranch house as a gift for Ingersoll. On the eighth they left for the rail depot at Raton. There they ran into a committee and a band. "The citizens insisted on my making a little speech. I did say a few words" (Dear Folks, Leavenworth, March 13, 1884, L.C.). Rumors that he might speak had spread, and the little station was packed with people sitting and standing. Territorial Governor Hadley introduced him with as fine a compliment as could be expected (from a politician) as "the man who can make the presentation of sentiment, whether it is true or not, represent the grandest ambition of mankind." Ingersoll accepted "this kind and generous demonstration" not for himself but for "the great cause of free thought that is in some slight degree represented by myself." All over the country people were abandoning the cruel dogma of eternal punishment, which balanced a few hours of life against an eternity of pain. He restated his life-long mission: "That frightful doctrine I made up my mind to do what little I could to destroy. No matter whether my utterance might be popular or unpopular—whether anybody agrees with me or not—I have made up my mind to do what little I can, while I live, to put out the fires of hell, and I have the happiness to state tonight that there is very little fire in that location now." This reception itself illustrated how the times have changed, he continued. In a former age he would have been mobbed; earlier, imprisoned; still earlier, burned at the stake. He was not only a freethinker; he loved America:

> In religion I am for allowing every human being to think for himself, and I exercise that luxury for myself. I have also another religion, and that is the religion of patriotism. Do you know that we hardly imagine how great and magnificent our splendid country is? If you think for a moment you will see that there is not a land beneath the sun like ours, where the children of the poor man have an equal chance in the great race of life with the sons and daughters of the rich. . . . [He was proud] of every part of our broad continent, where the flag of our country floats and is honored. I think it is our duty to raise all our children to be patriotic, to be lovers of their country, to believe above all things in the United States of America. (*Raton Comet*, March 14, 1884)

In letters back home to the Farrells and the other "Dear Folks," dashed off in snatches of free time, Ingersoll conveyed the spirit of his travels. "Mother is sleeping and Eva and Maud are reading. It is now about seven o'clock and as soon as Mother wakes we will go to supper" (Feb. 20,

1884, L.C.). "We have had a famous time. The girls have been happy every minute and so has Mother and the subscribed" (Springer, N.M., March 21, 1884, *Letters*, 534). He was concerned for the folks back home. "Tell Grandmother not to get anxious—not to worry. The Indians are all dead and the road agents are in the penitentiary" (Feb. 21, 1884, To Sue, Kansas City, L.C.). He wrote of lecture schedules (almost every day in a different place), good houses almost everywhere (though not so good in New England where unemployment was heavy), cordial receptions by audiences and townsfolk, and weather conditions. The railroad companies, appreciating the travel business awakened for many miles around by an Ingersoll tour, often let the family ride free (go "ded hed") in private luxury cars. In sightseeing adventures they explored the countryside, visiting White Pass and Clear Creek Canyon. He saw beauty in town and country and in waters on the horizon. At Mesilla the dried grapes were "better than any raisins I ever ate" and he ordered five cases of the wine, "absolutely pure and 8 years old" (*Letters*, 53). They took a four-mile walk at night in the boundless desert. In Santa Fe the girls went shopping for Indian dishes, blankets, bead-work baskets, and other curios, and at Las Vegas Hot Springs "we all took hot baths, the best in the world—and we all felt as though dirt had left the world." At the Dorsey ranch bold Eva rode a horse, cautious Maud a mule. The girls "pet every dog they see for Rust's sake" (Rust was the family's Irish setter).

Typical, even to the strain of morbidity, is the letter to Eva and Maud (he and Mrs. Ingersoll were alone on this trip) from New Haven dated May 14, 1884.

> I think Mother will go off from New York. So you will see her tomorrow evening. I know that you are lonely & that it is a little selfish of me to take Mother away. Sometime we may be well enough off to live together. About that time we may lose you. Something is always wrong. Ride out every day. Enjoy every moment while you are young and before the old man of the sea, Responsibility, gets on your backs. Enjoy the flowers and the sunshine while you can. The flowers will soon fade and clouds will soon darken the days to come. Get all out of every moment that you can. I want you to be happy every second. . . . [The faithful scribe corrected himself in a postscript.] Mother says that you need not expect her until you see her. (*Letters*, 535)

It was a presidential election year. In due time Cleveland the Democrat would defeat Blaine the Republican, and for the first time since 1860 the Republican party would be swept from the White House. For Ingersoll the political year 1884 would be important not for what he did but for what he did not do: He made no political speeches, not one. To him the political contest was a sham, and he had an unalterable private grievance (which he kept private) against Blaine.

By 1884 Ingersoll had come to the mindset that no issues separated the parties, that the Republicans could not keep on belaboring the dead Confederacy (he had done his share with the bloody shirt), that no great persons were on the political horizon, and that there was no role for him in the charade. He was still, however, a renowned free-speaking pundit on politics, more than on religion; he could not shed his identity. As the election year opened, reporters besieged him with political questions. He brushed them off almost roughly (he was not always the perfect interviewee): "Oh, I don't want to talk about that. I am sick of it. That subject doesn't interest me. It is really such a silly question. The available candidates are like a lot of polliwogs in a small pond" (*Denver Daily News*, Jan. 17, 1884). "Sit down," he welcomed a reporter to his hotel suite in Chicago, "but, for heaven's sake, don't talk to me about politics. It is all trash and amounts to nothing. Ask me anything about religion and hell, but let me off of politics" (*The Times*, Feb. 2, 1884).

When reporters persisted, he tried to turn them off with jokes or witty remarks. Who would be the Republican candidate? The man who got the most votes; or, since he was not a theologian, he had no gift of prophecy and could not tell; or, if he announced the name in advance many persons would be unhappy. Arthur had no chance; Blaine's intentions were not known. He did have a good word for Blaine, nonetheless—"a man of ideas, of action" (*Denver Tribune*, Jan. 11, 1884). What should the Democrats do? "Well, the best thing for the Democrats to do is to wait until we nominate, and then nominate the same man" (*Chicago Times*, (March 20, 1884). Whom would they nominate? His answer pointed up the absurdity of seeking differences between the parties. "I have not the slightest idea. I have not paid any attention to the subject. It will be difficult to find just the man. He ought to believe in free trade and vote for protection. He should have been against the war and for [the] Union. He should believe in hard money and unlimited currency. He should be down on monopolies and at the head of several himself" (*Buffalo Express*, May 19, 1884).

In Chicago a reporter interrupted him at dinner in the hotel dining room. Between bites and swallows he analyzed the public unconcern about the coming election. The pool of popular apathy was "tideless, waveless, ebbless." It was "marbled over with the frog-spit of indifference." This indifference of the people was no cause for alarm, as politics had ceased being important. "If there was any danger to our interests—I will take a little more of that milk, if there was any danger of free trade, any danger of the destruction of our industries, the interest of course would be great and intense and universal, but nobody believes that the democracy can succeed in so changing the capital and industry of the country; for these reasons there is no interest" (*Chicago Daily Inter-Ocean*, March 20, 1884). He himself was inclined to sympathize with the general inertia: "Whoever is elected the country is safe enough. The grass will grow and the sun will rise and set, and things go on about the old way" (*Buffalo Courier*, May 19, 1884).

When asked directly who was his candidate Ingersoll answered with a wisecrack: "The dark horse." The reporter went along; would the dark horse win? "The dark horse seems to have the inside track at present and as in the last election will be successful" (*Topeka Capital*, March 15, 1884). At last he stated his preferences. "I like two men for that position. I like [Postmaster General] Gresham because he was a soldier [a minus mark for Blaine], an honest judge, and because he is a level-headed man of spotless character and of real ability. I admire Judge Harlan of Kentucky, because he had the courage to stand by the Civil Rights bill, because he is a great lawyer, a broad, comprehensive, and splendid man. Either of these men could carry the entire strength of the party, heal all factions, and give the country honest administration." At the same time he scoffed at the idea that if Blaine were nominated he could not win. (*Bradford* [Pa.] *Era*, May 21, 1884).

On his own role in the coming campaign Ingersoll was vaguely negativistic. He had orated for every Republican president since 1864— Lincoln-Johnson, Grant, Hayes, Garfield-Arthur. He was a Republican fixture, a party mouthpiece. Surely he could be counted on to mount the stump for the Republican ticket in 1884? Would he take an active part? He answered flatly, "Not at all," but then hedged. "Of course I shall feel interested in the result, but I do not expect to take an active part. I have about retired from politics, what little I have had to do in that way, and while I shall do all possible to help the Republican campaign, I can't say that I will do any campaign speaking" (*Topeka Capital*, March 15, 1884). Two months later he was more firm in negation but still equivocal. "I take but little interest in political matters. There is really no great question at issue, no great principles at stake. Politics had drifted into mere personalities. I care but little about the matter. Of course I am a Republican and want that party to succeed, and I believe that it will. Besides the wish I am willing to do what little I can to help" (*Buffalo Courier*, May 19, 1884).

All this aside, Ingersoll would most likely have accepted selection as a delegate to the Republican convention. The party in the District of Columbia, a black enclave, in whose routine business he had not participated, passed over him. At least one black publication reproached them for this disgrace. "This action does them no honor," the *Louisiana Standard* cried out, for "Ingersoll is the best friend of the Negro. . . . When the Supreme Court's civil rights decision sent a wail over the land, covered it with gloom, made every friend of liberty weep and filled every Negro cabin with dire forebodings Ingersoll was the only white man to raise his eloquent voice in protest against the iniquitous decision and plead the cause of humanity. The Negro Race will miss him at the National Convention" (undated clipping, L.C.).

Ingersoll was undecided as to whether he should attend the convention at Chicago as an observer and persuader. The old issues that had made the party sublime had been settled to the satisfaction of the people, and the pioneers were dead or tired. The Republican party like the Democratic party was trying to please everybody, so both conventions and campaigns would be hollow. The Supreme Court had turned the "wards of the nation" over to "the tender mercy or cruel negligence of the States." Still he had not given up hope. "If we can nominate a real Republican at Chicago, one really in favor of protecting citizens at home—one who believes in the Thirteenth and Fourteenth Amendments, and is in favor of a tariff for revenue and reasonable protection, then we will have an enthusiastic and successful campaign, otherwise it will be simply a scramble for office" (*Truth Seeker*, June 7, 1884).

With some misgivings Ingersoll went to the convention. There he had no influence on issues and candidates. In spite of the efforts of friends he was not invited to address the convention. An Ingersoll philippic against the Civil Rights decision might have galvanized the delegates into reviving the pristine splendor of the party as the party of freedom and might even have changed the course of history (certainly as far as the black population was concerned). A by-product might have been the complete enlistment of Ingersoll in the campaign, no matter who the candidate might be. Nothing of the kind happened. The apathy of the people was reflected in the apathy of the convention. Excepting one or two generalities about equal rights the proceedings of the 1884 convention emit not an inkling that the Republican party was tied by history to the black race, that the Supreme Court had dealt the cause of human rights a heavy and intolerable blow, or that the party faced a crisis of conscience and commitment. Ingersoll must have listened with wry amusement as the nominating speech by Judge West of Ohio for Blaine heaped laurels on the Plumed Knight of the Republican party. "Through all its conflicts, from the baptism of blood on the plains of Kansas to the fall of the immortal Garfield, wherever humanity needed succor or freedom needed protection or the country a champion, wherever blows fell thickest and fastest, there in the foreground of the battle was seen to wave the white plume of James G. Blaine, our Henry of Navarre" (*Official Proceedings of the Republican National Convention*, 104). Blaine easily beat Arthur for the nomination, and the Plumed Knight set forth with derring-do on a tired steed carrying a blunt lance.

Ingersoll was a loyal Republican. Before the world he greeted the nomination of Blaine with liberal if measured praise. Blaine was chosen, he said, not by the politicians but by the rank and file. He would make a better president than Garfield, as he had more executive ability. He was a real American, representing the progressive spirit of the country. "He is strong on foreign affairs, would protect our citizens abroad and enlarge our foreign trade, his personal reputation has survived all aspersions. The Democratic party should never hold·office until it is civilized enough to respect the rights of all citizens." Did Ingersoll have any doubts of Republican success? "Of course. Nothing is certain, but my judgment is that we will succeed, but it will require work and lots of it." The parties were equally strong; the Democrats still held the solid South (*Truth Seeker,* June 21, 1884, quoted from *New York Mail and Express*).

Having paid his respects to the party and its nominee Ingersoll had gone as far as he would go. Plenty of work might be required but none would come from him. It was to Blaine that he had said in 1878: "Before leaving this world I would like to see a man of genius in the White House and you are the only chance I know" (Muzzey, *Blaine,* 133). But that was before Star Route. Ingersoll had answered Blaine's call for help in 1868, 1876, and 1880. Now when Blaine needed him most, he was not available. Blaine would soon learn that the chicken had come home to roost.

On June twenty-second Ingersoll was in Cincinnati lecturing on "Orthodoxy." A reporter gushed over him: "Bob Ingersoll embodies in that great big six feet one or two frame more hospitality and good nature to the square inch than a regiment of ordinary men." On the key question Ingersoll gave the Republican cause a damp blanket. "Asked whether he was going to do any political work between now and November, he said he believed not, because it gave him more pleasure to fight the Church than to fight the Democrats, and besides there was no important issue between the parties. If there was, he would go on the stump for Blaine and work as long as he was able" (*Enquirer,* June 23, 1884). He would make no speeches, not one, for Blaine. The reporters, knowing him well, could hardly believe him. When a reporter in Cleveland challenged him to a bet that he would sooner or later mount the stump for the Republican ticket he smiled and declined. He knew himself better (*The Herald,* June 28, 1884).

Ingersoll undertook a long lecture tour, the longest of his career, into the wide open spaces of the Far West. From early July into October the Ingersolls—Robert, Mrs. Ingersoll, Eva, and Maud—journeyed in a wide broken loop from Omaha to Los Angeles, through Iowa, Minnesota, the Dakotas, Montana, Washington, Oregon, and California. In·some ninety days the nominal head of the family delivered about sixty-five lectures, the nonlecture days spent in trains or in sightseeing. The lectures were all on freethought, repeat performances but new to most of his audiences—"Liberty of Man, Woman, and Child," "What We Must Do To Be Saved," "Orthodoxy." Nothing prevented Ingersoll from inflaming Republican rallies along the course, nothing but his own mind.

Having resolved the political problem in personal terms Ingersoll did not brood about it. Politics was part of the human comedy; it could be observed without emotional involvement. He had not been on the Pacific Coast since 1877. In good health and exuberant spirits he renewed acquaintance with sights and sounds and old friends, enjoying preaching freethought night after night to enraptured crowds and enriching the family coffers. His whimsical epistles to the "Dear Folks" back home reflect the vicissitudes of the pilgrims' progress. He began with a bang. From Leonie City, July 10: "We are all alive and well. The weather has been very warm. At Des Moines about 97°—same day 100° Omaha, and it is no slouch today. I have done very well in spite of mercury and Old Sol. My share at Des Moines 400 [dollars]—at Omaha 350—and here it will be at least 600. So you see that we are not losing any thing" (To Farrell, L.C.). At Garrison, Montana, all the rooms at the hotel were occupied, and Mrs. Ingersoll and the girls slept on cots in the "parlor," Ingersoll, Baker, and an assistant on the floor. "Well, we talk of you all a hundred times a day. We love you all, and we are lonesome without you. We want to see your faces and hear your voices every day. We miss you at table and all the food tastes a little bitter without you" (Aug. 1, 1884, *Letters*, 537). From Butte City, Montana, August second, he encapsulated the hurly-burly of travel with good humor. "Nothing new—the same old story—packing and unpacking. What time does the train leave? Is the baggage checked? Where are the umbrellas? What time do we get there? Did you order us to be called? Where is the pass? What has become of Baker? What is the difference between town time and railroad time? Which is the best hotel? What is the train stopping for? How do you like our country? Is this your first visit? Who has the checks? What is the bill?" (L.C.). Also from Butte he wrote to his housekeeper of long standing, Sue Sharkey. He regretted that he did not take her along. "I know that you are as lonely as a dollar in a poor man's pocket and that it was hardly fair to leave you in Washington" (Aug. 2, 1884, *Letters*, 538). From Spokane, August sixth:

> Spoke here last night. Mercury 100° in the shade. We did a splendid job in the way of perspiring. Had a good house and my shirt collar wilted. We leave today for Walla Walla. The people here think this the greatest country in the world and they sincerely pity the poor wretches who live on Madison Square and Boston Common. They enjoy what they call freedom. The scenery between this place and Missoula is very beautiful and impressive. We passed along the shore of Lake Peu D'Oreille—the most beautiful sheet of water we ever saw. It is pronounced here *Peu doray*. Nothing can be more enchanting than this lake surrounded by mountains rising about three thousand feet above its water. The whole scene was like fairyland. (L.C.)

Wherever he went Ingersoll was among friends. He was among enemies too, of course, but the enemies did not materially affect the prevailing welcome. "We have had a wonderful experience," he wrote home from Garrison, Montana. "I find that this wild country is full of my friends. They know me here just as well as they do in Illinois" (Aug. 1, 1884,

Letters, 537). Eva went horseback riding with Jesse Seligman of the banking family and Miss Woods, daughter of the chief justice of the Montana Territory. The *Daily Herald* in Helena felicitated the visitors: "Col. Ingersoll and family today have been the recipients of many calls from the people of Helena, not a few of whom are personal friends and acquaintances who have met them in Washington and shared the splendid hospitality of their Capital home. We are glad that with the Colonel came wife and daughters—as charming people as ever blessed a husband's and father's household—to look at these mountains and share in the wonder-looking of a northwest visit. We greet their coming and regret their going" (July 30). In San Francisco they found their hotel suite filled with thousands of flowers, on the table in the parlor a spray of flowers and evergreens spelling WELCOME (To Farrell, Sept. 4, 1884, L.C.).

It was not flowers, flowers all the way. Canada provided an ambivalent reception. It had been planned that while in the Far Northwest Ingersoll would speak at the new Theater Royal in Victoria, British Columbia, on "Orthodoxy." There he encountered "Orthodoxy" in a very concrete form. First the authorities denied a meeting permit on the ground that the newly remodeled building was a fire hazard. However, the requisite corrections were made and the permit was granted. On the night of the lecture, one-third of the theater having already been filled, the police arrived to declare that the buildng was still a fire hazard and the meeting could not be held. Councilor Boyd and a Mr. James Fell, among others, vehemently protested the stifling of free speech. As a local paper put it, "The latter gentleman, after warmly venting his opinion of the interference, withdrew to find the Superintendent of Police. Councilor Boyd and others meanwhile made no effort to conceal their contempt of the unexpected step which had been taken" (*The Daily Times*, Aug. 29, 1884). When the police stopped the sale of tickets some people dashed around the sides and climbed in through the windows, helped by those already inside. The police definitively announced that the absence of another side door made the assemblage unlawful, whereupon the gallant building manager and an assistant hacked down an old boarded-up side door. Official opposition collapsed and the meeting went on. It was summer and the ardent audience did not complain of the doorway without a door (Interview, *San Francisco Daily Post*, Sept. 16, 1884).

The lecture halls—auditoriums, theaters, opera houses—on the Pacific coast, whether seating four hundred or two thousand, were usually packed "from pit to dome" for Ingersoll appearances. Neither blistering heat nor torrential rains nor the dread of damnation discouraged the multitudes who came for what might be the one chance in a lifetime to hear the great iconoclast as he condemned the old gods and preached the religion of humanity. The journalists, who had not seen Ingersoll since 1877, renewed their love-feasts with him. The newspaper accounts are a garland of praise and pleasure, love of the balding fat man with the twinkling eyes, in rapture at his performance. We dip almost at random. Walla Walla: "Ingersoll is not half as bad as he is painted. We remember, when a little boy, our religious teachers led us to believe that this man, of whom we had heard so much, was a wicked, infamous being, an enemy to religion, to civilization, to happy homes, to progress, and to humankind. Instead of this we find him to be a great, ruddy, good-natured old gentleman, with noble, exalted ideals, and the courage to express them. A man who instead of endeavoring to direct the human family into a pathway leading down to hell, is spending the last days of his brilliant life in an effort to bring man and woman to a higher plane of usefulness and happiness. From the time Col. Ingersoll took the stand until the last word fell on reluctant ears, poetic eloquence flowed from his lips like water from a fountain" (*Sunday Epigram*, Aug. 11, 1884). Sacramento: "When he throws out question after question for his imaginary orthodox opponent to answer, and moves with slow and measured step across the stage, one is apt to see in him a resemblance of a grizzly bear. Not that there is any suggestion of ferocity in his manner. It is the manifestation of power that impresses his listeners at these times. Never is there harshness in his voice or bearing. Even in his strongest invective there is a certain mildness and gentleness. The bitterest pill that he administers to orthodoxy has a sugar coating" (*Daily Bee*, Sept. 12, 1884).

"Colonel Ingersoll is with us again," sighed the weekly *San Franciscan*. "He comes, as usual, to make money, to delight the ungodly, to trouble and exasperate the elect, to weaken the faith of many who would fain believe, and to make unbelief fashionable among the young." The editor deplored the inevitable prospect of an immense audience greeting blows against the church with storms of applause. Alas that the audience would not be of the vicious element but well-dressed and well-behaved people who read and think and lead decent lives. There might be among them some cranks and "hard cases," some pious folk painfully come to hear the enemy, some of the more brainy church people whose faith requires a foundation of reason, while the majority of church members would consider it a sin to attend an Ingersoll lecture or to read newspaper accounts of it. The *San Franciscan* cried,

> What manner of men are the preachers that they let this apostle of infidelity go swaggering through the land, sneering at their faith, and taunting them as if they were pygmies and he a giant? Are they afraid of him? Do they think that his brain is better than theirs? Or do they despise him so much that they think him not worth fighting? If so, they blunder sorely. Ingersoll's work is not to be neutralized by silent contempt. He is a power, a great power. Undoubtedly he has shaken the belief of many thousands, and his daily books and pamphlets are shattering the faith of more. It is no answer to Ingersoll to say that his assaults are nothing new. They are new to ninety in every hundred

of those who listen to Ingersoll, and are as powerful for harm to the church as if they came fresh from the lips of Voltaire, Hume, Paine, Gibbon, Buckle, Lecky, Huxley, or any of the great men at whose heels Ingersoll trots, letting off his fireworks. . . . Who among them [the local ministry] has the pluck to go up against this loud, defiant, and self-confident traducer of God's word and ridiculer of his people? The clergyman who shall so successfully expose Colonel Ingersoll's sophisms, disprove his logic, and meet his wit and eloquence with equal brilliancy of thought and style, would not only lay the Christian church, and all who incline to belief in the faith of their fathers, under a great debt of obligation, but fame and fortune will be his. (Sept. 13, 1884)

Two weeks later the *San Franciscan* published a candid though anonymous response from a local minister. In effect, as in a court of law, the respondent pleaded no contest. After all, Ingersoll was "the greatest orator and the finest rhetorician that speaks the English language. No man now living can stand up against him." The editor's call for a champion of the faith must be as bootless as would have been the cry of an ancient Greek for an opponent worthy of Demosthenes. The interlocking of editor and minister in helpless despair was so complete that one might suspect a freethinker behind it.

In San Francisco Ingersoll met again with his cousin Mrs. Sarah Cooper, a liberal-minded social worker. On September fifteenth Mrs. Cooper and her daughter Hattie took the Ingersolls and Mrs. Baker on a tour of the Jackson and Stanford free kindergartens. The children sang songs of welcome and thanks for gifts, and the visitors praised the craft work and drawings. "Comment was freely expressed by the visitors, and the venerable Colonel himself [now fifty-one] seemed almost a child again, so completely was he imbued with the spirit of the scene" (*San Francisco Morning Call*, Sept. 16, 1884).

Mrs. Cooper told Ingersoll about a Mrs. Mary Merchant. The woman's young son had died and she was agonizing over his fate in the hereafter. Mrs. Merchant was a churchgoer. Could Ingersoll comfort her? He would try. His letter to Mrs. Merchant (which unfortunately is not included in the *Letters* or *Works*) is a little masterpiece akin to Lincoln's letter to Mrs. Bixby in the context of patriotism (Sept. 27, 1884, L.C.). He blends old ideas and phrases from his storehouse of rational compassion into a balm for all mourners, believers and unbelievers. He knows that he cannot lessen Mrs. Merchant's grief and anguish but perhaps he can do something to drive fear out of her heart. "If there is a God, let us hope that he is good; and if he is good, the good have nothing to fear." He had heard that her son was kind and generous. Like begets like, and kindness evokes kindness; her son would find kindness wherever he may be. "You would not inflict endless pain upon your worst enemy. Is God worse than you?" No human being knows anything beyond the grave. All the churches know no more about it than an anthill. "Let us have courage. Under the seven-hued arch of hope let the dead sleep. . . . Look to your own heart and believe what it says, and wait with patience and without fear for what the future has for all. . . . I wish I could say something that would put a star in your night of grief—a little flower in your lonely path; and if an unbeliever has such a wish, surely an infinitely good being never made a soul to be the food of pain through countless years."

Mrs. Merchant immediately responded to "Dear Colonel Ingersoll." Her gratitude overflowed. "While I will not doubt the existence of a God, I feel that I can rest my grief-stricken heart on his goodness and mercy, and you have helped me to do this. . . . I am writing while people are talking about me, just a line to thank you from the bottom of my heart for the comfort you have given me today. You great, good man, I see the traces of your tears all over your letter, and I could clasp your hand and bless you for comfort you have given to my poor heart" (MacDonald, 54).

What about politics? It was impossible to ignore it. Although Ingersoll proudly asserted in the privacy of the family that he had not read the party platforms or any of the campaign speeches he could not cut off his inveterate interest in the quadrennial spectacle in which he had played so prominent a part so many times. He watched the current encounter between Tweedledum and Tweedledee with amusement. Competing doggerel highlighted the personal differences between the candidates. Cleveland had fathered a child out of wedlock, and Blaine had been accused of sexual improprieties in his youth and still had not freed himself of the charge that he had sold his vote in Congress. So the Democrats in torchlight parades chanted:

> Blaine, Blaine, James G. Blaine
> The continental liar from the State of Maine.

And the Republicans countered:

> Ma! Ma! Where's my Pa?
> Gone to the White House,
> Ha! Ha! Ha!

Ingersoll wrote to Clint from Portland: "They are very anxious to know how I stand about politics. I tell them that I am not going to take any part. The story about Cleveland is a settler and the ones about Blaine are rather salty. Both the candidates are a little tainted with original sin and both seem to have suffered from the 'thorn in the flesh.' It is a nasty business and the principal issues in the campaign will be fornication and adultery. Great country!" (Aug. 13, 1884, L.C.).

To insatiable reporters Ingersoll firmly reiterated that he would not participate in the campaign. He was not a politician, he held no public office and wanted none, and he owed no debts to be paid on the stump. Had there been a vital issue between the parties he would have entered the fray. A reporter was not satisfied. Did the Colonel mean that no great issue was at stake? Yes, that was it exactly. "If it were a matter of personal liberty, I should take part. If the Republican party had stood by the Civil Rights bill, I would have taken part in the present campaign." Could he still be counted on as a Republican? "Certainly I am a Republican" (*San Francisco Daily Evening Post*, Sept. 16, 1884).

The long western tour ended with a bang. Ingersoll wrote from Los Angeles to "Dear Folks, I lectured here last night—had a splendid house and everybody happy. We leave in two hours—2 P.M.—for the ranch. We will be there Saturday or Sunday. Everybody wants to have me stay and lecture again. This is the way in every town. So you see 'Ingersollism' is growing" (Oct. 9, 1884, L.C.).

The Ingersolls, all of them, had earned a good long rest in their newly built ranch house in New Mexico. The train from Los Angeles brought them to Las Vegas, where there was a layover, but no incognito peace. A local reporter-friend pounced upon them at dinner in the depot dining room and noted everything they did and every word that fell from the great man's lips.

> The big man got up and said "howdy," and all three of the ladies smiled pleasantly and called the scribe by name. "We have been to California," said the Colonel, "and we are now en route to the ranch house all fixed up for us and we will live at home there for two months. Oh yes, if I lecture in Las Vegas you shall be my manager. Thanks (to the waiter), don't mind if I do" and he helped himself to another piece of chicken. "Tariff is the main point in the political canvass now. No sir, made no speeches this campaign. Hello, Brundt, how's the springs (and up he jumps and shakes hands with Charley Brundt, of the springs). Yes, sir, you've got to settle these land grant titles before New Mexico can come before the world in her proper and prosperous light. Of course the Democrats claim that Cleveland will be elected. Did you ever see an election where they didn't claim everything and get nothing? Send me *The Optic* for a couple of months. Want to get acquainted with your way of doing things." He walked up to the counter, paid his bill, not claiming to be a railroad man, and taking Mrs. Ingersoll by the arm and followed by the two young ladies entered the Pullman palace. Smart? Why, he's the smartest man in the United States today, and as nature made him you find him always. Some men forget that one man is as good as another as long as he does right, but Robert G. Ingersoll never does. (The article was headlined NATURE'S MASTERPIECE. *The Daily Optic*, Oct. 11, 1884)

On October twelfth a free public barbecue feast welcoming the Ingersolls, probably engineered by Dorsey, was held in Springer. At tables in the central square several hundred persons partook of two big steers roasted in an open pit before them, bread, and coffee. Their stomachs well filled, the celebrants repaired to the courthouse to hear a free lecture by Ingersoll. The courtoom had been decorated with evergreens, a military band from Fort Union played, and cattle bosses and cowboys piled in to fill up the physically available space, sitting on seats, railings, and tables, or standing side by side. Ingersoll delivered his favorite lecture, "Liberty of Man, Woman, and Child," spicing his generalities with local references, the crowd "answering his every mood with smiles, tears, or uproarious laughter, according as he swayed their souls with the pathos or humor of his remarks, and interrupting him with frequent outbursts of applause in manifestation of their unqualified delight." Finally everyone so inclined could shake hands with the guest of honor (*The Trinidad Review*, n.d.).

From the new ranch house next to Dorsey's, named Maudeva for the girls, Ingersoll invited the Farrells for a visit, all expenses paid. Sue had been coughing; it would be good for her health. "We have nothing to do but to enjoy ourselves. We walk and ride, read and talk, eat and sleep—look at the shadows upon the undulating plains" (To Sue, Oct. 16, 1884, L.C.). The Farrells were unable to come, so Ingersoll said that he would hurry home if it would not offend Dorsey, who had taken so many pains to make a place for them. Maybe next year the entire household would be together in Maudeva. "I know that Sue Sharkey would enjoy the melodious song of the coyote" (To Sue Farrell, Oct. 23, 1884, *Letters*, 538; To Sue Farrell, Oct. 27, 1884, L.C.).

At the hour of truth, with the election returns coming in state by state—a confused household at Maudeva. "We hardly know whether to laugh or cry and are not quite certain which side we are on" (To Dear Folks, Nov. 6, 1884, *Letters*, 179). Then it became clear that Cleveland had won. "Blaine is busted." Ingersoll's second letter to his brother-in-law puts on record, though in a private communication, his real feeling about Blaine. It moves in a crescendo of gloating. As a party regular he was disappointed at the outcome; on the other hand he found comfort in the thought that the party had been punished for not taking a stand against the Supreme Court on civil rights. He did not forget to laugh at the ministers, most of whom had supported Blaine. "The only persons for whom I am really sorry are the 600 preachers who called on Blaine to assure him of the support of Jehovah & Co.—I hate to have the old firm disappointed." He was a little glad that the New York vote was so close. "I feel way down in my gaiters that I could have carried the state for Blaine, and it occurs to me that Blaine will have a like impression in his mind.—Of course it is wrong to be a little malicious, but I am growing that way as I get older. Blaine has reached the end of his career. I wish sometimes he had allowed me to be his friend—in other words—I regret that he is not the man I once thought he was. And yet—after thinking the election all over—of the effect on the country—taking into consideration the way the leaders have always trated me, the verdict of my heart is 'Glad of it' " (Nov. 6, 1884, L.C.; *Letters*, 181. The *Letters* omits Ingersoll's personal grievance against the party, "taking into consideration the way leaders have always treated me," supplying asterisks).[1] He will enjoy seeing the old Republican guard take a back seat. "Let them R.I.P. The atty for the Defs [defendants] in the Star Route trial has his revenge." The attorney, not the defendants.

Cleveland's popular margin in New York State was a mere 1,149; nationwide, a mere 62,689. If an itinerant Ingersoll had mounted stumps for Blaine, would the scales have tipped the other way?

On November eleventh Ingersoll wrote to Clint: "I also enclose an article from the Denver News—a Democratic paper—about Dorsey and myself. I like that and I hope that it will meet the eye of Mr. Blaine. The mills of the gods are somewhat slow, but they grind 'exceeding fine' " (L.C.). The *News*, in a post-election analysis, discussed ironically how deeply pained Ingersoll and Dorsey must have felt at Blaine's defeat. Dorsey, Blaine's partner in corruption, had made him Secretary of State [hardly true] and had reenforced his presidential possibility by buying the election of 1880 in New York and Indiana. Ingersoll of the great "Plumed Knight" speech was the most useful man of honor who was ever deluded into supporting him. Instead of respecting his debt of gratitude to Dorsey and Ingersoll, Blaine tried to make a scapegoat of Dorsey in the Star Route prosecution and subjected Ingersoll to the ordeal of the defense (*Denver Rocky Mountain News*, Nov. 9, 1884). In his letter Ingersoll took no offense at the unflattering words about Dorsey. He had campaigned with Dorsey and had no illusions about the practical politician's role in the Garfield victory.

In the ensuing months reporters swarmed around Ingersoll for analysis of the Blaine disaster. He was glad to oblige. His own abstinence? He assured them that there had never been any rupture with Blaine, that no unpleasant words had ever passed between them. "I took no part in the campaign; first, because there was no very important issue, no great principle at stake, and, second, I thought that I had done enough, and, third, because I wanted to do something else" (*Topeka Commonwealth*, Nov. 21, 1884; *Works*, VIII, 216). He set out a litany of reasons why Blaine lost. On the black question Ingersoll appears to have been self-contradictory: The nation as a whole was not sympathetic to the black and yet the party should have come out strongly for civil rights. He was gentle with the Reverend Burchard, whose history-making libel of the Democratic party as the party of rum, romanism, and rebellion handed the Catholic vote to the Democrats. "I think though that it is time to let up on Burchard. He has already unloaded on the Lord" (*Cleveland Plain Dealer*, Dec. 11, 1884; *Works*, VIII, 223).

And what a golden opportunity Blaine ruined when he sat down with the captains of industry and finance—Gould, Vanderbilt, Russell

Sage, and the like—at Delmonico's (the purple press would label the banquet "Belshazzar's Feast"). What a superb moment to extol the Republican party as the party not of the rich but of all the people! "I would have given $50,000 had I been Blaine, to have been invited to that dinner at Delmonico's." He demonstrated what he would have done. He would have spoken on the labor-capital question, would have warned the capitalists that their safety and power lay in the welfare and contentment of the laboring classes. He would have pointed a finger at Gould or Vanderbilt and asked what were the great railroads of the country worth if they had to fight against the laboring men, to make bitter and deadly enemies of the wage earners? He would have lectured the banqueters on true morality, that real success in life is to be found in advancing the human race, not in building palaces and amassing fortunes. Capital should treat Labor with justice, honesty, and fairness, and should provide pensions for employees aged and enfeebled in its service. Ingersoll's might-have-been jeremiad struck his listeners with awe. "Thus," recorded one, "would Ingersoll have spoken had he been Blaine. Such are some of the ideas that he would have expressed, and from the eloquent way in which he uttered them while seated in a chair, in a hotel reading room, before an audience of fifteen or twenty hearers, he would have created something of a sensation at the feast of millionaires of the United States" (*Albany Daily Press and Knickerbocker*, Feb. 24, 1885). In his mind Ingersoll was not a Socialist, but in his heart he was. It is not incongruous that Debs adored him and his memory.

At Maudeva Ingersoll put together a new lecture, "Which Way," a mixture of his familiar arguments on reason and science versus superstition. It has its moments of authentic Ingersollism, of rollicking wit, epigrams, purple patches. On the "power" of prayer: "They often pray for the impossible. In the House of Representatives in Washington I once heard a chaplain pray for what he must have known was impossible. Without a change of countenance, without a smile, with a face solemn as a sepulchre, he said: 'I pray thee, O God, to give Congress wisdom.' It may be that ministers really think their prayers do good and it may be that frogs imagine their croaking brings spring" (*Works*, III, 422). A slogan for freethought: "Let the Gods take care of themselves. Let us live for man" (443). On the art of living: "The world is a great orange tree filled with blossoms, with ripening and ripened fruit, while, underneath the bending boughs, the fallen slowly turn to dust. Each orange is a life. Let us squeeze it dry, get all the juice there is, so that when death comes we can say: 'There is nothing left but worthless peel' " (445).

"Which Way" ends in a kind of cyclorama of human history, past, present, and future, its theme perfect for a histrionic display of the highest order. First were the ages of entrenched superstition with their peasant huts, robes of priest and king, barbaric rites, and persecution. "I see the victim on the rack, I hear the tendons as they break. . . . This was" (447).

Next came the present. The world was at war, thrones were crumbling, altars falling. Discoverers enlarged the world, inventors conquered nature, and teachers slowly were taking the place of priests. "This is" (448). Finally the popes and kings and priests would be gone, all the gods dead. A new religion would shed glory on mankind.

> It is the gospel of this world, the religion of the body, of the heart and brain, the evangel of health and joy. I see a world of peace, where labor reaps its true rewards, a world without prisons, without workhouses, without asylums for the insane, a world in which the gibbet's shadow does not fall, a world where the poor girl, trying to win bread with the needle, the needle that has been called "the asp for the breast of the poor," is not driven to the desperate choice of crime or death, of suicide or shame. I see a world without the beggar's outstretched palm, the miser's heartless, stony stare, the piteous wail of want, the pallid face of crime, the lurid lips of lies, the cruel eyes of scorn. I see a world without disease of flesh or brain, shapely and fair, the married harmony of form and end, and as I look life lengthens, fear dies, joy deepens, love is intensified. The world is free. This shall be. (448)

Refreshed by five weeks at the ranch and with a new message of hope and cheer in his baggage Ingersoll was ready and eager to resume the crusade for freethought. He and Mrs. Ingersoll started back home in mid-November. It was a slow journey at top speed through many stations for spreading the word (and reaping the profits). "I am to be at Topeka on the 19—Atchison 20—St. Joe 21, Kansas City 22, St. Louis 23—Springfield, Ill. 24, Jacksonville 25. That is as far as I know," (To "Dear Folks," Nov. 6, 1884, *Letters*, 179). Along the way he made engagements for, among other places, Evansville, Indianapolis, Louisville, Chicago, Milwaukee, Cincinnati, and Cleveland, filling out a standard itinerary for an Ingersoll tour of little more than three weeks.

In the public eye on- and offstage Ingersoll was an easy and juicy prey for the admiring press. He was tireless, and gave every reporter his full attention. "The colonel himself, though he has had very little rest for the past week, looked very bright and appeared in excellent spirits." How did he enjoy the trip to the Pacific Coast? "The very best." The ranch? "Perfectly happy." What did he think of the attacks by the ministers? Ah, that was a good one. "I feel a good deal as the girl did when the young man squeezed her hand. She said it didn't hurt her, and seemed to please him" (*Kansas City Journal*, Nov. 23, 1884). In Springfield a fearless but not unique local paper heralded the impending appearance: "Already the super-religious nose to advertise him. The surest way in the world to fill a house for Col. Ingersoll is for some blatant ass to go mouthing around about 'Pope Bob,' the 'blaspheming infidel,' and other choice garlands in which to entwine Ingersoll's name" (*Morning Monitor*, Nov. 26, 1884). In St. Louis a reporter observed that Lord

Dundas sat in one box, Governor Hedley in another (*The Republican*, Nov. 23, 1884). A reporter latched on to Ingersoll at the close of his lecture in Louisville. He sat down in a chair at a corner downstage and engaged in a rapid-fire exchange on civil service reform. It would not work, he said. Cleveland would find tricks in reducing the force and in rehiring that would sweep Republicans out and Democrats in. If a Republican was otherwise suitable, he would be rejected because he had long fingernails. "I don't think there will be a genuine enforcement of the law. We didn't enforce it, you know, and they won't" (*The Commercial*, Nov. 28, 1884).

An account in the *Chicago Tribune* reflected Ingersoll's attractiveness in the big cities, particularly to radicals of every description, almost all of whom were more than ready to claim him as their own, especially since he had not sullied himself by participating in the hollow Blaine-Cleveland contest.

> McVicker's Theatre was filled to overflowing yesterday afternoon, the attraction being Col. Ingersoll's new lecture entitled "Which Way." . . . The audience was more representative than fashionable. It was a sea of bright eager, attentive faces—an audience of which any orator might be proud. There were many women present, not that class of women whose diamonds sparkle, and whose ribbons flutter, and whose handkerchiefs exhale sweet perfume in the front pews of palace churches, but women of [Women's Rights activist] Belva Lockwood proclivities—women who had Rights (with a Big R), and who don't propose to be the "slaves of men or a tyrannical religion." As a rule they were plainly dressed, serious women—the kind that dudes don't attempt to fool with. The male portion of the audience was more representative. Socialists were there—the men who talk blood and anarchy on the Lake Front Sunday afternoons; bloated capitalists and horny-handed laborers were there; brazen infidels were there—men who spout blood-curdling blasphemy at "free thought" and "liberal league" gatherings on the West Side on Sunday evenings, and alack-a-day! there were good church-going deacons there also. (Dec. 1, 1884)

What about politics in the future? Ingersoll disparaged the boom for Blaine in 1888. "I have heard of counting chickens before they are hatched, but in this case the eggs have not been laid." How would the election affect the business interests? "Very little. . . . We all know that Democrats are about as fond of good times as other people. The capitalists will take care of themselves. You know that a dollar has—above all things—the instinct of self-preservation. During the election all kinds of disasters and horrors were predicted by each party in case the other succeeded, but nobody now expects the predictions will come to pass. I hope that Cleveland will make a good president; that his administration will be conservative and satisfactory to all sections. All I want is good government. I want the old ship to steer clear of rocks and breakers, and if that is accomplished I don't care who the captain is" (*Milwaukee Journal*, Dec. 1, 1884).

Always there was the tension between love of his crusade and love of his family. He wrote to his daughter Eva on December second, "Kiss that Maud for me. Now kiss her again, and tell her to kiss you for me— once more—that will do. I love you Eva—you are fairer, sweeter, purer, than any girl that ever leaped from Shakespeare's brain" (*Letters*, 504). And on December sixth: "Words cannot express the feeling I have for you and Maud and mother. You are the Trinity that I adore—all that I am capable of loving I love you. Give my love to all and kiss all for me. We will be together in a few days" (*Letters*, 540).

Back in Washington Ingersoll wound up the tour by lecturing on December fourteenth at the National Theater on "Orthodoxy." Posters advertising the lecture had been torn down and it was raining, but nevertheless the house was full. Several members of Congress were present. For the occasion Ingersoll included the section from "Which Way?" on the chaplin's prayer for the impossible (that God confer wisdom on the Congress). At this point the whole audience convulsed with laughter (*The Republic*, Dec. 14, 1884; *The National Republican*, Dec. 15, 1884).

On December twenty-sixth Ingersoll received a letter from one Isaac T. Dyer of Quincy, Illinois, challenging him to a debate on religion. The letter was not signed Rev. Isaac T. Dyer or Isaac T. Dyer, D.D., but the letterhead identified the correspondent as "Patentee of the Eagle and National Refrigerator." Ingersoll declined. Obviously, he wrote, Mr. Dyer was not interested in having hell abolished because he hoped to carry on business in the next world. "Biased as you are and must be by your business, prejudiced by your own interest, I think it hardly worthwhile to discuss the question of eternal fire with you" (Dec. 29, 1884, *Letters*, 271).

New Year's Day 1885 was gloomy in Washington. Dull and dreary clouds hung over the city, a chill in the air hinted of coming snow. Republican politicians were preparing to leave the scene of power for the first time since the Civil War. People were talking about the terminal illness of Grant, and not all were sorry for him. Blaine seemed finished. In tune with prevailing sadness or perhaps out of embarrassment due to nonparticipation in the campaign the Ingersolls did not make and receive calls; they hung a basket at the door for visitors to leave cards and be on their way. Sending a season's greeting to his brother Robert reflected the atmosphere of the capital city. Public office was a poor business. "I think of the men whom I have known and are now at the bottom of the ladder. The public is a kind of strumpet after all. Better a crust with contentment than a 'busted' politician without a crumb. It makes me glad, as I look around at the wrecks, that I was not popular enough to get office" (To John, Jan. 1, 1885, *Letters*, 182). The times were hard in Washington, but the family had plenty of coal and enough to eat—and more than that, "a thousand times more, love." He would resume lecturing on the eleventh, lecture every day thereafter for the rest of the month, take two or three days' rest, and return to the platform into May.

So he was in motion again, this meteor flashing across the the sky of America. In New York Ingersoll ran afoul of his polemic adversary, Reverend Talmage. Talmage was a zealot—in plain language, a bigot. Incensed at Ingersoll's free-and-easy tone in speaking of Jesus Christ, Talmage demanded that Ingersoll be gagged. The blasphemy laws should be enforced, he stated preemptorily. No issue of free speech was involved— good speech was legal, bad speech was not. "But I am asked, 'Don't you believe in free speech?' Yes, I believe in all kinds of freedom. I believe in driving horses, but not in driving over others. I believe in the free use of knives, but not in assassination. I believe in free speech, but not in the freedom of blasphemy. Freedom to do right but not freedom to do wrong. It would have been one of the grandest dramas ever enacted in the Brooklyn Theater if last Sunday evening my friend, Patrick Campbell, chief of police, a Christian man, had marched on the stage with a platoon of police and, laying his hand on the lecturer's shoulder, had said, 'In the name of the common law, in the name of the state of New York and the city of Brooklyn, stop! Stop here and stop now' " (*Truth Seeker*, Feb. 1, 1885, quoted from *New York World*).

With matching belligerence Ingersoll retorted in a lecture titled "Blasphemy" to a full house in the same theater. "Dr. Talmage wants to crush all infidels. There have been other times when it has been sought to crush the infidels. I want to tell him tonight, and all others like him, that day has passed. I want to tell him that all the churches in the United States can't ever crush us. That day has gone never to return. Superstition has caused too many tears; it has broken too many hearts; it has filled too many insane asylums; it has kept this world in darkness long enough. If they think they can crush free thought in this country, let them try it" (*New York Herald*, Feb. 23, 1885). The audience cheered and cheered again, and Chief Campbell was conspicuous by his absence.

In the hotel suite, with the usual reporters and people, pontifically and benevolently the oracle puffed away at his cigar and answered every question, the big and the little, the old and the new, seriously and/or humorously. What did he think of interviews in general? They could be a blessing, but if questions are impudent or trivial and answers are the same as the questions, they were failures. When the interviewer makes up both the questions and the answers "such interviews are always interesting, and, as a whole, the questions are to the point and the answers perfectly responsive" (*Cleveland Plain Dealer*, Sept. 5, 1885; *Works*, VIII, 240).

Why was he out of politics? The great questions of nationhood and liberty had been settled, he believed. The Supreme Court settled wrongly the rights of black citizens, but the Republican party submitted and so that was not an issue in the campaign. Only protection tariffs and office-holding remained. Not all Republicans favored protection, and not all Democrats opposed it. "On the other question—office—both parties were and are in perfect harmony" (*Iowa State Register*, May 23, 1885; *Works*, VIII, 237). Was he still a Republican? He stated his political creed. "I believe that this is a Nation. I believe in the equality of all men before the law, irrespective of race, religion, or color. I believe that there should be a dollar's worth of silver in a silver dollar. I believe in a free ballot and a fair count. I believe in protecting those industries, and those only, that need protection. I believe in unrestricted coinage of gold and silver. I believe in the rights of the State, the rights of the citizen, and the sovereignty of the Nation. I believe in good times, good health, good crops, good prices, good wages, good food, good clothes, and in the absolute and unqualified liberty of thought. If such belief makes me a Republican, then that is what I am" (*Cleveland Plain Dealer*, Sept. 5, 1885). Had an era of good feeling set in between the North and South? Yes. "We should stop thinking about North and South. We are one people, and whether we agree or disagree one destiny awaits us" (*New York Mail and Express*, March 10, 1885; *Works*, VIII, 230).

What was the source of the greatest trouble among men? He stated his religious creed. "Superstition. That has caused more agony, more tears, persecution, and real misery than all other causes combined. The other name for superstition is ignorance. When men learn that all sin is a mistake, that all dishonesty is a blunder, that even intelligent selfishness will respect the rights of others, there will be vastly more happiness in this world. Shakespeare says that 'there is no darkness but ignorance.' Sometime man will learn that when he steals from another, he robs himself—that the way to be happy is to make others so, and that it is far better to assist his fellow-man than to fast, say prayers, count beads, or build temples to the unknown" (*Iowa Register*, May 23, 1885). The Salvation Army arose because of the Church of England's indifference to the poor. "I don't suppose the Salvation Army will accomplish much. To improve mankind you must change conditions. It is not enough to work simply upon the emotional nature. The surroundings must be such as naturally to provide virtuous actions" (*Truth Seeker*, Sept. 5, 1885; *Works*, VIII, 248). Is the Catholic Church an enemy to republican liberty? "Every church that holds itself under greater obligation to a pope than to a people is dangerous to human liberty."

Pursuing the argument against superstition Ingersoll fired a brilliant broadside against the Christian Sabbath as hypocrisy.

The cars run Sundays, and out of the profits hundreds of ministers are supported. The great iron and steel works fill with smoke and fire the Sabbath air, and the proprietors divide the profits with the churches. The printers of the city are busy Sunday afternoons and evenings, and the presses during the night, so that the sermons of Sunday may reach the heathen on Monday. The servants of the rich are denied the privileges of the sanctuary. The coachman sits on the box outdoors, while his employer kneels in church, preparing himself for the heavenly chariot. The iceman goes about on the holy day, keeping believers cool, they knowing at the same time that he is making it hot for himself in the world to come. Christians cross the Atlantic, knowing that the ship will pursue its way on the Sabbath. They write letters to their friends knowing that they will be carried in violation of Jehovah's laws by wicked men. Yet they hate to see a pale-faced sewing girl enjoying a few hours by the sea; a poor mechanic walking in the fields; or a tired mother watching her children playing on the grass. Nothing endures, nothing ever will be more utterly absurd and disgusting than a Puritan Sunday. (*Truth Seeker*, Sept. 5, 1885; *Works*, VIII, 240)

Are evolution and revealed religion compatible? Could a man be an evolutionist and a Christian? "Evolution and Christianity may be compatible provided you take the ground that Christianity is only one of the links in the chain, one of the phases of civilization. But if you mean by Christianity what is generally understood, of course that and evolution are absolutely incompatible" (*New York Mail and Express*, March 10, 1885). Did he believe in the existence of a Supreme Being? "I do not believe in any Supreme Being who made the universe and governs nature. I do not say that there is no such Being—all I say is that I do not believe that such a Being exists. . . . This universe—embracing all that is—all atoms, all stars, each grain of sand and all the constellations, each thought and dream of animal and man, all matter and all force, all doubt and all belief, all virtue and all crime, all joy and all pain, all growth and all decay—is all there is. It does not act because it is moved from without. It acts from within. It is actor and subject—means and end. It is infinite; the infinite could not have been created. It is indestructible and that which cannot be destroyed was not created. I am a Pantheist" (*Philadelphia Times*, Sept. 25, 1885; *Works*, VIII, 240). Isn't the belief of the agnostic more satisfactory to the believer than that of the atheist? "There is no difference. The Agnostic is an Atheist. The Atheist is an Agnostic. The Agnostic says, 'I do not know, but I do not believe there is any God.' The Atheist says the same. The Orthodox Christian says he knows there is a God, but we know that he does not know. He simply believes. He cannot know. The Atheist cannot know that God does not exist." Would he lecture in the coming winter? "Yes, about the same as usual. Woe is me if I preach not my gospel" (*Cleveland Plain Dealer*, Sept. 5, 1885).

In his family letters there was no hint of messiahship, no cloak of Olympian wisdom on the nation's affairs. He accepted the hardships of travel whimsically. "I know," he wrote to Clint, "you are enjoying home better than the road. We had to get up this morning at 5. That would have made you happy. The weather was cool in Rochester last night. 6° below zero. The air was fresh and bracing. No malaria perceptible"

(Jan. 27, 1885, Bradford, Pa., L.C.). Mrs. Ingersoll was brave but not doing well; she would not stay the course. He gave his daughters paternal advice. "A moment lost can never be recovered—a joy lost is gone forever" (Jan. 22, 1885, Dear Girls, L.C.). He reported on his box office, the index of his popularity and financial success. The prospects in Portland were good. At seven o'clock the advance sale was over two hundred dollars; a "very good house"in Auburn (Portland, Me., Jan. 17, 1885, to Maud; Gloversville, N.Y., Jan. 22, 1885, L.C.). "I had a very enthusiastic audience at Salem. What would the forefathers have thought could they have heard such talk? I think that I am going to have a successful week" (Boston, June 22, 1885, Eva and Maud, *Letters*, 540).

He described the passing scene, the winter revivals, the young at play. "The winter in this country is the time for revivals, and in nearly every town they are having what they call an outpouring of the Holy Ghost—whatever that is. So in nearly every town they have a skating rink, and all the young people are crazy on rollers" (Rochester, N.Y., Jan. 24, 1885, Dear Girls, L.C.). In his hotel room in Portland he heard the boom-boom and rat-a-tat of an approaching band, looked out of the window, and saw a contingent of the Salvation Army on the march, cymbals, drums, and flag-bearer at the head, "and following in couples a dozen women and some twenty boys—all wading along in the slush and snow. A poor beggarly wretched-looking set, the boys among them not more than ten years old. Just as they got opposite my window they halted—and, one of the leaders cried out 'Now, all that have been saved shout "Amen" ' and thereupon they all cried 'Amen.' 'Now,' said the man, 'once more,' and the boys and girls yelled at the top of their voices 'Amen.' Then the cymbals clashed—the drums thundered—the man waved the flag and away they shuffled through the snow. All I could say was 'Is the world going mad?' " (Portland, Jan. 17, 1885, To Maud, L.C.).

In Pittsfield and Salem, where in olden times witches had been hanged and Quakers tied to the tails of wagons and whipped out of town, his imagination was vivid. He almost expected to see stains of witch blood on the streets, and was happy that he did not live in those times. "The more I think of these things the more I hate every form of religion. How cruel it all is. When we think how willing thousands and millions have been to kill their fellows to please a King, no wonder that they would do the same to please their God" (Pittsfield, Jan. 14, 1885, To Maud, L.C.).

On June twenty-second, for a moment alone and very lonely in his room at the Adams House in Boston, the weary, wayworn traveller yearned for a respite from the public life. He visualized a speedy transit of lecture engagements, then a family reunion and a blissful period at the beach. "We will have a lovely time this summer—riding—boating, walking, picnicking, and above all—being together. Now it is raining with all its might—but it is early—only a little while after ten. At five I go to Lawrence—then to Manchester, N.H.—then Fitchburg, Mass.; then Holyoke—Southampton, where Jonathan Edwards used to preach—then to Boston, then Fall River—then to Boston Monday morning to meet the sweetest girls, the dearest wife in all the world" (Boston, June 22, 1885, To Eva and Maud, L.C.).

Ingersoll had put the house of freethought in order. What about his own house? He had told a reporter early in 1884 that Washington was a beautiful city, a pleasant place in which to live, and that he expected to stay there the rest of his life (*Topeka Capital*, March 15, 1884). The election of 1884 had ended that prospect. He had turned his back on politics, and politics had walloped him. To the victorious Democrats he was anathema, to the defeated Republicans a deserter. His Washington law practice was drying up. What should he do? It was time to think afresh of his possibilities.

Practice law in another city? Serving clients, being at their beck and call, had become increasingly disagreeable. "Eva, I think, wants me to settle in New York, but I hate to practice law. It is a d----d small business. It is nothing to be at the head of the bar" (To Farrell, N.Y., Oct. 27, 1885, *Letters*, 543). Continue on the lecture circuit in freethought? He and his family were tired of it—and at any rate how long could it last? Had he not said his say, delivered his message? Was he not in danger of becoming a mere itinerant showman, living out of a suitcase and performing with declining power the same old act to smaller and smaller audiences, thereby bringing discredit upon the freethought movement that it did not need? (Not that this was an imminent likelihood.) He was buoyed by a sense that he was not losing his magnetism. "I lectured at Brooklyn," he wrote to Clint on November eighth, "and the rain poured and poured and came down in sheets and bedspreads and coverlets. You never saw a worse night, and yet we had a right good house. I do not believe my popularity ever had a severer trial. The folks went over with me and we met Mr. Conway [Unitarian minister and author of the trail-blazing two volume *Life of Thomas Paine*] and his family. I delivered a good speech for me and the people seemed enormously pleased" (L.C.).

Ingersoll began feeling out the law practice in New York. He was able to report to Clint on March twenty-fifth: "I am getting along all right in the law business and hope to do quite a stroke of business" (L.C.). Having plunged into the law, he could not readily withdraw. In July he began an important case, a minor sensation in New York. The American Rapid Transit Company had gone into receivership. The receiver leased its poles and wires to the colossal Western Union, which proceeded to tear them down. Ingersoll appeared in the Supreme Court of New York on behalf of the Bankers and Merchants Company, which had a proprietary interest in Rapid Transit, suing Western Union for injunction and damages. He slapped a chart on the judge's desk and traced the relationship between Bankers and Merchants and Rapid Transit and tore into Western Union's claim of title to the destroyed property. "If they belonged to the Western Union, why did they cut? The woman who was satisfied to have the baby cut in two to settle a dispute as to who owned it was not the mother." He won a preliminary injunction. The popular press headlined RAIDERS IN COURT and THE TELEGRAPH OUTRAGE (*New York Herald*, July 15, 16, 1885). Law could be more hectic, more insistent than the lecture circuit, but victory at the bar had its own sweetness. "I have had a devil of a time here, tried three suits this week here & I have succeeded in all" (To Farrell, July 31, 1885, L.C.).

Soon the family was with Ingersoll at the Hoffman House in New York preparatory to leaving for Long Beach. He checked his weight, a perennial problem. He was not a very fat man—he could not be compared to a three-hundred pounder like Speaker Reed of the House—but his excess pounds gravitated to his midriff, making him appear corpulent (incidentally, an easy target for caricature). " '211 lbs'—That is what the man said as I stepped off the scales today. '211 lbs' is what I said to the folks as we sat down to dinner. 'Don't fast any longer,' said Maud, 'you will be a living skeleton.' " Thereupon he decided to aim at two hundred, after which he would celebrate with a glorious feast. It would consist of:

"1. Potatoes—fried, not too hard.
2. Green corn—lots of butter
3. Cantaloupes
4. Hot biscuits and butter
5. More potatoes
6. More green corn
7. Some cantaloupes
8. Glass of cream
9. A little fried chicken with potatoes
10. Corn fritters with chicken gravy
11. Another cantaloupe"
(To Farrell, N.Y., July 29, 1885, *Letters*, 473)

At last the Ingersolls arrived at Long Beach, haven of rest and relaxation. On August fifth he wrote to Clint that the "cottage" was "quiet, cool—roomy, comfortable." He had been "busy as an ant in a hill that has been stepped on. We see daylight and all will come out right" (L.C.). Alas, it was not to be. Day after day legal business kept pulling him to the city "for stays and injunctions" (To Farrell, L.C.). The weather was capricious, uniformly unpleasant. "Yesterday I nearly roasted—today I nearly froze—tomorrow I expect to do both" (Aug. 25, 1885, L.C.). The weather continued frigid. He put on winter clothes and dreamed of hot whiskey punch. He would have to arrange a lecture program for the fall. "I must soon take to the road, and see what I can do in the old business." Perhaps, he hoped, the Ingersolls and the Farrells could spend two weeks in mid-September in the White Mountains. That too was not to be. His case in Cleveland took more time than expected. "Here I have been ever since last Saturday trying a d----d law suit. I never was so restless in my life. Fine vacation I have had. A few more summers like this and I shall take a rest in the winter" (To Farrell, Sept. 2, 1885, L.C.). On September fifth *The Truth Seeker* carried an Ingersoll interview on freethought; on September seventeenth he attended the Free Thought convention in Albany. He was being yanked hither and yon. The rhythm of work and rest had been his lifestyle, even during the rigors of Star Route, but his nerves were beginning to frazzle under the bonhomie.

For his autumn tour in "the old business" Ingersoll had prepared a new lecture, "Myth and Miracle." In it he reviews the universal phenomena of myths, laying them to primitive man interpreting the forces of nature as the workings of supernatural beings, and his belief in miracles as the interference of these beings into the normal processes of nature. "A myth is the idealization of a fact. A miracle is the counterfeit of a fact" (*Works*, II, 451). The great philosophers, scientists, and inventors—pioneers of freethought, astronomy, geology, the study of steam, of electricity—had at great sacrifice, including martyrdom, discredited superstition and its ally persecution. "Our fathers, some of them, demanded the freedom of religion. We have taken another step. We demand the religion of freedom" (490). Folksy wisecracks alternate with ornate rhetoric in the lecture, of course, which ends in a fervid millennial apostrophe cast in sacerdotal phrases:

> O Liberty, thou art the god of my idolatry: Thou art the only deity that hateth the bended knees. In thy vast and unwalled temples, beneath the roofless dome, star-gemmed and luminous with suns, thy worshippers stand erect! They do not cringe, or crawl, or bend their foreheads to the earth. The dust has never borne the impress of their lips. Upon thy altars mothers do not sacrifice their babes, nor men their rights. Thou askest naught from men except the things that good men hate— the whip, the chain, the dungeon key. Thou hast no popes, no priests, who stand between their fellow-men and thee. Thou carest not for foolish forms, or selfish prayers. At thy sacred shrine hypocrisy does not bow, virtue does not tremble, superstition's feeble tapers do not burn, but Reason holds aloft her inextinguishable torch whose holy light will one day flood the world. (491)

Mrs. Ingersoll was again with him on the road. She was a loyal but not very happy fellow traveller. It was dawning on the evangelist of liberty and the family that he was not treating his spouse fairly, but what could he do? "We are both well. I think Mother is rather tired of going about. It may be that I can stop lecturing in a little while. I hope so. Maybe we had all better go to Chicago. I can practice law, stay at home, and all can be happy" (Dear Daughters, Portsmouth, N.H., Sept. 24, 1885, L.C.). At September's end the elder Ingersolls met briefly with their daughters. Parting was painful. "After we left your Mother had a little cry in the carriage, and has talked about you ever since" (Newburyport, Mass., Oct. 1, 1885, *Letters*, 541).

On Sunday evening October fourth Ingersoll lectured at the Boston Theater, presenting "Myth and Miracle." "The audience," according to the *Herald*, "which greeted him greatly taxed the capacity of that spacious edifice." At the conclusion a reporter mingled with the departing crowd, noting bits of comment. "Well, you've at last heard Ingersoll. What do you think?" "Well, I could have got more satisfaction for one-fifth the money in a dime museum." "So could I. Ingersoll labored hard, didn't he?" "Yes, he did." A stranger broke in, "Not half as hard as you will, if you live long enough to understand what he said." At the sidewalk another pair: "I never knew before why people closed their eyes while in the act of prayer." "Didn't you? I never did either, but Bob can tell us all about it, can't he? I wonder how he found out all those things? Wonder if he'd tell us how much he got for howling an hour and a half tonight" (Oct. 5, 1885). Obviously attendance at an Ingersoll lecture was no sure sign of adherence to his doctrines.

Ingersoll had hoped that he and Mrs. Ingersoll might see their daughters briefly in Washington before he went on to Cleveland for the Ninth Annual Congress of the National Liberal League, scheduled for October ninth through October eleventh. It was not to be. He was so tied down with legal business that he had to stay in New York until time to go directly to Cleveland. Privately he fumed at the freethinkers *en masse*. They were dragging him away from the best thing in life, his family. "I wish that Secular Union—National League & all—in the place spoken of in the Bible. But I cannot get away from this horrible case. I leave poor Mother all alone at the Hoffman. I should think she would hate the place. . . . Maybe the day will come when we can live together. When the day will be filled with light—serene, tranquil—and we, intoxicated with each other's presence, will feel what heaven. is" (Dear Girls, N.Y., Oct. 8, 1885, *Letters*, 542).

The generalissimo of the freethought movement in America loved all the freethinkers but did not like many of them. They were continually pulling the Liberal League into the politics of dissent. As long as the League functioned within its traditional bounds for freethought and freedom of thought, leader and troops were in perfect unison. When, however, in 1879 the League had voted in opposition to moralistic laws curbing freedom of the mails, he had resigned, their divorce ending in a remarriage stronger than ever. In February 1885 the League voted to limit itself as an organization to its original purview and elected Ingersoll president. The main function of the October conference was to adopt a change of name formalizing the new-old approach as the American Secular Union.

As president of the League, Ingersoll had to be there. He arrived at the session already in progress on the last day and slipped into a back seat. Needless to say, he was instantly recognized and the members crowded around him to show their pleasure and reach for a handshake. The *Truth Seeker* said: "From the reception accorded Mr. Ingersoll at Albany, as well as at Cleveland, we hold the opinion that he is all but idolized by the great body of free thinkers." A motion was made to raise a campaign fund of $10,000. Ingersoll supported it. "There is no better cause, no grander object in this world than to get the fiend of fear out of the human mind." He pledged $250, remarking sotto voce that he was not jeopardizing his creditors. Immediately $940 was raised, and he threw in another $60, making an even $1,000 (Oct. 24, 1885).

"Speech!" "Speech!" He was ready. Proudly he declared that a free-thinker might not be elected as an errand boy in Congress or placed as a weathervane in the president's chair, but "the time has come when a man can express his honest thought and be treated like a gentleman in the United States" (*Works*, XII, 1883). He did not say that this was his own achievement (which it was). He stated the basic objectives of the freethought movement: an end to Sunday blue laws ("We want the Sabbath day for ourselves and families. Let the gods have the heavens."), taxation of church property, no public money for sectarian schools, no chaplains in the armed forces or the legislatures, no presidential procla-mation invoking divine assistance for some project or other. He lavished praise on all his newly elected fellow officers. He even had compliments for Wakeman, with whom he had frequently clashed: "an able, thoughtful, and experienced man, capable in every respect" (222). One of the new officers, the Englishman Charles Watts, had said of Ingersoll, "Let the truth be frankly written: In him is concentrated that which makes man noble and renders character sublime. He has the wisdom of the philosopher, allied with the simplicity of the child and the intellect of the giant molded with the sweet tenderness of woman" (*Truth Seeker*, Feb. 21, 1885). And young Samuel Putman, another new officer, later would say of Ingersoll's speech, "Those who listened to Ingersoll's introductory address Sunday afternoon enjoyed a most exquisite gem of extemporaneous speech. It came forth like a fountain from his irrepressible spirit and dashed this way and that way with impetuous bubbles of light, making rainbows of hope for all our hearts" (*Truth Seeker*, Oct. 24, 1885). The freethought movement in America closed ranks around Ingersoll for a while.

Ingersoll was still practicing law only sporadically in New York. He was restless, tired of living at a hotel. "Nothing new," he wrote to Clint on November third. "Weather chilly, dismal, apprehensive—What I mean by apprehensive is a feeling that something bad is going to happen. You know that there are such days—I want to get home. I want a good breakfast—something that tastes real good. I am tired of the Hoffman. All things taste alike. I am sick of the bills of fare—tired of ordering" (*Letters*, 442).

The Ingersolls explored the rush and roar, the sights and sounds, of the big city. They visited art galleries, and attended plays, operas, and concerts (*Romeo and Joliet, Carmen, The Mikado*, Beethoven's *Sixth Symphony*). Twice their friend Andrew Carnegie sent them free box-seat tickets for concerts at the Metropolitan. They walked about Gramercy Park and Madison Square and, as he reported, worked up an enormous appetite for dinner. They planned a boat ride up the Hudson: "We shall have a good lunch—that is the great thing—lunch!! How good it tastes—how delicious mixed with the scenery of autumn" (To Farrell, Oct. 23, 1885, L.C.). The vital juices were flowing. On reflection there was nothing in Illinois he cared to go back to. New York was a good place in which to live and Mrs. Ingersoll favored it. They would move to New York.

On November eighteenth the Ingersolls informed their "Dear Folks" that they had rented a furnished house at 101 Fifth Avenue. The scribe depicts it in glowing detail—the three floors, the two bathrooms and two washrooms on the second and third floors, the paintings, bronzes, and marbles, the grand piano and the two uprights, the library, and the basement with billiard table, kitchen, laundry. He jested about the neighborhood. "Judge Pierrepont lives next door. The widow of Marshall O. Roberts on the corner, Belmont next corner. It is one of the most aristocratic localities in New York. I say this for Sue's benefit." A postscript: "Mother is satisfied" (*Letters*, 476).

The Ingersolls quietly closed out their Washington life. The *Capital* informed its readers on November fifteenth that the family was moving "to the great Babylon of the new world, the city of New York." "He will be as much missed by his professional acquaintances here as his wife and family by their circle of society friends." Among the farewells was a note from Justice Harlan: "Dear Col. We wish you all much joy in your new home. Please make my best respects to the ladies. I shall never *dissent* from anything that conduces to your and their happiness" (Nov. 25, 1885, L.C.).

Note

1. In preparing Ingersoll's personal correspondence for publication, Mrs. Wakefield attempted to sanctify her grandfather's mode of expression by supplying the asterisks rather than risking any offense.

XI

"A' That and A' That"

The move to New York ushered in a period of crowded years. Ingersoll drew copious juice from the orange of life for the benefit of himself, the nation, and mankind. Eminently if not universally respected, he fought the war against revealed religion in dignified debate in Brahmin periodicals with the most distinguished opponents. When not impassioned at wrongs or entranced with visions of ideal freedom for America and the world, he laughed his way through this mortal existence, ever mindful of its inherent tragedy.

Ingersoll established a law office in the financial district. He had come to look down upon the practice of law as not worth his strife, but it was a living. He served his clients well and usually had more business than he could handle. His main concerns as a New York lawyer were with the routine problems of corporations (railroads, mines, telegraph, telephone, transocean cables), and claims against the American and foreign governments—like most legal business rarely of human interest beyond the immediate parties.

In the fall of 1885 Ingersoll made a special trip to Washington on what was to him really important business. A friend, Miss Mary Matteson, daughter of an exgovernor of Illinois, was in danger of losing her Treasury Department job in the Cleveland takeover. As Senator Charles Thomas, a member of the Democratic National Committee, happened to be entering the Willard Hotel Ingersoll stopped him. "Thomas," he said, "if you were not a Democrat I might acknowledge a hand of Providence in this meeting." He stated his client's anxiety and Thomas agreed to help. On the next day they had an audience with Secretary of the Treasury Manning. Ingersoll had not gone far into his emotional entreaty when the secretary had enough. Assuring him that her job was safe, Manning asked Ingersoll to please limit his future efforts to as few employees as possible, otherwise the new administration would be stymied in its personnel program. Thanking the secretary as for a great honor conferred upon him personally, Ingersoll picked up his hat and said, "Excuse me, gentlemen, but I must go right away and tell the good news to Mary." The secretary heaved a sigh of relief and remarked to the senator, "I can well understand the secret of that man's marvelous influence. He is intensely human" (Thomas, "Reminiscences of Ingersoll," *Truth Seeker*, Aug. 27, 1921).

Ingersoll made a strong beginning at the New York bar, notably in the suit against Western Union (as discussed in the previous chapter, pp. 231-232). Here was a case worth fighting on its own merits. Associated with ex-Senator Conkling against Joseph Choate and other leaders of the New York bar, he thrilled a packed courtroom with a jeremiad against the rapacious corporate giant and its head, Jay Gould. Rising to a climax he thundered, "The Western Union acts as though it owns the hemisphere. It looks on any rival as an interloper, as if it had itself a pre-emption not only of the United States but of the ocean as well." He confessed he could not keep his emotions out of this legal contest. "I admit that I have a feeling in this case. When I see power perverted, when I see it used to destroy and not to benefit; when I see a great corporation turn on another to crush it, I do have feeling. I want such a corporation to know that there is such a thing as law in the United States and that it is more powerful than any corporation" (*New York Herald*, May 26, 1886). Ingersoll would again have business with Conkling, this time as opposing counsel in a telephone patent hearing in Washington, where Ingersoll would parry Conkling's sarcasm with broad smiles of good humor (*The National Republican*, Feb. 13, 1888).

In the spring of 1886 Ingersoll left the aftermath of the Western Union case to his associates and repaired to Chicago, where truly earth-shaking events (to be known in history as the Haymarket Affair) were in progress. The Windy City had been in a chronic state of turbulence due to labor-capital warfare. Labor's struggle for unionization and an eight-hour day had been beaten back by strikebreakers and police; thousands of workers and their families had been thrown into the streets in the bitter winter of 1885-1886. The vacuum of leadership of the loosely connected workers had attracted a small group of revolutionary doctrinaires. During the McCormick Harvester strike, at a strike meeting outside the gates, August Spies delivered a low-key address urging the strikers to stand firm. Strikebreakers poured out of the factory and a fracas ensued. The police arrived in force and subdued the strikers with clubs and guns. In the melee one striker was killed and several other persons injured. Believing that six workers had been killed, Spies flung out a handbill carrying the headline "REVENGE! WORKINGMEN! TO ARMS!" In its original version the handbill contained the words, "Working-men, arm yourselves and appear in full force," but Spies insisted that he would not proceed if violence were called for. In further versions those terms were deleted.

The meeting, attended by several thousand, began as an ordinary speech-rally. Spies, Albert Parsons, and Samuel Fielden exhorted the strikers to militancy against capitalism, to armed resistance, to armed revolt. As rain fell, the speech-making was speeded up and the crowd was in fact dwindling away when a company of about two hundred policemen charged the speakers' stand and ordered the assemblage to disperse. Somebody threw a bomb into the ranks of the police, who opened scatter-gun fire. When the smoke cleared, one policeman and one civilian lay dead; shortly afterward six more policemen died of their wounds (as did three other workers). The authorities rounded up all the radicals in town and finally put eight on trial for complicity in murder—August Spies, Albert Parsons, Adolph Fischer, Michael Schwab, Samuel Fielden, Oscar Neebe, George Engel, and Louis Lingg. The bomb-thrower himself was never identified.

Amid the storm of denunciation against the defendants that swept the country the sympathy of a large liberal element was evoked. Able counsel from the colorful William Perkins Black, a prominent figure at the Chicago bar, was provided for the defendents. By mid-July, the jury had been selected and testimony was about to begin. The governor of Illinois at that time was once again Ingersoll's old friend and patron, Richard Oglesby. When Ingersoll called upon him, the governor could not or would not see him. However, Oglesby wrote: "I do not know anybody I would rather see than you. The next time you come to Springfield do not hesitate to call at the Executive Mansion and see me" (July 16, 1886, IHS).

On August nineteenth the case went to the jury. The judge had stretched the law of conspiracy through the breaking point so as to include incitement by abstract speech, and after merely three hours of deliberation the jury convicted all of the defendants, condemning seven to death and Neebe to seven years imprisonment. The defendants made overtures to Ingersoll to participate in their appeals. He declined. The prosecution had attacked the defendants as a gang of "atheistic foreigners" and Fischer had inferentially linked his cause with Ingersoll's when he addressed the court after verdict: "This verdict is a death-blow against free speech, free press, and free thought in this country." One minister of the gospel placed the entire blame for the tragic encounter at Haymarket Square upon Ingersoll as an enemy of the Bible and an advocate of anarchism (To Rev. Calvin T. Blackwell, April 29, 1887, L.C.). Ingersoll could not help the defendants by his conspicuous public association with their cause.

When all appeals in the courts had failed, Ingersoll promised the defense committee that he would make a private appeal for clemency to the governor. He said of Oglesby, "His instincts are noble and all his tendencies are toward the right. I have the greatest respect for him. The only fear I have is that he will be overawed by the general feeling—

by the demands of the upper classes" (To George C. Schilling, Nov. 3, 1887, *Letters*, 629). To avoid publicity the letter was hand-delivered to the governor by one of Ingersoll's daughters.

Ingersoll's letter to Oglesby is a masterpiece of persuasion, a patriotic document in the highest sense. Fully recognizing the "very great and very serious responsibility" resting upon the governor, his "Dear Friend," Ingersoll assured him that he would not recommend any course he did not consider right. He knew that the governor's decision, whatever it might be, would come from a sense of duty. Regardless of the guilt or innocence of these men, would their execution do good or harm to the country? Millions of men believed that the rich oppress the poor. Taking the lives of the defendants could intensify the widespread belief that they had not received a fair trial. "Blood has been dripping from every gallows, from every guillotine, and yet the agitation does not cease. The Nihilist still lives in Russia, the Socialist in Germany, the Communist in France, the Rebel in Ireland, and the Agitator everywhere. Force begets force; brutality is the parent of brutality." The defendants simply acted from principle (no matter how irrational), not against the individual, not for money, not for revenge. Extremists among the rich were crying for death, extremists among the poor for absolute pardon. Between them dwelt Mercy and Justice. "I have given you my views, and I beg of you, should there be any doubt in your mind as to what, under the circumstances, you should do, give the seven men the benefit of the doubt" (L.C.).

The nation had polarized pro and con on the fate of the convicted men; the cry for death was the louder. Ingersoll knew Oglesby to be a politician. Ultimately he weighed his options with an eye to the dominant sentiment in the community. Ingersoll's magnificent plea had little effect. Fortified by recommendations from the judge and the prosecutor, the governor commuted the sentences of Fielden and Schwab to life imprisonment (Lingg killed himself by exploding a dynamite cap in his mouth), and Spies, Engel, Fischer, and Parsons were hanged on November seventh. The case was officially closed (until 1893, when Governor Altgeld, the "Eagle That Is Forgotten," excoriated the trial as a travesty of justice and freed Fielden, Schwab, and Neebe). True to his letter Ingersoll did not break with Oglesby over the Haymarket Affair. After the execution he reflected on its long-range consequences: "The State simply furnished food for future agitation. If Caiaphas, the High Priest, had any sense, or if Pilate had had any authority, Christ would never have been crucified, and the Inquisition would never have been established in Spain" (Ingersoll to Martin H. Bovee, 1887, *Letters*, 630). (One cannot help wondering: If Ingersoll had been attorney general to Governor Oglesby during Haymarket, would the result have been different?) The men who died on the gallows have become enshrined as martyrs in the annals of class struggle.

On returning from Illinois in the summer of 1886 Ingersoll was afflicted with a growth on his vocal chords that caused torturous pain including the probe of surgery. The malady was widely publicized. The growth was benign and left only a slight hoarseness. In convalescence Ingersoll wrote jocular letters allaying the fears and dashing the prayers of those who thought his demise imminent. "Most people talk too much, so that I may at last be the gainer" (To Sue, Aug. 11, 1886, L.C.). A steady stream of requests for lectures poured in from all over the country. He refused them all, even after he was fully recovered. Sometimes he said that he was waiting for the clergy to catch up, but more often than that he was busy in the legal profession that sustained his family. "The fact is, that I have given the best part of my life in what is now known as the liberal cause—much more than I could afford—As the winter is coming on, I must do something for the ones who are dependent upon me" (To Converse Close, Dec. 4, 1888, *Letters*, 653). He did not say, because it was nobody's business, that his greatest pleasure was in being at home with his family and friends.

In the late summer of 1886 Ingersoll made time to take his wife and daughters for two or three weeks in a mountain resort. It was a dismal investment in relaxation. Rustic life in the hills was primitive—they had to check with the manager even for water to swallow a pill and for hot water to take a bath. They were all glad to get back home again at 101 Fifth Avenue. Even the dog Tiny, companion to Rust, barked with joy as he saw the house. And what a breakfast! "We had fried chicken and gravy for breakfast," Ingersoll drooled, "—lots of fried potatoes—tomatoes with mayonnaise dressing—skins all off—hot biscuits, plenty of butter—Coffee fit for the Caesars and Shakespeares of the world. We have peaches as large as your head—plums bigger than watermelons and watermelons as big as young worlds" (To Sue and Clint, Sept. 4, 1886, L.C.).

Ingersoll scanned the New York mayoral contest of 1886. It had been said—Ingersoll himself had said it—that if the laboring class was unhappy it had only itself to blame. It was in the majority and could remedy its ills at the ballot box. On the other hand it must realize that government itself could not bring about a fairer distribution of the wealth. The mayoral race addressed none of these national issues—the tariff, currency reform, or expansion. Ingersoll repudiated the Republican party for the first and last time since joining it. He came out for the Labor Party and its candidate Henry George.

After dining at Ingersoll's home his former manager, James Redpath, brought his letter of endorsement to the Labor Party rally of October fifth. Redath said that he would deliver the best and most eloquent speech of the evening, and thereupon he read Ingersoll's message to a breathlessly still audience eager for his support.

Ingersoll regretted that he could not make a speech in person because of his throat condition. He did not agree with all of Henry George's ideas on land reform but did agree with his concern for the workers. The times were on the march. The people must learn to rely on themselves and the rich must learn that they are responsible for the use they make of their wealth, that nothing is, in the long run, more extravagant than to set wages below a decent standard of living. The security of property depended on the contentment of the people. "Let that be destroyed, let the multitude be hungry, let them feel that they have been robbed, that the rich are their enemies, that wealth is a slave-driver, that capital is cruel and heartless—what then will the palaces be worth? The world must be governed by "science—that is to say, kindness guided by intelligence." The poor people would not docilely starve while the rich have more than enough food for all. "You cannot prevent a revolution by attacking new ideas as though they were wild beasts. Such a course produces revolution. . . . My sympathies are with the laboring men. The industrious should wear the robes and crowns and sit at the banquets of the world."

When Redpath finished reading, he asked whether he had not delivered the most eloquent speech of the evening. The audience responded with three cheers for Bob Ingersoll. In the final showdown George ran second to Tammany's man Hewitt and outdistanced the Republican candidate, young Theodore Roosevelt (*New York Leader*, Oct. 26, 1886).

Ingersoll's office was not quiet enough for the practice of law, but there was no alternative. He could not avoid being at the mercy of endless traffic from all directions, too much of it having nothing to do with the law. Devotees came every morning to refresh the place with flowers. Reporters, would-be reporters, friends, and strangers sat down to discuss politics, religion, or Shakespeare's heroines with their resigned captive to their hearts' content. Too many of his visitors wanted something—testimonials for their causes, investments in get-rich-quick schemes, recommendations for jobs, barefaced handouts, loans without interest or maturity date. He wrote to Clint, "Nothing keeps happening all the time. Same old crowd in the office, same disparity between numbers and fees. I am going at 9:40—will see Mackay—Stokes—Chandler—Townsend, John Anderson, and Kneeland sandwiched in between beggars of both sexes" (Aug. 21, 1889, L.C.). One such beggar told a reporter about her experience with Ingersoll. She was in desperate straits—out of work, penniless, nowhere to turn, spirit gone. Her minister shrugged her off. She turned to Ingersoll, her heart pounding, her head in a whirl. She was ushered into his inner office. They shook hands; he asked her to sit down, smiled cordially and said, "Let's see what is the trouble." While paying clients cooled their heels in the outer office he questioned her carefully and gave her fatherly advice. "I felt already enriched with his earnest, sympathetic words but before I left he voluntarily helped me substantially." As they were parting, he invited her to keep in touch and said, "Goodbye, success to you—and yes, I'll say God bless you." Her fortunes improved, and the crisis passed, Night and day she prayed, "God bless Bob Ingersoll" (*Free-*

thought, Feb. 2, 1889, quoted from the *New York Sun*).

At the office lunch was a social event. Ingersoll never ate alone if he could help it. He took along one or more visitors, clerks, or clients to share in steak or chops, terrapin or goose, while they listened with patience or pleasure to his discourses on any topic under the sun and the careless minutes passed (Baker, *An Intimate View of Robert G. Ingersoll*, 187).

Some visitors were entirely unwelcome. They came to save his soul, to exhort him to repent. One day Ingersoll was in his inner office conferring with a client on some important railroad business when a neatly dressed couple burst into the room and announced that they had come on "the business of your Soul, O great infidel." They fell on their knees and prayed to the Lord to save him. They chanted:

> United in King Jesus
> We'll send the cry along,
> For in his strength we'll battle
> And do our best to win.
> From Satan and his minions
> To Christ we'll bring him in.

The unrepentant sinner begged them to leave so that he could go on with his legal business but they would not budge, so lawyer and client left the building to continue the conference elsewhere. Later Ingersoll had his stenographer make up a sign on cardboard in big black letters:

NOTICE

I DON'T NEED SALVATION

All persons who wish to pray for me have
my permission to do so.

BUT

Kindly keep out of my private office until
after business hours.

ROBERT G. INGERSOLL

(*New York Herald*, Aug. 21, 1893; *Truth Seeker*, Sept. 2, 1893)

Ingersoll became a well-known figure on the streets of New York. As he walked the few blocks from his office to the El, people hailed him and there was handshaking. At the station he chatted with the newsstand operator and the ticket collector. On one rainy afternoon his friend Mrs. Mary H. Fiske, who wrote a column for the *Dramatic Mirror* under the appropriate name GIDDY GUSHER, was in a carriage waiting for a friend at the friend's door. Noticing a man seated in front of the church opposite, she dismissed him from her thoughts as a gin-mill habitué until he raised his haggard but sober face and turned imploring eyes to the pedestrians hurrying by. Three men, "sleek, well-fed," one in clerical garb, came out of the church, raised their umbrellas, said goodbyes, and went their separate ways, "as indifferent to the water-soaked wretch who leaned against their door-post as they would be to a bottle of cod liver oil in a drug-store window." Along plodded "a big man with a boy's face and a very small umbrella," bearing a mildly happy expression—"Robert Ingersoll, by the big unlighted torch of Liberty!"[1] Head bent, lumbering from one puddle into another, he passed the derelict, halted, retraced his steps, and, holding his umbrella carefully over the man, questioned him. Ingersoll had been going east. He helped the man up and held him by the arm as they went west. Ingersoll "was the finest-looking man in the United States that afternoon." She ended her column, "He has a wife and two daughters, and no doubt a few affectionate female friends, and I hope the next time they kiss that expansive countenance they will put in a dash of extra warmth for the sake of the GIDDY GUSHER" (New York Dramatic Mirror, Nov. 20, 1886).

As in Washington, so in New York the Ingersoll residence was not an island of seclusion. Mrs. Ingersoll held receptions on Fridays, and conducted a soup kitchen for the poor in the basement on Sunday mornings. On Sunday evenings the whole family, including the Farrells, were "at home." Invitations were not sent. Friends came and brought friends; everybody was welcome. The guests occupied the richly furnished library and parlor, chatted in small groups, partook of delicacies, and fell silent for the renditions of poetry and music. In New York the company was primarily from the performing arts. Luminaries of the stage attended: Joseph Jefferson, Lawrence Barrett, Edwin Forrest, Edwin Booth, Julia Marlowe, Minnie Maddern Fiske. Musicians were there, notably Remenyi and Anton Seidl, concert pianist and conductor of the New York Philharmonic. Some other guests were Moncure Conway (biographer of Thomas Paine), Charles Edward Russell (journalist, future man of letters, and prominent Socialist), Helen Gardner (feminist), Ella Wheeler Wilcox, and Courtland Palmer (wealthy radical). Among the makers and shakers were John Mackay of the Postal Telegraph, Senator William Clark of the Montana silver fortune, Henry George, Andrew Carnegie, Eugene Debs. The Ingersoll receptions were not freethought affairs, but freethinkers came, rich in ideas but poor in worldly goods. They enjoyed and were encouraged by personal contact with their prestigious leader.

Ingersoll was not trained in music and could not read music, but Charles Edward Russell (who would later write a book on the American orchestra) marveled at Ingersoll's analysis of technique in Beethoven, whom he rated below Wagner (Russell, Julia Marlowe, 166). The great Remenyi stayed with the Ingersolls when in New York and played at the receptions and small parties (*New York Dramatic Mirror*, Dec. 12, 1891). Returning home from an evening concert by the great violinist Brodsky, Ingersoll could not wait but had to dash off a note to "my dear Remenyi, Shakespeare of the violin." Brodsky has talent but "ah, my good Fiddler, you are a genius—the greatest that ever wrought from common air the throbbing melody of love. . . . It is now midnight. I will go to bed and hear in dreams the strains of passion" (Feb. 2, 1897, *Letters*, 447). On concert tour Remenyi lauded Ingersoll to reporters as one virtuoso describes another. "When he speaks his two words even, they have wings and soar away up into the heavens. And what a thoughtful, considerate man he is. Look at this telegram he sent me the other day: 'The house has been full of music since you left' " (*Detroit Free Press*, Jan. 23, 1892).

Some of Ingersoll's guests were eccentrics. Literally and figuratively they buttonholed him and poured their solutions for the world's woes into his inexhaustible ears. Russell asked him, "Why on earth do you allow yourself to be bothered with all these cranks, lunatics, and pariahs? Why don't you shoo them away?" Ingersoll defended his tormentors. "I had rather be bored than unkind. And if you come to that, what is a crank? Mr. A thinks that Mr. B is a strange fellow, a crank—a pest; he doesn't see how Mr. B. can be so strange. He forgets that by just so much as Mr. B. seems strange to him he must seem strange to Mr. B. and in fact on good grounds" (Russell, *Julia Marlowe*, 174).

Ella Wheeler Wilcox enjoyed the atmosphere of an Ingersoll soirée but found serious fault with Ingersoll himself. "Mrs. Ingersoll radiates happiness and content. She looks up into the beaming, jovial face of her husband with an expression that tells its own story—it is so full of happy gratitude and sweet affection." She quoted Ingersoll as saying to her: "'Life is a railroad train on which every person knows he must be killed. Maybe to-day, maybe tomorrow, but somewhere down the line he must meet his doom. Ah! I have no use for a world with death in it,' and the jolly face looked sad, the clear, honest eyes shadowed with pain as he spoke." To her his statement revealed "the folly and fallacy" of his ideas on the future life. She also said that he said *damn* too much ("Colonel Ingersoll at Home," *Truth Seeker*, No. 5, 1887, quoted from *New York World*).

Two writers of books on contemporaneous manners, Max O'Rell and James Bridge, devoted extensive sections of appreciation to the social circle at the Ingersolls. They struck the same note of inspiration emanating from his presence. O'Rell said: "Between midnight and one in the morning, the last visitors reluctantly depart. On the way home, you think of all the witty things that have been said, the arrows of satire that have been shot at hypocrisy and humbug, the ennobling humanitarian opinions that have been advanced; and though you may not feel converted, or diverted, or perverted by Ingersollism, you are sure to leave that home feeling full of good will toward all men and saying to yourself, 'What a delightful evening I have had'" (*Jonathan and His Continent*, 186). Bridge:

"It was an atmosphere of love, and no one could breathe it without absorbing some of its divine quality. If a church service is helpful in proportion it confers a spiritual uplift on its votaries, then a Sunday evening spent in the radiant presence of this great man, whose sunny optimism gave a warmth and comfort to all who came within its range, was at once a *sursum corda* and a benediction" (*Millionaires and Grub Street*, 172).

A key to Ingersoll's impact on his times and his enduring reputation, if any, is in his friendships with Andrew Carnegie and Eugene Debs. He had ties to each but belonged to neither. He admired Carnegie for his love of Burns (Carnegie was born in Scotland), his general skepticism, his contribution to creating modern industrial America, and his philanthropy. Young Debs looked up to Ingersoll for his free mind, his freethought, and his sympathy with the oppressed. And in each relationship, in different ways, liquor played a part.

An ardent opponent of prohibition, Ingersoll appreciated fine liquor as well as the evils of intemperance. In bouts of illness he welcomed alcoholic gifts from Carnegie, who sent one with a note: "Have just rec'd from Scotland direct the very medicine you need—Some of the oldest and best Scotch whiskey in the world—So the Sender pronounces it & he is one who has the right to know. So try it & dwell in your Mind upon Burns and the Heather as you sip & sip" (May 1891, IHS). Ingersoll wrote back, "I have not touched it—Both bottles are as they were. You must be present when they are opened. We four must have an evening —I mean Burns, Carnegie, the whiskey, and myself" (May 6, 1891, *Letters,* 377). On a later occasion: "I thank you for the two bottles of spiritual consolation—for a liquid I have held in high esteem since first I read the glorious line—'Freedom and Whiskey gang t-gither' " (Nov. 30, 1896, *Letters,* 563). When he heard that Carnegie was ill, he sent a get-well note. "We cannot spare you yet. The world needs such men as Andrew Carnegie, and he, to satisfy his own generous impulses, needs the world" (Nov. 29, 1897, *Letters,* 588).

Young Debs worshipped Ingersoll. To him Ingersoll was simply and literally the greatest man that ever lived, an opinion that he never toned down in spite of political differences. His whole family, he effused to Farrell, "loves him for his brave, noble, and manly defense of the right and his vigorous, necessary denunciation of the wrong, for his great, generous nature and because he has done more than any other man the world has ever produced, in any age, to improve the condition of common humanity and leave the world happier, better and brighter than he found it" (Nov. 3, 1889, L.C.).

Conversing in the office one day Ingersoll told Debs with tears in his eyes that he had come to hate going to work. So many needy called upon him and he could not help them all or have the heart to turn them away. He would stop doing business with his present shirtmaker if that sweatshop owner did not begin paying a living wage to his girls. Ingersoll had warned of the danger of revolution if the misery of the laboring classes was not relieved. Enlarging on the truth after Ingersoll's death, Debs wrote, "With the whole of his great heart he sympathized with working men and women who toil. Again and again in the most thrilling eloquence he appealed to the working class to assert its might and take possession of its own" ("Recollections of Ingersoll," *Pearson's Magazine,* April 1917).

Debs appealed to Ingersoll for help in his personal problem—drinking. Ingersoll referred him to his own physician, Dr. Robertson. When the Pullman strike (of which Ingersoll disapproved) broke out in 1894, catapulting Debs into national prominence, Dr. Robertson let it be known that he had treated Debs for alcoholism—or, in the phrasing of that day, dipsomania. In an interview, Ingersoll gently chided Dr. Robertson for breaking professional confidence, defended Debs as an excellent man and a sincere labor leader, asserted that he had never seen Debs under the influence, and refused to answer further questions (*New York Herald,* July 9, 1894; *New York Evening Sun,* July 9, 1894). Following the electoral campaign of 1896, in which Debs had spoken for Bryan, Debs notified Ingersoll of his conversion to socialism. Ingersoll jotted down some objections: "I rec'd the papers giving the acct of your new Republic—I know that you desire to make your fellow creatures happy. I am perfectly sure of that. But the great question is—Can you control people who cannot or will not control themselves?—There is still another—Will men who will not work themselves willingly work for others—Another still—Will the superior men voluntarily stand on a level with the inferior?" (June 5, 1897, IHS).

For Debs the note reflected the honest probing of a generous and independent mind on the problem of the distribution of wealth. Ingersoll groped for a solution but could not find it. Somewhere down the road of time a solution would be found based on intelligence and kindness. He began his public thinking on the question, as we have noted, with a phenomenal statement denying the existence of the class struggle in America: "There is no conflict and can be no conflict in the United States between capital and labor, and the men who endeavor to excite the envy of the unfortunate and the malice of the poor are the enemies of law and order." However, with thousands of men able and willing to work jobless, families starving in the streets, he warned his audiences about mass discontent becoming senseless revolt.

In "A Lay Sermon" delivered to the Secular Union Ingersoll urged capital and labor to shake hands and work together. He took as his text (for it *is* a sermon) Lear's beautiful soliloquy on the heath, embracing his fellow sufferers:

> Poor naked wretches, wheresoe'er you are
> That bide the pelting of this pitiless storm.

There had to be equity. The rich must give up some of their wealth for the benefit of the poor. "My sympathies are with the poor. My sympathies are with the workingmen of the United States. Understand me distinctly. I am not an Anarchist. Anarchy is the reaction from tyranny. I am not a Socialist. I am not a Communist. I am an Individualist. I do not believe in tyranny, but I do believe in justice as between man and man" (*Works*, IV, 223). On its side labor must exercise self-restraint. The first big strike would be the last for the forces of law and order would suppress it. Boycotts would not do, brute violence would not do. Only reason and goodwill on both sides would solve the social problem.

Ingersoll's article "Some Interrogation Points," written in 1887, is his most pragmatic statement on the labor-capital confrontation (*North American Review*, March 1887). Gone is the naivete of "Hard Times" and "A Lay Sermon." It was clear to him that classes with conflicting interests would exist until the world was truly civilized. Exploitation continued. "The large fish still live on the little ones, and the fine theories have as yet failed to change the condition of mankind." Law could not solve the fundamental injustices. The business of government was to repress violence and fraud, and to enforce honest contracts. It could ameliorate the condition of workers with such remedies as workmen's compensation, ventilation in mines, abolition of child labor, and making houses safe and food wholesome. And if the workers voted properly they could have judges who would not consider a combination of capital as "an exchange of ideas" and a combination of labor as a "conspiracy."

Ingersoll took a strong stand against socialism, which he saw as the extinction of liberty. A socialistic society would assign jobs; fix wages and prices; allocate food, clothing, and housing; and take children from their families, making every man a citizen of a penitentiary. "Socialism seems to be one of the worst possible forms of slavery. Nothing would so paralyze all the splendid ambitions and inspirations that now lead to the civilization of man." He called upon the workers to think for themselves, and to realize that they could not win their own liberty by destroying the liberty of others, that "every man has a right to choose his trade, his profession, his employment, and has the right to work when and for whom and for what he will" (*Works*, XI, 199).

The *Illustrated World's Fair* carried in its November 1891 number an article elicited from Ingersoll entitled "Effect of the World's Fair upon the Human Race." He hailed the inventors of the world as the benefactors of mankind and celebrated the American exhibits as object lessons for other nations of the achievements of the great Republic. "We want them to know that here, under one flag, are sixty-five millions of people and that they are the best fed, the best clothed, and the best housed in the world, and we want them to know that we are solving the great social problems, and that we are going to demonstrate the right and power of man to govern himself." And where was the world going? He did not use the word but his ultimate goal is plainly socialism. The article even begins to sound like a socialistic tract. In a typical Ingersollian effusion, a millennial dream, Ingersoll simply relates the solution to a transcendental order of being beyond the horizon. Only when those who do the work own the machines, "when they belong to labor instead of what is called capital; when these great powers are free to the individual laborer as the air and light are now for all; then, and not until then, the individual will be restored and all forms of slavery will disappear." In its context his solution is not connected with the pressing troubles of the day. It is a safe-and-sane firecracker, not another Communist manifesto.

In his correspondence Ingersoll had begun to confess that he had no program of action for "solving the great social problems." He generally favored the Republican party because it contained "the better elements" and because it was right on protectionism (To Traubel, Aug. 21, 1892, L.C.). He thanked Traubel, a Socialist, for the compliment but declined the role of leading a great movement of economic reform. He felt helpless when faced with the complex and variegated causes of the economic crisis. He detested Social Darwinism's "Plan of Nature," the survival of those with the strongest claws and largest teeth. "It may be that the distance from protoplasm to man was not so great as it will be from man to gentleman. And yet I am full of hope for the future, although I know that the day will not come until many centuries after I am dead. Yet I am willing and anxious to do what I can to lead people to think and to destroy the phantoms of superstition" (Aug. 17, 1893, *Letters*, 659).

Not so sanguine is his letter to his cousin Frank Gilbert, editor of the *Chicago Inter-Ocean*. He had no remedy for the current strike in Chicago. Men could not be forced to work; and strikes had done little good. Profit-sharing was unworkable since it was not balanced by loss-sharing. Government control would be slavery. The Labor-Capital problem included almost an infinity of factors of human nature, theories of money and government, production, transportation, exchange, and so forth. "A few thousand years of civilization may produce men wise enough to solve the question—but there are no such men now. And I have written enough to convince you that I do not know what to do" (July 24, 1894, *Letters*, 625).

Amusements

The Ingersolls were avid theatergoers, averaging more than two plays a week during the season. Ingersoll did not like the new realism, which he said exposed the bald and hideous and omitted nature's antidotes (Speech to Lambs Club, *New York Recorder*, March 4, 1891). At the seventh anniversary celebration of the Actors Fund Association he said, "I have an immense sympathy with the whole human race, and of that feeling, that spirit, the drama is born. People must first be in love with life, before they can think of worthily representing it" (*New York Herald*, June 6, 1888). On the stage he preferred the larger-than-life, the heroic, the triumphant, Wagner and Shakespeare. As he loved the theater, so he loved its people— actors, playwrights, producers. They were his friends and his clients. He shielded them from critics and creditors, lavished praise and constructive criticism on them, loaned them money, represented them as an organized group in legislative lobbies, and managed their probate estates. In his last home in the city, 117 Gramercy Park, he had a miniature theater built on the top floor where Eva, Maud, and their friends could put on amateur theatricals. When the young thespians complained that they often found the door locked as they arrived for rehearsals or other business, Ingersoll expressed surprise that they were put off by such an obstacle. One tyro tried to climb in a window and was arrested and briefly detained. It was said that Ingersoll took his time about getting the youngster out of this detention—an Ingersoll joke. The housebreaker was a future Secretary of State, Bainbridge Colby (*New York Herald*, Nov. 10, 1925).

Ingersoll felt a sentimental attachment to the memory of Madame Ristori of old Illinois days; there would never be another actress like her. In New York he frequently saw performances by another Italian genius, Eleanora Duse. Her fine performance, though in a comedy, moved him to tears. He said, "It was just too beautiful, it was hard to bear" (Minnie Maddern Fiske, *Truth Seeker*, Aug. 11, 1923). In Minnie Maddern Fiske and Julia Marlowe he perceived elements of greatness and he gave them strong support in their professional and personal lives. Mrs. Fiske would treasure his memory as "a priceless possession" (*Truth Seeker*, Aug. 11, 1923). She recorded: "In my humblest days in the theater I was never in a place too lonely for Ingersoll to seek me out. And I must have been one of many struggling beginners who found their inspiration and cheer in the understanding of Robert Ingersoll—the understanding of the rare critic." When her company producing *Twelfth Night* ran into a financial crisis, it was Ingersoll who rescued them (Mrs. Fiske to Ingersoll, March 28, 1892, L.C.).

Mrs. Fiske's husband, Harrison Grey Fiske, was a prominent drama editor and producer. One day the young couple burst into Ingersoll's office in a state of high agitation. They wanted legal advice—they got plenty of it. A newspaper had said unflattering things about Mr. Fiske, and they demanded redress. Ingersoll listened gravely to their story of outrage. If there was a twinkle in his eyes they did not notice it. He read the offending article carefully. "Let me see," said he, "this paper says you are so-and-so, well—are you that?" "No!" replied Fiske. "Very good. To continue. The paper goes on to say that you are so-and-so. Is that so?" "It is not so!" from Fiske. "Ah, I thought so. . . . Very well. And now—finally the paper says that you are so-and-so. Are you?" "No, I am not, sir!" "Ah!" from the Colonel, "so I understand. Very well. From what you tell me I gather that all the statements about you contained in this newspaper are lies. Is that right?" "Yes, sir, they are lies!" "Very good. You are in luck. Now see here, young man, all these things here are lies—but some day the paper may tell the truth about you, then where will you be?" Fiske dropped the case (Minnie Maddern Fiske, *Truth Seeker*, Aug. 11, 1923).

Ingersoll played an important role in making Julia Marlowe a fixed luminary of the American stage. On the evening of October 12, 1887, accompanied by his family, he went to the Star Theater expecting to be bored by this newcomer in a mediocre performance of Juliet. At her first word his attention riveted on her until the intermission. In the lobby, running into William Winter, dean of New York critics, he enthused, "What do you think of that? Isn't it wonderful? Isn't it glorious? Did you ever hear Shakespeare spoken like that?" Winter had not been impressed. "Poof! The Balcony Scene! Anybody can do the balcony scene. Wait till she comes to the Potion Scene. Then you'll see. She'll fail completely." Ingersoll exploded, "You critics make me tired. You sit in your little cells playing with your little fingers on your little yardstick and don't see anything else. I tell you a girl who can read like that is a genius, and you'll see the day when you'll have to acknowledge it." Winter was slow in relenting; it took him ten years to confess his error (Russell, *Marlowe*, 94).

The final curtain fell, and the Ingersolls went on stage, where he took Marlowe's hands in his, exclaiming that after many years of disappointment he had seen the Juliet of the script. From that evening until she reached the pinnacle of status he was her self-appointed guardian angel. When she went on tour he sent advance promotion to newspaper editors and other key figures along the route. To Murat Halstead, Cincinnati: "I want you to see her. Take my word for it that you will not feel that an evening has been lost" (Jan. 22, 1888, *Letters*, 431). To W. H. Caukins, Indianapolis: "It may be that you will say you are going to Washington to see the Inauguration—but if you have sense enough to remain at home, go to the theater and see the best actress on the stage" (Feb. 26, 1889, *Letters*, 432). He loaned her small bits of money, arranged for Charles Edward Russell to become her business manager, thanked her admirers for their praise, and defended her judiciously from criticism (a poor play, not a poor performance). He agonized when she was stricken with a near-fatal case of typhoid. When a newspaper critic disparaged both Ingersoll and Marlowe on Shakespeare he hastened to soothe her sensibilities. He didn't mind the "yawp" and it could not injure her, as all the fault-finders would soon be swearing that they had always considered her the greatest actress in the world (Ingersoll to Marlowe, Nov. 26, 1888, Russell, 136).

Marlowe spent part of the summer of 1889 with the Ingersolls in their spacious house at the seashore. Russell observed how association with the tranquil and culture-loving family enriched and elevated Marlowe, saving her from the calculating spirit of the commercial theater. Behind the house was an old barn, where Marlowe practiced dramatic parts. One day she was working on Imogene in *Cymbeline*. As she uttered the last line of Act III, Scene 4 ("Amen! I thank thee") a burst of applause startled her. The Ingersolls had slipped in, sat down on the rickety stairs, and had been listening raptly. Mrs. Ingersoll embraced and kissed Marlowe and said, "You have won," and Ingersoll added, "Make no mistake. You have a mouth especially shaped to speak Shakespeare" (Russell, 172).

That evening in the social circle Ingersoll recited Burns's "To Mary in Heaven," beginning "Thou lingering star with lessening ray." "Imogene sat forward in her chair to listen," Russell recalled. "It was the way she had always wanted to hear poetry read, not chanted, not sniveled, not trampled flat, but made into music with the touch of its meaning in every significant word, and tones changing with the changed feeling. . . . When the Colonel ceased she was looking at space through clouded eyes, and always afterward she would hear those resonant tones and faultless modulation" (173). On another occasion a professor of elocution lectured family and friends on how to recite Shakespeare's sonnets. As the professor pounded the life out of those matchless poems Ingersoll beamed, and Marlowe writhed. The professor gone, Marlowe was nearly hysterical. "Oh, read them, read them," she gasped, "that I may get the horror out of my mind before I try to sleep!" And she would not release him until he had read again all the verses that the professor had butchered (175).

Business as Usual

Ingersoll had withdrawn from the lecture circuit. Thousands of people missed him in the flesh on the platform. Had he lost interest in freethought? Had he—good heavens, or thank God—recanted? A correspondent reported a Methodist minister as saying that Ingersoll had regretted his assault on Christianity and prayed God for forgiveness. Ingersoll denied the minister's assertion passionately. "If I have any regret at all," he replied, "it is that I have not said more against the superstition called Christianity. . . . Tell your Methodist friend that he should wait until I am dead, because, as long as I have breath to speak, these lies will be denied" (To I. H. Peingle, May 24, 1887, *Letters*, 287; cf. to Joseph Stidham, Feb. 6, 1890, *Letters*, 316). There were more places to smash idols than the lecture platform. Every morning's mail brought a heavy load of letters on religion. The abuse, the threats, and prayers to recant went into the wastebasket. Serious and well-mannered messages pro or con received serious and well-mannered responses, although sometimes with whimsy. Patiently and at length he expounded the common theses of freethought.

He was guru to a multitude. He had opinions on almost every subject which were eagerly sought and freely given. He declared himself against vivisection, capital punishment, and the theory that Bacon was the true author of the Shakespeare canon. Would he define a true American? "He who gives to every other human being every right that he claims for himself" (To Charles A. Kinnear, Sept. 30, 1887, *Letters*, 186). Ingersoll had declared that suicide was an act free of supernatural taboos and a legitimate way to escape or avoid unbearable suffering. This view, though distorted by his critics, was framed in common sense. To a man contemplating suicide he recommended as alternatives the pleasures of a cool summer and acts of altruism. "No man should kill himself as long as he can be of the least use to anybody, and if you cannot find some person that you are willing to do something for, find a good dog and take care of him. You have no idea how much better you will feel" (To ***, June 2, 1890, *Letters*, 704). Dame Rumor, buzzing in a religious weekly, published that Ingersoll's only son had been addicted to cheap novel reading, and that he had gone out of his mind and was quietly taken to a private asylum, where he died. To the man who sent the clipping Ingersoll answered: "1. My only son was not a great novel reader; 2. He did not go insane; 3. He was not sent to an asylum; 4. He did not die; 5. I never had a son" (Baker, 120). A devout Christian expressed a hope to meet Ingersoll in Heaven. "You certainly will if you are there" (To F. Van Dresser, Feb. 21, 1887, *Letters*, 282).

Especially amusing was being on Baptist mailing lists. No, he would not contribute to rebuilding the Baptist church at DeLeon, Texas, blown down by the wind. He acquiesced in the will of the Lord, who had chosen to destroy that church. Perhaps the Lord was testing the faith of the Baptists in De Leon, in which case they should rebuild the church themselves. "My position is this: if the 'Lord God of Israel' wants a Baptist church in De Leon, let him change the wind and blow the old one back" (To the Committee, DeLeon, Texas, Aug. 7, 1886, *Letters*, 272). No, he would not contribute to putting a roof on the Baptist church under construction in Peoria. Since the Baptists believe in salvation by water, they should not obstruct "the means of grace" by a roof for the church. "The wetter, the better" (To Mark M. Aiken, Nov. 20, 1891, *Letters*, 321). Nor would he subscribe to *The National Baptist*. "I am a practical Baptist already—I take a bath every day, and consequently am not in need of your teaching. My System also has one advantage, that I use soap" (To Editor of *The National Baptist*, Dec. 18, 1891, Georgetown).

Courtland Palmer attained the age of forty-five on March 25, 1888. On such an occasion what could a man say to a friend about life's journey? For himself, Ingersoll wrote him, the milestones were drawing nearer together. Nooks and brooks beckon but he could not linger. "For as you know, a traveller cannot stop to rest and start again. To pause for a moment is to stop forever. The only inn is the one at the last stone, and one who rests there can never know fatigue again. I hope that your inn is far away, that the road leading to this room of peace is long—that it winds amid the sunny hills and shadowy vales—growing fairer and fairer to its close. And more than all, I hope that you will have for fellow-travellers only the ones you love" (March 25, 1888, *Letters*, 546).

In the summer of 1886 an aggressive freethinker named Charles B. Reynolds, said to have formerly been a Methodist minister, brought the gospel of freethought to northern New Jersey. Pitching a tent in Boonton, he expounded infidelism and distributed pamphlets jeering at Christianity. Local pulpits raised a hue and cry, and some of their parishioners broke into a Reynolds assemblage, pelted the speaker with stale eggs and vegetables, slashed the canvas, and ripped up the pamphlets. They searched in the wreckage for the disturber of their Christianity to dump him in the duck pond, but he had miraculously disappeared. Surfacing in Morristown, Reynolds held no further meetings but continued to distribute his offending pamphlets. For the latter offense indictments for blasphemy were handed down in Boonton and Morristown. A typical passage: "An all-wise, unchangeable God, who got out of patience with a world which was just what his own stupid blundering had made it, had no better way out of his muddle than to destroy it by drowning." For such unconventional utterances the statute provided a maximum penalty of two hundred dollars fine or twelve months imprisonment at hard labor or both. (It had never been enforced.)

Ingersoll undertook the defense. After several postponements due to his throat affliction, the trial was finally set in Morristown for May 19, 1887. Circuit Court Judge Childs presided, assisted by County Judges Munson and Quinby. Early in the morning of the nineteenth an immense crowd gathered at the courthouse hill and, when the doors opened, stampeded into the seating space, latecomers being left behind. Ingersoll and his clerk arrived at eleven o'clock. In the tumultuous greeting of the celebrated infidel-advocate nobody noticed the defendant slipping in behind him—an elderly gentleman who could not pay counsel but was dressed in frock coat and silk hat for the historic event (*New York Times*, May 20, 1887).

In questioning prospective jurors Ingersoll probed into any prejudice that might prevent a fair trial. One asked what the meaning was of prejudice. Ingersoll said, "I may not define the word legally, but my own idea is that a man is prejudiced when he has made up his mind in a case without knowing anything about it." The questioner admitted such conditioning in this mater and was excused.

When the prosecution had proved that the defendant had distributed the pamphlets in question, Ingersoll moved for a recess. "I do not know," he said blandly, "that I shall have any witnesses one way or the other. Perhaps after dinner I shall feel like making a few remarks." Judge Childs responded, "There will be great disappointment if you do not," and spectators nodded and murmured in agreement.

Of course Ingersoll would deliver an address to the jury. His "few remarks" filled the afternoon and the next morning. *Reynolds* was his most important case. The record of *Star Route* is but a relic of the passing day, of interest only to historians and aficionados of courtroom drama. Ingersoll's address to the jury in *Reynolds* should be a perennial resource in the ongoing struggle for freedom of the mind, for what Justice Black has called the Firstness of the First Amendment.

Ingersoll set the high level of the issue in his first sentence: "Gentlemen of the jury: I regard this as one of the most important cases that can be submitted to a jury." He then proceeded in some four hours of sustained eloquence to glorify freedom of the mind. He spoke as an old friend of the jurors who brought good tidings, "in a voice as gentle, soft, and persuasive as the honey-scented wind of Hybla" (*New York World*, May 20, 1887).

This case is important, Ingersoll said, not because it involves the right of an individual to be secure in person or property, but the right of every citizen in New Jersey to live like a free man. "The most important thing in this world is liberty. More important than food or clothes, more important than gold or houses or lands—more important than art or science—more important than all the religions is the liberty of man" (*Works*, XI, 59).

What is blasphemy? Blasphemy in one country is orthodoxy in another. If Morristown sent missionaries to Turkey who denounced the Koran and were put in jail, wouldn't it be said that Turkey needed more missionaries? And if the Turks would send missionaries here to denounce the Bible and were put them in jail, wouldn't the Turks say that Morristown needed more missionaries?

The constitution of New Jersey provides that "no person shall be denied the enjoyment of any civil right on account of his religious principles. . . . No law shall be passed to restrain or abridge the liberty of speech or of the press." In spite of this guarantee and the Christian precept to turn the other cheek Christians proposed to imprison every man who laughed at their religion, and in so doing would repeat the tragedy of Christ, who was crucified for breaking a blasphemy law.

The statute proscribes "cursing or contumeliously reproaching the Scriptures." Is it a crime to demonstrate that the Scriptures were adopted by a convention vote and to discuss the books put in or left out? "Does it make any difference whether or not you believe that a man was going through town, and his hair was a little short, like mine, and some little children laughed at him, and thereupon two bears came down and tore to pieces about forty of these children?" (75). Every man had a right to express his views on such matters and to use the arrows of wit and the smiles of ridicule. "Anything that can be laughed out of this world ought not to stay in it" (79).

Ingersoll turned a sharp lawyer's eye on the offending passages in Reynolds's pamphlets. What do they amount to but mere restatements of biblical accounts, that God felt anger, that he allowed the ancient Jews to practice polygamy, fornication, and incest, or innocuous notions that Christ as an infant kicked and flung about his arms? To condemn such utterances as criminally offensive would be to revert to the days of savagery and superstition.

Ingersoll returned to the concept of blasphemy, giving his own vibrant definition:

What is real blasphemy?
> To live on the usurped labor of others—that is blasphemy.
> To enslave your fellow-man, to put chains upon his body—
> that is blasphemy.
> To enslave the minds of men, to put manacles upon the brain,
> padlocks upon the lips—that is blasphemy.
> To deny what you believe to be true, to admit to be true
> what you believe to be a lie—that is blasphemy.
> To strike the weak and unprotected, in order that you may gain
> the applause of the ignorant and superstitious mob—
> that is blasphemy.
> To persecute the intelligent few, at the command of the
> ignorant many—that is blasphemy.
> To forge chains, to build dungeons, for your honest fellow-men—
> that is blasphemy.

Finally Ingersoll told his friends the jurors that they were the final judges on all the issues, that if they acquitted, no court could reverse their verdict. Furthermore, even if the judge instructed them that the law was constitutional, the words charged in the indictment were not blasphemous under the statute.

For the sake of your State—for the sake of her reputation throughout the world—for your own sakes—and those of your children, and their children yet to be—say to the world that New Jersey shares in the spirit of this age—that New Jersey is not a survival of the Dark Ages—that New Jersey does not still regard the thumbscrew as an instrument of progress—that New Jersey needs no dungeon to answer the arguments of a free man, and does not send to the penitentiary men who think, and men who speak. Say to the world, that where arguments are without foundation, New Jersey has confidence enough in the brains of her people to feel that such arguments can be refuted by reason. (115)

The courtroom audience continually broke in with cheers and applause. In vain Judge Childs banged and banged his gavel on the resounding marble; he could not repress them. In recesses and at the end enthusiasts gathered around the defense attorney. One old man said, "Mr.

Ingersoll, I am a Presbyterian pastor, but I must say that was the noblest speech in defense of liberty I ever heard. Your hand, sir, your hand" (*New York World*, May 20, 1887).

Judge Childs instructed the jury along predictable lines, saying that the blasphemy statute was an example of self-government in action, that it was outside their concern to inquire into its constitutionality, that they should acquit or convict in accordance with the law, and that they should not acquit by violating the law themselves.

After about an hour's deliberation the jury brought in a verdict of guilty. The sentence was nominal, a compromise among the judges— twenty-five dollars plus costs (estimated at seventy-five dollars). Ingersoll paid by his own check. The indictment in Boonton was still outstanding, however. When Ingersoll threatened that if the indictment was pursued, he would come down and convert the whole county to freethought, it was withdrawn. On May twenty-third he sent an additional payment of $18.21 and gibed, "When this is settled, I presume there will be joy in heaven and some Enthusiastic Angel of the musical persuasion will probably give to the Angelic choir the Morristown March" (L.C.).

While the Ingersolls were still living in Washington Dr. Henry W. Field, Presbyterian minister and brother of Associate Justice Field of the Supreme Court, had been a guest one evening. Like every other visitor Field was impressed by the charm of the family and the conversational brilliance of Ingersoll. Within the family circle believer and unbeliever discussed religion. Field quoted Ingersoll as having a dim view of human existence in general. "Life is very sad to me; it is very pitiful; there is not much to it" (*Works*, VI, 130). When Ingersoll's temper warmed up, little Eva Farrell patted him on the shoulder, saying, "Uncle Robert wouldn't hurt a fly."

In the fall and winter of 1887–1888 Field and Ingersoll engaged in a debate on revealed religion in the *North American Review*. The enterprising editor of the *Review* reached across the Atlantic and enlisted two additional spokesmen for orthodoxy—Gladstone and Cardinal Manning. The prestige of the forum and the caliber of his opponents attested to the fact that Ingersoll had attained full respectability on the highest levels, and the quality of his contribution could leave no doubt that his eminent adversaries had met their match if not their master.

In order to avoid misrepresentation Field sent the draft of his first article to Ingersoll in advance, and the two continued to confer on preliminary drafts (Interview with Fields, *New York Times*, Feb. 25, 1888). They had become and remained friends. Nevertheless, neither showed any restraint in lambasting the other personally and on doctrine.

Field averred that a country youngster coming to the city lured to drinking, gambling, and vice, might throw off the restraints of religion and family and fall into eternal ruin after attending an Ingersoll lecture, with its "caricatures of religion, with descriptions of the prayers and the psalm singing, illustrated by devout grimaces and nasal tones which set the house in roars of laughter and are received with tumultuous applause" (Works, VI, 139). He said that Ingersoll dishonored his parents when he repudiated the religion of his childhood. Ingersoll had a right to express his honest opinions but he could not fairly complain of ministers who inveighed against him as a monster since he spoke of them as knaves or fools. He should speak politely like Huxley and Spencer and then he would be more effective.

Ingersoll responded that he did not corrupt a young man by freeing him from superstition and impressing upon him the wisdom of living according to reason. He did not dishonor his parents by repudiating their religion any more than the first Christian or the first Presbyterian dishonored his parents. He would not take advice from his enemies on how to be more effective in fighting them. "A religion that is not manly and robust enough to bear attack with smiling fortitude is unworthy of a place in the heart or brain. A religion that takes refuge in sentimentality, that cries out, 'Do not, I pray you, tell me any truth calculated to hurt my feelings,' is fit only for asylums" (167).

Field also expounded familiar arguments on the reasonableness, comfort, and guidance of Christianity. He relied upon the traditional argument from design to prove the existence of God: The watch implies the watchmaker, the design implies the designer, the orderliness and beauty of the world imply the Creator. God is a mystery, but to deny him is to exchange one mystery for another, and, worst of all, it meant disobedience to God's law, "the highest moral restraint upon man." God's governance of the world was proved by the retributions of history. Evil receives its just desserts (he cited Lincoln's classic utterance that the horrors of the Civil War were divine retribution for the sin of slavery).

The world was not a playground for happiness but an arena for developing character with comfort from the divine Christ in times of trouble. He consoled the slave mother bereft of her children, who crooned:

> Nobody knows the sorrows I've seen
> Nobody knows but Jesus.

A mother mourns her son, her only consolation being her religious belief that beyond this life is another where she may once again clasp him in her arms. What could freethought offer? It was not essential to the Christian religion that a sinner shall suffer eternal punishment but he can never escape the spiritual consequences of his sin. "If his existence is immortal, are not the consequences immortal also?" (187). Field concluded: "No voice in all the ages thrills me like that which whispers close to my heart, 'Go with me and I will give you rest,' to which I answer 'This is my Master, and I will follow Him'" (198).

To Ingersoll, as to many others before and since, the argument from design was not persuasive. If the world is a wonderful thing and implies a designer, the designer must be more wonderful—implying another designer. "Nothing can be mysterious enough to become an explanation" (151). A God who inflicted pestilence, earthquakes, and cyclones upon the good and the bad and who permited the triumph of injustice through the ages could not be a wise and good God. As for retributions of history, what retribution had been dealt for the great and brave who died in dungeons? Was Lincoln's assassination itself a part of any divine plan of restitution?

Was it wrong to consider happiness rather than character development the goal of life? The Christian religion itself in the Book of Revelation looks forward to the day when there shall be on earth "neither sorrow nor crying, neither shall there be any more pain." Would Dr. Field tell the poor woman in the tenement, her eyes blinded by tears, trying to provide for her children, that God put such a burden on her that she might suffer and be strong? Did God let the noble and good languish in prisons, die on the scaffold or at the stake because he could save them but was restrained by love? Did he allow millions of his people to be slaves in order to be object lessons of virtue? If suffering patiently borne elevated character, how unfortunate were those who lead prosperous and happy lives without such crises of character. And what character development could there be for the millions who die in infancy? "You have had the goodness to invite me to a grave over which a mother bends and weeps for her only son," Ingersoll continued. "I accept your invitation. We will go together" (157). Assuming that the man was an unbeliever, Field must tell this woman that according to the Bible and the Presbyterian Confession of Faith her son would be going to hell. "This reverend gentleman" knew nothing of another world, but if God existed, he was a good God, always providing an opportunity to do right. If death were the end her son would not suffer. Ingersoll fired a shot at his favorite target, eternal punishment. "Nothing can be nearer self-evident than the fact that a finite being cannot commit an infinite sin; neither can a finite being do an infinitely good deed" (204).

What was right? What was wrong? There was no infinite Being who by his mere will made right and wrong. These two qualities were inherent in the nature of things, in the relations of acts and consequences. "Let me say it to you again—and let me say it once for all—that morality has nothing to do with religion. Morality does not depend upon the supernatural. Morality does not walk with the crutches of miracles. Morality appeals to the experience of mankind" (174).

Ingersoll asked whether the time had not come for a philosophy of human nature that viewed every human being as the creature of circumstances and forces beyond his control and so beyond his responsibility. Ingersoll had adopted the deterministic philosophy of nineteenth-century science. "After all, is it not possible that we may find that everything has been necessarily produced, that all religions and superstitions, all mistakes and all crimes, were simply necessities? It is not possible that out of this perception may come not only love and pity for others, but absolute justification for the individual? May we not find that every soul has, like Mazeppa,[2] been lashed to the wild horse of passion, or like Prometheus[3] to the rocks of fate?" (182).

"Let us banish the shriveled hags of superstition; let us welcome the beautiful daughters of truth and joy" (218).

As the title of his article indicates—"Colonel Ingersoll on Christianity: Some Remarks on his Reply to Dr. Field"—Gladstone limited his argument to a commentary on the Field-Ingersoll debate. Ponderously Gladstone hammered away at the details of Ingersoll's debate. He did not like Ingersoll's "denunciation, sarcasm, and invective," his lack of calmness and sobriety in treating solemn themes, or his assertions without proof. Ingersoll had bluntly charged Christianity with the cruelties of Jephtha and Abraham, but Christians were not obliged to approve of Jephthah's sacrifice of his daughter or Abraham's willingness to sacrifice his son, and Jephtha and Abraham were acting in accordance with the primitive morality of their times. Ingersoll ran two biblical quotations as one, called Shakespeare the greatest of the human race so far without defining greatness or comparing Shakespeare with Dante or Caesar, and apparently did not know that the greatest of Greek thinkers, Aristotle, had no perception of a future state. Ingersoll defended the expression of honest opinion, but no opinion, Gladstone contended, could be honest if influenced by prejudice or interest. Ingersoll criticized Christ for not producing a complete moral code for all times and places, but this would have been beyond the needs of his contemporaries, for whom he set forth only basic principles, including the indissolubility of marriage.

Gladstone contended that evolution and Christianity were not incompatible, for the grand design of the evolutionist implied a guiding hand, and modern scientifically minded thinkers like John Fiske believed in a divine force behind the universe. But who was truly competent to judge of such matters or to believe that the evil outweighs the good?

The ultimate questions of existence should be addressed with the common sense that is appropriate to the business of ordinary life, but there was a mystery of existence beyond common understanding. Gladstone dismissed Ingersoll with a grand eloquent gesture: "And whereas the highest self-restraint is necessary in these dark, but therefore all the more exciting inquiries, this rider [Ingersoll] chooses to ride an unbroken horse, and to throw the reins upon his neck" (253).

Ingersoll treated his right honorable opponent with due respect but not more gently than Dr. Field. "Many will regret that you did not give your views upon the main questions—the principal issues—involved, instead of calling attention for the most part to the unimportant. If we were discussing the causes and results of the Franco–Prussian war, it would hardly be worth while for a third person to interrupt the argument for the purpose of calling attention to a misspelled word in the terms of surrender" (301). If Ingersoll asserted conclusions without proof, so did Gladstone in assuming "the scheme of redemption" (which he did not prove). Solemnity in discussion should not lead to mental paralysis: "Humor should carry a torch, Wit should give its sudden light." In praising Shakespeare he was speaking only of the poet's intellect. "It never occurred to me that anyone would suppose I thought Shakespeare a greater actor than Garrick, a more wonderful composer than Wagner, a better violinist than Remenyi (284). . . . The real question was that if we could not account for Christ without a miracle, how could we account for Shakespeare?"

Is there moral government of the world? Why did the all-powerful God allow the cruel system of Old Testament days; the Fall in the Garden of Eden and the resulting condemnation of all mankind; the slaughter of the Waldenses and the Scotch Covenanters; the Catholics of Ireland; the victims of St. Bartholomew's Day and the Spanish Inquisition; the executions of Bruno and Servetus; all the suffering that has come "of ambition, of perjury, of ignorance, of superstition, and revenge, of storm and earthquakes, of famine, flood, and fire?" (292). If Christ did not answer the problems of all the ages his value has been exaggerated; in particular, when he sanctions the indissolubility of marriage he condemns many a woman to indissoluble bondage to a cruel and false man.

By honest opinion Ingersoll meant any opinion that a person really believed, regardless of any hidden motivation; that opinion is dishonest which is not a person's real opinion. "The poor sovereign of this pictured world is led by old desires and ancient hates, and stained by crimes of many vanished years, and pushed by hands that long ago were dust, until he feels like some bewildered slave that Mockery has throned and crowned" (298).

Although Ingersoll was opposed to all belief in the supernatural including mystic faith in a divine presence, he did not seek battle with modern-minded believers in God who did not look to revealed religion for guidance. Hence he disposed of references to such thinkers as John Fiske with a question aimed at orthodoxy: Who were the parents of Adam and Eve? Science would destroy the mischievous dogmas of the past, for "intelligence, guided by kindness, is the highest wisdom. . . . And, after all, it may be that 'to ride an unbroken horse with the reins thrown upon his neck'—as you charge me with doing—gives a greater variety of sensations, a keener delight, and a better prospect of winning the race than to sit solemnly astride of a dead one, in 'a deep reverential calm, with the bridle firmly in your hand'" (303).

The articles by Cardinal Manning and Ingersoll are both captioned "Rome or Reason," the Cardinal's subtitle "The Church Its Own Witness," and Ingersoll's "A Reply to Cardinal Manning." The cardinal was not interested in crossing swords with Ingersoll. His article is an abstract statement of Catholic doctrine: He asserted the divine legation of the Catholic Church as demonstrated by its unique role in history. He described its origin and growth, its universality, and its survival through the centuries. He further delineated the Church's "inexhaustible fruitfulness in all good things," its conquest of natural impulses by the doctrine of the indissolubility of marriage and by the celibacy of the religious orders (preserving the highest condition of man and woman), and, finally, the sanctity of the church unimpaired by the failings of some of its members. Having had his say, he departed.

Ingersoll responded with a blast. Dignified but impassioned he plied a heavy lash upon Cardinal Manning's institution, addressing the prince of the church in the third person. The history, universality, and survival of the Catholic Church were not signs of its supernatural being as the same story could be told of Mohammedanism. How many supernatural churches could there be? The spectacle of cardinals kneeling before the pope was not inspiring. The cardinals kneel to the pope, the bishops to the cardinal, the priests to the bishop, the lower orders to the priest, and all expect the laymen upon whom they live to kneel to them. "The man of free and noble spirit will not kneel. Courage has no knees" (363).

Have the popes, the vicars of Christ, been "the greatest of statesmen and rulers?" Ingersoll turned to Draper's *History of the Intellectual Development of Europe* for an account of the low moral tone of the papacy during the Middle Ages—the bloody feuds among rivals, the strangulations, maimings, and imprisonments, the fornications, the briberies, and the auctioning of the papacy itself. Surely these evil occupants of the papal throne were not selected by Christ but by men and men only, and "the claim of divine guidance is born of zeal and uttered without knowledge" (368).

Was the history of the Catholic Church "a record of inexhaustible fruitfulness in all good things?" The Catholic religion declared that salvation was possible only to believers, that all others would everlastingly perish. "If the creed is true, then a man rejects it because he lacks intelligence. Is this a crime for which a man should everlastingly perish?" (307). If this creed is true, any heretical thought, and freedom of thought itself, must be suppressed by any means. "It is impossible to forget the persecutions of the Cathari, the Albigenses, the Waldenses, the Hussites, the Huguenots, and every sect that had the courage to think just a little itself" (326). This has been the history of the Catholic Church. "It loaded the noble with chains and the infamous with honors. In one hand it carried the alms dish, in the other a dagger. It argued with the sword, persuaded with poison, and convinced with the faggot" (362).

Ever sensitive to matters of love and marriage, Ingersoll was most vehement in responding to the cardinal's views on celibacy and matrimony. Marriage was not a sacrament of indissolubility in the grip of any church but a civil contract born of mutual attraction. "To this contract there are but two parties. The church is an impudent intruder" (381). The dogma of indissolubility had trapped millions in hopeless wretchedness, filling their lives with agony and tears. Marriage, not celibacy, is the highest good. Nothing could be deeper and stronger than a mother's love, nothing holier, purer, than a mother holding her babe to her breast. "Celibacy is the essence of vulgarity. It tries to put a stain upon motherhood, upon marriage, upon love, that is to say, upon all that is holiest in the human heart. Take love from the world, and there is nothing left worth living for" (383). If human beings were to live according to the cardinal's conception of "the highest state," this generation would be the last. Why were men and women created? "The Cardinal ought to take the ground that to talk well is good, but that to be dumb is the highest condition; that hearing is a pleasure, but that deafness is ecstasy; and that to think, to reason, is very well, but that to be a Catholic is far better" (384).

Ingersoll and Huxley ("Darwin's Bull-dog") exchanged thoughts on his encounters with the prime minister and the cardinal. An unknown benefactor had sent Huxley copies of the *North American Review* containing the debates. Huxley sent Ingersoll a congratulatory letter. He had a low opinion of Ingersoll's opponents. Cardinal Manning was "a parlous wind-bag." "Gladstone's attack on you is one of the best things he has written. I do not think there is more than 50 per cent more verbiage than necessary nor any sentence with more than two meanings. If he goes on improving at this rate, he will be an English classic by the time he is ninety" (May 1889, *Letters*, 309). Ingersoll responded, "Your estimate of Mr. Gladstone is generous. It does not seem to me that he can live long enough to become a classic. . . . Your description of the Cardinal is perfect. I was greatly disappointed by both of these men. It is hard to have any respect for an intellect that in this age accepts the orthodox creed—I feel that the brand of intellectual inferiority is on the theological brain" (July 25, 1889, *Letters*, 310).

Ingersoll continued the debate on divorce with leaders of the religious establishment in the *Review* in 1889. Cardinal Gibbons, Episcopal Bishop Potter, and Ingersoll discussed, not in give-and-take but in independent articles, "Is Divorce Wrong?" (*Works*, VI, 397–429). Cardinal Gibbons opposed all divorce except legal separation as contrary to God's law in the Scriptures and counseled unhappy spouses to seek the grace to suffer and be strong from a higher power. Bishop Potter stated that opinion in his church was not uniform. A majority supported prohibition of absolute divorce, but a minority would allow it against a drunken and brutal husband. Ingersoll argued that marriage was the most important of all contracts, "the uniting of two mornings of hope to reach the night together," but it was only contractual and when either party failed to live up to its terms the innocent party should not be bound to it for the sake of God.

Ingersoll could not answer each of the scores of tracts that rolled off the presses against his criticism of orthodoxy. He believed that none of these remonstrances had any stature as a defense of revealed religion worth pondering. "I cannot afford to waste time on little priests, or obscure parsons, or ignorant laymen" (Macdonald, 69). One prominent adversary was Father Louis A. Lambert. The quality of Father Lambert's efforts may be seen in his response to Ingersoll's criticism of the slaughter of whole peoples as mandated by the God of the Old Testament ("Physical death is a trifling circumstance in man's immortal career") and especially on the Canaanites, "whom you beslaver with your gushing sympathy": "The unparalleled wickedness and filthy abominations of the seven nations of Palestine, commonly called Canaanites, were such as to render their national expulsion or extermination a just punishment and a useful lesson to other nations" (Notes on Ingersoll, 56). Ingersoll wrote on the flyleaf of a reporter's copy of Lambert's Notes, "I never thought it worth answering. I have read but bits of it and that little is poor and puerile" (E. M. Macdonald, 72). To E. M. Macdonald, successor to Bennett on The Truth Seeker, he explained, "I can't bother with such little fellows as Lambert. Let them bring on the pope, or a cardinal, and I will give him a whirl" (81).

Another popular offering in the same vein was The Mistakes of Ingersoll And His Answers, edited by J. B. McClure. This was a cunning compilation of pieces by Ingersoll and his critics that could be sold to both sides. In reply to a characterization in The Mistakes that he was a materialist Ingersoll remarked that he wrote of the world as he perceived it, so he might be better called a naturalist (To T. N. Mason, Dec. 11, 1883, Letters, 270). Clark Braden's Ingersoll Unmasked was a tissue of scurrilities noteworthy for its imagination and rhetoric. J. P. D. John's Did Man Make God, or Did God Make Man: A Reply to Robert G. Ingersoll was respectful: "His philosophy contains much that is helpful and elevating. It could not well be otherwise at those points in which he coincides with the philosophy of Jesus. But credit be where credit is due. I wish that much of his inspiration concerning justice, humanity, love, and liberty might take possession of the people" (13). John's argument is wistful: "If man made God the destiny of the soul is in the clods, but if God made man, the soul will find its destiny in the bosom of the infinite" (97). John's pamphlet came to be advertised as having elicited an acknowledgment that John was the only man who ever answered him. Ingersoll explained in a letter to Macdonald, "I may have written, or said, or both, that he was fair or decent, but it never occurred to me that he had really answered me" (April 5, 1898, Letters). An in-depth study of the literature against Ingersoll remains to be made (Cf. Stein, Ingersoll: A Checklist).

On May 8, 1888, the exclusive Nineteenth Century Club met in a private room at the Metropolitan Opera to hear a three-cornered symposium on "The Limits of Toleration." Ingersoll was joined by a prominent Catholic layman and lawyer, Frederick P. Coudert, and Protestant ex-Governor Stewart L. Woodford (who would later become our peace-minded minister to Spain before the outbreak of the Spanish–American War). Courtland Palmer, president of the club, who had arranged the debate, introduced Ingersoll as of the stature of Voltaire, Rousseau, and Victor Hugo in the French Pantheon.

Ingersoll contended that honest opinion was independent of the will and without moral fault; it was entitled to free expression. As he was among friends, he supported his theses with jokes. He told a story illustrating the uncontrollable processes of the mind. A man promised a Methodist minister a fine riding horse if he could recite the Lord's Prayer without thinking of anything else. "Our Father which art in Heaven, hallowed be thy name. Thy kingdom come. Thy will be done—I suppose you will throw in the saddle and bridle?" Coudert did not object to freedom of thought but denied a right to free expression. A word uttered is an act. If society believed that the tendency of a certain idea was to undermine its most sacred values, that society would be justified in attempting to suppress it by any means. He applauded the New Jersey judgment against Reynolds (while complimenting Ingersoll on paying the fine out of his own pocket). Woodford argued for freedom of the will and individual responsibility. Responding, Ingersoll attacked the doctrine of eternal punishment with a story. There was a Mexican who believed that Mexico was the only country in the world. A priest warned him that there was another country occupied by a man eleven or twelve feet high and that, if the Mexican denied his existence, this aggrieved individual would grab him and break every bone in his body. The Mexican refused to believe the priest. One day in his boat the unbelieving Mexican was caught in a storm and, after several days adrift, saw the shores of another country. As his boat reached land he knew that he was doomed—"sure enough," a man twelve feet high approached. The Mexican cried, "Master, whoever you are, I denied your existence—I did not believe you lived. I swore there was no such country as this; but I see that I was mistaken, and I am gone. You are going to kill me, and the quicker you do so the better, and get me out of my misery. Do it now." As the great man said nothing and just looked at him, the little fellow cried again, "What are you going to do with me because over in that other country I denied your existence?" "What am I going to do with you?" said the supposed God. "Now that you have got here, if you behave yourself, I am going to treat you well." With this sweet yarn, the gentlemanly exchange of views ended (*Works*, VII, 219–260).

The evening with the Nineteenth Century Club was the only time that Ingersoll ever engaged in a live debate on religion. The daily mail brought many challenges from unknowns eager to share the platform (and the proceeds) with the noted unbeliever. To be available for such entertainments with weak or eccentric opponents would be demeaning. He advised such challengers to read his lectures, to lecture or write against him, to acquire a reputation, and then challenge him again (To Rev. Robert

Monroe, Chicago, Ill., Dec. 29, 1884, L.C.). He was ready to debate any cleric of substantial standing, but he challenged none, and none challenged him. He was interested in debating Moody, but nobody ever carried the possibility beyond preliminary suggestion. When, however, the New York Free Trade Club formally challenged him via the American Tariff Protective League to debate Henry George on protection versus free trade he declined, pleading other engagements—which was surprising in a man who always found time for any public function of special importance. As it was a presidential election year, a strong argument for protection would have enhanced the Republican cause, which again listed Ingersoll among its ranks. Such a debate would have been an historic event (*New York World*, Sept. 10, 1888).

Friends became ill, friends died. In illness Ingersoll sent encouragement, in bereavement, condolence. There was a vogue among freethinkers to enlist Ingersoll as future eulogist. "To have Robert G. Ingersoll speak words of praise above the silent form is fame; to deserve those words is immortality" (*Boston Investigator*, Aug. 28, 1884). Reading from manuscript, an irrepressible tear or two trailing down his cheeks, he draped garlands of Ingersollian rhetoric on his departed friends. So for Elizur Wright, abolitionist and freethinker: "Maybe the longing for another life is but the prophesy forever new from Nature's lips that love, disguised as death, alone fulfills. . . . But this we know: Good deeds are never childless. A noble life is never lost. A virtuous action does not die. Elizur Wright scattered with generous hand the priceless seeds, and we shall reap the golden grain. His words and acts are ours, and all he nobly did is living still" (Dec. 19, 1885, *Works*, XII, 412). For Ida Whiting Knowles, friend: "There is this consolation: She can never suffer more; never feel again the chill of death; never part again from those she loves. Her heart can break no more. She has shed her last tear, and upon her stainless brow has been set the wondrous seal of everlasting peace" (Dec. 16, 1887, *Works*, XII, 415). For Courtland Palmer, dead at forty-six: "Farewell, dear friend. The world is better for your life. The world is braver for your death" (July 29, 1888, *Works*, XII, 448). For Mary H. Fiske, the "Giddy Gusher": "Her heart was open as the gates of day. She shed kindness as the sun sheds light. If all her deeds were flowers, the air would be faint with perfume. If all her charities could change to melodies, a symphony would fill the sky" (Feb. 6, 1889, *Works*, XII, 454). For Horace Seaver, freethinker: "When the day is done—when the work of a life is finished—when the gold of evening meets the dusk of night, beneath the silent stars the tired laborer should fall asleep. To outlive usefulness is a double death" (Aug. 25, 1889, *Works*, XII, 465).

Invitations to speak kept pouring in, but Ingersoll could not accept them all. "I am sorry that you did not write sooner, so that I would have time to prepare. All of my Fourths of July are now booked up to 1911" (To L. B. Bartholomew and A. L. Pierce, Nov. 5, 1887, L.C.). Roscoe

Conkling died on April 18, 1888. The New York Legislature planned a memorial service for the former senator, and the arrangement committee unanimously chose Ingersoll to make the address. Objection to the appointment by zealous religionists was muted because of the friendship between the two men (*New York World*, April 30, 1888). Ingersoll had liked Conkling as a man, though he disdained him as a politician. Undoubtedly Conkling was one of the most impressive figures of the Gilded Age. Much good could be said about Conkling, and Ingersoll said it to an audience of some three thousand legislators and citizens who packed the regular seats and the stage. "Roscoe Conkling—a great man, an orator, a statesman, a lawyer, a distinguished citizen of the Republic, at the zenith of his fame and power has reached his journey's end; and we are met here, in the city of his birth, to pay our tribute to his worth and work." Let us rise above the prejudices of mere partisanship, "the clouds that cling to mountains." How poor the world would be without the memories of the great dead. "Only the voiceless speak forever." Conkling inspires still with his courage, his personal honesty, his impassioned commitment to equal rights for the freedmen. "The cry of 'social equality,' coined and uttered by the cruel and the base, was to him the expression of a great and splendid truth. . . . He has left us with his wealth of thought and deed—the memory of a brave, imperious, honest man, who bowed alone to death" (*Works*, XII, 427-437). A motion was adopted expressing the thanks of the legislature for an oration which the *Albany Express* found no difficulty in characterizing "as effective as Demosthenes, as polished as Cicero, as ornate as Burke, as scholarly as Gladstone" (May 10, 1888). (Ingersoll could have done without the last comparison.)

Three weeks later the Grand Army of the Republic staged a mammoth celebration of Decoration Day in the Metropolitan Opera House. Among the guests of honor were a body of veterans in faded uniforms, here and there a grizzled mustache, an empty sleeve. The Army Band played "Marching Through Georgia" and other patriotic songs, Tetrazinni and Campanini sang arias from Faust, Rose Coghlan recited "The Charge of the Light Brigade" and "All Quiet on the Potomac," and the New York Choral Union contributed "The Song of the Vikings" and "Where Are You Going, My Pretty Maid?" Then the crowd, seated or standing in the aisles, listened to Ingersoll. He was the Voice of America, a redeemed nation, a real democracy, the United States. "We commemorate the great and blessed victory over ourselves—the triumph of civilization, the reformation of a people, the establishment of a government consecrated to the preservation of liberty and the equal rights of man." The heroes of the war vindicated the "human right of people and of all the people to make and execute the laws—that authority does not come from the clouds, or from ancestry, or from the crowned and titled." He reviewed the history of slavery in colonial days, its enshrinement in the original Constitution, and the Fugitive Slave Law—the mistakes of the past, a hideous dream. The nation was now united in freedom. "We are one people. We will stand or fall together. At last, with clear eyes, we see that the triumph of right was a triumph for all." Suitably, by request, he included the romantic "Vision of War" from his 1876 speech. He added a millennial vision of the fruits of victory—a country of happy homes, a world without thrones or kings or slavery, where Science makes Nature toil for man, a nation of peace without gibbets, where Labor reaps its just reward, where there are no misers or beggars. The audience cheered and clapped frequently and, as one reporter noted, "simply went wild at its end," stood up and sang "America" [New York Times, May 31, 1888; Works, IX, 437-454).

Ingersoll continued to be fair game for interviews and, though he may have grumbled softly at times, he really did not mind it. In the summer of 1887, on legal business in Cincinnati, he seemed to have a free moment in the federal courthouse. A reporter grabbed him; "What, if any, are the differences between the parties in the United States?" Very little. "Some Republicans believe in protection and some Democrats in free trade. A great many in both parties want offices, that is the great issue—probably the greatest issue is as to which party shall have the places. . . . Of course I like the Republican party much better than I like the Democrats, but there is nothing at stake, and I am not relying on those parties for the civilization of the country. Politics is a small factor in the great working of civilization, compared with the arts and the sciences—compared with education, and with the thousand influences tending to refine and elevate the race" (Post, June 11, 1887).

Later that same day in the reading room of the St. Nicholas Hotel a reporter from another paper found him smoking a cigar and at his ease. Protecting his sore throat from the cold he was wearing a heavy blue coat and kept his top hat firmly on his bald head. The reporter was timid but hopeful. "Have you talked so much today that you have nothing left to say to the Enquirer's readers?" "I really don't know anything to say to them that would be interesting." A pause—then the floodgates opened. His throat was improving; politics did not interest him; he had not seen Blaine since 1884; a man should take a stand for a cause, a principle, to which office-holding should be incidental; he enjoyed the theater and thought Joseph Jefferson was America's greatest actor. Had he been correctly quoted as saying that no great issue divided the parties? "That is a fact—there is no issue now except the offices. There was the Southern question, that's dead, a thing of the past." Did he have any sympathy with the bloody-shirt doctrine? "Not at all. The Southern people are all right now. There should be no more talk about Confederates and Brigadier Generals. The matter should be dropped." He was troubled about labor unrest; he favored Irish independence. The infatuated reporter concluded: "Colonel Ingersoll is a most fascinating talker and agreeable gentleman. He is very busily engaged just now and his practice reaches over a great party of the country. Last Monday he tried a case in New York, Friday one in Chicago, Monday he will appear in the New York court again" (*Enquirer*, June 12, 1887).

The practice of law, usually corporate law, was a living, but that was the best that could be said for it. Office routine was dull, and representing A against B in the courtroom seldom fun. It could hardly make the sky ring unless the client was a Charles B. Reynolds with empty pockets. Representing the new owners of Bankers and Merchants Company against the demands of bond holders, he wanted to know where the plaintiffs were when the company was fighting for its life against Western Union. "They took just the part the husband did in the fight between his wife and the bear—looked on and awaited the result." Appearing for Postal Telegraph and other companies before the Senate Committee on Interstate Commerce he raked over the old devil Western Union as reaching for a monopoly of lines on the Pacific Railroad, thereby preventing the benefits of competition (*New York Herald*, March 11, 1888). He represented the hotel owners of New York in their conflict with the city government over their claim of right to serve wine on Sundays. When he won in the State Supreme Court and the corporation counsel took the case to the Court of Appeals, Ingersoll surprisingly argued that this was a criminal matter beyond the jurisdiction of the corporate counsel. His opponent ex-Judge Davis cried foul. Ingersoll had broken faith, had promised not to raise that objection. As Ingersoll bristled, Davis put it to the court that his charge against Ingersoll was "a mere question of credibility." No, an infuriated Ingersoll shouted, "It is a question of a true or untrue statement." Judge Davis sneered, "To a man of your beliefs the sanctity of an oath may not amount to very much." Ingersoll rose in his place and roared, "Before I'd speak of the sanctity of an oath I'd tell the truth myself" and was ordered to sit down. As the session ended, he muttered sotto voce, "It always provokes me to see a man back up against his church," and at the door of the courtroom he said for all to hear, "I'll strip the mantle yet from the shoulders of that infernal rascal." The next day Judge Davis cited St. Paul on the meaning of "entertain," arguing that since angels do not drink, the word "entertain" in the statute did not contemplate dispensing alcoholic beverages. Ingersoll replied that he was not familiar with the drinking habits of angels but that the Scriptures report, "And when St. Paul read the sign of the three taverns he thanked God and took courage," which meant that he expected something beside cold water (*New York Herald*, May 19, 20, 1888). Ingersoll won the case.

In spite of his avowals that he was through with politics Ingersoll could not resist the gravitational pull of politics in the presidential election year 1888. There was talk of running him for president which he laughed off. Freedom of thought was not a burning national issue—much less, freethought. He belonged for better or worse to the party of freedom, hopefully the party of progress, the Republican party. There was a live issue, protectionism, and an outstanding candidate, Walter Q. Gresham. Gresham had excellent credentials: He was personally impeccable; he had risen in the Union army from private to general, had been a member of Arthur's cabinet, and was a federal circuit judge, careful and fearless on the bench and moderately sympathetic to labor. Gresham passed Ingersoll's test on freedom of thought and welcomed his support. Willy-nilly but surely without much inward resistance Ingersoll found himself a collateral leader in the pro-Gresham movement. Prior to the convention Ingersoll promoted the Gresham candidacy in contacts with party leaders and in press interviews.

The Ingersolls and their guest Dr. Robertson, the family physician, arrived in Chicago on June sixteenth and went that night to see *The Magic Slipper* at the Opera House. Their suite at the Grand Pacific became a campaign center. At almost all hours visitors piled in. War Veterans and elderly women occupied the chairs and the sofa; others sat around on the window sill, the table, and the edges of the white bed. Family meals were haphazard as Ingersoll huddled with groups in a corner and Mrs. Ingersoll and the girls held receptions at bedside. In hotel lobbies Ingersoll hob-nobbed with party leaders, ambled arm-in-arm with Senator Depew, and touted Judge Gresham as the strongest and least objectionable candidate available. On the twentieth Ingersoll stayed in at the hotel nursing a sore throat, his speech impaired but not cut off. He was feeling good. A reporter asked him what his business was in Chicago. Now that was a good question. "I came here to rest. I felt I needed quiet and wanted to come to Chicago. . . . I wanted to meet my old friends, I wanted to be in Illinois once more, and I wanted to give you this interview." What did he have against President Cleveland? "1. He was on the wrong side during the war. 2. He has abandoned the idea of one term. 3. He has given up on civil service reform. 4. He is a free trader. 5. He is a Democrat. 6. He is doing what he can to give the South the control of this country. 7. Because he is President. 8. Because I want another. There is one thing, however, that I have in his favor (and I say this because I want to show that I have no prejudice), we can beat him" (*Chicago Herald*, June 21, 1888).

Susan B. Anthony was at the convention, pressing for women's rights. One day she had in tow Alexandra Gripenberg, a social worker visiting from Finland. They had no tickets and were standing disconsolate in the lobby where tickets could only be had from scalpers for twelve to twenty-five dollars apiece. Suddenly from a corner there came into view, as Gripenberg would describe him, "a stout, light-complexioned gentleman with a white vest of enormous dimensions" working his way towards them. "Oh, there comes Bob," Anthony sighed in relief. "Now we don't have to worry. He will let us in." Ingersoll bowed and beckoned. "I am glad to see you, Miss Anthony. How are your plans going? Well, well, well, I'll do what I can for you. So you don't have tickets. Well, we'll see, we'll see." "Good day, Bob, how are you?" said Anthony. "I am very glad to see your daughters." He introduced his daughters. The girls bowed and smiled. "Children," said Ingersoll, "don't you know that you are talking with Susan B.?" "Oh, Aunt Susie!" they exclaimed. It was a very hot day and Ingersoll wiped his "homely but bold and rugged face" profusely. "How beautiful and cool you must have it in Finland," he effused. "I will have to move over there. Here everything is so wretched, every bit of it. All mankind is a mistake. It is best to start from the beginning. Go back to tails and coconuts." He winked slyly, kissed Mrs. Ingersoll (who had come in), his daughters, and two or three of their girlfriends, and said, "Miss Anthony, you'll get in, I promise that. You know, Miss Anthony, that I am a friend of woman suffrage. Did you say that you should have a deliberative voice in the meeting? Well, well, of course you should. It is a shame that you don't have it. But as I said, the existence of all mankind is a mistake, a stupid, wretched mistake." He smiled broadly and went into the convention. Instantly a man wearing the red badge of an usher came out and escorted the ladies to their seats (Gripenberg, *A Half Year in the New World*, 91–93).

As he was not a delegate, Ingersoll sat with the honored guests on the platform. On June nineteenth Frederick Douglass (referred to in the record as Fred) delivered a brief scheduled speech pleading in vain for a strong stand on black rights. Came cries of "Ingersoll!" "Ingersoll!" repeated day after day. On the twenty-second the chairman invited Ingersoll to address the delegates outside the official record. He was seated backstage, his chair tilted back, his eyes fixed on the ceiling, apparently oblivious. A look of surprise, a nominal show of reluctance, and he came forward.

Four ballots had already been taken. John Sherman was in the lead, and Gresham was second, third, second, and fourth. The delegates were tense, tired, the galleries on edge. Big, overpowering, perfectly poised, Ingersoll commanded the complete attention of some eight thousand people spread out before him. Charles Edward Russell would record "the silvery voice, the flawless and unhesitating utterance, the telling phrase, the best eloquence" (*These Shifting Scenes*, 120). The guest of honor immediately struck a note that was sheer pleasure. "Ladies and Gentlemen: I am a Republican. I belong to the greatest, the grandest, party ever organized by the human race." He wrapped the party in the flag, and picked up the bloody shirt that he had thrown away. "I want two patriots against two copperheads." Under the leadership of the Republican Party a high protective tariff would foster a scientifically-minded industrial society rather than a poor and ignorant supplier of raw materials for the great powers. "I am in favor of that party because it gave freedom not only to 4,000,000 people, but to thousands and millions yet unborn." He hailed the Republican party as the party of civilization, of education, of equality, of protecting the rights of the citizen, of the honest ballot. Then the bombshell: "Now, being a Republican, being for the Republican party, being for protection, wishing and hoping for success, I am in favor of the nomination of Walter Q. Gresham" (*Chicago Tribune*, June 23; Russell, *Shifting Scenes*, 122).

Ingersoll had assumed that since he was not making a formal appearance before the convention he was not bound by the rule that guest speakers should not show partiality to any particular candidate. Others felt differently, that he had abused the invitation. At any rate the speech precipitated a riot. First the Greshamites picked up their banners and marched, screaming, up and down the aisles. Then other factions followed suit shouting up "Harrison," "Alger," "Blaine," "Sherman." Delegates milled about on the floor, stood on chairs, and fists flew, everybody yelling at the top of his lungs, the chairman banging and banging his gavel in vain. For half an hour the bedlam grew worse and more dangerous, until a delegate with a big voice mounted the platform and began reciting "Sheridan's Ride." The crowd listened, calmed itself, and dispersed. Some commentators thought that Ingersoll had ruined Gresham's chances although Gresham himself did not think so. In her biography of him Mrs. Gresham proudly related that he walked by the suite of Senator Platt, the New York boss, whose overtures for a deal he had spurned, on the way to the Ingersoll rooms to thank Ingersoll (*Life of Walter Quinlan Gresham*, I, 593). Actually, Ingersoll's speech was no great help. The party leaders who break deadlocks rallied around the dark horse Harrison, who won on the eighth ballot. The *Philadelphia Call* opined: "It is nonsense to say that Ingersoll killed Gresham. He was not wanted by the bosses, and if killed at all his death took place before a ballot was taken" (June 25, 1888).

Ingersoll had done all he could to win the nomination for Gresham. Having failed, he did not sulk in his tent. Addressing a mass ratification rally at the Metropolitan Opera House on June twenty-ninth he outlined a program for the Republican party. It must return to its pristine glory as the party of Lincoln, the party of freedom. He advocated a high protective tariff as a temporary stimulus to developing a modern industrial society. "We want to rock the cradle [of infant industry] just as long as there is a child in it. When the child gets to be seven or eight feet high, and wears number twelve boots, we will say, 'Now you will have to shift for yourself.' What we want is not simply for the capitalist, not simply for the working man, but for the whole society. American labor does not receive a fair share of the nation's wealth. (*A voice:* "Under protection.") Yes, sir, even under protection. Take away that protection, and he is instantly on a level with the European serf." He posed the question, What has made America a great people? (*A voice:* "Freethought.") "Yes, Freethought of course. Back of every invention is freethought" (477). He turned to a side issue, the Republican proposal to repeal the wartime tax on liquor and tobacco. Prohibitionists had said that this would increase intemperance. Not so. When people find life valuable they do not sink into dissipation. "Do you know, I believe, as much as I believe that I am living, that if the Mississippi itself were pure whiskey and its banks loaf sugar, and all the flats covered with mint, and all the bushes grew teaspoons and tumblers, there would not be any more drunkenness than there is now!" (485). On the growing silver currency question his mind was in ferment. He declared himself a bimetallist, stating that silver, which the United States produced in abundance, should become a partner with gold in the nation's money.

The leadership of the Republican party automatically was counting upon Ingersoll for an all-out enlistment in the Harrison campaign such as he had given to every candidate of the party since Lincoln except Blaine. The National Committee hardly had to tell him that "the pressure on us for speeches is very great," and that he would be useful in doubtful states, on a full-time basis if possible, adding specially that he could begin right away at Rutland, Vermont (Aug. 21, 1888, IHS). They reckoned without their man. He had learned his lesson and had renounced political ambitions. He was not the divinely appointed lifeguard of a party with which in his heart he was not fully satisfied. He would speak at his convenience, not theirs. Rutland would have to do without him.

Vacationing at Saratoga Springs, where admirers and curiosity seekers gathered about him in his striking white summer ensemble, he readily consented to say a few words in the casino about politics. "I presume," he began, "that no one in the world is in a better frame of mind to discuss the political issues of the day than myself." Laughter. He hurried on. "I am not a politician. I want no office. I work just as little as I can and I am no mechanic." He proceeded to flog the South and the Democratic party in the spirit of the bloody shirt. The Democratic party said to let bygones be bygones because it could not defend its past, preferring to make promises about the future. "If a tombstone were erected for every mistake of the Democratic party, the Republic would look like a vast cemetery." The Democratic party was like the rooster proposing to the horse that they should not step on each other's feet. There was one important live issue—the tariff, "whether there shall be protection for American labor (*applause*) and not only protection for American labor but for the protection of American homes, of American ingenuity, of American brain" (*great applause*). The crowd joined him in laughing at his witticisms, including the Mississippi whiskey-fantasy, which he repeated (*Daily Saratogan*, Aug. 30, 1888; *The Saratoga Summer Season*, Sept. 2, 1888).

Ingersoll bounced back into the defense of Bankers and Merchants as well as U.S. Telegraph against creditor claims by Boston Safe Deposit and Trust. Appearing at the federal courthouse in Syracuse he was "the same smooth, round-faced, jolly Colonel" that he had always been, "sharp and witty," startling the judges with his favorite gesture of emphasis (from prewar days), shoulders thrown back, left hand extended, right hand raised as high as possible and suddenly crashing down on the left (*Syracuse Journal*, Sept. 5, 1888). On the streets of New York he was a radiant personality. Swinging down Wall Street in the early morning, "rosy-faced, bright-eyed, and buoyant," his new brown melton cape overcoat flung jauntily over his shoulders and flapping in the breeze, he looked "remarkably healthy, wealthy, and wise in these autumnal days" (*New York Evening Post*, Oct. 23, 1888).

The Republicans held a mass meeting at the Brooklyn Academy of Music on October thirty-first. Ingersoll was the principal speaker. The doors opened at seven o'clock, and the hall was packed in ten minutes. Thousands stood outside to catch his words and join in the acclamation. The chairman said, "Fellow citizens, it would be an abuse of speech for me to say that I will introduce to the people of Brooklyn the next speaker. You all know him well. I will only say to you that the next speaker is that prince of orators, that stalwart thorough Republican, Col. Robert G. Ingersoll." Bowing to the tremendous ovation Ingersoll went on to deliver a blend of nationalism, northern industrialism, and the Republican right of control. He contrasted Democratic vices and Republican virtues, covering every political topic of the day excepting currency. "The Republican party has a history—so has the Democratic party." The crowd was delighted when again he talked of Democratic mistakes and commemorative tombstones and compared the Democracy to the rooster seeking a compact with the horse. He lectured like a patient schoolmaster that protection was the foundation of a great society powered by the achievements of science and independent of the rest of the world. The high wages of American labor would always restrict American exports in the imaginary cooperative mechanism of the free traders, thus it did not matter how high protected prices were—all the money stayed here.

He welcomed immigrants but directed them to leave their native flags in the home country, as there was air enough in America for only the American flag. He tore into Cleveland for breaking his promise not to seek a second term, for contributing money to his own campaign, for hanging people in Buffalo while General Harrison was fighting valiantly at the front, and for denying pensions to Union soldiers, their widows and children. If there was any touch of the religion of humanity in his speech, it was both in his suggestion that in time of war the nation should draft wealth as well as men and in his declaration that the Republican party was the party of the workers' dream. "I would like to see them go up to men like Vanderbilt and say: 'We want $100,000,000 from you tomorrow.' I would like to see them go to such men as Jay Gould and say: 'How much have you got? We want it all.' " Proud of his independence from day-to-day politics—held no office and would take none—he was free to judge his party objectively. "I am with the Republicans because in my judgment they are right. I am with them because I believe there is something wrong in a country where those who do the least have the most and they who do the most have the least. And this world will never truly and really be civilized till all the workers of the world have the luxuries of the world." At the end the grateful applause went on for some ten minutes. Ingersoll bowed gracefully and made his way to the private entrance. From the opposition the *Brooklyn Daily Eagle*, among others, threw cold water on the performance, saying that Ingersoll talked up protectionism in a suit of English worsted and chuckled along in his speech at the clever way he was putting things. "His hoarseness stayed away, and he kept his huge heart thumping for humanity and the Republican ticket all the time" (*Brooklyn Daily Eagle, Brooklyn Standard Union, Brooklyn Times, New York Daily Tribune*, Nov. 1, 1888).

Having done his stint for the coming Harrison victory Ingersoll relaxed at the theater. On the election eve he was not among the politicians. The Ingersoll family was occupying a box at the Fifth Avenue Theater attending a performance of *The Rivals*, after which Ingersoll opined as the avid reporter took notes, "What strikes me as remarkable about Jefferson's Bob Acres is that he does not suggest by the remotest echo of a tone nor the slightest shadow of a gesture his Rip Van Winkle. He is a wonderful artist" (*New York World*, Nov. 7, 1888). On November tenth the Saturday Night Club gave a banquet at the Hoffman House celebrating American drama in the person of Dion Boucicault, the magnetic actor-playwright-producer. Among the celebrants were Carnegie, General Sherman, and Ingersoll, Sherman and Ingersoll joining the guest of honor in making a few remarks (*New York Sun*, Nov. 11, 1888). At the theater on the nineteenth he lavished praise on Julia Marlowe, Edwin Forrest, Joseph Jefferson, and other luminaries of the American stage in a monologue to friends so rich and spontaneous that a reporter could not help writing, "We are surprised when we see a person in these days of ledgers, mortgages, and stocks as natural as the grass that blows, as graceful as a bird in air, touched and glorified with the romance of all time" (*New York World*, Nov. 20, 1888).

People seeking jobs in the new Harrison administration called upon Ingersoll for help. He did what he could but warned them that he had little influence with the administration. He rejected any requests to knock at the door of the Department of State, where Blaine was once again secretary. "I am out of politics, and hence politicians have no use for me" (To George W. Roberts, Omaha, April 9, 1889, L.C.). "Your letter came like a breeze from the sea," he wrote to Judge Gresham, thanking him for continuing a case scheduled for the one-hundred-degree weather of July sixteenth. "I hope that you will be cool all summer, cool as the atmosphere of the White House to a man asking for an appt." (July 3, 1889, *Letters*, 553).

In January 1889 it was rumored that Ingersoll had applied for membership in the prestigious Players Club and had been blackballed because of his views on religion. The press rushed to his side. *The Sun* was outraged. "Elegant in manners, unexceptionable in habits, brilliant in wit, instructive in conversation, never obtruding any particular opinion where it was not called for, there is no man in this city who counts more friends among cultivated persons, or who is more cordially welcome wherever he appears." There was talk that he was not eligible because not an actor, but Elihu Root, General Sherman, and other nonactors were members. The reporter from *The Sun* found his smile "all cool and a yard wide." He had not applied for membership but was obviously chagrined at such treatment from alleged friends (Jan. 26, 1889). Joining in, *The Star* branded the rumor as untrue and an insult to the Club. "While the *Star* does not share Colonel Ingersoll's beliefs, it concedes that his fine character as a gentleman, his great originality of thought, his superior intelligence and the constitution of his country alike, separately and jointly, entitled him to hold and to express any religious beliefs he pleases, and those who seek to exclude him from enlarged liberty of association with men of equal intelligence and spirit are probably devoid of any of the virtues these terms imply" (Jan. 28, 1889). His friend and client Lawrence Barrett, a distinguished actor and member of the club, assured him that it was all a mistake and pressed him to apply for membership. He refused.

A trial civil or criminal is usually a grim encounter. Sometimes— with all respect to Judge Wylie—it smacks of comic opera, and the judge in spite of or because of his high-and-mighty stance is part of the comedy. If there was a seed of humor in the situation Ingersoll cultivated it. In February and March he was cocounsel for the defense in the Kerr trial. Thomas B. Kerr, treasurer of the Broadway Surface Railroad Company, was charged with a not uncommon transgression in the Gilded Age— bribing members of the Board of Aldermen for a franchise. Nobody expected a conviction. Word had it that Kerr had contributed heavily to the election campaign of District Attorney Fellowes, who assigned the main burden of the prosecution to raw recruits in his office. A principal witness against Kerr was Alderman Fullgraff (that was his real name), who testified under a pledge of immunity. In cross-examination he faced a past master at demolishing pious turncoats. Ingersoll rose, adjusted his glasses, rubbed his bald head, and cleared his throat. Fullgraff sweated. Ingersoll put the witness at ease and sweet-talked him into admitting that his memory was poor, portraying himself as an innocent who happened to attend meetings of the corporation without any evil intent and "fell from grace," as Ingersoll described his mishap, without preliminaries. In summation Ingersoll was merciless. "When a man who has committed [a] crime sincerely repents it; when in the innermost chamber of his soul he turns his back to the darkness and his face to the rising sun of truth; when the glistening tear drops of repentance jewel the cheek of shame, that is a holy moment. But when that man has been hailed and found and convicted with proofs of his crime, when this informer offers to sell his evidence in order to save his worthless self at the expense of his partners of crime, that man excites nothing but the contempt of all honest men."

The jury withdrew to deliberate, the courtroom tense with expectation. Ingersoll matched pennies with Fellowes. "I'll tell you a story, boys," and he was off with a yarn about the gold rush days in California. It was the law that if a man left his claim for ten successive days he lost entitlement. When a certain prospector became sick and took to his tent, an interloper sneaked in and perfected title. The original prospector sued. Speaking in the pompous tones of the judge Ingersoll declared that the law was absolute and that the defendant could not be legally ousted. The plaintiff jumped up and struck the defendant a blow behind the ear and knocked him to the floor. As the plaintiff pummelled and stamped on the defendant the constable rushed up to pull the litigants apart. "You, Sir," Judge-Ingersoll bellowed, pounding the desk with an imaginary gavel, "leave them alone! The law is the law, but if the gentlemen want to compromise, they mustn't be interfered with."

The verdict, finally, was not guilty and the courtroom went wild with joy. Judge Danielle was outraged. He flailed about with contempt citations. He turned a baleful glance towards defense counsel. Was Ingersoll involved in the disturbance? "I always behave," said Ingersoll. "Badly," sighed Fellowes (*New York World*, March 7, 1889; *New York Evening Telegram*, March 14, 1889; *New York Morning Journal*, March 25, 1889; *San Francisco Freethought*, April 27, 1889, quoted in *New York Sun*).

After the Kerr trial Ingersoll and his family went for a brief vacation to the Princess Anne Hotel at Virginia Beach. An extraordinary storm swept in, wrecking ships along the shore and blasting houses. Was the day of judgment at hand? "My mind was taken off the law business for at least 48 hours." The family motto was "never mind the weather, so the wind don't blow." Prudently his family decided to come home via the railroad, not water, when the trains would start running again. He himself preferred water; he would rather be drowned than smashed (April 8, 1889, Dear Folks, L.C.). Back in the city there were important letters to write. He has heard that his "dear old friend," Alvah Bishop of Dunlap, Illinois, was ill, at death's door. He wrote to Bishop that he regreted that he was unable to visit and hold his hand as he remembered Bishop's friendship and loyalty in the vanished years. "My heart goes out to you in your day of sickness and pain." Bishop had led a good and useful life, devoted to his wife, his children, and his country; he has nothing to fear in the beyond. "You have the serenity born of common sense—of natural philosophy—and this you will have to the peaceful end. . . . I love you for your goodness and for your constant kindness to my dear brother and myself. With hope and love" (April 15, 1889, L.C.). He sent twenty-five dollars to the Whitman Fund (L.C.). And he wrote to his client the street car executive, "my dear Friend Thomas B. Kerr, Esq." One Peter McCune had been a driver on the Seventh Avenue and Broadway Line for thirteen or fourteen years. Although he had joined the recent strike, he was not by nature militant, nor was he a member of the Knights of Labor. He had a wife and seven children, an eighth on the way. His eighteen-year-old daughter earned eight dollars monthly, his sixteen-year old daughter three dollars weekly. Could Kerr restore McCune's job to alleviate his family's suffering? (April 16, 1889, L.C.).

The Ingersolls spent part of the summer of 1889 as guests of their friend Henry Taber at Wave Crest, Long Island. How fast the summer faded, how swiftly life went out! "The dead leaves prophesy of winter— the funeral ceremonies of the year have commenced" (Aug. 20, 1889, To Farrell, L.C.). His attack of malarial fever had left—"gone dead—as the widow remarried—for the time being." Occasionally he went into town—"same old crowd in the office, same disparity between numbers and fees" (Aug. 21, 1889, To Farrell, L.C.). The family had been reading a novel about the evils of the Catholic Church. "How I hate a priest! But I am not prejudiced" (Sept. 2, 1889, To Farrell, L.C.).

On October first Ingersoll made a sentimental visit to his place of birth which he had left as an infant. He delivered a free lecture at the Yates County fair in Penn Yan, some ten miles below his native Dresden, providing an additional one day's wonder to the fruits, vegetables, flowers, fowl, cattle, quilts, embroideries, jams, cakes, pies, and such. Much that he told the eight thousand people spread out before him on the fairgrounds was a restatement of what he had told the farmers of Illinois in 1877— the necessity of home ownership, clean and beautiful dwellings, reasonable hours for work and rest, good cooking, cultural awareness. He did not discuss debts and foreclosures. It was a beautiful day and his spirit soared for Yates County and for America, the beacon of hope for mankind. This was the greatest country in the world, a land of equality and freedom. He cracked jokes new and old and everybody including Mrs. Ingersoll, Eva, and Maud laughed with him. He ended on a utopian dream blending the ideals of the French Revolution with the prophecy of the Book of Revelation.

> Let us congratulate each other again that we are citizens of such a great republic. I want to hasten the day when liberty will preside throughout the earth, when labor will be adequately rewarded, when there will be no more slavery, no more suffering, no more criminals, no more penitentiaries, nothing but happinesss. The only thing in the world worth living for is happiness. I want to see the day when liberty, fraternity, and equality, like the rings of Saturn, shall encompass and surround this world of ours. (*Yates County Chronicle*, Oct. 2, 1889)

The crowd responded with a vote of thanks and three cheers. The local *Vineyardist* was at a loss for words. "There is nothing that can compare with the original and the magnetic presence, voice, manner, and indescribable humor of the incomparable Ingersoll himself. He is a marvel of natural gifts, talents, and graces, and, whatsoever his religious views and opinions may be, there are but few better men today on the face of our little planetary world" (Oct. 2, 1889).

Three days later Ingersoll was a featured guest at a Delmonico banquet given by his client John W. Mackay (of the Postal Telegraph), where the ingestion of fish, oysters, and duck was refreshed by four kinds of wine and *sorbet a la Russe*. Ingersoll delivered a speech reported as "half-and-half honey and lard" (*New York World*, Oct. 6, 1889). On December 11 Ingersoll and Mrs. Ingersoll were inducted as members of the Goethe Society. Called on for a toast Ingersoll raised his glass to happiness as the only good, otherwise a fiend is behind existence, and added a compliment which the Society may not have relished, "I like you Germans who can be happy with a glass of beer and good mustard on your sandwich—and a band" (*New York Sun*, Dec. 12, 1889).

On November thirteenth Eva was married to Walston Hill Brown, financial entrepreneur, in a ceremony from which the public and the press were excluded (*New York World*, Nov. 14, 1889). Wedding announcements had been sent, and among the return greetings was one from the still dreamy-eyed friend in Terre Haute, Mr. Debs, on the pleasures of being a grandfather (Nov. 11, 1889, IHS). Eva's marriage brought a radical change in Ingersoll's lifestyle. He could not endure being separated from his daughter, and it may be surmised that she felt likewise about him. It was agreed that the Ingersolls would live with the Browns in their spacious home at Dobbs Ferry, twenty miles north of the city on the east bank of the Hudson, for half the year including summers and vacations, and the Browns with the Ingersolls in the city the other half— on one end commuter trains, tight schedules, and a relative isolation in the country, and on the other the convenience of work and pleasure in the city. Ingersoll had experimented with the arrangement and was not overjoyed at the constraints of Dobbs Ferry. "I am getting a little tired of the everlasting work. I am up at six—eat breakfast a little after seven—leave for the city at eight—get to the office at 9:30—leave for home 4:30—eat dinner at six and this is called life" (Letter to John, Oct. 18, 1889; Larson, 229). But he was willing to pay the price. (Did he ever wonder how he would preserve the unity of his family if and when Maud married? That would never be a real problem for Maud did not marry until after his death.)

The case of *Cammerer v. Muller* was a notorious breach of promise suit in which Ingersoll appeared for the defense. In that romantic era gold diggers could strike it rich by exposing their bruised hearts and receiving munificent awards of heart balm. The plaintiff was about thirty years old, the former object of her affections about sixty. Ingersoll may not have enjoyed needling Miss Muller but she was an obvious fraud and he played a cat-and-mouse game with her. Was she not troubled about all the bad things said about her in public? No, since they were all lies, they didn't bother her at all. Perhaps, he insinuated, nothing much bothered her and she was not really suffering from an injured heart. Didn't she know that Mr. Cammerer was a married man when he proposed to her and that she would have to delay her nuptial bliss until a divorce? Yes. "And so there you were a-waitin' with your heart all in a flutter for a whole year—satisfied that everything was all right and waitin' for the divorce papers and askin' no questions." Miss Muller sought damages of $100,000; the jury awarded her $12,000 (*New York Times*, Jan. 18, 1890). The verdict was reached on Saturday, and announced on Sunday, but although it was really a victory for the defendant Ingersoll routinely moved on Monday that it be set aside. The motion was summarily denied. Monday night Ingersoll was in Albany for a speaking engagement on the morrow.

Ingersoll had accepted an invitation from the New York State Bar Association to address its annual convention. Governor Hill, a Democrat, had invited him to stay at the Executive Mansion, but he preferred to bring his family and Walston and Eva Brown and take rooms at a hotel. The Bar Association had given him free range as to a subject, and he had chosen the problem of crime.

The hall was crowded with the officialdom of the legal system including Governor Hill and federal and state judges. They had not expected anything like the address, which bears the title "Crimes Against Criminals." Ingersoll may not have been the first theoretician of a modern deterministic penology, but his eloquent plea burst upon that captive audience like a thunderclap from a quiet sky. As he had argued with Dr. Field and Gladstone against eternal perdition for sins, so he argued with the legal establishment against the doctrine of punishment for crimes. He perceived all men as inescapably lashed to the wild horses of instinct and passion, and all behavior as the consequence of heredity and environment over which the individual had no control. "Is it not true," he asked "that the criminal is a natural product, and that society unconsciously produces these children of vice? Can we not safely take another step, and say that the criminal is a victim, as the diseased and insane and deformed are victims?" (*Works*, XI, 148).

It was high time, said Ingersoll, for the modern civilized world to abandon the spirit of the past in treating crime—torture, confiscation, degradation. The whipping post brands the whipper as well as the whipped. The death penalty did not prevent murder, but every execution hardened the public heart and lessened the sacredness of life. Poverty bred crime. He sketched a social program for prevention and alleviation: Schools should teach how to make a living, home ownership should be promoted by breaking down and subdividing large idle estates, prisons should not be like cemetaries where each cell was a grave, inmates should be allowed to earn by labor small sums to ease their readjustment to society, and reemployment should not be impeded by the stigma of having been a convict. On the other hand, criminals beyond correction should be segregated in isolated communities and not allowed to reproduce themselves. Ingersoll hammered away:

All the penalties, all the punishments, are inflicted under a belief that man can do right under all circumstances—that his conduct is absolutely under his control, and that his will is a pilot that can, in spite of winds and tides, reach any port desired. All this is, in my judgment, a mistake. It is a denial of the integrity of nature. It is based upon the supernatural and miraculous, and as long as this mistake remains the cornerstone of criminal jurisprudence reformation will be impossible. . . . [He concluded with a Buddhist prayer.] I pray thee to have pity on the vicious— thou hast already had pity on the virtuous by making them so. (166)

He left town a conquering hero, the plaudits of the local press behind him as "the eminent master of the harmony of language, the matchless word-painter, the great 'infidel,' who carries in his big heart more human kindness and rugged honesty that does many a man who parades the outward show of orthodox religion" (*Journal*, Jan. 21, 1890; *Express*, Jan. 22, 1890). (In the next generation Clarence Darrow, his disciple and critic, would make the same argument in his *Crime: Its Cause and Treatment*.)

In his compassion for the damned of society Ingersoll was a spiritual brother of Walt Whitman, who wrote:

> For me the keepers of convicts shoulder their carbines
> and keep a watch.
> It is I let out in the morning and barr'd at night.
> Not a mutineer walks handuff'd to jail but I am
> handcuff'd to him and walk by his side.
> Judge not as the judge judges, but as the sun
> falling upon a helpless thing.
> Not until the sun excludes you will I exclude you.

Ingersoll and Whitman were alike and different, the likeness outweighing the difference. Both were prophets of the religion of humanity. Whitman said in table talk, "I consider Bob one of the constellations of our time—of our country—America—a bright, magnificent constellation" (Traubel, "With Walt Whitman in Camden," V, 187). It was natural that the two would be drawn together personally. The Good Gray Poet was living out his last days in disabling illness and penury (brightened by pride in the growing recognition of his genius) in a plain little house in Camden, New Jersey, under the care of Horace Traubel, Philadelphia bank clerk and Socialist, whose monumental *With Walt Whitman In Camden* is a masterpiece of Boswellian biography. Some fifty or sixty devotees of the poet put on a supper party for Whitman on arriving at the age of seventy-two, and Traubel invited Ingersoll to attend. Coming from a strenuous day in courtroom and office, Ingersoll was as expected ready with a forty-minute encomium addressed to Whitman, who sat opposite him. The local press described his remarks in superlatives beyond the usual superlatives for exceptional Ingersoll performances. "It was probably, in its way, the most admirable specimen of modern oratory hitherto delivered in the English language, immense as such praise must sound" (*Camden Post*, June 2, 1890). Whitman, paralyzed and unable to rise from his chair, felt impelled to speak. He thanked the Colonel for his praise, the culmination of all commendations he had ever received, but he had to add that he did not share the Colonel's religious doubts; he believed in God and immortality. "For what would this life be without immortality? It would be as a locomotive, the greatest triumph of modern science, with no train to draw. If the spiritual is not behind the material, to what purpose is the material? What is this world without a further Divine prospect in it all?"

On June fifth Ingersoll wrote Whitman: "I can hardly tell you what pleasure it gave me to meet you, to look into your eyes, to hear your voice, to grasp your hand, and I thank you for the brave and splendid words you have uttered" (*Letters*, 390). He had received copies of the *Camden Post* praising him. He was sure Whitman was behind it, and he would repay with a fitting tribute. Nothing could have pleased Whitman more. "Your little note has touched the old man's heart" (Traubel to Ingersoll, June 8, 1890, L.C.).

It was decided that Ingersoll would deliver a benefit lecture for Whitman in the fall. Traubel undertook the arrangements but was soon overwhelmed by the rush of problems, particularly in finding a hall after the Academy of Music and the Union League Annex rejected his application. Vacationing with the Browns at their cottage in Elberon, New Jersey, Ingersoll sent encouragement. "Of course, I care nothing about the action of the directors of the Academy of Music or the Annex" (Letter to Traubel, Sept. 2, 1890, *Letters*, 391). He would send his secretary Baker to organize the project, advise on tickets, advertising, and so forth, and make advance payments. Perhaps the Horticultural Hall would be available. If a hall could not be found in Philadelphia, the lecture could be given in New York. "However, do not allow yourself to be annoyed or worried. It will all come out right enough. I have been through the same mill many times."

On October twenty-first Ingersoll delivered his testimonial to Whitman, "Liberty in Literature," at the Horticultural Hall. To an audience of some three thousand, Whitman seated among friends in a wheelchair on center stage, Ingersoll extolled Whitman as the pioneer poet of *Leaves of Grass* in 1855, the poet of the body and love, democracy, individuality, and humanity, a master of splendid rhythms whose "When Lilacs Last in the Dooryard Bloomed" would endure as long as the memory of Lincoln. He faithfully represented Whitman as believing in the divinity of all things and independently stated his own opinion that the ultimate questions are beyond the reach of the human mind. A correspondent wrote: "Mr. Ingersoll read from notes almost continuously, but this did not seem to make his hour's talk less interesting to the audience, which repeatedly cheered the orator" (*Cincinnati Enquirer*, Oct. 22, 1890). In cold print the address is not particularly impressive, consisting mostly of quotations from Whitman. But the audience loved the speaker and the subject-matter and they enjoyed the inimitable pleasure of hearing Ingersoll recite Whitman. Throughout the address Whitman sat calm, inert. When Ingersoll finished with, "We have met tonight to honor ourselves by honoring the author of *Leaves of Grass*," Whitman stirred and beckoned with his cane to speaker and audience. He had something to say from the chair. "Just a word, my friends, only a word. After all, the main factor, my friends, is in meeting, being face to face and meeting like this. I thought I would like to come forward with my living voice and thank you for coming and thank Robert Ingersoll for speaking, and that's about all. With such brief thanks to you and him, and showing myself to bear testimony—I think that is the Quaker term—face to face—I bid you all hail and farewell" (*Freethought*, Nov. 15, 1890, quoted from *The Truth Seeker*).

Although the testimonial was over, the socializing was not. The meeting adjourned, to be renewed shortly at the Lafayette Hotel on a smaller scale, where Whitman, propelled in his wheelchair, led a solemn procession down a long corridor to the dining room. The small company grouped close around the lecturer and the poet, awaiting their dialogue. Whitman and Ingersoll made a bizarre pair side by side: Whitman, his soft gray hat pressed down upon unruly white locks cascading over temples and ears upon his wide open collar, eyes watery and dim, beard flowing over his breast, hands tremulously holding on to the chair; Ingersoll, top hat before him on the table, wearing a light overcoat, smooth shaven, bald head shining, eyes fixed intently on Whitman for a cue. Ingersoll had a glass of apollinaris, Whitman champagne and bits of bread for dipping and chewing. Whitman spoke first. He read his translation of Munger's "The Midnight Visitor" on death opening all doors and asked Ingersoll, "Isn't that funny?" Ingersoll shrugged, said slowly, "I don't think there is anything funny about death. It's so sort of cold, so white. I don't like it." Whitman threw a challenge: "I believe religion has done more good to the world than harm." Ingersoll differed gently: "It might have done so had it only stuck to the good. It didn't, it taught what was mean and cruel," and he was off with the story of his boyhood, of how the evangelist consigned Lazarus to eternal bliss and Dives to eternal fire and thirst. His eyes popped with theatrical exaggeration as he relived his youthful dread of hell—"Bah! If religion had kept to the good of this life it might have done much less harm." Whitman persisted, "Sometimes it is better to soar." "No," said Ingersoll, "the reason why I like you, Walt, is that you have written for people here and now." Whitman raised a bony hand and said, "I think I have soared in the clouds a great deal, and—" "Yes, but you have taken lots of dirt up with you." As the party was breaking up, Ingersoll patted Whitman's hand and said," I hope you'll live many a year yet," at which Whitman sighed, "You might wish me something better than that" (*Truth Seeker*, Nov. 8, 1890, "After the Lecture," quoted from *The World*).

Messages passed back and forth between Ingersoll, Whitman, and Traubel, messages of love as Whitman faded. On December 21, 1891, Traubel wrote to Ingersoll: "Dear Colonel—I am afraid our dear friend has but a few days more of lease here with us on Mother Earth, have you the last word to send?" (L.C.). Ingersoll responded immediately with telegrams of concern and encouragement, which Traubel acknowledged: "Walt was profoundly moved & realizes the love and consideration out of which you spoke. . . . We rejoice to know that we can depend on you when the last note is struck" (Dec. 23, 1891, L.C.). Came another letter from Ingersoll, a comradely embrace to the master:

December 29, 1891

My dear Whitman,

I am glad that you have lived long enough to know that your *Leaves of Grass* will live forever—long enough to know that your life has been a success—that you have sown with brave and generous hands the seeds of liberty and love. This is enough—and this is a radiance that even the darkness of death cannot extinguish.

May be the end of the journey is the best of all, and may be the end of this is the beginning of another, and maybe the beginning of that is better than the ending of this.

But however and whatever the fact may be, you have lightened the journey here, for millions of your fellow-men. In the great desert you have dug wells and planted palms. As long as water and shade are welcome to the faint and weary, your memory will live.

Wishing you many, many days of health and happiness, and with a heart full of love,

I remain,
Yours always,
R. G. Ingersoll

(*Letters*, 396)

In March 1892 Traubel sent several reports that Whitman's condition was "helpless and hopeless," and Ingersoll answered with telegrams, a letter to Traubel (March 15, *Letters*, 397) and a letter to Whitman (*Letters*, 397) which was his last:

New York, N.Y.
March 24, 1892

My dear Friend:

I am pained to hear that you are suffering more and more, but was glad to know that your brave spirit has never been bowed—and that in all your agony your heart keeps sweet and strong.

I think of you a thousand times a day—and of the great good you have done the world. You have written such brave, free, and winged words—words that have thrilled and ennobled the hearts and lives of millions—that my admiration has deepened to obligation.

Again I thank you for your courage, and again I lovingly say farewell—and yet I hope to see you soon.

Yours always,
R. G. Ingersoll

Whitman died two days later, on the twenty-sixth. On the morning of the thirtieth the body lay on view in a plain oaken casket in the parlor, and between eleven and one o'clock thousands passed by. Moncure Conway cried, "How beautiful! How beautiful a face!" Ingersoll hurried in. He had resumed lecturing on freethought, starting with a tour in Canada, and had gone by train all night and all morning to join the procession to Harleigh Cemetery, where he was the last and main speaker to address the vast concourse of mourners.

Ingersoll's funeral oration over the "great man, the great American, the most eminent citizen in the Republic," is the finest effort of his many in this kind or on a par with the eulogies over his brother and "At a Child's Grave." He expressed the quintessence of Whitman—the free spirit no better or worse than others, the sympathy and charity for all, the absolute faith in "that divine democracy which gives equal rights to all the sons and daughters of men," the poet of Life, of Love, of Nature. He presented a consoling synthesis of harmony, assurance, and peace which in emphasis is more Whitmanesque than Ingersollian. "Today we give back to Mother Nature, to her clasp and kiss, one of the bravest, sweetest souls that ever lived in human clay. . . . He has lived, he has died, and death is less terrible than it was before. Thousands and millions will walk into the 'dark valley of the shadow' holding Whitman by the hand. Long after we are dust the brave words he has spoken will sound like trumpets to the dying" (Works, XII, 473).

The New York Herald wrote: "There was intense silence when Colonel Ingersoll arose, and in those glowing periods for which he is world famous scattered flowers of speech over the ashes of his friend. When the great orator had spoken—and his words dwell in the ear like rich music—there was nothing left to do but consign Walt Whitman to the tomb, and this was done without parade or ceremony" (March 31, 1892).

Two events in the aftermath: The loving friend in Terre Haute was grateful for a copy of "your beautiful oration over Whitman, which all of us have read and all agree is one of the noblest tributes man ever paid to man" (Debs to Ingersoll, April 8, 1892, L.C.). Traubel sent Ingersoll Whitman's "stained, eloquent hat—just as I recovered it from Walt's floor—and I am glad you are glad to have & to hold it. And I am glad, too, to know, as I do know, that your tender & growing love for Walt was a great rest and assurance to him in the later days of his life" (April 16, 1892, L.C.).

Notes

1. The Statue of Liberty had just been unveiled, on October 28, 1886, on Bedloe's Island in New York Harbor.

2. Mazepa (Ivan Stepanovich Mazepa-Koledinsky, 1644–1709) was a warrior-chief (hetman) of the Cossacks. In his poem "Mazepa" Byron tells how the young Mazepa, surprised in bed with the wife of a nobleman, was tied naked on the back of an unbroken horse and sent on a furious day-and-night ride traversing desert plain, wide river, and dark forest, until the horse dropped dead.

3. Prometheus, whose name means *forethought,* was given the task of creating mankind. Believing that men ought to be superior to the animals, he made them upright like the gods, gave them the gift of fire, and arranged that they should receive the meat from every sacrifice while the gods received the fat and bones. The Greeks thus considered Prometheus their savior, in part because he was condemned by Zeus to be forever chained to a rock, a helpless victim of the elements and the winged beasts of the air. The romantic nineteenth century thought highly of Prometheus *and* Mazepa.

XII

Intermezzo

Our pursuit of the Ingersoll-Whitman relationship to its end has taken us beyond other events in Ingersoll's career. We return to 1890–1891.

Ingersoll was in heavy demand as guest speaker at special events of civic organizations, a prize easily captured when available. Typical was the banquet at Delmonico's on December twenty-seventh where some 150 members of the Manhattan Athletic Club gathered to eat heartily and celebrate athletic living. The principal speakers were Ingersoll and his friend, Senator Chauncey Depew, the best-known after-dinner speaker of the period. Ingersoll sat at the head table chatting with the Reverend Dr. Maguire, but when it came his turn to speak he let loose with a barrage of Ingersollism on the good life. "I believe in the religion of the body—of physical development—in devotional exercise—in the beatitudes of cheerfulness, good health, good food, good clothes, comradeship, generosity, and above all happiness. I believe in salvation here and now— Salvation from deformity and disease—from sickness and pain—from ennui and insanity—the heaven of health and good digestion—of strength and long life—of usefulness and joy. I believe in the builders and defenders of homes." The athletes cheered him roundly: "Who is Robert G. Ingersoll? First in peace, first in war, first in the hearts of the M.A.C." (*New York Journal*, Dec. 28, 1890; *Works*, XII, 122).

Controversy is the spirit of American law, but when a lawyer tires of expending all energies on the claim of A against B or B against A it is hard to work up any zeal for an inevitably bitter contest. So it was with the Davis Will case in 1891. *Davis* is unimportant in legal history, but is important here because it involved Ingersoll, engrossing his time and sapping his nerves, but demonstrating once again his genius in the courtroom. The case involved the validity of a paper offered for probate in Montana as the last will and testament of Andrew J. Davis. The alleged will was dated 1866; Davis died in 1890. In 1866 Davis was an indigent resident of Iowa; by 1890 he had amassed a fortune in Montana mining property variously valued at between five and eighteen million dollars. The paper dated 1866, as it would operate in 1890, left the estate to a brother, John A. Davis, excluding the other next kin—brothers and sisters and their children. Blood being thicker than water, the aggrieved relatives engaged Ingersoll to lead their challenge to the alleged will. His fee would be $100,000 contingent on success. An otherwise obscure family quarrel in a mountain state drew nationwide attention because Ingersoll was involved in it.

On the way to Montana for the Davis case the Ingersolls arrived at Chicago on January thirtieth. Since Ingersoll never traveled incognito, reporters descended with a whoop upon "the untiaraed pope of America," who was "the same robust, good-natured Bob, although his hair, which does not grow on the top of his head, has whitened somewhat since his last visit to the Garden City." They were eager for his views on politics but he protested, "I am out of it, out of it"; then he took up their specific questions. What did he think of the Farmers Alliance? His instincts were all for it. "Of course the farmers are trying to help themselves. A man who depends on farming and has to pay 10 or 12 percent interest for money will find that he needs a good deal of help. I do not blame the farmers for trying to raise something besides corn. The Farmers Alliance will be an important factor in the next presidential campaign" (*Post*, Jan. 30, 1891; *Tribune*, Jan. 31, 1891).

He could not leave Minneapolis without responding to the St. Paul correspondent of the *Butte Miner*. What did he think of the money question? "I am a silver man. I believe in gold and silver and a free coinage. I want a dollar's worth of silver in a silver dollar and then the more silver dollars we have the better. Gold is the money of the creditors. The debtors want silver and I want both."[1] The *Miner* seized upon this not altogether pellucid remark as an endorsement of the silver cause. "Good for Ingersoll! With his active brain and broad mind he grasps the situation. He is too big intellectually to be controlled by the gold bugs, and although living in the atmosphere of Wall Street he champions the interests of the great west" (Feb. 4, 1891).

Stopping over in Minneapolis he wrote severally to the "Dear Girls" back home: "We leave at 4:30 for Butte. We have a good state room, and a dining car goes on all the way. There is no danger of starving." Nothing to report "except that we are well and that we love you and hope to see you in a few days. Without you the world would be a poor place." He was looking forward not to the big trial but to summer at Dobbs Ferry. "We will see the things grow and hear the hens cackle and the roosters crow—the dogs bark and the old cows low or loo" (Jan. 31, 1891, *Letters*, 563).

Arriving at Butte Ingersoll encountered a judge firmly conducting a narrow process of jury selection that favored those upholding the 1866 will. Ingersoll appealed against the judge to the Supreme Court of Montana in Helena. At Helena he was specially introduced to the judges, and the Ingersolls had lunch with Senator and Mrs. Harris and met old friends whom they had not seen since his 1884 lecture tour. The motion was argued the next day in the ceremonial courtroom, the largest available, so that the unprecedented audience for an appellate argument could see "the distinguished antagonist of the lamented Moses" in action. The court took the matter under advisement (*Helena Journal*, Feb. 5, 1891).

The inevitable reporter had urgent questions unrelated to the Davis case or "the lamented Moses." What did Ingersoll think of free coinage of silver? He replied that we produced more silver than the rest of the world and if silver was used as money the value of silver would increase. There was not enough gold in the world for its currency needs anyway. The creditor wanted dear money, the debtor wanted cheap money, and he himself wanted honest money. (He did not say what he meant by honest money but in the context he seemed to imply any monetary system that would benefit the debt-ridden farmers.) "I do not believe in the old prayer, 'Oh, God. Take care of the rich, the poor can beg.' The rich can take care of themselves. Governments should protect the poor and the weak, instead of passing laws for the benefit of the powerful and the rich." What did he think of the Farmers' Alliance? He replied that he was glad the farmers were organizing. America could not get along without the farmers, who worked early and late for the nation. "I want the farmers to have their share of the good things. The farmers ought to say their say, and stand by their convictions, and defend themselves. They cannot depend on the merchants and farmers to take care of their interests. They must take care of themselves." (*Helena Journal*, Feb. 5, 1891).

At the busy day's end Ingersoll found peace and comfort in writing to his daughters. He reported that he and their mother were in the best of health but would like to be home. "I want to play bezique with somebody I can beat. I feel that I am getting rusty on politics and music since I left Sue." (Mrs. Farrell was always trying to improve her brother-in-law's mind.) "Tell Walston that I am doing all I can for free coinage—just to help the New York bankers, just to protect them from themselves. I find that my ideas are all right in the West and I hope that they will capture the East in due time. . . . Well, I have to go to dinner. Mother is waiting—ready first." There was "no news to tell. Just the old story that we love you with all our hearts. Goodbye—kisses enough to cover your dear cheeks. Love to each and all. Yours forever Eva and Robert" (Feb. 4, 1891, *Letters*, 564).

A religious person might have thought it providential that Ingersoll was in Helena in early February 1891. The Speaker of the Montana House,

A. C. Witte, and his wife had recently died within a few days of each other of diphtheria, leaving two daughters, aged six and seven, in financial straits. Ingersoll discovered that he had time to compose and deliver a benefit lecture for the orphaned children on a plausibly safe subject which he had been working on for some time—Shakespeare.

Two days later every seat in Ming's Opera House was taken, including forty on the stage for dignitaries, among whom sat Chief Justice Blake of the Supreme Court of Montana. An escort committee led the speaker to the platform, where the chairman said that as no introduction was necessary there was an oppportunity "to give an ovation to America's master of English speech." The responding applause burst "like hail striking on roofs" (*Helena Independent*, Feb. 7, 1891). It was Ingersoll's first public appearance as lecturer in Helena in six years. Garbed in full formal dress, lecture notes in his left hand, he looked suddenly older, and a little heavier, with fewer hairs on the fringes. His bald head shone under the lights and his eyes beamed through round spectacles as he bowed and smiled at the welcome.

The Shakespeare lecture is loosely constructed—it is composed of an adverse critique of the theory that Bacon was truly the playwright (which was the rage in literary circles), a comparison of Shakespeare and Christ as two miraculous beings only one of whom asserted divine origin, recitations from the plays, and rhapsodies about the Bard of Avon ending in a tremendous conceit which would become illustrious in its own time:

> Shakespeare was an intellectual ocean whose waves touched all the shores of thought; within which were all the tides and waves of destiny and will; over which swept all the storms of fate, ambition, and revenge; upon which fell the gloom and darkness of despair and death and all the sunlight of content and love, and within which was the inverted sky lit with the eternal stars—an intellectual ocean—towards which all rivers ran, and from which now the isles and continents of thought receive their dew and rain. (*Works*, III, 73)

Ingersoll turned the pages of his manuscript with his left hand and kept his right hand firmly in his pocket except for slight gestures. He spoke in a conversational manner, but his resonant voice and perfect enunciation filled the hall, his plain and simple words and mobile features conveying a strong physical sense of the movement of his thought and emotion. "On frequent occasions when some extraordinary beauty of though illuminated his brilliant discourse, the audience would break out into applause, but their appreciation was also evidenced by a silent, close attention that from its breathless, intense character was no less complimentary" (*Helena Herald*, Feb. 7, 1891). The lecture was a success in every way, and $1,165 was collected.

In New York later in the month the Cigar Manufacturers Protective Association held their tenth annual banquet at Delmonico's. They dined from a special menu printed in French, received gold and silver toothpicks, and savored perfectoes and other cigars. Nine speeches were made, of which only the speech by their favorite cigar smoker was later printed in full in the *U.S. Tobacco Journal.* "Col. Robert G. Ingersoll was never in better mood for speech-making, and his effort was in his happiest vein. When he arose to speak the audience burst into unrestrained applause, and then everybody settled himself in his seat to listen to the best after-dinner talker in the world, bar none." He had been assigned a barren-sounding topic, "Facts," but he rambled on pleasantly, with jokes and wisecracks about facts and lies, virtues and vices, suggesting the occasional merit of lies and vices in an unhappy world. He ended, surely with tears in his eyes, on the theme of dying: "I hope that when you come to die you may never know the facts. I wish for you in that moment that Hope may be at your ear to whisper to you, 'Cheer up, old man, you're going to get well, you're going to get well.' May those be the last words that your dying ears may hear and that you may never know the facts in that supreme hour" (Feb. 28, 1891).

On scattered evenings he lectured, mostly on Shakespeare, in New York, Brooklyn, and several towns upstate. The *Rochester Herald* commented: "Colonel Ingersoll's lecture as delivered last evening was a glowing and eloquent tribute to the genius and ability of the Bard of Avon; and the large audience, not a few of whom had attended a Sunday evening lecture by a celebrated infidel only after silencing a qualm of conscience, listened in eager attention throughout the entire discourse, which lasted nearly two hours, and at its conclusion felt well repaid by the rich literary treat which had been afforded them" (April 20, 1891). In Rochester he was stricken with an inflamed appendix and was out of commission for a week under the care of Dr. Robertson. On recovering he gave his lecture "Liberty of Man, Woman, and Child" as a benefit for the New York Ethical Society, where "he was cheered to the echo" by an audience packing seats and aisles (*New York World*, May 4). He does not seem to have remarked on the administrators at Cornell who vetoed the law school seniors' request that he speak at commencement because—*mirabile dictu*—he was not a lawyer but an advocate! (*Oakland* [Calif.] *Tribune*, April 20, 1891). In spite of the temptations of the groaning board he was able to exercise a bit of restraint and could write to Clint, "We are all well—I lost a little flesh. Weighed today 225 lbs." (May 2, 1891, L.C.).

On May eleventh Ingersoll, Mrs. Ingersoll, and Maud arrived in Chicago on the way to Montana for the Davis case. At the hotel, from eleven to six, a continuous army of devotees besieged them. When "Pope" Bob turned an inquiring eye to some of these visitors, they had nothing to say except, "I think you are the greatest man on earth and I am pleased to meet you" (*Tribune*, May 12, 1891). At the Chicago Auditorium, where he was scheduled to speak on Shakespeare, bedlam prevailed among lovers of the Bard of Avon craving admission. (It is hard to believe, a century later, that a lecture on Shakespeare by anyone but Shakespeare's ghost could arouse such interest.) "What a gathering it was. They came like the rushing of a stream through a broken dyke. They surged and struggled and almost fought to get through the runways that led to the interior of the Auditorium. Before 7 o'clock in the evening every ticket in the box office was sold, and speculators were reaping a harvest on the sidewalk selling 'choice seats' at double prices" (Globe, May 13, 1891). In the hall the blind General Stiles introduced Ingersoll: "The orator of the evening has been a soldier, and is still a soldier fighting for freedom of intellect and untrammeled thought." The Washington Post reported that "as the Colonel stepped to the reading desk with manuscript in hand a tempest of applause swept from the top-most gallery of the theater to the stage as the thousands of heads swayed under its influence like fields of corn in a storm" (May 17, 1891). The lecture itself met with "applause that rippled and thundered, came in volleys, and broke out sporadically here and there" (Chicago Inter-Ocean, May 12, 1891). Some of the devout reassembled at the hotel, where Ingersoll regaled them until the early hours with his thoughts on George Jacob Holyoake and the cooperative movement in England, Gladstone, Shakespeare and poetry, and Mrs. Besant and theosophy (Journal, May 12, 1891). Pausing in Minneapolis Ingersoll wrote to "Dear Clint and Sue and the Baby" that "we had a great house in Chicago" and that they were "standing the trip very well—voice and appetite good" (May 13, 1891, L.C.).

The triumph in Chicago was repeated in other towns—Minneapolis, St. Paul, Duluth, Omaha—to and from Montana. When he spoke twice in the same town in two weeks, the reporter noted the difference between the low key of "Shakespeare" and the histrionics of "Myth and Miracle" (Minneapolis Tribune, May 30, 1891).

Reporters fell upon Ingersoll in the hotel suite, the hotel lobby, the theater where he had gone for relaxation, anywhere. It was vital to know where he stood on the agrarian problem, the monetary problem, the heresy trials of liberal ministers, Baconian theory. His heart had gone out to the farmers of the nation and their communities pressed against the wall by fixed debts and low prices of farm products, but when they organized politically to seek redress in low-interest government loans and inflated currency his enthusiasm waned. "The farmers ought to know that resolutions passed by political conventions raise neither corn nor wheat, neither can they affect prices. I do not believe that a government can make money by law any more than it can make good crops by law. The government cannot support the people. The people have to support the government" (Duluth News, May 27, 1891). No class should try to dominate the country; "all useful men should be brothers."

He was opposed to an infusion of silver into the currency above its actual commercial value. "We ought to have money that is good the world over. Back of every paper dollar ought to be a dollar's worth of gold or silver." (The silver currency movement to which he had once given his general blessing might begin to perceive in these animadversions that he would not be found in its ranks if it pressed for inflating the currency with over-valued silver.)

On the heresy trials that were convulsing the churches he sympathized with the defendants—Briggs, Swing, Bridgman—as moving in the right direction against the rigidities of the old religion (*Chicago Post*, May 11, 1891). As to Ignatius Donnelly, who combined agrarian radicalism and the Baconian theory, Ingersoll was not interested in public debate on Shakespeare v. Bacon. Donnelly's argument for Baconian authorship relied on the authenticity of a cipher, which he could sustain or not without Ingersoll's presence. Why not try to squelch Donnelly in debate? No, he was too good an advance agent (*Chicago Post*, June 21, 1891).

At Helena Ingersoll's clients did not absorb his mind. He was homesick, unhappy. He wrote to the Browns, "Another day nearer home. This is the first thought each morning." Helena was "the worst looking place in the world. . . . If we had an honest judge we would be absolutely sure of victory" (May 20, 1891, Carbondale). As the guest speaker at a Hotel Broadwater banquet speaking on "Our Visiting Friends," he was all good cheer and comaraderie. He told of how an old Kentucky minister, describing the delight of the heaven which awaited his hearers if they would join his church, exhausted all other superlatives and wound up, "Brethren and sisters, in short, it's a regular old Kentucky place." After the laughter he went on, "I suppose you are expecting in another world simply another Montana" (*Laughter and applause*). Then there was Mrs. Jones looking at the Apollo Belvedere in Rome. "That's the Apollo Belvedere, is it?" "Yes." "Well, give me Jones" (*Laughter and applause*). Waxing serious, he recalled the glorious epoch "when we were infinitely in love with justice, with liberty, and when we felt that we had given freedom to every man, woman, and child standing beneath the flag." He feared that trade and selfishness would make the nation small minded, saying, "People enough have come to this country, we don't want any more" (*Helena Independent*, May 23, 1891).

In late July, accompanied by Maud, Ingersoll returned on a slow trip to the trial court in Butte, pausing along the way at various towns for legal business and interviews with the swarming press. In Butte he plunged into a ordeal of combat and abuse in which he gave as good as he received. Leaders of the local bar, on their own turf before a friendly judge, mounted a formidable case for admitting the 1866 will to probate, but Ingersoll made an equally powerful assault on the instrument as a gross forgery. Win or lose, he was not happy. He wrote to John, "Here I am in the wild west trying that infernal will case." He was sick of the haphazard struggle. "Day by day I lose confidence in honest testimony. Ignorance, prejudice, malice, perjury, forgetfulness, stupidity, cunning and even honesty all combine to hide or distort the truth." It was "the greatest mining camp in the world—a town of saloons by the hundred . . . gambling establishments, and places for ignorant miners to enjoy themselves in beastly ways." He was "as lonesome as a polar bear at the equator. Wish I had never heard of Montana." Life was slipping away; he was wasting precious time in trivia. "August is here again and on the 11th I shall be 58. The years are flying fast, and—let 'em fly; but let us meet as often as we can." He wished he was rich, not always in debt (Aug. 1, 1891, *Letters*, 203).

The unhappy letter was written on Saturday. The next day would mark the six-hundredth anniversary of the independence of Switzerland. Earlier in the week Ingersoll had been invited by the William Tell Society to address the celebration. However, it was the first week of a trial involving the disposition of millions of dollars—a jumble of problems of law, fact, and persuasion. Evenings and weekends could be profitably spent in reviewing progress and strategy with associate counsel, or in taking a rest with Maud. It would have been common sense to decline the invitation. Ingersoll accepted.

On Sunday morning came the parade—a Union band in regulation uniform, marching detachments from the French Canadian Institute, the Cristoforo Columbo Society, the Krieger Verein, and the Turn Verein, six white horses drawing a wagon draped in Swiss and American flags and bearing the resplendent maidens Helvetia and Columbia, and the mayor and the council, some 5,000 people along the way cheering the procession (*Butte Miner*, Aug. 3, 1891). In the afternoon at the Columbia Gardens a local dignitary announced, "We have with us on this occasion at once the ablest and greatest champion of liberty in any form that the age has produced. I will not detain you longer with my feeble effort, but will introduce the man whose fame is as widespread as civilization itself, and whose eloquence is only exceeded by the kindness of his heart. I introduce Robert G. Ingersoll" (*Anaconda Standard*, Aug. 3, 1891). The speaker began on a high note: "Ladies and Gentlemen—We have met to celebrate one of those sublime events that history holds in her hand as a torch; one of those sublime events that has shed light on the whole civilized world." He went on with a dithyramb to freedom as the child of intelligence, to the heroes of ages past who languished in dungeons or died at the stake for freedom of the mind, to the struggle against the enduring superstition of divine right and for government by consent of the governed. He saluted the Civil War, as it had corrected in rivers of blood the decision of the Supreme Court that the man sitting on the fence could take the corn grown by the man in the field. Public schools should be amply supported by the public funds, every honest and industrious man should be able to live in his own home, and every person should have an equal chance to climb upwards. No man should feel at ease living in a palace while a few blocks away a poverty-plagued woman stitched and prayed that the angel of death might "with cold fingers touch her weary heart." All this would come to pass, he concluded in characteristic millennial style, under the reign of liberty in "the coming morning of the everlasting day" (Quoted in *Boston Investigator*, Aug. 19, 1891, from the *Anaconda Standard*).

On the next morning the family brawl was renewed in the court of law. The proponents having identified an alleged drafter of the will, Job Davis, now deceased, the opponents challenged the paper's excessive use of periods and capitalization and its misspellings as incompatible with the language skills of the purported author, and educated man and a judge. Of the three signing witnesses of the will only one, J. C. Sconce, was alive. He turned out to be relaxed and strong on the witness stand and supported by character witnesses. The challengers brought in neighbors to depict him as a notorious reprobate who dealt in counterfeit money, stole hogs, sheep, and harnesses, and killed another man's heifer in the woods. On Wednesday Ingersoll was stricken with a chill and had to be out of court for the rest of the week. On Sunday he and a party attended a play at Maguire's Opera House. (It was not a talented production, and the *Butte Miner* apologized for it [Aug. 3, 1891].)

On the eleventh, his fifty-eighth birthday, Ingersoll was depressed. The trial was not being conducted fairly. "The judge is a malicious and ignorant devil and is doing all in his power to defeat us," he told Clint and Sue. Butte was "an awful place to live. Two hundred & fifty tons of sulphur are burned in the air every day—it is suffocating, and yet some people are still alive. It is the most frightful place I ever was in." He was homesick. Two days previously he had told Eva to "go to Mother— look into her splendid eyes and tell her that I love her, and then give her a good hug and a long kiss for me" (Aug. 9, 1891, *Letters*, 566). Now he told his faraway daughter that she was a pure and perfect being, all her life the embodiment of all the virtues. "And so, my dear, dear daughter, on this my 58th birthday, I thank you with all my heart and love you beyond all words—Good night! Love and kisses to you and yours. Yours forever, Robert."

On that day two boxes of cigars arrived from the Browns. When he finished his supply on hand, he opened one of these gifts, savored the aroma, and as he puffed away he thought of Eva and Walston and how happy they were. "I hope that your troubles will all end in smoke & that you may ever be as serene as I was when smoking and thinking of you. I thank you both for having thought of me & for knowing me well enough to know that nothing could be more acceptable than the sacred leaves of Cuba" (*Letters*, 482). On his fifty-eighth birthday this unhappy man was the most popular person in Butte, an image of *bonhommie* to the whole town. When the infatuated *Miner* heard that the birthday had come and gone, it expressed surprise that no portents in the sky had signaled the event and extended greetings from the community. "Every citizen will join us in the wish that the colonel will live to round out his century as hale, as hearty, and as full of the milk of human kindness as he is today" (Aug. 15, 1891).

Ingersoll dominated "the d----d case" (To Sue, Aug. 28, 1891, L.C.)— expert testimony on disputed documents given, credibility of witnesses questioned, other will and their pertinence presented, possibility of forgery raised. He ridiculed opposing counsel, unnerving them. When he put one of his associates on the stand and questioned him about an investigation made in Chicago by a detective seeking possible witnesses to other wills, Senator Sanders objected on the ground of hearsay. Ingersoll snickered. Sanders spluttered that he had stood such abuse long enough, to which Ingersoll humbly responded that from the beginning of the trial he had been as polite as he knew how to be and that a lecture on deportment from Senator Sanders was "to say the least, refreshing." Since the detective had merely reported that he had discovered no witnesses, hearsay was not involved and the objection was overruled. Senator Sanders was plainly rattled. A few minutes later the court admonished him against lecturing to the witness. Another guffaw from Ingersoll, and Sanders groaned, "There, I am crushed again." Another guffaw, and Sanders heatedly protested that there was no need for laughter. Ingersoll smiled broadly and retorted, "Haven't I got a right to laugh at wit, even in the courtroom?" (*Butte Miner*, Aug. 14, 1891).

In his summation Sanders ripped into Ingersoll and his associates as foreign invaders who had treated the defendents and their counsel as "an aggregate of villains." "These strangers within our gates" had been graciously welcomed but had rendered themselves intolerable by their bad manners. He derided their experts and the inhabitant of Salt Creek, Iowa, (whom the prosecutors had brought in) as contrasted with the fifteen defense witnesses, any one of whom if believed would be sufficient, who had testified that they had seen the will and vouched for it. He assailed the one witness who had testified that he himself had drafted a later will but could not produce it and was not a lawyer—why would Andrew Davis have hired him? Sanders stated that compositional defects in the will were slight and did not militate against Job Davis as the author. He intimated that Ingersoll was a sinner and warned the jury against being seduced by this infamous advocate, described by the *Anaconda Standard* as "a man who was famous for his eloquence over two continents and in the islands of the sea, a man whose eloquence fittingly transcended that of Greece in the time of Alexander" (Sept. 5, 1891).

Ingersoll stood as the very model of an informed and sincere advocate fighting for the Truth, who could not and would not be defeated. He positioned himself next to the jury box, strode up and down as he talked, confronted individual jurors face to face, turned about at key points, and flung defiance at his adversaries. He reviewed the case in detail, marshalling an argument that must, he pleaded, irresistibly lead to the only verdict possible in accordance with common sense and justice, a verdict against the will. Being Ingersoll, he could not repress his wit, much to the delight of the spectators and the consternation of the judge. He made merry over all those witnesses who examined the disputed will over the years. He poured sarcasm on the witnesses attesting to Sconce's good reputation despite palpable facts to the contrary. "All these rumors, thick in the air, the bleating of sheep following him wherever he went, the low of cattle, and yet these people never heard it. Tried for stealing harness, they never heard of it" (*Works*, X, 552). He deplored the provincial prejudice that Sanders had dragged into the case. He had as many rights under the old flag in Montana as he had in New York and if any of the jurors came to New York he would see to it that they had as many rights there as in Montana. "I like Montana, too, and I believe the Montana people are big enough and broad enough not to have prejudice against a man because he comes from another State. Every State in this Union is represented in Montana, and the people who left the old settled States and came out to the new Territories dropped their prejudices on the way—and sometimes I have thought that is what killed the grass" (*Works*, X, 573).

The case was closed by Judge Woolworth, counsel for the defense. He especially stressed the fine reputation of Judge Trimble, one of the witnesses for the will, as an eminent lawyer and judge and as "a colonel in the war, carrying in his face the wound that he received in the defense of what Colonel Ingersoll says is the flag—the old flag." Well, he didn't go to the war, and get sick in the first battle, and come right home and get well and stay there. "That was not the sort of soldier that he was."

Ingersoll jumped up in fury.

INGERSOLL. Who did? Who did?
WOOLWORTH. Do you believe, gentlemen—
INGERSOLL. Wait one moment. Who did?
JUDGE DIXON. You were not interrupted when you were speaking.
INGERSOLL. If he tells a lie, I will interrupt him.
WOOLWORTH. I am sorry that the gentleman is so sensitive.
INGERSOLL. Ah, don't tell that then.

Woolworth ended his summation by saying that he intended no criticism of Ingersoll in that remark (*Inter Mount*, Sept. 5, 1891).

The jury froze in a deadlock—seven against the will, five for it. Under Montana law a majority of at least eight was required for a verdict—hence, the hung jury meant a mistrial. Considering circumstance and strategy in and out of the courtroom Ingersoll felt he achieved in the Davis stalemate a success as great as the acquittal in Star Route (To John, Sept. 20, 1891, *Letters*, 204).

The "d----d case" was over for the time being. Ingersoll fled from what he had called a sojourn in hell (To Sue, Aug. 28, 1891, L.C.). Well, it was after all just another case; he would not stew about it after the event. In Chicago the *News* reported, " 'Pope Bob,' healthy, spry, and genial, is again at the Grand Pacific" (Sept. 8, 1891). He brushed aside questions of politics and denounced the "countrified" idiots, the "donkeys" who would close the World's Fair on Sundays (*Chicago Post, Chicago Mail*, Sept. 8).

The rival Davis claims had culminated in six weeks of grueling trial with no winners. Years later the conflict was finally resolved by compromise on substantial terms for both sides. Ingersoll's fee of $100,000 had been contingent on breaking the will, but as he had not fulfilled the letter of his contract (he had simply made the bricks and built the fortress without which his clients would have received nothing) the ingrates felt that since they had paid him some $5,000 along the way they owed no more to him or his estate. (Mrs. Ingersoll sued and finally was awarded the full balance of $95,000 plus interest. [*New York Press*, Aug. 17, 1900])

In the fall Ingersoll was frequently on the move again. Lecturing in Chicago on liberty, in Cleveland on Shakespeare, he drew the usual enraptured audiences, standing room only (*Chicago Post*, Nov. 1, 1891; *Cleveland Plain Dealer*, Nov. 11, 1891). In Chicago he was introduced by Henry Demarest Lloyd, prominent social reformer: "A free thinker and a Puritan will speak to you tonight. You all have known and have loved him. You have heard him called 'Pope Bob,' but he is still the plumed knight of liberty. Emerson once said, 'Hitch your wagon to a star.' Tonight I ask you to hitch your wagon to a star and the name of the star is Robert G. Ingersoll" (*Chicago Post*, Nov. 1, 1891). In December, appearing as agent in the federal court in Toledo, he made a successful bid to buy the Cincinnati, Jackson, and Michigan Railroad for $150,000 (*Toledo Commercial*, Dec. 23, 1891). His unadvertised presence in Toledo did not pass unnoticed. "We couldn't let you out of the city," the *Commercial's* reporter cornered him, "without an interview of some kind." "Ah, well," he sighed, "I never try to escape the inevitable," and he was off with a stream of *bon mots* on politics, politicians, Ohio, and the Union.

At a dinner honoring Frank B. Carpenter for his painting *International Arbitration*, which would be a gift from America to England, Andrew P. White, who had been the founder and first president of Cornell, introduced Ingersoll as "a man who is admired and feared throughout the country. At one moment he smashes the most cherished convictions of the country, and at another he raises our highest aspirations for the future of humanity." Beginning by stating that he had no prejudices on the subject of art because he knew nothing about it, Ingersoll discoursed on art as the communion of souls, condemned the original Constitution for enshrining slavery, and favored liberal immigration and world peace through arbitration and international courts. Until the nations were civilized, however, this great peace-loving country was worth fighting for and should have the largest guns and the best navy. "We will just say: We want peace, and we tell you over the glistening leaves of this olive branch that if you don't compromise we will mop the earth with you." (He never minced words.) Colonel Ingersoll was proud of America and he was not a pacifist (*New York Press*, Dec. 1, 1891; *Works*, XII, 138).

The old year was dying and as December came the prospect was good for a relatively peaceful transition for Ingersoll into the new year. Friends joined the Ingersoll family at home in listening to Remenyi and his violin play Chopin, Schubert, and other masters (*New York Dramatic Mirror*, Dec. 12, 1891). On December nineteenth the *Telegram* published in its news columns a season's greeting from Ingersoll titled "A Christmas Sermon." The "Sermon" repeated his standard argument that Christianity brought a message not of joy but of eternal grief in an eternal penitentiary for most of the sons of men. Americans work too hard and should have more free days; Christmas should be a time for filling all hearts and homes with sunshine.

This little essay would have been long since forgotten if the champions of orthodoxy had not made an issue of it. In "Lies That Are Monstrous" the Reverend J. M. Buckley, with whom Ingersoll had tussled ten years before, denounced it as blasphemous and called upon the community to boycott the *Telegram* for tossing the offensive piece into its homes (*The Christian Advocate*, Dec. 24, 1891). Momentarily stunned, the *Telegram* retorted with a ringing defense of freedom of the press. "The *Telegram* wishes its friend Dr. Buckley to know that the days of the stake and witch-burning have gone by and that the *Telegram* cannot allow the torch to be applied to Colonel Ingersoll by so eminent a hand as that of Dr. Buckley" (Jan. 2, 1892). The confrontation flared. Almost every minister in town declared himself, the *Telegram* adding fuel to the fire. It opened its columns to letters pro and con, printed verbatim the pronouncements from the pulpit, and welcomed Ingersoll's responses. Ingersoll's articles cover ninety-one pages and take on more than a dozen clerical critics by name. The *Telegram* reported that the debate was the talk of the town and exulted that its circulation was booming, with every man going home on the commuter trains reading Ingersoll and his opponents in its columns.

The ministers of the city responding to "A Christmas Sermon" were almost to a man incensed by it, though there were notable exceptions. Dr. Talmage decried the assault on Christ: "Who has such an eye to our need; such a lip to kiss away our sorrow; such a hand to snatch us out of the fire; such a foot to trample our enemies; such a heart to embrace all our necessities" (*Telegram*, Jan. 16). Reverend Thomas Dixon and Dr. Madison C. Peters believed in freedom of speech, Reverend Dixon adding that Dr. Buckley took Ingersoll too seriously. "If God could choose Balaam's ass to speak a divine message, I do not see why he cannot utilize the Colonel. Give him rope" (Jan. 4, 5, 1892). Reverend W. H. Hillier shared with others the mainstream response of defense of the doctrines of free will, and eternal punishment: Every man had free will, but what he sewed he would reap. Reverend Hillier mocked Ingersoll's rhetoric: "Ingersoll cannot put out the fires of hell with the tears of pity" (Jan. 11, 1892). On the other hand, Reverend Peter M. Queen of the Dutch Reformed Church almost declared himself an Ingersollian. He admired "the picturesque and striking figure" of "the large-brained brave man" who was telling so much truth about Christianity. "The Christianity of Jesus Christ has been cruel, arrogant, bigoted, selfish. She has shed more blood to defend her doctrines than would float all the navies of the world" (Jan. 11, 1892). Reverend C. H. Eaton, Universalist, said, "He who attacks the doctrine of endless punishment as cruel or absurd is in my opinion more essentially Christian than he who defends it" (Jan. 7, 1892).

Dr. Buckley now hurled a medley of personal abuse: that Ingersoll attacked Christianity "for revenue only," that in his last moments on earth he would cower at the prospect of hell and recant like Voltaire and Paine, that he supported the circulation of obscene literature through the mails, that he had been procedurally unethical in his magazine debates with Black, Field, and Gladstone, that he encouraged indulgence in liquor.

Ingersoll pounced upon the opportunity to do battle in the press with the religious establishment as headed by Dr. Buckley, "who, as I understand it, is a doctor of theology—and I should think such theology stood in need of a doctor" (Works, VII, 342). "A minister says to me that I am going to hell—that I am bound to be punished forever and ever—and thereupon I say to him: 'There is no hell, you are mistaken; your Bible is not inspired; no human being is to suffer agony forever'; and thereupon with an injured look, he asks me this question: 'Why do you hurt my feelings?' It does not occur to him that I have the slightest right to object to his sentence of eternal grief'" (273). As to original sin, the mythical God of Christianity would have done better to drown the whole human race, not sparing Noah and his family, then start again in the Garden with a new pair of progenitors, give them the Bible and the Presbyterian creed, and keep the serpent out. According to Ingersoll men do not have free will but do as they must. If they do have free will and the all-knowing God knows that they will fail in the pursuit of salvation, then he is the one responsible. Human judges send men to prison to protect society and to allow them to ·reform, but there is no chance to reform in hell.

He set the record straight on the tranquil death scenes of Voltaire and Paine, who remained firm in their unbelief, and reviewed his battle against obscenity with the Liberal League. Turning to his magazine debates he pointed out that he had merely conformed to the directions of the publisher and that Dr. Field had become his friend. Yes, he had lauded choice whiskey and he even quoted himself: "Drink it and you will feel within your blood the star-lit dawns, the dreamy tawny dusks of many perfect days." He went further and admitted that he had even rhapso-dized about tobacco, which, again quoting himself, "when redeemed by fire, doth safely steal within the fortress of the brain and bind in sleep the captured sentinels of care and grief" (350).

Did Dr. Talmage intend by his trampling foot image of Christ to justify any and all religious persecutions of the past? Ingersoll paid respect to the man called Christ, a reformer and an infidel in his own day. "He was regarded as a blasphemer, and his life was destroyed by hypocrites who have done in all ages what they could to trample freedom and manhood out of the human mind. Had I lived at that time I would have been his friend and should he come again he will not find a better friend than I will be" (384).

The Buckley affair was only one incident in a crowded life during the early winter of 1891-1892. Nowhere so busy a man as he there was—legal business, a big party at his home for his friends in the theater, public dinners and after-dinner speeches, and lecturing all vied for his time (*Boston Home Journal*, Jan. 30). On January fifteenth, breaking bread with the Unitarian Club, he thanked them for their good sense in inviting him (*Works*, XII, 157). On the twentieth he spoke at Delmonico's before the Jewelers' Board of Trade, and on the twenty-first he drank from the loving cup with the Clover Club in Philadelphia (where he was greeted as Bishop Ingersoll) (*Philadelphia Ledger*, Jan. 22). On the twenty-fifth he socialized with the Police Association. The evening before he had lectured to a standing-room-only audience at Hammerstein's Opera House on liberty; the evening after he gave his lecture on liberty for the benefit of the Harlem Free Kindergarten Association at the Harlem Opera House, where, after speaking for an hour and a half, he was as fresh as when he began. He "appeared to be in the most happy mood, and this proved rather infectious to a portion of his audience, who laughed and applauded in turn when he spoke flippantly of the Deity, ridiculed the story of the Creation, and denounced the doctrine of hell as 'an infamous lie' " (*Harlem Reporter*, Jan. 29). The next day the Manhattan Liberal Club cele-brated the 155th anniversary of Thomas Paine's birth, and Ingersoll's speech was received with "laughter, applause, and tears" (*New York Press*, Jan. 30, 1892). After the speech-making Ingersoll and Moncure Conway held an impromptu reception on stage. A reporter noted that there were hundreds of pretty girls in the audience who knew all about Paine and threw farewell kisses to the beaming prophets of the free mind. The champion blasphemer of America was basking in idolatry.

Note

1. In 1873 Congress had demonetized silver, which the government had been accepting for free coinage in the proportion of 16 silver to 1 gold. Under

the narrow money supply based on gold alone, prices had declined, dollar incomes had fallen, fixed debts (mortgages, equipment, and such) became harder to meet, and forfeitures and collapses of rural communities were epidemic. (In 1877, in "About Farming in Illinois," Ingersoll had denounced the demonetization as a fraud that should be undone.) In the political struggle of the nineties free silver or free coinage meant that the government would again coin all silver brought to it at 16 silver to 1 gold valuation and would not charge for the manufacturing process. This would raise the price of silver on the commercial market and have an inflationary effect generally.

XIII

Quo Vadis?

Having settled with the New York ministers for the time being, Ingersoll returned to the lecture circuit. In February, accompanied by Mrs. Ingersoll and Clint Farrell, he set out on a three to four week tour crisscrossing the eastern half of the country above the Mason-Dixon line. He spoke in, among other places, Washington, Buffalo, Chicago, Cleveland, Cincinnati, Akron, Indianapolis, Detroit, and Erie. He stated his purposes to a reporter: "A few years ago my throat troubled me, and I did not lecture for some four or five years, but now I am perfectly well and expect to lecture more than formerly. I must give the clergy something to talk about and I must do what I can to civilize the creeds. I want the people to become good-natured so that they will discuss even religious questions with kindness" (*Cincinnati Enquirer*, Feb. 15, 1892).

There could be no doubt as to Ingersoll's enduring magnetism off and on the platform. On trains, at depots, in the supposed privacy of a box at the theater, he was fair game for the insatiable press and public. At the hotel he found himself in the usual continuous swirl of activity—chatting with politicians, friends, and strangers, sparring with reporters, signing autographs, writing answers to telegrams. Sometimes there was hardly enough time to sweep the company out, have a hasty dinner, and speed to the lecture hall.

Thousands of devotees who had languished in the desert of silence now swarmed to the revived fountain of oratory. Excepting when opposed by religious boycott, extremely bad winter weather, or competing attractions, Ingersoll spoke to overflow audiences. People eagerly paid speculators the sky-high price of two dollars a ticket. Improvised seating was provided on stage for scores or hundreds—all sorts of chairs, camp stools, sofas, boxes—anything a person could sit on. Standees were often exhausted after the endurance test of a two-hour lecture. A spell-bound audience knows no discomfort or fatigue.

As in the past the audience came in large measure from the literate public, middle and upper classes predominating. In Cincinnati "it was an assemblage of quality that drank in the elegance of the noted infidel; the most prominent families in the city were represented" (*Enquirer*, Feb. 15, 1892). In the Nation's Capital "at the theater entrance could be seen the drags and luxurious conveyances of the ultra fashionable world; while within, occupying every seat in the grand structure, was a class of beings whose faces showed the companionship of thought and good books" (*London Times*, Feb. 18, 1892).

For his return to the lecture platform Ingersoll had chosen innocuous subjects (Lincoln, Shakespeare, and the comparatively moderate "Liberty of Man, Woman, and Child"). If "Liberty" disturbed some with its critique of historical religion, it pleased all with its tributes to honesty, justice, kindness, married love, and the beauty of children. In "Lincoln" Ingersoll forgot what he had said about the Republican candidate in 1860 and the politician in the White House at critical junctures of the Civil War. His Lincoln is the Lincoln of legend, "associated with the enfranchisement of labor, with the emancipation of millions, with the salvation of the Republic" (*Works*, III, 123). Another reporter adopted Ingersoll's purple style as his own: "From his first sentence to his last, his address was a swift stream of eloquence; at times flowing between green and quiet banks, and anon dashing in foam among the rocks or breaking into rainbows as it plunged over giant precipices" (*Indianapolis News*, Feb. 19, 1892). After the lecture Ingersoll usually held a reception on the platform and, if his schedule permitted, repaired to home, club, or hotel party room, where over light refreshments he regaled his circle with banter, anecdotes, or an imitation of Mark Twain's Missouri drawl.

En famille Ingersoll was happy that his oratorical powers had not waned with disuse and that he could still draw the multitude. He wrote to Eva, "I am besieged day and night. I have had a real ovation everywhere. The people are anxious to hear me and the little trip has been a great success. I send you notices in the Indianapolis papers. All the house was sold in three hours after the tickets were put on sale" (Chicago, Feb. 19, 1892, Carbondale). And on the same day he joshed with Maud: "We are getting tired of going about the rainy drizzling world. It has been raining for several days but the houses have been full. I suspect people come in to get out of the wet" (L.C.).

Interviews with Ingersoll were republished far and wide; the country was hungry for his opinions on any topic. His return to the lecture platform coincided with a presidential election year, and reporters fell upon him for analyses and preferences but he was no longer "on fire" for politics. He was interested in poetry, not politics; his mind was on the banks of the Avon, not the Potomac; he would rather discuss Edwin

Forrest's interpretation of Lear and preferred listening to Remenyi on the violin to reading a presidential message. The tariff did not concern him personally, as he was not in trade; he would gladly take any money that was legal.

When reporters pressed, he asked that questions and answers be in writing to avoid misrepresentation. If the Republicans nominated a good man (not President Harrison, one term was enough for him), they would win. Would the Democrats nominate a candidate who would come out boldly for the free coinage of silver? "No sir, the Democratic candidate must come out boldly for reform, boldly against the Republicans— boldly against corruption, boldly against extravagance, boldly in a general way and the boldest and most general the better. . . . But after all it makes but little difference who is President. This country is a good deal like a splendid and prosperous cigar store, and it makes but little difference what wooden Indian is in front of the shop" (*Buffalo Enquirer*, Feb. 10, 1892). He elaborated on the theme. "But let us enjoy ourselves: we have a great country; the people are prospering; the towns are growing; the railroads are doing well; our soil is splendid; millions of children are going to school; millions of boys and girls are falling in love; several million papers are published every day. Ohio is full of statesmen, and it makes but little difference who the next president is—provided he is sound on the tariff and coinage" (*Cleveland Plain Dealer*, Feb. 12, 1892). (Who embodied such soundness he did not say.) A religious question: What did he think about the committee recommendation that the Presbyterian church eliminate infant baptism from its creed? "It is too comforting a doctrine to give up. What is to happen to all the infants damned under the old creed? It is just as reasonable to condemn infants as grown men and women. . . . All this damnation business is damned nonsense" (*Plain Dealer*, Feb. 12, 1892).

Ingersoll was hardly back in New York when a wide-eyed reporter broke in upon him at the office for sagacious comment on a current crisis. The clock makers were on strike at the same time the Fifth Avenue Church was planning to build an extension, to which Jay Gould had contributed ten thousand dollars. Should some of the building fund be given to the striking workers? The reporter said that the Reverend John Hall had brushed him off saying he had no time to discuss the matter, he was too busy with urgent church affairs. The reporter had found Warner van Norden, treasurer of the church's Extension Committee and president of the North American Bank. Van Norden had said that the clock makers had brought their trouble on themselves and that giving alms to the poor encouraged idleness and crime. He referred to his typist (the term then was "typewriter"): She had been brought up in a tenement house, but now earned two dollars a day and dressed better than the lords and ladies of olden times. The duty of the church was to save men's souls, and to minister to their bodies only incidentally. After all, happiness did not lie in the enjoyment of material things but in the soul. Why, at the Working Girls' Club the girls who have worked all day sang hymns and followed the leader in prayer. Anybody who wanted money should work for it since there was no lack of employment for real Americans.

What did Ingersoll think? He obliged by writing out a withering response, not against Hall and Van Norden personally, but against their ideas. Surely the reporter must have misrepresented Hall; the pastor could not have intended to deny the injunction of Christ: "Sell that thou hast and give to the poor." As to Van Norden, the striking clock workers did *not* bring their trouble on themselves; their wages were not sufficient to live on. A man without pity was an intellectual beast. Morality and goodness could be promoted only by changing social conditions.

> It is useless to give a hungry man a religious tract. Unemployment is caused by business conditions, over-supply of labor in an industry, competition. Yes, the girl earning two dollars a day dresses better than the lords and ladies of olden times—that is, of the Garden of Eden. Life is not worth living if the soul is without pity. . . . For my own part I would rather see the poor people eat than to hear them pray. I would rather see them clothed comfortably than to see them shivering and at the same time hear them singing hymns." (*Morning Advertiser*, March 8; *Works*, VII, 521)

Soon thereafter Ingersoll and Chauncey Depew were speakers at a celebration honoring Frederick Douglass and blacks in general. Ingersoll paid a glowing tribute to the achievements of the freedmen and their leader, his friend Douglass. Gesturing to Douglass he said, "He is one of the men who has done as much as any man living to civilize the people of the United States. I am a believer—not in God but in man. I believe in all the rights of the human heart and the human brain. No man is civilized who is not willing to give and who does not give to every other man the same right that he claims for himself. The same with races. Any race claiming to be superior should show it by acts of justice and kindness. No man is ever superior to the man he has robbed." He praised blacks for their patience and forgiveness: "The South has blossomed under your hands. You have raised everything in that country except hell," leading him of course, to urge them to think for themselves rather than thoughtlessly accept the white man's religion, whose biblical God sanctioned slavery. Depew, the perfect gentleman, recorded that Ingersoll was "master of the occasion and of his audience," but that he (Depew), though hating to contradict his friend, was constrained to declare that blacks owed their blessings to God (*My Memories of Eighty Years*, 321; *New York Sun*, March 15, 1892).

In late March Ingersoll went on a lecture tour to the provinces of eastern Canada. In Toronto the U.S. Consul introduced him: "I have the honor to present to you the man whose just fame in the advocacy of the expression of free thought is bounded by no continent, circumscribed by no sea, but reaches the utmost limits of civilization, 'the golden orator,' Robert Ingersoll" (*Mail,* March 29). (He broke this tour to speak at Whitman's funeral in Camden on the twenty-ninth).

In April Ingersoll presented his lecture "Myth and Miracle" at the Brooklyn Academy of Music to an overflow audience including Mayor Brody, "a gathering of well-dressed men and women who, as the great orator made his way through two and a half hours of witticism, logic, and poetry, showed its intelligence by grasping every point; in short it was an Ingersoll audience" (*Brooklyn Times,* April 4, 1892). They were more deeply moved than at a performance by Patti or Bernhardt (*Brooklyn Eagle,* April 4) and "a pin could have been heard to drop until with one will at the conclusion of the labored peroration the grand audience applauded until gloves bursted" (*Brooklyn Times,* April 4). Seated two rows from the stage was a reporter and his friend. The reporter, who attended every lecture by Ingersoll in the New York area, had told Ingersoll that the friend had never heard him. In the lecture Ingersoll directed all his energies on the friend, and the poor man almost fainted. The next day Ingersoll asked, "Well?" and the reporter answered, "He is as well as can be expected, Colonel," at which "a grim smile crossed his face. It meant volumes. If the public only knew that sunny-souled and juicy-hearted gentleman as he is in private nothing but violets and forget-me-nots would make the remainder of his road fragrant" (*Brooklyn Times,* April 9, 1892).

Father Thomas F. Ward was not interested in throwing violets and forget-me-nots to Ingersoll. He denounced the renting of the Academy to "so infamous a purpose as the dissemination of infidel doctrines" and rebuked the mayor and other public officials in attendance for giving aid and comfort to "a man who mocks at Christianity and despises God and Jesus Christ" (*Eagle,* April 4). The *Brooklyn Times* promptly shot a challenge back at Father Ward: "Let the Church gird itself to look squarely at the infidel and thus place itself in a position to do itself the highest justice in returning the infidel's blows" (April 4).

In April and early May, accompanied by Clint Farrell, Ingersoll lectured in various towns in Pennsylvania, upstate New York, Ohio, and in Washington, D.C., on Shakespeare and "Myth and Miracle." The reporter in Scranton described him: "The irrepressible agnostic is such a man as Julius Caesar liked to have about him. He is sleek and fat and looks as if he has what he delights in more than anything else, a conscience that doesn't trouble him and he can therefore sleep well o' nights" (*Tribune,* April 9). At his afternoon receptions he dashed off his opinions on the aspirants for the White House: Cleveland was the strongest Democratic candidate because the largest; Harrison had drawn four aces in his presidency and should quit while ahead; Gresham would make the best appeal to the electorate, particularly the urban workers. The lectures in the evening continued to win critical acclaim. On Shakespeare: "The sentences as they fell from his lips sounded like the cadence of an old sweet song" (*Wilkes-Barre Record*, April 15, 1892). On "Myth and Miracle": "That Mr. Ingersoll is eloquent is known to the world, and he knows as well as any man living how to tickle the fancy and to paint a thought. He kicks aside the thorns and strews life's pathway with flowers. He demolishes the creeds of Christianity and beatifies the ruins with the blossoms of common sense" (*Washington Post*, April 20, 1892).

When Ingersoll and Mayor Fellows walked on stage in Scranton the "large, intelligent, and enthusiastic" audience "went wild with delight" (*Scranton Tribune*, April 9, 1892). In Wilkes-Barre, an exception to the general rule of an overwhelming welcome, the hotel suite did not swarm with visitors, allowing Ingersoll to relax in the afternoon with a game of billiards and write out his opinion on the tariff. He was all for it—the higher the wall, the better.

> I am in favor of protection, because I prefer this country to any and all others. The great republic should be as nearly as possible self-supporting. We want to develop the ingenuity, the inventive genius of our people. . . . The more industries we have the more we will develop our brain, and the more intellectual we shall become. Let us make everything that can be made in this country. It is better to trade with each other than with aliens. Keep our money here, our gold and silver. Buy only what we must, produce and make what we can. (*Wilkes-Barre Record*, April 15, 1892)

A month later he would suggest a measure of restraint: "I am in favor of protection; of course I mean in reason. . . . I do want America to produce what America needs" (*Denver Republican*, May 15, 1892).

In Cincinnati the *Enquirer* said that "no man in the country is a more entertaining controversialist than Colonel Ingersoll. His opinions are always sought for, and he does not hesitate to give his views on any topic which may be of interest to the public." He had just come in the "cars" from New York and was tired, but he welcomed a steady stream of visitors all day including members of the Cincinnati Liberal Society (May 2, 1892). The next day he was in Columbus, where he greeted the reporters, "Well, I was well disposed of in the Queen City and here they [the reporters] are again." He was resting from the trip, he said, by walking to and fro in the room, "but if there was any exhaustion in his physique it was not discernible, the familiar clean-shaven rotund face and silver hair giving him the fresh and happy appearance which is characteristic of the nature of the man" (*Columbus Journal*, May 3, 1892).

In mid-May Ingersoll, Mrs. Ingersoll, and Maud began a two-week tour of the Midwest. He was traveling on legal business and also to lecture on Shakespeare and to deliver "Myth and Miracle." A stopover in Chicago to confer on the ongoing Davis case, and then on direct to Denver. That same evening, trying to relax in a "private" box at the theater, he "gracefully accorded" an interview which turned mainly on the silver question. "We are the greatest silver nation in the world," he said, "and I am in favor of silver money." Many nations had died, but none bore the epitaph, "died of too much silver. . . . I am afraid neither party will have the courage to take the right ground on the silver question. . . . I believe in the coinage of both [silver and gold] and I believe in keeping the proportion in such a way as to deal with perfect fairness between the debtor and the creditor" (The news account bore the headline SILVER BOB) (*Denver Republican*, May 15, 1892).

On the morrow socializing with old friends preceded the lecture on Shakespeare. He wrote happily to Walston and Eva Brown, "On Sunday I had the largest audience ever in the Opera House—over 500 people on stage. Everybody was delighted with the lecture. We left at 11:30 the same night for Las Vegas—had a pleasant ride—everything perfect." Ingersoll was in Las Vegas on legal business. The case was his own. He was grappling in court with Dorsey on the distribution of assets in the defunct Palo Blanco Cattle Company. His final judgment on Dorsey: "He is a great scoundrel" (To Eva and Walston, May 19, 1892, *Letters*, 568).

From Las Vegas he had to travel to Pueblo. Picking up his wife and daughter at Hot Springs he took the evening train, arriving in Pueblo at 11:30 P.M. A zealous reporter, amazed at finding himself the sole receptionist at the depot, greeted Ingersoll, helped with the luggage, got into the horse taxicab with the Ingersolls, and rode with them to the Grand Hotel. In the hotel lobby the reporter began his questions, but Ingersoll demurred. "My dear boy, I know you will excuse me from this interview when I tell you that the good wife and daughter are thoroughly worn out and that I am a trifle weary myself. A long ride in the cars and in this light atmosphere is exhausting." The reporter persisted, "Yes, but I did not understand who you said was your favorite candidate for the presidency." Ingersoll laughed. "You rascal, I am tired, but not too tired to say that if I had the power Judge Gresham would be in charge of the destinies of this country, so far as it is possible for the chief executive to be." Next the inevitable question; "And if silver what—" "That we cannot have too much of it." Ingersoll glanced at his wife and daughter waiting quietly at the far end of the lobby. He shook his fist at the reporter and "ran like a good-natured schoolboy to their side" (*Pueblo Daily Chieftain*, May 21, 1892).

In Las Vegas had come a telegram from the *Denver Times*: "To Col. Robert G. Ingersoll: The people here are anxious to hear your views on silver, which is a vital question to us all. Will you not devote a few minutes to this question during your lecture Sunday night?" (*Denver Times*, May 18, 1892). On May 15 Ingersoll had lectured in Denver on Shakespeare; six days later he came back with a lecture against Christianity. The town had not had enough of him, no matter the topic. "Colonel R. G. Ingersoll," said the *News*, "again enthused and delighted a great

audience at the Tabor Grand Opera House ,last night. The theme was
'Myth and Miracles,' and for more than two hours his auditors, filling
every seat from the pit to the topmost perch of the gallery, bent forward with absorbing interest as the great orator poured forth his thun-
ders against the church as it has existed in all countries and all ages
of the world. . . . Frequent and long continued applause testified to the
sympathy between listeners and speaker" (May 22, 1892).

Concluding his lecture Ingersoll added that he "would say one or
two words tonight on such vulgar things as gold and silver."

He proceeded to make an impassioned statement in favor of currency expansion, speaking like a populist. "I am as satisfied . . . as I live,"
he began, "that the few, the few who control the debts, the currency,
the money of the world—have combined, either consciously or unconsciously, to make the debtor pay more than the creditor has the right
to ask." In all ages the burdens of society have always been borne by
the weak. "Who goes to the [war] front? The millionaires? Not one. Who
goes? The great presidents of corporations? The bankers? The men who
preside over our great vaults of gold? Not much!" America had never
had enough money to conduct the nation's business, and the demonetization of silver had worsened the situation: "The less money the more
misery." The few should not have the right to magnify their power by
keeping money scarce. The audience burst into applause when he
proclaimed, "I want the free coinage of all the gold you can dig out of
the mines and crevices of the rocks and I want the free coinage of all
the silver you can win from the mines of America. If any people are
not willing to accept American silver, we will not trade with them. . . . It
would be a thousand times better for us if we never bought another
thing from Europe." Clearly, though in general terms, he seemed to have
enlisted in the agrarian revolt against the eastern establishment.

Back home to Dobbs Ferry, lecturing along the way to a few crowded
houses in Topeka, St. Joseph, and Kansas City on Shakespeare, in Indianapolis on myth and miracle. Addressing "the wealth and culture of
Kansas City" on Shakespeare—a poet dead in his grave for nearly three
hundred years—"what an audience, what attention, what applause, what
absorbing and delighted interest!" (*Kansas City Star*, May 27, 1892). ·

In interviews he warned that the common people were on the march:
"The farmers and laborers have got to thinking a little. In other words,
the masses are beginning to see how things go. They have finally discovered that people do on the land much as the fishes do in the seas—
the big ones eat up the little ones and the little ones are thinking of
combining themselves, and the Republican party has got to take that
into consideration at Minneapolis" (*Chicago Inter-Ocean*, May 29, 1892). What
did he think of the Methodist Conference at Omaha holding that "laymen" in church literature did not include women? "I am glad of it. The
women support the church. They fry the chickens for the preachers and

bear the burdens. I think they will soon see that the church is of no use to them. A religion in which women do not occupy the highest place is a poor affair" (*Kansas City Star*, May 27, 1892).

Spending the summer at Walston, his son-in-law's rustic estate in Dobbs Ferry, Ingersoll could look back on a half year in which he had proved the durability of his talents and popular appeal, had enjoyed refreshing skirmishes with the preachers, and had spread the message. While having a good time he had also made money. His random records show the following net lecture receipts from February through June: Chicago (two lectures), $3,540; Cleveland and Akron, $1,300; Toronto, $399.47 cash, $400 check; Brooklyn, $520; Washington, $900; Cincinnati, $1,100; Denver, St. Paul, Kansas City, and Indianapolis, $4,580—remarkable figures on attendance, considering that the top price of admittance was $1.50 (Acct. Book Beginning March 28, 1889, L.C.).

Best of all, he was with his family. Unfortunately birthdays came only once a year. What a celebration, his fifty-ninth, on August 11, 1892! "Well, we got through the birthday without incident and wound up with fried chicken, a magnificent mushroom omelette—fried potatoes—lima beans—green corn, cantaloupe—peaches and cream, coffee and ice cream, and champagne. This morning we are all alive. Rust [the dog] wanders and acts uneasy—like a candidate while the convention is in session— but he will be all right in a few days." Stone (a neighbor), Walston, and Ingersoll played eleven games of 41. "Stone won one game, Walston *one*— and I won 9!!!" (To Clint and Sue, Aug. 12, 1892, L.C.).

His friend Mr. Debs in Terre Haute (not yet a national firebrand) had sent a birthday telegram, and Ingersoll responded with avuncular advice.

> Each moment is a bee that flies
> With swift and unreturning wing,
> Giving its honey to the wise
> And to the fool the poison sting.

I hope that you and yours will have honey all your lives. We all send best regards to your father and mother—to your sisters—and to Mrs. Debs and yourself" (Aug. 12, 1892, *Letters*, 570).

Ingersoll took no part in the 1892 presidential contest between Harrison (seeking reelection) and Cleveland (a comeback to power). "My God! What a choice we have. It is terrible to choose one when we hate both— Think of marrying the girl you hate the least—that is my situation" (To Clint and Sue, Aug. 19, 1892, L.C.).

Letters poured in, responses poured out—encouraging fellow thinkers of freethought, expatiating on the black cause, on clerical bigotry, on the impossibility of proving the existence of God or immortality, on Conway's *Life of Paine*, and on Ingersoll's own minor *bête noire*, compulsory Sabbath observance.

Most people imagine that Sunday should be kept sacred by not doing anything on that day for the good of man, but by devoting your entire time in the worship of God—that is to say, in doing something for God. There is nothing a man can do for God, as God needs nothing; but there are many things we can do for our fellow-men because many of them are in constant need. All days should be for the good of man, and that day in which the most people are really happy is the best day. (To A. E. Ganning, July 15, 1892, *Letters*, 332)

On the surface there may have been jovial affirmations, but underneath, defeat and sadness. Ultimately, inevitably, the paths of glory and of happiness lead but to the grave. Judge Gresham had lost a brother. Ingersoll sent condolence. "How poor the world is growing. I know what it is to lose a brother—one that was dearer to me than my own life— and so my sympathy is yours. How little and worthless everything seems in the presence of death—and how withered and shrunken seem the little ambitions—the longings for place and power" (July 13, 1892, *Letters*, 569). As he sat in a rocker on the veranda and looked across the trees to the river Ingersoll was melancholy. "The river Time flows on." The antics of the barnyard reflected evanescence and futility. "The chickens are getting along as usual. The old Plymouth Rock rooster—he of the injured leg— is still lingering on the stage and like an old beau paying his attentions to the opposite sex—The hens avoid him as though they believe his intentions dishonorable. Thus it is and ever was with one who seeks to increase the happiness of others" (To Clint and Sue, Aug. 30, 1892, *Letters*, 483). A refrain: "The days are going. The sands of Time are eager to reach the desert of the Past" (Clint and Sue, Aug. 23, 1892, L.C.).

In October the Buffalo Real Estate Exchange provided "a great treat" free of charge to real estate men attending a convention and to the general public—it had engaged Ingersoll for a lecture. Ingersoll spoke on one of his earliest themes, "Progress," a performance filled with "magnificent flights" (*Commercial*, Oct. 6, 1892). The next day, in Chicago, he refused to comment on Gresham's conversion to the Democratic party except to say that Gresham was a high-minded man. "We live in an epoch of small things; when the sea is smooth a poor sailor will do"; he favored protection and Harrison against Cleveland on principle (*Chicago News*, Oct. 7).

At the Chicago Auditorium Ingersoll delivered his lecture on Voltaire for the first time. The tremendous audience attested to his enduring popularity in Chicago—some five thousand people occupying every seat from pit to gallery, another thousand in impromptu seating on the stage, and still another thousand standing crammed in the foyer. Ingersoll stuck close to his manuscript but he was in good voice and "had evidently lost none of the old-time power in swaying the feelings of his audience at will" (*Chicago Tribune*, Oct. 9). High passion tumbled out in a torrent of words. On death-bed recantation by unbelievers:

> Why should we think that the brave thinkers, the investigators, the honest men, must have left the crumbling shores of time in dread and fear, while the instigators of the massacre of St. Bartholomew; the inventors and users of thumb-screws, of iron boots and racks; the burners and tearers of human flesh; the stealers, the whippers and the enslavers of men; the buyers and beaters of maidens, mothers, and babes; the founders of the Inquisition; the makers of chains; the builders of dungeons; the calumniators of the living; the slanderers of the dead; and even the murderers of Jesus Christ, all died in the odor of sanctity, with white, forgiven hands folded upon breasts of peace; while the destroyers of prejudice, the apostles of humanity, the soldiers of liberty, died surrounded by the fierce fiends of God. (*Works*, III, 233)

And purple prose for Voltaire: "From his throne at the foot of the Alps, he pointed the finger of scorn at every hypocrite in Europe. For half a century, past rack and stake, he carried with brave hands the sacred torch of Reason, whose light at last will flood the world" (248). Later in October, on Ingersoll's motion, the court dismissed a petition seeking an accounting from Walston Brown, his son-in-law, receiver of the Rochester and Pittsburgh Railway, of two million dollars in assets. Not a week later was the first day of the Coles will trial, with press and public in attendance. The decedent, Elizabeth Coles, had excluded her brother Edward from any share in her three million dollar estate. Ingersoll, appearing for Edward, sought to break the will as the product of an unsound mind. Grasping and drawing back his lapels, he addressed the decedent's servants by their first names as he developed an image of the lady of the house as one who put clothes on the Venus de Milo, gave her servants short rations, accused them of poisoning her, and had a furious temper. However, evidence was lacking to conclusively demonstrate that Miss Cole was unbalanced (*New York Evening Advertiser* and *Sun*, Oct. 27, 1892; *New York Telegram*, Nov. 3, 1892).

On October twenty-ninth Ingersoll lectured on Voltaire in Milwaukee. Returning through Chicago with a heavy cold and impaired vocal chords, he uncharacteristically barred all comers from his hotel suite while taking remedies. He wrote a note for the bellhop to show would-be visitors: "I am booked to lecture tonight on 'Myths and Miracles' and I am waiting for a miracle to restore my voice" (*Chicago Inter-Ocean*, Oct. 3, 1892). The standing-room-only crowd at McVicker's Theater was not disappointed, as the slightly hoarse voice easily carried the sweeping message of ridicule through the large hall (*Chicago Times*, Oct. 31). The *Inter-Ocean* quoted, "As long, however, as the myths remained in poetry they were beautiful, but when the priests got hold of them and told them as facts, they became stupid, brutal, and infamous. Samson's strength was supposed to be in his hair. If that theory is true, I wouldn't have strength enough to stand," and he meditatively patted his "dome of thought, smooth as it is and devoid of hirsute adornment" (Oct. 31). Back in New York he lectured to a standing-room-only crowd at the Broadway Theater on Voltaire. Expressing the agony of a torture victim under the religious terror of the old regime, his voice dropped almost to a whisper—the audience leaned forward and concentrated on every word. Leaving the theater an old man proclaimed to all and sundry, "Ah, it's the same old Bob Ingersoll. He hasn't changed a bit" (*New York Sun*, Dec. 12).

The trial of Frank S. Gray against Col. Elliott F. Shepard provided a three-day circus for the New Yorkers who flooded Part II of the Supreme Court (*New York Sun*, Dec. 14; *New York Herald* and *Journal*, Dec. 16). Ingersoll's client Gray, discharged as manager of the *Daily Mail and Express*, was suing owner Shepard for $18,145 on breach of employment contract. Gray contended that he had been fired because he refused to carry a bribe of $5,000 to the Police Commissioner (required by terms of a printing contract). Shepard countered that Gray had been an incompetent, a drunkard, and an adept in profanity and blackmail. The holiday audience guffawed continually as "New York's most distinguished infidel, Colonel Robert G. Ingersoll," cross-examined its "most assertive Christian, Colonel Elliott F. Shepard." Judge Parker brought his ivory gavel down twice at the spectators and threatened to clear the courtroom. He warned Ingersoll about violations of decorum. Ingersoll responded with utter baby-faced amazement and called upon opposing counsel to endorse his innocence. He toyed with the defendant, insinuating that Shepard intended to add the bribe to the bill.

INGERSOLL. Then your intention was that the city should pay your commission?
SHEPARD. My intention was to instruct Mr. Gray—
INGERSOLL. No, no. Was it your intention that the city should pay your commission?
SHEPARD. It was not in my mind. I had no intention about it. Now you are going into a process of reasoning—

From Ingersoll came a smile oozing poisonous goodwill: "No, you might not be at home there" (*New York Sun*, Dec. 14). The judge ruled that the letter from Shepard to Gray that had enclosed the $5,000 "commission" belonged for evidentiary purposes to the employer (*Evening World*, Dec. 17). So limited, the jury held for the defendant.

On New Year's Day Ingersoll delivered his revivified old lecture, "Progress," to a packed house at the Broadway Theater; on the sixteenth he addressed a similar crowd in Washington on Voltaire. On the twenty-second, in Detroit to deliver "Myth and Miracle," he held court in his suite at the Cadillac Hotel. A reporter there described him: "The colonel is coming along into the 60's [he would be sixty on August eleventh] and looks it. But his vigorous mentality shows itself in every movement, every utterance, and an aggressive activity shows him to be a man of great stamina, great resource and great self-confidence (*Detroit Free Press*,

Jan. 23, 1893). On the next day in Chicago, he appeared before Judge Gresham on a railroad rate case, and, it being two days short of Robert Burns's birthday, his lecture that evening was on Burns. It was heavily patronized by Chicagoans of Scottish descent. He recited Burns's poems with full respect for their Scotticisms and extolled the bard of Afton for having put Scotland on the map of nations. Strangers in the audience clapped each other on the back and felt good about being brother Scotsmen (*Chicago Times*, Jan. 24, 1893).

A few days later, Blaine died. Ingersoll prefaced his lecture with a tribute to his Plumed Knight: "Today my heart goes out to the wife, the children, and to millions who mourn for the one they loved" (*Cleveland Plain Dealer*, Jan. 28, 1893). He sent condolences to Mrs. Blaine, and she responded warmly. The next day no callers were admitted to the Ingersoll suite. He did not want to talk about Blaine (*Cincinnati Enquirer*, Jan. 29).

In February Ingersoll appeared before the Court of Appeals in Albany, New York, laden with exhibits, to argue on behalf of a client for a $500,000 award for work done on the new Croton Aqueduct. In New York there was always time to be a man about town, particularly at the theater, where he and his family attended first-night performances and he vouchsafed his affirmative criticisms. He was particularly impressed with the down-to-earth genius of the great Eleanora Duse, and he attended every play during the season in which that worthy successor of Madame Ristori appeared (*New York Morning Advertiser*, March 14, 1893). Occasionally he lectured in New York and nearby towns on Shakespeare, Lincoln, and "Liberty" to overflow crowds, receiving in New York and Baltimore the extraordinary plaudit of curtain calls.

In late April, encouraged—if he needed encouragement—by his booming popularity, Ingersoll embarked on a lecture tour in eastern Canada, upstate New York, Ohio, Indiana, and Missouri, scheduling appearances in fourteen cities in nineteen days (*Truth Seeker*, April 22, 1893). In Canada, although the subjects Burns and Shakespeare were innocuous enough, (he even was introduced in Hamilton by the U.S. Consul) the reception was poor, the audience numbering about six hundred in Toronto, three hundred in Hamilton, and in London "one tenth the size of that which faced Rev. T. DeWitt Talmage, the famous preacher, some weeks ago" (*London Advertiser*, April 24, 1893). Reporters' impressions alternated between "rare treat" and "platitudes oft repeated always in the superlative degree" (*Toronto Mail*, April 21; *London Advertiser*, April 24). Back in the States he was on friendlier ground, addressing thousands rain or shine on Lincoln and Shakespeare. "Colonel Ingersoll has lost none of the personal magnetism that has held the millions of his fellow countrymen spellbound" (*Cincinnati Enquirer*, May 1, 1893).

In Terre Haute Mr. and Mrs. Ingersoll entered the opera house for the evening's lecture on Shakespeare escorted by Mr. and Mrs. Debs, and after the lecture Debs entertained the Ingersolls with a supper party at the Terre Haute. To reporters Debs gushed over the four generations living happily under the Ingersoll roof, and, turning to social issues, he opined that Ingersoll had "some powerful views, which he has never seen fit to make public" and would soon proclaim in "the greatest of all his efforts" (*Terre Haute Gazette*, May 8, 1893).

This statement was made only one year before Debs bounded into national headlines as leader of the Pullman strike; he would wait in vain for the earth-shaking declaration. Perhaps he mistook sentiment for action. Ingersoll would never take the lead in a radical movement in national politics. His social revolution was not for today or tomorrow but in some far-off day in the womb of time. Ingersoll was moving away from his May 1892 Denver statement applauding social action for social ills. Reforms were imperative but had to come from a change of heart. "Civilization is the only cure for the existing evils. I believe that in time the world will become so civilized that no man can be happy while another man is miserable" (*Lincoln* [Neb.] *News*, Oct. 25, 1893). Loving America as the hope of the world, he was beginning to look upon populism as a prescription for disunity and disaster. "Its platform is a collection of chimeras—of exploded theories—remnants and rags of socialism—the enslavement of all by the government under the idea that the government will support the people," whereas the government was a pauper, a consumer, not a producer, and should stick to its task to "protect us from foreign foes, enforce honest contracts and keep the peace" (*Kansas City Times*, Oct. 23, 1893). The free trade embraced by the radicals was fine for a family of nations imbued with brotherly love, where one bought the cheapest and sold for the most "but so long as the world is divided by these national lines and the conditions differ internally in different countries, it is the part of wisdom to take care of ourselves" (*Rockford Republican*, Oct. 29, 1893). Ingersoll was expressing his disagreement with the spearhead of the nineties' radicalism.

If the United States, with all its faults, was the hope of the world, it followed that the expansion of the republic would be a blessing to mankind. In the early nineties Hawaii (then also known as the Sandwich Islands) was ripe for the taking. The Hawaiian population consisted of some five thousand whites (led by sugar planters descended from American missionaries) and an underclass of about eight thousand Polynesians, Chinese, and Japanese. When Lilliokalani ascended the throne in 1891, she suspended the limited constitution that favored white supremacy and established an autocracy aimed at curbing the foreign influence. The American minority, emboldened by the American minister and by American marines in the streets of Honolulu, deposed the queen, set up a provisional regime, and offered the islands for annexation to the United States. Succeeding Harrison in the White House, Cleveland assailed the coup as a blatant violation of international law and withdrew Harrison's treaty from consideration by the Senate. Ingersoll immediately joined the popular clamor for annexation. The islands "would be of vast importance to us in time of war, also if we wished to trade with China and the far east" (*Rochester* [N.Y.] *Times*, April 25, 1893). Of course, he said, the wishes of the natives should be consulted. However neither the queen nor the provisional government were thinking about them, and other foreign powers were hovering in the seas to profit from the confusion. Ingersoll denounced Cleveland's opposition to annexation as unconstitutional, un-American, illogical, and absurd. The people of the Islands, he was sure, wanted to belong to us, and it was not for Cleveland to destroy provisional republics and restore kings and queens to their thrones. Having satisfied himself on the Sandwich Islands in favor of the white cabal as representing the entire population, he rhapsodized on a future United States as the sole nation on the North American continent: "I am in favor of growth. Canada is coming to the great Republic. Cuba and her sister colonies should be under our direction, and it seems to me that the time must come when from the Isthmus to the Arctic there will float but one flag. All this should be accomplished, not by fire and sword, but simply by allowing the great forces to take their course" (Letter to the *New York Journal*, Nov. 19, 1892, *Letters*, 210). (Unfortunately the great forces turned out to be armies and navies.) Ingersoll spent a day with his old friend Secretary of State Gresham in the Arlington Hotel in Washington, arguing for annexation. Gresham remained firm in opposing imperialism (*New York Advertiser*, Jan. 8, 1894).

In the summer of 1893 headquarters were at Walston in Dobbs Ferry, Ingersoll's haven of happiness. But the outer world pressed in. Brother John's wife died, and Robert's letter of condolence reflected as usual his abiding well of sadness at the meaningless tragedy of existence. "How the days and years fly away! In a little while, on the 11th of next month, I shall be sixty years of age, and only a few days ago I was a child. What a riddle it all is. Life and death, who can tell us what they are? And what is all this for—this living—this labor and hope and love—this gold and poverty and after all this death? Who can tell? Who can guess?" He cried, "My dear Brother, we must meet as often as we can. We must not waste our lives apart" (July 18, 1893, *Letters*, 571).

On occasional visits to the office, arriving by the commuter train and the elevated, it was fun pontificating to the press through cigar smoke on business conditions, Cleveland's errors, Republican chances, silver, and expansion. But suddenly there was too much time to do so. Legal business was drying up in the general hard times. "There is nothing doing at the office—just enough to pay the expenses—we will have to go into the talking business in a few months. As soon as you come home we will make the arrangements" (To Clint and Sue, June 4, 1893, L.C.). While relaxing at Saratoga he delivered "an intellectual, literary, and dramatic feast" on Shakespeare to nearly two thousand people in the great Convention Hall, where "for over two hours the jolly lecturer commanded the closest attention of his large audience" (*Saratoga Democrat*, Aug. 9, 1893). Solicitations to lecture came pouring in from all over the country. No need to worry about his drawing power in "the talking business."

Early in October Ingersoll began (at a slower-than-usual pace) a three to four weeks' lecture tour of Ohio, Indiana, Kentucky, Illinois, Iowa, Kansas, Nebraska, Missouri, and Michigan. He was accompanied by Maud, who gazed at him with adoration, smiled at his witticisms, and nodded sagely at his profundities. He was a patriot on Lincoln, a popularizer on Shakespeare, and an iconoclast on "The Gods," "Myth and Miracle," "Liberty of Man, Woman, and Child." Whatever his subject, everywhere the halls were packed or well filled, the audience enthralled and liberal in applause (in Kansas City thirty-eight such thunderclaps according to the *Star*), as he held their sensibilities in his grip. "At times his voice sank to the mellow and whispering cooing of a ring dove, and then rose to the furious energy of a lion when disturbed in his lair" (*Cincinnati Tribune*, Oct. 12, 1893).

Off the platform he was at the beck and call of the eager press as in the hotel suite he interrupted a game of backgammon with Maud or at the theater opened the door of his box, ready for the cue to expatiate on all sorts of current issues—Cleveland's mistakes, the virtues of protection, the naivete of free trade, the folly of populism. The black question? The law ought to forbid white people from entering Negro cars, said Ingersoll; there were two kinds of people in the world, the clean and the unclean, and the clean should not be compelled to sit with the unclean. The problem would be solved by amalgamation in a few years—about five thousand years (*Louisville Courier Journal*, Oct. 9, 1893). What did he think about the political situation in New York City? "I know but little about New York politics. The city belongs to Tammany Hall, and Tammany Hall is controlled by the saloon and the cathedral, by the spirituous and the spiritual" (*Indianapolis Sentinel*, Oct. 14, 1893).

Ingersoll traveled to Boston for a lecture on Shakespeare, a lecture almost entirely devoid of antireligion, and his famous peroration, which in no sense had anything to do with religion, evoked a prolonged and deafening volley of applause. Having left the stage, he bowed acknowledgment from a box (*Boston Journal*, Nov. 13, 1893). On the next Sunday he received quite a different recognition from the Reverend William Brady, who had not attended the lecture. Reverend Brady warned against the malign influence of the spellbinder: "His splendid presence, his audacious daring, his exuberant imagination, his florid rhetoric, his abundant eloquence and his reckless treason to the high court of this universe have made him the idol of the infidelity of this commonwealth." As a watchman on Zion's tower Reverend Brady felt impelled to cry out to all Boston against this madman, who was a million times more dangerous than a mad dog or a wild bull. "Brothers and sisters," he exhorted his congregation, "when you go out of this meeting and meet an infidel, do as the Irishman does—hit him with a shillalah." This incredible onslaught elicited only a sad smile from its target. Ingersoll simply chided Reverend Brady for bad manners. He himself never assailed persons, only ideas (Letter to the *Boston Herald*, Nov. 20, 1893, reprinted in *Boston Investigator*, Nov. 29, 1893).

Once again in New York the law offices at 20 Nassau Street were filled with a crowd of visitors who had no professional business with Ingersoll and had come for chit-chat during office hours. A zealous reporter posed a question to the party: How did they feel about Thanksgiving? Julia Marlowe said that she was thankful that she was permitted to play in Shakespeare's plays. Ingersoll did not share her unclouded mood. He was afraid that the Lord might be misled by those in authority. The times were bad, thousands of workers were unemplyed, farm prices were low, merchants were going crazy because they could not sell or collect, and thousands had died in storms on the high seas. If he thanked God for the good things, what should he say about the bad things? "All I can say is that I am glad that things are not worse, and sincerely hope that they will be better" (*New York Press*, Nov. 30, 1893). More congenial to some of his countrymen would be his response a month later to a request for a general New Year's message: "All I have to say about the years is that I hope they will hurry by as fast as possible until we get a Republican administration. I want good times" (*New York Herald*, Dec. 31, 1893).

In December and January Ingersoll appeared frequently on the lecture platform in the city and its environs as far as New England and the District of Columbia. There was no point in keeping regular hours at the law office. "We are all well and that is all the news there is. Times as hard as the heart of John Calvin. No business—nothing going on. No law—all men live in perfect peace. The future does not look much better than the present" (To John, Jan. 29, 1894, *Letters*, 571).

At the end of January Ingersoll, accompanied by Mrs. Ingersoll, started on a crowded month-long lecture tour of the central states. Arriving in Chicago they spent the day in their suite at the Grand Pacific receiving friends and reporters, the latter immediately busy in jotting down as hot news his routine blasts at the Cleveland administration. To a reporter from Philadelphia he let go against the income tax: "I think it is tax on brains. I don't wonder Cleveland favors it. Why, there is no more sense for the Democratic party to tax Cleveland because he is fat" (*Philadelphia Press*, Feb. 2, 1894). (Later he would endorse the theory of the tax but deplore its invitation to perjury and inquisitorial meddling in private affairs.)

The Western Society of the Army of the Potomac was holding its fifth annual banquet that evening at the Grand Pacific. They invited Ingersoll for an after-dinner speech. He was of course, available. Standing under a facsimile of General Meade's headquarters banner, on one side a life-size eagle wreathed in silver laurel and on the other the Stars and Stripes, Ingersoll thanked the veterans for the invitation and launched into an encomium of the heroism and tears (always tears) that had saved the Republic and set a people free. He heralded expansion of the land of liberty to embrace the whole continent and the Sandwich Islands, and he urged support of the Republican ticket in the fall election. There was a motion to make Ingersoll an honorary member. Everybody rose and cheered, and it was so ordered (*Chicago Inter-Ocean*, Feb. 2, 1894; *Chicago Record*, Feb. 4, 1894; *Works*, XII, 165).

In his lectures Ingersoll discoursed variously on his current themes, Lincoln, Shakespeare, "Mistakes of Moses," "Liberty of Man, Woman, and Child," and "What Must We Do To Be Saved." He was in a fallow season for subjects and ideas but not for militancy and magnetic attraction. In the dead of winter people came in droves. In Davenport, Iowa, a patently Democratic newspaper said, "Ingersoll is a man to conjure with. Few other single men, few companies of actors of national fame, few stars operatic, dramatic, or tragic, could have drawn a thousand of Davenporters from the family fireside last evening. In carriages, in sleighs, in street cars, and on foot they made their way to the opera house, and not one was there who, at 10 o'clock, wasted a regret on money or labor expended. Such an oratorical event is offered but a few times in a generation. When offered, it must not be despised" (*Democrat*, Feb. 13, 1894). Even when the magnetism wore off and people reverted to the faith of their fathers they looked back on the infidel with grateful affection. "Tears come unbidden to our eyes and laughter wells up unannounced to our lips, as he wills it. Wonderful and potent is the power which only one man in several generations possesses. But *cui bono?* What doth it profit to tear down the superstructure which has within it so much of value to humanity? Ingersoll could make an audience believe black is white, but that does not make it so" (*St. Paul News*, Feb. 19, 1894).

In February Ingersoll went to Peoria. He had visited his old hometown privately once or twice but not in his role as public citizen since 1878. He explained that so many of his friends had died, coming back felt like going to a funeral. Soldiers under his command, members of the free-thinking Turn Verein, in-laws, old clients, friends, and townsmen gathered about him in a continuous reception at the National Hotel, built on the site of his former home. Handshakes to every one within reach: "Good luck to you." He shouted into the ear of his old friend Alvin Kidder, "Are you as deaf as ever?" Kidder answered with a lusty, "Deafer." In the evening people formed a long, orderly line outside the box office of the opera house, and swiftly filled every seat in orchestra and balcony, every chair on the stage, and every inch of standing room. "Ladies and gentlemen," the lecturer began. His voice quavered. "Old friends and neighbors," and he was off on the wonders of Shakespeare. The performance defied description. "The 'myriad-minded' man was described as only such a consummate master of language as Col. Ingersoll could describe him. For two hours the audience hung upon his words, swaying between laughter and tears, with frequent bursts of applause; and when at last the lecture closed many were surprised that it was so short until they looked at their watches. After the lecture Col. Ingersoll held an impromptu reception on the stage" (*Peoria Transcript,* Feb. 9, 1894).

A week later the itinerant lecturer went through a very busy day in Minneapolis. One evening Ingersoll gave his lecture on Lincoln, after which he spoke at a banquet of the State Editorial Association. He spoke jokingly, saying that the journalists overpraised as many persons as they underestimated, so the balance of truth was in their favor. He then seized the opportunity to make his standard argument for the protective tariff as the foundation of a great modern state: "If we buy a ton of iron rails in England and pay $20, how does the account stand? The United States, one ton of rails; England, $20. If we buy the iron rails here and pay $30, how does the account stand? The United States now owns one ton of rails and $30 too" (*Minneapolis Journal,* Feb. 16, 1894). Back in the hotel he was at last able to finish the letter to the folks back home which he had been writing in dabs all day. "After the lecture Mother and I attended a banquet of the editors of the State and I made a little speech" (Dear Girls, Feb. 15, 1894, L.C.).

At home and on the road Eva Ingersoll was not just a gracious hostess for "Pope Bob's" levees. She was also something of a gadfly or a foil, breaking into his volubility with agreement and occasionally challenge. In their suite at the Hotel Julien in Dubuque he was holding forth on the nature of agnosticism, "the knowledge that we cannot know our origin nor our destiny, nor imagine an Infinite Being. In the days of barbarism men believed in divine original and immortal destiny, and nowadays they are Methodists or Catholics by accident of birth. When men get more sense, they will see no signs that man's fate is other than the fate of the mosquito. Prayer is of no avail. The lightning falls on the just and the unjust in accordance with natural laws." Mrs. Ingersoll spoke up, "Didn't God make mosquitoes too?" The response was immediate if not quite to the point. "Yes, but who has guessed immortality for the mosquito?" He went on. "The Bible says that the fear of God is the beginning of wisdom; agnostics say that man gets sense when he ceases to fear a god he cannot comprehend and ceases to guess the solution of a problem which the limitations of his mind make it impossible for him to solve." Again Mrs. Ingersoll: "But they speak now not so much of the fear of God as of the love of God." A perfect cue. "And," he settled the matter, "is it any more rational to love than to fear a God of whose existence you can have no knowledge?" (*Dubuque Telegram,* Feb. 13, 1894). To his visitors in Minneapolis he blasted the Cleveland administration as causing the current depression. What did he think of Cleveland on Hawaii? "It was the most abominably absurd mistake ever conceived," then, lowering his tone, "but I do not want to go into detail about it." Mrs. Ingersoll explained, "My husband does not like to talk about this matter. Mr. Gresham is a very dear friend of his and it is a sore point with him." Ingersoll rounded off, "I fear he will have to suffer for the sins of Cleveland, for which I am devoutly sorry" (*Minneapolis Tribune,* Feb. 16, 1894).

On other levels traveling on lecture tours with her husband was an ordeal for Mrs. Ingersoll. Under ideal conditions making more than twenty stops in a month at places located here and there in six states could hardly be conducive to a sense of well-being, less so in an age when only a few routes could be traveled by train, and all other conveyance between and within towns was by horse-drawn vehicles. It was no fun getting up at 5:00 in the morning, having breakfast at 5:30, and plowing with baggage by taxicab through snow-covered streets to the depot, or arriving at the depot at a quarter to one and having to wait for a late train. From Superior to St. Paul was a debilitating all-day trip, from Chicago to Bay City a poor variation by night. Robert himself, as we have seen, appreciated fine food but had a robust if not ravenous appetite and often enjoyed a big after-lecture snack of cold ham, a small pitcher of cream, and so forth. Eva was fastidious, refusing to accept much of the food provided by the hotels. It was not easy to attend the lectures night after night and always appear enthusiastic as her wonder-working husband injected new life into more-than-twice-told tales. Occasionally if possible she slumped out of sight into the recesses of a box—the only person dozing or asleep at the lecture! But she was with Robert; that was the main thing. He put the best face on the matter, writing to his daughters, "We had a good long ride in a slow train along the Mississippi and felt all tired out. Mother stands the trip very well and is in good spirits— but wants to get home and keeps talking about you and the babies" (Dear Girls, Dubuque, Feb. 14, 1894, L.C.).

Despite the travails of touring, once back home Ingersoll was soon itching to take to the road again. He wrote to Traubel, "I had a splendid time in the West—fine weather—fine houses and the people pleasant. I am going a little South—Richmond, Knoxville, Chattanooga, Memphis, Nashville, and St. Louis. I start on Monday next. Will lecture on Shakespeare at most places" (March 8, 1894, *Letters,* 400). On the same day he also wrote to Elizabeth Cady Stanton, who had scolded him for not being more active in the women's cause. He told her that he believed women should have the same rights as men, but he had had other fish to fry. He had through it more important to get superstition out of her mind than a ballot into her hand, and he did not want to create a negative image of her movement on account of his religious opinions. "Rest assured," he concluded, "I am on your side and will vote your way and will give you aid and comfort— and let you do the speaking" (*Letters,* 707).

For Ingersoll to venture upon the lecture platform in the South even in 1894 took almost as much courage as leading a cavalry charge at Shiloh. The South nursed a litany of grievances against him: He was a Union veteran; he had waved the bloody shirt, he was a Republican; he advocated a high tariff and "sound" money; he was the Anti-Christ, the "Pope Bob" of infidelity; his skill on the platform could lead the unwary into damnation. In the winter of 1892–1893 an invitation to lecture in Atlanta had died aborning because of a storm of protest led by the local clergy. And to lecture on Lincoln was not to be thought of. Ingersoll had felt a lack of adherance in the small towns on Shakespeare, but that was the only subject reasonbly available to him for his first intellectual foray into the South. It was a fragile instrument.

Riding the rails to Richmond, the Ingersolls arrived on March twelfth in good shape but exhausted. "The hotel here is good—we have lovely rooms and a good bath and Clint is in the room next to us & doors between—so, you see, we are well situated here" (Dear Girls, March 14, 1894, L.C.). Throughout the tour he found the people hospitable everywhere, especially in Memphis. "Col. Moore who used to be in Congress gave a reception for Mother and I at 6 in the evening. We met a couple of hundred men and women and they all seemed delighted— We had a fine house and everybody was pleased. The hotel keeper refused to let me pay my bill" (Springfield, Mo., March 19, Dear Girls, L.C.). Along the way the local clergy kept up a drumbeat of boycott, but that was to be expected. So, too, were the strains of travel. Leaving Richmond at 11:30 in the evening after the lecture, they rode the five hundred miles to Knoxville through the night and into the next day. On another leg of the journey they reached Nashville at 7:20 in the evening, rode in a horse taxi to the hotel, and Ingersoll shaved and changed his clothes and got to the theater at 8:05!

The lectures were completely popular. In Chattanooga rain and thunder intimidated some possible hearers concerned for their comfort or nervous about the portents from above, otherwise the "Standing Room Only" signs would have been posted. In Memphis the orchestra was packed to the door and over a hundred persons sat on the stage. As in the North, "the gathering was representative of the society, literary and scientific circles of Richmond" (Richmond Dispatch, March 14, 1894) and "the culture and intelligence, both pagan and Christian, of Knoxville filled Stark's last night from pit to dome, to listen to the greatest orator of this country, Col. Robert G. Ingersoll." The Chattanooga News went all-out in encomium: "It was a bewildering, pyrotechnical display of brilliant, burning words and thoughts to which the human voice and gesture only can do justice. It is not in the province of a newspaper article to give more than an idea of the magnetic flights of matchless eloquence to which the great orator soared" (March 16, 1894). Even as in the North, of course, a strong but tempered dissent was registered by one voice: "If Ingersoll were not famous, he would be classed as an orator going into decline." His age was telling, his voice was losing its resonance, he was no longer extraordinary, but "sufficient of the fire, force and impressiveness remain, however, to make him more than interesting, and even the loss of elocution is often forgotten in the pearls of language that drop from his lips" (*Chattanooga Times*, March 16, 1894).

Off the lecture platform Ingersoll was available for interviews. He was at his ease, answering all questions as freely and vigorously as in Chicago or New York. In Chattanooga a reporter asked whether the Christian church was gaining ground. No, it was not. Preachers frequently apologized to him; they didn't want him to think that they were idiotic enough to believe the doctrines of their church (*Chattanooga News*, March 15). On the train from Knoxville to Chattanooga a vigilant reporter was there, notebook in hand. Did he believe that the present depression was due to the extravagance of the people? "No, no, I do not," he exclaimed, banging his fist down on his knee. The trouble was that American ingenuity exceeded its consumption, the machinery making more things than could be used. "The rich spend too little; the poor too much." Was he an atheist? No. The atheist said that there was no God. "I do not declare there is no God, but neither do I declare that there is a God. I don't know. You understand me?—I don't know. How am I to know? What teaches me to know there is a God? It is a question beyond my intelligence. . . . Look here! I hate Christianity the most because it sells sin on a credit. It says that you can sin and be forgiven. Nonsense! Who is going to forgive us? Our punishment follows our crime. We can't escape it. The effect is inseparable from the cause. If we live right, we are happy; if we live wrong we are not happy. It is an invincible law." Christianity was not the religion of charity. Christianity took the moral code, tacked on miracles and atonement, and said "Behold Christianity." "Now, if you take Christianity away from morality, you will find that what is left is better than when Christianity adorned or rather deformed it." Put God in the Constitution? Whose God, Presbyterian, Methodist, Universalist, Unitarian, Catholic, the god of the Deists? "I think that if God were put in the constitution there would not be any room for the people" (*Chattanooga Times*, March 16).

Rounding out his tour in Missouri and Illinois Ingersoll enlarged his choice of subjects to include "Liberty of Man, Woman, and Child," and "What Must We Do To Be Saved." After the lecture in Decatur, Illinois, a reporter calling upon him at the hotel, where he was glumly partaking of dry toast and tea, confessed himself a Democrat. "Good God, young man," Ingersoll expostulated, "are you not afraid you will be eternally damned? I'm sorry for you, indeed I am, but there is no hope" (*Decatur Post*, March 23).

The Republicans were holding a convention in Danville, Illinois. Ingersoll attended and made a speech glorifying the party of freedom and progress. He had been, he said, a Republican from the beginning, because it favored freedom for the teritories (a revision of history by the Democratic candidate of 1860). He banged away for protectionism and for factories as the indicia of a great civilized state and slammed at Cleveland's handling of the "Hawaiian question" as "the most disgraceful bit of diplomacy in the history of the nation." ·The convention adopted resolutions favoring annexation of Hawaii and denouncing Altgeld for freeing the imprisoned Haymarket defendants (*New York World, Danville News,* March 24).

From 1894 to 1896 Ingersoll's principal activity was lecturing. He said, "I practice law when I feel like it, and I feel like it less and less every year. I prefer to lecture on religious—perhaps you'd call them irreligious—subjects" (*Pittsburgh Press,* April 18, 1896). Time and time again he mounted the platform in New York and its environs and he left the city on tours ranging from two or three days to six weeks through the eastern half of the United States. He was the most visible personage in the East and the best known throughout the whole country.

Ingersoll refreshed his message with new titles and occasionally with new arguments or new flourishes of rhetoric. In his most frequent lecture at this time, "The Foundations of Faith," he restated his assault on the Old Testament fables, the Old Testament God, the miracles and the contradictions in the New. "Ministers ask: Is it possible for God to forgive man? And when I think of what has been suffered—of the centuries of agony and tears, I ask: Is it possible for man to forgive God?" (*Works,* IV, 261). To the perennial challenge of what he would substitute as a guide in place of the old religion he gave a sparkling declaration of the good life in accordance with secular values:

> To love justice, to long for the right, to love mercy, to pity the suffering, to assist the weak, to forget wrongs and remember benefits—to love the truth, to be sincere, to utter honest words, to love liberty, to wage relentless war against slavery in all its forms, to love wife and children and friend, to make a happy home, to love the beautiful in art, in nature, to cultivate the mind, to be familiar with the mighty thoughts that genius has expressed, the noble deeds of all the world, to cultivate courage and cheerfulness, to make others happy, to fill life with the splendor of generous acts, the warmth of loving words, to discard error, to destroy prejudice, to receive new truths with gladness, to cultivate hope, to see the calm beyond the storm, the dawn beyond the night, to do the best that can be done and then to be resigned; this is the religion of reason, the creed of science. This satisfies the brain and heart. (290)

In "Some Mistakes of Moses" Ingersoll had inveighed against the Pentateuch in the light of science and humane values; in "About the Bible" he drew upon the higher criticism to emphasize errors and inconsistencies in the Old and New Testament, attack trinitarianism, and portray Christ as a human being with human limitations. The lecture mixes anecdotes and personal adventures in the world of thought with satiric humor and flamboyant rhetoric. On the doctrine of eternal perdition, his major villain in Christian orthodoxy, he proclaimed: "While I have life, as long as I draw breath I shall attack with all my strength, and hate with every drop of my blood, this infinite lie" (*Works*, IV, 22). Humanity should banish from its mind "the winged monsters of the night." Only then "we can civilize our fellow-men. We can fill our lives with generous deeds, with loving words, with art and song, and all the ecstasies of love. We can flood our years with sunshine—with the divine climate of kindness, and we can drain to the last drop 'the golden cup of joy' " (67).

It is not to be supposed that the Christian ministry lined up as a phalanx against Ingersoll the monster whom they would have burned at the stake if they had the power. Some ministers treated him with respect, particularly in the large cities. The ministers faced a dilemma not without its farcical aspects: Should they attend the lectures and learn first-hand what Ingersoll contended so that they might rebut him intelligently on Sunday, or should they stay away as they exhorted their congregations to do as a religious duty? Many ministers attended Ingersoll's lectures with notebooks in hand and, being there, found themselves willy-nilly joining in laughter at his wit and enthusiasm for his tributes to justice and intellectual honesty. One unfortunate minister, Reverend Milburn of Indianapolis, who ventured into an Ingersoll lecture, was censured by some of his parishioners (*Fort Wayne Journal*, March 31, 1895.) In Grand Rapids a Reverend Fairchild had delivered a scathing sermon against Ingersoll on the text that the fool hath said there is no God. Reverend Gibson took his fellow minister to task for forgetting St. Paul's admonition "not to render reviling for reviling but contrariwise blessing," charging that the worst foes of Christianity had been its professed friends. Gibson agreed with Ingersoll that there were substantial objections against creationism, and said that the belief in an anthropomorphic God was a self-evident absurdity. Belief in God, he said, rests upon a spiritual perception and not upon looking at the stars (*Grand Rapids Herald*, Jan. 26, 1896).

In Washington, when Reverend Blagden, author of a scurrilous pamphlet on Ingersoll, urged forcible outlawing of his lectures, it was Reverend Mackay Smith who rebuked this "self-appointed champion of truth," saying "the clergy of this city, as well as the laymen, are quite able to do any 'denouncing' when it is called for. But they do not believe in any such methods. They believe in givng Mr. Ingersoll, like any other man, a fair field in a free country" (*Washington Post*, Dec. 12, 1894). In a national religious magazine, *The Non-Sectarian*, Reverend Sunderland asserted that Ingersoll's factual criticism of the Bible was "exactly in line with the teaching of the most trustworthy, reliable, and reverent biblical scholarship of the present day" (Condensed in *Public Opinion*, May 30, 1895).

Though opinions might run high an Ingersoll lecture never erupted into chaos. Confrontation with orthodoxy or the police never came to a show of force. Occasionally the house buzzed with a hiss of disapproval; the ubiquitous drunken heckler popped up and Ingersoll regularly dubbed him a real Christian, but he knew when to leave the field. In Columbus, as Ingersoll was concluding "What Must We Do To Be Saved," a woman seated in the parquet broke out, "I hope your hand will wither." "Which hand?" he asked. As the audience made shushing sounds to her, she yelled, "I challenge you to a debate." Moderating the audience Ingersoll suggested a time for a debate. She did not answer and he left the stage. She then addressed the departing crowd with hurrahs for herself and Jesus Christ, her husband (*New York Sun*, March 19, 1895). Lecturing on the Bible in Indianapolis he declaimed, "I would rather go to hell than live in heaven with the Biblical God," at which a little, well-dressed woman cried in a shrill voice that carried all over the house, "You're getting there fast enough." Ingersoll looked directly at her, said "That's where I am, my good woman," and, after pausing for effect, "That remark shows that you are gifted with the gentle spirit of the great Jehovah" (*Cincinnati Enquirer*, March 30, 1895). In Belleville, Illinois, as Ingersoll was discoursing on liberty, a Dr. Washington West entered quietly, an Oxford Bible under his arm. Dr. West walked softly down an end aisle towards the foot of the stage, where he kneeled before a chair on the stage and silently prayed. Ingersoll did not interrupt his discourse, but glanced at Dr. West in a markedly compassionate way, which amused the crowd. Dr. West prayed for a while and then yielded without protest to an employee of the opera house, who led him away (*Belleville News Democrat*, April 29, 1896).

Reporters, overwhelmed by the Ingersoll phenomenon, declared that one could not appreciate the miracle of an Ingersoll lecture without being physically present, although one reporter almost surmounted the barrier to communication. Four thousand people in the vast Chicago Auditorium leaned forward as Ingersoll, on the Bible, worked up to a climax that Christ was a human being with ordinary human limitations.

> When Ingersoll reached the words "He did not know" a great sigh went up from the mighty audience. There was an instant of silence, and then a storm of applause that rose and surged and echoed from stage to top gallery. The hand-clapping died away, then rose again, this time a great burst of cheering accompanied it. Ingersoll stood there silent, flushed, trembling with emotion. He perhaps, like his hearers, knew that he had just achieved one of the great triumphs of a life that has been crowded with triumphs. Men who have heard him time and again in the years past shook their heads gravely and said he had never done anything so wonderful, so superb, and so full of deathless eloquence. (*Chicago Times*, Oct. 14, 1894)

Was it all a charade, this rapport with multitudes? Would it vanish into thin air like the smoke from an Ingersoll cigar, leaving religious orthodoxy impregnable, undiminished? Did the fact that he never entered the pantheon of American superheroes render Ingersoll's career without consequences? "You and I," a reporter fancied Ingersoll saying to his audience, "are very daring persons. We think advanced thoughts while most of the world is wrapped in superstition. It takes courage to think these thoughts, therefore you and I are brave." To this reporter Ingersoll's appeal to these brave souls was not in his infidelism but his advocacy of justice, mercy, and happiness. They would not take kindly to a speaker of equal talent who challenged such transcendent values as mere imaginings (*Minneapolis Sentinel*, Nov. 23, 1895). Was he only a strolling player, nothing more? "It cannot be told, from the laughter and applause, how many accept the eloquent and humorous speaker for more than the entertainer of an evening. It is an age that enjoys humor, persiflage, and fun. The comic Blackstone has become heavy, and we have had a comic guide book, 'The Innocents Abroad,' a comic history of England by Bill Nye, and burlesques on C. Columbus's discovery of America, and may listen and laugh at comic readings of Bible stories and keep on believing the stories" (*Terre Haute Express*, April 28, 1896). On the other hand, a reporter in Grand Rapids rhapsodized: "One thinks of the exclamation of Caius Cassius, over the scene of Caesar's assassination, 'How many ages hence shall this our lofty scene be enacted o'er in ages yet unborn, in actions yet unknown.' So with Col. Ingersoll in future ages there shall come flowery tributes to his eloquence, his generosity to humanity, his dedication to a religion which makes all loved as equals" (*Herald*, Jan. 6, 1986). Who can measure the influence of Paine and Voltaire? Who can measure the influence of Ingersoll?

In interviews on the politics of the nineties he belonged to the Republican party. Hard times were due to the Democratic administration. The people were tired of "looking at idle factories, at chimneys without smoke, at furances without fire, at men without work, at men without food." Everywhere excepting the South he saw the current "running our way." The people wanted a strong dose of protectionism. Free trade was unrealistic, worse than useless, as there were no foreign markets for exports to offset the damage done by the liberal flow of goods into America. "We manufacture nothing that we can sell at a profit in England, France, Germany, Belgium, or any country in Europe. The market in Africa is worth nothing to us, we have very little interest in Asia, very little in Japan, and less in the islands of the Pacific. America is the best market for what America can manufacture, and we cannot afford to desert our markets for what they call the markets of the world." But he was clearly separating himself from some radical trends with which he had once shown sympathy when he said that the laboring man had learned that he could not injure his employer without injuring himself (*New York Evening Advertiser*, Oct. 22, 1895).

Looming ever larger on the horizon was the money question. Ingersoll would become a leading exponent of the Republican theory of money, teaching the nation the ABC's of finance on Republican principles. Did he still favor the free coinage of silver and would it come about without international agreement? "No, this country cannot alone keep silver on the basis of 16 to 1 as good as gold. If silver is remonetized—and I sincerely hope it will be—it must be done by the great nations acting together" (*Cincinnati Enquirer*, Nov. 19, 1894). He inveighed against the idea then abroad that the government could support the people. It was all wrong. The government "collects alms in a high-handed manner, but it is a pauper. It produces no wheat or corn, some pork, it may be, but nothing it can sell. Consequently it is a consumer, not a producer. We might as well try to live on our hired men or on the inmates of the poorhouse as to depend on the government for support" (*Cedar Rapids Republican*, Jan. 18, 1895). He repeated in Omaha and Duluth what he had said in Cedar Rapids: "All our money, paper or silver, should be kept as good as gold, and no more paper should be issued and no more silver coins than can be redeemed in gold. The government cannot make money. If the government can make money, why take silver? Why not take copper? Why not take iron? Why not take paper?" (*Duluth Tribune*, May 7, 1896, reporting an interview in Omaha).[1]

Ingersoll fired away at the Democratic party, poured his acid wit over it. "I think that the Democratic party has demonstrated that it has neither the intelligence nor the cohesiveness necessary to govern the country. They are divided among themselves. . . . They have no definite policy and they recognize no leader" (*Biddeford* [Me.] *Journal*, April 13, 1894). Whom should the Democrats nominate? The best thing they could do would be to wait until the Republicans nominated and then nominate the same man (*New Orleans Status*, Feb. 18, 1895). Or perhaps they should go back to Andrew Jackson (*Rochester* [N.Y.] *Herald*, March 11, 1895). Among the Republican hopefuls he expressed preferences for House Speaker Reed or McKinley.

When Bryan—like the young Ingersoll a glamourous newcomer out of the West—was nominated, Ingersoll immediately put him down as not a man of thought and not capable of filling the office. McKinley was bound to win. What did he think of Cleveland's silence? "I think Cleveland appears at his best when he is silent" (*Burlington* [Vt.] *Free Press*, July 27, 1896).

Nonetheless, Ingersoll rejected overtures to add partisan politics to his lecturing. He had been approached with assurances of great profits to get up a lecture titled "The Mistakes of Grover," but had refused. His political speaking was not for sale (From F. E. Johnson, Feb. 24, 1894, L.C.).

Ingersoll's drumbeat for law and order drew kindly but earnest protest from some who said that he was wrong in religion and in politics. "He thinks the salvation of souls lies in Ingersollism and the salvation of the country lies in republicanism. His partisanship leads him to the most ridiculous assertions in discussing politics, just as we fear his zeal leads him astray when discussing more sacred things, but the colonel is always interesting" (*Oswego* [N.Y.] *Palladium*, May 1, 1894). Or that he was right in religion but wrong in politics: "As the great preacher of the doctrine of unrest, of doubt, of inquiry, he has undoubtedly accomplished much good. He has done more than any other man of his time to make the churches more tolerant. His great theme is liberty—liberty of thought, of speech, of enterprise, of labor, of religion—liberty of everything but trade and commerce. With regard to these he is as bigoted as McKinley himself" (*Minneapolis Times*, Jan. 12, 1895). And what about buying American products and keeping the money at home? This called for a bit of sarcasm. "Bob does not put the case in its strongest light. If we buy a jack-knife in England for a dime we have the jack-knife and they have the dime. If we pay $2 for a jack-knife manufactured in America we have both the jack-knife and the money. It will be observed that in this case the protected manufacturer and the small boy have $2 between them besides the knife" (*St. Louis Post Dispatch*, March 27, 1894). Ingersoll's economics were ridiculed in Dubuque. " 'Bob' Ingersoll may know something about 'The Mistakes of Moses,' but he knows little or nothing about political economy. Ingersoll says that money is like blood in the body; it must be good or the nation will not prosper. 'Everybody knows that however good the quality, the quantity of blood must be ample or the body will be debilitated,' and of making money out of paper, 'Why not?' " (*Dubuque Tribune*, May 12, 1896).

In the summer of 1894 Maud, overweight and out of sorts, went on a vacation trip with the Farrells. Robert saw them off at the station in New York and immediately wrote to Maud—surely she would be interested: "After I left you I walked down to 33rd Street and took the elevated for the office, stayed there until 2, and reached Dobbs Ferry at 3:43" (Aug. 30, L.C.). Every day for the next four days he sent her missives laden with fatherly advice on diet and the good life. "Keep your *end up*. Take rides and have plenty to *eat*. Eat toast—tomatoes, beans, lettuce, cabbage, etc., so that you can come back well and happy" (Aug. 31, L.C.). He philosophized on his obsessive theme—the passing season, the brevity of life. "Summer has gone—only a week ago the snow melted from the fields, and now the leaves are touched with the colors that tell of death—well, we cannot stop or stay the time. We will enjoy the journey as best we can" (Sept. 1, L.C.). "*Be sure and eat enough*. Take walks and drives and picnics. Clint will get the horses and you pay for them. Have the best time you can. Of all things we ought to be economical of time. If we are not happy the time is lost. The unenjoyed moment is lost forever. So be happy all the time" (Sept. 3, 1894, L.C.).

On the road his letters to the family reflect the salesman of ideas, his successes and disappointments. "Only a moderate week. Times are hard" (Boston, Dec. 1, 1894, Maud, L.C.). Two days later things were much better; he was always popular in Boston: "Yesterday the weather was awful. Snowed all day, streets full of slop, and I thought the theater would be empty—but to my astonishment the house was packed—full from pit to dome—magnificent house, the audience was wonderfully enthusiastic. So I had a marvelous success" (Dec. 3, 1894, Maud, L.C.). On the tenth he reported from Providence, "We had a fine house last night—full from bottom to top," but he was more interested in home-coming, as he says to Maud, "Only two days more and then I shall hold you in my arms. I hope that you are all well and enjoying yourselves. Go to the theater, the opera, all you want—do not be afraid of spending money—*Get good seats.* Take the best care of yourself. Throw your arms back 50 times every morning" (Dec. 10, 1894, L.C.).

He was not tremendously popular with all audiences. "The subject here was Shakespeare, a poor subject for this place. It might as well have been on Spinoza—or Neo-Platonism" (Texarkana, Tex., Feb. 4, 1896, Dear Girls, L.C.). The ministerial boycott did not trouble him. "In nearly all the towns the preachers have warned their flocks against me—advised them to keep away and in most places they started counter-attractions, 'mite' societies, and prayer meetings and sociables but I have had good houses" (St. Paul, Jan. 12, 1895, Maud, L.C.). As he went through Ashtabula, Greenville, and Vandalia, scenes of his childhood, he mused on the old days "when I was young and full of hope" and on the sadness of looking back: All the members of his original family were dead except John and himself (St. Louis, April 27, 1896, To Mrs. Ingersoll, Carbondale).

Love, always love. "I long to be where you are," he wrote to Eva, "to see your face, to hear your voice—to feel the clasp of your hand and your lips on mine. You and dear Maud and dear Mother fill my heart with perpetual joy. Yes, and the dear babes fill full the measure of my happiness. . . . After all, I am the most fortunate of men. I would not change places with any man that lives" (April 29, 1896, L.C.). Even when unhappy memories came to mind, his love of life shone through. He wrote to his wife, "Thinking over the vanished past makes me feel old and almost sad. But I have had much joy. The past is secure. Nothing can rob me of the happiness I have known in your arms. We will live and love as long as we can and drain the cup to the last sweet drop. . . . Dear love, sweet lover, I long to be in your arms. I love you with all my heart" (St. Louis, April 29, 1896, Carbondale).

In the summers Ingersoll had begun random lecturing at parks, fairs, and other recreation areas. He gave full meausure, two hours, on the Declaration of Independence, Lincoln, and liberty to audiences ranging from three or four hundred to several thousand. The crowds tended to be volatile, and some people, their curiosity satisfied, got up before the end and moved on to other attractions. His most congenial business arrangements were with the Spiritualists, who shared his denial of eternal damnation and were glad to feature him profitably at their summer outings.

One July evening, having delivered a lecture under Spiritualist auspices, Ingersoll was relaxing on the wide veranda of the Grand Hotel in Lily Dale, near Buffalo. The ubiquitous reporter described his face as beaming with contentment, as he had well spent a good day and earned eight hundred dollars. A man who turned out to be a Spiritualist came along and struck up a conversation as the reporter took notes.

SPIRITUALIST. Mr. Ingersoll, what was there in that story a clergyman is said to have told you, that you were knocking away the crutches from cripples in your attacks on orthodoxy?

INGERSOLL. Another canard. They tell all sorts of stories on me, you know. But I say, don't you think it was an admission on their part when they called their adherents "cripples"?

SPIRITUALIST. Well, we have the consolation of knowing that we live again, crutches or no crutches. We don't need any such support.

INGERSOLL. Ah! Where!

SPIRITUALIST. Why, in the summer land, in our Spiritualists' heaven.

INGERSOLL. But where is it located? Point me out the latitude and longitude of it.

SPIRITUALIST. All around us, one place. Other spheres, the evolutionary ones, are higher up.

INGERSOLL. I don't see how that would benefit us. I am satisfied with this world; that is, I have to be satisfied with it. Such an existence as you describe might please some but I don't know as it would me. . . . I don't know as I would care to live forever. What do you expect to do there?

SPIRITUALIST. Work, progress, evolve, and study conditions.

INGERSOLL. Work, eh? I thought when we got through with this world we took a rest. Why do you want to work in such a heavenly place? Isn't it all bright and fair up there? And why progress for all eternity, what good will it do? That's what I want to know.

SPIRITUALIST. Progress seems to be your keynote, Colonel. What about the Darwinian theory, the floaters on "the shoreless seas" and "the man in the dugout" from whom we sprang?

INGERSOLL. True, but all that argument was for men's progression in this world. When we get "up there" I anticipated that we would spring with one bound on that higher place you speak about. As far as I am concerned, I am having my share of work in this world. I don't want to labor in the next. In fact, I don't see how I am going to put in any time over there. There are some folks who could spend a couple of million years holding prayer meetings and enjoy it. But I couldn't. In fact, I think I should want to die again long before the expiration of that time. Where is the soul? Did you or anybody else ever see it?

SPIRITUALIST. Our trance mediums have seen a soul. They have sat at the bedside of one who is "passing over," and just as the breath was leaving the body have distinctly seen a substance they knew was soul taking flight. This fact has been demonstrated over and over again.

INGERSOLL. I can't believe it. I refuse to believe anything of that kind without proof. The idea that, as soon as a man's breath leaves his body, the soul flops out like a chicken's head and flies off into space to find a lodgment where there's harps and haloes. Too much for me. (*Buffalo Express*, July 15, 1896)

In the winter of 1894–1895 it was announced that Ingersoll was projecting a second series of lectures in the Deep South. As usual, ministers along the route mounted thoroughgoing boycotts. In Atlanta the *Journal* circulated a synopsis of Ingersoll on the Bible to the local ministry and solicited their opinions. The ministers who responded could hardly find words to express their hatred and contempt. Reverend Walker Lewis was ominous. "Can it be that there are men in this city who, for the money to be gotten out of this man's coming, are willing to inoculate Atlanta with the virus that he brings? They have even greater right, morally, to import smallpox or diphtheria to help trade. Let them uncover and then stand for votes or favor." Reverend R. J. Brigham characterized Ingersoll as "an infidel desperado," "the paid oracle of the barrooms, the bawdy houses, and the gambling dens," "vilest of all living lepers," and waved his own bloody shirt, gray stained with red, for the lost cause: "Let his lying assertions about our Confederate heroes be published in advance of his lecture in Atlanta, and before he asks our people to believe what he says about our Lord and Savior, let him prove what he has said about the best men and women of the South." Reverend L. R. Strickler inveighed against Ingersoll as the would-be destroyer of civilized society and asked, "Would we have better homes, better schools, better institutions and laws, a better civilization, a better morality, a better people, a better world? It is for intelligent people to decide how much encouragement such a man should receive." Reverend R. V. Atkisson pointed with pride to the map of the world: "England, Scotland, Germany, Canada, and the United States of America are the most prosperous people, enjoying the best government, with the largest personal liberties to be found on the face of the earth, and these very nations have been developed with an open Bible in the hands of the people." He assailed Ingersoll's exposition of the higher criticism as second-hand and reckless. "As he never does anything by halves he exaggerates these views and tries to popularize them." Finally, Rabbi Leo Lerch said that the great scientists whom Ingersoll admired believed in God (*Atlanta Journal*, Dec. 23, 1894).

All of which was quite a build-up for a lecture scheduled on Shakespeare! Ingersoll was not looking for a head-on confrontation with orthodoxy in the Bible Belt but lectured mostly on Shakespeare and occasionally on a watered-down "Liberty." Audiences took it well. "The statements were not presented in a manner that showed any conviction on the part of the speaker or attempt to give conviction to his hearers. The Colonel laughed, and the audience laughed, and everybody went away feeling satisfied that they had realized what they went for—they had seen and heard Robert G. Ingersoll" (*Jacksonville Citizen*, Feb. 11, 1895). When he entered a hall and took off his hat he was immediately recognized. Tumultuous applause escorted him to the platform, but there were no sell-out, standing-room-only crowds. In mid-winter, with religious-political boycott in the air, it was hard to leave home and fireside for a lecture on Shakespeare. Audience size fluctuated. In Savannah it was "very large and intellectual" (*Press*, Feb. 7); in Macon "unexpectedly small" (*Telegraph*, Feb. 9); in Chattanooga "an audience that made up in appreciation what it lacked by reason of the snow-storm—numbers" (*Times*, Feb. 10); in New Orleans, "Notwithstanding the fact that he had to contend with several other first-class attractions, the audience which he faced when he ascended the platform at 8 o'clock numbered between 1200 and 1500 persons, and was made up of the highest society and the most intelligent and cultured people of the city" (*Times Picayune*, Feb. 19, 1895).

Ingersoll's reception in Atlanta demonstrated the potent grip of the ministers upon the community. Only about five hundred people attended the lecture, and no ministers were recognized. The audience consisted of "good average people who went to hear the great infidel because of his distinguished reputation." They were somewhat disappointed at his inoffensive appearance and his low-keyed manner in discussing Shakespeare (*Journal, Constitution*, Feb. 14, 1895). At times in his lectures Ingersoll ventured into lukewarm criticism of Christianity, at which some people stirred uneasily while others applauded, and it was suggested that he might have drawn larger audiences if he had spoken more strongly. As always, though, the press could not resist the magic of Ingersoll on the platform. His lecture "was the rarest treat of poetic thought and exquisite word painting ever delivered to an Augusta audience. His words reached the highest pinnacle of thought, and soared above the clouds of the commonplace until one was lost in the delights of the rarer atmosphere of his undoubted intellect" (*Augusta Chronicle*, Feb. 8, 1895). The next day in Macon a local paper was saying, "Every word stood out as a bold stroke of the brush, and finally, when it seemed that the painter had exhausted all the colors of his palette one would look again to see other and more beautiful tints created. Again and again he carried his hearers to the highest pinnacle of thought, enabling the busy men and women before him to dwell for a time in the rarefied atmosphere of intellect and look down on the wondrous world of William Shakespeare, while they listened to the lecturer pointing out the beauties of that realm" (*Macon News*, Feb. 9).

Nonetheless, the press in Columbia (the *Sun* and the *State*) stood outside the circle of acclaim. To them Ingersoll was a washout, "did not impress his audience last night as an orator or anything more than a pretty speaker." "Not only in our judgment but in that of many others, Col. Ingersoll lacks flexibility of voice, aptness of gesture in the fire of oratory. His quotations were badly done—he was ungraceful and inept in his movements." These assaults drew a sharp rebuke from the *Macon News*: "We are assisted in identifying the species of animal responsible for this attack by calling to mind one of Aesop's familiar fables, for surely the ears were never more in evidence than in their complaints" (Feb. 10, 1895).

In the hotel in Augusta a nervous reporter found "the infidel" studying his notes for the evening's lecture. Ingersoll put down his notes, smiled a greeting. "Reporters, as a rule, are not shy, but having a life-long training to abhor all that was 'evil,' the scribe felt a little shaky. He had expected to find an ogre, and instead it was a man. This man, too, was far from the ideas of Ingersoll pictured in the reporter's mind since childhood. He did not even look wicked, and certain it was he didn't have horns. He was no different from the rest of the old gentlemen one sees every day, except that he looked satisfied. There was a merry little twinkle in his eye, and his snow-white hair softened the ruddiness of his complexion." Ingersoll expressed surprise that the local ministry had raised a hue and cry against him. If God was on their side, why were they afraid of one bad man? Would God allow him to defeat the saints? He denied the rumor that he had once said that the South should be wiped from the face of the earth (*Augusta Chronicle*, Feb. 8, 1895). On the train enroute from Augusta to Macon, a group having gathered about him in the smoking compartment, he was asked about the conspicuously hostile ministers in Atlanta. He laughed. It was an old story, a case of evolution, the baboon from whom men sprang showing up now and then. Why couldn't the preachers preach for intellectual hospitality? All were together under the same blue sky; why shouldn't we be happy and make the best of life? Why did the preachers flaunt eternal pain and damnation and then go to the legislature for laws to protect their creed? (*Atlanta Constitution*, Feb. 9, 1895). In New Orleans Ingersoll's lecture at the Washington Artillery Hall was a great success. The crowd gazed admiringly at "the splendid, portly figure and the ruddy good-natured face" and listened in rapt attention to his analysis of Shakespeare "except when irrepressible laughter was brought out by the extremely witty words which at times fell from the speaker's lips, or when some noble utterance struck them in all its force they responded with applause" (*New Orleans Times Picayune*, Feb. 19, 1895). The next morning Ingersoll was up early, had a cup of *cafe noir*, and took a walk through the French Quarter. Back at the hotel about nine he devoted himself to a hearty breakfast "with an appetite begotten of the consciousness of being at peace with all the world." He invited the reporter to sit with him and between bites extended his compliments to "the fair women and brave men" who had treated him so warmly (*New Orleans States*, Feb. 19, 1895).

On one thing Ingersoll was coy. What reception in general had he received in the South? "What I expected." What had he expected? "Just what I got" (*Augusta Chronicle*, Feb. 8, 1895). In fact he was disappointed. He had expected brickbats with bouquets, but he missed the big crowds and the comforts of the North. "We have been cold all the time except at St. Augustine," he wrote from Atlanta to "My darling Maud." "The houses have been rather poor, and most of the hotels very bad. Rooms cold and food the same. I am not in love with the South!" (Feb. 4, 1895, L.C.).

After three weeks in Dixieland Ingersoll was back in New York and comfortably ensconced in his warm bed at 11 A.M. An unexpected visitor, his current agent C. A. Davis, arrived in a panic. Trouble was afoot in Hoboken, New Jersey. When billboards about town had been placarded with notices that Ingersoll would lecture on the Bible, four local minsters called upon Mayor Fagan to prohibit the meeting as a violation of the blasphemy law. After some conversations among the mayor, the police chief, the corporation counsel, and the landlord it was concluded that Ingersoll could not be prevented from holding the meeting but might be prosecuted for any blasphemous utterances. What should he do? Ingersoll knew the New Jersey statute from his unsuccessful opposition to it in the Reynolds case eight years before. Now he himself was the target. He laughed, said he would think about it, and went back to sleep (*Pittsburgh Dispatch*, Feb. 24, 1895).

The meeting was held as scheduled. The publicity ("Hoboken is making as ass of itself" [*New York Recorder*, Feb. 24, 1895]) had assured an enthusiastic audience that crowded the hall to the doors. Mrs. Ingersoll and Maud were there, seated at the rear of the stage out of public view. Police were conspicuous, on guard against intellectual crime. Ingersoll, at his happiest as a public citizen, put on an *opera bouffe*. A hundred years ago, he began, some savages in New Jersey enacted a law prohibiting all people from thinking and discussing more than one side of a question, and prescribed imprisonment (why not burning at the stake?) for those who exercised their reason. Fortunately the enlightened State Constitution permitted him at least to speak in spite of "the bigotry and fanaticism of those who are taught by the Scriptures to love their fellow-men and be merciful." He hedged his criticisms of the Bible with comical disclaimers: "This is what infidels say." "I am simply repeating it to you." "Mind you, I am not giving my opinions." "Mind you, I don't say that the Scriptures are not inspired. On the contrary, I admit that they are—in New Jersey" (*Boston Journal, Jersey City Journal*, Feb. 25, 1895). But he did not hold back his thoroughgoing contempt for his inquisitors: "They are a pretty mean bunch of men, by the way. Now they know that I'm going to roast and blister and broil all through eternity. But these sanctified swine are not satisfied with that; they want to see me in the penitentiary here" (*Jersey City Journal*, Feb. 25). He professed his religion of liberty, "which is hated by kings and priests, [as is] liberty, the breath of progress, love, and joy, the sunshine of all that is good and just and glorious." The police had no instructions on how to handle this double-talk, and they did nothing. The Hoboken inquisitors, ashamed or bewildered, took no further action. The New York papers went after them. "Put him in the stripes of a convict, say the ministers of Hoboken, then he'll know whether there is a God or not!" (*New York Morning Advertiser*, Feb. 25, 1895). "If religion must enforce its creed by law, then the less religion we have the better for all of us" (*Brooklyn Eagle*, Feb. 26, 1895). There was groaning in the

Garden State. "Hoboken—unhappy Hoboken—is again being gouged by the New York press" (*Hoboken News*, Feb. 25, 1895). The ministers inadvertently had helped Ingersoll strike a blow for intellectual freedom.

On a lecture tour in the Midwest accompanied by Mrs. Ingersoll and Maud, Ingersoll returned to Peoria in September, 1895. He had come to lecture on Lincoln and to participate in the veterans' reunion at Elmwood. He spent a couple of days communing and reminiscing with old friends, neighbors, and comrades at arms. A reporter at the perpetual reception in the hotel could not fail to be charmed. "He was born in sunshine and expanded in light. The hand of time has touched him lightly, and life is to him a harvest of good things" (*Peoria Journal*, Sept. 4, 1895). All sorts of questions were thrown at him in writing, and he answered. Philosophizing on the inevitably of old age and its disabilities, he said that it was hardly worth while to commit suicide in order to die young. He felt well, slept soundly, had a good appetite, and found life worth living. He declared that he was a bimetallist but that America must conform to the gold standard until the great nations remonetized silver. Church property should be taxed, and public schools should be completely secularized. The country was in very good condition and the American worker lived better than the nobility of recent days.

The Elmwood reunion of six regiments from central Illinois turned out to be a personal gala for Bob Ingersoll, Colonel of the Eleventh Cavalry from Peoria. The day was bright and clear. Arriving at the depot with a contingent of Peoria veterans, Ingersoll was greeted by a reception committee and a thirteen-cannon salute. He marched under a veterans' escort through a town decked with flags and bunting, a picture or bust of the Colonel in every shop window. In the reviewing stand he sat with two members of Congress, the mayor of Elmwood, his old friend Clark E. Carr, and other dignitaries. Some 2500 veterans headed by the Eleventh Cavalry marched briskly by the stand, every man doffing his hat as he passed. In the park 150 little girls were spread out in a Living Flag, and a male chorus sang a special song for the occasion, "Ring Out O' Bells":

> Welcome now that leader fearless,
>   Free of thought and grand of brain,
> King of hearts and speaker peerless,
>   Hail our Ingersoll again.

Several oldtimers and dignitaries made brief speeches before Ingersoll. Introducing him, Mr. E. H. Brown reminded the audience how Ingersoll had electrified the meeting at Rouse's Hall on the eve of the Civil War with "the startling declaration that from that night forth there was going to be one free man in Illinois if there was never another to the end, that all America knows how grandly that pledge has been kept, but comparatively few have any conception of what that mighty brain, that one great brave heart, that one free and gentle spirit have done for him and freedom and happiness in the past thirty years" (*Inter-Ocean*, Sept. 6, 1895).

As Ingersoll came forward to the front of the stand "a mighty shout" went up and everybody joined the Living Flag children in waving banners furiously. After further bursts of applause there was silence. Ingersoll spoke. Never a man for making a short speech when a long one would do, he held the crowd in his grip with an hour and a half of grandiloquent oratory and sensational statistics on the nation's growth, saying that it took a million dollars a day to build the railroads. "I want you to think what that means. All that money had to be dug out of the ground. It had to be made by raising something, or manufacturing something. We did not get it by writing essays on finance or discussing the silver question. It had to be made by the ax, the plow, the reaper, the mower, in every form of industry, to produce these splendid results." (After the speech Ingersoll walked through the crowd to shake hands, giving rise to the groundless rumor that a pickpocket had relieved him of some checks and a roll of bills amounting to $250.)

Later in the afternoon Ingersoll addressed the veterans' assembly in farewell. He said that old friend were the best friends, as unlike new friends they wanted nothing. He loved Illinois where he first practiced law and found people "willing to waste time" listening to him. He liked the country better than the city; he might spend the evening of his life in the Illinois countryside. He embraced his comrades in their common glory. "The men who saved the first Republic and who founded the first free nation of the world—that is enough for us. Have we done our part well in the drama of life, then let the curtain fall and the orchestra stop playing." Now a salute, both serious and whimsical, to freedom of the mind: "Some people do not enjoy the delight of having free lips and speaking their honest thoughts. It is a great thing to feel that your mind and imagination are free. No one has enjoyed his freedom more than I have. And if there is another world, I will be free there and if I do not like the administration I will say so. . . . I wish you good-bye and wish you good-luck" (*Elmwood Gazette*, Sept. 12, 1895).

At the celebration Ingersoll had made a long speech and a short speech. In the evening he made another long speech—a lecture on Lincoln at the Grand Opera House. He came unattended. "There was no possibility of an introduction," observed the *Herald* (Sept. 6), "for none was needed." As the orator bowed to the applause the *Herald* reporter compared the new Ingersoll to the old. "There is more rotundity to the figure than there once was, and a greater amplitude of bald spot, but the eye has not lost any of its twinkle nor the features any of their benevolence." At the conclusion the reporter marveled at the modulated voice, the word painting, the rhetoric of vivid contrasts. "There may be some men who can give a more correct analysis of the character of Lincoln, but there is no one now living who can give a more poetic one."

At the depot waiting for the train Ingersoll was approached by an old veteran who grasped his hand and said, "Col. Ingersoll, I am glad of the opportunity to take you by the hand before I die." To which Ingersoll replied smiling, "Don't die! Comrade, don't die" (*Peoria Transcript*, Sept. 6, 1895).

A Conversion?

The orthodox community, far from joining in with such eulogies, decided to take action. It dawned upon some devout Christians in Cleveland that only a miracle could bring the iconoclast to heel, and they proceeded to assist in its coming into being. Evangelical organizations in that city— the Christian Endeavorers, the Epworth League, the Salvation Army, and others—combined to call upon God for a conversion of Ingersoll. It was agreed among these groups that, wherever their members might be on Thanksgiving Day, November 28, 1895, they would fall on their knees at the exact moment of noon and pray to God to move "the wayward Ingersoll" to "the straight and narrow path." Some local ministers disapproved of the project. Conversion, they argued, could not come about without a preliminary change of heart; God could not convert the devil against the devil's will; their prayer would probably fail and Ingersoll would exploit the failure in further argument against the church. Nevertheless, the earnest believers persisted, and at the appointed moment the town was churned up in a hundred places as some three thousand Christian Endeavorers, several hundred Epworth Leaguers, and every soldier of the Salvation Army fell upon their knees and prayed for Ingersoll's conversion. At the Salvation Army mass meeting a well-known local character named Joe the Turk, dressed in glaring red suit and holding aloft a paper parasol, implored the Almighty to demonstrate his power: "I believe it, I believe it, O Lord. We have an arch-enemy who is traveling over the country. He is working against Thee. He is working against us, O Lord. We have all faith in Thee. Thou art all-powerful and holdest everything in thy hands. Answer this, our prayer." Cries from the crowd filled the air: "Amen," "Bless the Lord" (*Philadelphia Record*, Nov. 29, 1895).

The sophisticated press of the country watched the spectacle in Cleveland with irreverent amusement. The *Record* also reported that many Christian Endeavorers were attending a football game on Thanksgiving Day. When the local team scored a touchdown at exactly twelve o'clock, the moment passed without religious expression. The *Washington Times* sadly shook its head: "It is not to be expected that persons unaccustomed to prayer as Ohioans are can at once acquire such facility as would enable them to accomplish so notable a work as Col. Ingersoll's conversion" (Nov. 28, 1895). In New York the *Post* denounced the Cleveland enterprise as a "studied insult," and the *Journal* advised Ingersoll "to follow the example of the historical coon in the tree that, observing Davy Crockett below with a rifle, said, 'Don't shoot! I'll come down' " (*Post*, Nov. 29; *Journal*, Nov. 30). The Evansville, Indiana, *Journal* frankly took sides with Ingersoll. "The praying people of the country have all been on their knees conjointly of late to effect the conversion of Col. BOB INGERSOLL, the agnostic chief. This is all very well and it is to be hoped they will succeed. BOB INGERSOLL is much too good a man to be left to go to perdition out of hand. The fact is that his charity and kindness to his fellow-men might well be imitated by some of the Christian brethren; [his benevolence] really seems as like the spirit the Savior taught that if the world did not know what a wicked man INGERSOLL was they might mistake him for a sample of first-class Christianity" (Dec. 1, 1895).

While the crusade for his conversion was running its course in Cleveland, Ingersoll was on an extensive lecture tour in the Midwest. On November twenty-ninth Ingersoll was in Lincoln, Nebraska. Did he care to comment on the Christian Endeavorers and their prayers for his salvation? "No," Ingersoll snapped, "I do not wish to say anything on that subject" (*New York Recorder*, Nov. 30, dispatched from Lincoln).

As reporters along his travels would not let the subject rest, however, he opened up gradually upon it. He regarded the praying Clevelanders as good, honest people who meant well and he did not want to say anything that would hurt their feelings. "If the god to whom they are offering their prayers has the power to convert me, I'm here to be converted," but he could not help asking why would a God with such power send millions to eternal torment "when he could convert them by the power of his word?" (*Des Moines State Register*, Dec. 6, 1895). Perhaps God had not yet made up his mind on Ingersoll. "Oh, we will have to wait and see what will be done. I suppose that God is too busy yet with the people's prayers of thanksgiving of last week and has not got around to that yet. . . . If the prayers are effective then the Endeavorers ought to go after Grover Cleveland. His message sounds like he needed it" (*New York Advertiser*, Dec. 4, dispatched from Minneapolis). He did not know of any prayers that had ever been answered. "I suppose that prayer is born of helplessness. It is a wish addressed to the unknown. I feel about as I did before the prayers were made. . . . "(*Davenport Republican*, Dec. 7, 1895).

Back in New York in mid-December he found in his office a stack of mail from the Christian Endeavorers and a reporter from the *Sun*, whom he assured he would like to finish out his days without the consolation of hell. Was he annoyed by the Christian Endeavorers taking such a public interest in his conversion? "Dear me, no, they meant it kindly and for my own good. The only difference of opinion that we have is that I believe this world is natural and they believe that is is supernatural, something that was constructed by sleight of hand." Suppose, the reporter asked, he were converted, what then? A mock expression of terror passed over

Ingersoll's face. He would be unhappy thinking of how people would be separated from their loved ones, some going to hell, others to heaven (Dec. 14, 1895). A month later, at home, smoking a cigar and preparing for the theater, he dismissed the whole affair by comparing himself to the girl who, when asked why she allowed the boys to press her hand, said that it pleased them and did her no harm (*New York Tribune*, Jan. 22, 1896). (This was a favorite expression of his for his more kindly critics.)

On January tenth Ingersoll was in Kalamazoo, Michigan, to lecture on Lincoln. Before the lecture friends took him on a tour of the People's Church, whose minister was Miss Caroline Bartlett. They informed him that this church was nondenominational and imposed no religious creed for membership. They showed him an institution equipped with parlors, reception rooms, study rooms, a library, a kitchen, and a dining room. Ingersoll was delighted, and midway in his lecture that evening he digressed to extol the People's Church. "It is the grandest thing in the State, if not in the United States. If there was such a church as that near my house I would certainly join it, if permitted." His statement caused a sensation, and some of the ecstatic members of the People's Church said that the prayers of the Christian Endeavorers were being answered through their creedless fellowship (*New York Herald*, Jan. 12, 1896, dispatched from Kalamazoo). On January thirteenth the *New York Journal* carried explanatory letters by Miss Bartlett and Ingersoll. She quoted from the People's Bond of Union: "Carefully desiring to develop in ourselves and in the world honest, reverent thought, faithfulness to our highest conceptions of the right living and love and service to our fellowmen, we join ourselves together, trying to help one another in all good things, and to advance the cause of the pure and practical religion in the community. We base our union upon no creedal test, but upon the purpose herein expressed and welcome all who wish to join us to help establish truth, righteousness, and love in the world." Writing from Toledo Ingersoll praised the absence of creed and the receptivity to Jews, infidels, agnostics, and even orthodox Christians. "I like that church."

What did the clerks at Ingersoll's law office think of his conversion? A reporter came to find out. Within three days of his Kalamazoo lecture the office held a jumble of letters and telegrams two feet high clamoring about it. Congratulations on being converted—congratulations on not being converted—what had he said? —what did he mean? —please answer by return mail giving full particulars. Answering this barrage was "a confounded nuisance" for the clerks. "What is this church he is converted to now?" one of them asked. "A kitchen or something, isn't it?" (*New York Commerical Advertiser*, Jan. 13, 1896).

Only a mystic poet could imagine Ingersoll's endorsement of the People's Church as expressing a conversion to Christianity. Certainly the smalltown ministers along the lecture route harbored no such fantasies. Although the subject at Adrian, Michigan, was not religion but Lincoln, the local preachers exhorted their flocks to stay away, and clusters of singing missionaries along the streets to the meeting hall exerted more than music and persuasion to discourage attendance. Nevertheless, he had "a good crowd," and lashed away at people who claimed for themselves rights that they would deny to others (*Detroit Tribune, St. Louis Globe Democrat,* Jan. 14, 1896). The *Adrian Messenger* was not intimidated by the ministers. Its reporter wrote, "Those Christian people who stayed away for fear of having their religious views exhibited on the canvas of Ingersoll's ridicule simply missed a great treat." On the debit side the reporter noted that the speaker looked like "a thoroughly over-fed gourmand" and that his voice had lost some of its power, but then the upswing: "He painted pictures with the English language as the master painter touches the canvas and transforms it into a golden sunset, a rosy morning, or with the swiftness of thought transforms the scene to the gentleness of a dewy spring-time eve, or the wild and picturesque grandeur of the lightning flash and the thunder roll in a summer storm. Here he was master" (*Adrian Messenger,* Jan. 15, 1896).

The news of Ingersoll's impending visitation threw Alliance, Ohio, into a dither. "A number of the pastors in the different churches throughout the city took occasion to refer to the Colonel's coming in anything but complimentary terms" (*Columbus Dispatch,* Jan. 14, 1896). (The *Dispatch* headlined this notice AN AD FOR INGERSOLL.) Not all the churchgoers in the small towns were frightened away. Ingersoll spoke in Findlay, Ohio, on the Bible and "in spite of the fact that all of the minsters in the city urgently requested the members of their congregations to remain as far away from the opera house as possible, fully 3,000 people listened to the noted orator" (*Cincinnati Enquirer,* Jan. 19).

In late February and in March Ingersoll took to the lecture platform in upstate New York, Massachusetts, Connecticut, and Rhode Island. His hosts were friends, his spirit exuberant, the press notices superlative. Rochester greeted him as an old friend. "Certainly the profession of infidelism seems to agree with Col. Robert G. Ingersoll. Hale and hearty as ever, vigorous in speech and gesture, lucid in thought, fearless in attack, infectious in humor, brilliant and beautiful in poetic flights and rhetorical ornamentation, forceful in argument, fertile in illustration, persuasive in oratory, this celebrated atheist logician last evening entertained a large and intelligent audience at the Lyceum eliciting round after round of applause at the telling points in his discourse and holding unabated the interest of his hearers until the end" (*Herald,* Feb. 24, 1896). A Danbury, Connecticut, paper concluded, "It is certainly not in Col. Ingersoll's nature to mince matters" (*News,* March 27, 1896). The *News* attributed the small audience to bad weather and (this was Yankeedom), "the admission tax of a dollar a head."

During a three week tour of the Midwest Ingersoll spoke on Saturday evening in Milwaukee on liberty, in Chicago on Sunday morning at the

Church Militant on "How To Reform Mankind," and that evening at McVicker's Theater on "Why I am An Agnostic."

What was going on? A church sermon in the morning, an infidel diatribe in the evening? Exactly. Like the nonsectarian People's Church in Kalamazoo the Church Militant in Chicago, led by Dr. John Rusk, had separated from the Fullerton Presbyterian Church because the Militants believed that Christianity was revealed in proper living and social concern. When it was announced that the Militants had invited Ingersoll to speak from their pulpit, the Women's Christian Temperance Union, which owned the building, prohibited the meeting. The Militants stood firm and moved to new quarters at the Columbia Theater. The inaugural service in the new house of God would be a lay sermon by the leading unbeliever in America.

The Church Militant encountered no difficulty in making the Ingersoll appearance a social event of prime importance. Admission was by card only. When the theater was packed to the point of suffocation by some three thousand persons a crowd estimated at one thousand remained at the door tryng to get in. On the stage were distinguished representatives of business, the professions, and the literary life of Chicago, nearly every judge of the trial and appellate courts, several county officials, delegations from colleges, law schools, and medical schools of city and suburbs, and some retired ministers (New York Herald, April 13, 1896). Among the dignitaries listed to attend at least one was memorable—Clarence Darrow (Chicago Record, April 14). Ingersoll and Dr. Rusk entered from the wings arm in arm and were greeted by a general burst of applause mixed with a few murmurs of discontent. The guest of honor was assigned a thronelike chair with gold-colored legs center stage.

The liturgy began with music and proceeded to the invocation, a recitation of the Lord's Prayer in unison, a reading from the tenth chapter from Luke (the parable of the good Samaritan), and the singing of "Nearer My God to Thee" and "America." The big man in the center nodded approval of the reading from Luke, but otherwise did not participate. He turned his ruddy face up and studied the ceiling decorations; his collar and neck-band were not comfortable and he fidgeted with them. He was also expressionless as Dr. Rusk introduced him mixing prayer and benediction, praising his life of usefulness to humanity, praying that he might enjoy health and happiness with his family and that "the arms of the Father be about him and his loved ones to the end." Dr. Rusk brought congregation and speaker together: "No matter whether a man believed in God or not, if he expounded the truth, then the truth was there and God was there" (New York Sun, April 13).

Calmly and candidly Ingersoll stated his radical difference with Christian belief. He had no faith in the supernatural, which belonged to the childhood of the race. "All that is, is natural. All is naturally produced. Beyond the horizon of the natural man cannot go" (Works, IV, 118). And beyond such argument for scientific method Ingersoll did not go. The *Chicago Times Herald* complimented him on being "as magnanimous as his audience" (April 13, 1896). He advocated international arbitration, humane treatment of criminals, diffusion of home ownership, harmony between labor and capital, and public education. He did not discuss the political issues of the day, nor is the address a primer of personal ethics or a manifesto for social change. At its conclusion the applause was loud and long, people waving hats and handkerchiefs, and the service ended with the congregation singing "The Tie That Binds" (*Waterbury American*, April 13, 1896).

Ingersoll was the big news that Sunday in Chicago, the subject of many sermons throughout the city. The *Tribune* (April 13) published five of these sermons. Unlike their brethren in the small towns the Chicago ministers regarded Ingersoll as a respectable antagonist, and so did not indulge in personal abuse. Dealing with Ingersollism in general rather than the Church Militant address being delivered the same morning, they reflected a gamut of ideas and moods held by the leaders of Christian thought. Dr. H. W. Thomas praised Ingersoll for believing in reason, truth, respectability, love of man, and liberty, and for his "noble patriotism" and "high morality." He laid the blame for Ingersoll's asperity on thoughtless and unkind ministers who fanatically defended what was objectionable in the Christian tradition. Reverend Dr. Hollis said that both the agnostic and the Christian see only part of the truth and that only "when we rise to the throne of God" would his majesty and goodness be understood. Then all would exclaim, "We have heard of thee by the hearing of the ear, but we have heard only the whispering." Dr. Henry assured his congregation in pounding phrases that agnosticism was "a doctrine of despair—a huge religious nihilism condemned by science, contradicted by experience, rejected by revelation, and discredited by morality." Reverend Danforth contended that religion was not out of date and standing still, that there was progress. This progress consisted not in altering basic principles but in deeper study of the Scriptures and in the applied Christianity of building schools, hospitals, and homes for the forsaken and "those little ones whom Jesus took in his arms and blessed."

Special attention is warranted by Dr. Herson of the First Baptist Church. Speaking on the topic "The Savageness of Scripture" he undertook to justify the ways of God to man as found in the Old Testament. He discovered the beneficent hand of God in instances adduced by Ingersoll as evidences of the monstrous cruelties of the biblical Jehovah. The man stoned to death for picking up sticks on the Sabbath, presumably to make a fire? The context shows that this gathering of wood was not a case of necessity but a presumptuous and defiant act meriting such punishment as General Dix decreed in the Civil War: "If any man hauls down the flag shoot him on the spot." The children's playful remarks to the bald-headed prophet and their punishment of being devoured by bears? These "children," as prominent Hebraists attested, were actually adult hoodlums, and their contempt for God's ambassador was contempt for God. "If a United States Ambassador be treated with indignity we regard no punishment as too severe, but God's ambassador may be assailed with impunity." The butchery of the priests of Baal? "They were not mere theologians but debauchers of morals and subverters of the government of which the God of Israel was the head, and so were traitors and anarchists." Slaughter of the Midianites and Canaanites by Moses and Joshua? They were a mass of putrefaction that defiled the atmosphere of the whole earth. "The best thing that could have happened to the antediluvian world was to sweep the Canaanites from the face of the earth. This was not savagery but mercy." (What can be temperately said of this pronouncement from the pulpit except Paine's dictum that belief in a cruel God makes cruel men?)

Once again in New York he delivered more lectures, took his family to the theater, and gave more interviews. He liked the Church Militant; its members were trying to make the world better. "To the extent that they rely on their own efforts they are right; to the extent that they rely on praying, they will fail." Among the Republican candidates for President, McKinley was ahead, although he himself leaned to his friend Reed. At any rate, the next President would be a Republican. "Am I as much in favor of protection as ever? Oh, yes indeed; if anything, more. I am ultra protectionist. I am more of a protectionist than most of the protectionists are themselves" (*Pittsburgh Dispatch*, April 26).

Lecturing in New York on "Why I am An Agnostic," "his keen sarcasms and shafts of irony were roundly applauded, and neither ancient dames with hairs of snow nor their grand-daughters spared their hands in displaying their appreciation of the 'noble infidel' " (*New York Advertiser*, April 20). Then on the lecture circuit again, and everywhere the same dichotomy—ministerial boycott but meeting halls usually packed or well filled. In Carthage, Missouri, where he was scheduled to speak on "Liberty," a local correspondent reported to the *Topeka Capital* that the ministerial alliance had issued a card urging Christians to stay away, and that "the sale of seats is unprecedented." The *Capital* headlined the article IS INGERSOLL RABID? (If he was not rabid, he was certainly contagious, as his audiences were imbued with his spirit.) In Omaha, on "The Foundations of Faith": "The celebrated agnostic spoke to an appreciative audience. His every point was caught and applauded almost before he could finish the phrase in which it was clothed. There was no dullness in the audience and as there was certainly none on the stage Colonel Ingersoll may felicitate himself upon his success" (*Omaha Bee*, May 6, 1896).

On May third, the train from Pittsburg, Kansas, pulled in at Kansas City at 5 o'clock in the afternoon, bearing Ingersoll, Farrell, and a current managing assistant. At the Coates Hotel Ingersoll took a nap before the lecture at the Coates Opera House. The house was packed with a "representative" audience including many prominent citizens and their families. A meticulous reporter noted that the orator was not as "spry" as in former years, "but this is due as much to the accretion of adipose tissue under his vest as to the advance of old age" (*Kansas City World,* May 4). Though a picture of health and good humor the speaker moved cautiously about the platform, his famous voice trembled occasionally, and more than once he swallowed a trochee. Nevertheless, voice, gesture, facial expression, and bodily movements combined for a superb presentation; the audience was more than satisfied. "The lecturer dealt very little with sarcasm or ridicule, although his bits of humor on the Trinity, the Savior, and Jehovah would have been apt to have made orthodox people wince somewhat. There seemed to have been few of such people in the audience, for all such pieces of pleasantry were greeted with marked applause" (*Journal,* May 4, 1896). After the lecture people came on stage for an impromptu reception. A reporter for the *Times,* probably on special assignment to bring back Ingersoll's views on politics no matter what it cost, tried to get his exclusive attention. Ingersoll was a bit irritated. "What do you want to interview me on?" he asked. "Politics? Well, McKinley will be nominated on the first ballot. No doubt of it whatever. Sure thing," and he turned to shaking hands with the swelling crowd. The reporter persisted: "Will you be there, Colonel?" "Will I be where?" "Why, at St. Louis when McKinley is nominated." "Me? I'll be at home smoking. That's all I've got to say," and the interview was over.

More fortunate was a reporter for the *Star* the next morning. "Pope Bob," as the reporter called him, was only having breakfast with Farrell and the managing assistant in the hotel dining room—as always a good moment to barge in and grab some of his attention. The salivary juices flowing, Ingersoll had started on a piece of broiled chicken, and an egg-cup with sliced boiled eggs on the side. The reporter fired a question: Who would be the next President? "Why, McKinley of course." Next: Who would be the Democratic nominee? Ingersoll repeated the question slowly and turned a thoughtful face to the food. Addressing the eggs he stirred in a pat of butter and a few shakes of salt and pepper. From the interviewee's deliberative manner the reporter awaited a searching and profound statement. Ingersoll tasted the eggs, found them to his liking. Suddenly—"Huh! Democratic nominee? Why, my young friend, it's of no more importance than a nomination in the Figi's [sic] islands." Ingersoll turned to the chicken, examined it for a new point of attack, and then as if awakening with a start. "The Democratic party will split at Chicago. Who cares?" A mouthful of the chicken. "It doesn't make any difference whether the Democratic party splits or not." Would the Democratic party be destroyed? "Huh!" he replied, scooping into the eggs. "You can't destroy the Democratic party. Nothing can destroy the Democratic party." What would the Republican platform be? "Gold, just plain gold," as he wiped his mouth with the napkin. What would the

Republican silver men do? "Don't know. Who cares?" After an uncomplimentary reference to Cleveland he assessed McKinley. "McKinley will
be the next President. He will be a good President. He was a good soldier,
he was a good congressman, he was a good governor, and he will be
a good President. Nothing very brilliant—just good. He has advanced
by regular steps, has always done well." Who would be Vice President?
"Why bother me about Vice President? Nobody cares about Vice President.
He doesn't amount to anything except annoy the President by wanting
to step into his shoes." Chicken and eggs gone, Ingersoll sighed. How
was his health? "My health is too good, entirely too good." Later in the
morning Farrell told the reporter than Ingersoll was "annoyed" by his
growing flesh and keen appetite, that he weighed 260 pounds and was
reminded of it every day when putting on his shoes, and that he ate
only a hearty breakfast, a light lunch at 2 o'clock, and nothing else until
the next morning. (Nevertheless, three days later in Des Moines, as he
discarded his cigar and was about to go on stage, he inquired whether
the hotel dining room would be open on his return [Des Moines Leader,
May 7, 1896].)

Passing the time while waiting for the train to St. Joseph, where
he would lecture that night, Ingersoll chatted with a group of friends
including Dr. J. E. Roberts, minister of All Souls' Unitarian Church. When
he stepped into his carriage, he reached out for a firm handshake with
Dr. Roberts and said, "Goodbye, my friend." Dr. Roberts replied, "Goodbye,
I love you" (Kansas City World, May 4). As the carriage rolled away a reporter
asked Dr. Roberts, "Did you try to convert him?" "Convert him? Convert
him?" Dr. Roberts exclaimed, heavily sarcastic. "He don't need conversion.
I wish all men were like him. He is the greatest apostle of liberty and
reason and fraternity. He is a pillar of goodness and kindness in the
world!" (Kansas City Star, May 4, 1896).

In June Ingersoll sent his application and five-hundred-dollar membership fee to the Ardsley Club, an elite society in Dobbs Ferry to which
his son-in-law Walston Brown belonged. The executive committee rejected
him and returned the fee. It was a personal affront, but Ingersoll affected
to take it lightly: "I think I am the lucky one. I got my money back"
(New York Tribune, June 23, 1896). Brown resigned from the club.

The put-down by the Ardsley Club was but a minor irritant in pleasant
summer days at bucolic Dobbs Ferry. Robert wrote to John on June thirtieth
that the roses were gone, new flowers taking their place. The weather
was perfect, it being the coolest June he could remember. Everybody
was in perfect health, and he was fighting the weight problem. "I am
not quite as fleshy as when I saw you last. I weigh about 240—did weigh
a few weeks ago 259½ [not 260 as Farrell had said]. I eat nothing but
meat, cucumbers, asparagus & lettuce. Am hungry night and day!" He
would soon be speechifying again. "On the 4th I am to make a speech
at Lake Pleasant, Massachusetts. On the 12th in Canandaigua—about

20 miles from Buffalo, on the 19th at Greenwich near Saratoga. On the 20th at Burlington, Vermont. Aug. 2 at Atlantic City—about two hours from Philadelphia. On the 9th, 16th & 23rd at Lake Pleasant, Mass. I forgot one place. I am to be at Bradford Pa. on the 13th this month. So, you see that I am to do some preaching and some traveling." It looked as though McKinley would win, and that would be a good thing. The people were tired of the Democrats and Cleveland, "a pudding-headed failure." He closed, "Give my love to each and all. Take good care of yourself. We must meet next winter. I enclose a few farthings. I love you. Robert" (*Letters*, 215).

McKinley was nominated in June. A month later the youthful Bryan ("prairie avenger, mountain lion") made his great Cross of Gold speech, capturing the Democratic party and its nomination (and soon the Populist nomination) with Ingersollian phrases beginning, "I come to speak to you in defense of a cause as holy as the cause of liberty—the cause of humanity," and ending, "You shall not press down upon the brow of labor this crown of thorns; you shall not crucify mankind upon a cross of gold." It was no longer politics as usual, no longer a question of choosing this or that cigar-store Indian. The electorate was presented its first great issue since 1860. The debt-ridden agrarian forces of the South and West were banging at the door of the industrial and financial East with a revolutionary program for monetary expansion. Ingersoll had passed the point of no return and flatly decried the insurgency. "The people of the United States are fairly sane," he said to a reporter, "and they are sane enough to elect McKinley. This is the richest and most prosperous country in the world and we ought to be honest." If Bryan were elected, a panic would follow. Gold would go out of circulation, the nation would be dishonored with its credit gone as government and railroad bonds fell to their value in commercial silver. "For the first time in our history we would know what hard times really are" (*Burlington* [Vt.] *Free Press*, July 27, 1896).

On September nineteenth he wrote to brother John from Dobbs Ferry. The family were all well; things were going along as usual; everybody believed McKinley would win. "I think that Bryan has no chance. He talks but he does not think" (*Letters*, 215). He expressed no interest in taking an active part in the campaign. He was not a politician; he had no ax to grind. If there was a role for him in the momentous contest now unfolding, it must seek him out. (It may be reasonably assumed that he was itching for a call.)

Presumably, when Ingersoll was writing to his brother on the nineteenth, he had not yet received the letter from the Republican State Central Committee of Illinois dated September seventeenth. The Republicans of Illinois were frantic. Altgeld was making a strong bid for a new term as governor and he might help carry Bryan into the White House. "Voicing the sentiments and the great desires of the Republican party in this State, for the first time in many years we send to you the message to 'come over into Macedonia' and help us" (IHS). Ingersoll accepted, but with a show of reluctance, quipping that he did not think there was any danger in Illinois, for Bryan was making all the speeches McKinley needed (*Chicago Tribune*, Sept. 28, 1896). It was finally decided that Ingersoll would make one speech in Chicago, then hit Galena, Galesburg, Bloomington, and Peoria. He would not have to share the platform with any other speaker. Requests poured in from other parts of the country but he turned them all down except New York. Screams of protest from the disillusioned. If he spoke for the gold standard, the enemies of liberty would rejoice, and his friends would be pained (Oct. 3, 1896, L.C.). Perhaps the time had come to turn his picture to the wall (To Ingersoll, undated, L.C.). Among the plaudits was a letter from his cousin Frank Gilbert, editor of the *Chicago Inter-Ocean*. "It is high time," said Gilbert, "for the American people to put a stop to the jeopardizing of business for campaign purposes" (Sept. 27, 1896, Kittredge, 183). A truly remarkable statement.

Prior to his speech in Chicago Ingersoll shared with Depew and other Republican leaders the balcony of the Union League Club and viewed a parade of the Business Men's Sound Money Association, 100,000 strong, taking four or five hours to pass any one point (*Inter-Ocean*, Oct. 3, 1896). Came the day of the great Ingersoll speech in the colossal tent on Sacramento Avenue and Lake Street. The tent had been designed to seat 12,000 but some 8,000 more packed in and occupied the remaining space. Outside thousands ebbed and flowed against the canvas until prevailed upon to adjourn a block away. Inside were Republicans, Democrats, Populists, all in contentious whirls. Three policemen assigned to keep order got wedged into the crowd and had to fight their way out to call for reenforcements. The sounding board at the rear of the platform trembled from the pressure of the crowd, a gasoline lamp hung up front on a pole swayed crazily, and the air was aquiver with the possibility of disaster. Ingersoll came on the platform escorted by the customary collection of office-holders seeking reelection. In his introduction the chairman referred to the Civil War as a heated encounter that melted away the shackles of slavery, and called upon patriots to save the country from the new assault by disorganizers, anarchists, and other professional troublemakers. Then: "My duty is to introduce to you one whose big heart and big brain are filled with love and patriotic care for the things that concern the country he fought for and loves so well. I now have the honor of introducing to you Hon. Robert G. Ingersoll" (*Inter-Ocean*, Oct. 9). As the crowd cheered, Ingersoll took off his slouch hat and coat and came forward. Midway in his first sentence the crowd burst into new tumult that lasted ten minutes. Then, suddenly, silence.

Ingersoll's opening words, once the crowd would let him get them out, were a masterpiece of persuasion.

Fellow Citizens: Again we are on the field of battle where thought contends with thought—the field of battle where facts are bullets and our arguments are swords. Again we appeal to the good sense, the con-science, to the patriotism of the American people. . . . This is our country, and we are responsible for what our country does. Every citizen has a right to think on the issues and to exercise his sovereign right to vote according to his conscience, wherever his conscience may lead him.

He said that three great issues faced the American people: money, the tariff, and government by law or the mob. As he elucidated these issues the crowd laughed and applauded continually, though there was some heckling that he beat down without difficulty.

On the money question Ingersoll the schoolmaster expounded the orthodox bullion value theory: Money was a product of nature, and must be found, created. "There are many statesmen going over the country, making speeches from the tail end of trains (*laughter*), and not one of them knows what a dollar is" (a crack at Bryan, who pioneered elec-tioneering from cabooses all over the country while McKinley stayed on his front porch in Canton, Ohio). A dollar was 23.22 grains of gold. Whether there were silver dollars or even paper dollars, the silver or paper used must be worth a dollar in the market. An honest dollar could not be made of fifty cents worth of silver. The idea that the government could create money out of nothing was as absurd as perpetual motion or the fountain of youth. If the government could make money, why not make it out of paper? Why pay taxes? (*A voice from the crowd:* "Free coinage will bring prosperity.") Would it? Ingersoll did not know. "I am not a prophet nor the son of a prophet, and perhaps not a very profitable son (*laughter*) but I can see into the future as far as any Populist" (*laughter*). Free silver would drive out gold, and the value of government bonds, of promissory notes, of fixed incomes and pensions would be cut in half. There would be a general panic.

Ingersoll framed the tariff issue: Should we keep the American market for ourselves or give it to the world? A manufacturing country was a great country, while a country that produced only raw material was a poor country. America needed protection in order to become a great country, in order to keep American wages high. The free traders spoke of opening the markets of the world. What they really wanted was to bring American wages down to the level of other countries. " 'The markets of the world!' We want our own markets. I would rather have the market of Illinois than all of China with her four hundred millions. I would rather have the market of one good county in New York than all of Mexico. What do they want in Mexico? A little red calico, a few sombreros, and some spurs. They make their own liquor and they live on red pepper and beans. What do you want of their market?" (*Works*, IX, 560). (This passage was added in New York.)

Finally, the United States was governed by law not the mob. It could not solve its domestic problems by the torch and the bludgeon. Labor and capital must become civilized and learn to respect each other's legitimate interests. The right to physical security extended to all, the lowest and the highest. If the states [under Democratic rule] could not protect their citizens from lynching, the Federal Government must do so. Ingersoll accused the Democrats of trying to poison the poor against the rich. "Why should we envy the rich? They never drank any colder water than I have. They never ate any lighter biscuit or any better corn bread. They never drank any better Illinois wine, or felt better after drinking it, than I have; than you have" (569). Do not divide this country into classes. The rich man who helps his fellow man deserves honor and respect.

"This is a Government of the people and by the people, a Government of law, and the laws should be interpreted by the courts in judicial calm" (571). The president must lay the mailed hand of the Republic upon the mob, must prevent the stopping of trains, burning of bridges, shooting of engineers. "The law is the supreme will of the supreme people, and we must obey it or we go back to savagery and black night." (573).

Finally, Bryan was not a tried man. He had no logic, no imagination. "His brain is an insane asylum without a keeper" (573). "When Major McKinley was fighting under the flag, Bryan was in his mother's arms, and judging from his speeches he ought to be there still" (574).

The *Chicago Tribune* headlined its story:

FIRED BY COL. BOB
Twenty Thousand People Stirred by Ingersoll
CLIMAX OF TENT CROWDS
Enthusiasm of West-Siders Goes Almost Beyond Bounds
CHEERS FOR HIS READY WIT
Logical Appeal to Sense and Conscience of Voters
EXPOSES FALLACIES OF BRYAN

The speech was printed and distributed in thousands of copies. On the cover a picture of Ingersoll at his most magisterial, above him INSPIRES TO LOYALTY! Loyalty to what? The Republican party? The Gold Standard? Wall Street? The United States of America? No matter, they were all the same.

In Galena on the ninth Ingersoll received several telegrams from Chicago signed by members of Congress running for reelection (and by other party candidates and functionaries) imploring him to come back to the Windy City to make a speech in the stockyards district on October twelfth. The fate of Republicanism in Illinois seemed to hang in the balance: "You can do more good than all the other speakers combined and will give us the next United States Senator and two Congressmen" (L.C.). The extra speech, they assured him, would be no great strain—he would have two whole days with nothing to do after speaking in Galena, and

after the second Chicago speech a whole day before his Galesburg
engagement. He agreed. In Galena he spoke to a crowd of 7500 and
7500 more tried in vain to get into the tent. On the twelfth he repeated
his speech with slight variations in Chicago in a tent on Halstead Avenue
and Twenty-Ninth Street. This crowd of some 14,000 was rather tough
and boisterous, with many Democrats among them, and Ingersoll fenced
continually with hecklers. Several shouted as with one voice, "Silver,"
and Ingersoll shot back, "I am just as much for silver as you are, and
more, too, because I want more of it in a dollar," and his partisans whooped
and cheered. Ingersoll was not the only speaker soliciting votes in the
streets of Chicago that day. His friend Eugene Debs, still and always
his friend, not yet a Socialist, addressed several mass meetings in support
of Bryan and free silver (*Chicago Tribune* and *New York World*, Oct. 13).

In Bloomington on October fifteenth an early morning report to Maud
and Eva: "We left Galesburg yesterday—came through Peoria—but did
not stop—We go there tomorrow. The weather is perfect and there is
the greatest crowd in Bloomington to-day that the town ever saw—I shall
speak to acres of people this morning—Oglesby meets us here and will
speak in the evening. Mother and I are perfectly well and my voice is
perfect. All I can say is that I love you both with all my heart and strength.
We send love and kisses to you both and the babes—Kiss each other
for me. Love to all in the house. Yours forever, Robert" (*Letters*, 216).

Among his old friends in Peoria Ingersoll held a reception in the
lobby of the National Hotel and a band played. A tabernacle had been
erected on Globe Street seating fifteen thousand. That number got seats,
and there were just as many standing outside. As the crowd poured into
the tabernacle Democratic pickets handed them leaflets containing quotations from Ingersoll's record in favor of silver coinage. One of the
managers of the meeting had obtained a leaflet and gave it to Ingersoll.
Without examination he put it into his side pocket. In the tabernacle
he faced a vast assemblage, Democratic leaflets fluttering in their hands.
He took it out of his pocket and read it aloud. "It is true; I made this
speech, but at the time I did not know that it was necessary for a dollar
to be as big as a pot lid," a question-begging exaggeration but seemingly unanswerable. The crowd—that is, most of them—applauded glee-
fully and settled down to enjoy a two-hour speech on the virtues of
Republicanism as only their most distinguished townsman could make
it (*Peoria Journal*, Oct. 17, 1896; William E. Hull, Speech at Interment of
Ashes, Aug. 4, 1923, L.C.).

Ingersoll's public espousal of McKinley for president made him a target for brickbats from all directions. Old friends as well as some old
enemies trod upon him in the press. An open letter in the *St. Louis Dispatch*
dated October 11, 1896, rebuked him in tones of anguish at betrayal:
"My friend, you have stood eloquently for untrammeled religious and
political liberty. Now how can you raise your voice to boom railroad,

coal mining, manufacturing, and other great corporations and trusts, in their work of coercing their employees to wear the McKinley label and attempting bribery of their votes through free pilgrimages to Canton?" A cartoon showed Miss Silver throwing into a trash bin Ingersoll's "I love you" missive after he sent Miss Gold a note penned "I am yours forever" (Denver Republican, Sept. 23, 1896). Some Democrats persisted in the old and futile effort of disparaging his politics because of his irreligion. The Philadelphia Item on October 13, 1896 ran a cartoon depicting Ingersoll and McKinley arm in arm on the platform, and cried out, "WILL A CHRISTIAN NATION STAND IT? BOB INGERSOLL, THE NOTORIOUS INFIDEL, Supporting McKinley on the same Political Platform." From quite a different viewpoint other opponents denounced the alliance of Ingersoll and the clergy against the people. A cartoon in the St. Louis Post Dispatch entitled POLITICS MAKES STRANGE BEDFELLOWS drew Ingersoll and Archbishop Ireland in bed together under a portrait of Mark Hanna, on its border IN MARK HANNA WE TRUST (Oct. 16, 1896). The Chicago Dispatch of October 24 presented parallel columns: On the left, BOB THE SINNER proclaiming HELL AND THE DEVIL EXIST ONLY IN CHILDISH FANCY, with ministers commenting, "Outrageous! shocking! blasphemous!!! Out upon the scoffer! Come, brothers, let us flee this ungodly man"; on the right, BOB THE SAINT: HELL AND THE DEVIL EXIST ONLY IN THE DEMOCRATIC PARTY, and the ministers: "What lofty thought! What glowing eloquence!! Go it, dear Robert, sic it to the Anarchist, Knock out the Repudiators with one of your sublimely eloquent upper-cuts!"

The Denver City World took Ingersoll to task for urging that the demonetization of silver could not be corrected. "Is there no such thing as righting a wrong? No remedy, forsooth. The remedy is in the hands of the people who have suffered all these years, the people who are the bone and sinew of the nation, the salt of the earth" (Oct. 15). In Peoria itself the Journal maintained that while precious metals were a work of nature, money was a work of art, a creature of law. It was government that defined a dollar as 23.22 grains of gold, and government could change the figure. The Chicago News made fun of Ingersoll's declaration that McKinley was more patriotic than Bryan in the Civil War. "Colonel Ingersoll's charge is indeed a serious one, and we do not see how Mr. Bryan can avoid making some sort of an explanation. The people have a right to know why a candidate for the presidency should loaf around home, resting in his mother's arms, when the Union was threatened with dismemberment" (Bryan was five years old when the war ended) (Oct. 13).

It was painful to see his old friends turn their backs on him and even ridicule him. Ingersoll defended himself in the household of freethought. On October twenty-fifth the Secular Union of New York put on a celebration for two distinguished British rationalists, Charles Watts and George W. Foote. "From personal acquaintance with most of the

Liberals in the audience," *The Truth Seeker* observed, "we should think that nine-tenths of them will vote for free silver next Tuesday, but those of our friends who have been saying and thinking hard things of Colonel Ingersoll would have learned a lesson in good nature by listening to the thunderous welcome he got from all when the chairman asked him to say a few words. The audience forgot its politics and everything but the presence of the greatest man this country has produced. He might have been advocating a single standard of diamonds for all they cared." The primary question for freethinkers, Ingersoll declared, was whether you had a right to be honest. "Is it right to tell what you think, or must you tell what somebody else thinks and pretend that you think that way? That is all." He reaffirmed that he wanted to be a citizen of the world and that he was the brother of every man everywhere, "in the shadow of the Pole and of the burning Afric sands," who wanted to be free. The world would become truly free and civilized when men did away with superstition. The audience loved the bringer of the dream. He was their shining leader who had gone astray, but they loved him just the same (Oct. 31, 1896).

On October twenty-ninth the McKinley League held its final rally of the campaign at Carnegie Hall, adorned for the occasion with flags, bunting, decorative shields, and gigantic portraits of McKinley and Hobart. It was an unusual mass meeting for the elite, with admission by ticket only. All the seats were occupied, mostly by men in evening dress and women in "brilliant gowns." There were some unscheduled moments of amusement when speakers quoted Scripture and one raised an arm "in the name of Almighty God." Ingersoll beamed as the audience laughed and tittered. The chairman introduced the speaker: "There is no intelligent audience under the flag or in any civilized country to whom it would be necessary for me to introduce Robert G. Ingersoll." Ingersoll rose slowly and advanced to the front. The lectern had been removed so that he could stride freely up and down the platform. When the applause ended, he launched into a rip-roaring rendition of his Chicago speech, augmented by platform displays of numbers and diagrams. It was, unbeknownst to all, the grand finale of his career as a political orator, the last campaign speech he would ever make (*Works*, IX, 536).

On November first, three days before the election, Ingersoll wrote to his cousin Frank Gilbert: "Dear Frank, Well the battle is almost over." He had "great confidence" and "great *fear*," for "the result is so important that in spite of my reason I am nervous." He hoped that he had done good, not harm. The campaign in New York was winding down. "Last Thursday night at Carnegie Hall I had a great meeting here—the last of the campaign in this city—Yesterday we had a magnificent parade— Eight hours in passing—tremendous, multitudinous, countless as the leaves—almost endless" (IHS). Nevertheless, the election was close—the electoral margin wide (McKinley, 271; Bryan, 176), but the popular margin narrow (McKinley, 7,035,638; Bryan 6,467,946). The sovereign majority had voted for business as usual.

For Ingersoll the Republican success in 1896 was the greatest achievement of American patriotism since the North had triumphed over the South. Not that it would bring in the millennial sunshine of the religion of humanity, but it would do for the time being. Sanity and honesty had been vindicated; the natural processes of renewal in a free enterprise system could restore prosperity. On election night, as the returns came in and it became clear that McKinley had won, he wrote letters of hallelujah to John and to Frank Gilbert:

> Dear Brother,
> Well, the battle is over and the most important victory since 1860 and 1864 has been grandly won. I am delighted beyond measure—delighted that the hosts of hatred have been defeated—that the multitude of malice has been scattered, and that all the insane reformers have been overwhelmed. Now we are going to have good times—prosperity—progress—plenty of work, good wages and enough to eat. The country has been saved from repudiation & dishonor. The people are capable of self-government.
> Every drop of my blood is glad.
> Love to each and all.
>
> Yours forever,
> Robert
> (Nov. 4, 1896, *Letters*, 217)

To his cousin: "The honor of the Republic is unstained as a star" (Nov. 4, 1896, IHS).

Ingersoll had planned to be in Chicago in mid-November to lecture and to attend the Free Thought Congress. Even before election day he had cancelled these appointments as he feared confrontations. "There seems to be a great deal of feeling among people who call themselves free thinkers," he wrote grimly to Samuel Putnam, "as to the position I have taken on the money question and many of them seem to think that I am, for the sake of money, expressing views that I do not honestly entertain. It seems that most of these people are for the free coinage of silver and really believe that all who disagree with them are the enemies of the poor and all who toil. Under these circumstances I hardly think I would be welcome at Chicago. It seems to me that I had better stay away." He concluded, "I have great feeling about this matter. It is bitter to find that you cannot depend on your friends. Please consider this as strictly confidential, as I do not wish to add fuel to the flames" (L.C., Nov. 28, 1896). The colonel and his troops had marched in different directions to different drummers and now stood at different stations.

Note

1. It would be presumptuous in a chronicle of this kind to take sides in the political contest of 1896, in which the electorate divided almost fifty-fifty at the polls. One need not, however, be an expert in finance and government to state for perspective some simple truths. An "honest" dollar does not depend upon its metallic base if any but on its contribution to a stable price level. History has shown Ingersoll wrong on his metallic theory of money and on the incapacity of government in a free society to deal with economic problems. Within a hundred years of Ingersoll's death the United States went off the gold standard, his financial Rock of Ages, without consulting other countries, and the dollar became simply a piece of paper not redeemable in any metal, finding value in government fiat and supply and demand, and the economic system did not collapse. And from its cornucopia the national government serves the felt needs of the nation in myriad ways including social security beyond Ingersoll's imagining. "True," Ingersoll might respond, "but this cornucopia is the product of a national debt beyond imagining in my own time."

XIV

"A Necessary End"

The career of Robert Ingersoll is a classic example of the insufficiency of freethought (secular humanism) as a total guide to social action. All freethinkers are opposed to belief in supernaturalism and subscribe in theory to freedom of belief and freedom of expression, democracy, and the scientific method. This is a sufficient program unto itself so far as it goes, but many in the movement in Ingersoll's time and later have tried to press their fellow secularists into agreeing with them on other issues that they consider of equal or greater importance. On reflection freethinkers appreciate that there is no imperative in secular philosophy for believing or not believing in free love, free trade, free silver, or, for that matter, free enterprise, and American freethinkers recognized this truth when, under prodding by Ingersoll and others, they changed their organizational name from the National Liberal League to the American Secular Union. But man does not live by logic alone, and in the heat of the Bryan-McKinley encounter some freethinkers denounced as traitors men like Ingersoll who could not in conscience believe in populism any more than in revelation.

Although Ingersoll distanced himself from any people who had accused him of selling out to other interests, he still had many friends and admirers among the leaders as well as the rank and file of the freethought movement. *The Truth Seeker*, the nearest thing to an official organ of the Secular Union, had opened its columns to Populist letters but had been neutral in the contest for the presidency. It regularly announced his continuing lecture schedule, published enthusiastic reports about his lectures and interviews, honored him as the undimmed star of freethought but Ingersoll kept out of the movement as such. Declining an invitation to attend the Free Thought Conference in Chicago in 1898, he wrote in a letter marked

Confidential to his young friend Samuel Putnam, "The Congress does not need me. You will have a success and that is enough. You have my best wishes. I admit that I have been wounded and I know that there is no sudden cure" (Nov. 6, 1898, L.C.). Perhaps that particular Congress did not need him, but the freethought movement needed him as its sounding board and he needed it as a political influence. (Surely had he lived longer, there would have been a reconciliation).

Ingersoll's break with organized freethought did not impair his standing as the country's leading attraction on the lecture circuit. Although his audiences came from all ranks of life, the majority that poured into his meetings were not League or Union members, bitter-end agrarians, or urban workers imbued with socialism. They were of the professional classes, liberally educated business men, comfortable rentiers, and public officials. They enjoyed a bright literate lecture whether or not they agreed with it. Ingersoll was at the zenith of his popularity and he remained there until the end of his life.

On November 13, 1896, Ingersoll lectured to a crowded house in Janesville, Wisconsin. Half through his discourse, swinging into his characteristic gesture, he raised his right hand in the air and started forward to slap it down into his left hand. Suddenly he stopped, his face twisted into an expression of pain. The audience laughed—this must be some Ingersollian stage business. They sat back for the punch line and the crash of palm on palm. Nothing of the kind happened. The pain was real, shooting up his right hip, almost taking his breath away—he was having a cerebral hemorrhage. The pain subsided, he explained that this was no stage trick, but proceeded to the finish. Farrell wanted him to cancel the rest of the tour and return home immediately; he refused and continued to lecture for another week until his condition worsened. In Chicago his cousin Frank Gilbert took him to Dr. Frank G. Billing (*New York Sun*, Dec. 14, 1896).

Dr. Billing diagnosed Ingersoll as having a weak heart and an enlarged liver, prescribed complete rest and a light diet, and strongly advised him to return home for treatment. Dr. Billing confided to Gilbert, "If the Colonel heeds nature's warning it will add ten years to his life. If he does not he will die. There will be no halfway business about it. He will either be better than ever or nothing. It will take time to reach the point of absolute recovery but he can get there if he will" (Gilbert to Ingersoll, June 19, 1898, L.C.). Back in New York Dr. Robertson put Ingersoll to bed and barred all visitors except family for an indefinite period.

The English freethinkers Foote and Watts, having finished their lecture tour in the States, were preparing to return to England. They could not leave America without paying respects to Ingersoll. Knowing of his condition, when they arrived at the house they had expected only a brief visit with the family, but Ingersoll sent down word that, doctor's order or no, he would see them. The time was set for the next afternoon.

Meanwhile the Browns took Foote and Watts to the theater, where they saw the great Richard Mansfield "wasting his talents in a trumpery play," as Foote recorded. Eva apologized for the poor play, saying she had hoped they could see Mansfield in *Richard III*. The party proceeded to the Ingersoll home, where the Britishers took supper with Mrs. Ingersoll, the Browns, Maud, and Clint, Sue, and Eva Farrell. Foote noted the striking contrast between the Ingersoll daughters, the delicate blond Eva and the brunette Maud, more robust but "not without a certain sweetness."

On Tuesday afternoon Foote and Watts met with Ingersoll in his bedroom. They found him looking better than they had expected, at ease and with good complexion, complaining of his inability to control his nerves and emotions but still showing his sense of humor, the twinkle in his deep gray eyes. They chatted about hotels, and Ingersoll mentioned an establishment much frequented by English travelers because "the uncomfortableness reminded them of home." Then there was the hotel that hit him with a frightfully high bill for three days' stay. He went to see the manager. "I told him that I did not want to buy the hotel, and asked him when he expected the other two installments. The manager knocked off some forty dollars." Ingersoll then gave his guests some practical advice on managing their future lectures in the States. The visitors had planned to take up only five minutes and rose to go. "What's the hurry?" asked Ingersoll. "What time's that? You've got more than half an hour and you're not going until the time's up." So they stayed for another minute or two, said goodbye, goodbye, and went downstairs for another half hour with the family before finally taking off. "Outside on the sidewalk," Foote ends his account, "I looked at Mr. Watts and said, 'What a beautiful family!' and the very same words were on his lips too" ("Mr. Foote's Letters from American" *The London FreeThinker*, Jan. 3, 1897).

Ingersoll resumed lecturing on January 28, 1897, in Boston, not as the beginning of a tour but as a single foray. All over town for the past three weeks Dwight Moody and Sam Jones had been holding revivals. Ingersoll was not looking for any confrontation with them although Jones would be evangelizing in the afternoon in the Boston Theater where Ingersoll would hold forth in the evening. A Reverend Deming suggested a debate between Ingersoll and Jones and invited Ingersoll to attend the Jones revival. Ingersoll declined. He said that Jones was too emotional, inclined to hysteria, and did not represent a distinct system of theology (*Lynn Item*, Jan. 25, 1897). The *Taunton Herald* agreed with Ingersoll's decision, saying that the messages of Christianity should not depend on a battle of wits on the platform (where incidentally Jones was no match for Ingersoll), and that the essence of Christianity lay in the imitation of Christ, which Ingersoll, though a "man of great intellect," could not assail (Jan. 25, 1897). Instead of going to the revival Ingersoll took a nap, and he and Mrs. Ingersoll were entertaining some friends when the reporter for the *Journal* joined the group and "was kindly received in that genial, cordial way wherein lies the secret of the Colonel's great personal magnetism" (Jan. 25, 1897).

That evening the Boston Theater was packed for Ingersoll, every seat and every foot of standing space occupied. A man connected with the place told a reporter that in the last thirty years it was the biggest audience he had ever seen within its walls (*Boston Globe*, Jan. 25, 1897). To one reporter Ingersoll did not seem at his best. He showed signs of age and enfeeblement and had lost weight. He read the two-hour discourse on "How to Reform Mankind" from manuscript, occasionally putting the paper down as he emphasized important points "with body, mind, and soul" (*Boston Traveller*, Jan. 25, 1897). Some hotheads in the crowd would have welcomed salty allusions to the evangelists but none were made. "The lecturer, nevertheless, was in excellent voice, and the audience showed appreciation by their hearty applause. Indeed, Messrs. Moody, [and] . . . Jones might have felt sad if they had seen the appreciation shown by a cultured Boston audience of some of the most caustic onslaughts on the doctrines they were preaching so earnestly" (*Boston Post*, Jan. 25, 1897). It was a typical great Ingersoll crowd as found in the big cities of the North, in full rapport with him, excepting one or two dissenters "acquainted with 'hard-stuff' dispensaries."

In February, responding to an invitation from the *The New York Journal*, Ingersoll wrote a short piece which that paper blazoned with boldface headlines: USE YOUR SENSES, CRIES INGERSOLL. Sub-headlines called upon the ministers to open their eyes, read their Bibles, and think as they read. If they did so they would surely follow the current trend of disbelief in the inerrancy of the Scriptures. He cited the findings of the higher criticism revealing the Bible as a jumble of contradictory texts written at various times long after the events narrated, and asked whether it was necessary for salvation to believe such fables as that David raised five thousand million dollars for building the temple or that Jonah lived in the whale. He also prepared his new lecture, "The Truth," an argument for intellectual self-reliance. Every man should pursue the truth in accordance with his reason. "To love the truth, thus perceived, is mental virtue—intellectual purity. This is true manhood. This is freedom. To throw away your reason at the command of churches, popes, parties, kings or gods, is to be a serf, a slave" (*Works*, IV, 73)..

In late February Ingersoll was back at full steam but with moderated pace on the lecture trail. His illness had slowed him down from his usual program of riding on the bumpy rails all day or all night and making two-hour speeches every evening. From late February to late May he undertook no extensive tours but lectured in New York and its environs, making short trips far and wide in the northern and eastern sections of the country. Free evenings on the road he spent at the theater or opera if available. He lectured most often on "How to Reform Mankind" and "Truth," occasionally on "Why I am an Agnostic," and once on Lincoln.

Having tested the waters, so to speak, in Washington, Baltimore, and Philadelphia, Ingersoll arrived in Chicago on March 6. No forum had been more hospitable to him in the past than the Windy City, and his stump speeches for the Republican ticket in October had not diminished his overall attractiveness. On the first night in Chicago he went to the theater, but not before answering the exigent questions of the press. He repeated for the nth time that the only rational way to coin silver was to put a dollar's worth of silver at the market price into the silver dollar. "The currency question is settled, has been really buried. All talk now is after the funeral" (*Chicago Tribune*, March 7, 1897). He said that he would be lecturing on the morrow at the Columbia Theater on "Truth," but he felt that his work in the religious field was nearly done; liberalism was invading the pulpit.

On March 8, 1897, Ingersoll delivered for the first time his lecture on "Truth." It drew the largest audience in any Chicago theater since the World's Fair of 1892. "The theater held the concentrated essence of all the admiration which has Ingersoll as its idol and Chicago as its home. Fashion was there, and people from the humbler walks of life were not absent. From the stage, where the eye had leave to roam from the top of the highest gallery to the row where on other nights the orchestra would have been found, not one seat could be found that had not an occupant" (*Chicago Chronicle*, March 8, 1897). The crowd waited for nearly half an hour until it grew restless, but then the speaker materialized from the wings, his bald head shining in the lights, and edged his way in a thunder of applause through the dense crowd seated on the stage to the reading desk. True to tell, the man they saw was not the rambunctious gladiator of October. His well-worn dress suit hung loose on a frame wasted by illness, his face had lost its plumpness, and he lacked the old-time vigor, but an Ingersoll below par could still give the crowd more than its money's worth. Without introduction or small talk, he set his manuscript on the desk and launched into a characteristic address in which the most audacious barbs were the most vigorously approved. The opening ovation "was typical of many that afterwards interrupted his utterances as the two hours of applause and merriment that followed the one trod upon the steps of the other" (*Chronicle*, March 8).

On March 11, having come back to Chicago after a triumphant lecture in Milwaukee on "How to Reform Mankind," Ingersoll took his ease in a rambling interview with cousin Frank Gilbert's *Inter-Ocean*. He talked of his love for Wagner and how he had enjoyed the opera last night. He praised Chicago's growth. He was ironic about "the real pious men" who ran some of the local newspapers. (The *Times Herald* had apologized to its readers for reporting his lecture but had devoted several columns to the prospective fight between "the good Corbett and the orthodox Fitzgibbons" who were getting ready to "attack juglars and noses, break jaws, blacken eyes and peel foreheads in a few days to settle the question of who can bear the most pounding.") He planned to deliver a few lectures until about the first of May, then "take a good long rest and play with the children." While he lived he would do what he could to eradicate superstition and the fear of eternal pain. He believed in international arbitration rather than warfare, "in settling disputes like reasonable, honorable beings. All that war ever does is to determine who is the stronger. It throws no light on any question, advances no argument." He liked McKinley's inaugural address, especially its denunciation of lynching. He had two positive reasons for thinking good times were on the way: "One of my reasons is that McKinley is in, and the other is that Cleveland is out" (March 12, 1897.)

The departing stormy petrel had two additional reasons for feeling good about his Chicago sojourn. He had called on Dr. Billing "and he said I was getting along the best kind and it would not hurt me to lecture" (Monmouth, March 9, 1897, Carbondale). And he had shown that he could still ruffle the feathers of orthodoxy. On March 8 a Baptist minister, P. S. Henson, spoke on the text, "God so loved the world that he gave his only begotten son that whosoever believeth in him shall not perish but have eternal life." Dr. P. S. Henson asserted that this simple message is the sum of all sound theology and the man who believes it is a Christian and will go to heaven. "According to that blatant blasphemer who last night talked before a lot of idiots who paid a dollar each to hear a man tell them what they didn't dare to say themselves, we should drop that belief in a God. If his claims were true I would go mad" (*Chicago Post*, March 8, 1897).

Mrs. Ingersoll, matronly but younger than her husband, was now always with him on the road. She was manager, valet, hostess, nurse, monitor, and one-person claque. She held her husband to no more than two lectures a week. He had shed much weight during his illness, so she brought along sewing materials and in free moments shortened the collars of his shirts. She administered his medicine, which he accepted meekly. To visitors in the suite she effused about their wonderful grandchildren—Eva, the fourth Eva in the extended family; Robbie, the second Robert—and showed their pictures. She participated in the give-and-take of discussions with visitors. The female reporter for the *Toledo Blade* calling upon them found "a vision of sweet domestic peace and contentment," Mrs. Ingersoll reading a magazine, Ingersoll puffing away at an after-dinner cigar. Magazine and cigar were put aside and the three embarked on chit-chat on all kinds of subjects including Shakespeare, women's rights, and the roles of chance and opportunity in human affairs. Another caller came to the door and the *Blade* reporter had to leave, feeling sorry for her readers that the delightful flow of thought had been cut short (*Blade*, April 20, 1897).

Mrs. Ingersoll had a manner of saying, "You didn't mean it that way, did you, Robert?" and then shaping his ideas to her own (*Indianapolis Sentinel*,

March 13, 1897). Interviewed in Louisville Ingersoll said that twenty-five years ago, even fifty years ago, some contemporary preachers would have been considered heretics. Mrs. Ingersoll interjected, Wouldn't twenty-five years more nearly cover the case? He smiled, saying he wanted to give a wider margin (*Louisville Commercial,* April 19, 1897). Entertaining a group in Kansas City he blurted out, "Oh, nature is a fool!" Mrs. Ingersoll had been chatting in a corner with Dr. Roberts, pastor of All Souls' Church. She looked up sharply, reprovingly. Ingersoll held his ground. "Yes, I say nature is a fool. Now wait" (shaking a lead pencil at her), "don't talk to me about nature's cures. Why, nature left to herself tries just as hard to kill you as cure you." "Why, how true," everybody said, and the object of their agreement leaned back and laughed "deeply and sonorously" (*Kansas City Star,* April 13, 1897).

From city to city members of the press perceived the prophet of infidelity in accordance with their biases, or the conditions of the moment, or the expectations of their publishers. To one reporter he seemed on the verge of falling apart: "He is showing quite plainly the weight of years, and is growing old in both appearance and activity. He does but little walking about and takes all the rest he can when at his lecturing points. He looks worn and weak and utterly tired out" (*Kansas City Journal,* April 13). To another he seemed altogether different. "Col. Ingersoll has lost none of the vigor that those who have attended his lectures know so well. In appearance he has not changed; he is round and rosy as the priests he abuses for their preying on the idiocy of the people to get their living" (*Toledo Commercial,* April 21). A third reporter was perhaps nearer to the truth. "There is no question about the fact that the great agnostic is growing old, but he is growing old magnificently. . . . When in Kansas City before, Colonel Ingersoll's face was as red as a brick, his cheeks stuck out, and his girth was tremendous. Since then he has dieted and now eats only vegetables and white meat—no beef—and has put off sixty-three pounds. Hence his figure is now more broad-shouldered than gross, and his face has become Ingersollian again" (*Kansas City Star,* April 13).

Ingersoll's return to the lecture circuit in 1897 was a great success. Waves of communion in freethought flowed back and forth between idolatrous crowds and the wonder-working prophet. "Everything else aside," marveled the *Kansas City Times,* "Robert G. Ingersoll is an interesting fellow. Few men alive—that is, simple, ordinary American citizens—could have filled the Coates house as it was filled last evening, to hear nothing but a talk. When the white-haired 'pagan' walked upon the stage last evening the house was filled from foundation to rafter beams with an intelligent-looking sympathetic audience with applause continually tingling at its finger-tips" (April 14). Not that every lecture was a standing-room-only event, scalpers furiously buying and selling in the lobby or on the sidewalk, with mesmerized crowds and curtain calls befitting luminaries of the stage, but many were such and most were at least well attended. And almost always after the lecture there were impromptu receptions wherever people clustered as the speaker was on the way out. He had begun to decline invitations to late-night talk-fests, though; he had to return to the hotel and go to bed.

Among newspaper reports, the *Louisville Journal Courier* agreed that his return was a success, and it vibrated with the sheer pleasure of hearing Ingersoll time and again, no matter what he said or how often he said it. "Those who have heard Mr. Ingersoll speak before heard little that was new last night in his own peculiar logic, especially as to his ideas on religion and social problems. But the magnificiently modulated voice still held the audience, his old theories were clothed in new and magnificent metaphors and similes, while the simplicity of his choice of words and expressions full of color had the same charm as of old" (April 19, 1897).

As usual Ingersoll was described as "one of the most approachable of men" for interviews. No reporter ever left his presence with an empty notebook, as the interviewee had something to say on almost any question (*Louisville Commerical,* April 19, 1897). The reporters invariably found him "the same genial gentleman as in former years, brimming over with a combination of jokes, hospitality, and irreverence" (*Indianapolis Journal,* March 14, 1897). Among the highlights of his offhand remarks in early 1897: The silver senators were wasting their efforts; the silver question was settled. Good times were on the way; all the nation needed was confidence (*Colorado State Journal,* March 16). There were four distinct stages of man: youth and hope, strength and accomplishment, memory, and old age. The man was fortunate who dies at the zenith, avoiding old age, the period of senility. As for himself, "I am very happy. I do not fear death any more than I fear sleep. I do not believe I shall become a convict in the penitentiary of a compassionate God." Did humanity need reformation? "Yes, it does. There is too much poverty, too much ignorance, too much vice, and too much crime. The only way to reform the world is to develop the brain. We want intelligence enough to find out the true conditions of happiness. Labor ought not to be satisfied with the rags and the crusts. There is enough in the world for all if properly distributed. We want to get rid of war and superstition" (*Kansas City Star,* April 13). "Most of the orthodox preachers today are ashamed to preach their creeds. The fires of hell have nearly gone out, and the climate of the place is quite salubrious. Sensible ministers are giving up miracles, giving up the inspiration of the Bible, doubting the existence of the devil, and even growing a little uncertain about God" (*Louisville Commercial,* April 19).

In Cleveland on a stopover, news of Ingersoll's presence got around town and soon his suite was stormed by visitors. As the reporter for the *Plain Dealer* entered, "the eminent lecturer" was in a chair smoking an after-luncheon cigar. Mrs. Ingersoll emerged from a curtained alcove holding a medicine bottle and a spoon, saying "You had better take this now, or I'll surely forget it." She measured out a few drops; Ingersoll "demurred not." The interview ranged over a wide variety of subjects, Ingersoll writing down his answers lest he be misquoted. The discussion turned to his favorite *bête noir*, observance of Sunday laws, and he was off.

> It always gives me pleasure to see the Sabbath broken. On that day I love to hear the violins and see the boys and girls dancing. I love to hear the music in the parks, love to see the bathers in the surf, love to see people on their wheels, love to see little children gathering flowers, love to see people sailing, love to see them playing golf or ball. All this is so much better and sweeter than going to church, hearing horrible hymns in horrible tunes, horrible sermons about the harps of heaven and the tortures of hell. Away with the sacred Sabbath, say I. "Man was not made for the sabbath."

The ministers want every place closed on the Sabbath except the churches. What then? "The people will go to church as the man went home. A man was staggering home about two o'clock in the morning. His poor wife said, 'John, how could you come home at such a time?' And John replied, 'Mary, the fact is, every other place is shut up' " (*Plain Dealer*, April 6, 1897). It was as if the ministers had nothing more important to do than keep tabs on Ingersoll. The assault on Sabbath observance could not be dismissed with a shrug or a smile; it had to be rebuked from the pulpit. The Reverend Ward Beecher Pickard of the Epworth Memorial Methodist Episcopal Church had his scale of values: "The Anarchist of the Haymarket is not as dangerous as this American-born bomb-thrower, who would lead the American Youth to purposely and persistently break the law of the state" (*Plain Dealer*, May 10, 1897).

Dwight L. Moody and Robert G. Ingersoll were the salient figures on the opposite ends of the religious spectrum. Nonetheless, they treated each other gently. "Colonel Ingersoll," said Moody, "has a great many noble qualities" and was right in opposing shams (*Springfield* [Mass.] *Union*, April 16, 1897). And Ingersoll said, "I have no doubt that Mr. Moody intends to do right. I have confidence in his sincerity." Neither challenged the other to debate, and no entrepreneur pursued its possibility. In St. Louis Moody said, "So he's going to lecture here on Truth, is he? Well, that is what I have been preaching for thirty years. I preached it last night in my sermon on Sowing and Reaping" (*St. Louis Post Dispatch*, April 9, 1897). Ingersoll had already declared himself as to Moody's mindset. How can one explain the "amazing credulity" of men like Moody who believed in the Jonah story in the century of Humboldt, Darwin, Huxley, Spencer, and Haeckel? And sowing and reaping—just desserts? Christianity was not based on belief in just desserts. Christianity blamed all men for the sins of Adam and promised forgiveness to every sinner via the goodness of Christ—if, that is, the sinner was fortunate enough to meet a revival preacher and repent before dying. In the Christian hereafter there was no room for deserving well or ill. "In the orthodox heaven there is no mercy, no pity. In the orthodox hell there is no hope, no reform. God is an eternal jailer, an everlasting turnkey" (*Chicago World*, April 2, 1897).

Moody spoke in St. Louis on April 8, Ingersoll on April 12. The *Globe Democrat* was evenhanded in reporting on the two speakers, though almost partial to Ingersoll.

> Last week people flooded [the] Music Hall to hear Dwight L. Moody glorify the Bible, arouse the ministers to higher spiritual life and effort and call sinners to repentance. Last night people paid $1.50 to hear 'Pope Bob' pick the Bible to pieces, making brutes of its expositors and preach 'the religion of usefulness and enjoyment.' The audiences were both compliments to two men of wonderful power, but they were as different as the poles. There was none of the correctness, none of the hallelujahs and amens of the Music Hall meeting at the Olympia. The audience was three-fourths composed of men, and all seemed to be there merely to be amused. Col. Ingersoll gave his new lecture, 'Truth.' It was witty, epigrammatic, abounded in irony, ridicule, and sarcasm and was occasionally lighted up with one of those prose poems which make even the reader thrill. It was such a lecture as only Ingersoll can prepare—such a one as the audience expected and the people were satisfied. (April 12, 1897)

Next stop Kansas City. Browsing through the newspapers Ingersoll discovered that at least two ministers had bidden him not welcome. He blasted away at them through the ever-grateful press. No, he said of Dr. Northrop's accusation, he did not advocate suicide as an easy way out of the loss of possessions beyond hope of replacement. "I have said, and I repeat it now, that when a man is of no use to himself and can be of no use to others, when his days and nights are filled with agony, when he is being devoured by a cancer or suffering from some terrible disease, then he has the right to end his life. I do not believe there is a man of real goodwill in this world who does not agree with me." His other clerical adversary, Dr. Coombs, was "filled with the true Christian spirit" in lying about him. Ingersoll had never said that in ten years no more churches would be built. "I did say some twenty years ago that I would make orthodox ministers ashamed to preach the dogma of eternal pain, and so I will." Did men need a sense of duty to God in order to be "honest, generous, and loving"? No, God himself recognized no superior; how, then, could *he* be good? Did Ingersoll rob man of a Father? This "Father" withheld rain and killed his children with famine, swallowed them with earthquakes, drowned them with tidal waves, and rent them with cyclones. "For my part, I would rather be an orphan than have such a father. The trouble with Dr. Coombs is he does not think, and he is, I am afraid, a little prejudiced against me." One religious institution in Kansas City against which Ingersoll could have no complaint was the Salvation Army. To them he was an erring brother, for whose conversion lovingly they prayed. All over town their little detachments went marching through the streets, shaking and slapping their tambourines, chanting hallelujahs to the skies, adjuring the lost soul to turn to the path of righteousness and walk in the footsteps of Jesus. Ingersoll might well be grateful to the Army for its expression of love—and for the city-wide publicity which guranteed a standing-room-only audience at the evening's lecture (*Journal*, April 13, 1897).

After Kansas City Ingersoll lectured in Kentucky, Ohio, Indiana, upstate New York, New York City, and Pennsylvania. The paen of praise was renewed everywhere. The *Evansville Courier* (April 17) and the *Toledo Blade* (April 21) simply cribbed the language of the *St. Louis Globe Democrat*. All agreed that "the lecture was witty, epigrammatic, and abounded in irony, ridicule, and sarcasm." According to the *Pittsburgh Dispatch*, "Few dramas of strong dramatic purpose recently witnessed on the stage of the new Grand Opera House have more completely absorbed the attention of the audience than did the lecture on Truth delivered there last night by Colonel Robert Ingersoll. One might add that few comedians have so legitimately mined their laughter and applause" (May 30, 1897).

During brief stays in New York Ingersoll could always find time to answer such of his heavy mail as was thoughtful, temperate, and worth answering. A minister had sent him a copy of his sermon on Christ and salvation. Ingersoll replied that he had no desire to be a Christian or to be "saved." Mankind could know nothing of origin and destiny and should devote itself to this life. If there is another life and it is good, so much the better. "All this talk about Christ being God and about the fall of man, the atonement and the redemption of true believers, is to me nothing but superstition. . . . Each man should live according to his ideal, be of use to himself or others" (To Mr. Haskett, Feb. 2, 1897, *Letters*, 339). To an author who had sent him a copy of his book on religion he had replied that he did not believe in the supernatural, adding that Christ had said some beautiful things, some awful, some foolish, and some heartless. No man, Jesus Christ or anyone else, could be a perfect model for all time. "Nature has not yet produced a man that the world can safely follow. The greatest man has had some weakness, some fault, some flaw, some prejudice. No man on all questions rises above his generation, so let us follow justice—not the man whom we call just. Principles are above persons" (To William Evans, Davenport, Feb. 20, 1897, *Letters*, 340).

To a fellow seeker of the truth who could find no answer to the riddle of existence he replied that no one could know the absolute. "Our life is a little journey from mystery to mystery. We emerge from darkness and are lost in night and must give our attention to the journey." As for himself, "I know that the walls cannot be scaled, and so I adorn my cell, cultivate patience, cheerfulness, and above all else courage. I know that virtue is the mother of happiness and that vice breeds grief, failure, and despair. This knowledge is enough for this life. If there is another it is enough for that" (To Mr. Wertheimer, May 27, 1897, *Letters*, 348). What was greatness in oratory, Colonel? "A great orator must have passion, intelligence, enthusiasm, wit, humor, pathos, logic, imagination, an impressive presence, a thrilling voice. He must be painter and poet, dramatist and orator. In his brain must flame the torch of reason" (To Mr. D. Rohan, Feb. 7, 1897, *Letters*, 212). No better description could be written of his own performance.

Occasionally on the road and at home Ingersoll was able to indulge his loves of the theater, music, and good company. One night after the theater a few friends gathered at the Ingersoll home and Anton Seidl, conductor of the New York Philharmonic, played Wagner on the piano. On the morrow Ingersoll expressed thanks. "Your presence charmed and honored us all, we felt that the impersonation of music in its highest, deepest, intensest, and most perfect form was with us. We know that the Master was present" (April 2, 1897, *Letters*, 452). The next day he was writing thanks again, this time to Harrison Grey Fiske, who had given the Ingersolls tickets to Mrs. Fiske's performance of *Tess*. "We were all overpowered last night. Mrs. Fiske was marvelous. Her acting was perfect. Every tone, every gesture was pathetic, dramatic, artistic, tragic, and even her laughter was filled with tears." He did think, though, that perhaps the ending was a little weak. Ingersoll offered a few Shakespearean phrases for Tess to utter to heighten the pathos as she was being led to her doom (*Letters*, 434).

While vacationing in the summer Ingersoll kept a finger on the pulse of the nation and spoke out when he felt that words might do some good. His friend Charles Broadway Rouss, the blind merchant, who in his perpetual darkness cried "Good! Good!" or "Beautiful!" or "How true!" at higher moments in Ingersoll's lectures, had sent him an account of the dedication of a monument to the Confederate dead. Ingersoll responded on a note of reconciliation. He was the determinist and the patriot with charity for all. "People who are in a real sense philosophers know that individuals and nations act as they must." It is foolish to question the sincerity of men who are willing to give their lives for a cause. "The past is beyond change. Let us live for the present and the future. Our country was divided and the division was necessary. It is now one, and I believe that there are patriots enough under the flag to keep it so. Long life to the Republic! Long life to you!" (*Winchester Times*, June 16, 1897).

A major strike for higher wages and shorter hours was raging in the bituminous coal fields of western Pennsylvania, Ohio, Indiana, and Illinois. Ingersoll proclaimed his support for the strikers. Their living conditions were intolerable. It would be easy to determine how much the miners needed for wholesome food, decent clothing, rent, and the care of their families. The employers denying such a wage were not civilized. "I do not blame the miners for striking. They must strike or starve. All I blame them for is for not acting together. Every miner in the United States should strike, and then if they demanded only the reasonable they would succeed" (*New York Evening World*, July 16, 1897). (In the end the miners prevailed on every demand.)

The newspapers were telling of the triumphant progress of the New York Philharmonic in Europe. A letter of congratulation to Seidl was obviously in order. "We clapped our hands and shouted 'Bravo.' We, the Browns, the Farrells, the Ingersolls, raised the roof. We kept our eyes on you in London, at Bayreuth. We kept our ears open and we heard the marvelous melodies—the divine harmonies—the floods and tempest and passions and we saw the many colored domes as you played Parsifal and Tristan" (July 27, 1897, *Letters*, 453).

On November 25, 1897, in Chicago Ingersoll introduced his "Thanksgiving Sermon." The "Sermon" was developed from previous short pieces into a forty-eight-page argument on whom to thank for what on Thanksgiving Day. Man had progressed from savagery to civilization. He owed nothing to the church, which had resisted the pursuit of knowledge and better conditions, preaching the vanity of earthly things and persecuting the real benefactors of mankind. He owed nothing to the monstrous God of the Bible, since it was Nature itself that inflicted pain with floods, diseases, and so forth. The inventors of pins and matches did a thousand times more good for humanity than all the founders and ministers of religion. "I thank Humboldt and Helmholtz, and Haeckel and Buchner. I thank Lamarck and Darwin—Darwin, who revolutionized the thought of the intellectual world. I thank Huxley and Spencer. I thank scientists one and all." He thanked "the heroes whose dungeons became shrines—the heroes whose blood made scaffolds sacred—the heroes, the apostles of reason, the disciples of truth, the soldiers of freedom—the heroes who held high the holy torch and filled the world with light. With all my heart I thank them all" (*Works*, IV, 208).

In the fall 1897 Ingersoll began a series of lectures through several states in the eastern half of the country. He spoke on a variety of his familiar themes—"Truth," "How to Reform Mankind," "Liberty," "The Bible," "Why I Am An Agnostic," and sometimes Lincoln or Shakespeare—averaging about two lectures a week, changing the subject almost every time from city to city, and delivering at each place his usual full-measure of Ingersollisms for nearly two hours. An Ingersoll appearance had become a standard community experience, a *déjà vu* event, the participants frozen in time, so to speak—the ministers and their faithful parishioners distressed and obstructive, the crowds streaming into the meeting halls, the spellbinder perhaps slower a bit in speech and movement but still the inimitable purveyor of Ingersollism, the reporters excited by the lectures and interviews and looking over their shoulders at their publishers.

Change the names of places and the newspaper accounts could have been written in any large city. In Detroit: "Col. Robert G. Intersoll faced an audience that filled every part of the Empire Theater when he stepped upon the stage at 8 o'clock to tell why he is an agnostic. Men conspicuous in professional and commercial circles were present with their families, and altogether in point of wealth and learning it was a fine audience and one that in part at least was in sympathy with the famous orator, judged by the frequent outbursts of hand clapping" (News, Nov. 22, 1897). In Chicago: "He held a *levee*, which was constantly augmented. Cards came up in stacks and no caller was turned away" (Chronicle, Nov. 25, 1897).

"The Colonel is a bit depleted in avoirdupois as he approaches his three score years and five, but his wit is iridescent as ever. Always willing to answer questions about anything" (Cincinnati Enquirer, Nov. 12, 1897). But there were limits of endurance even for him. "Now you see," he pleaded in a hotel lobby, "my daughter has rung for the elevator. If you will fire away at me with your questions I will say yes and no to them until the elevator door is open to receive us." When that happened Ingersoll said, "I like the newspaper men and am always glad to see them. Good night," and the Ingersolls disappeared (New Haven Palladium, Oct. 20, 1897).

What did the reporters learn? In Grand Rapids: What did he think of the political situation? He felt that the Republican party was on the biggest wave, with the tide running its way and the wind with the tide. The unemployed and discontented were going back to protection and prosperity. "The furnaces will be filled with fire and the chimneys with smoke and the pockets of the people with money" (Herald, Oct. 16, 1897). In New Haven: Would the coming New York City election have a national bearing? "Ha! Ha! Bless you, no. Not any more than the rotting of a codfish in Glocester." What about the big registration? It indicated interest, not a trend. "Of course, it gives you boys something to write about, eh!" Seth Low was a good man but Ingersoll would vote for his friend General Tracy, "an out-and-out Republican, and so am I" (Palladium, Oct. 20, 1897). In St. Louis: What did he think of the Cuban situation? The United States should recognize the belligerency or independence of Cuba, and drive the Spanish patrols off the seas. "There is no danger of a war between the United States and Spain. A country that cannot whip Cuba had better let the United States alone. We are in no more danger of a war with Spain than we are of being overrun by the Esquimaux [sic]" (New Orleans Times Democrat, Nov. 10, 1897, quoted from St. Louis interview).

In Cincinnati: What did he think of the McKinley administration so far? He liked it. "I think McKinley a careful, sensible, and safe man. He will do nothing in pyrotechnics—nothing for display. I want him to take decided action in favor of Cuba, and I think he will." What did he think of the future of silver? "It will go into spoons, forks, yachting cups, teapots, urns, statuary, and small change." Whom did he consider the greatest

Americans? In the realm of invention—Edison. The best actress in modern plays was Minnie Maddern Fiske. The best poet, among blacks, was Paul Lawrence Dunbar. "I am not certain about the rest." Had the Sermon on the Mount ever been equalled as a human production? "Oh, often, many times over. Some of it is good, and some of it silly, laughable. The best of it has been said often before" (*Enquirer*, Nov. 14, 1897).

In Detroit: What did he think of the Rev. H. S. McCowan of the People's Church inviting Emma Goldman to speak in his pulpit? Ingersoll replied that all anarchists were crazy and should be confined as lunatics. To hang them would be to make them martyrs and to promote their cause. Like Emma Goldman, society believed in self-defense, but, unlike Miss Goldman, he held that imperfect government should be improved, not destroyed. The trouble with marriage, an institution that Miss Goldman would abolish, was not in the institution but in the folks who were not civilized. "Love does a great deal of harm, but we do not wish to abolish love, because it is the source of nearly all there is of happiness." Reverend McCowan was "a courageous, honest, and hospitable man." He had done no harm. "The people who heard Miss Goldman know how idiotic are her ideas" (Correspondent for *Topeka State Journal*, Nov. 24, 1897). In Chicago: What did he think of vegetarianism? He did not approve of killing animals, but he recognized that he was inconsistent in eating them after they were killed by somebody else. Personal plans? "I never was in better health. I shall stay here two days. I will not attend a football game because I do not like feats of strength." What might he say on Thanksgiving, on which he was scheduled to speak in the Auditorium? Wait and see—but "I think the people have some cause for gladness that Mr. Cleveland's administration is ended and Major McKinley's is a year old" (*Times Herald*, Nov. 24, 1897). The Auditorium was a mammoth structure, and a storm was sweeping the city, so some of the expected audience stayed home. "Yesterday, the weather was awful—same today. Had a fair house—$2500 gross" (Nov. 25, 1897, To his daughters, L.C.).

In January 1898 Ingersoll began a series of lectures through the South, New England, and the Midwest. He was back to the marathon pace of his prime; no missionary ever labored with more devotion. He pounded out his message full steam almost every evening to a different crowd. Starting out in the South Ingersoll made substantial gains in confronting the animus of the establishment there. In Atlanta the papers were hostile but not the people. Of Atlanta he wrote to his daughters: "I had a fair audience and the people were very enthusiastic and applauded the most radical things. The papers here are orthodox—narrow, bigoted, provincial, and devout. They think they know their readers but I think the readers are far more liberal than they are" (Atlanta, Jan. 25, 1898, L.C.). A local freethinker enthused about Ingersoll and magnified the crowd: "We have had an intellectual feast. Colonel Ingersoll lectured here on Jan. 25 to a large and appreciative audience. The night was cold and wet, but he had a full house just the same. The lecture was just such a one as was needed in these moral diggings. The Colonel did the church people up in good style" (Quoted in *Truth Seeker*, Feb. 19, 1898). Callers at the hotel suite poured in and out *en masse* incessantly. "Some—many of the best people in the town—called on us and the rooms were so full all day that we could hardly get time to eat" (To daughters, Savannah, Jan. 28, 1898, L.C.). The suite, reserved and decorated in advance on orders from their New York friend, Dr. Bell, was filled with flowers and had on one wall a banner inscribed in big red letters "Love is the only bow on life's dark cloud" (Jan. 29, 1898, L.C.).

In New Orleans it was easy to believe that almost everybody in town was an Ingersollian. Speaker and audience were in perfect harmony. "No man can be paid a higher compliment," said the *Picayune* (Jan. 31) "than was to be found in the personnel of the vast audience which last night listened to Robert G. Ingersoll."

A man familiar with New Orleans could glance over the audience and see hundreds of faces prominent in all the walks of life here. . . . It was a composite of rare intelligence, ranging from butterfly society to men and women of weight and character and force. It was possibly an audience of more eager attentiveness than ever greeted the great Booth on his greatest night. Not a word was lost. So anxious was the concourse to catch every word that fell from the orator's lips that the audience was impatient at the enthusiasm. It could not repress and cried down its own applause every time it burst forth, fearing that the speaker would begin again before the applause had quite subsided.

A women's rights convention one thousand strong was being held in the hotel and the Ingersolls were invited to attend. Surely he would be asked to make a speech. What could he say? That women were entitled to equal rights plus the right to be protected? That men were oaks, women vines, children blossoms? That was not exactly what the partisans of Mrs. Stanton and Miss Anthony had in mind. The Ingersolls gracefully declined, as they had bought tickets for the theater (To his daughters, Feb. 1, 1898, L.C.). When, however, he was invited to address the Press Club he consented. In his brief remarks he praised the press as the destroyer of ignorance and provincialism and the Sunday newspaper as a relief from the old-time Sabbath observance. He disapproved of sensational crime stories as promoting crime and prying into private affairs. "I have no complaint to lodge on my own behalf, for I have no private affairs" (*Works*, XII, 210). "I do not know that I have anything else to say except that I wish you all good luck and sunshine and prosperity, and enough of it to last you through a long life" (212).

On the prospect of war with Spain Ingersoll had been partly right. There was no likelihood that the decrepit empire would declare war on the robust young republic, but he did not envisage that the republic might declare war on the empire. The American ambassador to Spain, Stewart L. Woodford (with whom Ingersoll had once engaged in gentlemanly debate on the limits of toleration), assured President McKinley that the Spaniards were prepared to grant every essential demand of the Cuban insurgents without engaging in hostilities. To no avail. Imperial interest, yellow journalism, and moralistic zeal were sweeping the nation in a clamor for war and nothing less. President and Congress yielded to the popular demand and on April 20 war was declared. Whether or not the Spanish-American War was "a needless War" (James Ford Rhodes) or "a splendid little war" (John Hay), it was certainly a popular one. Writing their history nearly forty years later Morison and Commager could still say, "No one who lived through them will forget those gay days of 1898. With what generous ardor the young men rushed to the colors to free Cuba, while the bands crashed out the chords of Sousa's 'Stars and Stripes Forever' " (*The Growth of the American Republic*, II, 331).

On April 30 Ingersoll came to Chicago to lecture on liberty. The great city was vibrating with the national fever. Although the nation was hardly holding its breath in expectation of his pronouncements, the local press corps—the *Chronicle*, the *Times Herald*, the *Inter-Ocean*, the *Tribune*—made a beeline to their oracle. Ingersoll was ready, as usual. He waved the star-spangled banner against the regime of bigotry and tyranny. He denounced Spain as a bankrupt nation of bullfights and superstition, matadors and priests, perpetrating cruelty and persecution through the ages that culminated in the atrocities in Cuba. Until there was an international tribunal to adjudicate international disputes force must be met with force, evil with justice. "I never was as proud of this great republic as I am now." The outcome was certain: America had greater resources than Spain, and the other European nations were too occupied with their own problems to interfere. Every citizen should be willing to carry his equal burden in the war. Should women serve as nurses in the army? "No, I think that men are better nurses for men" (*Truth Seeker*, May 21, 1898, composite of interviews).

In his lecture that evening Ingersoll departed from his text to drape his most fervid rhetoric upon the Cuban revolution and the American response. "Oppressed, assassinated, starved, Cuba fell on her knees and stretched out her hands towards the great republic, imploring aid. We looked at her pallid face and form wasted by famine, and anger moved us to redress a wrong. The great republic drew the sword of war and said to Spain, Take your hands from the throat of this victim. Your flag shall no longer pollute the air of the western hemisphere." He blessed the war against Spain as "the first war declared on earth by human beings for the salvation of humanity." It was "the holiest of all wars" (*Truth Seeker*, May 21). That was what the crowd wanted to hear, they burst into full roar. In the audience was Franklin Steiner, a prominent freethinker, who marvelled at the sheer commerical success of the lecture. "Contrary to my expectations (for the excitement over the war was intense), he had McVicker's Theatre full. What man on the American platform can command the crowds at the price. A generation has grown to maturity since he startled the world with his eloquence. Other lecturers on different subjects have come and gone, but he remains fresh, vigorous, and more popular than ever" (*Truth Seeker*, July 9, 1898).

While in Chicago Ingersoll was extolling the struggle of bleeding Cuba, in far-off Manila Bay Admiral Dewey was smashing to rubble the ancient Spanish fleet without losing a single American. Ingersoll waxed ecstatic. "Just read of the great victory by Dewey—it gave me hysteria. Good! Grand! Glorious!!! It looks as though the war was about over—Poor Spain!" (*Chicago*, May 1, 1898, L.C.).

As the war sped along to its foregone conclusion, the nation was at loggerheads over what was to be done with the Spanish possessions. Naturally Ingersoll joined the discussion. He had definite, positive ideas. The war was fought for freedom, so the settlement must be for freedom. This meant that Cuba should be, as promised, free, but that America should hold onto the Philippines for the benefit of the Filipinos. It was our duty to civilize them, not with preachers but with teachers, not with churches but with schools. It had been said that the Constitution did not allow for holding colonies or dependencies when there was little prospect of their becoming states of the Union. The same argument had been made against the acquisition of Louisiana, Florida, the Mexican territories, Alaska, and Hawaii, each of which had enriched the nation. He had never revered the Constitution completely. If that document stood in the way, change it. "It is a very easy matter to make a constitution, and no human happiness, no prosperity, no progress should be sacrificed for a piece of paper with writing on it, because there is plenty of paper and plenty of men to do the writing, and plenty of people to say what the writing stands for." The Philippines would ultimately be free, Puerto Rico should permanently belong to us, and in due time Cuba would come in voluntarily. Looking ahead, the United States must always be friends with England, our natural partner. "I think that the Englishspeaking people are to rule this world" (*Truth Seeker*, Aug. 27, 1898; *Works*, XII, 273).

By November the nation was in the mood for celebration. The Lotos Club in New York gave a banquet in honor of Rear Admiral Schley, who had commanded the operations at the battle of Santiago de Cuba that duplicated Dewey's feat in Manila Bay. All day the admiral's two-star pennant hung and fluttered outside the club on Fifth Avenue, and in the evening some three hundred military officers and prominent citizens, including Stewart L. Woodford and Captain Alfred T. Mahan (the famous advocate for sea power) gathered for the festivity. The dining room was decorated with the Stars and Stripes and the company received a souvenir menu embellished with images of signal pennants and the admiral's flagship

the *Brooklyn*. Speeches were made. Lotos Club President Carpenter introduced Ingersoll: "Gentlemen, we come now to one of our fellow-members,
a dear old fellow-member, who doesn't come here quite as often as he
should, but when he does come we place him among the clergy and
the others. Now, if you please, we will place him in the pulpit. I call
on Col. Robert G. Ingersoll." Ingersoll began, "Mr. President, Gentlemen
of the Club—Boys" and proceded to tell funny stories, swelling with pride
at belonging to the great Anglo-Saxon race that was whipping Spain.
He lauded Dewey and Schley for achieving the most wonderful naval
victories of all time, Anglo-Saxon triumphs of courage. He ridiculed the
fallen foe and his religion. "The Spaniards sprinkled the holy water on
their guns, then banged away and left it to the Holy Ghost to direct
the rest. I thank Admiral Schley for having enriched my country, for
having added a little to my own height, to my own pride, so that I utter
the word *American* with a little more unction than I ever did before, and
the old flag looks a little brighter, better, and has added glory" (The Ingersoll
of the Spanish–American War was typical of most of his fellow citizens—
a super-patriot, an ultra-American, even a racist) (*Times*, Nov. 27, 1898;
Works, XII, 18).

To his lecture offerings for 1898-1899 Ingersoll added a new topic,
superstition. This lecture is a synthesis of Ingersollisms from the viewpoint
of the supernatural. He defined superstition as belief without evidence.
Everyone was prone to superstition. Primitive men were frightened by
hostile events in nature, and the clergy arose, professing a mission to
intervene with the powers behind nature. In religious dogma good and
bad angels vied for the mastery of mankind, and belief in evil angels,
in the devil and his cohorts, was the foundation of Christianity. Ingersoll
described the mystery of life in rhythm and imagery: "We watch the
flow and ebb of life and death—the great drama that forever holds the
stage where players act their parts and disappear; the great drama in
which all must act—ignorant and learned, idiotic and insane—without
rehearsal and without the slightest knowledge of a part, or of any plot
or purpose in the play." Popes, cardinals, bishops, priests, monks, nuns,
friars, and saints were enemies of education and freedom and had brought
darkness where they had prevailed—to Spain, Italy, and Portugal in
particular. Men had wasted their lives in studying the Bible, as they could
not agree on what it means.

There is little humor in "Superstition," but there has to be some in
almost every Ingersoll production (except funeral orations), something to
bring the matter down to earth. He laughed at believers in the literal
inerrancy of the Bible. "They are like the janitor of an apartment house
who refused to rent a flat to a gentleman because he said he had children.
'But,' said the gentlemen, 'my children are both married and live in Iowa.'
'That makes no difference,' said the janitor. 'I am not allowed to rent a
flat to any man who has children' " (*Works*, IV, 373). He derided selective

thanksgiving to God, no matter who was saying thanks. "Only a few days ago our President by proclamation thanked God for giving us the victory at Saratoga. He did not thank him for sending the yellow fever" (324).

Science was the real redeemer, savior, and hope for mankind.

> It will put honesty above hypocrisy, mental veracity above all belief. It will teach the religion of usefulness. It will destroy bigotry in all its forms. It will put thoughtful doubt above thoughtless faith. It will give us philosophers, thinkers, and savants, instead of priests, theologians, and saints. It will abolish poverty and crime, and greater and nobler than all else it will make the whole world free. (399)

In the last series of lectures of his life, beginning in Cleveland on October 8, 1898, Ingersoll showed that he could still attract and charm the large crowds as of yore. Orthodox ministers tried to bury him prematurely; The Truth Seeker rejoiced in his continuing success. "The halls are more than filled at every town, and at Cleveland some six hundred were turned away. . . . The indications are that the people desire to hear the 'corpse' and the ministers who have been assuring their flocks that Colonel Ingersoll's popularity is waning are invited to make note of it for future reference" (Jan. 21, 1899). Hailing his visit in advance the Chicago Tribune said, "Col. Ingersoll is perhaps the best known man in the United States. He is liked by everyone, he is a whole-souled, genial, homeloving gentleman, and in Chicago where he will lecture tomorrow evening in the Columbian Theater every seat is already sold." However, the inroads of time could not be denied. "The colonel is advancing in years, although he is hale and hearty, and it is not unlikely that this will be his last season on the lecture platform." The paper also observed that ticket prices had been reduced to seventy-five cents and fifty cents for the orchestra, fifty cents for the balcony, twenty-five cents for the gallery (Oct. 25, 1898).

The reporter in Toledo mused on the Ingersoll phenomenon. People of all classes and ages had poured into the meeting hall, sitting in some tension at one another's unfamiliar company as they waited for "a man whose name is, perhaps, as widely known in Christendom as that of any other personage living or dead." The tension dissolved and the crowd was as one as the speaker stepped out from the flies. He bowed to the welcoming ovation and walked briskly to center stage, notes in hand. He beamed at the audience through his glasses and without ado began, "What is superstition? Superstition is the child of ignorance and the mother of misery." He cracked a joke; the surprised audience guffawed and giggled; he paused, chuckled, and went on. There were recurrent passages of sentimentality. He refered to the birds, the flowers, music, and the sweetness of human love. Here a minister listened deep in thought, there a minister looked angry. Most of the audience was enthralled, "supremely satisfied," and through it all ran the thought (the reporter's thought?)

"it was all delivered at so much per" (*Bee,* Jan. 15, 1899).

On January 21 Ingersoll arrived in Kansas City. It happened to be a day after the death of a friend of olden times, Mrs. Mary Bowman, whose husband had shared law offices with Ingersoll in Shawneetown nearly fifty years before. Ingersoll sent flowers and spoke at the cemetery. "This is a time when we can weep with those who held her dearest, for their loss is our loss, and one of the flowers which make the world sweeter and brighter will be hidden away when all is done today" (*Truth Seeker,* Feb. 11, 1899).

His friend and ally Dr. Roberts had left Unitarianism and started a Church of This World. On the twenty-second Dr. Roberts preached a sermon at the Coates Opera House on "The Sign of the Cross," how Christianity had transformed the gentle and forgiving Jesus into an instrument of judgment and eternal pain. That evening, speaking on "Superstition," Ingersoll concluded an attack on the churches,

> But I believe I can detect the faint dawning of light in utter darkness. Today I listened to a sermon. I do not often listen to a sermon, but I listened to one today here in this place. I heard and in the faces of the intelligent audience present I saw a newborn tolerance of thought and of intelligence and of fact. I was delighted. I was listening to Dr. Roberts of the Church of This World. . . . The Church of This World is the best and most enlightened church in this country today. Dr. Roberts is the greatest man that stands in the pulpit in this country today. [A moment of silence and then scattered "wildest applause."] (*Truth Seeker,* Feb. 11, 1899, from the *Kansas City Times*)

In "Superstition" Ingersoll had said that belief in the Devil was the keystone of the arch of Christianity. Some ministers responded that the devil of Scripture was not a real being but a personification of evil. In what was to be his last standard public lecture, "The Devil," Ingersoll answered his answerers. Tracing the origin of belief in devils to prebiblical times he said that Scripture was clear that it was the devil in the shape of a serpent that tempted Adam and Eve into the Fall of Man. If the serpent in the Garden was not the real devil, were Adam and Eve real? When Christ was reported as driving deaf and dumb devils out of the body of a man, was it to be supposed that these devils did not have other physical characteristics? Ingersoll had no kindness or courtesy for the personification argument. "Any clergyman who can read the Bible and then say that devils are personifications of evil is himself a personi-fication of stupidity or hypocrisy" (*Works,* IV, 400). He was further outraged at how Christian doctrine disposed of infants who died without baptism. "These babies were pure as Pity's tears, innocent as their mother's loving smiles, and yet the makers of creeds believed and taught that leering, unclean fiends inhabited their dimpled flesh. Oh, the unsearchable riches of Christianity!" (396). Like an eighteenth century *philosophe* he asked why the devil caused the Crucifixion when he knew that it would lead to the salvation of man and why he undertook from his arch-enemy God the assignment to torture the damned in hell. In the brain of science there was no room for devils. "No man of sense in the whole world believes in devils any more than he does in mermaids, vampires, gorgons, hydras, naiads, dryads, nymphs, fairies, the Fountain of Youth, the Philosopher's Stone, Perpetual Motion, or Fiat Money" (402).

A valedictory tone pervades "The Devil." It was time to restate fundamentals. He had been charged with fighting a man of straw. No, he had been fighting a real substantial force, "the Supernatural—the dogma of inspiration—the belief in devils—the atonement, salvation by faith— the forgiveness of sins and the savagery of eternal pain" (406). The real man of straw stood in the pulpit beside the preacher, holding in his upraised hand a club, the "creed," his menacing shadow falling upon the open Bible. This man of straw silenced Professor Briggs, Professor Smith, Father McGlyn, Professor Swing, and Reverand Thomas, blocking liberalization of the Presbyterian Creed. If the cruel and absurd dogmas of the New Testament could be eliminated, how wonderful it would be to believe that the remainder is true, that God existed and loved humanity. "To know that the loved ones dead are not lost; that they still live and love and wait for you. To know that Christ dispelled the darkness of death and filled the grave with eternal light. To know this would be all that the heart could bear. Beyond this joy could not go" (413).

"The Devil" concludes with the *Declaration of the Free,* eighteen sestets expressing the creed of reason. The Declaration does not resonate like *The Rubaiyat* or Tennyson's *In Memoriam* or even some passages in Ingersoll's lectures. It is a forthright statement of ideas. Those whose minds were free lived lives without falsehood, without belief in God, Hell, or the devil. They accepted the possibility that life may end in a dreamless sleep. They had no masters on the land and no king in the air. They regarded cyclones and earthquakes as acts of fate without purpose, thought, or plan. Life was joyous and free. They rejoiced in love's sacred flame, friendship's glow, and the miracles of art. They believed that the hands that help were better than the lips that prayed. In the last stanza, perhaps the most imaginative, Ingersoll still retained for himself a glimmer of hope—not faith but hope—in Immortality.

> Is there beyond the silent night
>   An endless day?
> Is death a door that leads to light?
>   We cannot say.
> The tongueless secret locked in fate
>   We do not know, we hope and wait.

Ingersoll kept up a heavy flow of correspondence with his family, the most important people in his life. From day to day there was very little to report to Maud and Eva, but he had to write and they had to read—his letters were a lifeline of love on both sides. "Well, Goodbye, I am going to bed—then will take a cold bath—dress, smoke, and lecture—and think of you" (Savannah, Jan. 28, 1898, L.C.). His lectures lost nothing in being delivered again and again even though he hardly shared the enthusiasm that he inspired. "Nothing wonderful happening. We go along the same every day—lecture—go to bed—get up—eat, pack the trunk—take the train—so it is over and over" (Paris, Tex., Feb. 12, 1898, L.C.). Trains still ran true to form—elegant but uncomfortable and boring—and Ingersoll's rides were frequently all day or all night, likely as not starting at the crack of dawn or at midnight, with failed connections, delays, and tedious layovers. "Here we are waiting for the train to Taylorville. We got up this morning at a quarter to six—left at 7:30—arrived here at 9:00 and here we have to wait until 4—So, you see, we are having a good time" (Decatur, Ill., March 19, 1899, Carbondale). The hotels in the small towns were hardly more than plain farm houses. In one there was no facility for a bath: "A day without a bath is wasted—a dead loss" (Fitchburg, Mass., Feb. 23, 1899, Carbondale). Conditions were even worse in another: "No bath—bed that sinks in the middle—pillows the size of pin-cushions—towels as large as postage stamps—soap made of wax and sand—Everything first class" (St. Louis, Mo., March 12, 1899, L.C.). However, such tribulations were usually forgotten in the general hubbub of popular acclaim. "The people are exceedingly hospitable and they seem really glad to see us. My lecture is the talk of the town" (New Orleans, La., L.C.). Hostile ministers were amusing rather than disturbing. In Marion, Ohio, alerted by advance publicity, "the Christians" arranged for afternoon and evening services by Moody on the same day. "Those who heard him in the afternoon came to hear me in the evening. We met a good many pleasant people" (Ft. Wayne, Ind., Dear Girls, April 30, 1898, Carbondale). In Carlinville, Illinois, the ministers persuaded the newspaper to refuse all Ingersoll advertisements (Carlinville, Ill., Jan. 14, 1899, L.C.). As lecturing was his business, Ingersoll assayed the size of crowds—fine, grand, good, or fair. Noting the small audience at Williamsport, Pennsylvania, for his lecture on Shakespeare he remarked, "The Life and Adventure of Genl. Tom Thumb would be a better subject—nearer to their thoughts" (March 21, 1898, L.C.).

Other relatives were not overlooked. Two new persons had joined the family—Eva Brown's children Eva and Robbie, upon whom the grandparents doted. The elder Ingersolls enjoyed the drawings and scribbled expressions of love from their grandchildren. Never a man in a hurry, Ingersoll found time on the road to write long, loving letters to Eva and Robbie, who were too young to apprehend the messages without help from older people. From Hot Springs he said that he and Grandma were glad for their love and would soon be telling them about their travels "over the prairies and bridges and through the forests and the towns and cities." It was a beautiful day "and Grandma and I are going to take a walk. The sun is shining and the sky is blue as Robbie's eyes and as bright as Eva's smile." When they all got together he would give them baked apples and "lots" of whipped cream (Feb. 16, 1898, Carbondale, 72). He gave special attention to his older brother John, the physician in rural Wisconsin. Congratulating John on reaching the age of seventy-four he said, "Well, keep on—hang to the willows. When the limbs break grab the roots. I am going to stay just as long as I can." He was glad that John was going to take some whiskey as a stimulant and sent him ten dollars for it, quoting a friend, "There is no bad whiskey, but some is better" (Oct. 23, 1897, *Letters*, 588). Later he sent John some of his own strychnine and nitroglycerine tablets, to take one after each meal. "Well, dear brother, do take care of yourself. Eat eggs. Eat bacon, drink milk, and take a cup of coffee in the morning" (Dec. 1, 1897, *Letters*, 589). (It is hard to tell who was the older, who the younger, who the doctor, who the patient.)

A bird of a different feather was Mrs. Clinton Farrell, née Sue Parker, Mrs. Ingersoll's sister. One shouldn't patronize her! She was always correcting her famous brother-in-law on public issues. He thought she deserved one of his epistolary gems, and he let her have it.

Dear Sue,
Clint says that you are not very well. Let me beg of you to take the world easy. You see that you had on your back the Spanish war all summer—and that was quite a load. Then you had to manage the Army and Navy and that increased the burden. Besides you had to feed the soldiers—give medicine to the sick—run the hospitals and superintend transportation. In addition to all this you had to keep McKinley straight. Now you have the treaty to ratify and peace to make with the Filipinos and Cubans. This is too much for a young woman suffering from nervous prostration. Then you have looked after the churches and preachers, the Dreyfus case, and the German Emperor. May I beg of you to take a rest and let the world drift—your mind is too active—you think and work too much. Go to sleep for my sake. If you wake, turn over and go to sleep again—then take another nap—lay down, stretch, and drift off again—I love you and I love you *well*. Read this and go to sleep.
Yours always,
Robert
(Champaign, Ill., Jan. 25, 1899, L.C.)

The *Weltschmerz* at the core of his being recurred; life ended in dusty death. There was no balm in Gilead. His son-in-law Walston Brown had lost a brother. "I know just how you feel, for I have gazed upon a brother's pallid face. . . . Well, we are all hurrying on the last step—to the silence" (May 29, 1898, *Letters*, 592). On a rainy day in Chicago he had a rare moment of solitude and his mind wandered back to his father's deathbed in the long ago, thirty-seven years in the past, to his integrity and sad life (The Girls, May 1, 1898, *Letters*, 592). When his brother John died, Ingersoll wrote a bitter-sweet letter to John's daughter Mary. "He whom you so dearly loved—if conscious—would wish you to be happy now. Death seems terrible, frightful, awful, and yet if there were no death, there would be no love. The fear, the certainty of loss feeds and makes sacred the flame of love. Every life is a tragedy, and we know what the end must be." He gave her some practical advice: "Get interested in the little things of life. Write some every day—read a little. Talk with your neighbors—keep the horror out of your heart. Well, goodbye. I love you, Robert" (July 1, 1898, *Letters*, 593). His New Year's greeting (and he would not live the new year out) was cheerless: "My dear Dr. Bell: This is the end of the year. The last sad grains of sand have reached the desert of the past. Today the cradle—tomorrow the coffin—a tear and a smile" (Dec. 31, 1898, *Letters*, 421).

Ingersoll and his friend Dr. Bell—Dr. Ralcey Husted Bell—would soon have another cause for melancholy. In the summer of 1897 Ingersoll had a long courtesy session at the White House with President McKinley and in the fall his nephew John, Clark's son, was appointed consul at Copenhagen (*New York Sun,* July 29, Oct. 10, 1897). Dr. Bell also aspired to a consulship and Ingersoll did his best to help him. On March 10, Ingersoll reported to Dr. Bell that he had met again with the president, that the president had given him a card instructing Secretary Day of the State Department to place Dr. Bell. Secretary Day, in his presence, had summoned the Chief of Consular Service, who said that there was no current vacancy worth anything and so Day promised Dr. Bell the next vacancy worth $1500-$2000 (L.C.). In May 1899 Ingersoll informed Dr. Bell that there was a vacancy in Valencia; was he interested? He was, and Ingersoll applied for the appointment, probably quoting optimistically from Matthew, "Ask and it shall be given you." But Matthew was wrong. On May 8, Secretary John Hay, who had succeeded Day, sent Ingersoll the bad news: The president had given the Valencia post to somebody else. Hay squirmed to soften the blow. "The text you quote reads in the revised version, 'Ask and you shall receive information.' I have been here seven months and have never yet been able to do anything for a friend—and I do not know when this lack of ability has annoyed me as much as it has today" (L.C.). Again, and for the last time, though not for himself but for a friend, Ingersoll had a golden apple from the political Hesperides in his grasp when it was snatched out of his hand.

From summer 1898 to summer 1899 Ingersoll lectured extensively in the eastern half of the country as only part of his activity. Nothing could stop his absorption in the problems of the nation and the world. (His satiric portrayal of his sister-in-law could apply to himself.) He was at the beck and call of any cause that interested him. In spring 1899 news got around that he would be the first speaker at a fund-raising entertainment for actors' relief and soon the Fifth Avenue Theater was packed to the doors as "the special star" arose (*The World*, March 24, 1899). He was the strewer of flowers, the master of pathos. Everyone, he said, was a traveler on the street, in the train, or on the ship, all doomed to be struck down by Death, the inevitable assassin. The people of the theater gave us a better world, where mirth held carnival, villains failed, and virtue was its own rich reward. Shouldn't the children of the stage be helped when wreaths fade, leaves fall, and "failure sadly sups on memory"? And when they die there should be friends "to lay their breathless forms away and on the graves dump flowers jeweled with the tears of love." The lesson of this meeting was the lesson of usefulness. "The hands that help are holier than the lips that pray" (*Works*, XII, 204). In May he spoke for the Paine Bust Fund and gave a benefit lecture ("Liberty") for the relief of sick and indigent veterans and their families.

During the year Ingersoll wrote some notable nonlecture pieces. The *Boston Investigator* solicited his views on "What Would You Substitute for the Bible as a Moral Guide?" In their June second number he argued that a sound morality could not be based on supernatural authority and the jumbled records of primitive people but rather on a rational inquiry into human needs and the conditions for happiness. "What then is or can be called a moral guide? The shortest possible answer is one word: Intelligence" (*Works*, XI, 543). In the spring of 1899 Governor Rollins of New Hampshire issued a Fast Day proclamation exhorting the people to resist the decline of religious belief and the loss of its restraining influence. Ingersoll applauded the decline and the loss. No intelligent modern person, he said, could believe in Christian orthodoxy. He was particularly scathing on the vicarious atonement. "The old belief that he was actually God—that he sacrificed himself unto himself—that he deserted himself; that he bore the burden of his own wrath; that he made it possible to save a few of his children by shedding his own blood; that he could not forgive the sins of men until they murdered him— this frightful belief is slowly dying day by day." And how did the restraining influences of religion work when salvation by faith exonerated the sinning believer and sends the virtuous unbeliever to hell? The restraints of religion had brought darkness to strongly religious countries, "reduced Spain to a guitar, Italy to a hand organ, and Ireland to exile" (*Works*, XI, 555).

Ingersoll and De Witt Talmage contributed Memorial Day messages to the *New York World*. Ingersoll's war fever had abated. He thanked Dewey and Schley, and supported the investigation of food management and medical treatment in the armed services, but could not estimate whether the victory was worth the price. He mourned for the heroic dead: "On Memorial Day our hearts will blossom in gratitude as we lovingly re- member the brave men upon whose brows death with fleshless hands placed the laurel wreath of fame." Talmage prayed that there be no more war and that the Spanish government "be scourged and hung up for the world's indignation" for its "high crimes against God and humanity."

Ingersoll kept up his extensive correspondence. A friend invited him to an evening of billiards. Sorry, he could not accept; he had to be in Boston. Billiards, billiards, did they not symbolize the human experience? "The fact is that the whole world is a table, we are the balls, and Fate plays the game. We are knocked and whacked against each other—followed and drawn—whirled and twisted—pocketed and spotted, and all the time we think that we are doing the playing. But no matter, we feel that we are in the game and a real good illusion is after all, it may be, the only reality that we know." And what kind of player was that Fate that controls us? He believed that "Fate is a careless player—that he is always a little nervous and generally forgets to chalk his cue. I know that he has made lots of misses with me" (To Mr. Ranney, Feb. 17, 1899, *Letters*, 595). A neighbor had sent him a box of cigars. He lit one, felt good, and was grateful; he had a friend and was not forgotten. Tobacco meant the pipe of peace, the essence and aroma of friendship.

> Tobacco is social. It has in it the clasp of comradeship—the soul of confidence. It is a medium of mental exchange. The doctors say that it shortens life. But the longer life is without it, the worse it is. The preachers say that its use is wicked. The only reason they have for saying so is that it gives us joy. For my part I had rather smoke one cigar than hear two sermons. In fact I had rather chew "green twist" than read the best chapter in Leviticus. [His memory drifted back to "the dear, dear departed days" of boyhood, when the old women smoked pipes at the fireplace.] But whether smoking shortens life or not, whether it puts my soul in peril or not, I send you a thousand thanks for the box of temptations—temptations from which my sincere prayer is not to be delivered. I love temptations. (To Orlando J. Smith, April 14, 1899, *Letters*, 485)

An author had sent him a copy of his book that affirmed belief in immortality. Ingersoll's response, dashed off at Walston Brown's banking office less than a month before his death, is the final distillation of his views on the subject. Complimenting the author on his rational approach and his rejection of the argument from Scripture, Ingersoll wrote that if there is a God of infinite wisdom and compassion there may be a better world than this; on the other hand, God let injustice triumph here, why not hereafter? "Certainly God will be no better then than now." There was no evidence that the world was created by wisdom or compassion or that men differ from trees in their possibility of immortality. Yet the yearning of the heart could not be entirely dismissed. "Love and hope are universal. As long as men love and as long as they hope, there will probably be in heart and brain the splendid dream of immortality." In this world "after joy comes grief, and after day comes night; and it may be there is some world where after grief comes joy, and after night comes day" (To Edward R. Johnes, June 25, 1899, *Letters*, 352).

Ingersoll did not expect that the summer of 1899 would be his last even though he knew that he had developed angina pectoris (he had not told his family, pledging the doctors to secrecy) and might die at any moment. He knew that he could put little reliance on cousin Frank Gilbert's assurance of June 19, 1898 that a "ten years' lease has been signed, sealed, and delivered" (L.C.). He would be only sixty-six in August; to all inquiries about his health he answered, "All right." He planned to visit England in the fall, not for an extended lecture tour, but to see friends on the way to the Wagner festival at Bayreuth. He hoped to be again in California. If Death was his obsession he was not afraid of it and it did not seem imminent. It was an inevitable event in the cycle of nature, of birth, growth, and decay, not to be dreaded even if hated. He could say with Shakespeare's Caesar:

> Of all the wonders that I yet have heard,
> it seems to me most strange that men should fear,
> seeing that death, a necessary end,
> will come when it will come.

Yet he could not avoid feeling that he might be at the end of the road, that it might be time to sum up. Writing to a California correspondent he lived again the good times he had when lecturing on the Pacific coast. He was glad that his friend "is as cheerful in the evening as in the morning. . . . I am beginning to think that the dusk is far better than the dawn." For himself he was satisfied. He knew that he must submit to nature and that the world went on without concern for him and his. He knew the real values of life and had pursued and enjoyed them: "To enjoy today—without regard for the loss of yesterday or fear for to-morrow—this is real philosophy and you seem to have it. Your life has been a success. You have loved and been loved. You have been blessed in wife and children—and you have lived in the heart of that perfumed place called home. That is enough. I feel that I have had my share— and so I am content" (To Mr. Holladay, July 11, 1899, L.C.). Nor had he any regrets or second thoughts about his lifelong warfare against religious orthodoxy. One correspondent had sent him compliments and good wishes on the fight and he was grateful. "You are right in thinking that I have not changed. I still believe that all religions are based on falsehoods and mistakes. I still deny the existence of the supernatural, and I still say that real religion is usefulness" (To Clinton J. Robins, July 13, 1899, *Letters*, 354).

Ingersoll's last public lecture, "What is Religion?," was delivered before the American Free Religious Association in the Hollis Street Theater, in Boston, on June 2, 1899. It is a synthesis of familiar Ingersollisms on the growth of religion. Religion, he said, arises in primitive subservi-ence to the concept of an all-powerful creator and lord of the universe amenable to propitiation or prayer. The evils of the world, in nature and in human history, proved that if there was a god he was not good or did not have the power to do good. Some modern believers said that there was a force that worked for "righteousness" and had implanted conscience in the human soul. This trend to "righteousness" was only the natural result of trial and error; conscience inhered in mankind as a natural fact. Religion had been a curse wherever it has prevailed, including our Puritan forefathers. "On the door of life they put the crepe of death" (*Works*, IV, 493). Reasoning from the indestructibility and everlastingness of force and matter, Ingersoll took the leap from agnosticism to atheism. "It follows as a necessity that no God exists." In the peroration Ingersoll called upon his audience "to forget all gods, their promises and threats, to feel within your veins life's joyous stream and hear the martial music, the rhythmic beating off your fearless heart," and to "make a palace for the soul. This is real religion. This is real worship" (507–508).

He had more to say in this last message, however, as he was still concerned about social problems. He had discovered that the root of all social disorders lay in overpopulation by what in a later age we have come to call the underclass. "The real question is, can we prevent the ignorant, the poor, the vicious from filling the world with their children?" (593). The solution was plain and simple—a voluntary stop of procreation. "Science, the only possible savior of mankind, must put it in the power of woman to decide for herself whether she will or will not become a mother" (505). Having the knowledge of preventing birth, the worthless people would of their own accord stop having children, none of whom they wanted anyhow. Then someday there would be no such people around. Then Utopia! "When that time comes, the prison walls will fall, the dungeons will be flooded with light, and the shadow of the scaffold will cease to curse the earth. Poverty and want will be childless. The withered hands of want will not be stretched for alms. They will be dust. The whole world will be intelligent, virtuous, and free" (506). What can be said of this vision, so contradictory to the emphasis on social conditioning in "A Lay Sermon," "Crimes Against Criminals," and "How to Reform Mankind," so absurd on its face?

Wearied of his travels, feeling his mission in freethought done, and yielding at last to homesickness (especially for his grandchildren), Ingersoll was turning from the lecture platform to the courtroom for his living and for relief. The Russell estate case occupied him during most of June 1899. It was the kind of case he liked, for it had to do with love and marriage. He could smile, he could chuckle, his eyes could moisten. In this case he challenged the validity of a prenuptial agreement whereby the prospective groom, aged seventy-five, gave his future bride, aged fifty, $5,000, supplemented (it was alleged) by an oral promise to provide "liberally" for her in his will, and she renounced the right of dower in his estate (which she was legally entitled to). In his will, however, Russell had left his widow only a thousand dollars' worth of stock as her entire legacy in an estate valued at $250,000. Ingersoll claimed the right of dower as waived under false pretenses. His final argument, delivered without notes and preserved only in the stenographer's unedited record shows him in full command of law and facts, logic and banter. Was the Russell romance a mere business deal between an aged pair, subject to *caveat emptor?* Oh no, it was a union of love, at least as far as she was concerned. He had to tell a story. There was a black woman, 125 years old, who, when asked at what age a woman ceases having thoughts of love, answered, "I don't know, honey, you will have to ask somebody older than I is." He twitted the opposing counsel on the allurements of a woman twenty-five years his junior. He chided the late husband on having concealed knowledge of his assets from the object of his courtship, to whom he owed the highest duty of good faith. "The affection that man has for woman is, in my judgment, the holiest and most beautiful thing in nature; the affection that woman has for man—that affection that we call love—has done all there is of value in the world. It has civilized mankind; made all the poems, painted all the pictures, and composed all the music" (*Works*, 589–601). The judge took the case under advisement and after Ingersoll's death decided against him, holding that the agreement was honest and that Mrs. Russell was bound by it (*New York Press*, Aug. 17, 1900). Sometime in June Ingersoll visited a new client, the Kimelis Motor Company, of Wilmington, Delaware, to become acquainted with their inventions in railroad engineering. A photographer materialized. The subject lit a cigar, held it in the fingers of his left hand, put his right hand on his hip, and directed. "Ready, aim, fire!" A showman to the last (*New York World*, July 29, 1899).

In the war with Spain McKinley negotiated a treaty which provided for the independence of Cuba and the annexation of the Philippines. Both the Filipinos and the Cubans had armies in the field fighting for independence. In the debate that divided the nation on acquiring the Filipinos as an alien race under indefinite subjugation Ingersoll had sided with the administration. After the treaty squeezed through the Senate and the American army entered the islands for takeover, reports came back of American troops duplicating the Spanish atrocities in Cuba. A wave of revulsion swept the country, Ingersoll along with it. He would not say with Mark Twain that the white stripes on the flag should be painted black and the stars replaced with skulls and crossbones; that was no way to speak of Old Glory. But he was sorely troubled. In his last interview he affirmed that he was an expansionist and wanted all the land that America could honestly get. "But I do not want the Philippines unless the Filipinos want us." The whole business of supplanting the Spanish had been stupidly handled (*The North American* (Philadelphia), June 22, 1899). His last letter, written the day before he died, denied authorship of a tough-minded article attributed to him. He *had* said (he had said it many times), "I have one sentiment for soldiers—cheers for the living, and tears for the dead"—but all the rest was by someone else. He positively did not want the Philippines if the Filipinos did not want us. The record must be kept straight (To Editor, *Clarion*, July 20, 1899, *Letters*, 218).

On July 20, 1899 at Walston, Ingersoll spent the evening playing billiards. At about ten o'clock he went out on the piazza with Clint Farrell. He sat in his rocking chair smoking a cigar and looked over the grass and flowers and through the trees to the majestic river a mile away. "This is a beautiful world," he said (*New York World*, July 22, 1899).

Some seven years later, in order to quash the inevitable rumors about a deathbed recantation, Mrs. Ingersoll, Mrs. Farrell, and Sue Sharkey issued an affidavit describing his last hours (*Truth Seeker*, March 21, 1906). During the night of July 20 he had an attack of acute indigestion and slept poorly. He came down to breakfast, then sat on the piazza reading and chatting with his family. At about ten thirty he said he would lie down and rest a little. Mrs. Ingersoll accompanied him to their bedroom and stayed there while he slept. At about one forty-five he awoke and sat in his chair to put on his shoes. Miss Sharkey and Mrs. Farrell entered. Mrs. Ingersoll said, "Do not dress, Papa, until after luncheon; I will eat upstairs with you." "Oh, no," he replied, "I do not want to trouble you." Mrs. Farrell spoke up: "How absurd, after the hundreds of times you have eaten upstairs with her." He looked up laughingly at Mrs. Farrell as she turned to leave the room. Mrs. Ingersoll said, "Why, Papa, your tongue is coated. I must get you some medicine." "He looked up at her with a smile, and as he did so closed his eyes and passed away without a struggle, a pang, or even a sigh." Medical efforts were futile.

The body lay on a bier in the parlor. The widow and daughters, sitting on opposite sides, kept vigil for five days. Sometimes Mrs. Ingersoll waved a fan over the body; Eva and Maud pressed the folded hands. From all walks of life all over the world came the messages of condolence—fifty telegrams one day, a hundred the next, letters in bundles. Some of the messages were from clergymen. The American Federation of Musicians grieved for "one whose whole nature grasped the true beauty of our noble art" (*Truth Seeker*, Aug. 5, 1899).

On Tuesday afternoon there was a private funeral at the residence. As the mourners (including several blacks who had worked for Ingersoll in Washington), arrived at the railway depot in Dobbs Ferry, they were met by carriages and taken up the hill through a dismal rain to Walston. The straggly procession looked like a line of pilgrims on the way to a new shrine. The body and the bier had been moved to the bedroom where Ingersoll had died. Flowers were everywhere. He was dressed in his night clothes and a white winding sheet, his eyes calmly closed, a faint smile on his lips, head pillowed on a mass of pink sweet peas, arms folded on his breast. Festoons of flowers hung over the bier.

Excepting the widow and daughters the mourners stood about. The funeral was all Ingersoll, the chosen jewels of a lifetime. Professor John Clark Ridpath read the *Declaration of the Free*, including

> We love no phantoms of the skies,
>> But living flesh,
> With passions soft and soulful eyes,
>> Lips warm and fresh,
> And cheeks with health's red flag unfurled,
>> The breathing angels of this world.
>
> The hands that help are better far
>> Than lips that pray.
> Love is the ever gleaming star
>> That leads the way,
> That shines, not on vague worlds of bliss,
>> But on a paradise in this.

Major Orlando J. Smith read the creed of the good life from "The Foundations of Faith": "To love justice, to long for the right. . . , to love the truth. . . , to love liberty. . . , to wage relentless war against slavery in all its forms, to love wife and child and friend. . . , to cultivate courage and cheerfulness, to see the calm beyond the storm, the dawn beyond the night, to do the best that can be done and then to be resigned— that is the religion of reason, the creed of science. This satisfies the brain and heart." Dr. John Lovejoy Elliott of the New York Ethical Society read the eulogy of Robert's beloved brother Clark, containing "Life is a narrow vale between the cold and barren peaks of two eternities. We strive in vain to look beyond the heights. We cry aloud, and the only answer is the echo of our wailing cry. From the voiceless lips of the unreplying dead there comes no word, but in the night of death hope sees a star and listening love can hear the rustling of a wing." There was no music, no eulogy. The mourners filed by the bier for a final view and left into the darkened hall. Blind Charles Broadway Rouss, led by an attendant, passed his hands over the features and said, "Well, perhaps he is better now, no one can understand it." Mrs. Ingersoll touched his arm. "He wanted you," she said, "to place your hand upon his heart." She lifted the pall and guided his hand.

Two days later Mrs. Ingersoll released the body for cremation. The ashes were deposited in a vase of bronze on a porphyry base, trimmed with cypress and laurel and inscribed, *"L'urne garde la poussière, le coeur le souvenir"* ("The urn guards the dust, the heart the memory").

The national reaction to Ingersoll's death was a continuation of the love-hate atmosphere in which he had lived. From the White House not a word. In New York City the St. Nicholas Orchestra of forty musicians ended their program on July 26 and July 27 with Ingersoll's favorite piece,

Siegfried's Funeral March from *Die Gotterdamerung*, "as a token of their affection and gratitude for his patronage of the arts and for his material support of this orchestra, he having been the largest subscriber thereto" (Flyer, L.C.).

The thousands who had flocked to hundreds of meeting places over the nation and had applauded him as the resplendent champion of their unbelief could not find any publications outside the freethought press to proclaim their enduring commitment. The magazine *Public Opinion*, seeking a cross section of published opinion on Ingersoll's influence, cited one voice for him (*Freethought Magazine*) and four against (*North American Review, Catholic World, Review of Reviews*, and *Bookman*). In the *North American Review* Dr. Field, a warm friend and ardent opponent, said that he had been personally assured by the great scientist Lord Kelvin that Paley's argument from design could not be refuted; hence the ground was sinking under the feet of the advocates of atheism. "They will have their little day and then fade away in the distance, and be seen no more, while the truths of Christianity will abide forever. This makes an end, so far as I can see, of the fear or the hope that the followers of Ingersoll, feeling deeply, as well they may, the loss to them by his death would make an organized body of agnostics, not only to preserve his memory, but to perpetuate his belief or unbelief. But you cannot make a party of one man, nor a creed out of mere negations." Dr. Henry A. Bream in the *Catholic World* was disdainful. "We notice this man because of the harm he did and tried to do, not because of any great quality that he possessed. His career as a soldier was very short; while his career as an anti-Christian lecturer was too long for the good of his own soul, and for the faith of the many half-educated people who listened to his speeches or read them in print, laughed at his jokes, and took his caricatures of Christian doctrine for solid arguments against them."

In the *Review of Reviews* Dr. William Hayes Ward pronounced Ingersoll "the most brilliant propagandist of unbelief since Bradlaugh," who, however, "had attracted only nominal believers in Christianity, and had not touched the real Christian doctrine at all." Yet Dr. Ward could not deny his charisma: "His appeals for freedom, for honesty, and his personal example of what is beautiful in domestic life have, I believe, more permanent influence than his sometimes violent attacks on popular faith. Those who have heard him will remember longest his exquisite oratory and will give him credit for the loyalty to truth he professed." Professor Harry Thurston Peck in the *Bookman* said that Ingersoll had lessened his possible influence by his bad manners. "If Colonel Ingersoll honestly and conscientiously believed that it was his duty to shake the faith of Christians, to refute their error and to tear from them a belief that he supposed a false one, then at the very least he should have respected the sincerity of their convictions and have laid his hand upon them gently and with reverence, and not burst into the sacred silence of their devotion with the raucous bellowing of an itinerant stump-speaker and the clowning of a vulgar mountebank." On the other hand, in the *Freethought Magazine* Professor David T. Ames lauded Ingersoll as the greatest benefactor of humanity in the nineteenth century: "No other man has done so much to emancipate the human race from the grinding, impoverishing, and dwarfing thraldom of religious creeds and bigotry."

Searching for avowals of freethought in the newspaper accounts *The Truth Seeker* found two. The *De Kuyter* (N.Y.) *Gleaner:* "He has left an impress upon the age in which he lived that time will not dim, rather as years roll on will his influence roll on with his influence widened and strengthened." And *The Stockton* (Calif.) *Daily Record:* "The age does not fully appreciate, but as the religion of superstition and impulse and passion gives way and the religion of intelligence, of love and justice is developed he will be appreciated as a hero, and it is a grand compliment to the intelligence of the present age that he was not also a martyr."

One need not have been a freethinker to mourn the passing of Ingersoll. He had been a darling of the press and they treated him lovingly. The editorial in the *Chicago Tribune* is a poignant threnody over their fellow Illinoisan who had been such a popular visitor in the Windy City over the years. "To all Americans who have heard and seen Robert G. Ingersoll on the stump or the platform—and their name is legion—the news of his departure from this world for another, which he had no faith in, will be a surprise and a shock. They will feel that they have lost an old familiar friend whose wit has made them shriek with laughter and whose pathos has unsealed the fountains of their tears" (July 22, 1899). Likewise the *Washington Post:* "Ingersoll was happy in his death as befits the man whose life had been beautiful" (July 27, 1899). The *Trenton American* admired "the courage with which he confronted the whole world of religious thought and uttered and maintained his belief without fear or favor. . . . It is to be said for the credit of the cult that in all this broad land there are very few jackasses engaged in kicking the dead lion." The *New York Sun* embraced him, rebuking the clerics who had consigned the dead unbeliever to hell: "That is an awful assumption of omnipotent authority by a human being."

> Let men rather dwell on the virtues of Robert Ingersoll—his superb courage, his beautiful family life, his justice, his loving kindness. Death silenced in him a voice whose eloquence was sweet as music and a heart filled with humanity—with that sentiment which the Founder of Christianity himself has extolled as the chief of virtues, which the believer, seeing in him, the Infidel, may be the more impelled to imitate as he proceeds to work out his own salvation with fear and trembling. (*Truth Seeker*, Aug. 5)

Even in deploring or minimizing his influence the publications defending orthodoxy could not suppress their sense of his personal radiance.

So the *Christian Advocate* said: "This man of splendid gifts went through the world, laughing as he went, knocking the crutches from under the arms of the lame, the glasses from the eyes of those who saw but dimly (reckless whether the blow fell upon the eye itself), and the cordial from the lips of fainting pilgrims" (*Truth Seeker*, Aug. 12, 1899). And the *Atlanta Constitution:* "He went hither and yonder, rosy and rotund, spouting forth with a broad smile his illogical but poetic denials, always jovial, always in good humor, and occasionally making desperate but boyish efforts to be eloquent at the expense of Christian belief" (July 24, 1899).

Two days after his death a score of ministers in Chicago told the *Tribune* what they thought of Ingersoll. They varied in style and substance but all agreed that Ingersoll wasted his talents and did not understand the truth and comfort of religion and that Christianity was stronger than ever (July 24). In New York his old adversary Talmage said that the Ingersoll "incursion" had done good inasmuch as it made people read or reread the Bible and appreciate the inspired word of God, the religion of John Adams, Daniel Webster, William Seward, William Gladstone, of Goethe, Tasso, Spenser, Bunyan, and other great writers. "The most popular institution on earth today is the Church, the most popular book is the Bible, and the most popular man is Jesus. . . . Farewell Robert G. Ingersoll! Hail, thou word of God, which liveth and abideth forever" (*Atlanta Constitution*, Aug. 6). Contrarily, Moody declined to comment on Ingersoll. It was for God to judge. Ingersoll had been driven to infidelity by abuses in the church (*Chicago Tribune*, Aug. 24).

At the memorial meeting in Denver, Senator Thomas of Colorado, political opponent and personal friend, said that Ingersoll's character "was as nearly perfect as it is possible for the character of a mortal man to be. . . . None sweeter or nobler had ever blessed this world" (Kittredge, 495). In Peoria John S. Starr remembered how in 1860, having just suffered defeat as the Democratic candidate for Congress, Ingersoll attended a party rally held to consider affiliation with the Confederacy and, in an impassioned speech, swung it into support for Lincoln. "I say with pride that Robert G. Ingersoll showed himself to be the greatest patriot in the United States" (MacDonald, 162). At a Chicago meeting Clark Carr said of his old friend, "He was the boldest, most aggressive, courageous, virile, and the kindliest and gentlest and most considerate and loving man I ever knew" (Kittredge, 495). Here Clarence Darrow struck a discordant note. He began as a true believer in freethought.

> Robert G. Ingersoll gave his life, his splendid energy, his matchless eloquence, to the cause of humanity. . . . Most of the prizes sought by men passed him by. He gained fame and honor of some sort, but had he been content to follow the mob and prostitute his great genius for honors and profit, no prize in the gift of the American people would have been too high for him. [But] I do not mean to say that Robert Ingersoll never squirmed in the great fight. He loved the applause of

mankind, as we all do, and there were times when, I think, he wavered. . . . Ingersoll believed in liberty as far as the church was concerned, but on political questions he was seemingly color blind. The older and more venerable a political superstition, the more he would cling to it. (*Truth Seeker*, Aug. 20, 1899; Sept. 8, 1900)

Right or wrong, it was the wrong place, and there were boos and hisses.

Three disparate men known to history sent condolences. Mark Twain wrote to Eva Farrell: "Except my daughter's, I have not grieved for any death as I have grieved for his. His was a great and beautiful spirit; he was a man—all man from his crown to footsoles. My reverence for him was deep and genuine; I prized his affection for me and returned it with usury" (Quoted in *Truth Seeker*, Aug. 11, 1923). Andrew Carnegie regretted that he had lost contact with Ingersoll in recent years and praised him as "right on every issue," including the Philippines after what had seemed to Carnegie the anti-imperialist a bad start. He was pleased with the tenor of the press notices which gave Ingersoll his due, "one of the great characters of modern times and the greatest of orators, a true friend of the people. . . . I am so sorry for you and your daughters, but remember you had such a husband and they such a father" (To Mrs. Ingersoll, July 26, 1899, L.C.). Eugene Debs wrote immediately to the family. "All our family unite in profound and loving sympathy. Millions mourn with you your great bereavement" (*Chicago Tribune*, July 23), and later declared,

The name of Robert G. Ingersoll is written in the Pantheon of the world. More than any other man he destroyed religious superstition. Like an electric storm he purified the religious atmosphere. With rare courage and brilliant ability he applied himself to his task and won an immortality of gratitude and glory. He was the Shakespeare of oratory—the greatest the world has ever known. Ingersoll lived and died far in advance of his time. He wrought nobly for the transformation of this world into a habitable place, and long after the last echo of detraction will be silenced his name will be loved and honored and his fame will shine resplendent, for his immortality is fixed and glorious. (Quoted in *Truth Seeker*, Oct. 21, 1899)

To Mark Twain and Carnegie Ingersoll was a friend, but to Debs he was a human god: "I have never loved a mortal as I have loved Ingersoll," he said. "Not a day passes that I do not think of the Colonel; his loving, living presence is still with us" (To Clinton Farrell, Jan. 17, 1900; Feb. 27, 1900, L.C.). On August 11, 1903, the seventieth anniversary of Ingersoll's birth, he wrote to Farrell, "This day is holy in our calendar" (L.C.).

Dr. Roberts said that thirty years ago a man did not dare to declare himself a freethinker; if he owned a copy of *The Age of Reason* he kept it hidden. "And then there came unannounced, unsuspected, unheralded, a minister's son, a man with courage, a man equipped with imagination, armed with wit, panoplied with logic, adorned and beautified with rhetoric and humor." He had made a revolution. Now millions stood up and proclaimed their commitment to freethought (*Truth Seeker*, Dec. 14, 1907). Traubel said that Ingersoll's opposition to socialism came from inadequate knowledge, that socialism would not suppress but free the individual, and that Ingersoll's criticism of social inequities put him in the Socialist camp (*Montreal Star*, March 25, 1912).

Ingersoll did not convert the nation or even a large part of it to freethought. Orthodoxy remained the dominant faith of the millions. The clergy was overstating the facts when they said that he had not destroyed the religion of the people. Consider a hypothetical average American man of the 1890s: He runs a farm or owns a shop or works in a factory. He is married, has two children. He votes Democrat or Republican, knows little of nineteenth-century science and the higher criticism, and is a regular churchgoer. He has heard about Ingersoll or may even have heard Ingersoll on the Fourth of July, on the stump, or in a lecture hall. He applauds Ingersoll as the celebrant of "The Stars and Stripes Forever." If he votes Republican, he applauds Ingersoll the more; if he votes Democrat, it is not because he dislikes Ingersoll. If he has ventured to attend an Ingersoll lecture he may have enjoyed with some unease the sparkling play of wit, poetry, and pathos. He senses rightly that in the final analysis Ingersoll's title to remembrance or oblivion depends upon his role as the champion of freethought. But this American cannot enlist in that cause. He cannot cut away from his spiritual moorings and societal pressures into the flight for freedom; he marches in the ranks of Christian soldiers. If literate and fair minded he might say of Ingersoll, "Handsome of person, persuasive of tongue, a clear, logical reasoner, and a deep student of literature, law, and politics, he had every requisite for a successful career. Brave, generous, truthful, charitable, and patriotic, he had the power to sway the reason of men and win their hearts. He was in all his dealings a living example of the Golden Rule. He was a devoted husband, a kind father, a generous neighbor. Love was his religion, home was his heaven." He would hasten to add, though, that for all his excellences, Ingersoll was a failure. "His fatal flaw was not that he was an unbeliever, but that he paraded his unbelief and sought to destroy the faith of others. He tried to tear down the dearest possession God has given His children, and offered nothing in its place. Therefore is this man's name, which should have been placed on high, written in sand" (*Philadelphia Times*, quoted in *The Literary Digest*, July 30, 1899).

Mrs. Ingersoll lived to the age of eighty-two, promoting social causes and preserving the memory of her husband. She died on February 2, 1923. The funeral at the Gramercy Park residence was conducted by Dr. Elliott. Among the mourners present were Julia Marlowe and E. H. Sothern, Senator (Dr.) Royal Copeland, and Professor Muzzey. Messages came from, among others, Albert Bigelow Paine, Hamlin Garland, Eugene Debs, I. Newton Baker, Minnie Maddern Fiske, Ellen Glasgow, Henry Mott Osborne, General Nelson A. Miles, and Dr. Roberts. Dr. Roberts wrote: "My sympathy for yourself, and congratulations for your mother. If there is another life, she is now with him whom she worshiped and adored. If there is not, her longing and lonely heart will know loneliness and longing no more forever" (*Truth Seeker*, Feb. 17, 1923). The body was cremated.

On May 4, 1923, the ashes of Robert and Eva Ingersoll were interred on a knoll in Arlington Cemetery. Senator Copeland spoke of the graciousness of Mrs. Ingersoll, and William E. Hull recalled how Ingersoll captivated the Republican rally in Peoria in 1896. Charles Edward Russell—journalist, biographer, musicologist, Socialist—told of how as a fledgling reporter he called upon Ingersoll at his home and found him in his library reading Shakespeare. Having received his answer to some political question Russell rose to leave. "Wait a minute," said Ingersoll, "have you ever considered carefully the Queen Mab speech in *Romeo and Juliet?*" Proud young Russell sat back to be bored, and after an hour appreciated how little he had understood the play.

> He has taken his place with all of the great souls that from the beginning of man's slow ascent from the jungle have braved the current of unthinking opinion, and stood forth for light and the great advance, with Arnold von Winkelried and Nathan Hale, with Voltaire and Humboldt, with the Gracchi and Rienzi, with Bruno and Huss, with them he shares the immortality of great dreams and great devotion. . . . Because of him, millions of men and women today that knew him not have less of fear and more of serenity, less of the tyranny of dogmatism and more of the priceless liberty of thought and speech, less of grief and more of joy, less of darkness and more of light. (L.C.)

In time a stone cutter came and inscribed on the oblong block Ingersoll's words: "Nothing is grander than to break chains from the bodies of men—nothing nobler than to destroy the phantoms of the soul." The colonel and his lady were together in the mystery of death in the arms of their beloved Republic.

References

Collections

Georgetown University Library (Georgetown), Washington, D.C.
Illinois State Historical Society Library (IHS), Springfield, Ill.
Library of Congress (L.C.), Washington, D.C.
New York City Public Library, New York, N.Y.
University of Southern Illinois (Carbondale), Carbondale, Ill.

Writings

Ingersoll, Robert G. 1903. *Works*. Dresden edition. Clinton P. Farrell, ed. 12 vols. New York. The Dresden Publishing Co.
Ingersoll, Robert G. 1951. *Letters*. Eva Ingersoll Wakefield, ed. New York. Philosophical Library.

Bibliography

Stein, Gordon. 1969. *Robert G. Ingersoll: A Checklist*. Kent, Ohio. Kent State University Press.

Biographies

Smith, Edward G. 1904. *The Life and Reminiscences of Robert G. Ingersoll*. New York and London. The National Weekly Publishing Co.
Kittredge, Herman E. 1911. *Ingersoll: A Biographical Appreciation*. New York. The Dresden Publishing Co.
Rogers, Cameron. 1927. *Colonel Bob Ingersoll*. New York. Doubleday, Page, and Co.

Kleber, John E. 1939. *The Magic of His Power: Robert G. Ingersoll and His Day.* Unpublished dissertation, University of Kentucky.

Cramer, C. H. 1953. *Royal Bob: The Life of Robert G. Ingersoll.* Indianapolis and New York. Bobbs-Merrill Co., Inc.

Larson, Orvin. 1962. *American Infidel: Robert G. Ingersoll.* New York. The Citadel Press.

Other Books

Avery, Lillian D. 1926. *A Genealogy of the Ingersoll Family of America.* New York. F. H. Hitchcock.

Blaine, Mrs. James G. 1908. *Letters.* Harriet Blaine Beale, ed. New York. Duffield and Co.

Braden, Clark, ed. 1900. *Ingersoll Unmasked.* Lexington, Ky. Blue Grass Printing Co.

Bridge, James H. 1931. *Millionaires and Grub Street.* Rpt. 1918. Freeport, N.Y. Brentano's.

Bryan, William Jennings. 1971. *The First Battle.* 2 vols. Rpt. 1896. Port Washington, N.Y. Kennikat Press.

Carr, Clark E. 1908. *My Day and Generation.* Chicago. A. C. McClurg & Co.

Darrow, Clarence. 1922. *Crime: Its Cause and Treatment.* New York. Thomas Y. Crowell Co.

Depew, Chauncey. 1924. *My Memories of Eighty Years.* New York. Charles Scribner's Sons.

Douglass, Frederick. 1893. *Life and Times.* Boston. DeWolfe, Fiske, and Co.

Ferry, Abby F. 1928. *Reminiscences of John W. Farwell.* 2 vols. Chicago. F. R. F. Seymour.

Gresham, Matilda. 1919. *Life of Walter Quinlan Gresham.* 2 vols. Chicago. Rand McNally & Co.

Gripenberg, Alexandra. 1954. *A Half Year in the New World.* E. J. Moyne, trans. Newark, Del. University of Delaware Press.

Hayes, Rutherford B. 1964. *Diary of a President.* Rpt. 1924. T. Harry Williams, ed. New York. D. McKay Co.

Henry, Robert S. 1944. *"Fust With the Most" Forrester.* Indianapolis and New York. Bobbs-Merrill Co., Inc.

Hubbard, Elbert. 1911. *Little Journeys to the Homes of Great Americans.* "Robert G. Ingersoll." East Aurora, N.Y. The Roycrofters.

John, J. P. D. 1898. *Did Man Make God, or Did God Make Man? A Reply to Robert G. Ingersoll.* Indianapolis. F. Caldwell.

LaFollette, Robert M. 1913. *Autobiography.* Madison, Wis. The Robert M. LaFollette Co.

Lambert, Louis A. 1883. *Notes on Ingersoll.* Buffalo, N.Y. Catholic Publishing Co.

———. 1898. *Ingersoll's Christmas Sermon.* Akron, Oh. D. H. McBride & Co.

Macdonald, E. M. 1911. *Col. Robert G. Ingersoll As He Is.* New York. The Truth Seeker Co.

McClure, J. B., ed. 1898. *The Mistakes of Ingersoll and His Answers.* Chicago. Rhodes and McClure, Publishers.

Morison, Samuel E. and Commager, Henry S. 1937. *The Growth of the American Republic.* 2 vols. New York. Oxford University Press.

Muzzey, David S. 1934. *James G. Blaine: A Political Idol of Other Days.* Port Washington, N.Y.: Kennikat Press.

O'Rell, Max (pseudonym of Paul Blouet). 1889. *Jonathan and His Continent.* Mme. Paul Blouet, trans. New York. Cassell and Co., Ltd.

Official Proceedings of the National Republican Conventions of 1868, 1872, 1876 and 1880. 1903. Minneapolis, Mn. Charles Johnson, Publisher.

Official Proceedings of the National Republican Convention of 1884. 1903. Minneapolis, Mn. Charles Johnson, Publisher.

Paine, Albert B. 1912. *Mark Twain, a Biography.* 3 vols. New York and London. Harper and Brothers.

Plummer, Mark A. 1984. *Robert G. Ingersoll: Peoria's Pagan Politician.* Western Illinois Monograph Series, No. 4. Macomb, Ill. Western Illinois University Press.

Russell, Charles E. 1914. *These Shifting Scenes.* New York. Hodder and Stoughton.

———. 1926. *Julia Marlowe: Her Life and Art.* New York. D. Appleton & Co.

Sherman, Edgar J. 1908. *Some Recollections of a Long Life.* Boston. Private printing.

Smith, Theodore G. 1925. *The Life and Letters of James Abram Garfield.* 2 vols. New Haven, Conn. Yale University Press.

Stevenson, Adlai. 1909. *Something of Men I Have Known.* Chicago. A. C. McClurg & Co.

Talmage, Thomas DeWitt. 1890. *Trumpet Peals. A collection of timely and eloquent extracts from the sermons of Reverend T. DeWitt Talmage including Demosthenian phillippics against Ingersollian infidelity.* Collected and classified by L. C. Lockwood. New York: Bromfield.

Traubel, Horace. 1964. *With Walt Whitman in Camden.* Vol. V. Gertrude Traubel, ed. Carbondale, Ill. University of S. Illinois Press.

Twain, Mark. 1917. *Letter.* Arranged with a Comment by Albert B. Paine. 2 vols. New York and London. AMS Press.

Articles in Magazines and Newspapers

Angell, Donald E. 1966. "Ingersoll's Political Transition—Patriotism or Partisanship?" *Illinois State Historical Society Journal,* Vo. LIX, No. 4, Winter.

Blanchard, George C. 1910. "A Reporter's Notes. Recollection of Ingersoll and Golden Days." *The Truth Seeker*, April 2.

Debs, Eugene V. 1917. "Recollections of Ingersoll." *Pearson's Magazine*, April.

Foote, George W. 1897. "Letters from America—XII, The First Shadow." *The London Freethinker*, Jan. 3.

J. H. Undated clipping. "The Apostle of Unbelief: An Englishman's View of Ingersoll." *New York Times*, (L.C.).

Meek, Basil D. 1924. "Ingersoll's Military Career." *The Truth Seeker*, Aug. 9.

Plummer, Mark A. 1980. "Goodbye dear Governor, You are my best friend." *The Private Papers of Robert G. Ingersoll to Richard J. Oglesby, 1867-1877.* Illinois State Historical Society Journal, Vol. XXIII, No. 21, Summer.

———. 1980a. "Robert G. Ingersoll on Leeks and Onions in the Holy Land." *Illinois Quarterly*, Vol. XL, No. 1, Fall.

———. 1980b. "Robert G. Ingersoll and the Sensual Gods: An Unpublished Letter." *Western Illinois Regional Studies*, Vol. 1, No. 2, Fall.

Thomas, Charles S. 1921. "Reminiscences of Ingersoll." *The Truth Seeker*, Aug. 27.

Underwood, B. F. 1905. "Recollections of Colonel Ingersoll." *The Progressive Thinker*, Nov. 11.

Wilcox, Ella Wheeler. 1887. "Colonel Ingersoll at Home." *The Truth Seeker*, Nov. 5. Quoted from *New York World*.

Index

Since Ingersoll is the focus of each reference herein, he is not separately treated, likewise his principal places of residence (Peoria, the District of Columbia, New York City, and Dobbs Ferry) are omitted.

www.ingramcontent.com/pod-product-compliance
Lightning Source LLC
Chambersburg PA
CBHW021826090426
42811CB00032B/2036/J